The Matchcover Collector's Price Guide

1st Edition

by
Bill Retskin

with contributions by

John Williams

Published by:

WorldComm®
a division of Creativity, Inc.

Asheville, N.C.

Publisher: Ralph Roberts

Executive Editor: Kathryn L. Hall

Production Editor: Melody A. Grandy

Cover Design: WorldComm®

Interior Design and Typesetting: Bill Retskin & WorldComm®

Printed in the United States of America

10 9 8 7 6 5 4 3 2 1

ISBN 1-56664-036-9   Library of Congress: 93-060795

The opinions expressed in this book are solely those of the author and are not necessarily those of WorldComm.

WorldComm—a Division of Creativity, Inc., 65 Macedonia Road, Alexander, North Carolina 28701, (704) 252-9515—is a full-service publisher.

Trademarks

Names of products that are suspected of being trademarks or service marks are capitalized. Use of a product or service name in this book should not be regarded as affecting the validity of any trademark or service mark.

Although this is the first matchcover price guide published for worldwide distribution, the current values listed here should be used only as a guide. *The Matchcover Collector's Price Guide, 1st Edition*, is intended as a flexible starting point for the matchcovers listed here, and prices may vary in different sections of the country. With any kind of paper ephemera, condition is king. The prices in this book are quoted, and in some cases have been adjusted, as mint condition value. Neither the authors, editors, or WorldComm© assumes any responsibility for losses or damages incurred as a result of consulting this publication. This book is intended as a guide only.

References to *The Matchcover Collector's Price Guide, 1st Edition*, are made from research material and all information is copyright © The Retskin Report, 1993.

The address below currently serves as a clearing point for correspondence regarding matchcovers as generated by this book. An application form for *The American Matchcover Collecting Club* appears in this volume, and new collectors are encouraged to join this organization. U.S Bulk rate, $10.00, U.S. and Canadian First Class, $15.00, Overseas Rates, $25.00. Members receive *The Front Striker Bulletin*, a subscription newsletter dedicated to the history of matchcovers, the match industry, and matchcover collecting; a member's roster with addresses, phone numbers, and categories; four valuable national political matchcovers; a membership card; and discounts on services, books, matchcovers, and custom match books. When inquiring about matchcover activity in your area, when seeking information about collections for sale, or when requesting estimates on collections or estates, please include an SASE for a prompt reply. All correspondence will be answered if you send an SASE.

The authors and associated editors have researched the sources used in this book to ensure the accuracy, validity, and completeness of the information provided. We assume no direct or indirect responsibility for omissions, errors, inaccuracies, or other inconsistencies found herein.

This book was conceived, written, typed, laid out, and edited by Bill Retskin, with contributions by John Williams. Other publications by the author include *The Matchcover Collectors Resource Book and Price Guide*, *The Front Striker Bulletin*, *Matchcovers of the 1939 New York World's Fair*.

Additional copies of this book may be ordered from:
The American Matchcover Collecting Club
Bill Retskin, Editor
PO Box 18481
Asheville, NC 28814-0481
(704) 254-4487
Softbound: $16.95 (plus postage: $3.25 U.S. ,$5.25 Canadian, $7.50 Overseas)
Hardbound: $24.95 (plus postage: $4.00 U.S., $6.00 Canadian, $9.00 Overseas)

For my mother,
Mimi Retskin,
who always saw the light

I would also like to thank the following people who made special editorial contributions to this book: John Williams, Jim Moffett, George Sparacio, Bill Thomas, Rich Semko, Wanda Lee Nunery, and Sheila Wilkins.

I would also like to thank the current membership of **The American Matchcover Collecting Club** who have supported *The Front Striker Bulletin* and the **AMCC/FSB** Auctions. They include (in alphabetical order):

Herb Abelson, Jeff Ackerman, Bruce Ackerman, Joel Acus, Robert E. Adamski, David A. Ainsworth, G.B. Albertson, Mary J. Albrecht, Don Allen, Edgar D. Allen, William Allgood, Frank C. Ambrogio, Andy Anderson, Bette Anderson, Robert Anderson, Paul Anthony, Rich Apgar, Ralph Arnold, Gil Arseneau, Robert J. Astle, Roland Austin, John Baeder, William Barilla, Sr., Mary K. Barker, Jack Barnes, Bob Barnes, Muriel Barr, Bill Bassett, Joyce Bauer, Ned Bayer, Ron Beach, Mike Beatrice, Bob Beaty, Robert L. Beck, Al Beckwith, John J. Behr, Larry Bell, Jim Bell, Henri Benard, James Benes, Pat Bennett, Tom Benson, David Berger, Stuart Bergman, Henry C. Bernhardt, Renee M. Betchyk, Keith Beynon, Joyce Biliczky, William Bilsbarrow, I.L. Bittinger, Mike Blaisdel, Mary M. Blakesly, Joseph W. Blewitt, Art Blinick, J.G. Bliss, Jr., James A. Bodnar, Betty Jane Boian, Mary K. Book, Thomas E. Borchers, Frank A. Borracci, Bob Borton, Don Boucher, Robert O. Bowman, Peter Bowman, John D. Bowman, Fred J. Boyle, Philip Bracewell, William Bradfield, Brenda Bradley, Carolyn Brady, Ralph D. Brann, Walt Bransford, W. Earl Brenneman, Charles Bressler, William J. Brickelmaier, Jr., W.D. Broadway, Sandi Brockway, Jerry Brotman, Richard B. Brown, Everen T. Brown, Randall Brown, Russell J. Brown, Jane Brown, Gail Brown, William C. Bryant, Nancy J. Brzezinski, Richard S. Buck, Roy Buckley, Ernest W. Bueschel, Elma B. Bull, Bernie E. Burnell, Joe Burnett, Delbert L. Burt, Charles F. Busnuk, Brian Butko, Helen Byers, Michael D. Byers, B. Ray Byrd, Ruth V. Bywater, Donald A. Caldwell, Clem Campbell, Tom & Mary Campbell, Thomas D. Campbell, Lance Campbell, Robert W. Carlson, Trudy Carubia, Jim Caruthers, Reginald Case, Robert L. Case, Felix Caste, Jr., Rita Chabot, Louis Cherny, Jr., Susan L. Chirico, Lou Choquette, Bob Cirillo, Dante Citraro, Richard C.B. Clark, Jimmy Clarke, John G. Cocharo, Orville L. Cody, Gene Collins, Scott Conkle, Bob Connison, Earl H. Conrad, Edith Cooper, Maureen Coral, Gregory Corrales, Audrey Corsino, Georgia Corvino, Richard Cote, Ben Cother, Harry Counceller, E.J. Coury, Danny Creedon, Thomas Crenshaw, Teresa Crider, Joseph Crocetta, Alexander Crucioli, Larry Cummings, Tom Curry, Cheryl Curtis, Carl Cushing, Ben D'Addario, Rob Dalton, Robert Dandeneau, Jeannette Danford, Bill Danley, Carl Davenport, Ben Davis, Jr., Joe De Gennaro, Linda Deibler,

Ron Del Greco, Michael J. Demshock, Harold Denfield, Glenda K. Dennison, David L. Derrick, David M. Dickinson, Everett Diefenbach, Dick Dietzel, Barbara Dixon, Joan J. Dobbins, John Dockendorf, Linda Doelle, Myrtle Drevlow, Diana Drowley, Ben Druckerman, Karen Dubinski, Armand A. Dubois, James Duffy, Sandra Dulla, Bud Duncan, Bruce Dwyer, Jonathan Dyer, Jeff Eastland, Harry O. Echols, Marc Edelman, DeWolfe Edward, Stephen E. Edwards, Glen Edwards, Katherine N. Eggleston, Robert A. Eichel, Barbara Eisenberg, Ronald Eitel, Helen Eitel, Robert Ellenberger, William W. Ellis, Mary L. England, Michael Estock, William R. Evans, Doug Ewen, Jr., Mary Faneuf, Francis Fasciano, Mike Faulkner, J. Scott Fawcett, Ray Featherstone, Kelly Fennell, Hugh Ferguson, Eugene P. Fink, Marie Fischer, Gery Fisher, Wilbur P. Fiske, James T. Flaherty, John Flara, Charles P. Flaugh, Charlotte A. Floyd, Pat Flynn, Thomas Flynn, William J. Foehlinger II, Louis Fols, Barbara B. Folsom, Bob Footlick, Thomas Foran, Robert G. Forbes, Murray Ford, Janet Forester, Mike Forney, Tony Fortunato, Gary Foster, Barry C. Foster, B.R. Fraley, Bob Franz, Harry Franzen, Tom Frederick, Harvey Freeman, Nina Friedman, Tim Frier, Tracy Frischkorn, Carol Frizzell, Nicholas A. Fronduto, Cheryl Frost, David Frost, Kenneth Fuller, Claude Gadoury, Shirley Gadwell, Marie Jeanne Gagnon, Carl Gainer, Matt Gajewski, Bernice Gardner, Melvin Garrett, Arthur Garringer, John W. Gentleman, Billie Gerred, Larry Gerson, Charles Gilbert, Jr., Pat Giroud, David Glenn, William Glosser, Robert A. Glover, Charles R. Goley, Jr., Bob Goodyear, Daniel L. Gore II, Kurt Gotsche, Paul W. Gramlich, Alan Grant, Tom Gray, Lillian Greek, Richard L. Greene, Robert Greenlee, Virginia Gregg, Donald Grepke, Ronnie R. Griffin, Tom Griffin, Frederick Griisser, Sr., James Groblewski, Irwin E. Gross, Matthew T. Guihan, Robert Guliano, Josef Gurvich, Bunny S. Hackmeyer, Rick Hagberg, David Hampton, Scott R. Handler, Harold Hankes, Ray Hanson, John E. Hardy, Barbara Harlow, David M. Harris, Deelano J. Harrison, John P. Hart, Jane Hathaway, Mike Haywood, George A. Heffernon, Jim Heim, Gloria Hellinger, Phil Hemstock, Wayne Hendrickson, Douglas Henley, Michael Henneman, Sibyl F. Henshaw, Scott M. Herman, George Hersey, Robert Heskett, David Hess, Mrs. Russell Hetrick, Mike Hickey, Edward Hickey, Gisele Hill, Charles Hill, Emily Hiller,

Richard E. Hilty, Jr., Frank Hinze, Frank Hoak, Walter Hoffman, Edward Hoffman, Frank A. Hoffmann, David Holcombe, Bill Holman, David E. Holschbach, Gary Hong, James D. Hopson, Marc Horn, Ephraim Horowitz, Neal Hospers, Michael L. Hothan, Mike Hubbard, Bill Hubbard, William E. Huber, Bobbie Hufford, Bernard Humphrey, C. Luther Hunt, James Hunter, Bob Hurd, Vernon G. Hutfless, Gloria Ibold, Richard W. Jackson, Bonny J. Jackson, Donald Jacobs, Jan James, Stephen Jeffres, Janet Johnk, Floyd Johnson, Robert A. Johnson, Robert E. Jones, Peter R. Jones, Bob Jones, Betty Jordan, Edward J. Kabala, Rick Kaljas, Alan Kaplan, Frank Q. Kaspar, Bill Katzker, Lenny Kaye, Michael J. Kelly, Jr., Roger Kemp, Howard Kessler, Joanne Kessler, Barbara Kieffer, Sheldon Kielmeyer, Al Kilburn, Robert Kim, Laurie King, Rudy Kirchgassner, Ruth Kirkpatrick, Victor Kitching, Susan Klarnet, Sal Kluger, Robert Koerner, Joseph Kolodziej, Anthony V. Komsa, Richard D. Korns, Joe Kovacs, Allen Kramer, Frederick Krantz, Chris Kreiger, Adeline Krol, Elwood E. Krzyske, Paul Kummer, Henel K. Kurtz, Steve Kuryk, Ellie Kusiak, Thomas F. Labeska, Chuck Ladouceur, Rawland Lamoy, Wyatt Landesman, David Landy, Ronald Lang, Gary Lau, Brian C. Laura, Kevin Lawson, Chris Lee, Kevin K. Leino, Harry L. Leister, Arthur Lewis, Bob Lincoln, A. Bruce Lindquist, Edd Little, Michael J. Lochman, Sigmund C. Loikits, William Longenecker, Burt Loring, John L. Lucas, Bruce Lucker, Philip Lunn, George Lux, Kevin Macomber, Betty Madher, William B. Mahaffey, Wally Mains, Thomas Malloy, Alkei Manuel, Edgar Manuel, Jr., Arthur Manwaring, Anna Mae Marner, Donald G. Marquette, Lester Marshall, Jr., Larry Martin, Paul Martin, Genny Mathis, James A. Matthew, Carrol Mazur, Warren A. Mc Conchie, Jack Mc Donald, E.J. Mc Guire, Karl Mc Neill, Donna McClellan, Jack M. McKittrick, Jerry D. McMillan, K. Meek, Roger H. Meier, George Menge, Toby Messmer, Brian Meyer, Cameron Jon Meyers, Ronald Miastkowski, Earl V. Mick, Erich Miethner, Ralph Mills, John J. Modrusic, Jim Moffett, John Monson, Robert A. Montgomery, H.G. Moody, Frank Moon, J.T. Moore, Florence Morrisey, Bill Morrison, A. Morse, A.V. Mosca, Lothar Mueller, Ian Murphy, Pat Muster, Jacob H. Myers, Ruth Myers, Robert C. Nehotte, Ron Nelson, Wayne C. Nelson, Robert E. Nelson, Marie Nemec, Pierre Neveu, Robert E. Newnham, John Nichols, Bill S. Nielsen, Cobbs Nixon, George H. Nold, Grace E. Norcross, Judy Norman, Ed Novick, Wanda Lee Nunery, Ruth Nycum, Bill Nye, Denis O'Brien, Roberta O'Quinn, Louise Ogilvie, Robert Oliver, Edna A. Olson, George Olszewski, David Origlio, Ellsworth Ott, Lin Overholt, Carol Owens, Tom Pace, Kernis Pantsari, J.B. Parks, Clem Pater, Elizabeth Patterson, Raymond C. Patton, Mary F. Peeling, Brenda Pelletier, Mike Pender, Verlin E. Perry, Betty C. Petersen, Jim Peterson, Ben Peterson, Thomas L. Peterson, Dot Peterson, Claudia W. Pettine, Manny Phillips, Don Phillis, Jean-Guy Pichette, Billijo Piper, Lewis Pittell, Joan E. Plunkett, Robert Podeswa, Joseph A. Pollard, Louise Poorman, David Pophal, Mike J. Porcelli, Mac Porter, Gary W. Potter, George Poulsen, Dea Powell, Jean Powers, Mike Prero, Duane Pruitt, Elma Purvis, Jeff Puschnig, Edward Pyatt, Scott Qualley, John Qualters, Gregory Quina, Phil Quint, Eileen Ragsdale, Bruce A. Randall, Connie Randolph, Marcia Repanes, Peter Repoli, Jessica Retskin, Joe Richards, Ray Richardson, Mike Richmond, Robert L. Riel, David Riel, Alice Riel, Stephen Rigelsky, Lucky Riley, Julius Ritchie, John C. Rizzo, Gertrude Robinson, Santos Rodriguez, Jr., Patrick E. Rogers, Leland Roll, Pam Romaniak, Herman Rosen, Edward P. Rousher, Terry Rowe, Paul Roy, Murry A. Ruggiero, Fred Rumplik, Dennis Russell, Daniel Saks, James Samatuzski, Michael Samuels, A.A. San Miguel, Jr., Tina A. Sanborn, Jim Sannerud, Don Sarver, Merle Sass, Michael C. Savage, La Verne Schlegel, Armin P. Schmalz, Thomas E. Schmelzle, Bob Schmelzle Jr., Jackie Schmidt, Ken Schneider, Steve Schooley, Rex Schultz, Bernard Schwartzman, Edward Scott, George C. Scott, James E. Sekavec, Richard Semko, Lorenzo Semple, Jr., Larry Seymour, Floyd Shade, Michael D. Shannon, Janet L. Shannon, Barney Shapiro, Mike Shapiro, Philip H. Sharpe, Seymour Shedlow, Chester Shott, Al Shpil, Norman F. Sieh, Robert Simpkins, Mike Simpson, Ilene Singer, Addie L. Singleton, Ed Skrocki, John Slade, Carol Smart, Lyle & Penny Smith, Howard S. Smith, James A. Smith, Bill Smith, Oleta Smith, Kirby F. Smith, Robert O. Smith, Steve F. Soelberg, Frank Solla, John W. Spangler, Thurman A. Spangler, George Sparacio, Carl Sporkmann, Ron Spykerman, Joseph Stanek, Ronald Stankovitz, Don Steinbach, Bob Steiskal, Thomas Stephen, Martin P. Stephen, Ed D. Stephens, Clarke Stephens, Sharon Stepp, Ralph D. Stern, Susan Stinson, Betty E. Stokes, Christian A. Stoldal, Bill Stone, Neal Strebel, Betty Streusand, Helen Striker, Irvin C. Strohm, Jr., Dwight M. Stuckey, Roy H. Sunday, William Sundstrom, Nina Swanson, Richard C. Swanson, Connie Swenson, Fred Swick, Jim Swisher, Al Sylvia, Mildred Sypher, John S. Taber, John A. Takahashi, Suzanne Talbot, Mike Tate, Allison Tatum, Jeff Tauber, Hersey D. Taylor, Mort Thaler, Richard Thompson, Stephen Thompson, Elizabeth Thompson, Walter G. Thomson, John W. Throne, Kathie Tietze, Joseph Tortis, Verna Troxel, Morton Trupp, David Ullery, Ronald Ulrich, Glenn Underwood, Richard J. Urban, Thomas Valachovic, Berry Van Leer, Carry van Tol, Howard B. Vanderslice, Pete Varvis, Ginny Vaughter, Doug Vetter, Ray Vigeant, Steve Visakay, James Vislosky, Wayne W. VonSeggen, Mike Walker, Donna Walker, George L. Wallace, Eugene Walter, Charles Walter, Jr., Iain K. Walton, Robert C. Wanamaker, Nicholas Ward, Mark Warda, Dorothy Webster, Theron Weeks, Sr., Richard Weisler, Irvan

Welch, Harriet Wentico, Alan Wernimont, Terry W. Wheatley, Elmer E. Whitlatch, Laurette Whittle, Fay Widdicombe, Gregory M. Wikan, Richard A. Wikenhauser, Jo Wilding, Nathan Willensky, John Jay Williams, Michael Williams, John Williams, Dorothy Williams, Sally Wilson, Earl G. Wise, Francis Wise, Judi Wittwer, Chester Wojciechowski, Al Wolf, Gerald J. Wolfley, Marie A. Woller, John Woods, Bob Wright, George J. Yarrish, Tony S.W. Yeong, Karl Youck, Phil Yurcak, Lauren Michelle Zaremby, Howard J. Zaremby, Michelle Zaslavsky, Larry Ziegler, Al Zook, Don G. Zuck.

(as of May 1, 1993)

The Legendary Charles A. Lindbergh Matchbook

The 'Lindy' matchbook, as it is known in the hobby, was made to commemorate Lindbergh's historic 1927 trans-Atlantic flight. It was produced by the Lion Match Co. of New York City, and is also a Safety First.

There are at least three different versions of the Lindy known. All have the likeness of Lindbergh on the front, but different salutations on the back. One reads, "Joint Luncheon Chamber of Commerce of the State of N.Y. The Merchants Ass'n of New York in honor of Col. Chas. A. Lindbergh, Hotel Astor, Wednesday, June 15, 1927."

The matchbook auctioned by the American Matchcover Collecting Club (AMCC) in May 1992 stated: "Dinner to Capt. Chas. A. Lindbergh, New York City, Tuesday, June 14, 1927." (Note the difference in the dates.) Questions have been asked as to why the different dates, and most probably the answer is that there was more than one celebration held for the famous aviator. Lindbergh experts know all about this, I'm sure, but we're matchcover collectors, and it's enough to say that at least two, and probably more, matchcovers exist commemorating this famous celebrity.

Recent history surrounding the emergence of Lindbergh matchbooks is relatively exciting. In the early 1970s, a California buyer paid the astronomical sum of $150 for a Lindbergh matchcover at a convention auction.

Another Pennsylvania collector displayed his Lindbergh matchcover at a convention in the late 1980s, and was toying with the idea of asking $300 for his find. I saw that matchcover, and it looked as if it was picked up from the gutter. But, still, a Lindy none the less.

At this time, full book Lindys weren't even talked about, and conversations among the learned mentioned the existence (known in the hobby) of five, six, or nine, depending on which expert was holding the seminar.

At the 1991 Cleveland RMS Convention, Lance Campbell of Mary Ester, Florida purchased a near mint full book for $4,000.00. It had one stick missing and a gentle distress fold on the saddle. But to date, it was the finest example of the Lindy matchcover ever seen. (Remember, the 1970 California purchase was a matchcover, not a full book, as was the Lindy owned by the Pennsylvania collector.)

In the May 1992 AMCC mail auction, a Lindy was auctioned from the estate of the late Jack Gerson. It had four sticks missing but otherwise was mint. In this case, as well as the Cleveland sale, the 65 year old lettering on the back had faded, and was barely legible. The mail auction listing asked for a minimum bid of $2,000 and showed an estimated value of $3,500. This matchbook sold to a California collector for an undisclosed price. It is safe to say that it didn't realize the extraordinarily high price as the Lindy in the Cleveland sale, but remember, Cleveland was a

live auction—The AMCC Auctions are held through the mail.

When it rains, it pours. Just after the Cleveland convention, a New Hampshire businessman inherited a Lindy from a customer, reportedly at no charge. Some people are very lucky. He had already had a Lindy reportedly worth $900, but the condition was good to fair.

In mid-1993, the most perfect example of a Lindy went to auction, again at the hands of the AMCC auctioneer and author of this book. Insofar as this article was written prior to the auction, there is no way of printing the sale price. (Write me and I'll tell you the rest of the story. Don't forget an SASE.) However, the estimated value was up there with the Cleveland purchase.

Quoting from an article by Lance Campbell, written shortly after the Cleveland auction: "I think there is a lot of interest in Lindbergh. I never particularly followed his career in general. I wanted the cover because I think it's the premier item available in the hobby right now. It's one of those legendary pieces. You can compare it with other hobbies, like the 1804 silver dollar in numismatics."

Table of Contents

Preface

When I wrote my first book in 1988, *The Matchcover Collectors Resource Book and Price Guide,* I was generally opposed to any book which regulated matchcover prices. Having been a collector and dealer for more than 25 years, I watched price guides change the face of once-great fun-filled hobbies.

A story related to me about the first pocket knife price guide written in mid-1970, told of a once prominent dealer and the method he used to determine prices for older knives.

He would ramble up to a dealer's table at a local flea market and ask, "How much do you want for that knife?" The dealer's horse-trading response reflected the kind of hat or shine on the boots of the person asking the question; high or low depending on whether the flea market dealer felt the potential customer could afford his price. The price was dutifully recorded and placed on a master list. When the list was long enough to make up a price guide, the author sent it to his publisher and the book was printed.

Several years later, when asked why he used this highly "scientific" method of price determination, he simply answered, "Well, that dealer could have been as right as you or I, couldn't he?" I rest my case about price guides.

Not all price guides are written using this kind of "scientific" procedure. There are many good price guides on the market, and some contain information that would take an author two lifetimes to evaluate, much less properly research and classify.

About This Matchcover Price Guide

This book was the largest research and typesetting project of my career as an editor. It was fun to write and I loved every minute of it. The approach I used to write *The Matchcover Collector's Price Guide, 1st Edition* was less scientific and more practical than the approach used by the knife dealer. First, over 10,000 actual prices were gathered from mail, live, and private auctions, private sales, and other negotiations. The prices realized were gathered into a database and classified according to category. Duplicate sale items were eliminated, and prices were rounded to the nearest quarter. Extensive research was used to determine key identifying phrases for sets and singles, and several category experts were asked to verify each category listing. The glossary was updated to include over 125 new items and over 175 changes.

I chose this method because I realized that for a first price guide on matchcovers, collectors needed an accurate and reliable price foundation. Had the author of the pocket knife guide written this price guide, I seriously doubt whether matchcover collecting could attain hobby-wide acceptance.

In addition, no fewer than four accomplished and experienced matchcover collectors, collectively representing a total of over 75 years of collecting experience, were asked to help edit the technical aspects of this price guide.

Don't accept any of the prices in this book as gospel. This is just a price "GUIDE" and should be used to give you an idea of where to start or end your financial decisions regarding purchases or sales.

Over the years, I have also discovered that the most disturbing point about price guides is the way people use them. Some swear by them and often imagine the word "Bible" inscribed under the title. Don't use this book to value your collection, either. These prices are mostly from auctions and private sales, and represent mint condition values only.

Introduction

What exactly are matchcovers and why do we collect them? Matchcovers are ephemera. *The American Heritage Dictionary of the English Language* says that ephemera is: 1. Something short-lived or transitory. 2. Printed matter of current and passing interest, such as periodicals, handbills, and topical pamphlets.

They could easily have included matchcovers in that definition, as probably more matchcovers have been printed than all other types of ephemera combined. Don't confuse ephemera with baseball cards, which were made only to be collected. Matchcovers had another purpose first and were originally meant to be discarded after use.

For tens of thousands of small businesses throughout America in the 1920s, 1930s, and 1940s, matchcovers were the principal means of advertisement. A local restaurant would open; the lights were turned on, the insurance was paid, a check was written for the first and last month's rent and the tables, silverware, chairs, plates, and food were ordered. A sign went up to attract neighborhood foot traffic but a wider appeal was soon needed. Radio may have been too expensive and television wasn't around. Newspaper ads were an alternative, but the owner of the restaurant needed more.

"Twenty little messages," as one match company's manual called them. "Every time your customer lights a match, he will think about your business." Orders flocked into match companies, and small businesses thrived. An initial case order of 2,500 books could soon lead to two, four, and ten case orders. The American matchbook led the way to inexpensive business promotion, and on the coattails of tobacco smoking, became the most popular form of American advertisement for over thirty years.

For the purposes of this book, I will use the term matchcovers to mean that which is collected. Many of us collect full books but for the sake of simplicity, I will stick to the term matchcovers, unless otherwise indicated. Matchbooks, of course, are what the businessman ordered, received, and gave away to promote his business. When collected, however, a majority of them are stripped, flattened, and kept in albums or displays. When stripped and flattened, matchbooks become matchcovers.

So why collect matchcovers? Besides having a historical interest to anyone who has ever watched a television commercial, they represent a period in classical advertising when America was just starting to grow commercially. Many have also sought them for their rare miniature beauty and fine detail. Famous magazine artists like Petty, Moran, Thompson, and Vargas were at one time matchcover designers.

American advertising had been in diapers for over a hundred years with print media the only advertising available. Around the turn of the century, an enterprising young salesman from the Diamond Match Co. took us from knickers and trousers, linking matchcovers to advertising. Simply put, his idea was to sell matchcover space to large advertisers. And it worked. For the next 60 years, we grew out of our trousers and into Madison Avenue type suits. We learned to walk and run and then fly, as more products, services, and businesses printed their slogans, messages and ads on matchcovers.

Today, that legacy still exists in American basements, attics, and garages. More matchcover collections haven't seen the light of day in 40 plus years than there are collectors in this country and Canada. Hundreds of thousands of restaurants, banks, and hotels have made matchcovers in their image, and for each, between 2,500 and 50 million were printed.

If you could put all the matchcovers in all the known collections in the United States in fifty Astrodomes, you wouldn't be looking at 5% of the collectible matchcovers still around today.

One final note. If you are new to the hobby, read the sections titled: How to Grade Matchcovers, For the Beginner, and Hints for New Collectors. They will save you hours of striking out in wrong directions and assist you in building a collection of which you can be proud.

How to Grade Matchcovers

General Notes:

When grading matchcovers, there are really only two major condition classifications—struck and unstruck.

Struck—As defined by the glossary at the end of this book, struck means any matchcovers whose striker surface has match abrasions caused by striking a match. There are degrees of these abrasions, and phrases such as "lightly struck" have recently become popular in hobby repertory.

Bobtailed matchcovers are those without strikers, and unless the matchcover dates prior to 1936, are usually not kept.

Keep a struck version of a matchcover if: (1) You are looking for an unstruck specimen to upgrade the current struck copy that you have; (2) One matchcover in a set is struck and you want to display the set in your album. Replace it and complete the set with an upgrade as soon as you can; (3) The matchcover is one which you have never seen before or of exceptional design or coloration. Keep the struck version until you can upgrade it; (4) The matchcover is from a defunct business, product or service and you sincerely do not think that you will come across an unstruck version. (5) You don't mind collecting struck matchcovers. Keep the struck version as a record but don't attempt to trade or sell it.

Unstruck—These are preferred in all cases and can be graded accordingly (note: flats or salesman's samples don't officially fall into the category of matchcovers).

CONDITION GUIDE:

The value of a matchcover is directly related to its condition, age, scarcity, printing originality and advertiser; but not necessarily in that order. One or all of these features may affect its desirability and therefore the value of a matchcover.

The condition of any matchcover should be the most important factor in determining its value. Insofar as this is a general condition guide (i.e. applicable to older and newer matchcovers simultaneously), no direct correlation can be made as to value at any level. Of course,

a near mint condition specimen would certainly be worth more than a Very Good or Fair example, but the value diminution should be rendered on a percentage basis.

Recent back strikers for example, should always be collected in as fine a condition as possible. Older front strikers, however, may not be found in Near Mint condition, eliminating the entire scope of this condition guide for that age group.

Use common sense when aligning your matchcover with this condition guide. Sometimes a Poor or Bad specimen of a matchcover is the only one in existence, and should be treated with the greatest respect.

(Note: In describing each condition, no attempt is made to cluster flaw types. One or several flaws might be present on any given specimen and any one flaw might relegate your matchcover to that level. Use common sense.)

MINT (MT): A pristine matchcover in irreproachable condition, unused, flawless and exemplary. There should be no visible marks or scratches and the corners should be sharp and the corners should be completely square. There should be no odor or mildew or discoloration due to staining or exposure to sunlight.

NEAR MINT (NM): Under close scrutiny, a minor flaw or two may be discovered and allowed. Very minor or yielding wear on the edges, with very light aging or only insignificant discoloration. This is especially true for older matchcovers which have been preserved in paper-page albums. There should be nothing strenuous to detract from its color or beauty.

EXCELLENT + (EX+): Like mint in appearance with no bends, creases, or rounded corners or edges. A very small loss of original luster is permissible. Light fuzzy edges and/or corners and some slight wear may be visible only upon close examination.

EXCELLENT (EX): A matchcover with minor defects which might include one or two scarcely detectable surface creases or gently rounded corners. These shortcomings should not be visible when the matchcover is viewed through its plastic holder. No evasive signs of gouging or chipping are permitted at this level.

VERY GOOD (VG): A matchcover which may show discreet handling but no abuse, layering or scuffing at corners or edges. A negligible crease or bend that does not detract from overall appearance may also be allowed at this level. Some retirement of gloss on the front may be allowed but no alterations. A borderline mildew odor is accepted at this level, but not enough to pinch the nostrils.

GOOD (G): A well handled matchcover with no purposeful abuse. Signs of notching, medium creases, and casual scuffing are allowed. The overall appearance should be good while the luster may be noticeably rough. At this level and from here on, new matchcovers drop off dramatically in value. Certain older front strikers will retain diverse amounts of value depending on scarcity and rarity.

FAIR (F): Wear is arresting. Medium to heavy creases, notching and layering of edges may be indisputable. Stains or inordinate scuffing on the matchcover front may blatantly detract from its appearance. The striker may show outright signs of light use, and harmful staple removal, as evidenced by gouging of the card stock, may also classify at this level. One or more sticks may be absent from a Feature matchbook. Cardstock may show clues of dry rot on the inside striker.

POOR (P): A shabby matchcover. Ostensible creasing with heavily worn edges and striker marks are common at this level. Complete loss of luster and exorbitant soiling or staining may also be prominent. This might still be a scarce matchcover and difficult to find in any other condition. A rank mildew aroma may emanate from the matchcover, so much so that it should not be integrated with others in your collection. Riffled matchcovers fall into this category.

BAD (B): Generally only collectible if extremely rare. The matchcover front may exhibit sustained abuse, loss of print copy, or exhibit a tear. The matchcover front may also be fuzzy due to moisture or excessive abrasions

and staining may obliterate the advertiser's logo. Cardstock may be dry rotted and ready to disintegrate if handled.

WORTHLESS (W): An item that has no redeemable qualities, something that you would not display regardless of rarity. Most bobtailed matchcovers fall into this category. (note: matchcovers in this category should not be thrown away, but sent to the Home for Bobtailed Matchcovers.)

(Editor's Note: It isn't possible to demonstrate a sample of each of the levels in this condition guide. Successive levels may be grouped since this system was not originally intended for ephemera. Use common sense in condition grading your matchcovers.)

Grading - Terms & Conditions:

Bobtailed (or Bobbed) - A matchcover that has had its striker removed. Such matchcovers will have no collector value.

Chipping - Refers to matchcover borders that are worn away. This condition usually appears with dark-colored matchcovers or older dark-gray card stock.

Crease - A wrinkle or flaw on the matchcover surface resulting from careless or deliberate mis-handling. Depending upon the severity of the crease, the value of the matchcover will be proportionately reduced. Creases can be categorized according to severity using the following:

Light Crease: A crease that is barely noticeable and minimal only upon close inspection. Light creases will not be visible when a matchcover is viewed through its plastic holder.

Medium Crease: A crease that is noticeable when viewing a matchcover at arm's length and with the naked eye. A medium crease may not detract from the overall appearance of the matchcover. This type of crease is obvious, but does not break the surface of the matchcover or the continuity of the design.

Heavy Crease: A crease that breaks through the face of the matchcover, often revealing the underlying card stock.

Ding (or Dent) - Slight damage to any of the edges of a matchcover, including a corner or striker edge.

Discoloration - Caused by exposure to prolonged sunlight or other heat discoloring processes.

Layering - The separation or peeling of one or more layers of matchcover card stock. This condition is most noticeable at the corners of the matchcover but can encompass the entire specimen. This condition is especially noticeable on early Mirro-Gloss finishes and is frequently caused by moisture.

Luster - The amount of glossiness or sheen on the front of the matchcover. Older matchcover insides have no luster, but exhibit a dull gray card stock. Newer shinekote card stock matchcovers have a slight luster on the inside, but none to compare with the outside or front of the matchcover.

Notching - Indentations along the matchcover's edges. Possible causes may be tight binding with rubber bands, fingernail gouging, gouging with a staple removal tool or mishandling matchcovers by shuffling. Notching is often caused when a matchbook is carried next to keys or other abrasive metal or plastic objects.

Odor - The natural odor of a matchbook has a slight air of sulfur but is not offensive to most noses. Mildew causes a bright and often eye-watering odor when growing in porous card stock.

Rippling - An overall condition concerned with the flatness of a matchcover. Matchcovers which have been exposed to moisture and quickly dried often ripple. This is due to the fact that the coefficient of expansion of the higher quality surface or front paper and that of the underlying card stock are different. Older rippled matchcovers are almost impossible to flatten.

Scratch (see Crease).

Scuff - A noticeable rub mark or abrasion on the matchcover's front which removes or dulls a portion of the gloss. Scuffs on the back of a matchcover might show tread or abrasive marks.

Stain - A change in the color of the matchcover caused by moisture or other contact with liquid.

Struck - A matchcover's striker that has been or shows signs of being used. The amount of use will impact the overall condition of the matchcover.

How To Use This Book

There are a few special notations that should be kept in mind.

Brackets ([ ]) around dates refer to the years of manufacture. When brackets are empty, dates are not known.

Please use the Legend on page 334 for references to abbreviations, both in the text and the price guide. These abbreviations have come about through trail and error. Other abbreviation systems exist in this hobby, however, this one is indigenous to The American Matchcover Collecting Club and this price guide.

Variations in state names (i.e. CA, Calif, California) as they appear in the description of a matchcover, are written as they appear in the address on the matchcover. The two letter current standard convention is used only when it is actually written that way. The relatively recent two letter standard abbreviations for states was the brain child of the United States Postal Service and should be used on all mail. However, many business entrepreneurs used abbreviations that came naturally.

The price guide was written as the result of tallies and price accumulations from live and mail auctions, as well as private sales. These prices are also quoted for mint/near mint condition singles and sets. As in any ephemeral hobby, condition reigns. Use common sense and this book as a guide, not a Bible.

(**Note:** The designs in the center of most pages in the non-price guide sections of this book are matchcover cut art from the 1940s, 1950s, and 1960s.)

FOR THE BEGINNER

What is a Collection?

Any good thesaurus will offer alternate forms of the word collection, to include accumulation, assembly, association, band, brood, clique, cluster, covey, group, team, organization, summation, assortment, selection, and variety.

The one alternate form of the word collection which we as matchcover collectors would be interested in, is accumulation, which means a mass or heap of anything. When you take an accumulation of matchcovers and put them in some kind of order, you have a collection. A collection can be an ordered accumulation of one kind or type of matchcover, or it can include several different categories, organized into albums, boxes, racks, or display frames.

Collections can be large or small, and are usually considered to be any organized heap of more than two of a single item. I have a collection of four triangle boxes and a collection of 3,500 Lion Wide Stick features. Of course the general term collection also means everything that you collect. "How big is your collection," means all of it.

Who are matchcover collectors?

Loosely categorized, there are three kinds of matchcover collectors. First, there are the casual collectors. Far outnumbering the other two kinds put together, their collections are more like accumulations. Fish aquariums, brandy snifters, shoe boxes, and potato chip cans often serve as repositories for matchbooks.

The second kind of collector is somewhat serious. They use albums, shoe boxes, or pickle jars (for full book collections), to keep matchcovers separated. Weekends are spent hunting new restaurants and hotels that offer free matches. Vacations are documented by picking up matches from every restaurant and vacation spot visited. The big difference between Mr. Casual and Ms. Almost Serious is that when they learn about organized matchcover collecting they say, "I didn't know anyone else collected those things." Is that you? Is that why you bought this book? Don't be bashful—I'll understand!

Finally, we graduate to Dr. Serious. This collector makes a habit of knowing as much about matchcover collecting as possible. He belongs to one or more local matchcover clubs and receives their newsletters. He is a member of **The American Matchcover Collecting Club** and receives his quarterly *The Front Striker Bulletin*. He participates in the FSB mail auction and has between 5 and 20 traders that he corresponds with. He slips a few flattened matchcovers into every letter he writes and knows the familiar hobby terms such as caddy, shucking, manumark, and footer.

It isn't difficult to move from Mr. Casual to Ms. Almost Serious to Dr. Serious in less than a year. Like any hobby, matchcover collecting takes time before you feel comfortable. A majority of serious collectors are more than willing to help newcomers advance in the hobby, and will often send loads of free matchcovers to beginners. Local clubs boast freebee tables at meetings, where new collectors can come and fill up a shopping bag in one sitting.

As you read through this book, you will become exposed to new terms and ideas. These terms don't have to be memorized, but like your sixth grade English teacher always said: "Use them three times and they're yours." She may have also told you that you don't have to know every book in the library—just where to find them. The author and editors hope you use this book as such a reference.

Patronizing us is like making love to a widow

YOU CAN'T OVERDO IT !

Just to answer a question that will sooner or later cross your mind, a majority of matchcover collectors are non-smokers. Matchcover collecting is a clean, safe way to learn about America, advertising, art, beauty, and history; and involve yourself in an inexpensive, fun-for-the-whole-family hobby.

What categories should I start with?

Beginners usually assign themselves the category titled General. With this category after your name in a trade letter or club roster, other collectors will know that you are testing the waters. You will receive a variety of matchcovers when you trade.

In another section of this book there is a list of do's and don'ts for the hobby, but there's one definition needed now. When a matchbook comes out of a box at a local restaurant, it is considered unused. In other words, it hasn't been struck and no matches have been removed. A used matchcover (shucked and flattened) is one which has had at least one match struck against its striker. For the full book collector, it means that at least one match has been removed.

When you trade with others, assume that they will only trade and accept unused matchcovers. If you ask and establish other levels of trading, that's fine. But don't start off on the wrong foot. Condition means everything, and nothing is worse than receiving a trade of 10 matchcovers, six of which have unsightly marks across the striker.

Are some matches easier to find?

Besides specific categories, types, and sizes, there is a philosophical side to this hobby that you should know about. Don't be scared—we aren't talking *deep*, just philosophical! We like to say that matches are either "easy" or "difficult" to find.

What exactly does that mean? Well, easy matches are available at most local club meetings and conventions. They are sent by traders from all over and several find their way into your trading box. Easy matchcovers are usually from large cities and popular vacation spots. They usually include restaurants, hotels, motels, and banks. There aren't specific matchcovers which fit into this category, but you will know them when you see them.

Example of an easy matchcover: About 7 years ago, an overrun of 40 cases of a specific restaurant was donated to the hobby. One case (2,500 matchbooks) of this design found its way to each local matchcover club and the matchcovers started appearing on every freebee table and at every meeting. Soon, traders were sending them off and everyone had one. It will take another ten years before this matchcover is desired again, and there is *no* question why it is called an easy matchcover!

Example of a difficult matchcover: In 1988, a 30 strike supermarket set appeared commemorating the 50 states. Collectors flocked to supermarkets and bought caddies of these matches, trying to get the complete set. This set didn't break well, meaning that it sometimes took 20 or more caddies to collect even 47 states. Collectors contacted other traders all over the country searching for the elusive three matchcovers. Two appeared in a mid western state. A few collectors made one or two sets, but hundreds of 49 matchcover sets are sitting on collectors' desks waiting for number 50. That is a difficult matchcover to find and will soon have a value above normal expectations.

No one knows if poor-breaking sets are planned by the match companies or not—who can say? One thing for sure—it gets people involved!

Remember also that about 50% of the matchcovers produced are not collectible. They include most vending machine matchcovers and matchcovers with 800-number hotels and motels. Any matchcover without an address is usually not desirable.

Matchcovers or full books?

Matchbook production and its use is native to the United States and Canada. Matchbooks are produced in a few foreign countries. Most matchcover collectors, however, see the rest of the world as collecting match box labels and skillets.

Many matchcover collectors save full books and some full book collectors hold onto matchcovers. For most usage, the terms are interchangeable.

So what's the big deal?

There is a difference. Matchcover collectors argue that flattened covers take up less room, are easier to handle, trade through the mail, and are less of a safety hazard. On the other hand, full book collectors insist that the hobby is *matchbook* collecting, and when you take the matches out you ruin their collectibility. There are two schools of thought, no doubt. But the savvy full book collector will usually assume a comfortable middle ground. Here's why.

From the beginning of the organized hobby, certain designs could only be collected as matchcovers and were never available to the public as full books. Edgar Perkins, noted matchcover historian and publications editor during the early days of the hobby points out that several U.S. Navy ships, hotels, radio stations, and foreign matchcovers were not obtainable as full books.

As pointed out earlier, space is another important factor. Over two hundred stripped 20 strike matchcovers can be stored in a caddy where only 50 full books fit fifteen minutes earlier. One statistic indicates that the ratio of matchcover collectors to full book collectors is about fifty to one.

When older full books are found in pristine condition, the wise matchcover collector will not try to shuck them and lay them flat. Years of exposure to light, air, and the natural aging of paper won't allow a clean recovery of the flattened matchcover. Only experience in handling older matchcovers can help determine this condition and only an expert would even attempt to shuck an older match book. If your choice is matchcovers, augment your collection with a side collection of full books. If full books is your direction, don't turn down interesting flattened matchcovers because you are a purist. Someday, you might want to trade those matchcovers for full books.

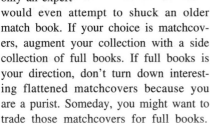

There is one exception. Although common practice years ago, it is considered sacrilege today to strip a Lion Wide Stick Feature. These gems from the 1930s and 1940s have brilliantly colored designs on the sticks, and although there is no easy way to display them, they are usually held in full book form, even by the most ardent matchcover collector.

Dispelling another myth might help you with your choice. Contrary to popular belief, full books don't present a fire hazard as long as the front flap is securely tucked in and they are safely stored. It takes a good hefty physical strike or temperatures of 300 degrees Fahrenheit be-

fore a common match will ignite. After all, why do you think they are called "safety matches?"

What size matchcover should I collect?

You mean there is a choice? Yes, once you had a choice, but if you are collecting only new matchcovers (made after 1987), there are only two general sizes that are still available, the 20 stick size and the 30 stick size.

When the formal hobby first started around 1940 or so, matchcover classification by size was considered an important club function. There was a national classification committee which determined the size of various matchcovers and offered proper naming schemes. Today, that committee and the Maytag repairman would make great poker buddies.

Two broad general categories were decided upon in those early days—standard and odd sizes. Standard matchcovers included 20 sticks, 30 sticks, and 40 sticks. Odd sizes represented all other sizes and shapes.

Some experienced collectors might take exception with the term "standard" or "regular" as being applied to 20 stick, 30 stick, and 40 stick sizes. Originally, only the 20 stick was given this classification; however, with the growing popularity of the other two sizes (especially the 40 strike or "Royal Flash" during World War II), the term grew to encompass all three sizes. Today, the terms are used interchangeably.

Another variation within 20 stick full books comes from the fact that prior to World War II, a longer match was needed to light either of the two predominant forms of tobacco enjoyment—the pipe and the cigar. There were four match companies producing these "tall" matches: Universal Match Co., Federal Match Co., Star Match Co., and Diamond Match Co. Although the widths of the matchcovers were relatively standard, the flattened tall matchcover ranged from 4 7/8" to 5" in length.

After the war, soldiers returned to the United States smoking cigarettes. Along with this popular attitude toward cigarette smoking came the vending machine which made cigarettes more convenient and accessible for the fast-growing, hungry American market. The taller match was no longer needed. The size of the matchcover therefore shrank as a quicker light was used for cigarettes. Although shorter matches were made prior to the war, The Ohio Match Co. of Wadsworth, OH, was the first match company to be granted size patents and vending machine rights. Other major matchbook companies soon followed suit and the "tall" matchbook was eliminated forever. Since the mid 1940s, the regular size 20 stick matchcover measured 4 5/8" x 1 1/2."

Odd size matchcovers?

Well, there were several, and they were introduced on the market for a variety of reasons. I've already mentioned the 40 strike size which became popular after 1937 with the introduction of the Royal Flash line by Universal Match Corp.

It measured twice the size of the modern 20 stick matchcover and contained twice as many matches.

Military service Royal Flash also became a popular collecting category during the early 1940s. With over one thousand different military 40 strike designs to collect and post war production booming, it looked like the 40 strike matchcover would always be with us. International Harvester Corp. printed over eight thousand different matchcover designs. They must have been thinking of us collectors!

The popularity of the 40 stick size was obvious. It offered advertisers more than 22 square inches of advertising space, double that of the 20 stick. The result was beautifully designed, colorful advertisements which stand today as miniature masterpieces.

Universal Match Corp. was the leader of the 40 stick matchcover revolution until Diamond Match Co. entered the race in the mid 1940s with a single 40 stick design featuring one oversized staple. Collectors differentiated between the 40 stick (by Diamond Match Co.) and the Royal Flash (by Universal Match Corp.). The quality and advertisement design were about the same.

One 40 stick size error, known as "Siamese Twins," isn't really a 40 stick matchcover. Popularized by a design for the U.S.S. Louisville, it was never really accepted by collectors.

The Lion Midget was probably the first real odd size matchcover to be discovered by early collectors. Measuring 1 5/8" X 1 1/8" and in the same proportions as its 20 stick uncle, it was originally designed for the popular clutch purse used by the newly emerging smoking

American woman.

Although the term Midget was a Lion Match Co. trade name, it was soon adopted by collectors as the generic name for any matchcover in this size category. Both Ohio Match Co., with its "Juniors" and the Diamond Match Co. tried to enter this market. The flattened matchcover measured 3 1/2" X 1 1/8". All three companies issued a combined total of over 7,500 designs. During World War II, O.P.A. (Office of Price Administration) staple sanctions excluded production of this matchcover size from American factories.

In competition with Lion's Midget, Universal Match Corp. came out with the 10 stick matchcover. It was exactly half the width of a 20 stick, but just as tall. This popular size came along at about the same time as the Royal Flash. As with the Midget, O.P.A. and World War II staple restrictions temporarily halted production during the war. Prior to 1941, around 2,000 10 stick designs were known. This 10 stick size continued in popularity until Universal Match Corp. ceased production in 1987.

If there was a *Pinnacle of Matchcover Design Award,* it must go to Lion Match Co. for its popular Feature, 21 Feature, and 30 Stick matchcover designs.

The 21 Feature took its name from the fact that it held three rows of seven sticks each of a wide stick match that was easily printed. The Feature held three rows of five sticks each. Both the Feature and the 21 Feature were the most complete and fulfilling esthetic experience ever encountered by a matchcover collector. The wide, flat sticks were usually masterfully decorated with three, four, and five color images.

During World War II, O.P.A. sanctions against decorated match sticks forced Lion Match Co. to convert its artistic endeavors to the 30 Stick match. Stick widths reverted back to the pre-war size, and designs continued to be printed on the sticks.

Thin stick printed designs are not called Features, but are known as Printed Sticks. There is no comparison between printed sticks and Features. Some printed sticks are handsome, but the viewer is constantly reminded of the coarse, rhythmically undulating pattern of the rows of match sticks. No such illusion exists when viewing Lion Wide Stick Features. Overpowering designs and meticulous attention to the detail and palette dominate whatever shallow separations appear between the sticks. At first sight, one is taken back by the fact that the design and color patterns are so rich, full, and lively.

Lion Corp. of America, formerly Lion Match Co., is still producing Wide Stick Features. However, the craftsmanship and production technique can never equal the splendor and attention to detail of early Features.

Another magnificent contribution to matchcover collecting is one of my favorite categories, the Lion Match Co. Giant. This matchcover offered the advertiser over 30 square inches of advertising space per side, and was the largest matchcover that could be comfortably carried in pocket or purse. Measuring 9" X 3 3/8" (flattened), early Giants had up to four rows of matchsticks, while most later Giants contain only one.

Lion Giants have the same wide stick style as the 21 Feature and came with both printed and unprinted sticks. Giant Features always had wide printed sticks, with designs repeating themselves on single matches, panoramic views of seaside resorts or powerful hotels, or combinations of daring five-color art and bold lettering. This is another full book that collectors like to keep un-stripped. Although production was not curtailed during World War II, only "Seasons Greetings" Giants were allowed during the conflict.

A number of other odd size matchcovers were popular among collectors. The Action Match by Universal Match Corp. was introduced around 1940 and is considered a "flash in the pan" design. Less than twenty varieties were made for this style and it was considered experimental for its time. The predominant feature of the Action Match added disc-shaped "wings" on either side of the saddle, lending it a "satchel-like" appearance when opening and closing.

Another Universal Match Corp. design was the Adverap. More than a matchcover, it was a box-shaped contraption which fit snugly over a standard cigarette pack. Identified as early as 1940, both the Adverap and the accompanying matchbook were printed with the same advertisement.

Pullquicks and pull matches were produced during the 1930s and 1940s. Both worked on the concept of quickly pulling the match out of a paper holder, simultaneously striking it on a hidden striker inside an individual cell. However, any hesitation in striking the match often proved disastrous, and their popularity lasted only a few years.

Among the very large matchcovers were the 100 stick and 200 stick souvenir designs. Super Giants were also made for a while, measuring 4 3/4" x 15 1/2" (flattened) and contained 240 match sticks.

Another infrequently collected oddity is the Spinning Wheel. Due to the overwhelming number of matches in the case (approximately 500) and the absence of commercial advertising on most known specimens, it is understood that the Spinning Wheel was probably used for prayer ceremonies in churches where candles were part of the offering.

The extremely rare Hummingbird measures 1" X 1/2", and held eight match sticks. It is not known what the original purpose was in making this tiny matchbook; however, it may have been a novelty store item and was collected only as an oddity or peripheral.

Finally, Edgar Perkins offers the following in an early essay on matchcovers. "The mastodon of Hitlerian Germany was 11 1/2" x 4 3/4", with side green wooden panes and oversized red match tips. Holland had a similar type along the general idea of the "giant", consisting of two rows of ten matches each; the panes being 7/16" wide."

How do matchcovers differ?

As in any production item, variations appear when repeat orders are made. Matchbooks manufactured months or years apart for the same business, service, or product, will often show a variation in the address, phone number, color, or style of the design. Advertising directors change, styles vary, and new approaches are used to attract different customers. There are also a few variations which should be kept in mind when asking yourself, "Is this restaurant matchcover different from the one I got last year?"

Some differences: (alphabetically):

Abrasive Color of black, brown, and gray were the pre-1960 abrasive colors. Today, mostly black is used.

Alignment or positioning of the copy. Read each matchcover you are comparing several times. Sometimes, only one word is different.

Color shade variations are not considered differences, but different base colors are.

Design variations, yes, but the changes must be readily noticeable.

Freaks include mostly miscuts and misprints. These are usually collected as a separate category and should not be put in with your regular category.

Inside Variation must be different regarding design or copy.

Mis-cuts as mentioned before are a separate category and not a legitimate variation.

Off-shade due to color change in sunlight is not a valid variation.

Paper Stock detected either by color or finish is acceptable. Older stock was thicker gray and light gray, while modern matchcovers are printed on thin white shinekote.

Perforation concerns mostly Royal

Flash postcard matchcovers and are not a legal variation.

Reversals in sets of two are considered legal variations.

Rubber Stamp Imprints placed either on the front of a stock matchcover or inside are not considered a true variation.

Scored Saddle on older matchcovers is not a permissible variation, due to slight variations in matchcover manufacturing machinery.

Size changes are permissible, especially when the same design appears on a 20 stick and 30 stick matchcover.

Streaks Across the Abrasive on older matchcovers is not a permissible variation due to chemical imbalance in the striker solution.

Style of Lettering or Copy change is legal, even if only one word or phone number changes.

Texture is considered permissible, if the same design is made on a Pearltone and Filigree, for example.

Thickness of Cover Stock is not usually allowed, as this was an industry wide standard regulated by production periods and availability of materials.

Tip color changes are acceptable between serials in older matchcovers.

Width of Abrasive is all right if it measures more than 1/16" (or 1.5mm).

Wording is acceptable if in the advertising copy itself and not in the manumark. Purists do not agree with this point.

Special cases may arise that I have not covered here, and when in doubt, ask. The only silly questions are those that are not asked. Most experienced collectors will help you in determining variations.

Always send an S.A.S.E. (Self Addressed Stamped Envelope) with your request and a few quality matchcovers for their trouble.

What is a salesman's sample (flat)?

The friction flat (flats) or salesman's sample, refers to cardboard matchcover material before it becomes a matchcover. Flats were used by company salesman as samples in making commercial matchcover sales, and they are currently not considered a collectible matchcover. Flats, however, were chosen from the production line and were probably the finest example of the run.

Flats were also used in salesman's sample books to represent colors, textures, designs, union labeling, and size. Special salesman's sample books were popular when new lines were added to regular production. These special, smaller salesman's pamphlets contained friction flats and were often left with the customer for their inspection.

From the beginnings of the hobby, collectors feared that some flats might not represent real businesses, services, or products. Not that they were fakes, but they were actually dummies, *not* actual matchcovers from real businesses. In some situations, therefore, fictitious companies, products, or services could be put in the design for special sales presentations. This idea struck fear into the hearts of early collectors and early protectors of the hobby.

New collectors should respect these early trepidations and take some time to learn to identify friction flats. As no collector should ever dictate how you should set up your collection, some suggest that friction flats can be used as fill-ins until the real matchcover comes along.

As a matchcover historian, I have several thousand older flats which I use for purposes of study and reflection. Early fears prevailed that unscrupulous collectors would try to staple and crease flats, passing them off as real matchbooks. Early hobby vigilante groups insisted that all flats be destroyed regardless of their age, color or design. Collectible matchcovers must have machine creases, staple markings and a striker before any serious collector will call it a matchcover.

Today, older flats can be considered as proofs. Pristine images of the best that came off the matchcover production line, they are deemed perfectly collectible, but not permissible to pass off as matchcovers. It will take years of re-thinking the purposes of matchcover collecting before old timers concede this point. As novices in this hobby, I ask you to use your best judgment and consider the source.

How big is your collection?

Numbers have both amused and astounded collectors since man put an extra flint in his hide rucksack. "How big is your collection?" is a frequent question posed by non-collectors and novices alike as numerical advantages hold a psychological spell over the masses. Maybe it is because a bigger score than your opponent means a win. In collecting matchcovers, however, it is quality rather than quantity that counts.

It is nice to say you have 10,000 matchcovers in your collection instead of 1,000, but is there any need for a figure like 10,481? Several matchcover collectors go through the process of counting their entire collection every year. Making sure that 10,481 is correct, and not 10,487.

So, I ask you again, "How many matchcovers do you have?" With an answer of five, fifty, or one hundred and fifty thousand, non-collectors "oh and ah" profusely. No matter what I say, I can't win! Any number that can't be immediately counted is large. For collectors, it is often a basis to compare their counts against, but in the end, what does it matter?

One collector is rumored to have seven million matchcovers, but not all different. Seven million matchcovers is a stack just under 28,000 feet tall, or 5.3 miles high. That many matchcovers would fill a room 24 feet long by 24 feet wide by 24 feet tall and weigh just over 15 tons. Now *that's* enough numbers for a while—let's get down to honest-to-goodness *quality* collecting!

The only number that is important is "one" . . . your first matchcover. If you don't already have it, send a large, #10 size S.A.S.E. to The American Matchcover Collecting Club, PO Box 18481, Asheville, NC, 28814, and I will rush you a few to start your collection. There is never any charge; I just want you to enjoy this hobby.

How did matchcover collecting begin?

On July 7, 1989, I had the privilege of receiving a phone interview from Bob Oliver, who at that time, was the only known living matchcover collector who attended opening day of the 1939 New York World's Fair. Now 83 years old and living in Mira Loma, CA, he returned several times, once on Sunday, May 7, 1939, with his friend Henry Rathkamp, namesake of the first real matchcover club, The Rathkamp Matchcover Society.

Retskin: Did every pavilion have matchcovers?

Oliver: Not every pavilion or exhibit had matchcovers, but we checked them all. Most of the restaurants had matchcovers and were glad to give them to us.

Retskin: What about peripheral matchcovers, you know, those not directly affiliated with the Fair?

Oliver: Pavilion and exhibit covers were actually picked up on the Fair grounds. For the others, I scoured the city for covers with some connection to the Fair.

Retskin: What were they called?

Oliver: When a matchcover has two different categories (i.e. a hotel and a Fair cover) it's called a conjunctive.

Retskin: How were you received when you asked for matchcovers on the Fair grounds?

Oliver: We were received with open arms, everywhere. You see, this was a new thing—they never heard of matchcover collecting. After all, they had matchcovers there for the primary purpose of advertising.

Retskin: What would you ask for?

Oliver: Well, we didn't ask for what they call "a caddy" today. We just asked for some matchbooks.

Retskin: Did you ever get a caddy?

Oliver: Most matchbooks at the Fair were wrapped in cellopaks, in twos and fours, or dozens, like the Blue and Orange Set. The Blue and Orange Set were mixed, and didn't come out separately.

Retskin: So how did you get a set?

Oliver: You didn't get them all when you bought a package. You had to buy umpteen packages until you found a complete set. The Fair sets came packaged ten or twelve to a package.

Retskin: When did you get your sets?

Oliver: When the Fair first opened, I got the Silver Set by buying cellopaks.

Retskin: What about the Blue and Orange Set?

Oliver: Not when the gang went there (May 7th). I got those later.

Retskin: Do you know why they came out with the Blue and Orange Set?

Oliver: They were non-metallic and were cheaper to print, so they abolished the silver. Why they had different colors, I have no idea.

Retskin: Possibly because they were the Fair colors, Blue and Orange? How many times did you go to the Fair?

Oliver: Well, once with the group, but several times by myself and I had also been there before on opening day with Richard Powell, the writer.

Retskin: What was it like on opening day?

Oliver: On opening day it was brand new because fairs weren't common place to anyone. Six years before they had had one in Chicago, but it was new to us. A lot of frivolity prevailed, should I say. People were happy.

Retskin: What do you remember most about the Fair?

Oliver: The thing I remember most

about the Fair was that huge statue on top of the U.S.S.R. building. They made two different matchcovers from that place. Here's a funny story about that statue. A couple of years ago I read that they found that statue in the basement of a New York building, abandoned for years. It was discovered, and someone put two and two together and figured out what it was. The Russian government bought it and had it shipped back to Russia. As I remember it, it was very impressive, a very huge statue. Their ad in the 1939 Official Guide was for propaganda purposes. Remember, this fair took place just before World War II broke out; that happened just a few months later. It happened during the Rathkamp meeting on Labor Day weekend. So here we were in a neutral country, war hadn't started here yet.

Retskin: What else impressed you about the Fair?

Oliver: Well, I saw the King and Queen of England at the Fair, to publicize the British Pavilion.

Retskin: Which pavilion or exhibit impressed you the most?

Oliver: Not a pavilion, but I was quite impressed with the railroad exhibits. They had whole trains there on tracks. Like the Royal Scot, an English train that went from London up to Glasgow.

Retskin: Were you ever at the Fair at night?

Oliver: A few times. There were different color lights and large searchlights everywhere.

Retskin: What about the people— what kinds of people were there?

Oliver: I remember mostly families, as they had a large population to draw from in the New York area.

Retskin: Where did you live in New York?

Oliver: We lived on Austin Street in Forest Hills, right next to the Fair Grounds. It was a dead end street when we lived there. All of a sudden, they opened the street down to where Grand Central Parkway would be and these huge dump trucks would go by, 24 hours a day with land fill so they could fill in the dump for the Fair. When they threw the dirt into the dump, the rats came out of the dump—that's one reason we moved from Forest Hills to Jamaica.

Retskin: So your family was actually a casualty of the Fair?

Oliver: Yes, we had to move out of there. The vibrations from these trucks shook the house, night and day. It went on for months.

Retskin: How did you feel about the $ .75 Fair admission price?

Oliver: I have a mint admission ticket from the Fair. I will send you a copy. Seventy-five cents wasn't bad.

Retskin: How did the 1939 New York World's Fair help the hobby?

Oliver: It contributed a lot of nice covers to the hobby, but that's all. Clubs and collectors were around for years before. Blue Moon started in 1934, and I was president of Blue Moon.

Retskin: How about the influence of the 1933 Chicago Fair on collecting?

Oliver: Not too great, but for those who lived in the area, it was fine. For us, Chicago wasn't too easy to get to. We didn't have cars that could make that kind of a trip, and the roads. . . The Chicago Fair only had local impact.

Retskin: What about United Matchonians?

Oliver: Blue Moon and Matchonians were originally label clubs. So you see, there's really no connection.

Retskin: So what influence did either Fair have on matchcover collecting?

Oliver: Well, it was nice in that they came out with complete sets and established a new category for collectors that they didn't have before. Another interesting thing is that I never saw a Chicago Fair set until after I had been to the New York Fair and got the (New York) Silver Set. I wouldn't have even seen the Chicago set except that old Doc Wilson went there and picked some up.

Retskin: In the ad that ran in the June 1939 Matchonia—how could you sell that Lion Midget set for 30 cents? How many did you pick up at the Fair?

Oliver: Well, I went at different time and got more when I needed them. I lived 10 minutes away from the Fair so I could go any time I wanted to.

Retskin: What did they cost at the Fair?

Oliver: I think each set, the Midget and Giant set, cost about $.15 a set. I could replenish the stock any time I wanted.

Retskin: And what about outside the city?

Oliver: Well, then you had to scrounge. It was pot luck. I covered the whole city practically, with some other people.

Retskin: Just in the hotels or from the street also?

Oliver: No, the gang never did that. Oh yes, there was one, Paul Schaefer—he didn't care if the cover was used or unused. So if he saw something on the street, he'd just pick it up.

Retskin: Any other impressions or feeling about the Fair?

Oliver: I enjoyed being there with the group. It was fun for all of us. We really didn't know then what we had started, but we knew we were having a great time and getting lots of new covers. The Fair was a new concept—you had the World of Tomorrow and how things would be in the future.

Retskin: What about the scarcity of Fair covers today?

Oliver: From time to time I find singles, but the sets are very scarce. When you find a complete Silver Set, or for that matter, several Blue or Orange covers, you really have something there.

Retskin: Was Lion the official matchcover company for the Fair?

Oliver: No, they weren't, but they did a lot of advertising with the Fair logo on it. They were the only match company to advertise themselves using the Trylon and Perisphere.

Retskin: Was the collection that you gave me a complete set of the New York World's Fair covers?

Oliver: No, I can't say if it was complete— all I can say is that that's all I know of. Just like the recent article I wrote on Diamond Manumarks, a new one will probably come out of the woodwork when you print this.

Retskin: Thanks, Bob, for your help with this report.

Oliver: Well, I just hope it helped and people will enjoy reading your work.

Before the formal beginnings of the hobby, there were several hobby and matchcover publications available to the infant hobby. A 30 year old Bob Oliver published his recollections of the beginning of the hobby in an article which appeared in the June 1939, *Matchonia & Hobby Advertiser.*

The second article appeared in June 1939 issue of *The United,* Vol. III, No. 10. The front page of this publication shows a photo of six original collectors including Paul Schaefer, Henry Rathkamp, Frank Ryan, " M i d d i e " Middlebrook, Bob Lockard, and Bob Oliver. This article was written by Bob Lockard. In the following, all spelling, grammar, and punctuation have been left as both Bobs wrote them, more than 50 years ago.

(Please note that the number of individuals purported on this expedition vary from account to account.)

Article 1: The recent match cover collectors' convention in New York is now only a memory but one which will live long in the minds of all who attended it. The gathering of the clans began in Penn Station at eight in the morning on Saturday, May 6th. Even though most of them had not met before, each could recognize the other by an eager raring to go gleam in his eye! The writer was soon joined by Paul Schaefer of Egypt, PA.; Frank Ryan of Somerton, PA.; Robert Lockard of Philadelphia and Harry Rathkamp of Newport, RI. The five of us rushed right from the Brooklyn Navy Yard where we went aboard all the ships there and also obtained covers from some of the shore stations near-by. Then time out for lunch on Sands Street and some naval conjunctive covers.

Mid-afternoon found us bound for

Jamaica, L.I., and the swappingist time it has ever been my pleasure to witness. All rolled up their sleeves and got right into the thick of it and every one added plenty to his collection. After dinner, we were joined by Messrs. Cherinsky and Middlebrook and the trading began anew and lasted far into the night. We finally broke it up at 2 a.m. in order to rest a bit before going to the World's Fair the next day. However, rumor has it that friend Schaefer got up an hour ahead of the rest of us and carefully scanned the streets of Jamaica for covers and did not do so badly either!

Then off to the Fair at ten and the hunting began in earnest. We had the good fortune to locate three different official Fair sets by Lion—one of four midgets, one of four regular size covers and the other consisting of four giants. Several of the later were autographed by all and mailed to other collectors. A number of Fair conjunctives were found too and will doubtless find their way to the albums of many of you readers. It is a fact that all of us saw more of the sidewalks and streets than we did of the exhibits and 'tis well known that "the Carpetbagger" did very nicely for himself and went away with the bag filled! The boys finally had to tear themselves away in order to catch their trains and boats but decided to hold another meeting perhaps late this summer. So, all interested in this will kindly get in touch with the writer.

Several collectors wrote their regrets. Ted Shumon sent his by air mail from Chicago and we also had word from Bill Eisenhart, Art Rogers, Harvey Flood,

Tom Jackman, Max Rosenberg and Roscoe Yorgey. The pass word for the convention was "Youse Crahooks"!

On page ten of that issue, Bob took out two classified ads, one relating to 1939 New York World's Fair matchcovers:

"NEW YORK WORLD'S FAIR match covers for sale." Two complete sets by Lion, consisting of 4 midgets and 4 regular size—both for 30 cents. Giants (when in stock) at 20c each. Fair conjunctives, 5c each. Service covers at a nickel each. Bob Oliver, 84-38 Charlecote Ridge, Jamaica, L.I.

Article 2: Was It Worth It? At the instigation of Bob Oliver, seven booklet match cover collectors met in what is believed to be the First concerted get-together, ever attempted in the hobby. At 8 a.m., May 6th, Bob Oliver, Henry Rathkamp, Frank Ryan, Paul Shaefer and your correspondent met at the Penna. R.R. Station in New York City and started on a general match cover collecting tour by visiting the Brooklyn Navy Yard where new covers were secured for the U.S.S. Ships Seattle, Ellet, Somers and Warrington, and a promise of a supply of covers from the Dunlap.

Then a visit through Navy Village for conjunctives and, prey tell, what is a Naval collection worth without a cover from the Oval Bar or Leo's Bar both located in the world famous Sans Street, and what is a naval Conjunctive worth without the autograph of "Irene" the Navy's girl friend.

Then to Bob's home in Jamaica where there took place the swappingest time ever staged. If there is any doubt as to this statement "yust awsk Louie." In the evening "Middie" Middlebrook and Cherinsky joined the party and the trading and bartering started anew. And what a host and hostess, this Mr. and Mrs. Oliver are, and we must also include Mrs. Pomeroy, Mrs. Oliver's mother, and the youngest of them all, little Joyce.

To bed at 2 a.m. and up again at 8 a.m., Sunday morning. Now I'm wrong as a certain party arose at seven and with his trusty carpet bag, walked about five miles through the streets of Jamaica- -the early bird after the worms?—No, my friend, after the good old World's Fair conjunctives dropped the night before.

Then to the Fair at ten and the hunt started anew. There we found four new Giants, a set of four midgets, and a set of four regular size covers, all by Lion. Several conjunctives were purchased, borrowed or just stolen. Let it be said in passing that at least one collector may not be able to tell you much about any exhibit higher than his knees, but it is a definite fact that he missed nothing below his knees and the carpet bag was full.

In the evening the boys started to wend their tired but happy way homeward, but before doing so arrived at the conclusion that it should not be an end but the beginning of a series of conventions and while no place was definitely decided upon, invitations were offered for the next one to be held in either Philadelphia or Newport some time this coming fall. It may seem far off but I'm sure we would all welcome suggestions as to location from you, my reader, and it is hoped that

wherever and whenever the next convention is held, many more collectors will be present with us. Please try won't you? At least your suggestion will be appreciated.

Ted Shuman sent his regrets by air mail, but wished the convention a success. Bill Eisenhart, Tom Jackman, and Harvey Flood, and the Yorgey's (Roscoe and Helen) also sent their regrets for not being able to be present, and their kind comments were certainly appreciated, and it can be said we drank a toast (or many of them) to their presence in spirit.

Surely you can now answer the question, "Was it worth it?"

How do I join a matchcover club?

At last count, there were approximately 30 local matchcover collecting clubs in the United States and Canada. Most of them are located in metropolitan areas, but through their publications all are accessible from anywhere.

Officers and addresses change regularly, so please allow this book to act as a clearing house for information about matchcover clubs. Write to me and include a large #10 size S.A.S.E. for information about any matchcover collecting clubs in your area.

In the traditional manner, most clubs have a board of officers, a constitution and bylaws, and they conduct regular meetings. Most publish a regular newsletter and, when finances permit, hold an annual swapfest for their local members.

It is especially important to choose your club affiliation carefully, and for the

95% of the nation's matchcover collectors who do not live near a local club, choose your membership by evaluating its newsletter or bulletin.

Most clubs invite general memberships as long as you have a minimal interest in the hobby. One club offers a club store in which they sell collecting supplies such as pages and albums. Another club specializes in hotel and motel matchcovers. Still another features a pictorial catalogue of the famous girlie sets and singles beginning in the late 1930s. If you decide to stick with matchcover collecting you might want to sample a few clubs to see how you like them.

Matchcover newsletters are published for two distinct collecting tastes. First, you have the social newsletter. It is usually filled with local, newsy comments and stories, less related to matchcover collecting than to the social environment of the local stalwarts who fortify the meetings and do most of the work. Who died, who moved to a different town, birthdays, anniversaries, parties, vacation talk, who's in the hospital . . . the list goes on.

This kind of newsletter is an important link among friends and collectors in different towns. The social newsletter, however, is usually lacking in hobby content and is frequently devoid of any new matchcover information. Unfortunately, most of the local clubs produce this kind of publication.

The second kind of matchcover newsletter is what I call a true hobby newsletter. Although not truant in social detail, its editor is aware of his or her responsibilities of informing the membership about the hobby. Information about the current match industry or historical events relating to matchcover collecting

are featured. Editors of this type of hobby newsletter work diligently for their membership and it is well worth joining such a club just for its publication.

This book is sponsored by one of the finest clubs in the country, **The American Matchcover Collecting Club.** *The Front Striker Bulletin,* published by the author of this book, is such a publication. Conceived and dedicated to the hobby and the match industry in August 1986, *The Front Striker Bulletin* delights in a membership base of over 650 serious collectors internationally.

The purpose of *The Front Striker Bulletin* is to publish information for serious matchcover collectors, abrogating some of the time consuming formalities of officers, a constitution and bylaws. The AMCC is governed by a board of advisors and an editor.

What about the newsletter?

Let's take for example any local club. The XYZ Matchbook Club maintains a club roster of say, 100 members. It has approximately 25 local members who regularly attend meetings and other club functions, and another 75 members around the country who just receive its newsletter.

The job of editor, therefore, is probably the most important single responsibility that a club member can have. The editor is responsible for writing, editing, and collecting matchcover information. Frequently, he performs layout functions and liaison operations with the printer, spending long evenings stuffing and addressing envelopes. After the stamps are licked, he mails the newsletter and then sits and waits for comments and letters from the membership.

Every club editor has a similar responsibility to his club. Too many editors complain that they do not get any help from the membership. "Send articles and information about collecting in your area," is their plea. Recommendations, reminders, and suggestions are repeatedly sent to members, but, for most part, club editors receive little fulfillment.

Start your own matchcover club?

Great idea! Glad you thought of it!

There are no restrictions about starting your own club. You should get a separate checking account, and, as a non-profit organization, you can apply for a state non-profit number. In many cities, banks will not charge a service fee for a non-profit organization.

A good place to start is at your local library. In order to minimize start-up expense, ask your local library if you can use a community meeting room for your club function. Plan on a Saturday meeting of about two hours and secure a date from your library coordinator. After all, you are a non-profit community organization, interested in the public welfare.

The only restriction that a library could place on club meetings is that your activities must be open to the public, and, after all, what better way to attract new collectors? You should leave the meeting room clean and follow the eating and smoking rules of your library.

Next, place a small ad in the personal column of a local or city newspaper nearby. The ad might say: "Matchcover

Collecting! A great way to meet new friends. Men and women, boys and girls. Come on down to your local library this Saturday at 2:30 P.M.—bring your matches!!"

Go to local schools, recreation centers, the court house, and supermarkets and ask them if you can put up a notice. Restaurants and some businesses in your area may allow a small 8 1/2" X 11" flyer in their window. Send the flyer to your local radio station, and ask them to announce your meeting during their community service segment. If this is the first matchcover club in your community, you may get invited to talk to a radio personality on the air about your activities.

Another way to attract attention to your club and hobby is to make up a display of your favorite matchcovers. Put your name and phone number at the bottom of the display and try to put it in a prominent place, like a bank lobby or a restaurant waiting room. People will be attracted by your ingenuity and the novel idea of a matchcover club.

Get to the library early on the appointed day. With their permission, place a few signs around the library so that people will know where you are meeting. If you are a beginner and don't have a collection, turn your meeting into a round table discussion. Go around the room and ask everyone who they are, if they are a collector, and if they have ever held a club office before. You will be amazed at the responses.

At this point, your job may be finished. As coordinator of this effort, you may be elected president so be prepared for more work. Once your officers are established, contact your local Chamber of Commerce for information about running meetings and advertising your club through their services. If you decide to have a formal meeting agenda, a Sergeant-at-Arms and a copy of Robert's Rules of Order will come in handy. If you want to make it an informal, social kind of meeting, then forget about Robert's Rules and just have fun.

What about dues? How much should you charge? Of course, no one can tell you what to charge, but most local clubs charge between $4 and $10 yearly for membership and their newsletter. The dues should reflect on the kinds of services offered by the club. One local club boasts the lowest dues in the hobby, and puts out a social one-page newsletter that never changes. In contrast is a nationally known West Coast club that puts out a monthly newsletter packed with matchcover information and some social news.

To cover printing and mailing costs for a quarterly newsletter, I suggest a starting yearly dues fee of $3 to $4. If you have money left over, you might want to subsidize your annual Christmas meeting dinner or buy a club matchcover.

You mean we can have our own club matchcover? Sure you can! Besides sales of regular orders of matchcovers for business, special occasions, hobby clubs, etc., **The American Matchcover Collecting Club** offers a service to print a case of matchcovers for any new member or start-up club at a discount. A case of matches (2,500 books for the 20 stick size or 2,000 books for the 30 stick size) costs less than you think and is a great way to advertise your club. Send a large #10 S.A.S.E. to **The American Matchcover Collecting Club** for full details

and prices.

Be sure to get everyone's name, address, and phone number for your mailing list. Start with a simple, one page newsletter. Play up the great time you are having at your meetings. Make others interested in your events. Talk it up and carry on like there is nothing better then a matchcover meeting among friends.

Plan matchcover outings. Get a group of collectors together and drive to another part of town. Walk up and down the streets going into every restaurant, hotel, bank, etc. asking for matchcovers. Gather as many as you can and divide them among your club at the end of the day.

As your club grows, you may want to venture out to a local restaurant and include dinner with one of your meetings. Christmas is a great time to have a big fall gathering. Plan some special events, like a raffle, an auction, a grab bag, or special games.

Investigate this route carefully and always be aware of your budget. In metropolitan areas, hotel meeting rooms can be very expensive even if you promise them 25 or so paid dinners. In less populated areas, hotel managers may be very willing to throw in a few extras in order to attract new faces to their facilities. When in doubt, contact local fraternal organizations and ask them how they arrange for dinner meetings.

One final note. The American Matchcover Collecting Club maintains a database of over 6,000 matchcover collectors nationwide. Our demographic survey is free (for a large #10 S.A.S.E. of course) to new start-up clubs. Send me the ZIP code range for your area, and I will let you know of any collectors from your town that I have on my listing. Some might be advanced collectors and can assist with the organization of your club or help you find quality matches.

Starting a matchcover club can be fun and filled with rewards. Ask questions and be careful not to bite off more than you can chew. Matchcover collecting is a very friendly and fun-for-the-whole-family hobby.

Who are matchcover collectors?

A mid-1980 survey of local club members tried to discover a composite of the average matchcover collector. Of course, this composite doesn't fit anyone exactly and may fit no one you know who collects matchcovers, but it is the most recent survey taken and I would like to tell you about it here.

We aim at..... PLEASING YOU ---- and hope we hit the mark !

The results are as follows: The average matchcover collector is an American white male, 51 years old, whose favorite category is Hotels/Motels, and who has been collecting for an average of 12 years.

He has approximately 30,000 matchcovers in his collection, belongs to seven local matchcover clubs, and trades with at least 28 other collectors.

Before selling your collection or jumping to any rash conclusions as far as the matchcover hobby is concerned, male collectors outnumbered female collectors by about three to one.

Why is this so? Is there something about matchcovers which are more attractive to males? The study shows no apparent answer for this question. Longevity statistics would suggest that females should dominate this figure, but that wasn't the case.

Ages ranged from 12 years old to 90 years old, with the average at 51 years old. A quick eyeball survey of any matchcover collecting function (Christmas party, swapfest, convention, etc.) will show that a majority of collectors are older. Could the aggregate of the hobby disappear with the passing of one generation? Probably not. Surely, the hobby will continue, even after this generation relinquishes its collections to the next fold of young collectors, but in what numbers?

One theory debating this apparent generation problem indicates that matchcover collecting is a time-consuming hobby, and that only older individuals, who have raised their children and finished their careers, have the time to devote to collecting. If, in fact, this assumption is correct, then there should be a steady flow of new collectors ready to garner and persevere the hobby.

For many, category selections come from life experiences. The average enthusiast collects in at least 16 different categories. In order of importance were the categories of : hotels and motels, girlies, small towns, Holiday Inns, restaurants, banks, old matchcovers, and Chinese restaurants.

The first two categories mentioned are shoo-ins. There are more hotel and motel matchcovers than in any other collectible category, and they are relatively easy to obtain. The second choice should be obvious. Over the years, categories have grown in popularity and then faded. In recent years, both older matchcovers and military matchcovers have enjoyed a resurgence in collecting popularity.

"Experience is the best teacher", said one worldly philosopher. Collecting longevity averaged about 11.6 years, with beginners admitting to less than one year in the hobby while some boasted to more than 50. Most surveyed said five years.

The average size of a collection was approximately 30,000 matchcovers, ranging from under 1,000 to over 1,000,000. It is an accepted fact that volume isn't everything and frequently can be misleading. For example, a general collection of 100,000 matchcovers might render a comparatively poor selection, possibly being laden with nationals, easy matchcovers, or struck matchcovers. However, a Holiday Inn collection of 22,000 different matchcovers might prove to be an outstanding endowment.

Some collectors only belong to their local club, not bothering with other local clubs or the national society. A majority, however, belonged to several clubs ranging from 2 to 24 members, with seven being the average.

The survey goes on to indicate that in recent years, trading has become a tenuous area. Collectors surveyed say that they trade with an average of 28 people yearly, although this is considered to be an inflated figure. Serious trading and casual inclusion of a few matchcovers in a friendly letter are not the same. Active traders tend to return the survey, lending further suspicion to its accuracy. At least 50% who responded trade with less than five traders or none at all.

Not surprisingly, a whopping 42% identified their biggest gripe with the hobby as having to do with trading. Nine percent lamented the "non-participation" of members, so the 42% figure may represent the same complaint.

Complaints lodged against trading centered mainly in two areas: (1) the unwillingness of others to respond to requests for trades, and (2) the limited quality of matchcovers received. The hobby has been struggling with this problem for years. Recently, however, inroads have been forged, and the future of trading looks better than ever.

In addition, the survey provided the following. Lists were used by about 65% which helped collectors in two important ways. (1) Lists enabled the collector to keep track of collection needs and (2) assisted them in requesting future trades. The constant influx of unwanted material can therefore be eliminated through the creation of an active "want list."

More than 88% of those surveyed said they buy matchcovers from time to time. Approximately 68% sell matchcovers as well. This is of particular interest because there is a current controversy raging in the hobby over the commercial selling of matchcovers. Commercial sales have been small but very active since the mid-1930s, but still people ask, "Is it ruining the hobby?"

New collectors tend to use purchases as a method of quickly building quality collections and trading stock. Casual selling by collectors is one method of recouping expenses. A few collectors sell professionally and the non-collector dealer has been around for a while.

Regarding displays, the survey indicated that participation is low among local club members. Reflecting a national norm, over 60% would rather watch than participate. Constructing and preparing displays take time and effort but can be rewarding when complete. Some complain that it takes time away from collecting. Display contests enjoyed by a few will always afford members the opportunity to show off favorite matchcovers and receive deserved recognition from peers.

Whether you happen to fit the norm or not, this hobby is what you make of it. Tailor it to your specific needs, and don't let it get the best of you. It should afford you endless hours of pleasure and satisfaction. There is ample room for individual likes and dislikes, peculiarities and idiosyncrasies. Matchcover collectors are a breed unto themselves. That's what makes this hobby so rich and fascinating!

HINTS FOR NEW COLLECTORS

Airline Collectors:

Airline matchcover collectors may be puzzled when trying to identify the airline or country on the matchcover. What is LAN, or LOT, or KLM? Venture out to a local travel agency and ask for an outdated copy of their monthly "OAG" book. It's a thick book with many airline schedules, and it has a page that identifies every airline by its three letter code. On that page you will discover that LAN is a Chilean airline, LOT is a Polish one, and KLM is a Dutch airline.

The American airline industry has recently banned smoking. It is likely that you will find that the airlines have cut back on matches. Ask friends who travel abroad to save matches for you.

Auctions:

Matchcovers don't regularly come up at general auctions. When they do, be sure to inspect them first. Odor, brittleness, and wear has a lot to do with the value of a collection. This is a very tricky way to purchase matchcovers.

If you have the opportunity to participate in a matchcover auction, try to sit next to an old-timer. Keep your eyes wide open and make notes for later discussion.

Prior to the start of most live matchcover auctions, there is a viewing period when you can look over the lots. The usual rules of most general auctions apply to matchcover auctions. In general, auction bids are made by hand or facial movements. If you are not bidding, it is best to sit very still. Don't make eye contact with the auctioneer unless you are bidding on a lot.

Boxes (flattening and collecting):

Boxes can be prepared for collecting in a number of ways. Boxes can be mounted by opening the glued seam on one edge with an Xacto knife and laying them flat. Some use the "scrunch" method. Even if you want to keep the box and tray intact, it is usually best to discard the match sticks.

Boxes can be mailed a number of ways; scrunch the box flat after the tray has been removed. Press the box flat, the same as you would a matchcover. Some collectors display boxes in their original shape, with or without the tray. Although bulky for transporting, this method shows the box in its original form. An opened, flattened box (a Universal American Ace or the Diamond Pocketbox) will fit in the album pages made for 30 strike matchcovers. Many foreign boxes will not fit existing matchcover album pages so you will be forced to cut your own slits on a blank page or use photo corners.

Categories & Types:

Matchcover collecting categories are as numerous as people's interests. If you enjoy airlines, or semi-clad pin-up models, or crocodiles, those are *your* categories.

Cover types are not the same as categories. Type means the kind of matchcover and most types are designated by the manufacturers. Universal used to make many types, such as Cameos, Jewels, Jewelites, Matchoramas, Matchtones, etc. Lion Match Co. was famous for Giants, Midgets, Contours, and Features.

So if you have a group of matchcovers with lobsters on them, some might be Uniglos, some Features, and some just regulars. When collectors tell you that they collect Sheratons, patriotic, blacks, Jewels, Filigrees, and Features, they mean that the first three are categories and the last three are types.

Combos:

Combo collecting is popular in many hobbies and can relate to any group of collectibles. Matchcovers are just one of them. Any time you find a matchcover or matchbox, along with a related item (e.g. napkin, swizzle stick, writing stationery, sugar pack, ball point pen, postcard, etc.) you have a combo. Combos are usually mounted together and relate to a central theme (e.g. hotels, banks, etc.).

Conjunctives:

Conjunctive matchcovers are those which contain advertising of two or more advertisers, such as the old airline matchcovers that had Chiclets ads on the back. Another example is a matchcover from Kuwait Airlines with Kent cigarettes advertised on the back. The inside of many European hotel matchcovers have airline ads which often go undetected.

Not strictly a conjunctive, matchcovers can fit into several categories at the same time. For example, if you had a Jewelite matchcover with a real color photo, advertising the U.S. Marines, and it had a filigreed surface, the matchcover is a Jewelite, a Matchorama, a Service and a filigree! The manufacturer's logo inside could read Jewelite, or Matchorama, or nothing at all.

Courtesy Among Collectors

The matchcover collecting hobby has some generally accepted courtesies that most collectors try to practice. These courtesies are not difficult, and are mostly common sense.

Whenever you write to a fellow collector, send along a nice matchcover or two. When trading by mail, try to adhere to your trader's collecting preferences. Lists are frequently exchanged and trading stays in the designated areas. If you can't trade within your trader's category, say so and try to make up for it in a later trade.

With regular traders, find out what kind of matchcovers they will accept if their primary choices are unavailable. Determine if they want matchcovers with minor variations, such as manumarks or striker color and size.

The phrase "quality matchcovers" means Cameos, foilites, Jewels, Jewelites, Matchoramas, and other preferred types. These are distinguished from run of the mill matches such as Willie's Bar or Miss Kitty's Saloon.

Crystal Mounts:

These are plastic sleeves made for stamp collectors, but are also great for protecting matchcovers. There's one size that fits our 20 strikes perfectly.

Custom Matchbooks:

If you are having matchbooks made up for a wedding, bar mitzvah, meeting, convention, swapfest, or whatever, take the time to print up an oversize sketch of exactly what you want. The hobby has a few collector/salesmen who will help you. The American Matchcover Collecting Club is one such organization, offering discounts to members on custom matchbooks.

If you venture to a local advertising specialty business, make sure the salesman's order says "per sketch attached." Keep a copy of your sketch, proofread the final product, and if a mistake is encountered, don't hesitate to insist on a new order.

Displays:

Matchcover and match box displays are attractive in the home, office, or meeting hall. Matchcover conventions, swapfests, and local meetings often offer prizes for creative displays.

Plan convention display sizes carefully. If you fly to meetings or conventions, build your display so that it fits into your largest piece of luggage, or can be folded to do so. Cover it with clear plastic or something to protect it from careless accidents.

In your home, display matchcovers under glass, on a coffee table or on a lamp shade. Crafty collectors like to decorate purses, briefcases or other carrying cases with matchcovers.

Matchboxes can be displayed several different ways. You can open the glued seam, flatten the box and display it as you would a matchcover. You may leave the box intact and mount it on a board, with or without the match tray.

Displays are also used for promoting the hobby. Make up a colorful, eye-catching display, and place it in a bank or library lobby. Show your name and phone number so interested folks can call for more information. Newspapers are often interested in doing feature articles about collectors. You'll get inquiries and matchcovers.

Experienced Collectors:

As a beginner, you might ask yourself, "Should I contact an established collector who lives nearby and ask to see their collection?" Most collectors will be glad to show you their matchcovers. The best way to learn is to ask questions and see as many matchcovers as you can. Trading, club meetings and conventions are also suggested.

Flattening Matchcovers:

Flattening takes pressure, applied by squeezing or by weight. Cut some pieces of 1/4" plywood or particle board to the same size as 20 strikes and Jewel matchcovers. Furring strips can also be used, cut to 5" sections. Sand lightly to remove sharp edges and splinters. Next, assemble between 50 to 75 stripped matchcovers, all the same size. (The 5" furring strip works well for 20 strike and 30 strike matchcovers.) Alternate them (front and back) and stack them striker-up, striker-down. (First one, striker up, face up; lay the next matchcover on top of it, striker down, face down.) Stack them neatly and square the corners. Make a sandwich with two pieces of plywood and wrap three heavy rubber bands around both ends and the middle. Be sure the rubber bands don't crimp the edges of the matchcovers. Standard C clamps can also used; however, don't make them too tight, especially with older matchcovers. When flattening newer matchcovers, set them aside for a day or two. Older matchcovers may take up to two weeks to flatten.

Don't moisten matchcovers or treat them in any way.

One word of caution. Older matchcovers are made of un-coated stock and may have picked up moisture over the years. The strikers are also less stable and may stick to the neighboring matchcover if the C clamp is too tight. Experiment with a few matchcovers first.

Foreign Matchcovers:

Foreign matchcovers can be confusing unless you are a linguist. For example, most Swiss matchcovers are printed in German, but the manufacturer's logo says "Zurich" and that's your clue. Belgian matchcovers are usually printed in French, but the manufacturer's logo says "Bruxelles." You'll have to decide whether to categorize your foreign matchcovers by advertisement or by where they are made. There are matchbooks that have matchcovers printed in England, matchsticks made in Japan—and they advertise an Israeli Hotel! Place them in what categories you want, but be consistent so you can find them again.

Full Books vs. Matchcovers:

Almost from the start, you have to make a decision as to which will be your main method of collecting . . . matchcovers or full books. There are pros and cons to each. Most of us collect the empty matchcovers.

Matchcovers are easily sorted, stored, traded, mailed, boxed, and handled. Full books are more difficult to store and must be carefully packaged when shipping. Matchcovers display well and the entire outside can be seen with one glance both in the hand and in a display.

Full books are the original example of what the customer ordered and the manufacturer produced. Some purists insist on perfect examples for their collections. They display the form and size of the

original matchbook. For example, demonstrating the difference between tall pre-1939 Federal Match Co. matches and post-1940 Federals is best seen with full books.

The disavantages of full books—there is the exaggerated fire hazard, the bulk in storage, and extra weight in shipping.

One caveat, however, must be kept in mind. The attraction for Lion Features is the stick design, and no matchcover collector would ever intentionally strip a Feature . . . hopefully, at least not after reading this book.

Another thing to keep in mind is that some matchcovers were never distributed as full books. The only existing case was stripped and distributed through the hobby as a flattened matchcover. No matchcover collector will refuse full books, and no full book collector should turn down flattened matchcovers.

Gathering Matchcovers:

The question is often asked, "How do I find matchcovers to collect?"

Matchbooks are advertising, and they do no good sitting in the merchant's storeroom. If you don't see matchbooks in restaurants, hotels, banks, etc., ask for them. Ask for a box of matchbooks. Nothing ventured, nothing gained. Remind the manager that you are helping him advertise his business by spreading them around your area.

If you hear of a firm going out of business or changing its name or location, offer to take all of their matchbooks off their hands.

Pay attention to big events coming up that might result in matchbooks or matchboxes. Many banks, for example, distribute a special Christmas matchbook in early December. Town celebrations might yield a special matchcover or box. Business promotions such as anniversaries use matchbooks to help celebrate.

Other suggestions for places to get matchbooks are hotels, restaurants, bars, banks, realtors, hair salons, newspapers, funeral homes, radio and TV stations, supermarkets (of course you have to buy them in a supermarket) and other local businesses. You can always buy a stockpile from an estate or buy cases of overruns from a matchbook manufacturer.

Enlist relatives who travel to gather matches for you. Teach them to ask for a whole box of matches. Remember, the worst that can happen is a shopkeeper will say "No!." Practice your sales pitch on a buddy and have him critique your approach.

Write to an out-of-town business for their matchbook, but send along an SASE (a self addressed stamped envelope). It is wise to send a sample of an empty, flattened matchcover to show them how to send theirs back. Mention that if they prefer not to remove the matches, they can wrap the matchbook in a piece of aluminum foil.

When requesting a whole box, send a caddy mailer and enough postage, but remember to call it a box, not a caddy. A caddy mailer is a foil-lined carton, just big enough for a standard box of matches.

Lists:

A number of matchcover clubs and some specialty collectors produce numbered lists of known matchcovers in specific categories. They include Jewels, Jewelites, sports Jewelites, American Ace boxes, etc. Anyone can make up a list, but it's useless if it's not properly updated. Lists can be a big help if you want to collect all the known Jewelites, or

whatever.

Lists are not manufacturer approved, therefore there is no assurance that they are complete and accurate. Most lists can be purchased for a copying charge and postage. Once you have a list, you can make your wants known by sending a selection of numbers to traders, instead of describing each matchcover in detail.

Mailing:

A copy of all USPS mailing regulations can be obtained from your local postmaster at no charge. Ask for Section 124.

The USPS has a surcharge for First Class letters that are over one quarter inch thick, weighing one ounce or less. If you exceed this weight, the surcharge doesn't apply.

Enclosing 20 or so regular 20 strike size matchcovers in a letter will make it too thick to avoid the surcharge, so try the following: Make two stacks of ten matchcovers and wrap each with a strip of paper. Tape the two together (side by side) and place in an envelope. They fit neatly and your letter is now less than one quarter inch thick.

Use the less expensive Third Class rate when sending a sizable quantity of matchcovers. You can also place a letter in a Third Class package.

Match boxes are a little more difficult to mail. If you mash a box flat and place it in an envelope, it has a tendency to upright itself and jam the cancellation machines. Try this. First, open the glued seam of the box, using a sharp, curve bladed Xacto knife. Then press the box flat. It will be the same size as a 30 strike matchcover.

Manumarks vs. Logos:

The word "manumark" is a hobby term only. It is the copy printed at the bottom fold of the matchbook. The manufacturer doesn't call it a manumark, but a footline. Sometimes the manumark (footline) is the name of the ad agency instead of the manufacturer.

A logo is the trademark symbol of a firm. Matchbook manu-facturers place their logo inside, near the staple. Logos and trademarks such as Giant, Owname, Colgate, Uniglo, etc., are copyrighted. A Lion Match Co. Feature is truly a Feature, but a similar-looking matchbook made by another manufacturer can't be called a Feature.

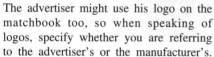

The advertiser might use his logo on the matchbook too, so when speaking of logos, specify whether you are referring to the advertiser's or the manufacturer's.

Money:

A question frequently asked by new collectors is: "If I write to a collector for a matchcover, and he is not a regular trader, should I send money, an SASE, matchcovers—or what"? Send some matchcovers or an SASE, or both, but do not send money. If you don't know what that person collects, choose a special matchcover like a Jewel, Cameo, foilite, etc. Never send a national or a "ma & pa" diner type—you may not get an answer.

Mounting:

The question often comes up, "How should I mount my matchcovers?" In years past, slotted paper pages were the rage. They came in 20 strike, 30 strike, 40 strike and uncut (make your own size cut). They are still sold today.

Within the last 10 years, however, plastic page manufacturers have seen an increase in demand for matchcover pages and several types are on the market. Some have opaque centers so only one side of the matchcover shows. Others are true clear plastic pages, so interesting insides can also be viewed.

For more information on suppliers, contact **AMCC**. Please include an SASE.

Mounting 10-Strikes:

Ten strike match-cover pages can be purchased commercially. Another way to mount 10 strikes is to insert two 10 strike matchcovers into the slots normally used for a 20 strike match-cover. You can also cut a diagonal slit at the top and bottom of the page, where the 10 strike matchcovers come together; then insert one matchcover corner into the top slit and the other match-cover corner into the bottom slit.

Sewing plastic pages is another way to custom design 10 strike pages or any size pages.

Mounting Odd-Sized Matchcovers:

If you are using paper pages, use an Xacto knife to cut slots for odd-sized and odd-shaped matchcovers. Enlarge an existing slot if possible. Often, older matchcovers are wrapped in cellophane so that their corners won't be separated by the slots.

Mounting for Displays:

First, flatten the matchcovers. Glue will work, but decreases the value of the matchcovers and is not recommended. Some collectors use transparent photo corners which can be purchased in camera stores. Stamp hinges also work, but use two per matchcover so they won't turn in the display. Purists won't trade or buy matchcovers with any glue or markings on the back, so keep this in mind when making up any display. Cover your display with clear plastic to protect it against damage or loss.

When is a Matchcover "Different?"

There are no published rules concerning this subject and no solid body of opinion among serious collectors. If an advertiser releases a matchcover that is totally different from an earlier one, there is no doubt that it is a new matchcover. But what if it's not *completely* different?

Perhaps a minor color change or new phone number has been added. Is this considered a new matchcover? Sure it is, because you can see that there has been some change. At what point, then, does this change not count as a new matchcover?

As in other hobbies, the line forms and the opinions split. Purists on the one side and the "what-the-heck" people on the other.

When an advertiser orders a matchbook for his business, he doesn't specify the size or color of the striker. He could care less what the manumark says, he is only interested in his advertisement. When repeat orders are made, the manufacturer may not use the same size or color striker, but is bound to keep the integrity of the message.

It should also be remembered that repeat orders may be made on different machinery or in another plant, adding another variation factor.

Repeat orders frequently have small differences, such as size and color of the striker or manumark wording. The purists say, "Hey, that's a new matchcover, because there's no period after the "Co" in Diamond Match Co. on the manumark!",

or some such small difference.

Most serious collectors will say the matchcover is different if that difference is noticeable without microscopic examination. Technically, the purists are correct, but there is a difference between having fun and working at having fun. Most matchcover collectors are not impressed by a collection which addresses several pages of the same basic matchcover showing microscopic differences in each.

What about using Computers?

The answer to this question is simple. Which would you rather spend more time with . . . your matchcover collection or your computer? Some collectors count their collections yearly. Others don't feel comfortable unless they list every matchcover in their collection on paper. Why? If you are answering the call of the obsessive perfectionist within, there's no better way to give vent to this urge than with matchcovers. However, if you want to have fun with your hobby, forget the computer.

Old Matchcovers:

Old, as applied to matchcovers, is a relative term and highly subjective. It is regularly misused by antique and collectibles dealers, and can be your cue to keep your guard up.

How do you tell an old matchcover? A WWII matchcover might be old to a relatively novice collector, but to a venerable senior, it's a "yesterday" matchcover! Beat up and grubby doesn't automatically mean "old," but there are clues.

When applied to U.S. manufactured matchbooks, rear strikers are fairly new, and front strikers are usually pre-1975.

The nature and quality of the printing is also a clue. Most old matchbooks had a somber gray inside. Today's matchcovers have slick insides and are made from coated, polished white stock. Be careful, as there are new matchcovers that are being made from "recycled" paper, and are dark brown, thus appearing older. Old matchbooks were great for setting the points on your car as they were nearly all sixteen one-thousandths of an inch thick. Today's matchcovers are much thinner, making matchcover point-setting obsolete.

A rusty staple can also be a clue to age. Look for matchcover information, such as phone numbers with named prefixes; the absence of ZIP codes or the use of ZONE numbers; price changes—and hotels advertising rooms for $2.50 *must* be old! Today, you will rarely find prices on hotel or restaurant matchcovers. Things change too quickly.

Covers advertising doctors or dentists are also older, as today's professional ethics forbid such advertising.

Be careful of recent matchcovers that attempt to look old, such as the "Vote For Calvin Coolidge" matchcover produced by an East coast nightclub. Play detective and ask yourself, "Could this matchcover have been made thirty or forty years ago?"

Stripping Matchcovers:

The preferred tool is a small pair of needle-nose pliers with a narrow channel or groove at the tip to catch the staple. Grip the staple back with the pliers and pull gently, twisting the pliers half a turn. If the staple has become part of the striker, as with many older Diamond Match Co. matchbooks, first carefully unbend the ends of the staple from the opposite side.

Even wiggling these ends until they snap off sometimes helps. Turn the matchbook over and grip the staple back with the groove of the pliers. The staple will come out much easier.

If no pliers are available, however, a tool-less method can be used. Insert the thumbs between the two combs of match sticks, prying them apart as if opening a book. The staple pulls through the back of the matchcover and the rear match row. This method only works with newer matchbooks and should be avoided with older matchbooks.

One occasion to be very fire conscious is when you are stripping matchcovers. Put cigarettes away. Keep a glass of water near by. Don't toss unwanted matchcovers into the same wastebasket with discarded sticks. The odds are very much against it, but strikers can rub against a match and then.... Bag and close discarded match stems before putting them into the garbage. They may be thrown out along with your weekly garbage pick-up.

Rubber Bands:

Rubber bands can be your best friend and your worst nightmare. First, never use heavy rubber bands on an open stack of matchcovers or matchbooks. Any crimping made by the rubber bands will lower the collectible value and beauty of the matchcovers.

If you are storing matchcovers for a long period of time, don't use rubber bands. Rubber bands will deteriorate and will often stick to the top and bottom matchcovers. One good idea is to cut matchcover size cardboard pieces to layer the top and bottom of each rubber banded package of matchcovers.

Sets & Series:

A set is two or more related matchcovers made and issued at the same time. True sets exhibit different scenes, themes, or pictures. The same copy or scene on various color stocks is called a color set.

Manufacturers used to have stock sets of four or more different matchcovers depicting safety rules, girlies, hillbillies, wildlife, etc. These matchcovers had blank fronts used for imprinting. There are non-advertising sets and some collectors have personal sets made yearly for conventions and swapfests. Some foreign countries are known for their matchbook sets, but they, too, are becoming scarce. A relatively common example of a set is The Antique Pistols Set, which can be gathered by opening two or three supermarket caddies (if you're lucky).

A series is made and issued over a period of time. One good example is the gold Cameo Apollo matchcovers, a series commemorating the Apollo missions.

Shopping Lists:

A list of tools for the hobby might be helpful. In alphabetical order they include: adhesive tape (single and double sided), album pages, aluminum foil, art board (colored), art eraser, blank preference cards, C Clamps (2"), calendar (monthly planning), cardboard cartons, club dues dates, desk lamp, draftsman's compass, duct tape, Elmer's glue, envelopes, file folders, fire extinguisher, furniture scratch remover, letter opener, lighter fluid, magic marker, magnifying glass, masking tape, metal can with lid, mounting corners (photo), needle-nose pliers, paper clips, plastic drawers (in racks), plastic wrap, plywood strips, pocket calculator, postage stamps, postal rate schedules (domestic and international), postal scale, postcards, protractor, push pins, return address labels, rubber bands, ruler, or cellophane, scissors, shoe boxes, stamp hinges, Stanley razor blade knife, stapler, stationery, strapping tape, telephone index, three ring binders, tweezers, white out, Xacto knives.

Covers and albums are the basic ingredients, but there are other helpful items. Get a set of Xacto knives at your local hardware store or hobby shop. These will be helpful in extending slits in album pages to accommodate oversize matchcovers, and are also used for parting slits to insert matchcovers.

A small postal scale is helpful in avoiding overweight letters when answering trades. It also helps to get the most number of matchcovers into a one-ounce letter.

A magnifying glass can be helpful. Try one of those binocular—like glasses that strap around the head made by OptiVisor or some other company. This will leave both hands free to work. Several rubber stamps: First Class, Photographs Do Not Bend, and a name stamp. Using the word "Matchcovers" on your return address stamp may mislead postal workers into thinking there are full matchbooks inside.

Sorting for Trades:

Here is just one of several methods of controlling the "In & Out" flow of matchcovers and trades. When a trade comes in, leave the matchcovers in the envelope until you are ready to reply. That way, you don't have to remember who sent what—the trader's name is still on the envelope.

The matchcovers then go into a holding box labeled TO BE SORTED. When the box is nearly full or whenever you feel like it, sort the matchcovers into separate piles. Major divisions might include; FOR ME and FOR OTHERS. The former should fit into your categories and will be checked against your collection at a later time.

The latter goes to others, either because you don't collect the category or already have it. They may be further subdivided into CATEGORIES and PEOPLE. Using a plastic nuts & screws chest of drawers, each trader has his or her own drawer, along with numerous category drawers. The trader's categories are cross referenced on index cards. Several of these plastic chests can give you a lot of room for sorting.

Mail and trades can then be answered quickly and efficiently. Regular trader's matchcovers are easily found and sent with your regular trades. General collectors usually get an assortment picked at random. For traders who collect several categories, select one or two of their preferred categories, and try to choose some other categories the next time.

Stock vs. Non-Stock:

In stock car races the cars are right off the shelf, while at Indy and at Grand Prix races, cars are non-stock, and specially made. So it is with matchbooks.

For example, Holiday Inn prints thousands of standard, stock matchcovers. Each individual Inn has its own name imprinted inside, but the parent company controls the outside design. Some Holiday Inns spend extra money and have special, non-stock matchcovers made with name and locale on the outside.

Super Market Sets:

Every supermarket sells boxes (caddies) of matchbooks. Some have nice drawings on them. It can take several caddies to assemble a complete set. Single supermarket matchcovers are also collected, so don't cast them aside. The difference between a set and a series isn't always apparent.

Supermarket sets "break" well or not so well. Sometimes, looking through ten caddies won't complete your set. If this happens, ask your traders for help.

Things not to do:

You know not to chew garlic before swapping kisses, but here's a few hobby No-No's which might come in handy. (1) Don't send used or bobtailed matchcovers in trade, unless you have previously arranged to do so. (2) National advertising matchcovers are never desirable trades. Get permission first. (3) Carefully weigh all outgoing trades. Recipients shouldn't have to pay postage due. Invest in an inexpensive postal scale. (4) Never ask for a "caddy" of matches (a manufacturers term which means nothing to a merchant). Instead, ask for a box of matchbooks. (5) Don't be bashful about asking collectors for their opinion or advice—it's free, and you are free to ignore it.

Trading:

Not all matchcover collectors trade. Some don't like to trade, others can't trade, and some may already have enough traders. If you want to trade, decide on what you want and what you can offer. Determine how many traders you can handle, a few regular traders or many slower ones. Prepare a shotgun form letter stating your wants and enclose a few nice matchcovers. Be sure to say that the matchcovers are a gift and not an unsolicited trade. Your gift will also show that you know how to flatten matchcovers.

State how frequently you would like trades and in what quantity. If you have a preference, regional club membership rosters normally list collector's categories. Ask prospective traders to pass on your request to others. Don't hold your breath waiting for 100% replies, because a shotgun doesn't down a duck with every pellet.

Once traders are established, don't be surprised if some send trades without a note. Others scribble something on the back of a grocery slip and a few write a fine letter to accompany their offering.

Used Matchcovers:

Someone once asked "Why do we collect only unused matchcovers?" Probably because our founders were neat, orderly guys who felt that a shiny new Rolls Royce was better than a dented, grubby one. Of course, there is no rule that says you can't collect used matchcovers; some collectors do. Just be sure to define your wants when you start trading with them.

With older matchcovers, it is sometimes impossible to find a mint specimen. The practical collector keeps a used matchcover until a mint condition specimen is found. This is called upgrading and practiced by most collectors. Collect whatever you want. and don't be influenced by those who collect what they are told to collect.

Value of Matchcovers:

What is a matchcover usually worth? Everything has a value of course, but a glass of water in the desert is worth far more than one at a kitchen faucet. Worth, therefore, is relative.

To a millionaire who wants your matchcover badly enough, it may be worth $100, but to an average guy, maybe only a buck. If you go to a flea market and see a bushel of matchbooks, try not to pay more than 1 cent apiece even if you find some great matchcovers among them. Most of them are likely to be junk, and it is difficult to determine that at a flea market. Flea market peddlers have little or no idea as to the real value of matchbooks, and they invariably ask inflated prices because they assume that OLD means valuable. Old doesn't mean valuable, it means old, especially with matchbooks. Bargain and haggle, if that's your style. A matchbook is worth whatever a willing buyer will pay.

FUR STORAGE and Repairing

VIP & Personalities:

This subject can be confusing for the beginner and there are different interpretations. VIP literally stands for Very Important Person and a VIP matchcover is one having the person's name and no advertising. Therefore, a governor's matchcover, or the President's matchcover, or Dolly Parton's matchcover, is a VIP.

A personality matchcover uses the name of a well-known person: Gene Autrey's Hotel, Pete Rose's Restaurant. A matchcover from Governor Ronald Reagan of California is a VIP; a matchcover reading Vote for Ronald Reagan for President is a Political, but one from President Ronald Reagan is, again, a VIP.

DRAW TRADE TO YOUR PLACE OF BUSINESS

This selling plan may be employed to advantage in many ways.

A merchant operating a general store, for example, might offer a discount of $1.00 on a purchase of $10.00, or more, in return for a $3.00 trade card, fully punched out. This often influences his customer to do all his trading at his store in order to get his card punched out. Then he is induced to make the purchase of $10.00 or more at the same store to get the discount. Thus the storekeeper will have stretched a sale of 50c, or so, up to $12.00, or more.

Others might offer a reward of some kind in the way of money or merchandise for having one of these tickets punched out. And this plan is an effective trade builder, too. In lines where competition is keen it often persuades a customer to trade at the one place exclusively to get these rewards. After he has won a reward or two his dealing with the one place of business is likely to become a habit . . . particularly if quality, price and service are right.

Return this cover, fully punched out and have your suit pressed FREE at—

KENWOOD CLEANERS
438 E. 47th Street

CUT NO. 956   Punches out $5.00

Above "ad" suggested for Cleaners

When fully punched out turn in this cover for a FREE grease job at—

HAYNES' GARAGE
First Ave. & Highway 66

CUT NO. 957   Punches out $10.00

Above copy shows use by Filling Stations

A REAL TRADE STIMULATOR

"Punch Ticket" advertising is a real trade stimulator.

In some lines it makes advertising book matches do double duty at the same low cost. Just like regular advertising book matches, each book tells your story TWENTY TIMES. And it REPEATS that message every time the customer lifts the cover and presents it for a "punch-out."

Above all, it encourages that exclusive trading habit that every storekeeper desires so much and which pays so well in volume sales and profits.

WE DO NOT SELL PUNCHES

Many merchants already have punches which they use in their business. Those who do not have them can obtain them at practically any hardware or stationery store. A good one can be secured at very small cost.

We do not sell punches.

Page 212

(above) Page 212 from an early 1960s Matchcover Salesman's Sample Book.

Matchcover Price Guide

Airlines

Airlines—Any matchcover with an airline or air services related advertisement to include meals, airports, lessons, cargo handling, etc. There are about 3,000 airline matchcovers and boxes known from about 500 companies such as Pan-Am who printed sets. The most difficult group to find is the 118 matchcovers from the 1940s Chiclets Peppermint Candy Coated Gum Company, used as conjunctives with several airlines. Another popular set is the 1977 Pan-Am New Zealand Movie Set.

Airlines

1C,20S,FS A.C. Co., At Your Service, Greater Pittsburgh Airport, shows terminal (B) MN/WE 6.50

1FB,30S,FS Air West (F/B) (BE/GN) 5.00

4C,40S,FS Artcraft Engineering Mfg. Co. Old Airplanes, 2 photos on each 8.00

5C,40S,FS Artcraft Engineering Mfg. Co., (B/W) photos of two jets or Bombers on Ea ... 5.00

5C,40S,FS Artcraft Engineering Mfg. Co., show Air Force planes on F & B 5.00

1C,20S,FS,FL Al Green Enterprises Inc, Friendship Int'l airport, MD, plane (F) (DGN/LGN) 5.50

5C,40S,FS Set from Artcraft Eng. Mfg.,Co., photo (F/B) of jet planes 12.50

5C,40S,FS Artcraft Engineering Set #1 [1953] Charles Lindbergh..-First Commercial Mail Plane-First Transcontinental Airplane Trip-Kitty Hawk-Will Rogers 10.00

5C,40S,FS Artcraft Engineering Set #2, Type 1 [1955] no dots either side of manumark, Convair Sea Dart-Douglas F4D Skyray-North American F 86 Sabre Jet-North American F 100 Super Sabre-Northrop.. .... 5.50

5C,40S,FS Artcraft Engineering Set #2, Type 2 [ ] 2 dots either side of manumark, Convair Sea Dart-Douglas F4D Skyray-North American F 86 Sabre Jet-North American F 100 Super Sabre-Northrop.. .... 8.00

30C,20S,FS Australian Airlines Issues, assorted 4.00

1C,20S,FS Berz Flying Service, Berz Airport, Birmingham, Mich (RD/WE) 3.25

6C,20S,BS BOAC Airlines, British Flag (B) 6.00

6C,20S,FS Great Britain, Africa-Asia-Australia-The Caribbean-Europe-North America, Type 1, long covers, (RD) BOAC (B) 6.00

6C,20S,FS Great Britain, Africa-Asia-Australia-The Caribbean-Europe-North America, Type 2, short covers, (RD) BOAC (B) 2.00

6C,20S,FS Great Britain, Africa-Asia-Australia-The Caribbean-Europe-USA/Canada, Type 3, [1956] (BE) BOAC (B) 10.00

6C,20S,FS Great Britain, Africa-Asia-Australia-Europe-South America-USA/Canada, Type 4, small flag (B) 1.00

6C,20S,BS Great Britain, Africa-Asia-Australia-Europe-South America-USA/Canada, Type 5 .... 2.00

2FB,20S,FS BOAC, part of Fly BOAC set, large letter BOAC (DBE/BK/YW/WE) (B) from Asia and U.S.A./Canada 1.75

2FB,20S,FS BOAC, part of BOAC set, small letter BOAC (DBE/BK/YW/WE) (B) from Australia and Asia 2.25

6FB,20S,BS BOAC, all printed sticks, set or part of including USA/Canada, Europe, Africa, Australia, Caribbean, and Asia, BK border, British flag (B) country design (F) 2.50

8C,30S CP Air Set, 1-Boeing Jet 737, colorful 5.25

20C,20S,FS Braniff Air Set [1964], (S) says Enjoy Braniff, Bogota-Buenos Aires-Chicago-Chile-Colorado-Dallas-Houston-Kansas City-Lima-Mexico (2 covers)-Minnesota-Montevideo-New York-Oklahoma-Panama-Rio de Janeiro-San Antonio-Sao Paulo-Washington . 10.00

12C,30S,FS Braniff Air Set, Type 1 [   ] For a rare adventure.., Bogota-Buenos Aires-Chicago-Dallas-Lima-Los Angeles-Miami-New York-Panama City-Rio de Janeiro-Sao Paulo-Washington 7.50

12C,30S,FS Braniff Air Set, Type 2 [1963] (BN) striker, World's Fastest Jetliner, Bogota-Buenos Aires-Chicago-Dallas-Lima-Los Angeles-Miami-New York-Panama City-Rio de Janeiro-Sao Paulo-Washington 7.50

12C,30S,FS Braniff Air Set, Type 3 [1963] (GY) striker, World's Fastest Jetliner, Bogota-Buenos Aires-Chicago-Dallas-Lima-Los Angeles-Miami-New York-Panama City-Rio de Janeiro-Sao Paulo-Washington 7.50

12C,30S,FS Braniff Air Set, Type 4 [1963] (BN) striker, World's Finest Jetliner, Bogota-Buenos Aires-Chicago-Dallas-Lima-Los Angeles-Miami-New York-Panama City-Rio de Janeiro-Sao Paulo-Washington 7.50

12C,30S,FS Braniff Air Set, Type 5 [1963] (GY) striker, World's Finest Jetliner, Bogota-Buenos Aires-Chicago-Dallas-Lima-Los Angeles-Miami-New York-Panama City-Rio de Janeiro-Sao Paulo-Washington 7.50

7C,20S,BS Braniff Air Color Set, Type 1 [1966] has Atlas circle (I) at bottom, (BK/BE/GN/OE/PK/WE/YW) 3.00

7C,20S,BS Braniff Air Color Set, Type 2 [1966] doesn't have Atlas circle (I) at bottom, (BK/BE/GN/OE/PK/WE/YW) 3.00

1B British Airways (F), Benson & Hedges (B) manumark British made (RD/WE/BE) .. 2.25

9B CAAC Airlines 22.00

4C,30S,FS Canadian Pacific Air, Canada-Japan-Mexico-Rome/London, Type 1 [   ] Eddy Match Ltd. 3.00

4C,30S,FS Canadian Pacific Air, Canada-Japan-Mexico-Rome/London, Type 2 [   ] Vista-Lite 3.00

4C,30S,FS Canadian Pacific Air, Canada-Japan-Mexico-Rome/Amsterdam, Type 1 [   ] Eddy Match Ltd. 3.00

4C,30S,FS Canadian Pacific Air, Canada-Japan-Mexico-Rome/Amsterdam, Type 2 [   ] Vista-Lite 3.00

4C,30S,FS Canadian Pacific Air, Grant-Mann, SM35 to SM38, Hawaii-Rome-Vancouver-Japan, Type 1 [   ] large wording at bottom (I) 3.00

4C,30S,FS Canadian Pacific Air, Grant-Mann, SM35 to SM38, Hawaii-Rome-Vancouver-Japan, Type 2 [   ] small wording at bottom (I) 3.00

1C,20S,FS Capital Airlines, VIP Flights, (PE/WE) 5.00

1FB,24S Caravelle, Air France Boeing Jet Intercontinental, plane (F/B), Regie Francaise 3.25

1C,20S,FS,FL Chicago and Southern Air Lines, The Route to the Dixieliners (GN/YW) .. 7.50

72C,20S,FS Chiclets Gum w/Airline Advertising 70.00

1C,30S,BS Delta Airlines 50th Year, 1929-1979 .... 5.00

1FB,40S,RF The Douglas DC-6, plane (F) 2.75

1FB,20S,FS East African Airways, African shield (F), animals (B), printed sticks w/E. A. Airways 4.00

1B Eastern (SR/BE), metallic (F), Made in Sweden 3.00

12C,30S,FS El Al Set, Type 1 [1966], Universal Match Corp., New York, Acre-Ashkelon-Beersheba-Eilat-Haifa-Jaffa-Jerusalem-Nazareth-Safad-Tel Aviv-Tiberias-Zichron Yaacov 12.50

12C,30S,FS El Al Set, Type 2, Universal Match Corp., New York, Acre-Ashkelon-Beersheba-Eilat-Haifa-Jaffa-Jerusalem- Nazareth-Safad-Tel Aviv-Tiberias-Zichron Yaacov 13.00

12C,30S,BS El Al Set, Type 3, Superior Match, Acre-Ashkelon-Beersheba-Eilat-Haifa-Jaffa-Jerusalem- Nazareth-Safad-Tel Aviv-Tiberias-Zichron Yaacov 12.00

10C,30S,BS Finnair [   ], set........ 13.00

6C,20S,FS Grumman Aircraft [1944], Avenger TBF 1-Goose JRF 6B-Hellcat F6F 1-J2F-Widgeon J4F 1-Wildcat F4F 4.......... 15.00

1FB,30S,FS Lufthansa (wooden sticks) plane (B), logo (F), (DBE/YW/WE)............... 5.00

1C,20S,FS Mt. McKinley Airways, Inc, Anchorage - Seattle............ 6.00

1C,30S,BS National Airlines w/Face & Sun on B 1.00

1FB,20S,FS The Star (F), National Airlines, New York, Washington, Florida, Cuba (B) (DBE/WE)............... 5.00

1FB,30S,FS O'Hare Flight Kitchens, Inc, jet (F), (BK/GD)............. 2.25

1FB,30S,BS Ozark Air Lines (F), Ozark flies your way (B), satin finish,(RD/BE/WE) ... 2.25

14C,30S,FS PAA Set [1955], (I) Alaska-Australia-Canada-Europe-Hawaii-New Zealand-Philippines-South Africa-South America-The Mainland-The Orient-USA................. 7.00

15C,30S,FS Pan American on one line above striker Australia-Bangkok-England-Fiji-France-Hawaii-Hong Kong-Japan-Mexico-New Zealand-Philippines-Rangoon-Saigon-Singapore-South America, Type 1 [1956], 35,000 Pacific Crossings............ 8.00

15C,30S,FS Pan American on one line above striker Australia-Bangkok-England-Fiji-France-Hawaii-Hong Kong-Japan-Mexico-New Zealand-Philippines-Rangoon-Saigon-Singapore-South America, Type 2 [1956], Sleeperette Service 8.00

11C,20S,FS [1957], Pan Am Set, Argentina-Brazil-Central America-Colombia-Cuba-Mexico-Panama-Puerto Rico-Uruguay-Venezuela-West Indies........... 5.00

15C,30S,FS Pan American on 2 lines above striker Australia-Bangkok-England-Fiji-France-Hawaii-Hong Kong-Japan-Mexico-New Zealand-ThePhilippines-Rangoon-Saigon-Singapore-South America, Type 1 [1957], 40,000 Pacific Crossings 7.50

15C,30S,FS Pan American on 2 lines above striker Australia-Bangkok-England-Fiji-France-Hawaii-Hong Kong-Japan-Mexico-New Zealand-The Philippines-Rangoon-Saigon-Singapore-South America, Type 2 [1957], At Your Service 7.50

15C,30S,FS Pan American on 2 lines above striker Australia-Bangkok-England-Fiji-France-Hawaii-Hong Kong-Japan-Mexico-New Zealand-The Philippines-Rangoon-Saigon-Singapore-South America, Type 3 [1957], 1957-58 Calendar............ 7.50

15C,30S,FS Pan American on 2 lines above striker Australia-Bangkok-England-Fiji-France-Hawaii-Hong Kong-Japan-Mexico-New Zealand-The Philippines-Rangoon-Saigon-Singapore-South America, Type 4 [1957], 1958 Calendar 7.50

12C,30S,BS Pan Am Set, True Color by Lion Match, Brazil-Caribbean-England-France-Germany-Hawaii-Hong Kong-India-Italy-Japan-New York-Thailand............ 6.00

12C,30S,BS [1968], Pan Am Set, Diamond Color, Argentina-Australia-Brazil-Caribbean-France-India-Ireland-Japan-Samoa-Spain-USA (Pan Am Building)-USA (San Francisco) 6.00

1C Atlas Match, Pan Am 747 POP-UP, 747 complete (I), color photo of plane interior (F/B), ca. 1969 .... 22.50

11C,20S,FS Pan-Am Set, Argentina-Brazil-Central America-Colombia-Cuba-Mexico-Panama-Puerto Rico-Uruguay-Venezuela-West Indies Type 1 [1954], Pan American World Airways (B) 5.00

11C,20S,FS Pan-Am Set, Argentina-Brazil-Central America-Colombia-Cuba-Mexico-Panama-Puerto Rico-Uruguay-Venezuela-West Indies Type 2 [1957], Pan American and globe (B) 5.00

1FB,30S,FS Pan Am makes the going great.(F), Karachi, Dacca, Kawalpindi, Lahore (B) (WE/PK/BE) Pakistan manumark 5.00

1FB,20S,BS Pan Am International Flag Service w/logo (F), colorful rectangle design (B) 2.00

50C,20S,FS Pan Am Movies Set [1976] 90.00

12C,30S,FS Pan Am Set, Sleeperette Service, Australia-Europe-Hawaii-Hong Kong-Japan-New Zealand-Philippines-South America-Thailand-The Mainland-The Orient-USA, Type 1, Sleeperette 5.00

12C,30S,FS Pan Am Set, Sleeperette Service, Australia-Europe-Hawaii-Hong Kong-Japan-New Zealand-Philippines-South America-Thailand-The Mainland-The Orient-USA, Type 2, Sleeperette Service 5.00
1FB,30S,FS Pan Am, (SR/BE), Wish you were here. Tell Them. Phone w/Bell logo (I) 2.75
17C,30S,JWL Piedmont Set (minus Baltimore), Matchoramas, 17 different cities 9.25
14C,JWL,BS Piedmont Airlines, [1984], Boston-Chicago-Dallas-Dayton-Denver-Houston-Miami-New Orleans-New York-North Carolina-Orlando-Tampa-Washington, D.C. 4.50
18C,JWL,BS Piedmont Airlines, [1986], reservation number (I), Baltimore-Boston-Chicago-Dallas-Dayton-Denver-Hilton Head-Houston-Los Angeles-Miami-New Orleans-New York-North Carolina-Orlando-San Francisco-Tampa-Virginia-Washington, D.C. 8.50
10C,30S,BS,RAMA Piedmont Airlines, [   ], Boston-Charlotte-Dallas-Denver-Houston-Miami-Orlando-Philadelphia-Pittsburgh-Tampa 6.00
1C,20S,FS Piper, Wings for All America, colorful plains (B/F) 4.00
1FB,30S,FS Piper (F), Anderson Aviation Co., Inc. (B), (BK/GD, Piper ad (I) 4.00
6B Qantas Set [1963] 3.00
8B Qantas Set [1966] 4.00
9B Qantas Air [1967], w/birds, Australia-Europe-Great Britain-Japan-Mexico-New Zealand-Pacific Islands-South Africa-U.S.A. 28.00
12C,20S,FS Fly Safely Set [   ], Any plane..-Before take off..-Be sure..-Check and..-Don't start..-Don't take..-Judge your..-Remember that..-The safest..- Taxi slowly..-There is..-You need.. .... 3.00
1B SAS Scandinavian Airline (BE/WE) Made in Sweden by the Swedish Match Co. 2.75
1C,20S,FS Showalter Flying Service, Orlando, FL, Go Air Taxi 5.50
1B Swissair by Svenska Tandsticks AB, shows plane (LBE/WE/BK) (B) 2.00
1FB,30S,FS Tallmantz Aviation, Inc (F), Movieland of the Air Aircraft Museum (B), (BK/WE/RD)BE) 4.50
1FB,30S,FS TCA Trans-Canada Air Lines plane flying at night (F), Maple Leaf logo w/ plane (B) 4.00
1FB,10S,BS TWA, repetitive (RD/WE) design 2.00
6C,20S,FS TWA Set, Type 1 [1953], hostess in (BE) uniform, Chicago-Italy-London-Los Angeles-New York-Paris 3.50
6C,20S,FS TWA Set, Type 2, hostess in (GN) uniform, Chicago-Italy-London-Los Angeles-New York-Paris 2.75
1C,BS TWA 747 Popup, Made in Japan Pipo 1969 (WE) 15.00
1FB,24S UTA, Union De Transports Aeriens, Regie Francaise (PE/GN/WE) stylized route map (F/B), made in France 6.50
1FB,40S United Air Lines (B), The Chef's Gourmet Flights (F), triangular (RD) pattern (F/B) 4.50
1FB,40S,BS United Red Carpet Service, The DaCostos (F),(RD/WE/BE) 5.00
1FB,30S,FS Universal Machine Co, Fenton, MI, Jet Plane (F/B) 2.00
1FB,40S,FS Wien Consolidated Airline, jet (F), map (B), Alaska's First Airline Flying America's Newest Jet (S) 8.00
1FB,10S Western Airlines (RD/WE/BK) logo (F/B) 5.00
10C,MS,BS Airlines, assorted 8.00
10C,FS Airlines (mostly older), assorted 14.00
15C,MZ,MS Airlines, planes on most 22.50
11C,20S History of Aviation, pic & desc of older planes, partial sets 3.00

Americana

Americana—Sets and singles showing scenes from American history, mostly drawn.

4C,20S,BS Atlantis #1 Americana Stock Design [1981] 1.00

10C,20S,FS American Bridges Set [1961], Bayonne-Carquinez-Eads-Fort Pitt-Hell Gate-Mackinac-Minneapolis St. Paul..-San Francisco..-6th,7th..-Tappan Zee 10.00

5C,20S,FS Chicago #1 Americana Stock Design Set [1949] Carefree Days-Dangerous Situation-The Muskallonge-Thoroughbreds-Watch It, Gramp 1.50

6C,20S,FS American Scene Set #2, Type 1 [1966], D.D. Bean, (WE) paper, Shurfine, The Deep South-The Great Northwest-The Great Southwest-Jupiter Light-The Mississippi-'Stand Rock' 3.00

6C,20S,FS American Scene Set #2, Type 2 [   ], D.D. Bean, (GY) paper, Shurfine, The Deep South-The Great Northwest-The Great Southwest-Jupiter Light-The Mississippi-'Stand Rock' 3.00

6C,20S,FS American Scene Set #2, Type 3 [   ], D.D. Bean, (GY) paper, White Villa, The Deep South-The Great Northwest-The Great Southwest-Jupiter Light-The Mississippi-'Stand Rock' 3.00

6C,20S,FS American Scene Set #2, Type 4 [   ], Central Retailers, (WE) paper, Shurfine, , The Deep South-The Great Northwest-The Great Southwest-Jupiter Light-The Mississippi-'Stand Rock' 3.00

5C,20S,FS Superior #1 Americana Stock Design Set #1 [1941], For Safety Sake-Fresh Scent-Peaceful Valley-Sock It Gramp-Sporting Chance 1.50

5C,20S,FS Superior #2 Americana Stock Design Set [1942], Protect Our Children-Three Champions-Touchdown-When Action Counts-Winter Moonlight 1.50

5C,20S,FS Superior #3 Americana Stock Design Set [1943], The Alarm-Faith-Forward America-Leaders of the Air-Watch 'Er Fly Gramp 1.50

5C,20S,FS Superior #4 Americana Stock Design Set [1944], Catch 'Em Gramp-Defense of America-Our Heritage-Three's A Crowd-Vicious Outlaw 1.50

5C,20S,FS Superior #5 Americana Stock Design Set [1945], Happy Reunion-He'll Land It-Let Freedom Ring-Moonlit Peace-Watchful Waiting 1.50

5C,20S,FS Superior #6 Americana Stock Design Set [1946], Autumn Glory-Old Glory Is Born-On The Wing-Partners-Symphony In White 1.50

5C,20S,FS Superior #7 Americana Stock Design Set [1947], Buddies-Contentment-Knee Deep In Sport-Old Mill Stream-A Winter Sunday Eve 1.50

5C,20S,FS Superior #8 Americana Stock Design Set [1947], Fisherman's Luck-Happy And Carefree-A Hunter's Dream-A Pair of Winners-Winter Wonderland 1.50

5C,20S,FS Superior #9 Americana Stock Design Set [1948], All Pals-Fisherman's Paradise-On The Rise-Snow Covered Lane-What A Mess 1.50

8C,20S,FS Superior #10 Americana Stock Design Set [1950], Casey At The Bat-Cornered-Heart Breakers-Hooked!-Hunting Pals-The Old Salt-Surprise Visit-Wild Horse Canyon .. 1.50

8C,20S,FS Superior #11 Americana Stock Design Set [1951], A 'Reel' Fighter!-Curious Kittens!-Defenders of America!-Does It Still Hurt?-On The Defense!-Rear Action!-Safety Zone-Who's Fooling Who? 1.50

8C,20S,FS Superior #12 Americana Stock Design Set [1952], Buddies-The Expert-Happy Hunting!-Hip, Hip, Hooray!-Sad Parting-Sweet Adeline!-What A Life!-Yankee Clipper 1.50

8C,20S,FS Superior #13 Americana Stock Design Set [1953], Boxer-Double Trouble-The Future Champ-Great Dane-I'll Be Waiting-Shepherd-Terrier-When Seconds Count 1.50

5C,20S,FS Superior #14 Americana Stock Design Set [1955], The Day's Catch!-A Dog's Best Friend!-Excess Baggage!-Let's Get Going!-Nothing to It, Fellers! 2.00

5C,20S,FS Superior #15 Americana Stock Design Set [1957], Caught Speeding-Future Buddies-Hunting Pals-Take Your Choice-Thoroughbreds 2.50

5C,20S,FS Superior #16 Americana Stock Design Set [1959], Boxer & Cocker Spaniel-But Who Will Pitch?-French Poodle & Collie-Leap for Freedom-Unexpected Company 2.50

5C,20S,FS Superior Americana Stock Design Set [1966], Capitol-Iwo Jima-Liberty Bell-Lincoln-Washington 2.00

5C,20S,FS Superior Americana Stock Design Set [1967], Casey at the Bat-Double Trouble-Excess Baggage-The Old Salt-Rear Action 2.50
5C,20S,FS Superior Americana Stock Design Set [1973], Astronaut on Moon-Flag & Liberty Bell-Iwo Jima Memorial-Mt. Rushmore-Rocket lifting off 2.00
4C,20S,FS Superior Americana Stock Design Set [1974], Flag & Men-Flag & Statue-Liberty Bell-The Spirit of '76' 2.00
4C,20S,BS Superior, Americana Stock Design Set, Cadillac 1906-Reo 1906-Stearns 1910-Simplex 1912 Type 1 [1975], stock 1.00
17C,20S Americana Set, All 1 Color (YW) 3.00
5C,20S,FS Match Corp. Set #1 [1950], Cup Race-Indian Summer-Nature's Majesty-Nature's Paradise-Road To Home 1.00

Banks and Financial Institutions

Banks and Financial Institutions—Sets and singles which feature banks, savings & loans, credit unions or other financial institutions, not to include, however, title & trust companies. There are over 130,000 matchcovers known, alphabetically within city and state. Many older bank covers show interest rate tables. Banks were famous for Christmas matchcovers; however, most bank matchcovers are relatively dull in appearance.

8C,30S,BS,RAMA Albuquerque National Bank Set 2.50
1FB,CLK American Security Bank, Uncle Sam (F/B) 3.00
7C,30S Set of First National Bank in Eastern Arkansas 2.00
50C,30S,BS Credit Unions 3.00
100C,20S,FS Credit Unions 6.00
200C,20S/30S,MS Credit Unions 11.00
250C,30S,MS Credit Unions 13.00
50C,20S,FS Oklahoma Banks, assorted 4.00
8C,30S Columbia Savings & Loan Set 2.00
100FB,20S,FS Banks and Savings & Loan Institutions, assorted 22.00
25C,20S,FS Banks, Savings & Loans, and Credit Unions 6.25
8C,30S,BS 1st of Windsor, Universal set, same (F), different (I), cute bank messages . 5.00
35C,40S,BS Banking and Loan related financial institutions, assorted 18.00
50C,20S,FS Banks, different cities 10.00
500C,MZ,MS Banks, different cities 22.00
40C,30S,MS Matchoramas, Banks & S/L 8.00

Beer

Beer—One of the most popular categories, especially among beer can and brewery memorabilia collectors. Advertisements mention beer, ale, beer products, breweries or prohibition related issues (very rare). Beer brand name matchcovers are traditionally colorful and most mention the brewery and town. Restaurants often mention a primary beer sold within and these are also considered in the category. Stock beer matchcovers are numerous, in which a colorful beer logo appears on the back and the restaurant, tavern, or bar is mentioned on the front.

1C,20S,FS Alt Heidelberg Beer, Columbia Breweries, Tacoma, USA 4.50
1C,20S,FS Ambassador Beer, Newark, NJ 4.00
1C,20S,FS Atlantic Ale and Beer, 10 cents (BK,YW) 2.75
1C,20S,FS Atlantic Ale and Beer, 'Full of Good Cheer' 4.50
1C,20S,DQ Atlas Special Certificate Brew, Atlas Brewing Co, Chicago 12.00
1C,20S,FS Baltimore American Beer, American Brewery, Inc., Baltimore, MD 9.00
1C,20S,FS Blackhawk Topping Beer, Indian (F/B) (RD/YW) 3.75
1FB,20S,FS Blatz Beer, ad: Howie's Tap, Markesan, Wisconsin (WE/BN/RD) 4.00
1C,20S,FS Blatz Old Heidelberg Beer, ad: Thiede's Tap Room, Fond Du Lac, Wis (OE) 3.00
1C,20S,FS Breidt's Half & Half Beer/Ale, Elizabeth, NJ 4 .... 3.00
1C,20S,FS Bub's Beer, Peter Bub Brewery, Winona, Minn (RD/WE) 5.00
1C,20S,FS Buckeye Beer, bottle (B), waiter (F) (GN,RD,WE) 1.00
1C,20S,FS Budweiser, King of Bottled Beer, logo (B), sweet beer test (F) 2.00
1C,20S,FS Budweiser Beer, ad: C & A Tavern, Carlinville, Ill, phone 637L (BK) 3.25
1C,20S,FS Burgermeister Pale Beer, Burgermeister Ale (BE) 1.25
1C,20S,FL Burkhardt's Beer & Ale, large lettering (YW) 1.50
14C,40S,FS Anheuser-Busch, w/Horses & wagon (F), colorful, stock 7.00
1C,20S,FS Bushkill Ale and Beer, Bushkill Products Co, Easton, PA 3.00
1C,20S,FS Cadillac Beer, Cadillac Brewing Co, Detroit, MI, Universal Tall 12.50
1C,20S,FS,FL Capitol Beer, Pride of Missouri, dome in center 3.00
1C,20S,FS Carling Black Label Beer, can & bottle (B), label (F) 2.00
1C,20S,FS Carling's Black Label Beer (B), Taste of the Nation (F) 1.75
1C,20S,FS Carling's Red Cap Ale, Cleveland, O 4.00
1C,20S,FL Chester Pilsner Beer & Ale, Quaker pouring beer (RD/BK) 5.25
1C,20S,FS Consumers Ale, plant drawing (B), Consumers Brewing Co., Hillsgrove, RI . 4.75
1C,20S,FS Coors, Adolph Coors Company, Golden Colorado 3.00
4C,20S,BS (RD) Coors, (SR) Coors, Old Style, F.X. Matt Brewery Tour 6.00
6C,30S,BS Coors Set [   ] 3.00
1C,20S,FS Country Club Beer, ad: Farnam Liquor House, stock 3.00
1C,20S,FS Dixie 45 Beer, long neck bottle (B) 3.75
1C,20S,FS Dubuque Star Beer, Dubuque Star Brewing Company 4.00
1C,20S,FS Effinger Beer, ad: Tim's Tavern, Ithaca, Wis (F) 3.75
1C,20S,FS Ekhardt and Becker Beer, 'Ask for Steinie Beer' (S) 6.00
1FB,20S,FS Falstaff, Cavalier (F), long neck bottle w/glass (B) 5.00
1C,20S,FS Falstaff, Falstaff Brewing Corp., St. Louis, MO (S), shield logo w/lion (F/B) 2.50
1C,20S,FS Flock's Pale Lager, Dial 9171 Williamsport, PA 5.00

1C,20S,FS Fort Pitt Brewing Co., Pittsburgh, PA 4.00
1C,20S,FS,FL Genesee Horse Ale, photo of 12 Horse team & beer wagon, ad: Stow-A-Way, Stow, NY 13.50
1FB,20S,FS Gettelman Beer, w/Curt & Vi's Dutch Mill Tap, Milwaukee 12, Wisc ad (F), stock 8.00
1C,20S,FS,FL Golden Glow Beer, FL of bottle (GD) 3.00
1C,20S,FS Golden State Beer & Ale, man (B), elaborate crest (F) 1.25
1C,20S,FS Grain Belt Beers, Minneapolis 3.00
1C,20S,FS Drink Grand Prize Lager Beer, Aged for Months, Always Dependable (S) ... 3.00
1C,20S,FS Grand Prize Lager Beer, Texas Largest Seller 3.50
1C,20S,FS Grand Prize Lager Beer, bottle & glass (B) 2.25
1C,20S,FS Griesedieck Bros Premium Light Lagar Beer, St. Louis, MO (RD/BE) 12.00
1C,20S,FS Hamm's Beer, blonde w/glass (B), ad: Saliman Bros., Denver, Colo 6.25
1C,20S,FS Hamm's Beer, Theo. Hamm Brewing Co., St. Paul, Minn - San Francisco, Calif., stock 1.25
1FB,20S,FS Hamm's Beer, show bear rolling log (F/B) (BE/WE/RD) 3.00
1C,20S,FS Hanley's Peerless Ale, Bull Dog, Providence, R.I. (WE) 10.00
1C,20S,FS Hanley's Ale, bull dog (B) (RD) 8.75
1FB,20S,FS Heileman's Old Style Lager, shield (B), Cavalier (F), copyright 1947 .... 6.00
1C,20S,DQ The Hofbrau Rotisserie and Beer Garden, Boston Mass. 3.75
1C,20S,FS Huber Premium Beer, Jos. Huber Brewing Co., Monroe, Wis. 2.50
1C,20S,FS Hull's Beer, The Hull Brewing Co., New Haven, Conn 4.00
1C,20S.FS Jolly Scot Ale, Robert H Graupner, Harrisburg, PA., w/Scot (F) (RD/WE) ... 3.75
1C,20S,FS Kuebler Beer & Ale Porter, Easton, Penn 4.00
1C,20S,DQ Kuhn's Beer Inc, 'The Beer with a Cheer', made in Jamestown, NY, (F/B) (RD/WE/ BK) 11.50
1FB,20S,FS Lithia Beer, shows long neck and glass (F/B) 3.00
1C,20S,FS Lithia Beer, West Bend, WIS 3.00
1FB,20S,FS Manhattan Premium Beer, ad (B), blank (F) 3.00
1C,20S,FS Metz 75th Anniversary Beer, Omaha, Neb 3.50
1C,20S,FS Extra Dry Metz Beer, Omaha, NE, Shows Premiums, Coupon (I) 3.00
1C,20S,FS Metz Beer (B), Golden Spike Beer (F) 4.00
1C,20S,FS Hotel Miller, Milwaukee (F), Miller High Life Beer ad (B) 3.25
1C,20S,FS Miller High Life Beer, bottles in ice (B) 5.00
1FB,20S,BS Miller High Life (WE/RD/GD) logo (F/B) 5.00
1C,20S,FS Drink Harry Mitchell's Quality Lager Beer, El Paso, TX 4.25
1C,20S,FS Mitchell's Premium Beer logo (F/B), The Name Assures Quality (S) 3.25
1C,20S,FS Mitchell's Premium Beer, El Paso, Tex 4.00
1C,20S,FS Harry Mitchell Beer, ad: Dixie 'Drive Inn' Tucson, AZ 4.00
1FB,20S,FS Mt Whitney Beer, snowman (B), 'Brewed with California's Finest Water' 4.75
1C,30S,FS National Bohemian, 'I Love It' on footer 4.00
1C,20S,FS Nutmeg State Ale (F), Nutmeg State Beer (B), Eastern Brewing Corp, Waterbury, Conn 4.00
1C,20S,FS,FL Old Export Beer & Ale, bottle & glass in ad 3.00
1C,20S,FS,FL Old German Beer, Cumberland, MD 4.00
1C,20S,FS Old Michigan Beer, School pennant (B), glass & bottle (F) 7.25
1C,20S,FS Old Oxford Ale & Renner Youngstown Bohemia Beer 6.00
1C,20S,FS Old Reading Beer, The Old Reading Brewery, Inc., Reading, PA, drinker (B . 4.25
1C,20S,FS Drink Old Stock Beer (F), long neck bottle and tall glass (B), (RD) 4.25
1C,20S,FS Old Style Lager, ad: Rainbow Ballroom, Austin, MN 4.00
1C,20S,FS Oltimer Beer, Belleville, IL ad: Blue Moon Tavern, Jerseyville, IL 3.75
1FB,20S,FS Light Olympia Beer, cap (F), logo (B) 2.00
1C,20S,FS Pabst Blue Ribbon Beer (RD/BE on WE), stock 2.00
10C,20S,FS Pearl Beer Cattle Brands Set, numbered, Type 1 [1954], Universal Match 10.50
10C,20S,FS Pearl Beer Cattle Brands Set, numbered, Type 2 [1960], Atlas Match 9.00
10C,20S,FS Pearl Beer Cattle Brands Set, numbered, Type 3 Ohio Match 10.00

1C,20S,FS Pilot Beer, ad: Bridge Resort, Beaver Dam on County Trunk G, stock 3.75
1C,20S,FS A-1 Pilsner Beer, Arizona Brewing Company, Inc. 3.25
1C,20S,FS P.O.N. Beer and Ales, Newark, NJ 4.00
1C,20S,FS Potsi Beer ad: Nelson's Bar & Café, Muscoda, WI 4.00
1C,20S,FS Potosi Beer w/sandwich, glass and long neck bottle (B), ad: Mart's & Pete's,
    Hartland, Minnesota, stock 4.00
1FB,20S,FS Primator on Draught (F), Daisy Beer, Garden City Brewery, Chicago (B).. 6.25
1C,20S,FS Rainbow Beer & Dominion Pale Ale, St. Johns, NFLD 3.00
1C,20S,FS Drink Rainier Beer, San Francisco, Seattle (et al) 4.00
1C,20S,FS Regal-Amber Lager Beer, short bottle (B) (YW,RD) 3.00
1C,20S,FS Regal-Amber, Regal-Amber Brewing Co., San Francisco 4.50
1C,20S,FS Richbrau Beer, A Virginia Product (S), (F/B), Richmond, VA 4.25
1C,20S,FS Richbrau Beer, Home Brewing Co., Richmond, VA 3.00
1C,20S,FS Rocky Mountain Beer, Anaconda Brewing Co., Anaconda, MT 5.00
1C,20S,DQ Scheidt's Valley Forge Special Beer...Lagered in wood 1.25
1C,20S,FS Schemm Pilsner Beer, Saginaw, Mich 4.00
1C,20S,FS Schlitz Beer, (GY) striker 1.25
1C,20S,FS Schmidt's Beer, Detroit, Mich (RD,BE) 4.00
1C,20S,FS Senate Beer, Chr. Heurich Brewing Co, Washington, D.C. 4.25
1C,20S,FS Shiner Beer, Shiner, Texas 4.00
1C,20S,BS Sieben Brewing Company, (RD,BK,WE), stock 4.00
1C,20S,FS Sieben's Real Lager, 1466 Larrabee St., Chicago 3.00
1FB,20S,FS Stop for Stag Beer, triangular pattern w/ bottle, glass, stein (F/B) 4.00
1C,20S,FS Stag Beer, Griesdieck Western Brewery Co, Belleville, Ill 5.00
1FB,20S,FS Stag Beer (BK/RD/WE) square (F/B) 13.00
1C,20S,FS Storz Winterbrau Beer, long neck bottle (F) 3.75
1C,20S,FS Storz Triumph Beer, Storz Brewing Co, metals (B) 4.00
1C,30S,FS Stroh's name & logo (F), Since 1950 (B), (RD/GD) 3.50
1C,20S,FS 7Up, The Joyce Products Co, Columbus, Ohio (F), Washington Dub-L-Ex Beer ad (B)
    .... 4.00
1C,20S,BS Waukesha Beer, ad: Windlake Bowl, Weber (F) 4.00
1FB,20S,FS Weber Waukesha Beer (B), Erv Matti's Dine & Dance (F) 2.00
1C,20S,FS White Crown Beer and Ale, Akron, OH 6.00
1C,20S,FS Wooden Shoe Beer, Dutch people (F), shoe (B) 2.00
10C,20S,FS Beer Related, (inc. Storz, Metz, Falstaff, Schlitz) 15.25
15C,20S,FS Beer Related, (inc. Carling's, Pointer, Pabst, Robin Hood, Schmidt's) 18.50
10C,20S,FS Beer Related, (inc. White Crown, Richbrau, Senate, Signal) 12.75
15C,20S,FS Beer Related 10.00
10C,20S,FS Beer Related, (inc. Breweries, Brands, Mentions) 13.50
15C,20S,MS Beer Brands and Breweries, assorted 10.25
10C,20S,MZ,1B Beer & Brewery Related 7.00
10C,MZ,MS Liquor & Beer (3 boxes), assorted 6.00

Birds

Birds--A category of matchcovers whose main theme is birds. Both in sets and singles, this category includes supermarket sets and many foreign matchcovers.

5C,20S,FS Barton-Cotton Birds Set, Roger Tory Peterson, Barn Swallow-Bluejay-Goldfinch-Red Headed Woodpecker-Towhee 2.50

6C,20S,FS Ducks Set, stock design Baldpate-Bluebill-Canadian Goose-Mallard-Pintail-Wood Duck, Type 1 [1964] 1.00

6C,20S,BS Ducks Set, stock design Baldpate-Bluebill-Canadian Goose-Mallard-Pintail-Wood Duck, Type 2 [1977] 1.00

8C,20S,FS Barton-Cotton Birds Set [1956], Bevans Bullfinch-Emerald Cuckoo-Indian Kingfisher-Little Kingfisher-Solomon Island Fruit Pigeon-Turquoisine Superb Warbler-White breasted Swallow-Wire tailed Swallow 3.00

5C,20S,FS Barton-Cotton Birds Set [   ], Francis Lee Jacques Bluebird-Cardinal-Downy Woodpecker-Robin-Scarlet Tanager 2.50

5C,20S,FS Barton-Cotton Birds Set [   ], Fritz Hilton Baltimore Oriole A Dogwood 2.50

5C,20S,FS Birds Set [1953], Bluebird-Cardinal-Downy Woodpecker-Robin-Scarlet Tanager 1.00

10C,20S Ohio Blue Tip Birds, The Ohio Match Co., Wadsworth, Ohio - Made in U.S.A., ca. 1956 .... 3.00

11C,20S,FS Bird Set, 1957 Ohio Match Co. 3.25

10C,20S,FS Superior Set 5.00

Blacks

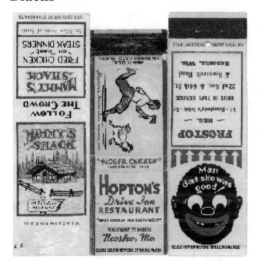

Blacks—A relatively recent collectibles category. These matchcovers feature any depiction of black people, to include drawings, photos, or symbols related to the American black position during any given period. They range from the mid 1920s, and names such as Mammy, Sambo, Picaninny, Topsy, Coon, Black Cat, and Pappy are often included in this category. Real photo matchcovers of blacks are relatively rare, but many have been collected. As in other areas of black memorabilia, prices are bound to increase.

1C,20S,FS Billings Club, shows couple dancing (F), Wednesday is Mammy Night (S), address (B) (YW/RD) 7.00

1C,20S,FS Black Cat, 557 West Broadway, New York, shows semi clad black woman singer (F), Dinner and Supper Continuous Entertainment (B), Lion Match Co. 7.50

1C,20S,FS Carolina Pines, Denners Daily 65c, 75c, 85c, Christmas mofig (B), Mammy w/poka dot babushka (GN/WE) 4.25

1C,20S,FS,FEA Connie's Inn, 48th St & Broadway, show 2 black entertainers in high hat & cane (F), show times (B), FEA 17.50

1C,20S,FS Coon Chicken Inn, 3 addresses (B), broad smiling black porter w/cap, red lips (F) (DBE/RD/BK), Universal Match Co. 12.50

1C,20S,FS Coon Chicken Inn, 3 addresses w/chicken (B), broad smiling black porter w/cap, red lips (F) (RD/WY/BK), Diamond Match Co. 12.50

1C,20S,FS Coon Chicken Inn, 3 addresses w/chicken (B), broad smiling black porter w/cap, red lips (F) (OR/RD/BK), Diamond Match Co. 12.50

1FB,20S Coon Chicken Inn, Black Bellhop (F), nice 14.00

1C,20S,FS Cotton Club, Broadway at 48th St., drawing of naked black natives dancing (B) 6.00

1C,20S,FS Dinah's Shack, Since 1926, Palo Alto, Calif, Mammy w/(RD/WE) polka dot scarf and hair babushka (BN/RD/WE) 5.00

1C,20S,FS Dixie Sandwiches, Malted Milk w/4 addresses in Denver, Colo (F), shows black man eating watermelon w/Dixie (B) (GN/BK), Universal Match Corp. 15.00

1C,20S,FS Dixie Sandwiches, Malted Milk w/2 addresses in Denver, Colo (F), shows black man eating watermelon w/Dixie (B), (GN/BK)Universal Match Corp. 15.00

1C,20S,FS Frostop, 22nd Ave & 64th St, Kenosha, Wis, shows stylized black face, large red lips, few teeth w/Man dat sho was good! on forehead (F), Star Match Co, St. Louis, MO (BK/RD/WE) 22.50

1C,20S,FS The Gilbert system Hotels, At your service in 35 Cities, shows black bell hop in (RD) uniform (F), services pictures (B), Lion Match Co. 10.00

8C,30S,BS Black Historical Series Set [1976], Bunche-Dunbar-Hansberry-Hurston-Jackson-King-Pickett-Robinson (stock) 4.50

1C,20S,FS Hopton's Drive Inn Restaurant, Neosho, MO (F), shows barefooted black male w/ hatchet chasing chicken, 'Nigger Chicken, Copyrighted 1938' (S), Diamond Match Co. 25.00

1C,20S,FS Kit Kat Club, 152 East 55th St, New York, show assorted black entertainers around name (F/B), Telephone ELd. 5-0543 (S) (LGN/WE/BK), Lion Match Co. 12.50

1C,20S,FS Lincoln Loan Service, Inc, Harrisburg, PA, Phone: 5219, shows two blacks throwing dice (B) (RD/BK/GN/YW) 12.00

1C,20S,FS Mammy's Chicken Farm, 60 W 52nd St, New York, shows Mammy w/chicken dinner (B) (GD/BK/RD/WE ....) 5.00

1C,30S,FS Mammy's Shanty, The World's Best Apple Pie, shows black woman washing clothing while black man sleeps (F), 7 blacks at table (B) 12.00

1C,20S,FS Mammy's Pantry, Brooklyn, NY, building (B), full length Mammy (F), Phone Main 4-9365 (S), (RD/WE) 4.00

1C,20S,FS Piccadilly, We Win Their Favor With Our Flavor, shows black child w/red lips and name (B), address (B) (GD/BK/RD) 25.00

1C,20S,FS Piccaninny, Famous for Barbecued Food, shows black child w/red lips and name (F), addresses (B) (GD/BK/RD), Lion Match Co. 17.50

1C,40S,FS Florida's Silver springs, Ocala, Fla, shows famous photo of 'A Skin Game' w/3 blacks playing crooked cards (B) 10.00

1C,10S,FS Topsy's Famous for Chicken, 'Eat with your Fingers' shows Mammy (F), (GY) striker 12.00

1FB,G,FS,FEA Twenty One, Bermuda, (SR/RD), name (F), black bartender w/cap & cocktail shaker across sticks 22.00

1C,20S,FS Uncle Remus Restaurant, Eatonton, GA, shows (BK/WE) photo of white bearded black Uncle Remus character (B), H.S. Brown, Proprietor (S) 7.50

1C,20S,FS O. Ray Watkins, Private Investigator w/photo of young black man (B), Rapid Bail Bonds w/address and phone (F) 5.00

Blades (Razor)

Blades—A popular peripheral collectible among razor blade collectors. There are dozens of sets and singles related to this category. Marlin Blades produced nine sets of six cartoon matchcovers in the mid-1940s and The Gem Razor Blade Company issued six sets of six matchcovers also during this period. More recent blade matchcovers are uncommon. This category loosely includes matchcovers advertising electric razors and depilatories. Although these matchcovers are considered nationals, they are found in most older collections and are a challenge to find.

15C,20S,FS Razor Blade advertisement, assorted 3.50

6C,20S,FS D.D. Bean Set #1 Gem Blades But I don't..-Gee, Ethel,..-I feel..-We waited..-You mean now..-You're a different.. .... 3.00

6C,20S,FS D.D. Bean Set #2 Gem Blades Gosh, Hubert,..-Hello, Mama,..-I think my..-I wouldn't..-You have no..-You're putting up.. .... 3.00

6C,20S,FS D.D. Bean Set #3 [   ], Gem Blades cartoons (I) But I've..-I enjoy..-What's cookin',..-You measure..- You're getting..-You're really. 3.00

1FB,20S,FS Gillette Blue Blades 1.50

6C,20S,FS Lion Set #1 [   ], Gem Blades cartoons on (B) Gosh, Herbert,..-Hello, Mama,..-I think my..-I wouldn't..-You have no..-You're putting up.. .... 3.00

6C,20S,FS Lion Set #2 [   ], Gem Blades cartoons on (B), Save Waste Paper on (I) But I don't..-Gee, Ethel,..-I feel..-We waited..-You mean now..-You're a different. 8.00

6C,20S,FS Lion Set #3 [   ], Gem Blades cartoons (I) But I've..-I enjoy..-What's cookin',..-You measure..-You are getting..-You're really... .... 4.00

6C,20S,FS Lion Set #4 [   ], New Gem Razor on (F) But I've..-I enjoy..-What's cookin',..-You measure..-You are getting..-You're really.. .... 3.00

9C,20S,FS Marlin Firearms Co, New Haven, Conn. razor blade (partial) set, cartoons (B) of each 4.00

6C,20S,FS Marlin Blades Set #1 Hey, Joe!..-I'll Be Glad.. -I'm Going..-It's Amazing..-My Client..-One Thing.. Type 1 [1945], Arrow Match 3.00

6C,20S,FS Marlin Blades Set #1 Hey, Joe!..-I'll Be Glad.. -I'm Going..-It's Amazing..-My Client..-One Thing.. Type 2 D.D. Bean, inverted manumark, 18 for 25cts 3.50

6C,20S,FS Marlin Blades Set #1 Hey, Joe!..-I'll Be Glad.. -I'm Going..-It's Amazing..-My Client..-One Thing.. Type 3 D.D. Bean, regular manumark, 18 for 25cts 3.00

6C,20S,FS Marlin Blades Set #1 Hey, Joe!..-I'll Be Glad.. -I'm Going..-It's Amazing..-My Client..-One Thing.. Type 4 D.D. Bean, regular manumark, 25cts 3.25

6C,20S,FS Marlin Blades Set #2 Four Customers..-He Keeps..-I Can Hardly..-It's Like..- Sorry, Dear..-You've Got.. Type 1 [1946], (WE) paper outside 3.00

6C,20S,FS Marlin Blades Set #2 Four Customers..-He Keeps..-I Can Hardly..-It's Like..- Sorry, Dear..-You've Got.. Type 2 [   ], (BE) paper outside 3.00

6C,20S,FS Marlin Blades Set #3 [   ], D.D. Bean Bailey's Getting..-Don't You..-Is The U.S.A...-I Won't..- Sorry To Quit..-You'd Think.. .... 4.00

6C,20S,FS Marlin Blades Set #4, Don't Ask..-He's Doubled..-They Say..-Why Can't.- (2 more) Type 1 [1945], Arrow Match 3.00

6C,20S,FS Marlin Blades Set #4, Don't Ask..-He's Doubled..-They Say..-Why Can't.- (2 more) Type 2 [   ], D.D. Bean 3.00

Boxes

Boxes—Any container made of several materials, used for holding or carrying matches. Popular types include Pocketboxes (8,000 varieties), Pocketbox Slims (3,100 varieties), American Ace (9,300 varieties) and Ultraslims (2,000 varieties). Other box types include Kitchen Boxes, Presentation Boxes, Penny Boxes, Wooden Boxes, Cans, Barrels, and boxes made of various other materials. Boxes were the earliest conveyance of matches and date back to the early part of the 1800s.

25B American Ace boxes, numbered mostly between 4,000 & 6,000 .... 12.00
25B American Ace boxes, numbered between 7162 - 7960 .... 15.50
5AA American Ace Boxes, All Rainbows 4.50
4B A Frame Box 2.25
Bellezas Series, set of boxes, Viajeros Type 1 36 luces, striker at end 2.50
Bellezas Series, set of boxes, Viajeros Type 2 Cont. Neto 36 luces, striker at end 2.50
Bellezas Series, set of boxes, Viajeros Type 3 33 luces, striker at end 2.50
Bellezas Series, set of boxes, Viajeros Type 4 38/40 luces, striker in middle 2.50
Bellezas Series, set of boxes, Viajeros Type 5 36 luces, striker in middle 2.50
Bellezas Series, set of boxes, Viajeros Type 6 33 luces, striker in middle 2.50
1B BLAZERS (Wind Proof) Matches by Diamond Shows Man on early bicycle says 'Light Only On The Box', Match heads are 5/8' long, small wooden box 10.50
1B The Blue Cross Box 2 1/2D, 1962 by Nitedals Match Co. Ltd 1.75
1B THE COAST MATCH by Diamond Match Co. (ca.1914) Non-Poisonous Double Dip (PK/BE)
    .... 7.00
1 book, Match Box Labels of the World by A.J. Cruse, soiled dust cover, (C) 1946 .... 50.00
12B Fortune Matches, each w/different fortune, assorted colors 3.00
9B Kitchen Box Set [1955], Ohio Match Co. At The Station-Band Concert-Country Kitchen-Country Store-Early American Fireplace-Harvest Time-Ranch Scene-Springtime-Winter Fun 4.00
1B Lenticular [1974-   ], Atlas Match Co., Bank of Douglas County 3.00
1B Lenticular [1974-   ], Atlas Match Co., Dallas Morning News 3.00
1B Lenticular [1974-   ], Atlas Match Co., Christmas design 2.25
1B Niagara Falls Lenticular, winking girl, Knickerbocker Fed Sav 6.00
1B Pocketbox, Mission: Impossible, Music by Lalo Schifrin, On Dot Records (F), Lenticular flashing 'Impossible' 7.50
15B Penny Box Set [1955], Ohio Match Co. Baseball Player-Bucking Bronco-Football Player-Golfer-The Hunt-1911 Maxwell-Old Time Rail Engine-Polo-Show Horse-Skiing-Sternwheel Steamer-Tennis Player-Trotting Horse-2 Boats-U.S. Constitu 7.00
6B Sainsbury's Safety Matches 1.50
1B Salvation Matches, Contain No Poisonous Phosphorus, Licensed Match, Approved Match Serial No. 1, (ca. 1871) 10.00
1B Triangle Box [1982] 5.00
300B Ultraslims, Diamond Match Co., numbered 35.00
16B World Wildlife Federation Boxes, Set #13 [1988], The Brothers von Wright, 2 sets of 8 boxes (average contents 190) in a presentation case 1850-1853-1854-1862-1866-1867-1868-1897
    .... 40.00
30B World Wildlife Federation Boxes, Set #10 [1984], Birds of Prey, 2 sets of 6 large boxes and 3 sets of 6 small boxes in a presentation case Large: Eagle Owl-Golden Eagle-Great Grey Owl-Merlin-Osprey-Peregrine Falcon Small: Goshawk-Gyrfalcon-Hawk Owl-Rough Legged Eagle-Snowy Owl-White tailed Eagle 35.00

16B World Wildlife Federation Boxes, Set #11, 25th Anniversary Set [1986], Panda, 2 sets of 8 boxes (average contents 190) in a presentation case Arabian Oryx-Bengal Tiger-Coral Reefs-Galapagos Giant..- Humpback Whale-Japanese Crane-King Penguin-Rafflesia 45.00

16B World Wildlife Federation Boxes, Set #12 [1987], Galapagos, 2 sets of 8 boxes (average contents 190) in a presentation case American Whimbreg-Cordia Lutia-Fig Cacti-Frigate Bird-Fur Seal-Giant Tortoises-Marine Iguanas-Red footed Booby 40.00

28B World Wildlife Federation Boxes, The Ark in Our Time [1974], 2 sets of 8 large boxes/3 sets of 4 small boxes in a presentation case Large: African Wild Ass-Arabian Oryx-Blue Whale-Hairy Rhinoceros-Orangutan-Polar Bear-Thylacine-Tule Elk Small: Galapagos Cormorant-Imperial Eagle-Rothschild's Starling-Whooping Crane 20.00

15B World Wildlife Federation Boxes, Set #7 [1981], Butterflies, Large: Aglois-Argyrinis-Delias-Morpho-Plebejus-Vanessa: Small: Aglais-Callimorpha-Cynthia-Ladoga-Polygonia-Vanessa, 2 sets of 6 large B/3 in a presentation case 35.00

30B World Wildlife Federation Boxes, Set #8 [1982], Birds of Paradise, 2 sets of 6 large boxes and 3 sets of 6 small boxes in a presentation case, Large: Le Loriot..-Le Manucode..-Le Nebuleux, Dans..-Le Nebuleux, Etalant..-Le Petit..-L'Oiseau.. Small: Barbu de la..-Le Barbu A..-Le Barbu Orange..-Le Barbu Rose..-Le Geai Blea..-Le Geai Peruvien.. .... 35.00

12B World Wildlife Federation Boxes, Set #9 [1983], Deer, Red Deer-Reindeer-Roe Deer 1 set and the presentation box, large and small boxes 22.00

1B Diamond Water-Resistant Matches, no ad, 'Sheds Water Like a Duck's Back', full of (RD)-tip stick matches, no zone or ZIP in address,(RD Diamond (F),(RD/WE/BE) 5.00

40B American Ace Boxes, Universal Match Corp. 4.50

25B, Universal Made in Japan, assorted themes 2.25

30B, Japanese Made, assorted themes 1.00

35B Miniature Boxes, assorted 20.00

60B Diamond Match [1959-present], Pocketboxes 7.50

50B Pocketbox Slims [1980-present], Diamond Match Co. 7.00

10B, Swedish Metallic Boxes, assorted themes 1.75

Cameos

Cameos—A premier category type, this style of matchcover often features an elaborate debossed design printed with metallic ink. Over 7,500 varieties are known and they have been collected from 1965, by number. The "Cameo" logo usually appears on the inside cover. The Cameo Box is usually not included in this category.

7C,30S,FS Cameos First National Bank, Eastern Arkansas 2.50

100C,20S,MS Cameos, assorted themes 19.00

15C,MZ,MS Cameos, Jewelites, & Jewels, assorted 4.00

50C,30S,FS,CA Cameos, assorted themes 8.00

Canadian

10C,20S, Canadian Animal Set, (BK/WE) 2.25
12C,30S,FS Arrow Shirt Set [1942], no tax imprint Cameron Highlanders..-Carleton & York..-
Hastings & P.E...- 48th Highlanders-Highland Light..-North Nova Scotia..-4th Princess
Louise..-Royal Canadian Regiment-Royal Montreal Regiment..-Scots Fusilie 1.00
20C,20S,MS British Columbia themes 4.00
1C,20S,BS 1867-1967 Canada Centenial, Kraft Foods (WE) 2.00
1C,20S,BS 1867-1967 Canada Centenial, Bulova, ad: Edmond Pariseau 4.00
1C,20S,BS 1867-1967 Canada Centenial, Parker's Dry Cleaners, (GD) 2.00
1C,40S,BS Canada Centenial 1867-1967, shows seals of 10 provinces 3.00
13C,20S,BS 1867-1967 Canada Centenial, assorted Thank You 4.50
1C,20S,BS 1867-1967 Canada Centenial, Zen Auto Parts, Hamilton, Ont, (OE) 2.00
20C,30S, BS Canadian Color Match, Vancouver, BC 4.50
5C,30S,BS Famous Composers, Canadian Set 2.00
4C,20S Dog Set, Strike Rite Match Ltd, Canada, muted tones 8.75

Canadian (Eddy Match Co.)

5C,30S,FS Canadiana Set [1969], Aerial View of Farmland-Fishing Port Scene-Guards on
Parade-Night shot of fountain-Night shot of new city hall 1.00
10C,20S,FS Animals Set, Beaver-Boxer-Coho-Eastern Brook Trout-Kitten-Raccoon-Red Fox-
Red Squirrel-Scotch Collie-The Thoroughbred Type #1 [1955], French and English ... 8.00
10C,20S,FS Animals Set, Beaver-Boxer-Coho-Eastern Brook Trout-Kitten-Raccoon-Red Fox-
Red Squirrel-Scotch Collie-The Thoroughbred Type #2 [1955], English wording only 2.00
10C,20S,FS Animals Set, Beaver-Boxer-Coho-Eastern Brook Trout-Kitten-Raccoon-Red Fox-
Red Squirrel-Scotch Collie-The Thoroughbred Type #3 [1959], (RD) maple leaf 2.50
142C,20S,FS Eddy Match Co. assorted sets and partial sets 3.00
9C,20S Nature Series, Eddy Match, birds 5.25
5C,20S,FS Birds Set Baltimore Oriole-Blue Jay-Cardinal-Red Headed Woodpecker-Screech Owl
Type 1 [1955], English and French wording (B) 4.00
5C,20S,FS Birds Set Baltimore Oriole-Blue Jay-Cardinal-Red Headed Woodpecker-Screech Owl
Type 2 [1956], English wording only (B) 2.00
5C,20S,FS Antique Cars Set [1956], Eddy Match Ltd, CN 5.50
6C,20S,FS Centennial [1967], Set #1, (BE) (S) Confederation Room-Montreal Skyline-Portage
& Main..-. Signal Hill-Stanley Park-Upper Canada Village 5.00
6C,20S,FS Centennial [1967], Set #2, (BN) (S) Bluenose II-Cattle Branding-Fort Walsh-Perce
Rock-Toronto City Hall-Victoria Harbour 5.00
6C,20S,FS Centennial [1967], Set #3, (OE) (S) Covered Bridge-Grain Elevators-Oil Rig-Peace
Tower-Red River Cart-St. Joseph's Shrine 5.00
12C,20S,FS Cities Series Set [1960], Agra-Berlin-Brussels-Cairo-Copenhagen-Istanbul-Lon-
don-Ottawa-Paris-Rome-Stockholm-Washington 4.00
12C,20S Cities Series, CN 2.00
9C,20S Nature Series, Eddy Match, All Flowers 2.00
10C,20S,BS Folk Art Set [1977] 2.00
6C,20S,FS Food Set #1 [1963], Fruit Salad-Hamburger and Corn-Pancakes-Strawberry Shortcake-
Turkey-Weiners and Bacon 1.50
5C,20S,FS Food Set #2 [1969], Dogwood Sandwich-Hamburger-Hot Dog-Sausage & Beans-
Steak 1.25
30C,20S,BS Four Seasons Set, color photo (F), Eddy Match Ltd, CN 7.00
10C,20S,BS French Woodcuts [1978], (BN) background, square designs, Eddylites 1.00
10C,20S,BS Japanese Family Crests Set [1978], (BK) background, circular designs 1.00

21C,20S,FS Locality Series Sets [1960], 7 sets of 3, 1) The Historic Ottawa: Champlain..-Early Traders..-Indians..; 2) Le Majestueux St. Laurent: Carre..-1534..-Le Sanctuaire..; 3) Ontario Vacationland: Famous 100..-Historic Fort..-Muskoka..; 4) Peninsula Highlights: Burlington's..-Niagara..-Rainbow..; 5) Seaway Scenes: High Level..-Kingston's..-Lake Freighter..; 6) Vancouver Island: BC Land..-Capt. James..-Fishing 7) West Coast Wonderland: BC's Fishing..-The Big..-Lions.. .... 3.00

20C,20S,BS Native Canadians Set [1975], Algonquin (BE (B)-Algonquin (YW/(B)-Beothuk-Black Foot (BE (B)-Black Foot (WE) (B)-Blood-Chinook-Chippewa (WE) (B)-Chippewa (YW (B)-Cree-Dakota-Eskimo (RD (S)-Eskimo (YW (S)-Haida-Huron-Kwakiutl-Northern Cree-Tils 2.00

3C,20S,FS Nature Series [1959], (BK): Duck-Fox-Owl, (GN):, (OE):, (RD): Fish-Grasshopper-Turtle 2.00

6C,20S,FS Nature Series [1961], (BE) (S): American Lotus-Marsh Marigold-Pine Grosbeak-Red Headed Woodpecker-Scarlet Tanager-Swamp Rose Mallow, Type 1 (WE) paper 3.00

6C,20S,FS Nature Series [1961], (GN) (S): Bohemian Waxwing-Meadow Rose-Red Crossbill-Sparrow Hawk-Striped Coral Root-Wood Lily, Type 1 (WE) paper 3.00

6C,20S,FS Nature Series [1961], (OE) (S): Blackburnian Warbler-Eastern Meadowlark-Fringed Polygala-Meadow Beauty-Rufous sided Towhee- White Water Lily, Type 1 (WE) paper 3.00

6C,20S,FS Nature Series [1961], (BE) (S): American Lotus-Marsh Marigold-Pine Grosbeak-Red Headed Woodpecker-Scarlet Tanager-Swamp Rose Mallow, Type 2 (CM) paper 3.00

6C,20S,FS Nature Series [1961], (GN) (S): Bohemian Waxwing-Meadow Rose-Red Crossbill-Sparrow Hawk-Striped Coral Root-Wood Lily, Type 2 (CM) paper 3.00

6C,20S,FS Nature Series [1961], (OE) (S): Blackburnian Warbler-Eastern Meadowlark-Fringed Polygala-Meadow Beauty-Rufous sided Towhee-White Water Lily, Type 2 (CM) paper 3.00

9C,20S Nature Series, CN (BN) 2.00

6C,20S,FS Nature Series [1965], 3 sets of 6, each has a different colored (S) (GN) (S): Audubon's Warbler-Black Capped Chickadee- Black Eyed Susan-Canada Violet-Downy Woodpecker-Purple Raspberry 7.50

6C,20S,FS Nature Series [1965], 3 sets of 6, each has a different colored (S) (BE) (S): Barn Swallow-Blue Jay-Common Purple Finch- Goats Beard-Grass Pink-White Trillium .. 7.50

6C,20S,FS Nature Series [1965], 3 sets of 6, each has a different colored (S) (RD) Saddle: Baltimore Oriole-Canada Lily-Golden Rod-Red Trillium-Waxwing-Wood Duck 7.50

6C,20S Nature Series, CN (GN) 2.00

12C,20S Nature Series, CN (OE) 2.25

12C,20S Nature Series, CN (WE) 2.00

3C,20S,FS Outdoor Series [1960], (RD) letter E (B) Set #1: Always keep..-Don't try..-Never dive.. .... 1.00

3C,20S,FS Outdoor Series [1960], (RD) letter E (B) Set #2: Make your..-This is not..-This looks.. .... 1.00

3C,20S,FS Outdoor Series [1960], (RD) letter E (B) Set #3: In emergency..-Never step..-Play safe.. .... 1.00

3C,20S,FS Outdoor Series [1960], (RD) letter E (B) Set #4: If vacationing..-Learn how..-Leave cleanly.. .... 1.00

3C,20S,FS Outdoor Series [1961], (GN) letter E (B) Set #1: If vacationing..-In emergency..-Make your.. .... 1.00

3C,20S,FS Outdoor Series [1961], (GN) letter E (B) Set #2: Always keep..-Don't try..-Play safe.. .... 1.00

5C,20S,FS Outdoor Series Set [1969], Camping-Curling-Golf-Sailing-Skiing 1.00

9C,20S Outdoor Series, CN 2.00

10C,20S,BS Pre-Columbian Designs Set [1977], circular designs, (BK) background 1.00

10C,20S,BS Pueblo Graphics Set [1978], (WE) background 1.00

3C,20S,FS Sailing Ships Set [1957], A Nova Scotia Schooner-The Atlantic Packet-The Lake Schooner 1.00

60B Canadian Scenes Boxes Set including 1) Alberta: Cable..-Calgary..-Klondike..-Lake..-Red Rock..; 2) British Columbia: BC Ferries-Burnaby-Opaben..-Steveston-Vancouver; 3) Manitoba: Fishing..-Manitoba..-Portage..-Water..-Whiteshell..; 4) New Brunswick: Campbellton..-Covered..-Farmer's..-Hopewell..-Provincial park..; 5) Newfoundland: Ferry..-Legislative..-Petty..-St. John's..-Signal; 6) Northwest Territory: Alexander..-Baker..-Mackenzie..-Muncho..-Yellowknife; 7) Nova Scotia: Container..-Downtown..-Halifax-Halifax..-Salmon..; 8) Prince Edward Island: Confederation..-Grahams's..-Green..-Horse..-Tuna..; 9) Saskatchewan: Batoche..-Fort..-Kimball..-Museum..-Ukrainian..; 10) Yukon: Dawson-Klondike..-Miles..-Sunset..-Whitehorse (see below)

60B Canadian Scenes Boxes Set Type #1 [1973], Sesqui on (S), manumark and address in small print 20.00

60B Canadian Scenes Boxes Set Type #2 [1973], Sesqui on (S), manumark and address in large print 20.00

61B Canadian Scenes Boxes Set Type #3 [1974], Eddy Sesqui on (S), added is Yukon: Arctic..
.... 20.00

30B Sportlites Set [   ] 4.00

22C,20S,BS Tarot Set [1973], numbered, Roman numerals The Fool-The Magus-The Sorceress-The Empress-The Emperor-The Pope-The Lover-The Chariot-Justice-The Hermit-The Wheel of Fortune-Strength-The Hanged Man-Death-Temperance-The Devil-The Tower-The Star-The Moon-The Sun-The Judgment-The World 3.50

50C,20S,BS U.S. Flags Set [1987] 5.00

10C,20S,FS Wildlife Set (1956), Bear-Belted Kingfisher-Canada Goose-Cocker Spaniel-Coyote-Golden Retriever-Porcupine-Rabbit-Rocky Mountains Goat-White Tailed Deer 2.00

12C,20S Winter Series, CN (WE) 2.00

3C,20S,FS Winter Series Set #1 [1959], (RD) letter E (B), Fir Cone-Holly Leaves-Snowflake (with dots) 1.00

3C,20S,FS Winter Series Set #2 [1959], (RD) letter E (B), Bells-Snowflake (without dots)-Tree (star on top) 1.00

3C,20S,FS Winter Series Set #3 [1959], (RD) letter E (B), Star-Tree-Tree Ornament 1.00

3C,20S,FS Winter Series Set #1 [1961], (GN) letter E (B) Fir Cone-Snowflake (with dots)-Tree (star on top) 1.00

3C,20S,FS Winter Series Set #2 [1961], (GN) letter E (B) Bells-Star-Snowflake (without dots)
.... 1.00

3C,20S,FS World Series [1958], Set #1: Belgium-Germany-Spain, 1A: (OE/ME) 1.00

3C,20S,FS World Series [1958], Set #1: Belgium-Germany-Spain, 1B: (RD/ME) 1.00

3C,20S,FS World Series [1958], Set #1: Belgium-Germany-Spain, 1C: (RD/LBE) 1.00

3C,20S,FS World Series [1958], Set #1: Belgium-Germany-Spain, 1D: (GN/BN) 1.00

3C,20S,FS World Series [1958], Set #1: Belgium-Germany-Spain, 1E: (YW/BN) 1.00

3C,20S,FS World Series [1958], Set #2: Canada (Eskimo)-Greece-Italy, 2A: (OE/ME) .. 1.00

3C,20S,FS World Series [1958], Set #2: Canada (Eskimo)-Greece-Italy, 2B: (RD/ME) . 1.00

3C,20S,FS World Series [1958], Set #2: Canada (Eskimo)-Greece-Italy, 2C: (RD/LBE) 1.00

3C,20S,FS World Series [1958], Set #2: Canada (Eskimo)-Greece-Italy, 2D: (GN/BN) .. 1.00

3C,20S,FS World Series [1958], Set #2: Canada (Eskimo)-Greece-Italy, 2E: (YW/BN) .. 1.00

3C,20S,FS World Series [1958], Set #3, Austria-Canada (Cowboy)-Holland (Holland in (RD))
.... 1.00

3C,20S,FS World Series [1958], Set #4, China-Mexico (World Series in (RD))-Scotland 1.00

3C,20S,FS World Series [1958], Set #5, France-India-Indonesia 1.00

3C,20S,FS World Series [1958], Set #6, Bulgaria-Poland-Yugoslavia 1.00

3C,20S,FS World Series [1959], Set #7, Finland-Holland (BE print)-Mexico W. Series: (BE) 1.00

3C,20S,FS World Series [1959], Set #8, Canada (R.C.M.P.)-Japan-Morocco 1.00

3C,20S,FS World Series [1959], Set #9, Albania-Denmark-Switzerland 1.00

3C,20S,FS World Series [1959], Set #10, Czechoslovakia-Hungary-Sweden 1.00

3C,20S,FS World Series [1959], Set #11, England-Greece(World Series in (BE)-Portugal 1.00

3C,20S,FS World Series [1959], Set #12, Algeria-Arabia-Italy(World Series in (BE) 1.00

1C,20S,BS 1867-1967 Canada Centennial, Northern Electric 1.25

4C,20S,BS Royal Canadian Legion, Branch 142, Dunnville, Ontario, color set 3.00
10C,20S,FS Canadian Geographic Facts, D.D. Bean, St. Cesaire, Que. 2.25
10C,20S,FS Canadian Geographic Facts, 1 from each province, Book Match Co. 2.00
11C,20S,FS Canadian Geographic Facts Set, Type 1, Book Match, Alberta-British Columbia-Manitoba-New Brunswick-Newfoundland-Nova Scotia-Ontario-Prince Edward Island-Quebec-Saskatchewan 3.00
11C,20S,BS Canadian Geographic Facts Set, Type 2, Book Match, Alberta-British Columbia-Manitoba-New Brunswick-Newfoundland-Nova Scotia-Ontario-Prince Edward Island-Quebec-Saskatchewan 3.00
4C,30S Canadian Artists Set of Indian Themes, colorful 4.25
6C,30S,FS Dept. of Industry & Commerce, Four-Color Saskatchewan 2.25
6C,30S,FS Department of Industry & Commerce, Saskatchewan, 4 colors 4.25
6C,30S,FS Dept. of Industry & Commerce, 4 color, Saskatchewan 1.50

Canadian (Military)

12C,30S,FS Army Set [1942] 14.50
1C,20S,FS HMS Kent, Guided Missile Ship, Commissioned Aug. 1963, Canadian 2.25
50C,20S,FS Royal Canadian Legion 2.50
25C,20S,FS Navy Ships, Canadian 25.75
8C,30S,FS Canadian Navy Ship Set, Grant-Mann 17.00
12C,30S,FS Navy Set [1942] 7.50
50C,20S,FS Canadian Navy Ships 23.00
50C,20S,MS Canadian Naval Ships 20.00
50C,20S,MS Canadian Navy Ships 18.00
12C,30S,FS RCAF Set [1942] 18.00
1FB,30S,FS Royal Canadian Navy, Bookmatch Mfg, w/CN tax stamp 7.00
11C,20S Ontario Welcomes You, D.D. Bean, Canada 1.00
11C,20S,FS Ontario Welcomes You [1957], Alexander Graham Bell..-Algonquin Park-Fort Wellington..- Grain Elevator..-H.B.Co...-Inner Gate..-Jack Miner's.. - Lift Locks..-Niagara Falls-Parliament..-Samuel Champlain.. .... 3.00
1C,20S,FS Canada Welcomes their Most Gracious Majesties, May 15-June 15, 1939, (B/W) photo (F) 2.50
1C,20S,FS Royal Visit/Visite Royale/1959 of Queen Elizabeth to Canada, Eddy Match Company Ltd, Canada 3.25
12C,20S,FS Quebec Set [1961], (BE) background 1.00
7C,30S,BS Canadian Radio Personalities, station (F), photo (B) 3.25
1C,20S,FS 1905-1965 Saskatchewan Diamond Jubilee, seal (F) 3.00
30C,20S,FS Tax Stamps, all with 1/5 tax imprint 22.50
2FB,30S,FS BC Telephone Co. Canada 1-(RD/WE), 1-(BE/WE) 2.00
50C,20S,BS Canadian Themes, assorted 3.00
5C,20S,FS Toronto Set [   ], Casa Loma,..-Centre Island,..-C.N.E. Grounds,..-Princess Gates,..-Toronto Skyline 2.00
4C,20S,FS Totem Series Set, The Bear-Graveyard Post-The Thunderbird-The Wolf, Type 1 [1965], (BK) striker, (WE) paper (I) 1.50

Canadian (Vista-Lites, Western Match Co.)

15C,30S,FS Set C-96 [1964], lettered, Sask. Travel Bureau 10.00
16C,30S,FS Set C-436, Bank of Nova Scotia Banff..-Brackley Beach..-Broadway Bridge..-Chateau Frontenac..-City View..-Harbour..-Lake Louise..-Legislative Bldgs...-Niagara Falls...-Parliament Buildings..-Peggy's Cove..-Skyline at Night, Montreal..-Skyline at Night, Vancouver..-The Town Clock..-Whitehorse..-Yellowknife.. Type 1 [   ], English captions 8.25

16C,30S,FS Set C-436, Bank of Nova Scotia Banff..-Brackley Beach..-Broadway Bridge..-Chateau Frontenac..-City View..-Harbour..-Lake Louise..-Legislative Bldgs...-Niagara Falls..-Parliament Buildings..-Peggy's Cove..-Skyline at Night, Montreal..-Skyline at Night, Vancouver..-The Town Clock..-Whitehorse..-Yellowknife.. Type 2 [   ], English and French captions 5.00

8C,30S,FS Set C-495, lettered, Type 1 [   ], Canada Iron 4.25

8C,30S,FS Set C-495, lettered, Type 2 [   ], Canron 4.25

12C,30S,FS Set C-575 [1967], Howard Smith Papers Charlottetown-Edmonton-Fredricton-Halifax-Quebec City-Regina-St. John's-Toronto-Victoria-Whitehorse-Winnipeg-Yellowknife 4.50

6C,30S,FS C-609, lettered, Saskatchewan 4.00

4C,30S,FS C-792 Klondike Days.. 3.50

5C,20S,FS Imprints Set [1963], SI-1 through SI-5 Antique Cars: 1911 Rolls..-1910 Ford-1921 Locomobile-1908/09 Mercedes..-1912 Mercer.. .... 5.00

5C,20S,FS Imprints Set [1963], SI-6 through SI-10 Vancouver: Queen Elizabeth Park-Vancouver Chinatown-Point Atkinson-Downtown Vancouver-Vancouver Harbour 2.25

5C,20S,FS Imprints Set [1963], SI-6 through SI-10 Vancouver: Queen Elizabeth Park-Vancouver Chinatown-Point Atkinson-Downtown Vancouver-Vancouver Harbour 2.00

5C,20S,FS Imprints Set [1963], SI-11 through SI-15 British Columbia: Stanley Park-Okanagan Beach-Peace Arch-Garibaldi Park-Rogers Pass.. 2.25

5C,20S,FS Imprints Set [1963], SI-16 through SI-20 Animals: Canadian Buffalo-Canadian Moose-Canadian Bear-Mountain Sheep-Squirrel....................................... 2.25

5C,20S,FS Imprints Set [1963], SI-21 through SI-25 Sport: Fishing-Golf-Water Skiing-Hunting-Winter Skiing 2.25

5C,20S,FS Imprints Set, SI-26 through SI-30 Glamour: Girl on towel-Girl in boat-Girl in tree-Girl by boat-Girl sitting on boat, Type 1 [1963], no caption for picture 3.00

5C,20S,FS Imprints Set, SI-26 through SI-30 Glamour: Girl on towel-Girl in boat-Girl in tree-Girl by boat-Girl sitting on boat, Type 2 Memories of Summer below picture 3.00

5C,20S,FS Imprints Set, SI-26 through SI-30 Glamour: Girl on towel-Girl in boat-Girl in tree-Girl by boat-Girl sitting on boat, Type 3 Memories of Summer in English & Fren 3.00

5C,20S,FS Imprints Set [1963], SI-31 through SI-35 Bar: Shanghai Sling..-Rye Egg Nog..-Gin Fizz..-Rye Alexander..-Vodka Martini.. .... 2.25

5C,20S,FS Imprints Set [1963], SI-36 through SI-40 Stampede: Cowboy in (BE) shirt-Cowboy in (RD) shirt-Chuck wagon race-Indian on horse-View of arena 2.25

5C,20S,FS Imprints Set [1963], SI-41 through SI-45 Rockies: Banff-Columbia Icefield-Lake Louise-Jasper Nat. Park-Maligne Park 2.25

5C,20S,FS Imprints Set [1963], SI-46 through SI-50 Niagara Falls: Horseshoe Falls-Falls at Night-The Floral Clock-Oake's Garden-Aerial View 2.25

5C,20S,FS Imprints Set [1963], SI-51 through SI-55 Toronto: Centre Island,..-Toronto Skyline-C.N.E. Grounds,..-Princess Gates,..-Casa Loma,.. .... 2.25

5C,20S,FS Imprints Set [1963], SI-56 through SI-60 Ottawa: Parliament Hill,..-'The Guards',..-War Memorial,..- Peace Tower,..-R.C.M.P. in Ottawa...................................... 2.25

5C,20S,FS Imprints Set [1963], SI-61 through SI-65 Quebec City: 'Bonhomme' Carnival,..-Quebec City..-Ste Anne De Beaupre-The Citadel,..-Changing of the Guard 2.25

5C,20S,FS Imprints Set [1963], SI-66 through SI-70 Ontario: Autumn Colors-Fort Henry-Summer Fishing-On the Beach-Autumn in the woods 5.00

5C,20S,FS Imprints Set [   ], SI-71 through SI-75 Quebec Province: Gaspé Sunset-Quebec in the Fall-St. Lawrence Shore-Along the Gaspé-Bake Oven 2.00

5C,20S,FS Imprints Set [1963], SI-71 through SI-75 Quebec Province: Gaspé Sunset..-Quebec in the Fall..-St. Lawrence Shore..-Along the Gaspé..-Bake Oven.. .... 2.25

5C,20S,FS Imprints Set [1963], SI-76 through SI-80 Montreal: Montreal Harbour..-Montreal at Night..-Place Ville Marie-'La Guinguette' Restaurant-Dominion Square 2.25

5C,20S,BS Imprints Set [1963], S.I.-81 through S.I.-85, Mailbox-Candles-Light-Noel-Greetings 2.25

5C,20S,FS Imprints Set [1963], SI-81 through SI-85 Saskatchewan: ? -Swift Current-Regina- ? - Lac La Ronge 2.00

5C,30S,FS Souvenir Matches, Western Canada Garibaldi Park-Okanagan Beach-Peace Arch-Rogers Pass-Stanley Park, Type 2 [   ], (BK) striker 1.00
5C,30S,FS Souvenir Matches, Western Canada Garibaldi Park-Okanagan Beach-Peace Arch-Rogers Pass-Stanley Park, Type 1 [1963], (GY) striker 1.00
12C,20S,FS Canada West Indies Trade Corporation 2.00

Canadian (Western Match Co.)

5C,20S,FS Animals Set, Vancouver, BC Canadian Buffalo-Canadian Moose-Canadian Bear-Mountain Sheep-Squirre 12.00
4C,20S,FS Canadian Artists, Vancouver, BC Indian Chief (facing front)-Indian Chief (facing side)-Indian Maiden-Indian Papoose, Type 1 [1965], (BK) striker, rough creamy paper (I) 2.50
4C,20S,FS Canadian Artists, Vancouver, BC Indian Chief (facing front)-Indian Chief (facing side)-Indian Maiden-Indian Papoose, Type 2 [   ], (GY) striker, (GY) paper (I) 2.50
5C,20S,FS Bartender Series Set [1969], Vancouver, BC Gin Fizz-Rye Alexander-Rye Egg..-Shanghai Sling-Vodka Mart. 2.00
5C,20S,FS British Columbia Set [   ], Vancouver, BC Garibaldi Park-Okanagan Beach-Peace Arch-Rogers Pass-Stanley Park 2.25
5C,20S,FS Western Canada Set Garibaldi Park-Okanagan Beach-Peace Arch-Rogers Pass-Stanley Park 1.50
4C,20S,FS Flowers Set Vancouver, BC Clematis-Dogwood-Lily-Orchid, Type 1 [1965], (BK) striker, rough creamy paper (I) 2.00
4C,20S,FS Flowers Set Vancouver, BC Clematis-Dogwood-Lily-Orchid, Type 2 [ ], (GY) striker, (WE) paper (I) 2.00
5C,20S,FS Historic Forts Set Vancouver, BC The Bastion-Fort Garry-Fort Henry-Fort Langly-Fort York, Type 1 [1965], (BK) striker, rough creamy paper (I) 3.50
5C,20S,FS Historic Forts Set Vancouver, BC The Bastion-Fort Garry-Fort Henry-Fort Langly-Fort York, Type 2 (BK) striker, (BN) paper (I) 3.50
5C,20S,FS Historic Forts Set Vancouver, BC The Bastion-Fort Garry-Fort Henry-Fort Langly-Fort York, Type 3 (GY) striker, (GY) paper (I) 3.50
4C,30S,FS Grant-Mann [1961-   ] SM3-6, British Columbia 2.00
4C,30S,FS Grant-Mann [1961-   ] SM7-10, Ontario 2.00
4C,30S,FS Grant-Mann [1961-   ] SM11-14, Alberta 2.00
2C,30S,FS Grant-Mann [1961-   ] SM15-16, Radium Hot Springs 1.00
2C,30S,FS Grant-Mann [1961-   ] SM17-18, Banff National Park 1.00
2C,30S,FS Grant-Mann [1961-   ] SM19-20, Jasper National Park 1.00
8C,30S,FS Grant-Mann [1961-   ] SM21-28, Royal Canadian Navy Ships 10.00
4C,30S,FS Grant-Mann [1961-   ] SM35-38, Canadian Pacific 3.25
4C,30S,FS Grant-Mann [1961-   ] SM43-46, British Columbia 5.00
4C,30S,FS Grant-Mann [1961-   ] SM47-50, Royal Canadian Navy Ships 5.00
2C,30S,FS Grant-Mann [1961-   ] SM51-52, Bartender Series 3.00
4C,30S,FS Grant-Mann [1961-   ] SM53-56, Vintage Cars 1.25
4C,30S,FS Grant-Mann [1961-   ] SM57-60, Antique Pistols 4.00
4C,30S,FS Grant-Mann [1961-   ] SM61-64, Canadian Artists 4.00
4C,30S,FS Grant-Mann [1961-   ] SM65-68, Historic Forts 1.25
2C,30S,FS Grant-Mann [1961-   ] SM69-70, Barkerville 2.00
2C,30S,FS Grant-Mann [1961-   ] SM71-72, Waskesiu 2.00
4C,30S,FS Grant-Mann [1961-   ] SM73-76, Totem Series 1.25
5C,20S,FS Montreal Set Vancouver, BC Dominion Square-'La Guinguette.'.-Montreal At Night..- Montreal Harbour..-Place Ville Marie 2.50
5C,20S,FS Ottawa Set Vancouver, BC Parliament Hill,..-Peace Tower,..-R.C.M.P. in Ottawa-'The Guards',..-War Memorial,..- 2.00
4C,20S,FS Antique Pistol set by Western Match Co. Ltd. 2.50
4C,20S,FS Antique Pistols, Vancouver, BC Colt..1874-English..1805-Le Faucheux..1862-Volca-nic..1856, Type 1 [1965], (BK) striker, rough creamy paper (I) 3.50

4C,20S,FS Antique Pistols, Vancouver, BC Colt..1874-English..1805-Le Faucheux..1862-Volcanic..1856, Type 2 (BK) striker, (WE) paper (I) 3.50
4C,20S,FS Antique Pistols, Vancouver, BC Colt..1874-English..1805-Le Faucheux..1862-Volcanic..1856, Type 3 (GY) striker, (WE) paper (I) 3.50
5C,20S,FS Rockies Set Vancouver, BC Banff-Columbia Icefield-Lake Louise-Jasper Nat. Park-Maligne Park, Type 1 untitled pictures...2.00
5C,20S,FS Rockies Set Vancouver, BC Banff-Columbia Icefield-Lake Louise-Jasper Nat. Park-Maligne Park, Type 2 pictures have titles... 2.00
4C,20S,FS Totem Series 1.00
65C,30S,BS Canadian, assorted themes.. 17.00
65C,30S,FS Canadian, assorted themes...20.00

Candy & Gum

Candy & Gum—Any matchcover advertising candy or gum, to include individual servings, candy companies, box candy or bubble gum. William Wrigley, founder of the Wrigley Chewing Gum Company, first put matchcover advertising on the manufacturing map with an order of 1 billion matchbooks around the turn of the century. This single order motivated match companies all over the country to modernize and enter the advertising market.

1FB,20S,FL Baby Ruth 5c, Curtiss Candies 6.00
1C,20S,FS Butterfinger, rich in pure DEXTROSE 2.00
1C,20S,FS,FL Dam Bar, 5c, 6,000,000 sold (SR/BK/RD) 2.00
1FB,20S,FS Enjoy Double-Mint Gum, Healthful Delicious 2.00
1FB,20S,FS Clark's Teaberry Gum 2.00
14C?,20S,FS,FL Wrigley Gum Series A-1097, B-8, B-69, B-126, B-170, B-254, B-336, B-391, B-419, B-419 A, B-468, B-495, B-495 A, B-630 .... 12.00
1FB,20S,FS,FL Wrigley's Spearmint, (BE/RD) w/GN arrow 4.00
1FB,20S,FS,FL Wrigley's Double Mint, (RD) w/(GN) arrow 4.00
5C,20S,FS Wrigley's Chewing Gum, assorted 7.00
1FB,20S,FS,FL Wrigley's Spearmint, (YW/BR) w/GN arrow 4.00
15C,20S,FS,FL Wrigley Gum Series A-442, A-456, A-515, A-516, A-521, A-576, A-601, A-606, A-617, A-644, A-683, A-760, A-783, A-850, A-885 .... 12.00
44C,20S,FS,FL Wrigley Gum Cartoons Set [1935-1936], A-905, A-906, A-907, A-908, A-910, A-911, A-912, A-913, A-922, A-923, A-924, A-925, A-926, A-927, A-928, A-929, A-955, A-956, A-957, A-958, A-966, A-967, A-968, A-969, A-973, A-974, A-975, A-976, A-984, A-985, A-991, A-994, A-995, A-996, A-999, A-1000, A-1032, A-1033, A-1034, A-1035, A-1062, A-1063, A-1064, A-1065 .... 30.00
13FB,20S,FS Chewing Gum & Candy related, assorted...10.00
15FB,20S,FS Older Gum, Candy, Nuts (Colorful), assorted 10.00
1C,20S,FS Jolly Jack 1/4 lb. 5 cents 2.75
1C,20S,FS Baby Ruth Candy, rich in pure DEXTROSE 3.00
1FB,20S,FS Delicious Tootsie Rolls, 1 cent and 5 cents, colorful 7.00
10C,20S,FS Candy and Gum ads, assorted 6.25

Casinos

Casinos—Matchcovers which advertise gambling houses or establishments that participate in legal gambling. Dating from the 1940s, most are from Nevada, and more recently, New Jersey. Over 2,500 varieties are known, and Casino collectors often include any matchcover depicting dice, gambling equipment, playing cards, or people in gambling attitudes.

5C,30S,BS Caesars Casinos in Atlantic City 9.00
47C,MZ,MS (one box) Atlantic City casinos 15.00
100C,MS Atlantic City Casinos, assorted 10.00
9C,MZ,MS Atlantic City resort casinos 3.50
85C,MZ,MS Atlantic City Casinos 18.00
25C,MZ,MS Atlantic City Resort Casinos 8.00
6C,20S,FS Circus, Circus Casino Set.. 8.00
10C,MZ,MS Lake Tahoe Casinos 2.75
20C,30S,BS Las Vegas Casinos 3.00
15C,30S,FS Las Vegas & Reno Casinos, assorted.. 4.25
40C,30S,BS Nevada Casinos... 5.00
3C,30S,BS Playboy Casinos in Atlantic City 7.50
90C,20S,MS Gambling Casinos, assorted 12.00
50C,MZ,MS Casinos, assorted themes 5.00
50C,30S,BS Casinos and Gambling Houses, assorted 18.00
10C,30S,BS Reno & Las Vegas Casinos, assorted 4.00
15C,MZ,MS Reno, LV, Lake Tahoe Casinos 15.00
15C,MS,BS Casinos, 5-Atlantic City Atlantis, 5-Trump, 5-Bally's 12.50

Civilian Conservation Corps

Civilian Conservation Corps—Over 500 different CCC Camp matchcovers are known, appearing between early 1933 and 1942. Most are green and yellow with the camp number and name appearing on the front. Collected by camp number, they are scarce and usually bring inflated prices.

1C,20S,FS Camp 134—220th Co. CCC, Canton, NY 2.75
1C,20S,FS Camp Co. 211, Camp S-102, Plattsburg, NY 2.75
2C,20S,FS Camps 220th Co., Canton, NY and 1387th Co., Elkton, VA 3.00
1C,20S,FS Camp 220th Co., Camps 134, Canton, New York 4.00
1C,20S,FS Camp 259th Co. Camp SCS -2(NJ), Freehold, NJ 2.75
1C,20S,FS Camp 259th Co., Camp SCS-2(N.J.), Freehold, New Jersey 4.25
1C,20S,FS Camp 259th Co, Freehold NJ 6.00
1C,20S,FS Camp Camp SP-36, 278th Co. CCC, Fairhaven, NY 2.75
1C,20S,FS Camp 310 Co. S-75-Pa., Hyner, Penna, scout (B), colorful 7.00

1C,20S,FS Camp 329th Co., S-51-Pa., Pine Grove Furnace, Penna 5.00
1C,20S,FS Camp 331st Co., S-116-Pa., Clearfield, Pennsylvania 6.00
1C,20S,FS Camp 333rd Co., NP-2-Md, Cabin John, Maryland 4.00
1C,20S,FS Camp 349th Co., P-63-Va., Big Stone Gap, Virginia 4.25
2C,20S,FS Camps 351st Co., Lyndhurst, VA and 331st Co., Clearfield, PA 8.50
1C,20S,FS Camp Co. 401, Marion, NC 4.50
1C,20S,FS Camp NC F-27, Co. 401, CCC, Marion, NC 'Oldest Company in 4th Corps Area' 3.00
2C,20S,FS Camps 1354th Co., Wellsboro, PA and 1355th Co., Gettysburg, PA 3.00
2C,20S,FS Camps 1420th Co., Fernandina, FL and 5483rd Co., Kerby, OR 5.50
2C,20S,FS Camps 1576 (Harding/Marion, OH) & 1587 (Tecumseh/Lafayette, Ind) 7.00
3C,20S,FS Camp Set from Company 1730, CCC, Camp Bunker, Bunker, Missouri 16.25
1C,20S,FS Camp Camp Westgate, 1915, Fallon, Nevada 2.75
1C,20S,FS Camp Co. 2214-V, Peekskill, NY 6.00
1C,20S,FS Camp Camp S-103, CCC Co. 2233 Veterans, De Ruyter, NY 6.25
2C,20S,FS Camps 2317 (Narbelt/Beltsville, MD) & 2335 (Glen Furney/Waynesboro, PA) 7.00
2C,20S,FS Camps 2319th Co., Sheffield, PA and 2335th Co, Waynesboro, PA 2.50
2C,20S,FS Camps 2335th Co., Waynesboro, PA and 2233rd Veterans Co., De Ruyter, NY 2.00
2C,20S,FS Camps 2351 (Ft. DuPont/Benning, D.C.) & 2384 (Stone Mountain/Moneta, VA) 9.00
2C,20S,FS Camps 2390 (Triangle/Salem, VA) & 2621 (City Point, Wis) 10.00
2C,20S,FS Camps 2690 (Hartwick Pine/Grayling, Mich) & 2748 (Black Hills/Pactola, SD) 10.00
2C,20S,FS Camps 2878 (Patroon/Center, TX) & 3363 (Edinburg, VA) 9.00
1C,20S,FS Camp Camp p-111, 3203rd Co. CCC, Averill Park, NY 4.25
1C,20S,FS Camp 3203rd Co., Averill Park, NY 6.00
2C,20S,FS Camps 3361st Co., Grottoes, VA and 3281st Co., Philipsburg, MT 3.50
2C,20S,FS Camps 3549th Co., Hedgesvile, WV and 3322nd Co., Beltsville, MD 2.50
2C,20S,FS Camps 3549 (Fairfax/Hedgesville, WV) & 3518 (Sand Run/Fairlawn, OH) .. 9.00
1C,20S,FS Camp G85, 6485, Winnemucca, Nev 2.75
50C,20S,FS CCC Camps [1933-1942], assorted 55.00
10C,20S,FS CCC Camps, [1933-1942], assorted 21.00

Christmas

Christmas—A very popular matchcover collecting category whose theme is Christmas or related winter festivities. Seasonally colorful and often highly decorated, Christmas matchcovers were made by businesses, banks, service establishments and product manufacturers. There are thousands known in all sizes, shapes and styles, a popular variety being the WWII Christmas Lion Giant Features (see Giant Features) which were the only Giants allowed to be produced during the conflict. Colorful Christmas matchcovers date back to the 1920s, and stock designs are plentiful.

3C,20S,FS Christmas Set [1939], Eddy Match Ltd., CN 5.00
9C,20S,FS Christmas Set (1958), Eddy Match Ltd., CN 3.00
4C,20S,BS Christmas Set [   ], Eddylites Carolers-Elf with brush-Sledding-Two people with presents 1.00
6FB,20S,FS Christmas Sleeve, NOEL, from Al S. Nelson 2.50
5FB,30S,FS Universal Christmas Set, ad: (I) Preble County Nat'l Bank, colorful 7.50

6FB,30S,FS North Pole, Home of Santa's Workshop, Matchoramas showing scenes of North Pole, NY 6.75

10C,20S,FS Toyland Set [1953], Bicycle-Doll-Green Hose-Horse Head-Man in shako-Stockings-Teddy Bear-Toy Pistol-Wheeled Toys-Wooden Soldiers, Universal Match Corp., 2.00

8C,20S,FS Christmas Carols set, no manumark 3.00

35C,MS,FS Assorted themes... 14.00

4FB,20S,FS Assorted themes... 7.00

16C,30S,MS foilites, Christmas themes 15.00

50C,MZ,MS Assorted themes 4.00

25C,MZ,MS Assorted themes 8.00

25C,MZ,MS Assorted messages and themes 5.00

4C,20S,FS Christmas Set [1956], Maryland Match, stock design Carolers-Children & Tree-Church Entrance-Fireplace.. 1.75

4C,20S,FS Christmas Set [   ], Panorama Set, Dickens Christmas..-God Rest Ye..-A Story Of..-God Bless... 5.00

6C,20S,FS Christmas Set, Panorama set, country name in (BK) Mexico-Italy-England-United States-Germany-Poland, Universal Match Corp., Type 1 [1949], (BK) FS manumark all capital letters 3.00

6C,20S,FS Christmas Set, Panorama set, country name in (BK) Mexico-Italy-England-United States-Germany-Poland, Universal Match Corp., Type 2 [1950], (BK) FS manumark mixed capital and small letters 2.50

6C,20S,FS Christmas Set, Panorama set, country name in (BK) Mexico-Italy-England-United States-Germany-Poland, Universal Match Corp., Type 3 [1950], (GY) FS manumark mixed capital and small letters 2.50

10C,20S,FS Christmas Set, Panorama Set, all words (BK) Ireland-Belgium-Mexico-Italy-England-United State-Germany-Switzerland-Sweden-France, Universal Match Corp., Type 1 [1951], no letters on either side of manumark.. 9.00

10C,20S,FS Christmas Set, Panorama Set, all words (BK) Ireland-Belgium-Mexico-Italy-England-United State-Germany-Switzerland-Sweden-France, Universal Match Corp., Type 2, Umc added to left of manumark 5.00

8C,30S,FS Christmas Set, 1795: Preparing the Feast-Roasting Apples..-Wild Turkey.. 1845: Christmas Calling-Making Candles-Open House.. 1895: Decorating the Christmas Tree-Viewing Scenes.. Universal Match Corp., Type 1 [1951], no dots either side of manumark, Close Cover Before Striking at bottom front 2.00

8C,30S,FS Christmas Set, 1795: Preparing the Feast-Roasting Apples..-Wild Turkey.. 1845: Christmas Calling-Making Candles-Open House.. 1895: Decorating the Christmas Tree-Viewing Scenes.. Universal Match Corp., Type 2 [   ], Umc to left of manumark and 2 dots right, Please Close Cover Before Striking at bottom front 2.00

4C,40S,FS Christmas Set [1955], Panorama Set, Santa & fireplace-Santa & reindeer-Santa in sleigh-Universal Match Corp. 2.50

6C,30S,FS Christmas Set [1957], The 12 Days of Christmas The First..-The Third..-The Fifth..-The Seventh..-The Ninth..-The Eleventh.. Universal Match Corp. 2.50

10C,20S,FS Christmas Set [1954], Ohio Match Co. lettered 335-A through 335-J, stock design Adeste Fideles-It Came..-Little Town..-God Rest..-Jingle Bells-'Twas the Night..-Coach & Horses-Greetings-Season's Greetings-Greetings of the season............................... 2.50

6C,30S,FS Christmas Set [   ], lettered 618-A through 618-F, stock design Greetings (on 1st 3), Season's Greetings (on last 3) 2.25

Clicks

Clicks—A specialized matchbook made in Italy and sold through the Maryland Match Corp. in America. Some versions were also made in the U.S. The matchbook has a curved end which clicks together to close. Clicks date back to the late 1940s and are popular today in European countries.

1FB Beau Nash Club, logo (F/B), wooden sticks 3.25
1FB Holsum Enriched Bread, colorful, Diamond Match Co. 2.50
1FB Kahili Bar, Princess Kaiulani Hotel, Hawaii, wood sticks (BK/RD/WE) 3.50
2FB no printing, test click-top books, one BK, one WE 2.50
1FB Newarker Restaurant, Newark Airport, wood sticks (BE/WE) 3.00
4FB Foreign w/Minerva tax stamp still in place - Wooden combs (all different) 4.00
5FB wooden sticks, assorted 3.00
20FB Maryland Match Co., assorted themes 20.00
3FB Maryland Match Co., restaurants 2.50

Cocktail

Cocktail—Several sets were produced in the mid 1930s to promote the consumption of hard liquor after the repeal of Prohibition. Lion Match Company had a set of 75 featuring 25 different popular mixed drinks on three varied background designs. The Hiram Walker Company issued at least 5 different numbered sets of 12 cocktails, plus a version was available where individual bars could put their own ad in a space on the front of the sets.

25C,20S,FS Lion Cocktails Set Type 1 [1935], rooster (F) Alexander-Bermuda-Bicardi-Brandy-Bronx-Clover Club-Eye Opener-Gin Rickey-Horse's Neck-Imperial-Liberty-Manhattan-Martini Dry-Martini Sweet-Mary Pickford-New Deal-19th Hole-Old Fashioned-Orange Blossom-Pick Me Up-Side Car-Soda-Three Little Pigs-Tom Collins-Whiskey Sour 20.00
25C,20S,FS Lion Cocktails Set Type 2 [1935], pouring from strainer (F) 15.00
25C,20S,FS Lion Cocktails Set Type 3 [1935], lemon peel in glass (F) 15.00
25C,20S,FS Lion Cocktails Set Type 4 [1935], hand holding shaker 12.00
75C,20S,FS Lion Cocktails Set, Type 1-2-3, full set 37.50
12C,20S,FS Walker Cocktails Set, numbered, Bronx Cocktail-Cablegram Cocktail-Canadian Club Sour-Manhattan Cocktail-Cowboy Cocktail-Colonial Cocktail-Tom Collins-Old Fashioned-Ink Street Cocktail-Mamie Taylor-Walker Gin Fizz-Dry Martini (see below)
12C,20S,FS Walker Cocktails Set, numbered, Type 1 [1934], (BK) background all the way left (I), New York manumark, longer cover than Type 21.00
12C,20S,FS Walker Cocktails Set, numbered, Type 2 [1934], (BK) background all the way left (I), St. Louis manumark, shorter cover than Type 1 .... 20.00
12C,20S,FS Walker Cocktails Set, numbered, Type 3 [1934], The Universal Match Corp. at left 20.00
12C,20S,FS Walker Cocktails Set, numbered, Type 4 [1934], Universal Match Corp. at left 20.00
12C,20S,FS Walker Cocktails Set, numbered, Type 5 [1934], FREE Universal Match Corp. at left 20.00
12C,20S,FS Walker Cocktails Set, numbered, Type 5A [1934], space (F) for dealer imprint 20.00
12C,20S,FS Walker Cocktails Set, numbered, Type 6 [1934], Universal Match Corp. FREE at left 20.00

Colleges & Universities

Colleges & Universities—This category mentions institutions of higher learning to include private schools and junior colleges. However, commercial colleges and correspondence schools are not included. Some have team schedules printed inside; however, those matchcovers are usually classified with Sports Schedules. College & University matchcovers often feature book stores, the primary source of most of this category.

1FB,20S,FS (dated) 1809-1959 Sesquicentennial Miami University, Oxford, Ohio (RD). 2.50
11C,20S,FS Yale University Set #1 [1939], Berkeley-Branford-Calhoun-Davenport-Jonathan
    Edwards-Pierson-Saybrook-Timothy Dwight-Trumbull-Yale 10.00
??C,20S,FS Yale University Set #2 [1947] 10.00
25C,MS,FS Assorted states and locations 12.50
295C,20S,FS Mostly from Northeast, assorted, album 55.00
15C,MZ,MS Assorted states and locations 8.50
200C,MZ,MS Assorted 42.50
650C,20S,MS Assorted, album 77.50
50C,MZ,MS Assorted 10.00

Colgate

Colgate—Designed by William Homer Colgate, Diamond Match Co. gave him his own division in the mid-1920s. Known as Group One, Colgate's designs included homey settings and later, he devoted numerous sets to the game of Bridge. Colgate invented an elaborate numbering system but left no record of the legend. Most Colgate sets and singles are collected by this number, which can be found on the inside.

2FB,20S,FS Colgate Bridge Series, Deco design, 1-PE, 1-OE 2.50
16FB,20S,FS Colgate, 'Let me live in the house...', in original celo pack, all same 5.00
50FB,20S,FS Horse/carriage silhoutte, sealed caddy, all the same 20.00
6C,20S,FS Design #1, [1932], initials, color set, each initial A-Z has a set, Colgate Custom Design
    logo (I), has no full length stripe (BE/GN/OE/PE/RD/YW) 2.00
4C,20S,FS Design #28, Throw A Stick, Type 1 [042038-12345], (BE/RD), numbered and titled
    set 2.50
4C,20S,FS Design #28, Throw A Stick, Type 2 [042038- 2345], (GD/OE), numbered and titled
    set 1.75

4C,20S,FS Design #28, Throw A Stick, Type 3 [042038- 345], (GD/OE), numbered and titled set 1.75

4C,20S,FS Design #101, Pictorial Matches Set, [071338-12345], numbered 4.00

4C,20S,BF Design #102, Pilgrim Settlers Set, [011940-12345], numbered 4.00

4C,20S,BF Design #103, The Hunt Set, [011940-12345], numbered................................. 4.50

4C,20S,BF Design #104, Knighthood Set, Type 1 [011940-12345], numbered 3.00

4C,20S,BF Design #104, Knighthood Set, Type 2 [011940- 2345], numbered 3.25

4C,20S,BF Design #105, Home Town Set, [011340-12345], numbered 3.50

2C,20S,BF Design #107, Ships Set by Gordon Grant, Type 1 [010439-12345] (BE/RD).. 1.75

2C,20S,BF Design #107, Ships Set by Gordon Grant, Type 2 [010439- 2345] (BE/RD)... 1.50

2C,20S,BF Design #107, Ships Set by Gordon Grant, Type 3 [   ], no scoring table (BE/RD) 2.00

2C,20S,FS Design #108, Reflection Set, Type 1 [110138-12345], numbered, (GN/RD) ... 1.75

2C,20S,BF Design #108, Reflection Set, Type 2 [010339-12345], numbered, (GN/RD) ... 1.00

2C,20S,BF Design #109, Old Fashioned Bouquet Set No. 2, [010439-12345], numbered . 4.00

2C,20S,FS Design #110, Buck Set, Type 1 [111838-12345], (RD/GN) numbered 1.75

2C,20S,BF Design #110, Buck Set, Type 2 [010339-12345], (RD/GN) numbered 1.50

2C,20S,FS Design #111, Cartwheel Set, Type 1 [112338-12345], numbered (RD/GN) 1.75

2C,20S,BF Design #111, Cartwheel Set, Type 2 [010339-12345], numbered (RD/GN) 2.25

2C,20S,FS Design #112, Sloop Set, Type 1 [110938-12345], numbered (RD/BE) 1.00

2C,20S,BF Design #112, Sloop Set, Type 2 [010339-12345], numbered (RD/BE) 2.50

4C,20S,BF Design #113, Pueblo Indians Set, [011339], numbered 6.00

4C,20S,BF Design #114, Romance of Ships Set, Type 1 [010439-12345], captioned and numbered 1.75

4C,20S,BF Design #114, Romance of Ships Set, Type 2 [010439- 2345], captioned and numbered 1.50

4C,20S,BF Design #115, Flowering Window Set, [012739-12345], numbered 2.50

4C,20S,BF Design #116, The Setter Family Set, Type 1 [121639-12345], numbered 2.75

4C,20S,BF Design #116, The Setter Family Set, Type 2 [121639- 2345], numbered 3.00

2C,20S,BF Design #117, Blossom Time Set, Cherry Blossoms & Forsythia, Type 1 [010339-12345], numbered 1.75

2C,20S,BF Design #117, Blossom Time Set, Cherry Blossoms & Forsythia, Type 2 [010339-2345], numbered 1.50

2C,20S,BF Design #117, Blossom Time Set, Cherry Blossoms & Forsythia, Type 3 [010339-345], numbered 1.50

4C,20S,BF Design #120, Crest Set, Type 1 [020239-12345] each initial A-Z has a set, (BE/GN/RD/YW) 2.75

4C,20S,BF Design #120, Crest Set, Type 2 [020239- 2345] each initial A-Z has a set, (BE/GN/RD/YW) 4.25

4C,20S,BF Design #120, Crest Set, Type 3 [020239- 345] each initial A-Z has a set, (BE/GN/RD/YW) 2.25

4C,20S,BF Design #120, Crest Set, Type 4 [020239-   45] each initial A-Z has a set, (BE/GN/RD/YW) 2.00

4C,20S,BF Design #121, Tom and Jerry Set, Type 1 [030139-12345], numbered, each letter A through Z has a set 2.25

4C,20S,BF Design #121, Tom and Jerry Set, Type 2 [030139- 2345], numbered, each letter A through Z has a set 2.00

2C,20S,BF Design #122, Bitter-Sweet & Bayberry Set, [070940-12345], numbered 1.75

4C,20S,BF Design #123, Trix Set, Type 1 [031139-12345], numbered 4.25

4C,20S,BF Design #123, Trix Set, Type 2 [031139- 2345], numbered 4.00

4C,20S,BF Design #124, Buddies Set, Type 1 [051739-12345], captioned and numbered 2.75

4C,20S,BF Design #124, Buddies Set, Type 2 [051739- 2345], captioned and numbered .. 3.25

4C,20S,BF Design #124, Buddies Set, Type 3 [051739- 345], captioned and numbered .. 3.00

4C,20S,BF Design #127, Dances of Many Lands Set, Type 1 [052939-12345], captioned and numbered 1.75

4C,20S,BF Design #127, Dances of Many Lands Set, Type 2 [052939- 2345], captioned and numbered 2.25

4C,20S,BF Design #127, Dances of Many Lands Set, Type 3 [052939- 345], captioned and numbered 2.25

4C,20S,BF Design #128, N.Y. World's Fair at Night Set, [070739-12345], captioned and numbered 15.00

4C,20S,BF Design #129, Peasants Set, [081540-12345], numbered 3.00

4C,20S,BF Design #130, The Minuet Set, [102042-12345], numbered 1.00

1C,20S,FS Design #131, no number or title on covers, Harlequin Single 1.00

4C,20S,BF Design #132, Hide 'n Seek Set, Type 1 [070840-12345], captioned and numbered 2.00

4C,20S,BF Design #132, Hide 'n Seek Set, Type 2 [070840- 2345], captioned and numbered 2.00

1C,20S,BF Design #135, Old Fashioned Bouquet Single No. 3, [112540-12345] (BK) 1.50

2C,20S,BF Design #136, Old Fashioned Bouquet No. 4 Set, Type 1 [112540-12345], numbered (BK/BE) 1.75

2C,20S,BF Design #136, Old Fashioned Bouquet No. 4 Set, Type 2 [112540- 2345], numbered (BK/BE) 2.00

2C,20S,BF Design #136, Old Fashioned Bouquet No. 4 Set, Type 3 [112540- 345], numbered (BK/BE) 1.50

2C,20S,BF Design #136, Old Fashioned Bouquet No. 4 Set, Type 4 [112540- 45], numbered (BK/BE) 1.50

1C,20S,BF Design #138, Harvard Single [101640-12345], (RD) 1.00

4C,20S,BF Design #139, American Milestones Set, Type 1 [101140-12345], numbered .. 1.75

4C,20S,BF Design #139, American Milestones Set, Type 2 [101140- 2345], numbered ... 1.00

4C,20S,BF Design #139, American Milestones Set, Type 3 [101140- 345], numbered .. 4.00

4C,20S,BF Design #139, American Milestones Set, Type 4 [101140- 45], numbered 2.00

4C,20S,BF Design #139, American Milestones Set, Type 5 [101140- 5], numbered 2.00

4C,20S,BF Design #140, Scottie Follies, [032541-12345], numbered 3.00

2C,20S,BF Design #141, Early American Set, Type 1 [011341-12345], numbered, each letter A through Z has a set, (BE/RD) 1.00

2C,20S,BF Design #141, Early American Set, Type 2 [011341- 2345], numbered, each letter A through Z has a set, (BE/RD) 1.00

2C,20S,BF Design #141, Early American Set, Type 3 [011341- 345], numbered, each letter A through Z has a set, (BE/RD) 1.00

4C,20S,BF Design #143, On the Alert Set, Type 1 [032541-12345], numbered & titled, w/Scotties 2.75

4C,20S,BF Design #143, On the Alert Set, Type 2 [032541- 2345], numbered & titled, w/Scotties 3.00

4C,20S,BF Design #143, On the Alert Set, Type 3 [032541- 345], numbered & titled, w/Scotties 3.00

4C,20S,BF Design #144, Mike and Ike Set, [032541-12345], numbered 2.00

3C,20S,BF Design #152, Crest Set, [011343-12345], numbered (BE/RD/WE) 1.50

1C,20S,BF Design #154, Old Fashioned Bouquet Set No.5, [121642-12345] 6.00

1C,20S,BF Design #155, Old Fashioned Bouquet Set No. 6, [121642-12345] 5.00

1FB,20S,FS Design #701, Laddies, w/2 Scotties, [1932] (BE/RD) 2.50

4C,20S,FS Design #702, Park Ave Set, [1932] (GN/OE/PE/RD) 1.00

2C,20S,FS Design #703, Bok Singing Tower Set, Type 1 [1932], Contract Bridge (GN/PE) 1.00

2C,20S,FS Design #703, Bok Singing Tower Set, Type 2 [1933], New Contract Bridge (GN/PE) 1.00

2C,20S,FS Design #704, Pedigree Set, Type 1 [1932], Contract Bridge w/Scotties (BE/OE) 2.00

2C,20S,FS Design #704, Pedigree Set, Type 2 [1933], New Contract Bridge w/Scotties (BE/OE) 2.00

2C,20S,FS Design #705, Park Avenue Set, Type 1 [1932], Contract Bridge (GN/RD) 1.00

2C,20S,FS Design #705, Park Avenue Set, Type 2 [1933], New Contract Bridge (GN/RD) 1.00

2C,20S,FS Design #706, Old Lace Set, Type 1 [1932], Contract Bridge (BK/PE) 1.00

2C,20S,FS Design #706, Old Lace Set, Type 2 [1933], New Contract Bridge (BK/PE) 1.00

2C,20S,FS Design #801, Pals Set, Type 1 [1932], Contract Bridge Set (BK/BE) 1.00

2C,20S,FS Design #801, Pals Set, Type 2 [1933], New Contract Bridge, Diamond in small print set, (BK/BE) 1.00

2C,20S,FS Design #801, Pals Set, Type 3 [1933], New Contract Bridge, Diamond in large print set, (BK/BE) 1.00
2C,20S,FS Design #810, Glendale Set [1932], (BE/PK) 1.00
2C,20S,FS Design #811, Charme Set [1932], (GN/PK) 1.50
4C,20S,FS Design #822, Bridge Match Set, Type 1 [1933] w/Scotties (BE/BN/GN/RD) . 2.25
4C,20S,FS Design #822, Bridge Match Set, Type 2 [1934], Diamond Match Co. w/Scotties (BE/BN/GN/RD) 2.25
4C,20S,FS Design #823, Bridge Match Set, [1933], (BE/BN/GN/RD) 3.50
2C,20S,FS Design #824, Hostess Set, [1933], (BK/OE) 1.00
1PQ Design #1208, [   ], no title or number, a PullQuick, (RD), package has title of Red Sails 1.00
1PQ Design #1212, [   ], no title or number, a PullQuick, (RD), package has title of Howdy 1.00
2C,20S,FS Design #1225, Full Dress Set, [1934], (GD/SR) 1.00
2C,20S,FS Design #1231, Coronet Set, Type 1 [1933] (BK/RD) 1.00
2C,20S,FS Design #1231, Coronet Set, Type 2 [1934], Diamond Match Co. (BK/RD) 1.00
2C,20S,FS Design #1232, Admiration Set, [1933], (GN/PK) 1.00
2C,20S,FS Design #1233, Roll Along Set, [1933], (BK/RD) 1.00
2C,20S,FS Design #1234, Retreat Set, [1933], (BE/RD) 1.00
2C,20S,FS Design #1235, Jack and Jill Set, [1933], (GD/SR) 1.00
2C,20S,FS Design #1236, Trumps Set, [1933], (GN/RD) 1.00
2C,20S,FS Design #1237, Shuffle Along Set, [1933], (BE/YW) 1.00
2C,20S,FS Design #1238, Quaint Set, [1933], (BE/YW) 1.00
12FB,20S,FS Design #1239, Bridge Matches, 'Waggies' in original celo pack, all the same (BK/MN) 5.50
2C,20S,FS Design #1240, Cosmopolitan Set, [1933], (GN/RD) 1.00
2C,20S,FS Design #1241, Park Avenue Set, [1933], (GN/RD) 1.00
12FB,20S,FS Design #1243, Bridge Matches, 'Pussy-Willow' in original celo pack, 2 sets (BE/GN/PK/YW) 6.25
2C,20S,FS Design #1244, Fifth Avenue Set, [1933], (GN/SR) 1.25
2C,20S,FS Design #1246, Old Top Set, [1933], (BK/GN) 1.25
2C,20S,FS Design #1247, Round Up Set, [1933], (GN/RD) 1.25
2C,20S,FS Design #1248, Irish Setter Set, [1933], (GY/RD) 1.25
2C,20S,FS Design #1249, Blue Ribbon Set, [1933], (GY/RD) 1.25
2C,20S,FS Design #1250, Hunt Set, [1933], (GD/SR) 1.25
2PQ Design #1251 [   ], no title or number, 2 PQ, (BK/RD), package has title of Steeplechase 2.00
2C,20S,FS Design #1252, Bok Tower Set, [1934], (GD/SR) 1.00
2C,20S,FS Design #1253, Sovereign Set Type 1 [1933], New Contract Bridge, (GN/RD) 1.00
2C,20S,FS Design #1253, Type 2 [1937], no title or number, same design as Sovereign, New International Scoring, (GN/RD) 1.00
4C,20S,FS Design #1256, Bridge Match Set, [1934], (BE/GN/OE/RD) 1.50
1FB,20S,FS Design #1256, Cat on Piano 2.75
4C,20S,FS Design #1257, Bridge Match Set, [1934], (BE/GN/OE/RD) 1.50
2C,20S,FS Design #1260, Saxony Set, [1934], (BE/YW) 1.00
2C,20S,FS Design #1261, Shaggy Set, [1934], (GN/RD) 5.50
2C,20S,FS Design #1263, Meadowbrook Set, [1934], (BK/RD) 1.00
2C,20S,FS Design #1264, Pickwick Set, [1934], (BE/VT) 1.00
2C,20S,FS Design #1265, New Contract Bridge Set, Type 1, [1934], (GN/R 1.00
2C,20S,FS Design #1265, Whiskers Set, Type 2, [1935], Contract Bridge Revised (GN/RD) 1.00
2C,20S,FS Design #1266, Park Avenue Set, [1934], (BK/RD) 1.75
2C,20S,FS Design #1268, Cherry Blossom Time Set, [1934], (BE/GN) 1.00
2C,20S,FS Design #1282, Ginger Set, [1935], (BE/OE) 1.00
2PQ Design #1286, [   ], no title or number set (BE/RD), package has title of The Invader 2.00
2C,20S,FS Design #1600-F, no title or number, package has title of State Flower, [1936] 1.00
2C,20S,FS Design #1601, Laddie Set, Type 1 [1934], (GY) paper (I), (BE/RD) 1.00
2C,20S,FS Design #1601, Laddie Set, Type 2 [1934], (BK) paper (I), (BE/RD) 1.00
2C,20S,FS Design #1603, Sampler Set, [040937-12345], (GN/YW) 1.00

8C,20S,FS Design #1604, Summer Sports Set, [031837-12345], 4-(GN) and 4-(SR), (GN): Deuce-Fore-Outward Bound-Tranquillity; (SR): Fisherman's Delight-High Dive-Riding the Waves-The Sport of Kings 3.00

52C,20S,FS Design #1607, no number or title on covers, [1936], Full 26 letter initial sets, packages have title of Goin' To Town, each letter A through Z has a set, (BE/RD), Scottie dog beside picket fence looking up at sign 40.00

4C,20S,FS Design #1609, Diary of Paddy Set, Type 1 [083037-12345] captioned set, A Fresh Start-Good Morning-Out of Bounds-So Tired 3.25

4C,20S,FS Design #1609, Diary of Paddy Set, Type 2 [083037- 2345] captioned set, A Fresh Start-Good Morning-Out of Bounds-So Tired 3.25

4C,20S,FS Design #1609, Diary of Paddy Set, Type 3 [083037- 345] captioned set, A Fresh Start-Good Morning-Out of Bounds-So Tired 3.25

2C,20S,FS Design #1610, Type 1 [082737-12345], no design number Old Fashioned Bouquet Set (BK/BE) 1.75

2C,20S,FS Design #1610, Type 2 [082737- 2345], Old Fashioned Bouquet Set (BK/BE) 1.50

2C,20S,FS Design #1610, Type 3 [082737- 345], Old Fashioned Bouquet Set (BK/BE) . 1.50

2C,20S,FS Design #1610, Type 4 [082737-   45], Old Fashioned Bouquet Set (BK/BE) .. 1.50

2C,20S,FS Design #1610, Type 5 [082737-   5], Old Fashioned Bouquet Set (BK/BE ...) 1.50

2C,20S,FS Design #1610, Type 6 [082737-   ], Old Fashioned Bouquet Set (BK/BE) 1.50

2C,20S,FS Design #1613, Type 1 [100137-12345], Colorful Mexico Set, titled, In the Market Place-The Potter 1.75

2C,20S,FS Design #1613, Type 2 [100137- 2345], Colorful Mexico Set, titled, In the Market Place-The Potter 1.00

2C,20S,FS Design #1613, Type 3 [100137- 345], Colorful Mexico Set, titled, In the Market Place-The Potter 1.50

2C,20S,FS Design #1613, Type 4 [100137- 45], Colorful Mexico Set, titled, In the Market Place-The Potter 1.50

4C,20S,FS Design #1614, Type 1 [020738-12345], Colonial Days Set, numbered 2.75

4C,20S,FS Design #1614, Type 2 [020738- 2345], Colonial Days Set, numbered 3.50

4C,20S,FS Design #1614, Type 3 [020738- 345], Colonial Days Set, numbered 2.00

2C,20S,FS Design #1615, Rascals Set, [01101237-12345], (GN/RD) 1.00

2C,20S,FS Design #1616, Type 1 [0110937-12345], Footsteps Set (GN/RD) 1.00

2C,20S,FS Design #1616, Type 2 [0110937- 2345], Footsteps Set (GN/RD) 1.50

104C,20S,FS Design #1617, no number or title on cover, packages have title of Crest, [1935], 4 sets of 26 letters each in 4 colors 50.00

4C,20S,FS Design #1618, Crown 4.00

2C,20S,FS Design #1618, Type 1 [022338-12345], Crown Set (GN) (F), (RD) (F) 1.75

2C,20S,FS Design #1618, Type 2 [1936], (I) blank, same design as Crown Set (GN) (F), (RD) (F) 4.00

52C,20S,FS Design #1621, Type 1 [1933], (GY) paper (I), The Diamond Match Co. in same size print as lines above and below, 26 letters each in 2 colors, Initial Bridge Matches (GN/RD) 40.00

52C,20S,FS Design #1621, Type 2 [1934], (GY) paper (I), The Diamond Match Co. in larger print than lines above and below, 26 letters each in 2 colors, Initial Bridge Matches (GN/RD) 40.00

52C,20S,FS Design #1621, Type 3 [1934], (WE) paper (I), The Diamond Match Co. in larger print than lines above and below, 26 letters each in 2 colors, Initial Bridge Matches (GN/RD) 40.00

1C,20S,FS Design #1621, Type 1 [031038-12345], Ships by Gordon Grant 3.00

1C,20S,FS Design #1621, Type 2 [031038- 2345], Ships by Gordon Grant 1.00

104C,20S,FS Design #1627, Type 1 [1935], 1 line Diamond manumark, 26 letters each in 4 colors, no number or title on covers, Crest design, (BE/GN/RD/YW) 50.00

104C,20S,FS Design #1627, Type 2 [1937], 2 line Colgate manumark, 26 letters each in 4 colors, no number or title on covers, Crest design, (BE/GN/RD/YW) 50.00

23C,20S,FS Design #1628, Type 1 [1932], Match Aristocrat logo (I), no number or title on covers, packages have title of Pictorial Matches, set 10.00

23C,20S,FS Design #1628, Type 2 [1933], New Contract Bridge scoring added, no number or title on covers, packages have title of Pictorial Matches, set 10.00

2C,20S,FS Package #1633, Roll Along Set (RD/?) 1.00

3C,20S,FS Package #1642, Landing of the Pilgrims Set, Type 1 [1934], no scoring table (I), (BE/ GN/RD) 1.00

3C,20S,FS Package #1642, Landing of the Pilgrims Set, Type 2 [1934], scoring table on (GY) background (BE/GN/RD) 1.00

3C,20S,FS Package #1642, Landing of the Pilgrims Set, Type 3 [1935], scoring table on (BK) background (BE/GN/RD) 1.00

2C,20S,FS Package #1646, Old Top Set (BK/GN) 1.00

4C,20S,FS Design #1657, Scotty Peek-a-boo Set, Type 1 [1935], no date (I), (BK) background, (BE/GN/OE/RD) 3.25

4C,20S,FS Design #1657, Scotty Peek-a-boo Set, Type 2 [100936], (BK) background, (BE/GN/ OE/RD) 3.50

3C,20S,FS Package #1662, Pére Marquette Set, Type 1 [1934], (BK) background, silver lettering (BE/GN/RD) 1.00

3C,20S,FS Package #1662, Pére Marquette Set, Type 2 [1935], (BK) lettering (I) (BE/GN/RD) 1.00

2C,20S,FS Design #1664, Pickwick Set 1.00

2C,20S,FS Design #1665. Whiskers Set 1.00

2C,20S,FS Design #1666, Park Avenue Set 1.00

104C,20S,FS Design #1667, Type 1 [   ] 26 letters each in 4 colors, no number or title on covers, Dog Looking at Sign Set (BE/GN/RD/TN) 50.00

104C,20S,FS Design #1667, Type 2 [   ], colors very light, 26 letters each in 4 colors, no number or title on covers, Dog Looking at Sign, (BE/GN/RD/TN) 50.00

2C,20S,FS Design #1668, Cherry Blossom Time Set, (I) blank (BE/GN) 1.00

8C,20S,FS Design #1672, Flower Series Set, [1936], American Beauty Rose-Apple Blossom-Carnation-Lilac-Mayflower-Mountain Laurel-Orange Blossom-Poppy-Rose-Violet .. 3.00

2C,20S,FS Package #1674, Pals Set [1936], (BK/BE) 1.00

8C,20S,FS Design #1683, no number or title (I), [1937], Pictorial Silhouettes on package, Adventure Bound-Before the Wind-The Catch-The Chase-Down the Field-Flight-Harvest Moon-Steeplechase, (BE)(2)-(GD)(2)-(GN)(2)-(RD)(2) 4.00

2C,20S,FS Design #1687, Gold Eagle Set [1936], (BK/RD) 1.00

1C,20S,FS Design #1688, Bok Tower, Type 1 [   ], no manumark 7.50

1C,20S,FS Design #1688, Bok Tower, Type 2 [   ], Diamond manumark 1.00

2C,20S,FS Design #1689, Royal Scot Set, [1936], (BK/RD) 1.00

2C,20S,FS Design #1690, Fifth Avenue Set (BK/RD) 1.00

2C,20S,FS Design #1693, Imperial Set, Type 1 [9-15-36-12345] (BE/RD) 1.00

2C,20S,FS Design #1693, Imperial Set, Type 2 [9-15-36- 2345], (BE/RD) 1.00

2C,20S,FS Design #1693, Imperial Set, Type 3 [9-15-36- 345], (BE/RD) 1.00

2C,20S,FS Design #1694, Silvery Lane Set, Type 1 [9-29-36-12345], (BE/RD) 1.00

2C,20S,FS Design #1694, Silvery Lane Set, Type 2 [9-29-36- 2345], (BE/RD) 1.00

2C,20S,FS Design #1694, Silvery Lane Set, Type 3 [9-29-36- 345], (BE/RD) 1.00

??,20S,FS Design #1697, no number or title (I), packages have title of Initial Matches, Regal, each letter A through Z has a set 1.00

8C,20S,FS Design #1698, Winter Sports Set, Bobsledding-Hockey-Ice boating-Skating-Skiing-Snorekjoring-Snowshoeing-Tobogganing set, 4-(BK) and 4-(SR), Series A 3.00

2C,20S,FS Design #1699, Mac Set, Type 1 [020837-12345], (GN/RD) 2.50

2C,20S,FS Design #1699, Mac Set, Type 2 [020837- 2345], (GN/RD) 1.00

2C,20S,FS Design #1699, Mac Set, Type 3 [020837- 345], (GN/RD) 1.00

20C,20S,FS Colgate Studios (Diamond), Part of Initial Set w/(ABCDEFGHJKLMNPSTW) 7.00

16FB,20S,FS Colgate, Harvard, (RD) in original celo pack, all the same 7.00

1FB,20S,FS Colgate Studios, ca. 1930, crest with initial 'L' (F), by Colgate (B) 1.50

9C,20S,FS Miown Set #1 [   ], pictorials, Auction Bridge table (B), (I) blank, logo at bottom (F) (BK/BE/BEGN/GD/GY)/(2)(GN/OE/RD)) 20.00

21C,20S,FS Miown Set #2 [   ], pictorials, Auction Bridge (B), Miown logo (I), Colgate Studios, 351 W. 52nd St. (BK/BE/BEGN/(2)(GD)/(2)(GY)/(4)(GN/OE)/(4)(RD)/(3)(VT)/ (2)(YW)) 40.00

21C,20S,FS Miown Set #3 [ ], pictorials, Auction Bridge (B), Miown logo (I), Colgate Studios, Grand Central Terminal (GD/VT/YW) + 18 others 40.00

21C,20S,FS Miown Set #4 [ ], pictorials, Auction Bridge (B), Miown logo (I), Colgate Studios Inc., Grand Central Terminal (BK/BE/BEGN/GD/GY/GN)/(2)/(OE)/(2)(VT) + 11 others 40.00

21C,20S,FS Miown Set #5 [ ], pictorials, no scoring table, Miown logo (I), Colgate Studios, Grand Central Terminal (BE)/(2)(GD)/(2)(GY)/(2)(OE)/(2)(RD)/(2)(VT) (2) + 9 others 40.00

21C,20S,FS Miown Set #6 [ ], pictorials, no scoring table, Miown logo and golf scorecard (I), Colgate Studios, Grand Central Terminal (BE/OE/YW) + 18 others 40.00

21C,20S,FS Miown Set #7 [ ], pictorials, no scoring table, Miown logo (I), Colgate Studios Inc. Grand Central Terminal 40.00

21C,20S,FS Miown Set #8 [ ], pictorials, no scoring table, Miown logo and golf scorecard (I), Colgate Studios Inc., Grand Central Terminal (BK/OE) + 19 others 40.00

20C,20S,FS Miown Set #9 [ ], initials, each initial A-Z, no scoring table, Miown logo)I), Colgate Studios Inc., Grand Central Terminal (BE/GN/OE/PE/RD/YW) 1.00

6C,20S,FS Music Lovers Series Set, Type 1 [11142-12345], numbered, Bach-Beethoven-Schubert-Brahms-Wagner-Tachaikowsky 6.00

6C,20S,FS Music Lovers Series Set, Type 2 [11142- 2345], numbered, Bach-Beethoven-Schubert-Brahms-Wagner-Tachaikowsky 4.00

1C,20S,FS Colgate Contact Bridge, 'Old Lace', ca. 1930 (PE) 1.75

6C,20S,FS Rainbow Set #1 [1930], each initial A-Z has color set, Rainbow Matchpack logo (I), Colgate Studios, 351 W. 52nd St. (BE/GN/OE/PE/RD/YW) 6.00

6C,20S,FS Rainbow Set #2 [1931], each initial A-Z has color set, Rainbow Matchpack logo (I), Colgate Studios Inc., Grand Central Terminal (BE/GN/OE/PE/RD/YW) 6.00

6C,20S,FS Rainbow Set #3 [1931], each initial A-Z has color set, Colgate Rainbow Initial Matches logo (I), full length silver stripe has colored borders (BE/GN/OE/PE/RD/YW) 6.00

6C,20S,FS Rainbow Set #4 [1931], each initial A-Z has color set, Colgate Rainbow Initial Matches logo (I), has no full length stripe (BE/GN/OE/PE/RD/YW) 6.00

6C,20S,FS Rainbow Set #5 [1932], each initial A-Z has color set, Colgate Rainbow Initial Matches logo (I), full length colored stripe has silver borders (BE/GN/OE/PE/RD/YW) 6.00

1FB,20S,FS Colgate Studios, ca. 1930, 'Pedigree' w/Scottie Dog (F/B 8.00

5C,20S,MS Colgate w/Scottie Dogs from different sets 12.75

16FB,20S,FS Colgate, Scotties at Play in original celo pack, 2 sets 22.00

1FB,20S,BF Colgate Studios, 'Romance of Ships (1)' ca. 1935 .... 1.50

1FB,20S,BF Sailing Ship (F/B), Colgate addr & Patent No. (I), no ad 2.50

1FB,20S,FS Colgate Studios ca. 1930, Silhouettes, Woman w/dog (RD) 1.75

9 sets Colgate Studios Issues [1924-1949] 7.50

15FB,20S,BF Diamond Match Co., Assorted, [1937-1943] 3.50

50C,20 Colgate Studios Issues, Assorted, [1924-1949] 26.00

Combos

Combos, 50 matchcovers and postcards 5.50

Combos, 175 covers and matching postcards 12.50

Combos, 100 matched postcard and matchcovers 22.00

Combos, 135 Holiday Inn covers and matching postcards 15.00

Reward Matchcovers were often used to increase sales. Details of the "contest" were printed inside the matchbook and cash, service, or merchandise prizes were often awarded for referring new customers.

Comic

Comic—Any matchcover single or set which features cartoons, cartoon strips, or comical (usually hand drawn) characters. This does not include comedy stars of motion pictures or television. A number of sets and singles feature cartoons on the inside, including the 1935 Wrigley Gum Cartoon Set, which features 43 different cartoons drawn by Art Heifant.

12C,CON,FS Bernad Creations Set, Made in (location) [1959], Bermuda-Brazil-Italy-Las Vegas-London-Madrid-Michigan-The Moon-Quickly by Rabbits-Russia-Spain-West Germany 15.00

12C,30S,FS Bernad Creations, Crazy Ads Set [1959], in original box Business Opportunity..-For Rent..-Forced to Sell..-Girls! Girls! Girls!..-Increase Automatically!..-Wanted Accountant..-Wanted Bookkeeper..-Wanted Clerk..-Wanted Short..-Wanted Student..-Wanted Talent..-Wanted Thirty.. .... 3.00

12C,20S,FS Bernad Creations, Droodles Set [1960], Roger Price Aerial View..-Cow on a Cold..-Early Bird..-Long Underwear..- Misguided Missile-Navel Orange..-Old Zipper..-Plunging Neckline..-Rocket Ship..-Rye Old Fashioned..-Sliced Golf..- Two Fat Ladies 5.00

12C,30S,FS Bernad Creations, The Lonely Ones Set [   ], Wm. Steig 'Chester, Admit..'-'I Don't Claim..'-'I Didn't Come..'-I Have My..-If You're..-People Are..-'Please! There..'-'Sorry Charlie..'-Why Pick..'-Will You Ever..'-You've Ruined..'-You Know..' 10.00

24C,30S,BS Dennis The Menace Set [1952], Anyone In Here..-Beat It, Sailor..-Billy, This Is..-Boy, This Is..Did The Light..-Here's Fifty Cents..-Hey, Mom! Bring..- I Caught It..-I Found 'Em..-I Lost Harvey's-..I Took A..-I Was A..-I'm Warning You..-It's The Sitter..-Nothing Special..Pssst! Is It..-Stick Him A..-Taking A Sunbath..-Tie My Shoe-Well, you're Getting..-Where's That Big..-Will You Please..+ 2 more 11.50

24C,30S,BS Fractured French Set [1950], (BK/WE) by Fred Pearson II & Richard Taylor, Adieu..-A la carte-Allons..-Carte blanche-C'est a dire-C'est pour rire-Eau de toilette-Endive-Faux pas-Femme de menage-Hors de combat-Jeanne d'Arc- Je suis..-J'y suis..-Legerdemain-Mal de mer-Mise en scene-Pas du tout-Piece de..-Pied a terre-Quelle heure..-Tant pis..-Téte a téte-Tout en famille 25.00

24FB Gag Set [1952] 5.00

6C,20S,FS Hy Kern (Hoffman Studios) [1939], Dog Follies Aw, Take A Chance..-Children, Meet..-Funny Place to Wear..- My what Pretty..-Some Service..-Wonder What Fifi.. 2.00

12C,20S,FS Hoffman Studios, NYC, Comic set w/dogs 15.00

10C,20S,FS Hoffmann Studio Dogs, 3-Zito, 7-Kern 8.00

9C,20S,FS Hoffman Studio Dog Series, 3 by Hy Kern, 6 by Zito 5.00

6C,20S,FS Zito (Hoffman Studios) [1939], Dogs, 45 etchings Hey! What's On..-I Don't See Why..-Ladies First-Oh! Mary's Back..-Only God Can Make..-Tables Turned 2.00

1FB,20S,FS Alcatraz 'World's Finest View of the Golden Gate' (F) (WE/BK) 3.75

1FB,20S,FS Leavenworth 'A Home Away From Home' (F) (WE/BK) 3.75

1FB,20S,FS San Quentin 'For a Few Days or a Lifetime' (F) (WE/BK) 3.75

1FB,20S,FS Sing Sing 'Spend Your Time Overlooking The Beautiful Hudson River' (F),(WE/ BK) 6.50

12C,30S,FS Match Grins Set [1952], Monogram of California College Boy..-Here's Something..- Hey, waiter..-Hey you..-Just in case..-No bones about..-She was just an optician's..-She was just a shoemaker's..-She's the kind..-So glad you..-We're So Glad..-Whadjya have to.. 7.00

12C,20S,FS Nebbishes Set [1959], Herb Gardner After I've Had..-I Am So Smart..-I Hate..-I Have An..-I Love You Too..-I Think We've..-I Want To..-Let's Stop..-Next Week..-No, I'm More..-So?-We've Got To.. .... 5.00

10FB,40S,FS Solid color w/comical saying on each 7.00

20C,20S,FS Stupid Inc. Set [1961], Caution! Flammable..-Feel sluggish?..-Fire eater's..-Help conserve..-Help stamp out..-I like you..-Light up..-Motorists' peek..-Murder, Inc...-Nero did it..-Open cover..-Quit your..- See the world..-These matches printed..-These matches rejected..-These matches the..-This has been..-World's champion..-You bring out..-You can earn.. .... 2.50

5C,20S,FS Trailer Set (BK/WE) cartoons Hold It! My mistake..-How to build..-I knew hauling..- You'll be happy to know..-You'll never catch me.., Type #1 [1955], (WE) paper (I) . 4.50

5C,20S,FS Trailer Set (BK/WE) cartoons Hold It! My mistake..-How to build..-I knew hauling..- You'll be happy to know..-You'll never catch me.., Type #2 [1960], (GY) paper (I) . 4.00

Country Clubs

Country Clubs—The themes of this category include country and golf clubs but don't include fraternal or social organizations. These match-covers come in all sizes. Often, country club restaurants, pro shops or golfing associations offer match-covers during special events. Older country club matchcovers sometimes printed a golf score card on the inside or back.

25C,30S,BS Assorted 8.50
25C,20S,FS Assorted 4.50
70C,30S,FS Country Clubs and Golf Clubs 35.00

265C,20S/30S,MS Assorted in Beach Album 22.50

1C,20S,FS Awase Meadows Golf Club, Okinawa, For The Best In Golf (B) 2.00

County Seats

County Seats--This category refers to matchcovers which come from a city or town where the court house of a particular county is located. Collectors try to collect a 20 stick matchcover with the name of the town and state on the outside, preferably on the front panel. There are approximately 3,200 such towns in the United States. The subject on the matchcover can be any business or event as long as the town and state are shown. Boxes are not preferred in this category.

450C,20S,FS Assorted 25.50

50C,MS,FS Kentucky & Tennessee towns, County Seats 2.00

15C,30S,MS Assorted 10.00

Dated

Dated—This category can mention dates in several different ways, however, the year is always present. A milestone date with a 25th reunion or 35th anniversary; a period date such as "From 1930 to 1965;" a full date (month, day & year), such as "Vote on November 8, 1935." Dated matchcovers do not include periods of known production (i.e. an Eisenhower Presidential matchcover must have been printed during his administration) or dates such as "Since 1910."

1FB,20S,BF Goldsmith's 75th Anniversary Year, dated 1945 (GY/BE) 4.00

10C,MZ,MS Dated with anniversaries, assorted themes 4.00

1C,20S,FS For Governor 'Turn to Page 1936' w/(BK/WE) photo (F), Blin W. Page w/record (B) 2.00

1C,20S,FS Jos. Swartz, Republican Candidate for Treasurer of Ottawa County, Primaries Sept. 15, 1936 (B), (BK/WE) photo of candidate (F), Merchants Industries manumark (RD/WE/ BE) 5.00

1C,20S,FS Elect Ted Kantor for Sheriff, Primary April 12th 1938 .... 2.50

1C,20S,FS Mary McEnerney, Democratic Candidate for County Commissioner, Election Nov. 8th, 1938 (F), (BK/WE) photo of older woman, double string of pearls, Vneck color 2.50

1FB,20S,FS Greater Oswego Exposition, [April 12-15, 1939], Compliments of Diamond Match (GD) 5.00

1C,20S,FS Re-Elect Lester S. Moll, Present Circuit Judge, Non-Partisan Election, April 7th, 1941 .... 2.75

1FB,240S,FS Winter Carnival, Ishpeming, Michigan, Feb. 21 & 22, 1942, shows 7 ads and photo of slopes 4.00

1C,20S,FS Howard V. Stephens for U.S. Senator, (BK/WE) photo (F/B), Republication Primaries August 1st, 1944 (S) 3.25

1C,20S,FS Re-Elect Judge Clayton W. Rose, Court of Domestic Relations, (BK/WE) photo (B), Election Nov. 4th, 1952 (S) 2.50

2C,20S,FS 1. Seattle Area Boy Scout Council Jamboree, Troop 15, July 1953; 2. St. Louis Boy Scout Council 7.50

1C,20S,FS American Right of Way Assn., May 21-26, 1967 .... 2.00

65C,MZ,MS Dated Jewels, Jewelites, Fairs, Cars, Banks, no weddings 12.00

20C,MS,FS Dated or Anniversary, assorted themes 4.25

Disney World & Disneyland

25C,30S,MS DisneyWorld [1971-   ], assorted themes 9.00
25C,MZ,BS Disney World and Disneyland 10.00
75C,30S,MS DisneyWorld [1971-   ], assorted themes 10.00
15C,30S,MS Disneyland and DisneyWorld 8.00
40C,20S/30S,MS DisneyWorld [1971-   ], assorted themes 6.00

Dogs

Dogs—A category of matchcovers featuring pictures, drawings or photographs of dogs. These may or may not include kennels, incidental scenes or drawings with a dog, or dog food products. Collectors in this category usually insist on a dog, drawing or photo, being the principal image on the matchcovers. Dog sets are popular, especially from foreign countries.

12C,30S,FS Diamond Set #1 [1968], 6 dogs each in 2 colors, Beagle-Collie-Pointer-Poodle-Setter-
Wire Hair Terrier 2.00
4C,20S,FS Diamond Set #2 [   ], 3 beagles-2 collies-2 Dalmatians-2 poodles, stock design 2.00
5C,20S,FS Match Corp. Set #1 (1950), Boston Terrier-Cocker Spaniel-Collie-Dachshund-
Pekingese stock design 1.00
6C,20S,FS Party Dogs Set [1951] Call me a taxi-Hmm!-Ping pong anyone?-She got it wholesale-
She's such an actress!-She snubbed me 2.50
4C,32S,FS Personality Pups Set (1951), Beau Brummel-Danny Doxie-Pampered Poodle, He-
Shore Leave.. .... 1.75
5C,20S,FS Superior Set #1 (1945), Blue Ribbon Dogs Boxer (YW)-Cocker Spaniel (full view)-
Great Dane (RD)-Shepherd (BE)-Wire Hair Terrier (full view) 3.50
5C,20S,FS Superior Set #2 [1946], Blue Ribbon Dogs, Cocker Spaniel (head view)-Collie-
Retriever-Setter-Wire Hair Terrier (head view) 2.50
5C,20S,FS Superior Dogs #3, [1947], ad: Milton T. Payne, Jr., Bryan, TX, match cover collector
.... 5.00
5C,20S,FS Superior Set #3 [1947], Blue Ribbon Dogs Boxer (WE)-Bulldog-Great Dane (BN)-
Shepherd (GY)-Terrier.. 1.00
5C,20S,FS Superior Set #4 [1948], Blue Ribbon Dogs Chihuahua-Chow-Pointer-Saint Bernard-
Setter 9.50
5C,20S,FS Superior Dogs #4, 1948, ad: Joseph W. Lemming, Adams, MA, match cover collector
.... 18.00
5C,20S,FS Superior Set #5 [1949], Blue Ribbon Dogs Collie-English Setter-Greyhound-Schnau-
zer-Spaniel 5.00

5C,20S,FS Superior Dogs #5, 1949, ad: Pop Leeming, Adams, MA, match cover collector 3.00
5C,20S,FS Superior Set #? [   ], stock design, Basset Hounds-Collie-English Setter-Schnauzer-
      Terrier 1.00
4C,20S,FS Superior Set #? [   ], picture (F), Basset Hounds-Collie-Setter-Terrier 1.00
4C,20S,FS Superior Set #? [   ], name & picture (F) Boxer-Collie-Great Dane-Terrier 1.00
6C,20S,FS Calo Dogs Set, Type 1 [1936], Universal Match Corporation, Boston Terrier-Cocker
      Spaniel-English Setter-Samoyede-Scottish Terrier-Wire Haired Fox Terrier 10.00
6C,20S,FS Calo Dogs Set, Type 2 [1936], Made in America added to manumark, Boston Terrier-
      Cocker Spaniel-English Setter-Samoyede-Scottish Terrier-Wire Haired Fox Terrier 10.00
15C,20S,FS Scottie Dog, assorted themes 8.00

Diamond Quality (other Quality and Safety First)

Diamond Quality—An early trademark used by the Diamond Match Co. between 1926 and 1936. It appears to have at least eight variations and was found on the footer (lower left portion of the front cover). DQs, as they are known, are rare and considered scarce in any condition. This "quality" trademark started a landslide of other company trademarks which eventually included Eddy Quality, Union Quality, American Quality, Empire Quality, Stone's Quality, and American Art Quality. Other footers of this period include Diamond Safety First, Lion Safety First, and Green Hat.

Diamond Quality

1C,20S,FS The Albert Pike Hotel, Little Rock, Ark 2.25
1C,20S,FS Albert Sheetz Mission Candies/Ice Cream 2.25
1C,20S,FS Allis-Chalmers Equipment, Drott's, Milwaukee, WI 1.50
1FB,20S,FS American Gas, globe (F), ad (B) 4.00
1C,20S,FS Compliments of American Red Cross 9.00
1C,20S,FS Hotel Anderson, English Coffee Shop, picture (B), Anderson, Ind. 3.25
1C,20S,FS MI-31 Antiseptic Mouth Wash 2.25
1FB,20S,FS The Army and Navy Club, Washington D.C., logo (F/B) 3.50
1C,20S,FS Arthur Feilchenfeld Hats, Caps, Gloves (B/W) photo of Arthur (F) 1.75
1C,20S,FS Athens Athletic Club, Oakland, Ca. (DBE/RD) logo (F) 3.50
1C,20S,FS Atlanta Hotel 2.25
1FB,20S,FS Atlantic White Flash gas (B), ad: McMichaels General Store, Monroe Co., PA (F)
      (BE/RD/BK) 2.50
1C,20S,FS Atlantic White Flash Gas, ad: Americus Hotel, Allentown, PA (F) 6.25
1C,20S,FS Hotel Auditorium, picture (B), Rates $2.00 and up 3.00
1C,20S,FS Auditorium Hotel, $2.00 to $2.50, Cleveland 4.50
1C,20S,FS B & B Steak Station, Cuyahoga Falls, O., drawing (B) 3.50
1FB,20S,FS B/G Sandwich Shop, Inc. (OE/BK/GN) 4.25
1FB,20S,FS Hotel Bancroft, Saginaw, Michigan, (BK/WE) photo 2.25
1C,20S,FS Bar-B-Q (B), Cabin Bar-B-Q, 'Bar-B-Q at its best', stock 2.75
1C,20S,FS Sea Food (B), the Barre Restaurant, Barre, VT, stock 2.00
1C,20S,FS Beech-Nut Gum (F), Marlboro Cigarettes (B), A. Schulte (S) 9.25
1C,20S,FS Belmont Restaurant, Wilkes Barre, PA and Alco Lunch, Pottsville, PA 2.50
1C,20S,FS Hotel Benson, Absolutely Fireproof 7.00

1C,20S,FS Hotel Benton, Pacific Hiway, US99W 2.25

1C,20S,FS A. Berkowitz Bar & Grill, Braddock, Pa., stock 7.25

1C,20S,FS,FL Berwind Pocahontas and New River Smokeless Coal (RD) w/(BK/WE) writing
.... 1.50

1C,20S,FS The Bienville, New Orleans, LA 2.25

1C,20S,FS Big Jo, Sells Best Because It Is Best 3.00

1C,20S,FS Home Cooking (B), A Bit of Sweden Smorgasbord, Portland, Ore, stock 3.50

1C,20S,FS The Blackstone Hotel, Chicago, Ill. 3.50

1FB,20S,FS Blossom Bloomers are designed for Comfort, Durability and Wear (F), bloomered
girl touching toes (B), logo (S), (BE/RD/WE) 10.00

1FB,20S,FS Blue Parrot Patio, Oak Park Ill, w/colorful Parrot (B) 7.50

1C,20S,FS Blue Pig Barbecue, open until 12 O'Clock 3.50

1C,20S,FS Blum's, Polk & California Sts., San Francisco, Cal. (shows two costumed dancers)
.... 3.75

1C,20S,FS,FL Blums Ice Cream/Candy/Pastry 3.75

1C,20S,FS Hotel Boise, Boise, ID 2.50

1C,20S,FS,FL Bouquet Cohn Cigar Company, San Francisco 7.50

1C,20S,FS Bowman's in Needham, Mass...For Good Food 1.50

1C,20S,FS Brace for Auto and Truck Loans, Glenn W. Brace, 2608 So. Figueroa St., Phone
Prospect 2001, Los Angeles 1.75

1C,20S,FS The Brass Rail, San Diego 3.50

1C,20S,FS Hotel Breakers, Cedar Point on Lake Erie, girl swimming (F), hotel (B), colorful 2.50

1C,20S,FS Hotel Broadview, Emporia, Kansas, Rates $2.00 and up, pictures (B/F) 1.25

1C,20S,FS Bromo-Seltzer (WE) top bottle (F/B) 3.25

1C,20S,FS Bromo-Seltzer Stock Design, bottle, (RD) top 5.00

1C,20S,FS Bromo-Seltzer, girls (B), stock, error 3.25

1C,20S,FS Brook Forest Inn, drawing of inn (B) in Brook Forest, Colorado - Six Miles Above
Evergreen on Cub Creek 1.50

1C,20S,FS The Brown Derby on Wilshire at Alexandria in Los Angeles (other addresses) 5.50

1FB,20S,FS Brown, Stevens & Fifield Inc Monuments (F), (BK/WE) photo of Hartford
monument (B) (BK/SR) 4.00

1C,20S,FS Bullock & Jones Co., San Francisco 2.00

1C,20S,FS ad: Cabin Bar-B-Q (F), stock Bar-B-Q (B) 6.75

1C,20S,FS Café Boulevard, Allston, Mass. 3.25

1C,20S,FS Café El Portal in San Francisco - Club Breakfasts, Special Luncheons, Afternoon Teas,
Special Dinners, Fountain Service, Midnight Supper 3.25

1C,20S,FS Calaveras Cement Co., San Francisco 2.75

1C,20S,FS Camell Brothers Café, Dallas, Texas 2.75

1C,20S,FS The Carpenter, Manchester New Hampshire 3.00

1FB,20S,FS Case de Vallejo Hotel (F), phone Valley 390 (S), rates & ad (B) 4.25

1C,20S,FS The Chancellor Hotel, Parkersburg, W.Va., picture (B), 220 Rooms, Modern-Fireproof
.... 4.00

1C,20S,FS Cheyenne Hotel, Colorado Springs, CO, stock 4.00

1C,20S,FS Chicago Town and Tennis Club, drawing of club (B), Briergate 1750 (S) 1.50

1C,20S,FS Chuckles Candy at Walgreen's .... ' 3.00

1C,20S,FS City Club, Jacob Schmidt Brewing Co 6.00

1C,20S,FS Claremont Country Club, Oakland, Calif. 5.75

1C,20S,FS L. Clark Conner, Auto Loans, Los Angeles 2.75

1C,20S,FS Hotel Clarke, Hastings, Nebraska, rates (S) 3.00

1C,20S,FS Hotel Irvin Cobb, Paducah, Kentucky (BK/RD) 2.00

1FB,20S,FS Coca-Cola (GN/RD/WE) small bottle (B) w/Refresh Yourself 12.50

1C,20S,FS Drink Coca-Cola - Refresh Yourself (drawing of 5 cent bottle on B) (S) says - A PURE
DRINK OF NATURAL FLAVORS 9.75

1C,20S,FS The Commodore Perry, Toledo, Ohio 4.25

1C,20S,FS Congress Hotel and Annex, Chicago, H.L. Kaufman, Pres., drawing (B) 5.00

1FB,20S,FS Consumers' Cooperative Services, Inc., 433 West 21st St., New York, logo (F), name (B) 3.00
1C,20S,FS Coon Chicken Dinner (F/B), Coon Chicken 50c (BK) 15.00
1C,20S,FS The Copley Plaza, Boston (et al) 4.00
1C,20S,FS Court House Restaurant, Celina, Ohio, BK 2.00
1C,20S,FS The Courtland & The McKinley, Canton, O. both pictured 5.00
1C,20S,FS House of Crane Oakland 'Candies and Frozen Things' - (drawing of crane stepping through cattails) 3.75
1FB,20S,FS Crane Co, Everything for Any Plumbing Installation Anywhere, Chicago, NY, Atlantic, City, San Francisco, (LGN/YW/BK) 4.00
1C,20S,FL Crescent Park, Riverside, R.I. 3.50
1C,20S,FS Crouse's Restaurant, Eaton, Ohio, stock 3.00
1FB,20S,FS The Cullen Hotel, Salt Lake City (BK/GN/RD) 4.25
1C,20S,FS Davenport Hotel, Spokane, U.S.A., picture (B) 3.75
1C,20S,FS De Met's Candies 'Meet me at De Met's' (DBN) logo (TN) background 1.25
1C,20S,FS,FL Demetre Barbecued Chicken Sandwiches, From Wilmette, chip on striker 3.50
1C,20S,FS Denver Country Club, Denver, Colo. 3.00
1FB,20S,FS Diamond Book Matches (F), Try us for a Shoe Shine (B) 2.50
1C,20S,FS Diamond Book Matches w/Comapny logo 2.25
1FB,20S,FS shows color painting of Horse w/Dixie (F), Horse farm w/fence (B), single line Diamond Match manumark (RD) 10.75
1C,20S,FS Doyle's Pharmacy, 17th Ave. & Grant, stock 1.50
1C,20S,FS Drake's Restaurant, New York City, colorful (F) 9.75
1C,20S,FS The Drake, The Blackstone - Distinctive Hotels in Chicago 5.00
1C,20S,FS Drakes Berkeley - Caterers and Restaurateurs - 2441-45 Bancroft Way, Berkeley - California, Salads/Sandwiches/Short Orders 5.25
1C,20S,FS Durbin's Restaurant, Hagerstown, Ind. (BK) 2.00
1C,20S,FS Eagle Hotel, Concord, NH, Opposite State Capitol, colorful 3.75
1C,20S,FS Economy Cleaners 'Suits 50 cents cleaned right' - 2319 W. San Carlos, San Jose, Calif. Just say COLUMBIA 1000 .... 1.25
1C,20S,FS The Edinborough Restaurant, Hartford, CT 3.00
1C,20S,FS,FL The Embassy Restaurant, 928 Fourteenth Street, N.W., Washington, D.C. 4.25
1C,20S,FS Emerson Hotel, Baltimore, Central Location 2.25
1C,20S,FS Eppley Hotels, bell boy (F), hotel (B), stock 2.00
1C,20S,FS Eppley Hotels, Hotel Fontenelle, stock 7.00
1C,20S,FS Ex-Lax, The Chocolated Laxative 1.50
1C,20S,FS Exchange Buffet, 1885, New York/Brooklyn/Newark 5.00
1C,20S,FS Fernald-Hackett Inc., Rochester, N.H. 2.25
1C,20S,FS Ferncroft Inn 670 San Vincente Blvd at Wilshire Phone Oregon 2658 - Our menu - Soup-Salad, Rhode Island Red Fryers, Lattice Potatoes.... .... 1.75
1C,20S,FS Feuer's Restaurant, Chicago, We Never Close 3.50
1C,20S,FS Field-Ernst Envelopes San Francisco, Los Angeles, Oakland (RD/BK/WE) logo, (GD) background 1.50
1FB,20S,FS Filene's Men's Store—Barber Shop—Restaurant 4.50
1C,20S,FS Florsheim Shoe, ad: The Florsheim Shoe Store, San Francisco, stock 3.25
1C,20S,FS Foster's Good Things 'TO EAT,' San Francisco & Oakland 3.75
1C,20S,FS The Franklin Fire Insurance Company of Phila., seal (F), (S) says - 'You May Delay But time Will Not' Benjamin Franklin 3.25
1C,20S,FS Frencroft Inn, 670 San Vincente Blvd at Wilshire 1.50
1FB,20S,FS The Gardner, Fargo, N.Dak, name (F), hotel (B), European Plan (S) 3.50
1C,20S,FS,FL Gateway Chain, four hotels (F) 3.50
1C,20S,FS Gene Comptons Quick Lunch Rooms - San Francisco, Oakland 'All Stores Open Day & Night' 2.50
1C,20S,FS The Hotel Georgia, Vancouver, BC 3.25
1C,20S,FS Hotel Gibbons, Dayton's Finest, picture (B) 2.00

1C,20S,FS The Golden Pheasant, San Francisco, bird (F) 4.75

1C,20S,FS Golden West Hotel, San Diego, Calif 4.25

1C,20S,FS Diamond Golf-Tee, no tees 10.00

1FB,20S,FS Diamond Golf-Tee Book Matches, full book without Golf tees, Golf bag (F) 12.00

1FB,20S,FS Diamond Golf-Tee Book Matches w/6 Golf (RD) Tees 75.00

1C,20S,FS,FL Green Grill, w/Chicago addresses, Chef (B) 3.00

1C,20S,FS Green Tree Business Men's Lunch 11 until 2 in Mt. Clemens, Mich. 3.25

1C,20S,FS Greenfield's Cafeteria 'Detroit's Best Popular Price Food' 1130 Griswold St., Self Service Restaurant 2951 Woodward Ave. 2.50

1FB,20S,FS Old Grist Mill Dog & Puppy Bread (BE/RD) 3.00

1FB,20S,FS Grosner's, Washington w/crest (F), hat, cane & gloves w/name, Men's Wear Stylists (B) 5.00

1FB,20S,FS H.D. Reese Inc Meats Poultry Cheese, 1208 Arch St. Philadelphia (GD/BK/RD) (F), large ham & box of bacon (B)... 6.00

1C,20S,FS Haas Candy San Francisco (BK/GD) (S) says - Geo. Haas & Sons, San Francsico, Est. 1882 .... 1.25

1C,20S,FS Hampden Grinding Wheel Co., Springfield Massachusetts - Oxide Aluminium and Silicon Carbide Grinding Wheels 3.50

1C,20S,FS Hotel Harrington, Washington, DC 2.25

1FB,20S,FS Hartford Accident & Indemnity Company (RD/BE)....................................... 2.25

1C,20S,FS, Henrici's Chicago, No Orchestral Din (Deco design) 2.50

1C,20S,FS The Henry Perkins, Riverhead, L.I. 2.50

1C,20S,FS Herb's Auto Repair Service, Buffalo, NY, stock.. 2.00

1C,20S,FS Hermann's Hamburgers Monterey, Calif. - Steak Dinners Sandwiches Beer on Tap (OE w/(BK) lettering).. 2.75

1C,20S,FS Sea Food, ad: Herzog's, Washington, D.C., stock... 3.00

1C,20S,FS The Hollenden Hotel, 1050 Rooms, Cleveland, Ohio (BE)............................... 1.75

1C,20S,FS Dine and Dance, ad: Hong King Lum, Sacramento, phone Main 1841, stock ... 4.00

1C,20S,FS Huntt's Inc. 'The Place to Eat' (slightly faded) - ON THE ARCADE - LYNN 'Our Specialty - Broiled Live Lobster' 1.50

1C,20S,FS Huyler's (candies) favored Since 1876 .... 4.75

1C,20S,FS Hygrade Frankfurters and Honey Brand Ham.. 6.75

1C,20S,FS Ice Cream, Chocolate, ad: City Grill, Honolulu, HI, stock 5.00

1C,20S,FS Ideal Fish Restaurant, Municipal Pier Santa Cruz, stock 2.50

1C,20S,FS Illinois Café..Always Open in Waukegan, Il.. 5.75

1FB,20S,FS Indiana Railroad system, train (F), High Speed Low Cost Electric Service .. 5.50

1C,20S,FS New Hotel Indio, Strictly Modern 'in nature's winter playground' Indio, Calif., drawing of hotel (B)... 3.00

1C,20S,FS Ingham's Restaurant, Franklin, Ohio (BE), stock 2.25

1C,20S,FS Ivins-Jameson Drug Company, Lebanon, Ohio, stock 2.00

1C,20S,FS Jack's Restaurant 615 Sacramento St. between Montgomery and Kearney Sts. PHONE GARFIELD 9854.. 3.75

1C,20S,FS Hotel Jamestown in Jamestown, N.Y. (300 rooms - 250 baths) 'The distinctive Hotel of The Chautauqua Lake Region' 4.75

1C,20S,FS New Hotel Jefferson, St. Louis, status (B)(GD)... 5.00

1C,20S,FS Josephson Operated Hotels (3 listed) (GN) 1.25

1C,20S,FS Julius C. Birch Inc. Cleaners and Dyers, All Phones OAKLAND 6620 E.J.Prasil, Pres... .... 2.25

1C,20S,FS The K, Billiards, Pocket Billiards, Snooker (GN/RD) 2.00

1C,20S,FS The Kentucky, picture (B), crest (F), Louisville, KY 2.00

1C,20S,FS The Famous Kernwood Café & Coffee Shop, Malden, Mass 2.75

1C,20S,FS Keystone coffee 'it's the flavor' (a DQ national) Highest Quality, Vacuum Packed 2.25

1FB,20S,FS King Edward Hotel, Toronto, 1000 Rooms, 3/16 excise tax paid 8.00

1C,20S,FS Koffee Kup Restaurant Geary at 18th Ave, San Francisco, Cal., store front (B) 2.00

1C,20S,FS Kolb's Restaurant, New Orleans, LA 3.00
1C,20S,FS Koolmotor, City Service Gasoline 4.00
1C,20S,FS Koppers Chicago Coke (RD) 3.75
1C,20S,FS Hotel La Fayette, Lexington, KY (RD) 3.00
1C,20S,FS Enjoy a real Cigar - La Insular Cigars 5 cents (drawing of full length cigar)(BE) lettering, (YW) background w/big cigar) 4.00
1C,20S,FS La Normandie, Cincinnati 3.50
1C,20S,FS Lamar Hotel, 160 Rooms, $1.50 Up, hotel (B) (PE/WE) 5.00
1C,20S,FS Laube Restaurants, Buffalo & Rochester 4.75
1C,20S,FS The Lee House, 250 Rooms, 250 Baths, Wash, D.C. 2.50
1C,20S,FS Levin's Auto Supply. Van Ness Automotive Products 6.00
1FB,20S,FS Liberty Lunch Co, 242 Northern Ave, Tel. Dev 6683, Sea Food w/lobster (B), colorful (stock) 4.25
1C,20S,FS Linco Ethyl Gasoline, ad: Lincoln Oil Refining, Robinson, Il (stock) 2.50
1C,20S,FS Lincoln Oil Refining Co., Indianapolis, Indiana (stock) 3.50
1C,20S,FS The Broad Lincoln, picture (B) 3.25
1C,20S,FS Hotel Lincoln, Indianapolis, Ind., 400 Rooms-Baths 3.25
1FB,20S,FS Restaurant Madrillon, Washington, D.C., A strikingly unique establishment (B), Peacock & Peter Borras, Host (F) 2.00
1C,20S,FS Maillards Restaurant (BK) 3.00
1C,20S,FS Maison Paul, San Francisco 2.50
1C,20S,FS Manhattan Restaurant, lobster (F), Harrisburg, PA (BK) 5.00
1C,20S,FS Hotel Marion, 500 Rooms, different photos (B/F), 500 Rooms 3.50
1C,20S,FS Marlboro Cigarettes, 20 for 20 cents 7.50
1C,20S,FS Matson Line - Oceanic Line - San Francisco-Los Angeles - Hawaii Oceanic Line - Hawaii, South Seas, New Zealand, Australia 1.25
1C,20S,FS The McCloud River Lumber Co, McCloud, California 3.50
1FB,20S,FS McKeever and Goss Realtors, Washington, D.C. (B), Mary A. Craig (F) .. 16.00
1C,20S,FS Medford Café - 9 High St. Tel. MYSTIC 6010 (drawing of front of café (B), (S) says - 'Always at your Service' 4.00
1C,20S,FS Hotel Miami, Dayton, O., picture (B), crest (F) 3.25
1FB,20S,FS Middishade Suits, Woodward & Lothrop, Washington, strong 3-man model graphic (B) 4.00
1C,20S,FS Eagle Mikado - The Yellow Pencil with the RED BAND 7.00
1C,20S,FS Milk of Magnesia Toothpaste, national 2.25
1C,20S,FS Miller House, Greenville, Ohio (stock) 4.00
1FB,20S,FS Hotel Mizpah, Syracuse, Samuel M. Corson, Mgr., Rates $1.50 up (S) 4.00
1C,20S,FS Model Hote, San Francisco 2.50
1C,20S,FS The Monson, St. Augustine, Fla. 4.00
1C,20S,FS Hotel Multnomah, Portland, ORE, indian (F), hotel (B) 6.75
1C,20S,FS Nan's Kitchen, Boston 3.50
1C,20s,FS Nathan's Restaurant - 272 Sutter Street - San Francisco phone EXbrook 6678'We serve nothing but STEER BEEF and MILK FED POULTRY' 3.25
1C,20S,FS,FL Nation Bell Brand 3.50
1C,20S,FS National Press Club, seal (F) 2.75
1C,20S,FS Nature's Remedy Vegetable Laxative 3.00
1C,20S,FS New Gables Hotel, Daytona Beach, Florida 5.50
1C,20S,FS New Hotel Indio, Indio, Calif, Hotel (B) 6.00
1C,20S,FS New Nicollet Hotel, Minneapolis, Moderate Rates 5.00
1C,20S,FS The New Pfister Hotel, Rates: $2.50 and Up 3.50
1C,20S,FS New Shanghai Café, San Francisco 2.00
1C,20S,FS Hotel New Weston, New York 2.50
1C,20S,FS The New York Athletic Club of the City of New York 4.25
1C,20S,FS Nofade Shirts, Boston Store 5.00
1C,20S,FS G.H. Nollen South Side Druggist, Newton, Iowa (stock) 4.25

1C,20S,FS Lake Norconiah Club, California 2.25

1C,20S,FS The Northwestern Casket Co. Funeral supplies, Minneapolis, Minn. (S) says - Redwood Caskets 5.00

1C,20S,FS O'Brien's 'The Finest Candy Store in America' San Jose - Refined Dining Service 2.75

1C,20S,FS Oakland's Finer Store (B), logo w/3 initials T, C, & P 3.50

1C,20S,FS Old Ben Coal, ad: Western Coal & Supply Co., Prospect 3400 (stock) 3.50

1FB,20S,FS Old Grist Mill Dog and Puppy Bread, wire hair terrier (F), Dog Bread box (B) (OE/BE,WE) 7.00

1C,20S,FS Old Overholt Rye Whiskey 5.00

1C,20S,FS The Oliver, 350 Rooms, pictures (F/B), 350 rooms 3.75

1C,20S,FS Olmsted Grill 1336 G Street - Washington, D.C. - Sea Food Steaks Chops - Broiled over Live Hickory Coals 5.25

1C,20S,FS The Olympic Club - San Francisco (RD) logo on (GD) background, drawing of building (B) 2.75

1C,20S,FS Olympic Hotel, Seattle, drawing (F) 3.25

1C,20S,FS The Owl Drug Co 6.00

1C,20S,FS Pacific Steamship Company 3.00

1FB,20S,FS The Palatine Hotel, Newburgh, NY, name & crest (F), hotel (B) 4.50

1C,20S,FS Panama Pacific Line, Coast to Coast 2.75

1C,20S,FS Hotel Paris, Westend Ave @ 97th, New York, 800 Rooms, Baths, Radios 5.50

1FB,20S,FS Parker Bridget Company (F), Nationally Known (B) (BK/WE/GD) 4.00

1C,20S,FS Hotel Paso del Norte - five minutes from Juarez, Mexico - Management Paul Harvey, Jack Chaney 4.50

1C,20S,FS Patriot Shoes, Star Brand Shoemakers (GN,RD,WE) 4.00

1C,20S,FS Hotel Peabody and Garage, Memphis 2.00

1C,20S,FS E.S. Peckham, Lackawanna Anthracite, Newport, R.I. 1.50

1FB,20S,FL,FEA Pelton's Garage, very colorful 2.00

1FB,20S,FS Pennsylvania Station in the Heart of New York City (shows station w/old cars (F)), train & plane (B), colorful 7.00

1C,20S,FS Penn Drake Oil, Free Crankcase Service (S), 35c (B) 5.00

1C,20S,FS Penn-Stroud Hotel, Stroudsburg, PA, crest (B)(RD/GD) 5.00

1FB,20S,FS Pennsylvania Railroad, terminal (F), train & The Liberty Limited (B) 2.00

1C,20S,FS The Hotel Perry, Petoskey, Michigan, no photo 1.25

1C,20S,FS Pete's Place, Leechburg, Pa. (stock) 3.50

1C,20S,FS,FL Phil Johnson Just Good Food, Northbrook, ILL 5.50

1C,20S,FS Hotel Piccadilly, New York, picture (B) (RD) 4.25

1C,20S,FS Hungry?, ad: Pick's Grill, Clarendon, VA (stock) 3.75

1FB,20S,FS,FL Pilsner Pale Beer, Gluek Brewing Co, colorful 4.00

1C,20S,FS Pipes, Hutchins' Drug Store, Winston-Salem, NC (stock) 2.50

1C,20S,FS The Plains Hotel, Cheyenne, Wyo., Indian (F) 5.25

1C,20S,FS Hotel Plankinton, Milwaukee, hotel (B) 4.00

1C,20S,FS Hotel Plankinton, Milwaukee, hotel (F) 4.00

1C,20S,FS Hotel Plaza, Union Square, San Francsico 1.50

1C,20S,FS Plee-Zing Treasure Hunt 2.25

1C,20S,FS The Portland Hotel, Portland, Oregon 7.25

1C,20S,FS Providence Biltmore Hotel 3.50

1C,20S,FS Post Exchange, West Point, N.Y. 7.25

1C,20S,FS Prima Rainbo Garden, Clark At Lawrence, Longbeach 2210 .... 2.75

1C,20S,FS Quaker State Oil Refining Co., Indianapolis, Ind. (stock) 2.00

1FB,20S,FS Raleigh Haberdasher (B), Washington's Finest Men's Wear Store (F) 4.00

1C,20S,FS The Raleigh, Washington, D.C. 2.00

1C,20S,FS Hotel Raulf, Oshkosh, Wis 2.00

1C,20S,FS Dr. Fred A. Raulino, Kay Jewelry Co., Glasses 2.25

1FB,20S,FS H.D. Reese Inc, Meats, Poultry, Cheese, Philadelphia, (OE/BK) 2.00

1C,20S,FS ad: Rendezvous Night Club Modesto, stock dancing couple (B) 4.00

1C,20S,FS Rendezvous Night Club, Modesto (stock) 2.25
1C,20S,FS Rexall Drugs, ad: Kinne's Pharmacy, Needham, Mass (stock) 3.50
1C,20S,FS MI 31 Solution, Save with Safety, Rexall Drug Store (stock) 4.75
1C,20S,FS Rexall, ad: Doherty's Drug Store, Olneyville Sq (stoc 3.25
1C,20S,FS,FL El Rey Asphalt Roofing & Shingles 2.25
1C,20S,FS Reymer & Brothers, Cigars, Pittsburgh, PA 2.50
1C,20S,FS Hotel Rieger, Sandusky, Ohio, Absolutely Fireproof (S) 2.25
1C,20S,FS Hotel Rio Del Mar, Rio Del Mar, California 2.00
1C,20S,FS,FL Rippe's Café, Seattle, Wash, crab 7.50
1C,20S,FS Ritz-Carlton Hotel - Boston 'Under The Same Management' 3.00
1C,20S,FS Ritz-Carlton Hotel, Boston, Lion's head logo (F/B) 4.75
1C,20S,FS Robak's Restaurant, Patterson, NJ, interior view (B), est. 1910 .... 5.00
1FB,20S,LIC E. Robinsons Sons Pilsner Lager, Scranton's Pure Beer, Patented Sept. 27, 1892, (Licensed Match), The Diamond Match Co., N.Y. (mint) 65.00
1FB,20S,FS Romolo Ragu Tomato Sauce, Cooked Ready for use, large (RD) tomato (F), same ad sideways (B) (RD/YW/BK) 4.75
1FB,20S,FS,FL Roy's Grill, 173 Court St, Rochester, NY, shows full length diner w/signs & name (BK/YW/RD) 8.25
1C,20S,FS Royal Recreation, Play Billiards, Dayton, Ohio 2.00
1C,20S,FS Hotel Sainte Claire Excellent Food - Coffee Shop 65 cents Luncheon $1.00 Dinner - Café $1.00 Luncheon $1.50 Dinner 3.00
1C,20S,FS Seafood, ad: Sam's Sea Food, Phone Garfield 9616 (stock) 2.25
1C,20S,FS Sardi's 'Eddie Brandstatter's New Restaurant' Hollywood Blvd near Vine - California's Most Magnificent Eating Place - Phone Hollywood 2131 .... 1.25
1C,20S,FS Scanlan's, Springfield, Ohio (stock) 3.00
1C,20S,FS Schaefer Equipment Co, Koppers Bldg, Pittsburgh, PA. 3.25
1C,20S,FS A Schulte, We Give United Coupons, Marlboro's 20 for 20c (B) 17.00
1C,20S,FS A Schulte Cigar Stores, From Maine to Texas, Marlboro's 20 for 20c (B) 18.00
1C,20S,FS A. Schulte, ad: Marlboro Cigarettes 20 for 20 cents 10.50
1C,20S,FS,FL Hotel Senator - Sacramento, Calif. 375 Rooms - 375 Baths 'Fireproof', showing capital and hotel 2.75
1C,20S,FS Hotel Seneca, Geneva, N.Y. (SR) 3.00
1C,20S,FS Service Restaurant, Greenville, Ohio (stock) 3.00
1C,20S,FS Seymour's Pharmacies 'Highest Quality - Prompt Service - Reasonable Charges' - Free Delivery Phone Your Wants 1.50
1C,20S,FS Shanghai Café Chop Suey, in San Francisco 4.25
1C,20S,FS Hotel Sherry, Chicago (BK) 4.00
1C,20S,FS Shevlin Pine Product - The McCloud River Lumber Co. McCloud, California - California White Pine and Sugar Pine 2.75
1C,20S,FS Shevlin Pine Product, Minneapolis, Minn. 2.25
1FB,20S,FS The Shoreham Hotel, Connecticut Ave, Washington, D.C., drawing 4.00
1C,20S,FS E.S.Shuck Hotel, 400 Rooms, 300 Baths 2.50
1C,20S,FS Sinclair Refining Co., Ad: Opaline Motor Oil, W.B. Mills, Eaton, Ohio 2.00
1C,20S,FS The Sinton St. Nicholas, hotel (B) 1.75
1C,20S,FS Hotel Sir Francis Drake, San Francisco 3.50
1FB,20S,FS Smoke Chasers, overcome breath odor (F), price & ad (B) 4.00
1C,20S,FS Snyder's Hotel and Restaurant, Versailles, Ohio (BK) 2.00
1C,20S,FS Southern Pacific Lines - 4 Great Routes, drawing of two people sitting in dining car (B) 8.00
1FB,20S,FS St. Charles Hotel, 200 Rooms, Rates from $1.50 (F), hotel & Pierre, S.D. (B) 5.00
1C,20S,FS St. Francis Yacht Club, San Francisco 4.00
1C,20S,FS Stan's Service Station, Albion, Michigan 3.00
1FB,20S,FS Hotel Statler, radio in every room 3.00
1C,20S,FS Hotel Statler w/list of cities, Radio in Every Room 5.75
1C,20S,FS Stats Operated Hotels (F), list of three locations (B) 7.25

1C,20S,FS The Fort Steuben, Steubenville, Ohio, picture (B) 2.25
1C,20S,FS Hotel Steward, San Francsico 2.25
1FB,20S,FS Stork Club, New York City (GN/RD/BK) 5.25
1C,20S,FS,FL Stratfield Hotel, large lettering, w/crest 3.75
1FB,20S,FS Tacoma Hotel @ Rainier Nat'l Park (BK/GN/RD) 5.25
1FB,20S,FS Tacoma Hotel, color drawing (B), at the Gateway to Rainier Nat'l Park, Associated
    Hotels logo (S), Tacoma logo (F), (BK/RD/GN) 5.00
1C,20S,FS Tanglefoot Stock Spray, Tanglefoot Fly Spray 2.00
1C,20S,FS Tarzan Triple Twist - Tarzan Twist Suite - two trousers $25.00 - Selix corner Eddy
    & Mason Sts., San Francisco, Cal. 3.50
1C,20S,FS The Temple Bar Tea Room, San Francisco 1.50
1C,20S,FS Wyrick's Movie-Teria Café - 1063 Market St. San Francisco - (F) Cadillac Dairy
    Lunches (on B) 2.00
1C,20S,FS Therese Worthing Grant Restaurant, 290 Park Ave. 3.50
1C,20S,FS,FL P U R E F O O D, Thompson's Restaurants 3.75
1C,20S,FS Thompson's Restaurants 'must be a good place to eat!' Famous since 1891, (S) says
    - Good Food - without delay 3.00
1C,20S,FS The Tiffin Restaurant - 16 West Washington St., Chicago 1.75
1C,20S,FS Toledo Parking Garage 3.50
1C,20S,FS The Toll House, Whitman, Mass. 2.00
1C,20S,FS Hotel Touraine, Boston, drawing of hotel (B) 5.00
1C,20S,FS Hotel Traylor, Allentown, PA, hotel (B), Radio in Every Room 5.50
1C,20S,FS Hotel Traylor, Allentown's Newest and Finest Hotel, Hotel (B) 4.50
1FB,20S,FS Tropical Garden Restaurant, New York City (RD) 3.25
1FB,20S,FS Tropical Tavern Restaurant, NY w/Christmas Church scene (B) (RD/BE/WE) 4.00
1FB,20S,FS United Cigar Stores, Melachrino Cigarettes (B), Wrigley's Gum (F) 4.00
1C,20S,FS United Cigar Stores Co. Beech-Nut Gum 6.00
1C,20S,FS United Hotels of America, GD 5.00
1FB,20S,FS Marlboro 20 for 10c (B), Paul Jones Cigarettes (F), United Cigar (S) 7.00
1FB,20S,FS Tobacco Yello Holder, diagram (B), United Cigar (S) 3.50
1C,20S Blot-r Match [1928-], Union Match 5.00
1C,20S,FS Accommodations (B), Utah Motor Park, Salt Lake City, Utah, 125 Modern cottages
    (stock) 5.25
1C,20S,FS Van Ness Automotive Products - Levin's Auto Supply Co. 'Everything for the Auto'
    .... 3.00
1C,20S,FS Van Orman Hotels, Four Hospitable Hotels 3.50
1C,20S,FS Vienna Restaurants, Atlantic City, N.J. 1.50
1C,20S,FS The Virginia Restaurant, 1413 Douglas St., Omaha, Neb 4.75
1C,20S,FS Virginia Tuberculosis Association (F/B) 4.50
1C,20S,FS The Waldorf Astoria, New York City, hotel (B) 4.50
1C,20S,FS Waldron - Master Cleaners and Dyers, (S) says - For Your Clothes Sake - PHONE
    MAIN 6351 .... 1.25
1C,20S,FS Walgreen's, ad: Peau-Doux Shaving Cream 2.25
1FB,20S,FS George Washington 1732-1932, Mt Vernon (B) 4.00
1C,20S,FS Hotel Washington, Washington, DC 1.25
1C,20S,FS 1732-1932, George Washington Bi-Centennial 5.50
1C,20S,FS,FL Wayflower Café, Cheyenne, WY. 2.50
1C,20S,FS Service, ad: Hotel Wellington, Omaha, Rates $1.25 to $2.50 (stock) 5.00
1C,20S,FS Frank Werner Co, Stetson Shoes 1.25
1FB,20S,FS White Pig Bar-B-Q, pig (F/B), (WE/BK/GN) 5.50
1FB,20S,FS White House Tea Room, Stroudsburg, PA, Phone 1057, Mrs. R.L. Burnett, stock
    Welcome (B), colorful 4.00
1C,20S,FS The White Spot, Beverly Hills, California 2.75
1C,20S,FS Whitehouse Inn, New London, Conn. Phones 5331-5332 .... 4.00
1C,20S,FS Service, ad: Whitelaw Hotel, 13th & T Sts., NW, Washington, DC, phone North 1741
    (stock) 4.25

1C,20S,FS Wisconsin Club, Milwaukee, picture (B) 1.50
1FB,20S,FS Woodward & Lothrop, Washington 3.00
1C,20S,FS Wyandotte Cleaning Specialists, Indian w/Bow (F/B) 2.50
1C,20S,FS,FL Yacht Club Straight Burbon Whiskey and London Dry Gin 3.25
1C,20S,FS,FL Yacht Club Whisky & London Dry Gin 3.25
1C,20S,FS Yellow Van, Anywhere, van (B) 3.25
1C,20S,FS Yoengs Chinese and American Restaurant, drawing of inside (B) 2.75
1C,20S,FS Young's Market Company, Los Angeles 2.00
25C,20S,FS Bobtails, assorted themes 12.50
1 caddy box only for 10 books, ca. DQ period (GN) 2.25
1 caddy box for 10 books, ca. DQ period, no matchbooks (RD) 2.25
1C,20S,FS THESE MATCHES ARE FOR YOUR USE OUTSIDE THE FACTORY, CARRY NO
      OTHERS SEARCH YOUR POCKETS, ALL MATCHES ARE PROHIBITED IN THE
      PLANT - CELLULOID CORPORATION (F) 5.00
1C,20S,FS Diamond Book Matches - CLOSE COVER BEFORE STRIKING MATCH - Extin-
      guish Match before throwing away (ad and logo for Diamond Matches (F/B)) 2.00
1FB,20S,FS Bromo-Seltzer for Headache (RD) top bottle (F/B), Bromo-Seltzer (S), wide striker,
      single line Diamond Match Co. manumark 15.00

Diamond Safety First

1FB,20S,FS Bromo Seltzer, gem mint condition, (RD) stopper 23.00
1C,20S,FS Clown Cigarettes, Diamond Match Co., clown (F/B) 35.00
1FB,20S,FS Safety First and Safety Always, ad: Diamond Book Match, single line large
      manumark, wide striker, ca. 1912, slight nick (F) 15.00
1FB,20S,FS Helmar Cigarettes, a few sticks broken, colorful 11.50
1FB,20S,FS New Process Clay Coated Folding Boxboard, Elkhart, Ind, colorful 4.50
1FB,20S,FS Standex Egyptian Blend Cigarettes, Equitable Bldg (B) 5.00

Lion Safety First

1C,20S,FS Abbott's Bitters Tones the Stomach 2.00
1FB,20S,FS ad: Ammonia Leak Detectors, Rahway, NJ 5.00
1C,20S,FS, The Armstrong Company, Boston, Mass, Dining Rooms, News & Cigar Stand 7.75
1C,20S,FS Hotel Astor, crest (F), hotel (B) 5.75
1C,20S,FS California Club, Los Angeles 4.75
1C,20S,FS Consolidated Hotels Inc., Los Angeles/Hollywood 5.25
1C,20S,FS Curtis Hotel, Lenox, MA 2.00
1C,20S,FS Davis Café Vallejo, Calif. Telephone 1858 .... 4.25
1C,20S,FS Omaha Elks Club Hotel and Café 2.25
1C,20S,FS Carl G. Fisher Hotels 2.25
1C,20S,FS Gaylord Inn & Gaylord Hotel 4.50
1C,20S,FS, Gilbert's Shoe Repair San Francisco, EXbrook 3735 .... 3.75
1C,20S,FS Happiness Restaurant, photo girl (F), Lion Match Co. 10.00
1C,20S,FS,FL Herbert's in San Francisco & Los Angeles 4.25
1C,20S,FS Hercules Gasoline has the Kick 2.75
1C,20S,FS M. Hoffman & Co., Bedford, Mass. 8.00
1C,20S,FS,FL The Italian Village, 425 W Eighth, Los Angeles, Phone: VA8594 .... 4.25
1C,20S,FS Joe's Grill, Berkley, Calif. (stock) 3.25
1C,20S,FS Lion Gaylord Inn, Jones St at Geary 6.00
1C,20S,FS Lou's Diner Mill Plain, Conn. Phone 3-9400 .... 4.25
1C,20S,FS Maryland Hotel, San Diego, Calif. 1.75
1C,20S,FS Midwick Country Club 2.25
1C,20S,FS Murray's Restaurants 'All Women Cooks & Bakers' 3.25
1C,20S,FS The Oceanside, Magnolia, Mass. 6.00

1C,20S,FS Palace Hotel, Missoula, Mont. (stock) 2.25
1C,20S,FS Hotel President, Lion Match Co., hotel (B) 6.00
1C,20S,FS Rippe's Café, Seattle, Wash., RD crab (B) 4.25
1C,20S,FS The Savarins Inc., Baltimore/Washington 2.25
1C,20S,FS Carl Wilke Cigarist, Sutter 8400 .... 5.00
1C,20S,FS Suwannee Hotel, St. Petersburg, Fla,. hotel (B) 2.25
1C,20S,FS Yellow Cab 5.00

Union Quality

1C,20S,FS The Aladdin Candy Shop, 211 Mass Ave, Boston, Mass (stock) 5.50
1C,20S,FS RCA Radiotrons, ad: B.M.& W. Service Station, N Baltimore, Ohio, Radiolas &
        Radiotrons (stock) 7.75
1C,20S,FS Cotton Club, Phone Schuylkill Haven 9411, club scene (B) 15.00
1C,20S,FS Drink Golden Dome Delicious Beverages (F), Fenway Pale Ginger Ale, Golden Dome
        Bottling Co., Boston, Mass, U.S.A. 11.50
1C,20S,FS The Hidden Door, 491 Lexington Ave, NYC, (OE/BK) 8.50
1C,20S,FS Francis Scott Key Hotel, Frederick, MD, drawing of hotel (B), muted tones . 12.00
1C,20S,FS Maritime Athletic Club, 2nd Annual Ball, dated: Nov. 17, 1928 .... 22.50
1C,20S,FS Niederstein's Restaurant, Lynbrook, L.I., map (B), (BN/RD/WE) 8.75
1C,20S,FS Powers' Asthma Relief 3.00
1C,20S,FS Union Match, Hotel Pullman, Newark, NJ 7.25
1C,20S,FS Silver Lake Inn on The White Horse Pike, Lobster (F), Lobster & Frog (B), colorful
        .... 12.50

English

8B Great British Achievements [   ], Concords-Conquest of..-The Four Minute..-The Hovercraft-
      Jodrell Bank-North Sea Oil-Water Speed..-The World Cup, average count 23 .... 5.00
16C,30S,BS Motoring Memories numbered (stock) 1907 Darracq-1912 Peugeot-1912 Hispano-
      1937 Austin-1914 Morris-1914 Vauxhall-1929 Ford-1922 Lancia-1924 Rolls-1929 Cadillac-
      1930 Delage-1930 Lanchester-1938 Triumph-1938 BMW-1937 Lagonda-1938 Packard 5.00
6B History of Banking [   ] 6.00
18B British Butterflies [1989], Cornish Match 5.00
10B Full City of Westminster Carnaby St, photo on each, London sights 10.25
4C,20S,FS Ceremonies of London, Beating The Retreat..-Chief Warder of the Tower-Yeoman
        of the Guard, Type 1, [   ], Contents 20 Matches 3.00
4C,20S,FS Ceremonies of London, Beating The Retreat..-Chief Warder of the Tower-Yeoman
        of the Guard, Type 2, [   ], Contents 20 Matches 3.00
1C,20S,BS Marriage of HRH The Prince of Wales and Lady Diana Spencer, 29th July, 1981, color
        photo of couple (F) 3.25
25C,30S,FS Restaurants, different British cities 2.75
35C,30S,MS Hotels, different British cities 3.00
17B Trophy Inns [1989], Cornish Match 5.00
4C,20S,FS Cries of London, Do You Want Any Matches?-Knives, Scissors & Razors to Grind-
        Old Chairs To Mend-Sweet China Oranges, Sweet China, Type 1, (BE) picture, Made in
        England manumark 1.00
4C,20S,FS Cries of London, Do You Want Any Matches?-Knives, Scissors & Razors to Grind-
        Old Chairs To Mend-Sweet China Oranges, Sweet China, Type 2, (BE) picture, Contents
        20 Matches Made in England manumark 8.00
4C,20S,FS Cries of London, Do You Want Any Matches?-Knives, Scissors & Razors to Grind-
        Old Chairs To Mend-Sweet China Oranges, Sweet China, Type 3, color picture, Cries of
        London on 2 lines 1.00

4C,20S,FS Cries of London, Do You Want Any Matches?-Knives, Scissors & Razors to Grind-Old Chairs To Mend-Sweet China Oranges, Sweet China, Type 4, color picture, Cries of London on 3 lines 7.00

1C,20S,FS Elizabeth R 1953 w/Crown (B), Her Majesty's Coronation 1953 (S), color photo (F) 3.50

1C,20S,FS Coronation Year 1953, Queen Elizabeth II, EIIR (F), pic (B) 3.25

1C,20S,FS Festival of Britain, 1951, Bryant & May, Ltd. 2.50

4C,20S,FS Gold Leaf Dogs [   ], Setter-Golden Labrador-Golden Retriever-Red Setter . 1.75

10C,20S,BS Grand National Winners, Specify 1971-Well To Do 1972-Red Rum 1973/4/7-L'Escargot 1975-Rag Trade 1976-Lucius 1978-Rubstic 1979-Ben Nevis 1980-Aldaniti 1981-Grittar 1982, Type 1, Bryant and May 5.00

10C,20S,BS Grand National Winners, Specify 1971-Well To Do 1972-Red Rum 1973/4/7-L'Escargot 1975-Rag Trade 1976-Lucius 1978-Rubstic 1979-Ben Nevis 1980-Aldaniti 1981-Grittar 1982, Type 2, Bryant and May, Canada 5.00

18B Hamilton Taverns [1989], Cornish Match 5.00

1C,40S,BS House of Commons 3.00

1C,20S,FS H.M. The King's Silver Jubilee 1935 .... 13.00

57B Last Steam Engines of the World 20.00

1C,20S,FS Her Majesty's Coronation [1953] 4.75

10B British Mammals [   ], numbered, Hedgehog-Rabbit-Bank Vole-Red Squirrel-Grey Squirrel-Fox-Badger-Otter-Red Deer-Roe Deer, average contents 40 .... 7.00

18B Match Play [   ], numbered, England's Glory 5.00

10C,20S,BS Military Swords, Cavalry Trooper's-Field Officer's-General Officer's-Guards Officer's-Highland Officer's-Infantry Officer's-Royal Air Force Officer's-Royal Artillery-Royal Naval Officer's-United States Navy, Type 1, Bryant and May 7.00

10C,20S,BS Military Swords, Cavalry Trooper's-Field Officer's-General Officer's-Guards Officer's-Highland Officer's-Infantry Officer's-Royal Air Force Officer's-Royal Artillery-Royal Naval Officer's-United States Navy, Type 2, Bryant and May, Canada 6.00

1C,20S,FS Their Majesties' Coronation [1937] 5.00

1B The Royal Wedding [7-29-1981], Cornish Match 5.00

10B The Marriage of HRH Prince Andrew and Miss Sarah Ferguson [23 July 1986], Wiltshire Match, Set #1, numbered 1-10, Made in Yugoslavia 5.00

10B The Marriage of HRH Prince Andrew and Miss Sarah Ferguson [23 July 1986], Wiltshire Match, Set #2, numbered 11-20, Made in Belgium 5.00

1C,20S,FS Royal Visit [1939], advertiser (B) 3.50

1C,20S,FS Royal Visit [1951] 2.00

1C,20S,FS Her Majesty's Coronation [1953] 5.00

1C,30S,FS Coronation Year [1953], Book Match Ltd. 5.50

1C,20S,BS Coronation Year, Strike Rite Type 1 [1953], blank (I) 1.50

1C,20S,BS Coronation Year, Strike Rite Type 2 [1953], Kings & Queens 1066-1547 .... 3.00

1C,20S,BS Coronation Year, Strike Rite Type 3 [1953], Kings & Queens 1547-1952 ...... 3.00

1C,20S,FS Their Majesties' Coronation 1937, color photo (F), Bryant & May 4.25

1C,20S,FS Souvenir Royal Visit 1954, Prince Phillip 3.00

1C,20S,FS Souvenir Royal Visit 1954, Queen Elizabeth 3.00

1C,20S,FS Royal Visit [1959] 2.75

4C,30S,BS The Royal Wedding, Andy and Fergi, dated 23rd July 1986 .... 5.25

6C,30S,BS Protected Eagles, numbered, White Tailed Sea Eagle-Harpy Eagle-Bateleur Eagle-Bald Eagle-Golden Eagle-Ornate Hawk Eagle, Type 1, [1978] 6.00

6C,20S,BS Protected Eagles, numbered, White Tailed Sea Eagle-Harpy Eagle-Bateleur Eagle-Bald Eagle-Golden Eagle-Ornate Hawk Eagle, Type 2, [1982] 6.00

10C,20S,BS Pub Signs, numbered, Royal Oak-Rose & Crown-The Bull-The Plough-The Chequers-The Bell-Red Lion-The George-The Swan-Pig & Whistle Type 1, [1979], has (I) printing 6.00

10C,20S,BS Pub Signs, numbered, Royal Oak-Rose & Crown-The Bull-The Plough-The Chequers-The Bell-Red Lion-The George-The Swan-Pig & Whistle Type 2, [1981], (I) is blank 6.00

10C,20S,BS Regimental Cap Badges [   ], Royal Hussars-Light Infantry-Royal Irish Rangers-Royal Scots Dragoon Guards-Royal Regiment of Artillery Institution-Brigade of Gurkhas-Royal Green Jackets-Royal Engineers-Royal Scots-Welsh Guards 2.00
200B Royal Navy Ship Badges 60.00
150B Scottish and Newcastle Inns 40.00
12C,40S,BS Sovereigns of England [1978], Henry 1-Henry II-Henry III-Edward I-Edward III-Henry VI-Henry VIII-Elizabeth I-George II-George III-Victoria-George V 20.00
17B Cricket Badges Set [   ], Derbyshire-Essex-Glamorgan-Gloucestershire-Hampshire-Kent-Lancashire-Leicestershire-Middlesex-Northamptonshire-Nottinghamshire-Somerset-Surrey-Sussex-Warnickshire-Worcestershire-Yorkshire Peter Dominic Wines 9.00
14C,20S,FS Cricket Players, Shepherd Neame 19.00
12B Coaching through the Ages [1989], Cornish 3.00
16B Cricket Badges 8.00
50B St. Georges Tavern Signs [   ] 25.00
12C,20S,BS Top Dogs, numbered Great Dane-Alsatian-Labrador Retriever-Old English Sheepdog-Irish Setter-Dalmatian-Cocker Spaniel-Welsh Corgi-Shetland Sheepdog-Fox Terrier-Miniature Poodle-Yorkshire Terrier, Type 1, [1977], 31-12-77 (I) 7.00
12C,20S,BS Top Dogs, numbered Great Dane-Alsatian-Labrador Retriever-Old English Sheepdog-Irish Setter-Dalmatian-Cocker Spaniel-Welsh Corgi-Shetland Sheepdog-Fox Terrier-Miniature Poodle-Yorkshire Terrier, Type 2, [1978], 30-9-78 (I) 6.00
12C,20S,BS Top Dogs, numbered Great Dane-Alsatian-Labrador Retriever-Old English Sheepdog-Irish Setter-Dalmatian-Cocker Spaniel-Welsh Corgi-Shetland Sheepdog-Fox Terrier-Miniature Poodle-Yorkshire Terrier, Type 3, [   ], (I) blank 6.00
60B British Military Uniforms [   ] 17.00
12B Victors in Battle [   ], numbered 10.00
12C,20S,BS Wild Animals of Britain [1976], numbered, Red Deer-Badger-Fox-Otter-Brown Hare-Rabbit-Grey Squirrel-Hedgehog-Stoat-Water Vole-Mole-Field Mouse 5.25
10B World Cup [1982], numbered, contents 48 .... 18.00
50C,20S,FS Miscellaneous British themes 4.75
50C,30S,FS Bryant and May, assorted themes 8.00
50C,20S,FS Bryant and May, assorted themes 5.00
75C,20/30S,MS Bryant and May, assorted themes 11.00

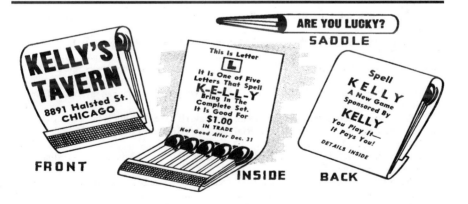

FRONT   INSIDE   BACK

The **Missing Letter Plan** was an incentive to bring more customers into a store. It was a plan that would make a store's name popular and attract trade to your place of business. To win a prize the book match user simply saves the book match covers until he/she has all the letters necessary to spell your name. Then he brings them in and gets his reward. It was advertised that: This plan should bring a growing number of patrons to your place by keeping your name and the new spelling game before them ... constant reminders of your name, your business, your product or your service.

Ex-Lax Jingles

Ex-Lax Jingles—A series of cartoon sets issued about 1935/ 1936 to promote the sales of Ex-Lax. Twelve cartoons comprise each set, and some drug stores had their store chain name on the saddle. To further complicate matters, each cartoon from each drug chain was produced either with no wording or with one of six different safety slogans on the inside. Several single matchcovers were also issued in the mid 1930s.

12C,20S,FS Jingles Set, Type 1A [1936], (BE) blank (I) 20.00
12C,20S,FS Jingles Set, Type 1B [1936], (BE) (I) slogan says Children Should Be 20.00
12C,20S,FS Jingles Set, Type 1C [1936], (BE) (I) slogan says It Takes More Time To.. 20.00
12C,20S,FS Jingles Set, Type 1D [1936], (BE) (I) slogan says Let The Traffic Lights.. ...... 20.00
12C,20S,FS Jingles Set, Type 1E [1936], (BE) (I) slogan says Let Us Have A New Deal.. 20.00
12C,20S,FS Jingles Set, Type 1F [1936], (BE) (I) slogan says Safe Drivers Are Life.. .... 20.00
12C,20S,FS Jingles Set, Type 1G [1936], (BE) (I) slogan says When Crossing Streets.. 20.00
12C,20S,FS Jingles Set, Type 2A [1936], (BE) (S) says 10 cts at all druggists, blank (I) 20.00
12C,20S,FS Jingles Set, Type 2B [1936], (BE) (S) says 10 cts at all druggists, (I) slogan says
Children Should Be 20.00
12C,20S,FS Jingles Set, Type 2C [1936], (BE) (S) says 10 cts at all druggists, (I) slogan says It Takes
More Time To.. .... 20.00
12C,20S,FS Jingles Set, Type 2D [1936], (BE) (S) says 10 cts at all druggists, (I) slogan says Let
The Traffic Lights.. .... 20.00
12C,20S,FS Jingles Set, Type 2E [1936], (BE) (S) says 10 cts at all druggists, (I) slogan says Let Us
Have A New Deal.. .... 20.00
12C,20S,FS Jingles Set, Type 2F [1936], (BE) (S) says 10 cts at all druggists, (I) slogan says Safe
Drivers Are Life.. .... 20.00
12C,20S,FS Jingles Set, Type 2G [1936], (BE) (S) says 10 cts at all druggists, (I) slogan says When
Crossing Streets. 20.00
12C,20S,FS Jingles Set, Type 3A [1936], (BE) (S) says Walgreen's, blank (I) 20.00
12C,20S,FS Jingles Set, Type 3B [1936], (BE) (S) says Walgreen's, (I) slogan says Children Should
Be 20.00
12C,20S,FS Jingles Set, Type 3C [1936], (BE) (S) says Walgreen's, (I) slogan says It Takes More
Time To.. .... 20.00
12C,20S,FS Jingles Set, Type 3D [1936], (BE) (S) says Walgreen's, (I) slogan says Let The Traffic
Lights.. .... 20.00
12C,20S,FS Jingles Set, Type 3E [1936], (BE) (S) says Walgreen's, (I) slogan says Let Us Have A
New Deal.. .... 20.00
12C,20S,FS Jingles Set, Type 3F [1936], (BE) (S) says Walgreen's, (I) slogan says Safe Drivers Are
Life.. .... 20.00
12C,20S,FS Jingles Set, Type 3G [1936], (BE) (S) says Walgreen's, (I) slogan says When Crossing
Streets.. .... 20.00
12C,20S,FS Jingles Set, Type 4A [1936], (RD) rectangle (B), Free! 12 jingle book blank (I) 20.00
12C,20S,FS Jingles Set, Type 4B [1936], (RD) rectangle (B), Free! 12 jingle book (I) slogan says
Children Should Be 20.00
12C,20S,FS Jingles Set, Type 4C [1936], (RD) rectangle (B), Free! 12 jingle book (I) slogan says
It Takes More Time To.. .... 20.00
12C,20S,FS Jingles Set, Type 4D [1936], (RD) rectangle (B), Free! 12 jingle book (I) slogan says
Let The Traffic Lights. 20.00
12C,20S,FS Jingles Set, Type 4E [1936], (RD) rectangle (B), Free! 12 jingle book (I) slogan says
Let Us Have A New Deal.. .... 20.00
12C,20S,FS Jingles Set, Type 4F [1936], (RD) rectangle (B), Free! 12 jingle book (I) slogan says
Safe Drivers Are Life.. .... 20.00
12C,20S,FS Jingles Set, Type 4G [1936], (RD) rectangle (B), Free! 12 jingle book (I) slogan says
When Crossing Streets.. .... 20.00
12C,20S,FS Jingles Set, Type 5 [1936], Katz Drug Stores on (BE) (S) 20.00

Fancy

Fancy—A limited category of matchcovers, many of which are not commercially produced. Limited production matchcovers have glued or attached items such as miniature musical instruments, animals, or pieces of cloth. They include Lenticular and most add-ons. Strictly speaking, however, commercial attachments, such as the Vicks cough drop in a box or Lincoln Penny attached to a matchcover by a matchbook company, may not be included in this category. This category is interesting but not widely collected.

1FB,20S,FS with plastic banjo glued to (GD) front, decorative only 3.00
1FB,20S, FS (WE) with plastic Thanksgiving turkey holding leaves (F) 2.00
1FB,20S,FS with Gold Metallic w/Violin Glued (F) 1.75
20C,30S,FS Fancy, assorted themes 6.00

Features (Contours)

Feature (Contour)—A Lion Match Co. trademark matchcover for a regular size (20 stick) matchcover with a custom die-cut shape. Often cut in the outline shape of the advertiser's product, the name Lion Contour Match appears on the inside. Over 1,000 varieties are known but these are not to be confused with the Universal Match Corp. design called Jewelites. Although not officially a Lion Feature, many Lion Contour matchbooks included Feature matches (See Features). A number of Lion Contours also had odd or spot strikers on the outside, further adding to their collectibility and value. This category can be kept either in matchcover or full matchbook form.

1C,20S,FS,CON Alabama Catering Service, pink orchid (F/B), phone (S), (BK/PK/GD), not FEA
.... 4.00
1C,20S,FS,CON AMSCO, American Mineral Spirits Company, no Lion markings, but CON (RD/
WE/BK/GY), not FEA 2.00
1C,20S,FS,CON Bob Murray's Dog House, no city, shows (WE) dog 'Butch' (F), (BK) dog (B),
map (I) (TN/WE/BK, not FEA 4.00
1C,20S,CON Box Car Fried Chicken, $3.49, Feeds 4 or 5 Hungry People, box car (F), drumstick
(B), not FEA 5.00
4C,FS,CON Cocktails Set [   ], Metalart Co. Manhattan-Martini-Old Fashioned-Whiskey Sour
.... 2.00
1FB,20S,CON The Embers, Chicago, ILL, chop (F/B), different address (F/B), not FEA 3.00
1C,20S,FS,CON Emil's Petit Hamburgers, Columbus, Ohio, building (F/B), steer (I), (GN/BN/
WE/YW) not FEA 2.00

1FB,20S,FS,CON ad: Frisch's Big Boy, Hamburger (F/B) 5.00
1C,20S,FS,CON Frisch's Big Boy, over stuffed hamburger (F/B), (BK/BN/WE/RD), not FEA
....6.00
1C,20S,FS,FL,CON Fruit of the Loom, October, 1953 (I), man's tee shirt & boxer shorts, DBE/
BE)WE), unusual, not FEA 5.00
1C,20S,FS,CON Geide's Inn of Long Island, Ft. Lauderdale, FL, w/ducks beside name (F/B),
ducks (I), phone (S), OE/BK/WE), not FEA 7.50
1C,20S,FS,CON Golden Slot Casino, Las Vegas, shows giant slot machine front of building (F/
B), address (I),(BE/YW/GD/BN, not FEA...4.00
1C,20S,FS,CON Hicks Gourmet Shop, The Fruit Shop (S), coach w/couple in period dress, (BK/
WE/RD), not FEA.. 12.00
1FB,20S,FS,CON ad: Hub Mail, Washington DC, shape of telephone.............................2.50
1FB,20S,CON Mister Kelly's, 1028 N Rush, Chicago, (BK) derby (F/B), (GN/BK), not FEA 3.00
1FB,20S,CON Lung Hau Lou Colonade Room, Chinese Restaurant, New York, large fan (F/B),
(RD/WE/BK), not FEA...3.00
4C,FS Signs Set [   ], Metalart Co., Dangerous Drinker-Drunk Ahead-Slippery When Wet-Stop
One Drink Limit 2.00
1FB,20S,CON Milliken fashion fabrics, same simple design (F/B), not FEA 2.00
12C,FS,CON Mottos Set [   ], Bernad Creations, Made In Bermuda-Brazil-Italy-Las Vegas-
London-Madrid-Michigan-The Moon-Quickly By Rabbits-Russia-Spain-West Germany .
....12.00
1C,20S,FS,CON The Parasol, Torrance CA, show parasol (F/B) (PK/WE/GD/BK) not FEA 12.25
1C,20S,FS,CON Pollack's Mink Farm, Pottsville-Lebanon, PA, (WE) mink (F), brown mink (B),
map (I), not FEA 6.50
1C,20S,FS,CON Ponte Vedra Club, Ponte Vedra Beach, Florida, oversized Golf ball (F/B), sea-
Horse logo (F), blank (I), not FEA...8.00
1FB,20S,FS,CON Printed Sticks, Chicken in the Basket 6.25
12C,FS,CON North American Soccer League Set [   ] 15.00
1C,20S,FS,CON Town View, The Master Champion, no city, shows home exterior (F), kitchen
interior (F),(GN/WE/TN, directions (I), not FEA...7.00
1FB,20S,FS,CON ad: Western Soft Nylon Monofilament, reel (F), fish basket (B) 5.00
600C,MS,CON Lion Contours, [1951-1991] (album) 300.00
35C,FS,CON Lion Contours, [1951-1991] assorted themes...45.00
50C,FS,CON Lion Contours, [1951-1991].. 27.50
1FB,20S,FS,FEA The Airline Showbar, Chicago, propeller w/Airliner on each stick, phone Del.
1169 (I) (DBE/WE/BN)...3.00

Features (15 Stick)

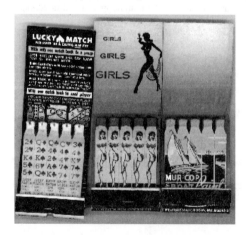

Features (15 stick)—A Lion Match
Co. trademark, this design was introduced
in September 1930 and is the fastest growing style matchcover collected today. One
to four color designs are printed on flattened wider match sticks in a combination
of panoramic, individual stick or mixed
patterns. The Feature is the finest example of design and beauty in the hobby.
Although some collectors take out the
comb and display it with a flattened
matchcover, the trend is to keep Features
in full book form. There are 15 sticks in each
book although early issues had only 10
sticks.

Features (15 Stick)

1FB,20S,FS The Airline Showbar, Chicago, propeller w/Airliner on each stick, phone Del. 1169 (I) (DBE/WE/BN) 3.00

1C,20S,FS,CON Allgauer's Restaurant, shows large (RD) lobster (F/B), no city 4.00

1C,20S,FS,CON Ben Gross Fine Foods, Irwin, PA, show restaurant awning w/glass, Since 1934, (BK/WE/TN) 2.00

1FB,20S,FS Café Bohemia, Chicago, grazing deer (F), 3 bears (B), each stick w/different entree 6.50

1FB,20S,FS Bond Tool and Die Co, 15453 West Parkway, Detroit, Mich. (SR/BE) (F), Minute Man w/For Safety Buy Bonds across sticks 10.00

1FB,20S,FS The Brass Rail, New York, hearth across sticks 11.00

1FB,20S,FS Broad Mont Café, nudes in glass on sticks 6.50

1C,20S,FS,CON Bryant Colorado Co, heating equipment, lucky match, show man w/pipe & dog (BE/RD/WE) 2.00

1FB,20S,FS Burke's Seneca Restaurant, Canandaigua, NY, Indian w/name (F), color Indian design (B), 2 Indians and name across sticks 7.50

1FB,20S,FS C and K Favorite Products, Quality Meats & Sausages Clauss & Kraus Inc, dancing hot dogs (F), cold cuts (F), different mean on each stick (DBE,YW,RD) 6.00

1C,20S,FS,CON Aug. Caruso & Sons Fruit & Veg. Distributors, colorful arrangement of fruits & veg. (F/B), (PE) background, all into (I) 2.00

1FB,20S,FS Columbia Homestead Association, 330 Carondelet St, New Orleans, LA (RD/WE) (F), FSLIC logo (B) slogan on sticks 3.00

5FB,20S,BS Cutty Sark Bar Game (WY/BK) combs different in each 7.00

1FB,20S,CON Davidson Transfer & Storage, colorful truck (F), different truck (B), colorful truck front across sticks 8.00

1C,20S,FS,CON Davidson Transfer & Storage Co., 2 different trucks (F/B), colorful, list of terminals (I) 4.00

1C,20S,FS,CON DiFederico's Lampost, New Paris, Ohio, photo of Joe (B), chicken basket (F) (RD/YW/GN/WE) 2.00

1FB,20S,FS Dine at Dinous, Chicago, Ill, coffee pot on sticks 6.00

1FB,20S,FS Edwards, Fifth Avenue, McKeesport, Pa., Schoble Hats logo (B), Schoble logo (RD/WE) across sticks 6.75

1FB,20S,FS English Terrace, Ft. Wayne, Ind, each stick a chef 8.00

1FB,20S,FS Five Sons Café, photo (B), one son on each stick 3.00

1FB,20S,FS,FL Frankfort & Cincinnati RR Co, full length train, route name on sticks, map (I) 10.00

1FB,20S,FS Frenchy's in Milwaukee, b/w cover w/fish, cover pattern across sticks 5.00

1FB,20S,FS Gus' Restaurant & Cocktail Lounge, Kansas City, MO, photo of bar (F), photo of lounge (B), sea food and name across sticks 6.50

1FB,20S,FS,CON Herco Products, shaped like a pipe, 27th Anniversary matchbook, (BE/OE), Calif firm, big 27th Anniversary across sticks 11.00

1FB,20S,FS Hillcrest Bowl, St. Paul, Minn, sticks shaped like bowling pins (BK/GN/GD/WE) 7.75

1FB,20S,FS The Hitching Post, 6 addresses (B), chef w/frying pan across sticks 7.00

1FB,20S,FS,ODD Strike at the seat of trouble, Buy War Bonds (F), Hitler w/striker on pants seat holding globe (B), each stick a bomb (RD/WE/YW/GN) 65.00

1FB,20S,BS The Holland Fountain Restaurant, Vancouver, Wash., (LBE/WE) two Dutch Children (F), ice cream cone on each stick 8.25

1FB,20S,FS Steve Hulburt, Freeport, Ill, each stick a suited man, CKB below 14.75

1FB,20S,FS L & S Package Store, 6524 E Northwest Hy, Loop 12, Dallas (BK/WE) (F), girl riding champagne bottle (B), girlie (I), each stick a liquor bottle 8.00

1C,20S,FS,CON Loffler Brothers Oyster House, Coral Gables, Florida, large top-hat lobster (F/B),(RD/BK/WE) 11.00

1FB,20S,FS Lowry's in Beverly Hills, logo & name (F), chef (B), each stick a chef w/alternating name and entree 8.25

1C,20S,FS,CON Macey's, Covington, KY, diamond ring (F/B) (PE/YW/WE) 12.25

1FB,20S,FS,CON Manero's Famous Steak House, Paramus, N.J., Tel. Oradell 8-1015 (S), chef w/ hat is each stick, colorful 9.25

1FB,20S,FS Melo-Cream Do-Nuts, Moline, ILL, name & specials (F/B), do-nut w/name and city across sticks 11.00

1FB,20S,FS Margaret Peterson's Melody Lane, San Francisco, colorful piano player on sticks, (B/W) photo Larry Larson, Westward Ho (I) 6.50

1FB,20S,FS Hotel Mishawaka, Mishawaka, Indiana (RD/BK (F), Northern Indiana's Small Hotel of Hospitality on Routes 20,331-33 (B), clock w/cocktail lounge ad across sticks 5.00

1FB,20S,FS Neuman's on the Plaze, Big Boy Bar-B-Q w/franks on sticks 13.25

1C,20S,FS,CON New England Oyster House, Coral Gables, Fla, large top-hat lobster (F/B) (RD/BK/WE) 7.50

1FB,20S,FS Pabst Blue Ribbon Beer, bottle (B), each stick shaped like a bottle, very colorful, 'The Beer of Quality,' below 18.50

1FB,20S,FS Pelican Restaurant, Sandusky, Ohio, pelican on each stick, w/restaurant name 8.00

1FB,20S,FS,FL Pelton's Garage, Bridgeport, Conn, (F) garage, tow truck w/name across sticks . 6.25

1FB,20S,FS Pinellas Industries, Inc., St. Pete, Fla, Concrete Truck on sticks 5.50

1FB,20S,FS Pretzer Paint Co., Cleveland, Ohio, (PE/YW/RD/BE) each stick is a colorful paint brush 9.25

1FB,20S,FS Prince Spaghetti House, Boston, Mass, chef w/spaghetti w/'Spaghetti at its best' across sticks 5.00

1FB,20S,FS Robertsons Cleaners, Dryers, etc., Sault Ste. Marie, Mich, sticks with dancing girls, plaid design 6.25

1FB,20S,FS,FL Sanitary Cleaners, New Canaan, Conn, (BK/PK), well-dressed women & men on each stick 5.25

1FB,20S,FS The Saxony, Miami Beach, Florida, hotel on sticks 4.00

1FB,20S,ODD Al Schacht, 'Clown Prince of Baseball, photo w/signature (F), striker on baseball diamond (B), baseball bat w/Al Schacht on alternate sticks 22.50

1FB,20S,FS Showboat Restaurant, Miami, FL, Showboat w/name (F), front of restaurant (B), sea food across sticks 3.75

1FB,20S,FS Casino St. George, St. George, Bermuda, table (F), fish or lobster on alternating sticks, name below 5.00

1FB,20S,FS Strike 'em Dead, sticks: Japanese soldier 12.25

1FB,20S,FS 'Time of Your Life' stage show, ghosts on sticks 11.50

1FB,20S,FS The Town House, Chicago, WG w/(BN) sign (F), inside scene (B), woman in hoop dress on sticks 4.50

1FB,20S,FS Trenton Radio Co., Morgantown, W.VA, logo (B), name of radio parts on each stick 8.00

1FB,20S,FS Triton Restaurant, four people in booth on sticks 2.50

1FB,20S,FS The Saint Tropics, Denver, CO, 'feelie' nude (F), silhouetted nude (I), building on sticks 8.25

1FB,20S,FS Pillsbury's Turk's Head Restaurant, Trenton/Princeton Phone 2188 (RD) 4.00

1FB,20S,FS The Mark Twain Hotel, Elmira, NY, Twain (F), hotel (B), cover design across sticks 10.00

1FB,20S,FS Union Oyster House, Boston, Fisherman on sticks 6.00

1FB,20S,FS,CON The White Spot, Route 3, Woburn, Mass, (BK/WE) 3.00

1FB,20S,FS White Fire Blackout Match Club, Is This Your Lucky Number? (blank space) (F), gasoline ad (B), each stick (RD/WE) is a White Fire Gasoline pump 7.25

1FB,20S,FS The White Turkey Inn, Display (I) 5.00

1FB,20S,FS Display (large bee), Womack Exterminators 8.00

1FB,20S,FS George Zahorsky's Five Sons Café, photo (B), five sons on sticks 2.25

Feature Combs--Often torn out or taken from used matchbooks, they are the reason Features are so popular. Not that the bulbs have been clipped on the second from the right. This was thought to prevent fires.

Features (21 Stick)

**21 FEATURE MATCH BOOK-PAT. L733.258-L839.845-6
LION • MATCH • CO., Inc. • NEW • YORK**

Feature (21 stick)—Exactly the same as the 15 stick Feature, except the match book contains 21 wide sticks. "21" Features, as they are also called, arrived later than the 15 stick feature. With three rows of seven sticks, no evidence has been found that there was ever a two comb (14 stick) "21" Feature made. "21" Features sometimes have display "pop-ups" inside. Above, a copy of the Feature manumark found on the inside.

"FEATURE"
Reg. U.S. Pat. Off.
MATCH BOOK
Made Exclusively by
LION MATCH CO., Inc.
250 W. 57th Street
New York, N. Y.
U. S. PATENTS Nos. 1839845-6
PATENTED IN CANADA - 1932
OTHER PATENTS PENDING

1FB,30S,FS Alexander's Shoes for Men, Hartford, Conn, shoes w/'Built in quality in Every Pair/ Alexander's' across sticks 3.75

1FB,30S,FS Arco Cravats, New York, (RD/BK) checker board pattern (F), each stick a different tie 10.00

1FB,30S,FS Armando's in Chicago, (RD/WE/BK) each stick a chef w/Armando across all 5.75

1FB,30S,FS Artists and Writers Club, Cleveland, OH, angle across sticks 4.00

1FB,30S,FS Bill's Clothes, (RD/GD/BK) name & addresses (F), ad message (B), man in suit or overcoat on each stick 5.75

1FB,30S,FS Budeke's, 418 S Broadway, Baltimore, MD (OE/BK/WE logo (F), can of Per-Ma-Lite paint (B), phone (S), each shaped stick a colorful paint brush 11.25

1FB,30S,FS Calumet Iron & Supply Co., E. Chicago, IN, name (F), name w/(We) Sell Everybody (B), (OE/BK/YW) 'We Sell Everybody' across sticks 6.50

1FB,30S,FS Calumet Iron & Supply Co, E. Chicago, Ind., 'We Sell Everybody' on banner across sticks 2.75

1FB,30S,FS Caruso's, Chicago, piano keyboard on sticks (RD/GD/WE) 7.50

1FB,30S,FS Cheney Studs, (RD/WE/BK) small Horse on each stic 5.00

1FB,30S,FS Cherry Creek Inn, Denver, CO, name (F), Red Slipper Room w/undershot of dancing girl, each stick a figural woman's leg 7.75

1FB,30S,FS Christmas Club, ad: Orange Cty Trust Co, Middletown, NY (B), colorful toy soldiers & Christmas tree on sticks 5.50

1FB,30S,FS Christmas Club, ad: Mechanics & Farmers Bank, Durham, NC (B), colorful toy soldiers & Christmas tree on sticks 8.00

1FB,30S,FS Churchill's Restaurant, each contoured stick is a spirits bottle, labeled . . . Gin, Ale, Wine, Rye, Beer, etc. w/name below 3.75

1FB,30S,FS Jack Dempsey's on Broadway 9.50

1FB,30S,FS The Frontier, 3765 Main St, Bridgeport, Conn, frontiersman w/wife & baby (F), river scene (B), conestoga graphic (I), The Frontier on each stick, (LBE,BN/WE) 7.25

1FB,30S,FS,FL Glass Bottles, each stick is a milk bottle 7.25

1FB,30S,FS The Golden Ox Restaurant & Cocktail Lounge, Kansas City, MO, (GN/TN) Golden Ox logo across sticks 6.00

1FB,30S,FS The Gotham Restaurant, Chicago, Ill, name across sticks 5.00

1FB,30S,FS Joe Gumin's Candlewick Inn, Hales Corners, Wis., each stick a candle, (BN/WE) 7.25

1FB,30S,FS The Helen Mar, Miami Beach (F/B), (BK/WE) drawing of hotel across sticks 4.25

1FB,30S,FS Hiram Walker's Canadian Club, et al, sticks tapered as Imperial Whiskey bottles 12.00

1FB,30S,FS Jo Jo Martinelli Restaurant, Cincinnati, OH, comic picture across sticks 11.00

1FB,30S,FS The Lantern Dining Room, Kansas City, restaurant sign w/name & 'next door to the Plaza Theatre' across sticks 3.50

1FB,30S,FS Hotel Last Frontier, Las Vegas, NV, Conestoga wagon (F), colorful bucking bronco w/rider (B), 3 Can-Can dancers across sticks 11.00

1FB,30S,FS Leslie House, (RD/WE) w/initial L, Leslie House w/initial across sticks 5.00

1FB,30S,FS Manahatta Sweet Vermouth, Indian (F), each colorful stick a contoured bottle of Manahatta, name below 10.00

1FB,30S,FS The Marine Midland, New York, sticks with printed address (SR/BE/WE) . 2.75

1FB,30S,FS Marine Transport Inc, line logo across sticks (RD/WE/BE) 4.00

1FB,30S,FS McCutcheon's Coctail Lounge, Niagara Falls, girl in swimsuit across sticks 8.25

1FB,30S,FS,FL Mickey's Steaks/Chops, POP-UP (I) of waitress, each colorful stick a contoured chef, 'Italian American Dishes' across sticks 13.50

1FB,30S,FS,FL Mickey's Villanova Restaurant, rest (F) full length, pop-up display of waitress (I), each shaped stick a chef, colorful 12.00

1FB,30S,FS Milano Pizza, Chicago, Ill, each stick has wording Milano/Pizzeria/Good Food 10.00

1FB,30S,FS,FL Modern Liquors, Washington, DC, each stick tapered link wine, beer, & liquor bottles 13.50

1FB,30S,FS Music Mart, Records, Magnavox TV (B), radio tube on each stick, 'Are Your Tubes All Lighting?' below 8.25

1FB,30S,FS Nautilus Hotel, Miami Beach, FL, (WE/OE) pool/cabana on sticks, hotel (B) 7.00

1FB,30S,FS New Dixie Lines Inc, Richmond, VA, terminal addr (B), truck w/company name across sticks 3.50

1FB,30S,FS Niagara Furnaces, name in (GN) (B), furnace w/name (B), name across sticks 6.50

1FB,30S,FS Hotel Norton, Detroit 26, Mich, hotel (B), 'Cocktails by Norton' w/champagne glass across sticks 4.00

1FB,30S,FS The Nut House, Des Moines, IA, Squirrel & 'Nuts to You' (F), squirrels (B), (RD/YW/WE/BE) name and squirrel across sticks 5.75

1FB,30S,FS Patsy's Italian Restaurant, New York City, initials across sticks 7.75

1FB,30S,FS Powell's Holland House, Dayton, Ohio, each stick is a tulip 7.75

1FB,30S,FS Power Equipment Co., Knoxville, TN, (BK/BW/RD) product names on each stick 7.75

1FB,30S,FS The Raleigh, Miami Beach, colorful drawing of hotel (B), colorful pool area drawing across sticks 3.75

1FB,30S,FS Red Skelton as The Fuller Brush Man, Raleigh 903 ad (B), Skelton (F/B), portrait (I), brush across sticks 75.00

1FB,30S,FS Rhode Island Tool Co., Providence, RI, caliper w/name (F), products (B), (BE/YW) each stick is a bolt and nut 7.00

1FB,30S,FS Rose & Percy's, 1630 Valley Blvd, Rosemead, Calif (BE/RD/BK) (F) w/names, colorful American Indian items display (B), special events & features on each stick 9.00

1FB,30S,FS Salem's Restaurant & Lounge, Akron, Ohio, food across stick 10.25

1FB,30S,FS The Sands, Las Vegas, NV, name (F), hotel (B), cowgirl (I), penguins on each stick w/Why be formal? Come as you Are! 4.75

1FB,30S,FS The Saxon Motels, Miami et al, AAA logo (F), addresses (B), (BK/WE) drawing of pool area across sticks 7.00

1FB,30S,FS The Saxony, Miami Beach, FL (B), logo and Bernard Kahn (F), (WE/GD/RD/GN) Hotel drawn across sticks 5.25

1FB,30S,FS Service Caster and Truck Co, Somerville, Mass, road w/'Indoor miles made easier, Service' across sticks 3.00

1FB,30S,FS,FL Silver Frolics, Chicago, FL nude w/'Silver Frolics' across sticks 11.75

1FB,30S,FS Snow's Laundry & Dry Cleaning, building (F), old delivery truck (B), (PE/WE) clothes line across sticks, snow man (I) 5.25

1FB,30S,FS Southern Coal Co., Inc, Memphis,(TN) Sentry 14 Coal logo (F), name and message (B), WWI sentry on each stick 10.50

1FB,30S,FS,FL Square Bottles, Glass Bottles, milk bottle (F), (MN/WE/YW) each stick is a milk bottle 7.00

1FB,30S,FS Thunderbird Hotel, Las Vegas, NV, colorful Thunderbird across sticks 6.00

1FB,30S,FS Trainer's Seafood, different sea food item on each stick (GN/RD) 6.00

1FB,30S,FS Taunton Inn, Taunton, Mass, (RD/WE/BE) logo (F) w/eagle, room, and grill names on each stick 2.50

1FB,30S,FS Tropics, Denver, nude feelie (F), hotel on sticks 6.50

1FB,30S,FS Walter's Flower Shoppe, Cleveland, O (B), 3 carnations (F), 2 carnations across sticks (stock) 5.00

1FB,30S,FS Weldex Universal Selling Co., Germantown, PA, can w/name (F), logo w/product message (B), YW/BE) Weldex across sticks 8.75

1FB,30S,FS West Coast Line, Inc., New York, steamship (F), ports of call on sticks 6.50

1FB,30S,FS,FL WNOW AM/FM/TV Broadcasting Service, WNOW & York, Pennsylvania across sticks 10.00

Features (Printed Sticks)

Feature (Printed Sticks)—Although not a feature, Printed Sticks are collected as a close first cousin to the Lion Feature. Designs are printed on normal 20 stick or 30 stick combs, but the rough undulated rhythmical pattern of the sticks tends to over take the image. Printed Sticks are also individually printed with a product or service name. Printed Sticks were made by several companies and not exclusively by Lion.

1FB,20S,BS Call Active for Photostats, (BK/WE) w/ addresses (F/B), Active Photo & Speed on alternating sticks, printed sticks 3.00

1FB,30S,FS,FL Albion Hotel, drawing across (O), ad (I), flowers across printed sticks . 3.50

1FB,30S,FS Alfred's Villa, Stenton Place & Pacific Ave, Atlantic City, (F), King w/kneeling chefs (B), name and products across printed stick (PE/WE/RD) 3.25

1FB,30S,BS Badcock Furniture, Mulberry, FL, map of Florida (F), Badcock truck (B), Badcock will Treat you Right, across printed sticks (BE) 2.75

1FB,20S,BS Beck's on the Boulevard, lobster (F) and across sticks, map (B) (RD/WE), printed sticks 2.75

1FB,30S,FS Bert Sanford, Thankful for your Tankful (F), Texaco & US Royal Tires (B), Van Nuys, California, name and services across printed sticks (LBE/RD/BK) 4.25

1FB,30S,FS Florasynth Laboratories, Inc, New York, logo w/name (F), addresses (B), Florasynth along every other printed stick (BK/RD) 3.00

1FB,30S,FS Hof Brau, San Francisco & Oakland, name (F), German Beer mug w/leprechaun (B), meals and side dishes across printed sticks (RD/BK/WE) 3.50

1FB,30S,BS Red Ivey's Automotive Service, Atlanta 5, GA, building (F), wheel balancing machine (B), services, name and address across printed sticks (RD/WE/BK) 4.00

1FB,20S,FS Lawry's The Prime Rib, Beverly Hills, logo (F), chef w/grill (B), Lawry on each stick, map (I), printed sticks 3.25

1FB,30S,FS Lone Star Bag & Bagging Co, Houston, Tex, plant (F), name & address (B), phone 2101 (S), products across alternating (BE/WE) printed stick 2.25

1FB,30S,FS New Joe's, Established 1928, San Francisco, logo (F/B), name and address along every printed stick, (BN/YW) 3.00

1FB,20S,FS New York & Suburban Federal Savings, 2 1/2 dividend ad w/map (B), services printed along alternating (BN/WE) printed sticks 2.50

1FB,30S,FS Preston, the 151 Line, name (F), truck (B), map (I), The 151 line along alternating printed sticks (OE/BN/WE) 3.75

1FB,30S,FS Preview Cocktail Lounge, Chicago, champaign glass (F), singer w/2 pianists (B), Preview along every printed stick, (RD/YW,WE,BE) 3.25

1FB,30S,FS Peoples Trust & Savings Bank, Indianola, Milo Locona, logo (F), bank (B), People's Bank East Side of Square across printed sticks (BK/WE) 2.50

1FB,30S,BS Rosie O'Grady's, New York City, name (F/B), Gibson girl (I), entertainment & services across printed sticks (GN/WE) 1.25

1FB,30S,FS Hotel Sahara, Las Vegas, name (F), man w/camel (B), ad: The Congo Room (I), front of hotel across printed sticks (BN/RD/WE) 4.00

1FB,20S,FS Yellow Pages, large Fingers Walking (F) and across printed sticks, logo w/saying (B), (YW/BK) 1.75

10FB,30S,FS Printed Sticks (not FEA) assorted themes 6.50

Flowers

Flowers—Any matchcover displaying flowers, both in a natural setting or in floral arrangements. An incidental flower in an advertisement may be included in this category; however, collectors usually want flowers that are the prominent feature of the design. Florists made popular use of this matchcover design. However, several supermarket sets feature different kinds of flowers with names.

10C,20S,FS Flowers Set (SR) color, name and picture (F/B) Anemone-Azalea-Camellia-Iris-Lily-Narcissus-Peony-Poppy-Rose-Violet 2.00

5C,20S,FS Barton-Cotton Set [1955], John Work Garrett.. Anemone-Carnation-Moss Rose-Portland Rose-Primula 2.00

5C,20S,FS Barton-Cotton Set [1955], Florence Titman Trumpet Daffodil-4 others 2.00

5C,20S,FS Barton-Cotton Set [1955], Kathleen Cassel Cardinal Flower-Flowering Dogwood-Jack in the Pulpit-Wild Lupine-Wild Rose 2.00

10C,20S Diamond Match Set, Flowers, (F/only) (DGN) background 2.00

10C,20S,FS Diamond Flower Set, Grocery, (DGN) background, (F) only 1.50

10C,20S,FS Garden Flowers Set #1, [   ], names on (F) Bearded Iris-Canterbury Bells-Cosmos-Daffodils-Darwin Tulips Louis IV-Giant Pansies-Oriental Poppies-Peony-Ruffled Petunia-Tea Rose Poinsettia, Type #1 [1953], olive (GN) 3.00

10C,20S,FS Garden Flowers Set #1, [   ], names on (F) Bearded Iris-Canterbury Bells-Cosmos-Daffodils-Darwin Tulips Louis IV-Giant Pansies-Oriental Poppies-Peony-Ruffled Petunia-Tea Rose Poinsettia, Type #2 [1953], (GN) 1.50

10C,20S,FS Garden Flowers Set #1, [   ], names on (F) Bearded Iris-Canterbury Bells-Cosmos-Daffodils-Darwin Tulips Louis IV-Giant Pansies-Oriental Poppies-Peony-Ruffled Petunia-Tea Rose Poinsettia, Type #3 [1953], (BN) 2.00

10C,20S,FS Garden Flowers Set #2 [1956], names (I), Bearded Iris-Columbine-Cosmos-Daffodils-Darwin Tulips-Dwarf Hybrid Dahlias-Giant Pansies-Hybrid Tea Roses-Petunias-Single Asters 3.50

5C,20S,FS Flowers Set [1956], Match Corp., Dahlias-Mixed Flowers-Orchid-Poinsettia-Roses 1.00

12C,20S,FS Flower Set [1955] Ohio Match Co. 3.00

10C,20S,FS Flowers Set (SR) color Type 1 [1956] Anemone-Azalea-Camellia-Cosmos-Crinum-Daffodil-Easter Lily-Iris-Orchid-Rose, Ohio Match Co. name (S) and picture (F) 2.00

8C,20S,FS Flower Set [1957] Ohio Match Co. 2.50

10C,20S,FS Flowers Set (SR) color Type 2 [   ] Anemone-Azalea-Camellia-Cosmos-Crinum-Daffodil-Easter Lily-Iris-Orchid-Rose, Ohio Match Co. name and picture (F) 2.00

foilites

foilites--Made exclusively by the Universal Match Corp. and usually 30 stick, portions of the front design are printed in colored metallic foil. Most are Christmas matchcovers with the word (spelled with a lower case f) appearing on the inside.

100C,30S,MS foilites, Universal Match Corp. 4.50
125C,20S/30S,FS foilites, Universal Match Corp. 11.50
10C,30S,FS foilites, Cadillac Ads 3.00
50C,30S,MS foilites, Universal Match 8.00
100C,20S,MS foilites, assorted themes 19.00
100C,30S,MS foilites, assorted themes 9.00
30C,MZ,MS foilites, assorted themes 5.50

Foreign (Australia)

8B Aboriginal Bark Paintings [1965], Federal Match Co. 2.00
48B Aboriginal Life Set [1970], Australia 2.25
48B All States Set, Type 1 [1970], Bryant & May 2.25
48B 150th Anniversary of W.A. [1979], numbered 3.00
8B Capital City Crests, Type 1 [1989], Scotch Buy, has safety warning 1.00
8B Capital City Crests, Type 2 [1988], Scotch Buy, no safety warning 1.00
8B Capital City Crests, Type 3 [1988], No Frills, no safety warning 1.00
8B Capital City Crests, Type 4 [1989], No Frills, has safety warning 1.00
8B Capital City Crests, Type 5 [1989], (BK/GD) 1.00
8B Capital City Crests, Type 6 [   ], Bi-Lo 1.00
8B Capital City Crests, Type 7 [1988] Home Brand, no safety warning 1.00
8B Capital City Crests, Type 8 [1989] Home Brand, has safety warning 1.00
8B Capital City Crests, Type 9 [1988], Payless 1.00
9B, Coats of Arms [1961], Federal Match Co. 1.00
48B Decimal Currency, Type 1 [1965], Bryant & May 3.00
42B Decimal Currency, Type 2 [1965], Federal Match Co. 2.25
48B Decimal Currency, Type 3 [1965], Western Australia Match Co. 4.00
12B Ancient Egyptian Series Set [1989], numbered, Home Br. 6.00
14B Everbrite [   ], Bryant & May 4.00
48B Explorers Set, numbered, Type 1 [1968], Bryant & May Australian Issue 4.00
48B Explorers Set, numbered, Type 2 [1968], Western Australia Match Co. 4.00
64B Australian Fauna, Type 1 [1974], Bryant & May 6.00

64B Australian Fauna, Type 1 [1975], Western Australia Match Co. 8.00
??C,30S,BS Flag Inns, numbered 4.00
64B Flags, Type 1 [1957], Bryant & May 6.00
64B Flags, Type 2 [1958], Western Australia Match Co 6.00
32B Commonwealth Games Set [1962], Western Australia Match Co. 6.00
32B Commonwealth Games Set [1982], Redheads 1.00
12B Commonwealth Games Set [1982], numbered, contents 25, CBC Bank, Hanna Match 5.00
64B Industry, Type 1 [1962], Bryant & May 3.00
64B Industry, Type 2 [1963], Western Australia Match Co. 5.00
64B Mythology, Type 1 [1963], Bryant & May 3.75
64B Mythology, Type 2 [1963], Western Australia Match Co. 5.00
42B Naval Crests Set [1967], numbered, Federal Match Co. 1.50
40B Olympic Games Set [1956], Bryant & May 14.00
12B Payless Superbarn Set [   ], Made in Indonesia, Common Scoter-Gadwall-Garganey-
    Goosander-Long Tailed Duck-Mallard-Pintail-Pochard-Red Breasted Merganser-Scaup-
    Teal-Tufted Duck 3.00
40B Primary Industries Set [1971], Australia Match 3.00
64B Progress and Industry Set, Type 1 [1962], Bryant & May 2.50
64B Progress and Industry Set, Type 2 [1963], Western Australia Match Co. 5.00
32B Queensland Centenary Set [1959], Bryant & May 3.00
11B Redheads Set [   ], Made in Sweden 2.25
42B Road Safety Set [1972], Federal Match Co. 1.00
12B Royal Wedding Set [   ] 7.00
2C,20S,FS Royal Visit Set [1954] 4.00
12B Royal Wedding Set [1981], Western Australia Match Co. 12.00
42B Rugby Players Set [1975], Australia Match 10.00
64B Sea Life Set, Type 1 [1966], numbered, Bryant & May 3.00
64B Sea Life Set, Type 2 [1967], Western Australia Match Co. 5.00
29SK Sign Language Set [1981], Bryant & May 3.00
4C,30S,BS Southern Pacific Hotels Set [   ] 2.00
16C,30S,BS Southern Pacific Hotel Corp., Type 1 [1984], Bryant & May 3.00
16C,30S,BS Southern Pacific Hotel Corp., Type 2 [1986], Hanna 3.00
32B Space Set, Type 1 [1970], Bryant & May 3.00
32B Space Set, Type 2 [1971], Western Australia Match Co. 3.00
64B Think Metric Set, Type 1 [1973], Bryant & May 1.75
42B Think Metric Set, Type 2 [1973], Federal Match Co. 1.75
64B Think Metric Set, Type 3 [1974], Western Australia Match Co. 4.00
42B Town Crests Set [1963], Federal Match Co. 2.25
64B Transportation Set [   ], Western Australia Match Co. 5.00
64B Transportation Set [1967], Bryant & May 5.00
8B Travelodge National Trust Series Set [1979], numbered 3.00
28C,30S,FS Travelodge Set 5.00
3B Travelodge Pacific Harbour Series Set, numbered 5.00
13B, Travelodge South Pacific Series Set [1979], numbered 2.25
9B Two Decades of Challenge Set, Type 1 [   ], Bi-Lo, contents 50, Gretel 1962-Dame Pattie 1967-
    Gretel II 1970-Southern Cross 1974-Australia 1977-Australia 1980-Challenge 12 1983-
    Australia II 1983-Advance 1983 .... 5.00
9B Two Decades of Challenge Set, Type 2 [   ], No Frills, contents 50, Gretel 1962-Dame Pattie
    1967-Gretel II 1970-Southern Cross 1974-Australia 1977-Australia 1980-Challenge 12
    1983-Australia II 1983-Advance 1983 .... 5.00
9B Two Decades of Challenge Set, Type 3 [1987], Here's Value, contents 50, Gretel 1962-Dame
    Pattie 1967-Gretel II 1970-Southern Cross 1974-Australia 1977-Australia 1980-Challenge
    12 1983-Australia II 1983-Advance 1983 .... 5.00
20B Vintage Cars Set [1983], numbered, Hanna Match 5.00

Foreign (Boxes)

155B French boxes from 8 different sets 33.75
1B Order Militar de San Fernando (Espana), large, double drawers (I) 2.00
10B Full City of Westminster Carnaby St, photo on each, London sights 1.25
7B Japanese Boxes w/semi-clad women 14.00
18B Peter Dominic World Wines, Cricket Badges 5.00
6B Old Danish Domestic Industries, small boxes in package 1.75
10B Old English Inn Signs 2.25
1B Industrial Metallurgica, one small spot (F), large w/4 small (I) 2.50
1B Medalla de Honor del Congress (Estades Unidos) large, double drawers (I) 7.50
1 BL RMS Safety Matches, Made in Russia 1.50
1B The Ship Box, 2 1/2D, 1962 by J. John Masters & Co. 1.75
1B Three Torches 2 1/2D, 1962 by The Union Match Co. Ltd. 1.75
1B Tiger Matches 2 1/2D, 1962 by Bryant & May 1.75

Foreign (New Zealand)

18BL 50 Years of Value Set [1983], Beehive skillets Capone-Farnsworth-Forbes-Gable-Harvie-
     Hepburn-Hitler-Kern-Kingsford Smith-King Kong-Koroki..-Lovelock-McCombs-Mt. Everest-
     Roosevelt-Royce-Vallee-Wells 10.00
6BL Puzzles, numbered Beehive skillets Type 1 [1981], (YW) 3.00
6BL Puzzles, numbered Beehive skillets Type 2 [1981], honey colored, puzzles on left .. 3.00
7B Great All Blacks Set Beehive skillets Griffiths-Hart-Kilby-Lambourn-Manchester-Mitchell-
     Sullivan Type 1 [1981] 5.00
7B Great All Blacks Set Beehive skillets Griffiths-Hart-Kilby-Lambourn-Manchester-Mitchell-
     Sullivan Type 2 [   ], no country indicated 5.00
6BL Puzzles, numbered Beehive skillets Type 3 [1981], honey colored, puzzles on right . 3.00
6BL Flower Set [   ], Carnation-Iris-Pansy-Rose-Tiger Lily-Tulip 3.00
4B Maori Rock Drawings [   ], numbered, parlour boxes 2.00
20C,20S,FS New Zealand Truth [   ], numbered 5.00

Foreign (Portuguese)

32C,20S,FS Aeroplanes Set 6.00
32C,20S,FS Aircraft Set 22.50
24C,20S Portugal Alem Da Europa Set, photo (F), single striker 14.50
28B Alphabet with animals A-Z plus two, drawing on each 19.00
24C,20S,FS Scenes of Angola & Mozambique Set 10.00
60C,20S,DS Armaduras Set, numbered 20.00
20C,20S,DS Astronautica Set, numbered 23.00
10C,20S,FS Banco de Angola Set, Views of Angola 10.00
10C,20S,FS Banco de Angola 5.00
12?C,20S,DS Birds Set, numbered, Fp (S) 10.00
24C,20S,FS Birds Set 30.00
15C,20S,DS Birds Set, Sol (S) 10.00
24C,20S,FS Book Os Lusiadas in 1574 Set, [1972], numbered 13.00
48C,20S,FS Bullfighters Set 27.50
19?C,20S,DS Cachimbos Set, numbered 10.00

24C,20S,DS Caminhos de Fatima Set, numbered 30.00
24C,20S,FS European Classic Cars, known as Portugese Car Set 12.00
24C,20S,FS Cavalry Set..9.00
40C,20S,DS Cidades do Continente.. Set, numbered 25.00
30C,40S,FS Cidades da Europa Set, numbered.. 10.00
16C,20S,DS Circuito de Manutencao Set, [1982], numbered 16 (RD) & 16 (BE) 25.00
20B Circus Characters Set, Fosforos Del Pirineo, S.A. 15.00
40C,20S,FS Coats of Arms Set 17.00
15C,20S,FS Antique Coins Set, Portugal Bank 25.00
20C,20S,FS Coleccao Fotografias Set 5.00
20C,20S,FS Views of Portuguese Colonies Set... 7.00
20C,20S,FS Views of Portuguese Colonies Set... 10.00
20C,20S,FS Costumes Set 13.00
24C,20S,FS Cowboy Cartoons Set 24..10.00
60C,20S,FS Crest of Foreign Lands Set, photo (F) 18.00
30C,20S,FS Ancient Stone Crosses Set [1972]... 12.50
12C,20S,FS Dancers Set.. 10.00
48FB,20S,FS Discoveries Set [1991]... 12.50
96C,20S,DS Walt Disney Set 50.00
24C,20S,FS Ditados Populares Set, drawing (F), numbered 7.00
48C,20S,DS Dogs Set, numbered 30.00
40B Set of Dogs Set, Fosforera Espanola No. 2 .... 27.00
24C,20S,FS Dolls Set (PK) 17.50
24C,20S,FS Dolls Set (YW) 170.00
24C,20S,FS Dolls Set (BE) 17.50
24C?,20S,FS Figuras Tipicas Set, numbered... 20.00
24C,20S,FS Figuras Tipicas Set, drawing (F), numbered 12.00
30C,20S,FS Flags and Views of Cities Set 20.00
30C,30S,FS History of Flight Set.. 20.00
12C,20S,DS Folclore Set, numbered 8.00
10C?,20S,DS Fotografias de Portugal Set, numbered number in tiny (BE) circle 7.50
10C?,20S,DS Fotografias de Portugal Set, numbered number in large (RD) circle 7.50
18C,20S,DS Gatos Set, numbered 10.50
26C,20S,FS Girls Set, 1 each letter of the alphabet 31.50
24C,20S,FS Gunfighters, Set... 10.00
24C,20S,DS Dress Helmets Set, numbered 25.00
24C,20S,FS Ancient Helmets Set 4.00
24C,20S,FS Ancient Helmets Set 9.00
24C,20S,FS Heraldry Set 18.00
24C,20S,DS Hippies Set [1973], crest (S) 15.00
24C,20S,DS Hippies Set [1973], no crest (S) 15.00
24C,20S,FS Horsemen Set 10.00
24C,20S,FS Horses Set 20.00
96C,20S,FS Humor no Cinema Set, [1975], numbered 24, each in 4 colors (BE/CM/PK/WE)
    Linder-Chaplin-Turpin-Keaton-Lloyd-G. Marx-H. Marx-Hardy-Laurel-Fields-Rooney-
    Santana-Silva-Costello-Abbott-Tati-Fernandel-Moreno-Hope-Kaye-Toto-Lewis-Terry
    Thomas-Sordi 20.00
30C,20S,FS Ladies and Letters Set 25.00
40C,20S,FS Love is ... Set (Set A) 25.00
40C,20S,FS Love is ... Set (Set B).. 25.00
60C,20S,FS Military Uniforms Set 40.00
10C,20S,DS Moneyboxes Set... 5.00
10C,20S,FS Moneyboxes Set 7.50
40C,20S,FS Monograms Set, 17th European Exhibition 57.00
10C,20S,FS Movie Stars Set 32.50

16C,20S,FS Nocturno Set 10.00
24C,20S,FS Occupations [1972] Set 12.50
9C?,20S,DS Humor nas Olimpiadas Set, numbered 10.00
20C,20S,FS Olympic Games Comics Set 10.00
20C,20S,DS Historias de Paddington Set, numbered 15.00
36C,20S,FS Paisagens Scenes Set 9.00
40C,20S,FS Patterns [1970] Set 11.00
40C,20S,FS Patterns [1971] Set 22.00
30C,20S,DS Pelourinhos Set, photo (F) 12.50
30C,20S,DS Pelourinhous Set, numbered 17.50
48C,20S,FS Ancient Pistols Set 37.50
24C,20S,FS Antique Planes Set 25.00
24C,20S,DS Racing Cars Set, numbered 15.00
20C,20S,FS Racing Cars Set 12.50
44C,20S,FS Rio Cigars Set, photo (F), ad (B/I) 14.50
32C,20S,FS Safety Signs Set 10.00
36C,20S,FS Sailing Ships Set 30.00
24C,20S,FS Scenes Set 18.00
15C,40S,FS Scenes Set 4.50
20C,20S,FS Scenes Set 22.50
14C,20S,FS Scenes Set 5.00
20C,20S,FS Space Set 14.00
90C,20S,DS Sports Personalities Set, numbered 50.00
24C,20S,FS Sports Set 27.50
90C,20S,DS Famous Sports Personalities Set 55.00
90C,20S,FS Famous Sports Personalities Set 42.00
32C,20S,FS Traffic and Safety Signs Set, numbered 13.00
24C,20S,FS Warriors Set 14.00
18FB,20S,FS Water Sports Set [1990] 15.00
72C,20S,FS World Clothing Set 15.00
32C,20S,DS WWI Aeroplanes Set, numbered 20.00

Foreign (South Africa)

8C,20S,FS Martell Set 3.00
4FB,24S,BS Royal Wedding Set [1986], Coat of Arms-HRH Prince Andrew-Sarah Ferguson-Westminster.. .... 9.00
60C,20S,FS Haig Scotch Whiskey Set 20.00
112C,20S,FS Cocktail Set 50.00
8C,20S,FS Agrolite Set 3.00
8C,20S,FS Animal's Set 3.50
672C,20S,FS History of Aviation Set, 112 different planes, each in 6 colors 300.00
8C,20S,FS Beckman Lager 5.00
28C,20S Veteran Car Series (parts of sets), Booklite Match Co., South Africa 5.00
8C,20S,FS Castle Beer Set 5.00
14C,20S,FS Flowers Set 2.00
120C,20S,FS History of South Africa Set (BK/BE/GY/PK) 90.00
8c,24S,FS Ricardo White Rum Set 5.00
8C,20S,FS Seven Seas Pure Cane Spirit Set 3.00
60C,20S,FS SPAR Set, Made in South AFrica 30.00
6C,20S,FS Foreign, Union Allumettiere S.A. Bruxelles (manumark) 3.00
??C,20S,FS Veteran Car Series Set 5.00
60C,20S,FS Waverly Blankets Set 30.00

Foreign (Singapore)

8C,40S,FS Chinese Art Series Set #1 [1972] Chinese Lanterns 2.50
8C,40S,FS Chinese Art Series Set #2 .... 3.00
8C,40S,FS Chinese Art Series Set #3, numbered 3.00
12C,40S,FS Jurong Bird Park Set #1, numbered, Serpent Eagle-Black Palm Cockatoo-Fish Owl-
    Scarlet Macaws-Crown Pigeons-Sulphur Breasted Toucan-Lady Amherst Pheasant-Pea-
    fowl-Flamingos-Parrots-Scarlet Macaw, Type 1 [1971] 6.00
12C,40S,FS Jurong Bird Park Set #1, numbered, Serpent Eagle-Black Palm Cockatoo-Fish Owl-
    Scarlet Macaws-Crown Pigeons-Sulphur Breasted Toucan-Lady Amherst Pheasant-Pea-
    fowl-Flamingos-Parrots-Scarlet Macaw, Type 2 [1972], reissue 6.00
12C,40S,FS Jurong Bird Park Scarlet Macaw-Secretary Bird-Gold & Blue Macaw..- Flamingos-
    Gold & Blue Macaw-Stanley Crane-Bittern-Toucan-Common Guinea Fowl-Crown Crane-
    Pelican-Black Swan Set #2 [1972], numbered 2.50
8C,24S,FS Malaysian Cultural Scenes Set [1970] 10.00
8C,24S,FS Singapore Scenes, [1970] numbered, Busy Section..-Aerial View..-Lighters or..-
    Nicoll Highway- Delicious Satay..-A Snake Charmer-Lovely Chinese..-A Malay.. ...... 3.00
40C,80S,FS Stamp Series Set [9/8/1970-24/1/1973], numbered and dated 30.00

Foreign (Spain)

26C,30S,BS Abecedario Animal Set [   ], lettered 5.00
2C?,20S,FS Aves Set 2.00
30B Spanish Bullfight Set numbered boxes, 3 line manumark 7.50
30B Spanish Bullfight Set numbered boxes, 2 line manumark 9.00
20B Estampas Taurinas, numbered 7.50
39C?,30S,FS Fiestas y ferias de Espana, numbered 9.00
100C,30S,FS Spanish Set, 4 color pictures with horses 2.50
26C,24S,FS Letters of the Alphabet Set 10.50
??C,20S,FS Perros de Raza Set 2.00
77C?,30S,FS Spanish Cities Set, numbered 10.00
6C?,30S,BS Serie Grabados 2.50
16C,30S,FS Spanish Towns, numbered 9.00
30B Typical Dressing of America, numbered 10.00

Foreign (Switzerland)

24C,20S,FS Alpine Flowers Set 4.00
15C,20S Swiss Set (ca. 1958), Swiss Views by Kandergrund Match Works, Switzerland 8.00
14C,20S Swiss Set, Veteran Cars 10.00
25BL Set w/Coats-of-Arms from Swiss Cities 2.50

Foreign (Miscellaneous)

24C,20S Forest Animals & Insects Set, drawing (F), dated & numbered 25.00
17C,30S Bell & Howell foreign distributors (stock) 14.00
1FB,20S,FS WWII Egyptian Customs Administration stamp holding book together, large V for
    victory (F/B), wide striker, unusual 12.00
10B 1975 Helicopters and Planes, Made in France 3.00

10B 1975 Early Planes, Made in France 3.00
10B French Territories, Made in France 3.00
10B Military Uniforms (flattened), Made in France 3.00
48C,24S,FS S.E.I.T.A. set, Made in France, color photo (F/B) 2.00
1C,30S L'Originale Alfredo, All'Augusteo/Il Re Delle Fettuccine, Made in France 2.00
10B Postage thru the Ages, Made in France 3.00
10C,20S,FS W. German Set, 'Henkel-Noses' 10.00
12C,24S,FS Surprising Amsterdam Set [   ], Central Station-Floating Flower Market-Harbor
    View + 9 others 2.25
12C,24S,FS Holland Promenade Set [1969], Aalsmeer-Alkmaar-Amersfoort-Amsterdam-
    Bennebroek-Friesland-The Hague-Rotterdam-Scheveningen-Volendam-Zaandam-
    Zandvoort 14.50
273BL Very colorful, assorted sizes, Made in India 65.00
20B Dress Attire E, Made in Indonesia 6.00
12B Goose Safety Matches Set [1990], numbered, Carnation-Daffodil-Dahlia-Gladiolus-Holly-
    hock-Iris-Oriental Poppy-Pansy-Peony-Rose-Tulip-Clematis, Made in Indonesia 5.00
14C,30S,FS Ireland Issues, Cities and Towns [1971], Made in Ireland 12.00
7C,30S,FS Powerscourt Gardens Set, Made in Ireland 10.00
4FB Pier 1 Japanese Fan Set, Made in Japan 10.00
40C,20S Cerillos 'La Paz, S.A., Made in Mexico, scenes 5.00
6C,20S,FS Morocco Tourism Set, Made in Morocco 3.50
6B Allumettes Streichholzer, Russian partial set, 1-large, 5-regular 12.75
24B Yugoslavian Dogs Set, numbered contents 40, Drava, Made in Yugoslavia 10.00
100C,MS Foreign, assorted themes 2.50
50B, Foreign, assorted themes 2.50
305C,MZ,MS Foreign themes, assorted, no Canada 20.00
10C,20S,FS Foreign themes, assorted 5.25
400C,20S/30S Foreign, assorted themes 50.00

Fraternal

Fraternal—A category mentioning fraternal and veterans organizations including VFW, Amvets and American Legion. Principal fraternal organizations represented in color sets and singles include Lions, Eagles, Moose, and Elks. There are over 2,750 Elks lodges known and thousands of matchcovers from the other organizations. The organization's logo usually appears along with the lodge number on the front of the matchcover.

50C,20S,FS American Legion Posts & V.F.W. 10.00
50C,20S,FS American Legion Posts, assorted posts 11.25
10C,20S,FS American Legion Posts, assorted posts 5.00
18C,20S,MS F.O.E. Eagles, assorted lodges numbered below 99 .... 7.00
19C,20S,MS F.O.E. Eagles, assorted lodges numbered 100 - 299 .... 9.00
24C,20S,MS F.O.E. Eagles, assorted lodges numbered 300 - 499 .... 12.00

240C,20S,FS Fraternal Order of Eagles (F.O.E.), assorted aeries 45.00
235C,MZ,MS Eagles and Moose, assorted lodges 45.00
985C,20S/30S,MS Fraternal Order of Eagles (F.O.E.), in album 57.50
13C,20S,FS B.P.O.E. Elks Lodges, all numbered below #10 .... 7.00
21C,MZ,MS Elks B.P.O.E. Lodge Nos. between 57 and 2227 .... 9.00
10C,20S,MS Set of Elk Lodge No. 2041, Pearl River, NY 3.00
8C,20S,FS, Elks Lodges, dated 1953-1968 .... 2.50
500C,20S, Elks Lodges, 500 of the first 1000 lodges 82.50
10C,20S,BS B.P.O.E. Elks Lodges, assorted lodges 4.00
50C,20S,FS Elks Lodges, different cities 15.50
200C,20S,MS Elks Lodges 38.00
50C,20S,MS Elks Lodges, all numbered, assorted 11.25
15C,20S,FS Fraternal, L.O.O.M. Lodges 3.00
1FB,20S,FS Grand Lodge F.& A.M. of New York, Masonic War Chest, ca. WWII 2.00
10C,20S,FS Loyal Order of Moose Lodges, assorted lodges numbered below 100 .... 6.50
15C,20S,FS Loyal Order of Moose Lodges, assorted lodges numbered 100 - 199 .... 7.00
35C,20S,FS Loyal Order of Moose Lodges, all numbered below 250 .... 12.00
20C,20S,FS Loyal Order of Moose Lodges, assorted lodges numbered 200 - 399 .... 10.00
20C,20S,FS Loyal Order of Moose Lodges, assorted lodges numbered 501 - 699 .... 10.00
15C,20S,FS Loyal Order of Moose Lodges, assorted lodges numbered 701 - 999 .... 10.00
200C,20S,FS VFW, assorted lodges 20.00
265C,MZ,MS VFW and American Legion, assorted lodges 37.50
160C,20S,MS Fraternal, assorted lodges 9.00
75C,20S/30S,MS Fraternal, assorted lodges 7.00

Front Strikers

Front Strikers—A general classification of matchcovers in which the striker zone appears on the front flap or at the end of the matchcover. The front striker era in matchbook production is generally considered to be from the mid teens to 1976 when the United States Government set guidelines to move the striker to the back of the matchbook. The industry fought the government decision, showing time and time again that the striker in the front posed no more threat than a back striker. But the government won its case, and today all matchbooks made in America have the striker on the back.

Most pre-1960s matchcovers are front strikers (left). In the late 1930s, a few companies experimented with back strikers (middle) but the idea was largely abandoned. Between 1966 and 1976, all American matchbook companies were regulated to place the striker on the back (right). Many foreign matchcovers still use front strikers; however, none are made in the United States or Canada.

75C,MZ,FS Front strikers, assorted themes 8.50
25C,FS,MS Front strikers, assorted themes 4.00
50C,20S,MS,FL Front strikers, assorted themes 15.00
20C,20S,FS Front strikers, assorted themes 12.50
50C,20S,FS Front strikers, assorted themes 13.00
50FB,20S,FS Front Strikers, assorted themes 3.50

Full Length

Full Length—Any matchcover whose message or advertisement runs the full length of the matchcover as a continuous design. Generally known as full lengths, specialists further break this category down into horizontal and vertical full lengths. Recently, an offshoot of this category has been mentioned as half-lengths, a matchcover in which the back shows a horizontal design or message, while the front reads vertically. These are also known as full view matchcovers and can be found as real photo, Matchorama, stock, drawn or designed.

1C,20S,FS Billie's Coffee Shop & Lounge, Monterey, show map of Monterey Bay area (GN/WE) 3.25

1C,20S,FS Carlo's, vertical FL nude in front of mirror 5.00

1C,20S,FS Carls, Where Flower meets Figueroa, (RD/YW) restaurant, period car parked, colorful 3.50

1C,20S,FS Champion Motors, Portland, ME, show (RD) Ford grill, very colorful 5.00

1C,20S,FS The Cloud Room, Portland, Ore, shows lounge w/large colorful mural behind bar 3.00

1C,20S,FS Federal Diners, Open All Night, stock of FL (GN/YW) diner 2.25

1C,20S,FS Foley's Liquors, San Francisco, (BK/WE) pen/ink drawing, 2 addresses, 2 phones 3.50

1C,20S,FS Foley's Liquors, San Francisco, (BK/WE) pen/ink drawing, 1 address, 1 phone, man w/(GN) hat 4.50

1C,20S,FS Gateway Diners, Rosslyn, VA, stock of FL (GN/YW) diner 2.25

1C,20S,FS Hiram Green Blended Whiskey, vertical FL, bottle, Federal Match Co. tall 5.00

1C,20S,FS Hy-Gate Diner, 901 R.I. Avenue, NE, stock of FL (GN/YW) diner 2.25

1C,20S,FS International Forwarding Co, I.F.Co. 1942, show (RD) boxcar FL, ad on side 3.00

1C,20S,FS Jackson's Royal Crown Diner, Kansas City, MO, diner as train, Deco front, (BK/SR) 4.50

1C,20S,FS Kentucky Boys, West of La Cienega, pen/ink drawing of front of restaurant (RD/BK/ WE) 3.50

1C,20S,FS Lamie's Tavern, shows vertical FL map from Boston, Mass to Portland, ME . 3.00

1C,20S,FS Look Magazine, with letters L-O-O-K on vertical FL, stylized 3.00

1C,20S,FS McBroome's Diner, Jewett City, Conn, stock of FL (GN/YW) diner 2.25

1C,20S,FS Mission Inn, Greensburg, PA, aerial drawing of Inn w/ grounds, colorful 3.25

1C,20S,FS Overnight Motor Transportation Co., w/truck & Polar Bear logo on side, very colorful 4.25

1C,20S,FS Paul's Diner, Mountain Lakes, NJ, drawing of diner w/sign (BE/WE) 2.50

1C,20S,FS Penn Diner, Wilkinsburg, PA, stock of FL (GN/YW) diner 2.25

1C,20S,FS Pineland Diner, Augusta, ME, stock of FL (GN/YW) diner 2.25

1C,20S,FS Port Authority, Travelogs WOR, Let's Go and See! w/car, fort & G. Washington (RD/ WE/BE) 2.50

1C,20S,FS Hotel Roanoke, Roanoke, VA, large period building, colorful design 3.50

1C,20S,FS Sleepy Hollow Tavern, Greensburg, (GN/TN) building, colorful 4.00

1C,20S,FS Suburban Ice and Fuel Co, LaGrange, ILL, show coal truck FL, colorful 4.50

1C,20S,FS Top Rail Western Entertainment, Los Angeles, CA, shops, large hitching post, mountains in background 3.00

1C,20S,FS The Tower Cocktail Lounge, drawing of lounge, colorful 3.50

1C,20S,FS Trailways, FL bus w/services listed (RD/BK/WE) 4.00
1C,20S,FS Triple XXX, Seattle Wash, photo of diner, (OE/BK) 3.25
1C,20S,FS Union News Company, shows Greyhound Lines snout bus, (BE) background 3.50
1C,20S,FS Wilson Blended Whisky, Quality Whiskey Since 1823, vertical FL bottle 2.25
1C,20S,FS Yankee Flyer, Nashua, NH, custom w/name on side (BK/RD/WE/BE), colorful 3.50
1C,20S,FS Zimair Trailers, Los Angeles, show trailer w/plane (SR/RD) 3.00

Funeral Homes

Funeral Homes—Any matchcover whose message or advertisement mentions funeral parlors, funeral homes or funeral accouterments, such as caskets, casket companies or ambulance services. Most funeral home matchcovers have a city, state and phone number. Few discuss the details of the process, but invite you to use their services when needed.

25C,30S,FS Assorted, different cities, Matchoramas 2.25
20C,MZ,FS Assorted, different cities 6.00
100C,20S,MS Assorted, different cities 14.00
20C,30S,MS Assorted, different cities, Matchoramas 4.00

Gas Stations

Gas Stations—This category includes all service stations either depicted in a drawing or by advertisement. Closely related are gasoline products to include gas, oil, lubricants, or garages. Tow trucks or gasoline trucks are usually considered in a category of their own. Early service station matchcovers have low digit phone numbers, another category not possible to represent here, but growing in popularity.

20C,20S,MS Amoco, assorted 5.25
15C,20S,MS Chevron, assorted.. 6.25
10C,20S,FS Esso, (RD/WE/BE), assorted (stock)... 6.00
40C,20S,FS Esso/Exxon stations 9.00
15C,20S,BS Esso, N/S, assorted 4.50
15C,20S,MS Gulf, assorted 4.00
15C,20S,MS Phillips 66, assorted 4.00
25C,20S,BS Quaker State Oil, assorted 6.00
15C,20S,MS Shell, assorted 6.25

15C,20S,MS Sinclair & Sunoco, assorted 5.00
15C,20S,MS Standard, assorted 5.00
15C,20S,MS Texaco, assorted 5.00
75C,20S,FS, Texaco service stations 15.00
5C,20S,FS Texaco Set [1953], stock design All Over..-Best Motor..-Don't Guess..-Hatful of..-
    Like Riding 4.25
1FB,40S,FS ad:American, ca. late 1930s, (RD,WE,BE), Universal Match Corp. 5.00
75C,20S,FS, Gas Stations, hillbilly stock designs 3.25
15C,20S,FS Service Stations and Auto Sales 6.00
25C,20S,MS Garages & Service Stations 10.00

Giants (Features & non-Features)

Note here that feature means printed sticks while non-feature means wide stick,
but unprinted.

Giant Features—Made only by the Lion Match Co. with its trademark on the lower inside (see above), Giants usually come with a single comb which may be featured or not. Double and triple combs are known, each printed with the same theme. During WWII, only Christmas Giants were allowed to be printed and comprise the majority of most Giant collections. Dimensions are 9 1/16" by 3 3/8" with the sticks measuring 3 1/4" X 1/4". Lion first made Giants in 1936 and they are still being made today.

1FB,G,FS,FEA American Legion, New York 1937 (F), dated, 'Up Fifth Avenue Again in 1937!'
    (B) 11.50
1FB,G,FS,FEA Aspergum, (B/W) photo of woman (F), (BE/OR) sticks 6.00
1FB,G,FS,FEA Atlantic States Gas Co, Electrolux Refrigerator (BE/YW) 4.50
1FB,G,FS,FEA Reading Premium Beer, logo on sticks 7.00
1FB,G,FS,FEA Bonat Café Washington D.C. - French Chef on sticks 5.50
3FB,G,FS,FEA Bonat Café, The Brass Monkey, Robert Hills' Chef's Inn 6.00
1FB,G,FS,FEA Bookbinders Sea Food House, lobster (F), fishermen on sticks 4.75
1FB,G,FS,FEA C&P Telephone Co, (knothole) 8.00
2FB,G,FS French Casino in Chicago (nude on Horse on B) and Bonat Café, Washington D.C.
    .... 10.50
1FB,G,FS,FEA Chancellor Clipper Ship, sea plane (F), Chancellor Hotel (B), sea plane & hotel
    name across sticks 15.00
5FB,G,FS Christmas Scenes, 1956 calendar on one (I), ads on all 5.00
10FB,G,FS Christmas Giants, assorted 22.50
1FB,G,FS,FEA Crab Orchard Brand Kentucky Straight Whiskey, some tears (I) 4.50
1FB,G,FS,FEA The Derby, Arcadia, Calif, horses coming out of hat (F), photo of Jockey George
    (The Iceman) Woolf, 1938 (B), each stick winners of 1935 thru 1947 Derby and jockey 37.50

1FB,G,BS T. Edwards, modern drawing (B), triple comb 3.00

1FB,G,FS,FEA 14th Annual Freedom Celebration, SOL (F), w/sleeve 10.00

1FB,G,FS Desert of Main at Freeport (camel on F) 4.00

1FB,G,FS French Casino, Chicago, Parisienne Revue, nude on horse back (B), French Casino & Girls—Girls—Girls printed on sticks 13.00

1FB,G,FS Feely type, woman w/large breasts combing hair. ad: Julian C. Cohen & Co. . 10.00

1FB,G,FS,FEA Gofkauf's 11th Birthday Sale, drawing of Goff & Kauf (F), map of NE & 85 stores (B), birthday cake across sticks, each stick a colorful candle 12.50

1FB,G,FS M.L. Goldman Credit Jeweler, Newark, NJ, (BE/WE), bride/groom (F) 2.00

1FB,G,FS,FEA Jax Best Beer in Town, Jackson Brewing Co., long neck bottle w/Christmas wreath across colorful sticks 22.50

1FB,G,FS Discover America w/Jose Jimenez, NBC-TV 2.00

1FB,G,FS Kessler, Smooth as Silk, Whiskey, bottle on each stick, single comb 3.25

1FB,G,FS,FEA La Casa Blanca, Ponce de Leon Residence built in 1523, scene (F), El Morro (B), Ponce de Leon Carnival w/soldier & 1937 across colorful sticks 15.00

1FB,G,FS,FEA Lande's of Denver, Cock 'n' Bull having cocktails (B), double row of sticks w/ Lande's of Denver on each 10.00

1FB,G,FS,FEA Longchamps Restaurant, sticks w/chef at top 5.00

1FB,G,FS Joe Louis vs. Max Schmeling, June 18, 1936, ad: Buick & NBC 78.00

1FB,G,FS,FEA Christmas Giant for Luchow's Wurzburger Hofbrau and Wine Restaurant, NY, stock 2.50

1FB,G,FS,FEA Manufacturers Trust Co, New York, Business Reply postcard (B) 5.00

1FB,G,FS,FEA,CON Manero's Famous Steak House, Paramus, N.J., Tel. Greenwich 8-0049 (S), chef w/hat is each stick, colorful 28.50

1FB,G,FS,FEA Manufacturers Hanover Trust, car loans 8.00

1FB,G,FS,FEA,CON ad: Miner Friction Draft Gear, colorful 6.00

1FB,G,FS U.S.S. Missouri, Ship (F), Seal (B) 10.25

1FB,G,FS Monarch Butterfly punchout (F), ad: Abbott Labs (B), wooden sticks, Italy ... 3.50

1FB,G,FS,FEA Municipal Pier, St. Petersburg, FL, pier (F), scenic points (B), each stick is Mountain Lake Singing Tower, colorful 12.00

12FB,G,FS New York Times Set, (BK/WE), drawing (F) each, inc.: The Lawyer, The Social Leader, The Gourmet, The Salesman, The Banker, The Actress, The Executive, The Sportsman, The Hostess, The Broker, The Clubwoman, The Advertising Man 27.50

1FB,G,FS Nirvana Indian Rest, writing on sticks 3.00

1FB,G,FSPF Lion Match Co. ad, New York City 5.00

1FB,G,FS,FEA Old Grand-Dad Bourbon 6.00

1FB,G,FS,FEA Pak-Mor Refuse Collection Units, truck (F/B), double row of sticks w/Pak-Mor on each 7.00

1FB,G,FS Parrot Jungle, Alligator & Birds (F/B), Parrots on Sticks, colorful 8.00

1FB,G,FS,FEA Personal Finance Co, Pine Bluff, Arkansas, Tel. 301, mis-cut (GD/OE) 3.50

1FB,G,FS,FEA Pollak Reinforcing Service, Rail Steel, Real Strength, man in bed (F), each stick a tapered bottle of Pabst Blue Ribbon Beer 15.00

1FB,G,BS Pope John Paul II, October 1979 w/original mailer, VIP 4.00

1FB,G,FS,FEA Public Service Electric & Gas Co., Burlington, NJ, Electrolux Refrigerator, (BE/ GD) 12.00

1FB,G,FS,FEA Baltimore & Ohio RR Seasons Greetings, Christmas Tree (F) 23.00

1FB,G,FS,FEA Baltimore & Ohio RR Seasons Greetings, Snowman (B) 17.00

1FB,G,FS Best Wishes...Baltimore & Ohio Railroad, train (F)) (RD) 3.00

1FB,G,FL Reagan on $100 bill, made in Japan 3.00

1FB,G,BS Tri-State Cardinal Matchcover Club, 48th RMS Convention Souvenir 2.00

1FB,G,FS The Rogue Matches of the Past, Vol. 1, No. 1 .... 2.75

1FB,G,FS,FEA Shell Oil (RD/YW), logo across sticks 6.00

1FB,G,BS Empire's 6-Bottle Carriers w/coke, Dr. Pepper, 7up, Nehi & Royal Crown 6-pack (B), sticks have name of carrier across each 12.00

1FB,G,FS,FEA The Stork Club, New York City (F/B), Stork Club on each stick 8.00

1FB,G,FS,FEA Studebaker, Smart to be seen in, Smarter to buy, dealer imprint area (B), Studebaker Dictator (YW) across sticks 15.50

1FB,G,FS,FEA Thompson Terminal Warehouses, Inc., Chicago, building (B) 3.00

1FB,G,FS,FEA Tropical Hobbyland, Alligator Wrestler (F), Chimp on Sticks, colorful .. 12.00

1FB,G,FS,FEA Venus Velvet Office Pencils, Venus (F), American Pencil Co. ad (B), each stick a Venus Pencil w/different writing degrees on each 13.50

1FB,G,FS,FEA Wearley's Sea Food & Steaks, lobster (F), fishermen on Sticks 4.75

1FB,G,FS,FEA 1939 New York World's Fair, T&P (F), Aviation Building (I) 20.00

1C,G,FS,FEA 1939 New York World's Fair, montage of Electrical, Railroad, Glass, & Pharmacy building (BE/WE) 10.00

1C,G,FS,FEA 1939 New York World's Fair, Mithrana (B), Canadian Pavilion (F), mostly (BE) w/(WE) 10.00

1C,G,FS,FEA 1939 New York World's Fair, Souvenir (F), Forecast of Transportation (B), very colorful 20.00

1FB,G,FS,FEA Bigger Coverage in the Yellow Pages 8.50

4C,G Zebra Lounge, Robert Hills' Chef's Inn, Town Tavern, The Hearthstone 6.25

5FB,G,FS Lion Giants, colorful sticks, assorted 13.00

1C,G,FS Model Match, Lion Match, Top Hat 6.00

1C,G,BS Model Match, Lion Match, Turnit Too 13.00

1FB,GPF,FS The Marble Cliff Quarries, dated: May 1, 1956 .... 7.00

1FB,GPF,FS Miracle Food Drive In ad 7.00

1FB,GPF,FS,fea Von Paris Moving Co., post card (I) 5.00

1C,GPF,FS,FEA Hotel Philadelphian (OE/WE/BN) 3.00

1FB,GPF,FS Yellow Pages ad 8.00

1FB,GPF,FS,FEA Yellow Pages, photo (F) 8.75

Girlies (Sets & Singles)

Girlies—One of the most popular, this category has its own club and includes singles, sets, and series of slightly clad women at various stages of undress, or nudes. The first sets were popularized by Superior Match Co. in 1938. Called Nudies in England, sets of from four to eight matchcovers com-

(Arrow #2 Set)

prise most of this category's offerings. Matchcover companies employed famous artists such as Elvgren, Thompson, Petty, Vargas, Moran and others to enhance their matchbook line. Girlie sets and singles come in sizes from regular up to Giant, includes a special 240-strike series from Canada. Hundreds of sets and thousands of singles are known. Several major stock girlie sets and series are collected with sayings from "Sandy Says" and "Terri Says." In the following listing, GMC stands for Girlie Matchcover Catalogue.

Advance & Arrow Glamour Girls

5C,20S,FS Set #1 [1942], A Reserved Seat-All Out For Victory-Anxious To Serve-Call To Arms-Thru The Port Hole, GMC p. 1 .... 10.00

5C,20S,FS Set #2 [1944], A Slip of a Miss-I Like to Play-Is My Chute too Small?-Things Are So High These Days-Will My Dreams Come True?, ad: Veteran's Shoe Rebuilders, York, PA, GMC p. 1 .... 22.50

5C,20S,FS Set #3 [1950], Have a Sip?-Have you a Boat?-Isn't it Hot?-Paint Me?-Play with Me?, GMC p. 1 .... 20.00

Allenco (New Zealand)

5C,20S,FS Set #1 [1974], studio and outdoor photos of nudes, GMC p. 40 .... 8.00

5C,20S,FS Set #2 [1976], studio photos of nudes, GMC p. 40 .... 7.00

5C,20S,FS Set #3 [1978], outdoor photos of blonde nude models, GMC p. 40 .... 7.00

American Match Co.

5C,20S,FS Set #1 [1962], A Beachcombers Delight-How About This?-Make Mine on the Rocks-These Straps are Always Breaking-The Water's Too Cold, modeled borders, GMC p. 3 14.00

4C,20S,FS Set #2 [1966], GMC p. 3 .... 3.00

5C,20S,FS Set #2A [1966], fifth cover added, all photos, girls in lingerie (not listed by GMC) 8.00

5C,20S,FS Set #3 [1973], girls in bathing suits, GMC p. 3 .... 3.00

Arrow Match Co.

5C,20S,FS Set #1 [1950], A Study in Photo Art (on each cover), sitting or reclining photo nudes, GMC p. 2 .... 17.50

5C,20S,FS Set #2 [1950], Scotty Says!: Go West Young Man-Always Vote!-Support The Community That Supports You—Drive Safely-Salute America See it First!, (drawings) GMC p. 2 .... 22.50

Atlantis Match Co.

4C,20S,BS Set #1 [1977], ad: Tilton Sunoco, Tilton, NH, nude photos, girls on beach, GMC p. 4 .... 5.75

5C,20S,BS Set #1A, [1977], negatives reversed, models face opposite direction, GMC p. 4 5.50

Atlas Match Co.

5C,40S,BS Set #1 [1975], ad: Every body needs milk, on each, Western Consumer Industries, GMC p. 51 .... 25.00

5C,40S,BS Set #2 [1975], ad: Milk has something for every body., Western Consumer Industries, GMC p. 51 .... 10.00

2C,20S,BS Set #3 [1983], Clicks Pool Hall, A Pretty Good Little Pool Hall, GMC p. 51 ... 6.00

3C,20S,BS Set #4 [   ], Clicks Pool Hall, GMC p. 51a 7.00

4C,20S,BS Set #5 [1990], Clicks Pool Hall, GMC p. 51a 7.00

Australian

3C,20S,FS Hanna Set #1 [1974], outdoor photos of nude models, GMC p. 45 .... 20.00

4C,20S,BS Hanna Set #2 [1976], Playgirls, nude models GMC p. 45 .... 8.00

6C,20S,FS Hanna Set #3 [1976], Playmates, outdoor photos of nude models on beach, GMC p. 45 .... 7.00

4C,20S,FS Hanna Set #4 [1980], Playmates, outdoor photos of nude models, GMC p. 45A 8.25

3C,20S,BS Australia Girlies #1, ad: K.J. & D. Burton Painting, outdoor photos of nude models, GMC p. 40 .... 15.00

Brown & Bigelow

Brown & Bigelow #3

Cuts from early salesman's sample books often shows girlie poses. The phrase "Girlie Matchcover" comes from the early days of the hobby and not from the manufacturers. In the early 1940s, it was never intended to be a rude or chauvinistic title.

4C,20S,FS Set #1 [1962], Coming right up-A good connection-Let's go-The right scale-Roxanne 5.00

4C,20S,FS Set #2, [1964] York Springs, PA, GMC p. 6 .... 5.00

5C,20S,FS Set #2 [1964], Bareback Rider-Coming Right Up-A Good Connection-Let's Go-Roxanne-Stenographer, GMC p. 6 .... 25.00

4C,20S,FS Set #3 [1965], GMC p. 6 .... 20.00

4C,20S,FS Set #4 [1966] The Finishing touch-A Near Miss-Wanted-Your Move, GMC p. 6 6.50

4C,20S,FS Set #5 [1968], GMC p. 6 .... 30.00

4C,20S,FS Set #6 [1969], GMC p. 6 .... 30.00

4C,20S,FS Set #7 [1969] Anchors A Wow-Heart Warming-Sleepy Time Girl-Stepping Out, GMC p. 7 .... 20.00

6C,20S,FS Set #8 [1970], GMC p. 7 .... 17.00

6C,20S,FS Set #9 [1971], GMC p. 7 .... 8.00

4C,20S,FS Set #10 [1972], GMC p. 7 .... 22.00

4C,20S,FS Set #11, [1973], GMC p. 7 .... 8.00

4C,20S,FS Set #12 [1976], GMC p. 8 .... 10.00

4C,20S,FS Set #13 [1976] 30.00

4C,20S,FS Set #14 [1977] 30.00

4C,20S,BS Set #15 [1978] Fresno, CA, 1978 RMS Convention, GMC p. 8 .... 11.00

1C,20S,FS Hilda Single #1 [1962], Touching her toes, GMC p. 5 .... 12.00

1C,20S,FS Hilda Single #2 [1962], Toasting marshmallows, GMC p. 5 .... 9.00

3C,20S,FS Hilda Set #1 [1963], Bathing-Looking in stove-Stomping grapes, GMC p. 5 37.00

3C,20S,FS Hilda Set #2 [1964], Looking in stove-Stomping grapes-Wearing (YW) hat, GMC p. 5 .... 9.00

7C,20S,FS Hilda Fat Girls series, #1, #2, #3, #4, #5, #6, #7, GMC p. 5 .... 45.00

1C,20S,FS Single #1 [1961], Irresistible, GMC p. 5 .... 9.75

1C,30S,FS Single #2 [1962], GMC p. 5 .... 7.00

1C,30S,FS Single #3 [1962], GMC p. 5 .... 5.00

Maid in Baltimore (Universal Match Corp. or as indicated)

3C,20S,FS #1 [   ] drawings by Earl Moran 14.00
1C,20S,FS #2 [   ] drawings by Earl Moran 8.00
1C,20S,FS #3 [   ] drawings by Earl Moran 8.00
1C,20S,FS #4 [   ] Diamond Match 7.00
1C,20S,FS #5 [   ] 12.00
1C,20S,FS #6 [   ] 10.25
1C,20S,FS #7 [   ] 7.00
1C,20S,FS #8 [   ] 13.00
1C,20S,FS #9 [   ] 16.00
1C,20S,FS #10 [   ] Diamond Match 9.00
1C,20S,FS #11 [   ] Diamond Match 6.00
1C,20S,FS #12 [   ] 10.25

Brazil

4C,20S,FS Set #1 [1956], drawing of semi clad models, GMC p. 41 .... 30.00
5C,20S,FS Set #2 [1956], drawings of semi clad models, GMC p. 41 .... 30.00

Bryant & May

6C,20S,BS Australian Set #1 [1980], Centrefold, photos of nude models, GMC p. 42 ... 10.00
6C,20S,FS Australian Set #2 [1981], outdoor photos of nude models, GMC p. 42 .... 14.00
3C,20S,FS Set #2A, salesman's blanks, color photos of nude models (F/B), GMC p. 42 15.00
5B Australian Set #3 [1983], Penthouse Angie-Carmen-Cheryl-Julie-Lillian, soft core, GMC.
        p.42A 20.00
4C,20S,FS Australian Set #4 [   ], photos of nude models, GMC p. 42A 7.00

Canadian

Canadian #4, 1954

5C,20S,FS Set #1 [1950], Strike-Rite Match Co., Beautiful Take Off-Over the Top-Rear Reinforcements-Ship Shape-Showing Form, GMC p. 36 .... 6.75
4C,20S,FS Set #2 [1951], Premier Match Co., Look What I've Got-Short on Sails-Sport Model-Up to Par, GMC p. 36 .... 9.75
4C,20S,FS Set #3 [1952], Premier Match Co., Figures Don't Lie-Good Pickins-Net Results-Plenty on the.., GMC p. 36 .... 6.00
4C,20S,FS Set #4 [1954], Strike-Rite Match Co., Debutante-Stop Sign-The Finishing Touch-What A Frame, GMC p. 36 .... 7.25

5C,20S,FS Set #5 [1955], Strike-Rite Match Co., Bottoms Up-Call Again-Come Back Soon-Come up and See Us-HiYa, (BK/WE) drawings, GMC p. 36 .... 20.00
5C,20S,FS Set #6 [1961], Strike-Rite Match Co., Barking Dogs Bite-Like My Brand-Losing Her Spots-Well Stacked-What's On Your Mind, drawings, GMC p. 37 .... 10.00
5C,20S,FS Set #7 [1962], Eddy Match Ltd, outdoor photos of models in bathing suits, GMC p. 37 .... 7.25
5C,20S,FS Set #8, Vista-Lite Type 1 [1964], pictures have captions, GMC p. 37 .... 8.75
5C,20S,FS Set #8, Vista-Lite Type 2, picture has Memories of Summer in English 6.00
5C,20S,FS Set #8, Vista-Lite Type 3, Memories of Summer in English and French 6.75
5C,20S,FS Set #9 [1965], Strike-Rite Match Co, Flying Saucy-Mars or Bust-Rocket Shape-Space Suited-Take Me to Your Leader, drawings, GMC p. 37 .... 2.00
5C,20S,FS Set #10, [1966] Eddy Match Ltd., outdoor photos of models at beach, GMC p. 37 9.75

5C,20S,FS Set #11 [1968] Strike-Rite Match Co., French-Greek-Polynesian-Scottish, drawings, GMC p. 38 .... 8.25

5C,20S,BS Set #12, [1969] Eddy Match Ltd, photos of models in bathing suits at beach, GMC p. 38 .... 7.75

5C,20S,BS Set #13 [1973] Eddy Match Co., photos of models in bathings suits at beach, GMC p. 38 .... 8.00

4C,20S,BS Set #14 [1974] Strike-Rite Match Co., studio photos of models, one at beach, GMC p. 38 .... 8.25

5C,20S,FS Set #15 [1976] Eddy Match Co., outdoor photos of semi-clad models, GMC p. 38 7.75

4C,20S,BS Set #16 [1977], Premier Match Co., indoor studio photos of semi clad models, GMC p. 39 .... 8.00

4C,20S,BS Set #17 [1978] Eddy Match Ltd, studio photos of semi clad models, GMC p. 39 6.75

4C,20S,BS Set #18 [1980] Strike Rite Match Co., studio photos of nudes, GMC p. 39..... 8.25

4C,20S,BS Set #19 [1981], Premier Matches Ltd, outdoor photos of nudes, GMC p. 39 . 7.25

4C,20S,BS Set #19 [1981] Strike Rite Match Co., indoor & outdoor photos of semi clad and nude models, GMC p. 39 .... 7.50

4C,20S,FS Set #20, [1981] indoor & outdoor photos of semi clad and nude models, GMC p. 39 .... 6.75

5C,30S,BS Set #21, studio photos of nudes, GMC p. 39A 7.25

Chicago Maids

Chicago Maid #1, 1939

6C,20S,FS Set #1 [1939], Bet on MaMa-Inflation-Lady in Distress-Mind Reader-Strip Poker-Television, GMC p. 9 .... 27.75

4C,20S,FS Set #2 [1941], A Hot Number-Plenty Doggie-Pretty Sporty-Thum Stuff, GMC p. 9 .... 15.00

7C,20S,FS Set #3 [1943], Catch On-Current Event-Knots To You-Little Wolf-Sit Down Strike-So Full Packed-Stop Sign, Brook's Cafe, Phone 55, Ringgold, GA., GMC p. 9 .... 9.00

5C,20S,FS Set #4 [1949], D'Amario A Belle With A New Ring-I Appeal-Oarful Situation-Stuck Up-Wow! What, A Year will Do, GMC p. 9 .... 15.00

6C,20S,FS Set #5 [1951], A Good Mixer-Fixin' Her Drawers-Oh! Dear I Forgot..-Ridin' the Range-What a Frame-Who will Second the Motion!, Castle Cigar Store, New Castle, Ind, GMC p. 10 .... 9.75

6C,20S,FS Set #5A [1951], A Good Mixer-Fixin' Her Drawers-Oh! Dear I Forgot..-Ridin' the Range-What a Frame-Who will Second the Motion!, Castle Cigar Store, New Castle, Ind, manumark Evans Print Co., different colors, (not listed by GMC) 9.75

6C,20S,FS Set #6 [1960], Failor's Frozen Food, Newville, PA., phone 118-J (S), GMC p. 10 4.25

6C,20S,FS Set #7 [1965] 7.00

5C,20S,FS Set #8 [1968] 8.00

Crazy Horse
12FB,40S,BS Set, different color photo of club stripper on each (B) 22.00
12C,30S,BS Set #1, GMC p. 51b 10.00
12C,40S,BS Set #2, GMC p. 51b 10.00
23C,40S,BS Set #3 .... 10.00

D'Amario (Superior Match Co.)
5FB,20S,FS Set #1 [1952], Come Over, Party's On!-Maid To Order!-Wanta Buy a Duck?-Young
and Kittenish!-Young Dog, Old Trick!, GMC p. 32 .... 6.00

D.D. Bean & Sons, Co.
6C,20S,FS Set #1 [1947], Mennen, For Extra Man Power..-Man Wanted..-Men, to see more..-
New! Especially for men..-Something for the boys..- Strictly for Men, GMC p. 52 . 15.00
4C,20S,FS Set #2 [1947], Pepsi-Cola Girls, one full length, GMC p. 52 .... 30.00

Diamond Match Co.

5C,20S,FS Set #1 [1957], Studio Cover Girls I'm Ropin' You In-Plenty on the Ball-She'll Get Her
Man-The Right Bait Gets Results-Well Equipped for Gold Digging, GMC p. 11 ..... 20.00
5C,20S,FS Set #2 [1959], Studio Cover Girls, no sayings, GMC p. 11 .... 4.00
5C,20S,FS Set #3 [1962], models in bathing suits, no sayings, GMC p. 11 .... 5.50
5C,20S,FS Set #4 [1968], models on beach, no sayings, GMC p. 11 .... 6.50
5C,20S,BS Set #5 [1974], models on beach, no sayings, GMC p. 11 .... 12.00
5C,20S,FS Set #5A [   ], models on beach, no sayings, GMC p. 11 .... 5.00
6C,20S,BS Set #6 [1978],models on beach, no sayings, GMC p. 12 .... 8.00

Economy Blue Print & Supply Co.
6C,20S,FS Set #1 [1951], all with 3 addresses inside, GMC p. 53 .... 40.00
6C,20S,FS Set #1 [1951] 5th cover only blank (I), may have been issued as singles, GMC p. 53
.... 40.00
6C,20S,FS Set #1 [1951] 1st & 3rd cover w/1 address (I), may have been issued as singles, GMC
p. 53 .... 40.00

Elvgren (Superior Match Co.)

Elvgren #1, 1938

5C,20S,FS Set #1 [1938], A Good Hook up-A Live Wire-Doctor's Orders-Man's Best Friend-Sure Shot, GMC p. 26 .... 20.00

5C,20S,FS Set #2 [1938], A Perfect Pair-French Dressing-In the Dough-Just the Type-Out on a Limb, GMC p. 26 .... 12.00

5C,20S,FS Set #3 [1939], A Peek A Knees-Figures Don't Lie-Free Wheeling-Sitting Pretty-Social Security, GMC p. 26 .... 12.00

5C,20S,FS Set #4 [1939], A Knockout-Ankles Aweigh-Forced Landing-Peek A View-Playing Safe, GMC p. 26 .... 13.00

5C,20S,FS Set #5 [1940], A Lad Her Problem-Disturbing Elements-Palette Able-Short on Sails-Thar She Blows, GMC p. 27 .... 8.00

5C,20S,FS Set #6 [1940], 'Jutht My Thize!'-Miss Placed Confidence-No Stares!-Sport Model-Station WOW, GMC p. 27 .... 8.00

5C,20S,FS Set #7 [1941], A Clothes Call-A Hitch in Time-Help Wanted-The High Way-What Ho!, ACME, Harrisburg, PA, GMC p. 27 .... 9.00

5C,20S,FS Set #8 [1942], Look What I've Got-On De Fence-Tail Wind-Toots and Saddles-Weight Control, GMC p. 27 .... 8.25

5C,20S,FS Set #9 [1943], Caught in the Draft-Foil Proof-Good Pickin's-Keep 'Em Flying-Up To Par, GMC p. 27 .... 8.50

5C,20S,FS Set #10 [1944], Belle Ringer-One for the Books-Plane View-Skirting Trouble-Tree for Two, Archway Café, Des Moines, IA, GMC p. 27 .... 7.00

5C,20S,FS Set #11 [1945], Is My Face Red-Net Results-Out of Control-Over Exposure-Sleepy Time Girl, GMC p. 28 .... 7.00

5C,20S,FS Set #12 [1946], A Good Tie Up-A Sailor's Dream-Sun Kissed-Swell Fit and Form-What Every Girl Should Know, Mary Jane's Restaurant, Marcus Hook, PA, GMC p. 28 9.50

5C,20S,FS Set #13 [1947], A Good Number-A Perfect Image-Hold Everything-Like My Slippers?-Sittin' Prett, GMC p. 28 .... 6.00

5C,20S,FS Set #14 [1947], A Pleasing Discovery-Bird's Eye View-Hang It All-The High Sign-What A Break, GMC p. 28 .... 12.00

5C,20S,FS Set #15 [1948], Glamour Girls A Clean Start-A Sweet Job-All Puckered Up-Ship Ahoy-Well Stocked, Knight's Service Station, Bridgeport, Conn., GMC p. 28 .... 7.75

European

5C,20S,FS Set #1 [1974], Germany, studio photos of semi clad models, GMC p. 43 ..... 30.00

5C,20S,FS Set #2 [1974], French, studio photos of semi clad models, GMC p. 42 .... 30.00

Federal Truck (Ohio Match Co.)

1C,20S,FS Single #1, [1947], girl and dog . 9.00
1C,20S,FS Single #2, [1946], girl and fishing creel
.... 25.25
1C,20S,FS Single #3, [1944], girl and tennis racket
.... 17.00
1C,20S,FS Single #4, [   ], girl and 2 dogs 25.25
1C,20S,FS Single #5, [1942], girl with fencing foil
.... 20.00
1C,20S,BS Single #6, [1941], drum majorette ...
.... 25.25
1C,20S,FS Single #7, [   ], girl with captain's hat
.... 25.25

French
6C,20S,FS Series Set #1 [1951], full length models, bathing suits, (not listed by GMC) 50.00
6C,20S,FS Series Set #2 [1953], photos (F/B) of each cover, studio setting, GMC p. 44   60.00

Glamour Girlie
5C,20S,FS Set #1, 1942, GMC p. 1, ad: Victim of Defense Program 12.00
5C,20S,FS Set #2, 1944, GMC p. 1 .... 15.00

Guy Gray
3C,30S,BS Set #1 [   ], nude models, color photos (I), ad (O), GMC p. 54 .... 35.00
3C,30S,BS Set #2 [   ], nude models, color photos (I), ad (O), GMC p. 54 .... 20.00
3C,30S,BS Set #3 [   ], nude models, color photos (I), ad (O), GMC p. 54 .... 20.00
3C,30S,BS Set #4 [   ], nude models, color photos (I), ad (O), GMC p. 55 .... 6.00
3C,30S,BS Set #5, [1979], nude models, color photos (I), ad (O), GMC p. 55 .... 8.50
3C,30S,BS Set #6 [1981], nude models (2 Western), color photos (I), ad (O), GMC p. 55   7.00
3C,30S,BS Set #7, nude models, color photos (I), ad (O), GMC p. 56 .... 10.00
3C,30S,BS Set #8 [1982], nude models, color photos (I), ad (O), GMC p. 56 .... 8.00
3C,30S,BS Set #9 [1983], nude models, color photos (I), ad (O), GMC p. 56 .... 10.00
3C,30S,BS Set #10 [1984], nude models, color photos (I), ad (O), GMC p. 56 .... 8.00
3C,30S,BS Set #11, nude models, color photos (I), ad (O), GMC p. 56 .... 10.00
3C,30S,BS Set #12 [   ], nude models, color photos (I), ad (O), GMC p. 56A 7.25
3C,30S,BS Set #13 [1989], color photos (I), ad (O) 6.00
3C,30S,BS Set #14 [1990], color photos (I), ad (O) 5.50
3C,30S,BS Set #15 [1991], color photos (I), ad (O) 9.00
3C,30S,BS Single #1 [   ], GMC p. 54 .... 20.00
3C,30S,BS Single #2 [   ], May I Help You? (I), GMC p. 54 .... 25.25
3C,30S,BS Single #3 [   ], GMC p. 54 .... 12.00
3C,30S,BS Single #4 [   ]... 15.00
3C,30S,BS Single #5 [   ]... 15.00
15C,30S,BS Girlies, colorful nude (I) each, assorted 22.00

Hollywood Models
12C,20S,FS Series 3 [1949], (not listed by GMC) 4.00
12C,20S,FS Series 4 [1949] 5.00

Lakewood Pipe

3FB,G,BS Set #1 [ ], color photos of semi clad model, GMC p. 57 .... 20.00
4C,FS,G Set #2 [ ], color photos of semi clad model, GMC p. 57 .... 20.00
5C,FS,G Set #3 [ ], color photos of semi clad model, GMC p. 58 .... 17.50
5C,FS,G Set #4 [ ], color photos of nude model, Indian and Western motif, GMC p. 58   30.00
1C,30S,FS Single #1 [1971], ad (F), nude model (B), GMC p. 58A 7.00
1C,40S,FS Single #2 [ ], ad (F), semi clad model (B), GMC p. 58A 25.00

Lion Match Co.

3C,20S,FS Set #1 [1951], pen & ink drawings, no sayings, GMC p. 14 .... 35.00
3C,30S,FS Set #1A [1951], single 17.50
3C,20S,FS Set #2 [1952], drawings, girls partying, GMC p. 14 .... 25.00
3C,20S,FS Set #3 [1953], ad: Frank & Henry's Bar & Grill, Lindenhurst, NY, GMC p. 14 .... 22.50
3C,20S,FS Set #4 [1953], pen & ink drawings,(not listed by GMC) 20.00
4C,20S,FS Set #5 [1955], Mm m m-Ready to Serve-The Right Number-Tan and Terrific, GMC p. 15 .... 8.25

4C,20S,FS Set #5 [1955], NCO Club, Buedingen, Germany, live drawings, GMC p. 15 .. 9.00
5C,20S,FS Set #6 [1970], photos of models, all semi-clad, GMC p. 15 .... 5.00
4C,20S,FS Set #7 [1970], same blonde model on each, different pose, GMC p. 15 .... 15.00
4C,20S,FS Set #8 [1977], same blonde model on each, different pose, GMC p. 15 .... 7.75

Mad Cap Maids (Match Corp. of American)

5C,20S,FS Set #1 [1939], A Bare Escape-Harem Scarem-Hot Dog-Sitting Pretty-The Bare Essential, GMC p. 18 .... 12.50
5C,20S,FS Set #2 [1941], Air Raid Siren-Bomb A Dear-Naughty Nautical-No Man's Land-Para Cutie, GMC p. 18 .... 10.00
5C,20S,FS Set #3 [1943], A Bumper Crop-A Cute Trick-l Can Cook Too-Like My Daisy?-Like My Formal?, GMC p. 18 .... 10.00
7C,20S,FS Set #4 [1949], Case Dis Missed-Cover Girl-Foot Loose-Glovely-See worthy-What A Frame-What's Cooking?, GMC p. 18 .... 7.75
7C,20S,FS Set #5 [1950], Closed Case-Cute Trick-Good Looking-Just Right-One for the Books-Outside Chance-Taking a Lacing, GMC p. 19 .... 8.75
7C,20S,FS Set #6 [1951], Doggy Affair-Hot Dog-Knit Wit-The Last Draw-Slick Trick-Tapering Off-Well Equipped, GMC p. 19 .... 9.50
12C,20S,FS Set #7 [1952], A Wicket Player-Crash Landing-Dog On It-Exposed-Hold That Line-Island Serenade-Limbering Up-No Privacy-Skip It-Smart Set-Snow Fun-Thin Ice, GMC p. 19 .... 12.00
12C,20S,FS Set #8 [1954], Barrelly Covered-Heat Wave-Honey Combed-Pace Setter-Pretty Doggie-Putting on the Dog-Reel Evidence-Shaping Up-Slip Knot-Some Pumpkins-The Pay Off-Upswept, GMC p. 20 .... 10.00
5C,20S,FS Set #9 [1955], Barbecutie-Blonde Venus-Lady Godiva-Pressing Need-Your Attention Please!, George Winters, General Insurance, Harrisburg, PA, GMC p. 20 .... 10.00
5C,20S,FS Set #10 [1957], Clean Sweep-Lambie Pie-Lucky Me-Sugar 'n Spice-Watch the Birdie, GMC p. 20 .... 5.00
5C,20S,FS Set #11 [1958], Do It Yourself Kid-Hula Lula-Play Ball!-See, Senor!-What's Cooking, GMC p. 20 .... 10.00
5C,20S,FS Set #12, [1959], studio photos of semi-clad models, no sayings, GMC p. 21 .. 7.00
5C,20S,FS Set #13 [1963], studio photos of semi-clad models, no sayings, GMC p. 21 .... 6.75

Maryland Carnival

4C,20S,FS Set #1 [1972], full length nudes, GMC p.59 .... 20.00
4C,20S,BS/FS Series Set #1A [   ], strikerr (B) on 3 covers only, GMC p. 59 .... 20.00
4C,20S,FS Single #1 [   ] variation, inverted picture, GMC p. 59 .... 12.00
4C,20S,FS Single #1A [   ] variation, smaller picture, GMC p. 59 .... 12.00

Merlin (Maryland Match Co.)

Merlin #1, 1940

5C,20S,FS Set #1 [1940], Beautiful Take Off-Over The Top-Rear Reinforcements-Ship Shape-Showing Form, ad: It's Great To Be An America, GMC p. 16 .... 14.00
5C,20S,FS Set #2 [1948], Baby Sitting-Bulls Eye-Keep Cool-What A Catch-What's Your Brand?, GMC p. 16 .... 12.75
5C,20S,FS Set #3 [1952], A Good Connection-Arabian Knight's Dream-No Trespassing-Seeworthy-Too Hot To Handle, GMC p. 16 .... 10.50
5C,40S,FS Set #3A [1952], A Good Connection-Arabian Knight's Dream-No Trespassing-Seeworthy-Too Hot To Handle, GMC p. 16 .... 10.00
5C,20S,FS Set #4 [1955], Barking Dogs Bite-Like My Brand-Losing Her Spots-Well Stacked-What's On Your Mind, GMC p. 16 .... 9.00
5C,40S,FS,RF Set #4A [1955], Barking Dogs Bite-Like My Brand-Losing Her Spots-Well Stacked-What's On Your Mind, GMC p. 16 .... 10.00
5C,20S,FS Set #5 [1962], Flying Saucy-Mars or Bust-Rocket Shape-Space Suited-Take Me To Your Leader, GMC p. 17 .... 7.00
5C,20S,FS Set #6 [1968], French-Greek-Polynesian-Scotch-Spanish, Greek & French (BE), other 3 no printing, GMC p. 17 .... 4.50
5C,20S,FS Set #6A [1968], French-Greek-Polynesian-Scotch-Spanish, Greek & French (BE), other 3 in (BK) (not listed by GMC) 4.50
5C,20S,FS Set #6B [1968], French-Greek-Polynesian-Scotch-Spanish, Scottish, Polynesian (RD), others (BE), GMC p. 17 .... 4.50
5C,20S,FS Set #7 [1974], models both nude and in bathing suits, GMC p. 17 .... 8.00
5C,20S,BS Set #7A [1974], models both nude and in bathing suits, GMC p. 17 .... 8.00
5C,20S,BS Set #8, [1980], models semi-clad, in door photos, GMC p. 17 .... 15.00
4C,20S,BS Set #9, [1981], outdoor nudes, GMC p. 17 .... 15.00

Niagara Falls

5B 3D Single Set #1, 3D boxes, GMC p. 60 .... 8.00
1B 3D Single Set #2, 3D boxes, GMC p. 60A 7.00
6B Set #1 [1975], 3D boxes, GMC p. 60 .... 30.00

Pacific Dancer (Canadian)

7C,20S,BS Set #1 [1991], different color photo of nude on each (F), name (I), GMC p. 60c   10.25

7C,20S,BS Set #1A, No. 5 Orange Canadian, different color photo of nude on each (F), name (I), by Pacific Dancer 6.50

Petty (Superior Match Co.)

Petty #1, 1948

5C,20S,FS Set #1 [1948], Hold the Phone-Hot as a Firecracker-Perfect Form for Fun-Pistol Packin' Mamma-Will You Bait My Hook?, GMC p. 29 .... 12.00

5C,20S,FS Set #2 [1949], A Hair Raising Line-Any Number—I'm Lonesome!-High, Dry and—Wow!-It's Way Over My Head-My Heart Belongs to Daddy, GMC p. 29 .... 10.00

5C,20S,FS Set #3 [1949], The Home Stretch-It's In The Bag-L.o.v.e.l.y to Look At!!!-Snug as a Bug-Well I'll Be Witched, GMC p. 29 .... 10.00

5C,20S,FS Set #4 [1950], Fast, like a Bunny!!-Here's Looking at You!!-Perfect Posture-Shorts and Sweet!-Undercover Gal', Paul Felker's Maple Inn, Route 522, Telephone 29-R-10, GMC p. 29 .... 10.00

5FB,20S,FS Set #5 [1951], Golf Ball Curves-Look Here—Admiral!-Swing High Swing Low!-Why—I'm Shocked!-Y.e.s., I'm Home, GMC p. 29 .... 11.50

5C,20S,FS Set #6 [1965], Golf Balls Curves-Perfect Posture-My Heart Belongs to Daddy-Well...I'll Be Witched!!—Will You Bait My Hook (not listed by GMC) 12.00

5C,20S,FS Set #7 [1966], (not listed by GMC) 12.00

5C,20S,FS Set # 8 [1967], Loverly to Look at!!!-Any Number, I'm Lonesome—Snug as a Bug—Hot as a Fire Cracker—Swing High-Swing Low! (not listed by GMC) 14.50

5C,20S,FS Set #9 [1968], Will you Bait My Hook?—Look here—Admiral!-My Heart Belongs to Daddy—Perfect Posture—Well...I'll Be Witched!! (not listed by GMC) 10.50

Regal Match Co.

4C,20S,FS Set #1 [1987], GMC p. 24a 8.00

5C,20S,BS Set #1, GMC p. 24a, ad: matchcover club related, AASCO manumark 8.25

Regal #5, 1962

Republic Match Co.

5C,20S,FS Set #1 [1966], studio photo of nudes, GMC p. 25 .... 8.00

4C,20S,FS Set #2A [1970], (GY) background, nude w/guitar is redhead, GMC p. 25 ...... 8.00

4C,20S,FS Set #2A [1970], (GY) background, nude w/guitar is brunette, GMC p. 25 ...... 5.00

5C,20S,FS Set #2a [1970], colored background, GMC p. 25 .... 6.00
4C,20S,FS Set #3 [1977], nude models, studio & outdoor poses, no sayings, GMC p. 25 6.75
4C,20S,BS Set #3A [1977], nude models, studio & outdoor poses, no sayings, GMC p. 25 6.00

Starline English
6C,30S,FS Set #1 [1970], (PE), outdoor photos of models in bathing suits, GMC p. 46. 40.00
6C,30S,FS Set #2 [1971], (OE), indoor and outdoor photos of semi clad models, GMC p. 46 12.00
6C,30S,FS Set #3 [1972], (BK), outdoor photos of semi clad models, GMC p. 47 .... 10.00
6C,30S,FS Set #4 [1973], (BN), outdoor photos of semi clad and nude models, GMC p. 47 12.00
6C,30S,FS Set #5 [1975], (PK), outdoor photos of semi clad models, GMC p. 47 .... 10.00
6C,30S,FS Set #6 [1977], (TN), outdoor photos of nude and semi clad models, GMC p. 48 12.00
6C,30S,FS Set #7 [1979], (OE), photos of semi clad and bathing suit models, GMC p. 48 12.00
6C,30S,FS Set #8 [1984], pale (YW), studio photos of nude and semi clad models, GMC p. 48
    .... 10.50

Superior Live Models (Superior Match Co.)
5C,20S,FS Set #1 [1958], A Penny for Your Thoughts-A Well Fitted Case-No Cause for Alarm-
    Packed with Ammunition-This is No Gamble, GMC p. 32 .... 12.00
5C,20S,FS Set #2 [1959], Double Trouble-Just a Country Lass-No Fair Peeking-Sailor Beware-
    Something Like This?, GMC p. 32 .... 6.00
5C,20S,FS Set #3 [1960], A Site for Sore Eyes-Control Yourself-Double Top Feature-Let's Yarn
    About This-Matched Beauties, GMC p. 33 .... 17.50
5C,20S,FS Set #4 [1961], Curves A Plenty!-Keep Your Distance-My Toes are Cold-Sitting
    Pretty-Star Spangled Beauty, GMC p. 33 .... 13.50
5C,20S,FS Set #5 [1962], Fun in the Sun-Just Laugh It Off-On Guard-On the Barrel Head-Toast
    of the Town, GMC p. 33 .... 5.25
5C,20S,FS Set #6 [1969], GMC p. 33 .... 7.50
4C,20S,FS Set #6 [1969], Aasco manumark (not listed by GMC) 5.00
5C,20S,FS Set #7 [1971], Playgirls, GMC p. 34 .... 9.50
4C,20S,FS Set #8 [1973], Playgirls, I'll Be Ready..-Room for Two-Sheer Nonsense-That's All
    Brother, GMC p. 34 .... 4.75
4C,20S,FS Set #8 [1973], Playgirls, I'll Be Ready..-Room for Two-Sheer Nonsense-That's All..,
    GMC p. 34 .... 3.50
4C,20S,FS Set #9 [1976], Playgirls, Bill's Army-Navy Sales, Athens, OH 45701, GMC p. 34 7.50
4C,20S,FS Set #9A [1976], negative reversed on (BE) cover, GMC p. 34 .... 5.00
4C,20S,BS Set #9B [1977], negatives as shown, GMC p. 34 .... 5.00
4C,20S,BS Set #9C [1977], negatives reversed on (RD) (YW) & (GY) covers, GMC p. 34 8.00

Taiwan
4C,20S,FS Set #1 (RD), same design as Sets #2, #3, & #4, models (B), first cover same as Set
    #2, close up of girl (F), GMC p. 49 .... 25.00
4C,20S,FS Set #2 (MN), same design as Sets #1, #3, & #4, models (B), first cover same as Set
    #1, close up of girl (F), GMC p. 49 .... 25.00
4C,20S,FS Set #3 (BE), same design as Sets #1, #2, & #4, models (B), first cover same as Set
    #4, close up of girl (F), GMC p. 49 .... 25.00
4C,20S,FS Set #4 (GN), same design as Sets #1, #2, & #3, models (B), first cover same as Set
    #3, close up of girl (F), GMC p. 49 .... 25.00
4C,20S,FS Set #5, same model in bathing suit, (F/B), GMC p. 49A 25.00
5C,20S,FS Set #6, same model (F/B), GMC p. 49A 20.00
2C,20S,FS Set #7, Yung Shun Match Factory, same nude model (F/B), GMC p. 49A 20.00
3C,20S,FS Set #8, full length photo of Taiwan model (B), close up of face (B), GMC p. 49B 20.00
4C,20S,FS Set #9, same model (F/B), GMC p. 49B 25.00
1C,20S,FS Set #10, unknown if single or from set, full length (B), close up of face (F), GMC p.
    49B 25.00

Thompson (Superior Match Co.)

Thompson #5, 1957

8C,20S,FS Set #1 [1953], A Baton Beauty-Anything on Tonight?-A Perfect Pair!-Hawaii, Here we Come!-Howdy, Amigo!-I'm Next, Stick Around-Pride of the Harem-Roped and Tied!, GMC p. 31 .... 10.00

8C,20S,FS Set #2 [1954], A Two Gun Gal!-Fit as a Fiddle-Look What I've Got!-Pardon my Back!-Short and Sweet!-Snow Daddy!-That Ain't Hay!-Things are Looking Up!, GMC p. 31 9.00

5C,20S,FS Set #3 [1955], An Orchid for Betsy-Best Foot Forward-Better Than Bare Skin-Look Here Pardner-On the Hit Parade, ad: Scotty's Fruit Market, Lansing, MI, GMC p. 31 9.25

5C,20S,FS Set #4 [1956], Glamour Girls Facing a Heat Wave!-In Perfect Shape!-South of the Border-Strictly for the See!-To Be.. or Not to Be!, GMC p. 32 .... 12.50

5C,20S,FS Set #5 [1957], A Hooked Lass-Anyone For Tennis?-My Good Neighbor Policy-That Old Black Magic-Where's My Swim Suitor?, GMC p. 32 .... 7.50

Universal Match Corp.

Silhouettes, Type 1, 1955

5C,20S,FS Set #1 [1954], Inviting-No Trespassing-Sitting Pretty-Slow Curves Ahead-Temptation 12.75

4C,20S,FS Set #2,[1955], colorful drawings GMC p. 35 .... 5.50

4C,20S,FS Set #2, silhouettes, Type 1 [1955], (BK/WE) 7.00

4C,20S,FS Set #2, silhouettes, Type 2 [   ], (BE/YW) 6.00

4C,20S,FS Set #2, silhouettes, Type 3 [   ], (RD/WE) 6.50

4C,20S,FS Set #2, silhouettes, Type 4 [   ], (DGN/LGN) 5.50

4C,20S,FS Set #2, silhouettes, Type 5 [   ], (BK/PK) 6.50

4C,20S,FS Set #2, silhouettes, Type 6 [   ], (BK/RD) 6.00

4C,20S,FS Set #2, silhouettes, Type 7 [1966], (BK/OE), UMC in front of manumark 5.75
4C,30S,FS Eljer Series Set #1 [1957], Girl exercising-Girl stepping out of tub-Girl in ballet pose-
Girl in Turkish pantaloons, GMC p. 61 .... 30.00
6C,20S,BS Titanoxer Set #1, [1952], National Lead Co. ad, last cover not a girlie, GMC p. 61 15.00

Girlies (Miscellaneous Sets)

8C,20S,BS The Fox Pub Girlie Set, different color photo of nude on each (F), blank (I). 10.00
100B Modes [1988], numbered, Bath Model Agency, England 35.00
8C,20S,FS Girlie Set #1, Made in South Africa 5.00
6C,30S,FS Singapore Set #1 [   ], photos of semi clad and fashion models, GMC p. 45B 15.00
4C,30S,FS Germany Girlies Set, GMC p. 44A 17.00
4C,20S,FS Japan Hand-Matchic DeLight Set #1 [   ], exaggerated drawings of nude, curled finger
(B), Distributed in Australia, GMC p. 45A 5.00
6C,20S,FS Jersey Set #1 [1940], He, Your heart's..-I'll look at..-Just for the fun..-Just say, Dear..-
My, what beautiful eyes you have..-Yes, Mr. Rich.., ad for Jersey Match Co (F), GMC p.
13 .... 12.50
432B Girls Names [1984], 108 names each with 4 designs (butterflies-flowers-hearts-stars)
Alice-Allison-Amy-Andrea-Angela-Ann-Anne-Barbara-Becky-Beth-Betty-Bonnie-Brenda-
Carol-Carolyn-Carrie-Cathy-Cheryl-Chris-Cindy-Connie-Dana-Dawn-Debbie-Denise-
Diana-Diane-Donna-Elizabeth-Gail-Ginny-Guest-Heather-Heidi-Jackie-Jan-Jane-Janet-
Janice-Jean-Jennifer-Jill-Joan-Joanne-Jodi-Judy-Julie-Karen-Kate-Kathy-Kay-Kelly-Kim-Kris-
Laura-Laurie-Leslie-Linda-Lisa-Liz-Lori-Lucy-Luv-Lynn-Margaret-Margie-Maria-Marie-
Marilyn-Martha-Mary-Mary Ann-Melissa-Michelle-Mom-Ms-Nancy-Natalie-Nicole-Pat-
Patricia-Patty-Paula-Peggy-Rebecca-Renee-Rita-Robin-Ruth-Sally-Sandra-Sandy-Sarah-
Sharon-Sheila-Shelly-Sherry-Shirley-Stephanie-Sue-Susan-Teresa-Terry-Tracy-Vickie-
Virginia-Welcome-Wendy 72.50
4C,20S,FS National Set #1 [1956], Alluring-Beauty Prize Winner-Jo Ann-Rosalie 40.00
4C,20S,FS Switzerland Set #1[   ], Marocaine Super 20.00
5C,20S,FS Ohio Vargas Girls Set #1 [1953], numbered 331-1, 331-2, 331-3, 331-4, 331-5, Vargas
signature on each, GMC p. 24 .... 25.00
8C,20S,BS Vivid Video 900 Girlie Set [1991], all (BK/WE), GMC p. 62 .... 12.00
100B MODES Girlies from Bath Model Agency w/name of girl(s) and their photographer on each.
All real photos - Complete Set 75.00
30B Glamour Girls [1988], numbered, Wiltshire Match Co., England 10.00
12C,20S,BS Turkish Set #1 [1956], very limited distribution in Instinye near Istanbul, 12/56
through 1/57. Twelve photos known, extremely rare, GMC p. 50 .... 200.00
5C,20S, BS Long Beach MCC, 19th AMCAL, Fresno, CA, 1974, AASCO Set 5.00
5C,20S, BS Terry Says, Stock Girlies, 4(I), 1(F) 5.00

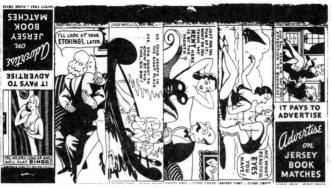

Jersey Matchcover Girlie Set #1, 1940. This complete set of six is unusual in that it advertises the matchbook company. Since the company name is on two matchcovers, it appears as if it was meant to be displayed as a set, and collecting numbers two through five wouldn't give you the name of the advertiser.

Girlies (Playboy)

4C,30S Playboy Clubs 1. Atlantic City, MN (U), 2. Atlantic City, SR, 3. Golden Steer, 4. Chat Noir.. 2.00

11C,20S,BS Playboy 25th Anniversary set, partial.. 8.00

7C,30S,MS Playboy (BK), 4 are personalized 4.50

2C,20S,BS Playboy 1. Playboy of Boston, BK, rabbit (F), 2. The Executive Hotel, Buffalo, (SR/BK/RD), rabbit (B) 1.75

4B Playboy Set #1 [   ], reclining nude on each, GMC p. 60B 30.00

19C,20S,BS Set, 1961, HMH Pub (I), cities on footer 10.25

19C,20S,BS Set (c) 1961 HMH Publishing Co (B) 15.75

19C,20S,BS Set, SR border (c) 1978 Playboy Clubs, Rabbit w/(RD) trim 30.00

25C,20S,BS Set (c) 1980, Playboy Club Int'l.. 28.00

21C,20S,BS Set #1 [   ], 1961 HMH Pub. Co. (I), Atlanta-Baltimore-Boston-Chicago-Cincinnati-Denver(2)-Detroit-Great Gorge-Jamaica-Kansas City-Lake Geneva-London-Los Angeles-Miami-Montreal-New Orleans-New York-Phoenix-San Francisco-St. Louis 17.50

17C,20S,BS Set, 20th Anniversary, (SR) set, cities on footer 1980 .... 18.75

20C,20S,BS Set #2 [   ], Playboy & Rabbit Head (I) Atlanta-Baltimore-Boston-Chicago-Cincinnati-Denver-Detroit-Gorge-Jamaica-Kansas City-Lake Geneva-London-Los Angeles-Miami-Montreal-New Orleans-New York-Phoenix-San Francisco-St. Louis 17.50

22C,20S,BS Set #3 [   ], 1961 Playboy (I), Strike (B)... at bottom (F) Atlanta-Baltimore-Boston-Chicago-Cincinnati-Denver-Detroit-Great Gorge-Jamaica-Kansas City-Lake Geneva-London-Los Angeles-Manchester-Miami-Montreal-New Orleans-New York-Phoenix-Portsmouth-San Francisco-St. Louis......................... 9.00

23C,20S,BS Set #3A [   ], 1961 Playboy (I), Close cover.. (F) bottom, Atlanta-Baltimore-Boston-Chicago-Cincinnati-Denver-Detroit-Great Gorge-Jamaica-Kansas City-Lake Geneva-London-Los Angeles-Manchester-Miami-Montreal-New Orleans-New York-Phoenix-Portsmouth(2)-San Francisco-St. Louis 9.50

15C,20S,BS Set #4 [   ], (BN) 1978 ... just above inside (S) bunny head on (B), (SR) color Chicago-Cincinnati-Dallas-Great Gorge-Lake Geneva-London-Los Angeles-Manchester-Miami-New York-Osaka-Phoenix- Portsmouth-St. Louis-Tokyo 10.50

19C,20S,BS Set #5 [   ], 25th anniversary logo (F), Chicago-Cincinnati-Costa Rica-Dallas-Great Gorge-Hawaii-Lake Geneva-London-Los Angeles-Manchester-Manila-Miami-Nassau-New York-Osaka-Phoenix-Portsmouth-St. Louis-Tokyo 12.00

17C,20S,BS Set #6 [   ], 20th anniversary (B), Chicago-Cincinnati-Dallas-Great Gorge-Lake Geneva-London-Los Angeles-Manchester-Manila-Miami-Nassau-New York-Osaka-Phoenix-Portsmouth-St. Louis.. 8.50

19C,20S,BS Set #7 [   ], 1978.. higher on (I), otherwise same as Set #4, (GY) striker Chicago-Cincinnati-Costa Rica-Dallas-Great Gorge-Lake Geneva-London-Los Angeles-Manchester-Manila-Miami-Nassau-New York-Osaka-Phoenix-Portsmouth-St. Louis-Tokyo   10.00

26C,20S,BS Set #8 [   ], 1980.. on (I), otherwise same as Set #7, Atlantic City-Buffalo-Chicago-Cincinnati-Columbus-Costa Rica-Dallas-Great Gorge-Lansing-Lake Geneva-London-Los Angeles-Manchester-Manila-Miami-Nagoya-Nassau-New York-Osaka-Phoenix-Portsmouth-San Diego-Sapporo-St. Louis- St. Petersburg-Tokyo 9.00

2B The Playboy Club, Made in Italy, Continental Match Co., Inc. LIC, NY 2.00

1B Diamond Pocket Box (SR/BK) Playboy Rabbit (F/B), no other markings 3.50

1B Playboy by Diamond Match Co., rabbit (F/B), (SR/BK) flattened 5.00

2C,30S,BS Playboy Hotel (RD) & Chat Noir, both Atlantic City, NJ 8.00

2C,30S,BS 1)Playboy Chat Noir, Atlantic City, NJ 2) Playboy Cabaret, Atlantic City, NJ   4.00
2C,30S,BS Playboy Club Golden Steer & Playboy Hotel, both Atlantic City, NJ 7.75
1FB,30S,BS Hugh M. Hefner's personal Playboy mc (BK/WE), rabbit (B) 10.25
1C,30S,BS Playboy, Kimberly Hefner (WE) 5.75
9C,20S,BS Playboy Club Set (partial), marked Marque Deposee (I) 6.75
1C,30S,BS Playboy Club, rabbit (F), nude (B), (BK/SR), no other markings 10.25
1B The Playboy Club (F), rabbit (B), for Continental Match Co., Inc., L.I.C., N.Y., made in Italy,
    appears to be early 7.25
1C,20S,FS Playboy Club, Portland, OR, (bk/we), rabbit (F) 5.75
1C,20S,FS Playboy Club, Portland, OR, bent ear bunny (F) 7.00
1C,30S,BS Salon Playboy, St. Jerome, France, bk/we by Eddy Match 5.25
1C,40S,FS Playboy VIP, Made in Italy, wooden sticks 6.50
2C,40S,BS Playboy VIP, personalized 2.50
3C,40S,BS Playboy VIP, all different 4.00
5C,20S,MS Playboy Clubs, assorted 10.00

Girlies (Numbered Singles)

Numbered singles (l to r) #429, #545, #473

1C,20S,BS No. 5, Melody Burlesk, (B/W) photo (F) 12.00
1C,20S,FS No. 26, Chesty Morgan, photo (F), Autograph (B) 14.00
1C,20S,BS,FL No. 28, Venus Theatre, drawing 5.00
1C,30S,FS No. 33, The Phone Booth, color photos (F/B) 5.00
1C,30S,FL No. 36, The Classic Cat, color photo 5.00
1C,30S,BS No. 40, Sodom and Gomorrah, color photo (B) 10.00
1C,30S,BS No. 41, Mitchell Bros. Theatres, color photo (F) 5.00
1C,30S,BS No. 63, Pussycat Theatres, drawing (F/B) 4.00
1C,40S,BS No. 77, Club Med 4.00
1C,30S,BS,FL No. 82, Club Super Sexe, Montreal, caped nude w/address (S) 5.00
1C,20S,BS No. 102, Mustang Ranch, drawing (F/B) 4.25
1C,20S,BS No. 103, Chicken Ranch Brothen, nude (F/B) 5.50
1C,20S,BS No. 104, Mable's Whorehouse, color photo (F/B) 12.00
1C,20S,FS No. 112, Pierros Café B.Y.O., photo of old fashioned nude (F), easelfront stand-up
    .... 7.00
1C,20S,BS No. 115, Wayne Eadie & Bob Borton, (B/W) photo (B) 2.25
1C,20S,BS,FL No. 120, Bocaccio Massage Studio 5.00
1C,20S,FS No. 123, Off Broadway 4.00

1C,30S,FS,FL No. 127, Starvin Marvin's Topless Go-Go, Wyandotte, MI, 48192, nude (important parts covered) 3.50

1C,30S,BS No. 129, MGM Grand Hotel Reno, Donn Arden's Hello Hollywood Hello!, nude dancer (B) 2.50

1C,20S,FL,BS No. 142, Club Med, color photo 2.75

1C,30S,BS No. 143, Filmores Exotic Dancers, drawing (B) 6.00

1C,20S,FS No. 149, gold 56 street, (B/W) photo (B) 4.00

1C,30S,FS,FL No. 151, Playgirl Club (I), photo of stage, GMC #151 .... 4.00

1C,20S,FS,FL No. 168, Tic-Toc Lounge-Bar, (B/W) photo of blonde, vertical 10.00

1C,20S,BS No. 173, Wayne Eadie & Bob Borton RMS '83 .... 2.00

1C,30S,BS No. 179, Mississaoga Tavern, Exotic Dancers (B), Mississaoga, Ontario 3.00

1C,20S,BS No. 189, Zanzibar on the Strip, nudes (F) 5.50

1C,20S,FS No. 198, Roaring 20's, photo (S), reclining nude (B), San Francisco 2.00

1C,30S,BS No. 200, Marilyn Monroe, drawing (F) 17.00

1C,30S,FS No. 204, Circus Circus, Las Vegas, NV, drawing (B) 6.00

1C,20S,FS Girlie Single No. 237, Minsky's Rialto Burlesque 10.25

1C,20S,BS Girlie Single No. 239, P.T.'s Showclub, Denver, CO 2.00

1C,20S,BS Single Girlie #240, 976-WETT Hot Talk, photo (F/B) 4.00

1C,30S,BS No. 252, Bar Sexe68, (B/W) photo (B) 4.00

1C,20S,BS No. 287, Cheetah III, girl w/cheetah (F/B), (BK/SR), GMC #287 .... 4.00

1C,20S,BS No. 289, 976-KISS, dial-a-porn, photo (F/B) 3.25

1C,30S,BS No. 330, Landing Strip 7.00

1C,20S,BS No. 352, Mary Kay Place 6.00

1C,30S,BS No. 362, The Grinder 5.00

1C,20S,BS No. 372, Runway 66, Adult Entertainment Niteclub, Mississauga, Ontario, drawing of showgirl (B) 3.00

1C,20S,BS No. 373, Club El Greco 4.00

1C,20S,BS No. 375, Golden Orange MC, drawing (F) 4.00

1C,20S,BS No. 376, Brass Rail Tavern, Toronto 4.00

1C,20S,BS Single Girlie #387, 976-6100 Hot Talk, photo (F/B) 9.50

1C,G,FS,FL No. 405, (B/W) photo, by Ray Schulz 1989 .... 7.00

1C,20S,BS No. 408, Hot Talk 970-GIRL, Call Me girl (F/B) 3.00

1C,20S,BS Single Girlie #410, Bermuda Tavern, Toronto, photo of dancer (F) 4.25

1C,20S,BS No. 412, Kitty's Guest Ranch, drawing (B) 3.00

1C,20S,BS Single Girlie #414, Fantasia Major Mack Hotel, nude (F) 3.00

1C,20S,FS No. 418, Beverly Hills Tropics, feelie 3.00

1C,30S,FS No. 429, The Tropics, big breasted girl (F), feelie 5.00

1C,20S,BS No. 433, Kit Kat Ranch, drawing (F/B) 3.00

1C,30S,BS No. 441, Condon Jewelry, photo of blonde (F) 3.00

1C,JWL,BS No. 447, El Torito's Rosa Corona 3.00

1C,20S,FS No. 452, Houlihan's 10.00

1C,20S,FL Single Girlie #460, Oasis, feelie nude blonde w/arms spread 12.50

1C,20S,FS No. 461, The Tropics, feelie 6.00

1C,20S,FS No. 462, The Tropic Hollywood, 'feelie' (F) 5.00

1C,30S,FS,FL No. 472, Silver Frolics, 400 N Wabash Ave, Chicago, nude sitting on globe 6.00

1C,30S,FS,FL No. 473, Bellevue Casino, Montreal, dark haired nude dancer w/Bellevue Casino 6.00

1C,30S,FS No. 474, Rube Kolker's All Girl Revue, Blue Room, arms-up nude (F/B), feelie 8.00

1C,30S,FL No. 476, Silver Palm, Chicago, blonde reclining nude 8.75

1C,20S,BS No. 486, Red Garter Casino, Wendover, NV, dancer (F) 4.25

1C,20S,BS No. 488, 970-8278 Call Me 2.00

1C,20S,BS No. 489, Hot Talk 970-7588 .... 2.00

1C,20S,BS No. 489, 970-7588, Hot Talk, photo (F/B) 9.00

1C,30S,FL,BS No. 508, 34th AMCAL 1989, (B/W) photo 3.00

1C,30S,BS No. 509, 49th RMS Convention, Phillu-Quebec MC 2.50

1C,20S,BS No. 537, Hawaiian Village 3.00
1C,30S,BS No. 551, Stardust, Las Vegas 4.25
1C,30S,BS No. 552, Stardust, Las Vegas 1.25
1B No. 568, The Flirt 6.00
1FB,G,BS,FL No. 827, Steve Kovacs & Larry Ziegler Girlie, 1990 RMS Convention tribute,
    topless (BK/WE) photo, nice 3.00
1C,40S,FS No. 1137, Navajo Truck Lines 6.00

Girlies (Miscellaneous Singles)
7C,20S,FS Melody Burlesk, photo (F) 39.00
1C,G,FS,FL Girlie, Ray Schultz 1988 convention mc 3.50
1C,40S,FS,RF Starlite Room, metallic finish w/nude (F), Chi Chi 4.00
14C,20S,BS singles from Melody Burlesk, photo (F), some nude 65.00
4C,20S,BS Superior Playgirl Halftones [1983], single issues 4.00
5C,20S,FS Scotty Says, Stock Girlies, 2(B), 1(I) 4.00
1B photo Lenticular (F), Los Oficios, shows blonde eating banana and standing near wall 10.25
1B photo Lenticular (F), Los Oficios, shows naked long-haired brunette lifting her shirt 10.25
1B photo Lenticular (F), Los Oficios, shows naked brunette lifting her bra, w/Tel 69 ..... 17.50

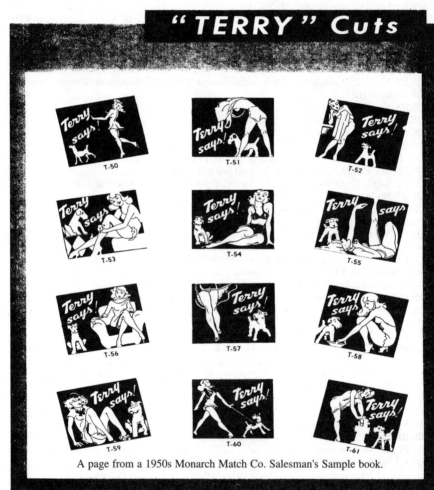

A page from a 1950s Monarch Match Co. Salesman's Sample book.

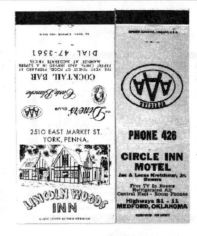

Hotels/Motels—This is one of the most widely collected categories with tens of thousands of singles, sets and series. Best Western alone boasts over 12,000 known matchcovers. The most popular hotel/motel collected is the Holiday Inn, with over 23,000 matchcovers recorded. This category can also include resorts, courts, guest houses, lodges, cabins, lodging inns, dude ranches, cottages and bed 'n breakfasts. Next to restaurants, this is the most popular category in the hobby. Beside hotel and motel singles, a popular sub-classification of this category is chain hotels and chain motels, of which Holiday Inn is considered one. Matchcovers printed by a hotel over a 50 years period isn't considered a set, but a times series.

(above) Several popular hotel matchcovers. (middle) Stock cuts for inside printing for hotel & motel matchcovers. (bottom) Back stock cuts for hotel & motel matchcovers, with a stock leader from a salesman's sample book (ca. 1950).

Cellophane Wrapping was popular for presentation matches. Popular sizes included six, eight and 12 books per sleeve. Any size matchbook could be cellophane wrapped.

Hotels & Motels

Canadian Pacific

24C,30S,BS C.P.H. Set #1 [1989], foil lettering, English set 4.00
24C,30S,BS C.P.H. Set #2 [1989], foil lettering, French set 10.00
24C,30S,BS C.P.H. Set #3 [1990], foil lettering, English set 4.50
24C,30S,BS C.P.H. Set #4 [1990], gold lettering, English set 5.50
24C,30S,BS C.P.H. Set #5 [1990   ] 1.50
24C,30S,BS C.P.H. Set #6 [   ] 1.50
24C,30S,BS C.P.H. Set #7 [   ] 1.50
24C,30S,BS C.P.H. Set #8 [   ] 4.00
24C,30S,BS C.P.H. Set #9 [   ] 4.00
24FB,30S,BS C.P.H. Set #10 [   ] 6.00

Delta Hotels

4C,30S,BS Set #1 [   ], Delta Hotels Man playing piano-Pears-Tennis player-Woman at pool edge
.... 1.00
4C,30S,BS Set #2 [   ], Delta Hotels, Expo 86 Man playing piano-Pears-Tennis player-Woman-
at pool edge 1.00
5C,30S,BS Set #3 [   ], Delta Hotels & Resorts 1.00
5C,30S,BS Set #4 [   ], Delta Hotels & Resorts 1.00
5C,30S,BS Set #5 [   ], Delta Hotels & Resorts 1.00
5C,30S,BS Set #6 [   ], Delta Hotels & Resorts 1.00
5C,30S,BS Set #7 [   ], Delta Hotels & Resorts, Saskatoon added (I) 1.00
5C,30S,BS Set #8 [1990], Delta Hotels & Resorts, Trois Rivieres added (I) 1.50

Four Seasons

30C,20S,BS Set #1 [1982], different color photo (F) of each 16.00
30C,20S,BS English Set #1 [1980], 1st line (I) shows Chicago (Ritz-Carlton) 4.00
30C,20S,BS English Set #2 [1981], 1st line (I) shows Four Seasons Hotels, 2nd line is New York
(The Pierre) 2.00
30C,20S,BS English Set #2A [1981], 1st line (I) shows Four Season Hotel, 2nd line is New York
(The Pierre) 4.75
30C,20S,BS French Set #2A [1981], 1st line (I) shows Four Season Hotel, 2nd line is New York
(The Pierre) 2.00

40C,20S,BS English Set #3 [1982], 2nd line (I) shows Montreal - Ottawa - Belleville 2.50
40C,20S,BS French Set #3 [1982], 2nd line (I) shows Montreal - Ottawa - Belleville 5.00
40C,20S,BS English Set #4 [1984] 5.00
40C,20S,BS English Set #5 [1984], 2nd line (I) shows Montreal - Ottawa 5.00
40C,20S,BS French Set #5 [1984], 2nd line (I) shows Montreal - Ottawa 5.00
40C,20S,BS English Set #6 [1985], 2nd line (I) shows New York (The Pierre) 5.00
40C,20S,BS English Set #7 [1986], 2nd line (I) shows Edmonton - Montreal 5.00
40C,20S,BS French Set #7 [1986], 2nd line (I) shows Edmonton - Montreal 5.00
40C,20S,BS Four Seasons English Set #8 [1987], 2nd line (I) shows Edmonton - Montreal - Ottawa - Toronto 5.00
40C,20S,BS English Set #9 [1987], 2nd line (I) Edmonton - Minaki - Montreal - Ottawa 5.00
40C,20S,BS English Set #10 [1987], 2nd line (I) Edmonton - Minaki (Ontario northland ..), Maui not shown 5.00
40C,20S,BS French Set #10 [1987], 2nd line (I) Edmonton - Minaki (Ontario northland ..), Maui not shown 5.00
40C,20S,BS English Set #11 [1988], 2nd line (I) Edmonton - Minaki (Ontario northland ..), Maui added 5.00
40C,20S,BS French Set #11 [1988], 2nd line (I) Edmonton - Minaki (Ontario northland ..), Maui added 5.00
40C,20S,BS English Set #12 [1988], first location is Minaki (Ontario northland resort), Chicago (1989) is on the right 5.00
40C,20S,BS French Set #12 [1988], first location is Minaki (Ontario northland resort), Chicago (1989) is on the right 5.00
40C,20S,BS English Set #13 [1989], first location is Minaki (Ontario northland resort), Chicago (1989) is on the left 5.00
40C,20S,BS French Set #13 [1989], first location is Minaki (Ontario northland resort), Chicago (1989) is on the left 5.00
40C,20S,BS English Set #14 [1989], Japan location is Tokyo Chinzan-So (1991) 2.00
40C,20S,BS English Set #15 [1989], Singapore date is 1991 .... 5.00
40C,20S,BS English Set #16 [1990], Singapore date is 1992 .... 3.00
40C,20S,BS French Set #16 [1990], Singapore date is 1992 .... 3.00
40C,20S,BS English Set #17 [1990], Singapore date is 1993 .... 4.00
40C,20S,BS French Set #17 [1990], Singapore date is 1993 .... 3.00
8B Set #18 [1990] 5.00

Holiday Inn

40C,20S Servico H/I 7.00
1C,30S,BS H/I #2, Alexandria, VA (B), The Hall of Presidents w/seal (F) 5.00
50B H/I (American Aces) [1952-present] 13.00
30B H/I Diamond Pocketboxes 7.00
12C,30S,BS H/I, Brians 3.00
25C,20S,FS H/I, Canadian 6.75
6C,30S,BS H/I, Canada, Ottawa 6.00
8C,30S, H/I N/S of Caribbean Island Resorts 3.75
20C,20S,FS H/I, some Christmas 15.00
4C,20S,FS H/I, Daytona Beach, four color set 4.50
1FB,24S,FS H/I Holidex, generic European Wooden Stick book, with instruction in German & English 3.00
1C,30S,FS H/I International Asia/Pacific (GN) 1.25
20C,MZ,MS H/I, foreign 6.00
35C,20S,MS H/I, foreign 11.00
11C,20S,BS Great Britain Set #1 [   ], (WE) map Birmingham-Bristol-Dover-Heathrow-Leicester-Liverpool-Marble Arch-Newcastle-Plymouth-Slough/Windsor-Swiss Cottage 5.00

8C,20S,BS Great Britain Set #2 [   ], (GN) map, 1700 hotels, Bryant & May, Aberdeen Airport-Bristol-Marble Arch-Newcastle-Plymouth-Portsmouth-Slough/Windsor-Swiss Cottage 5.00

9C,20S,BS Great Britain Set #3 [   ], (GN) map, 1750 hotels, Opening Spring 1983 below tel. Japan Matches Aberdeen Airport-Bristol-Glasgow-London/Marble Arch-London/Swiss Cottage-Newcastle-Plymouth-Portsmouth-Slough/Windsor ....:...... 5.00

7C,20S,BS Great Britain Set #4 [   ], (GN) map, 1750 hotels, Opening Spring 1983 omitted-Japan Matches-Aberdeen Airport-Bristol-Glasgow-London/Swiss Cottage-Newcastle-Plymouth-Slough/Windsor 5.00

10C,20S,BS Great Britain Set #5 [   ], (GN) map, 1750 hotels, Opening 1986 below/telephone, Bryant & May Aberdeen Airport-Bristol-Cardiff/Caerdydd-Glasgow-London/Marble Arch-London/Swiss Cottage-Newcastle-Plymouth-Portsmouth-Slough/Windsor 5.00

1C,JUP,FS Lebanon, Beirut 3.00

4C,20S,FS H/I 4-color set, Daytona Int. Speedway, Daytona Beach (West), FL 6.00

4C,20S,FS H/I 4-color set, Orlando, Florida 5.00

4C,20S,FS H/I 4-color set, Valdosta Georgia 5.00

1C,30S,BS H/I, Paris France 2.00

45C,20S,FS H/I (BK), assorted 4.50

50C,20S,FS H/I, N/S, assorted 4.25

4C,20S H/I, Cape Girardeau, MO, four color set 3.50

1FB,30S,BS H/I Golden Gateway, San Francisco, world map (B) 2.00

1C,30S,BS H/I, Grand Cayman 13.00

1FB,24S H/I International, reservation information (I) in German & English, wooden sticks (DBN/LBN/GD) 4.00

1FB,24S H/I Taberna Romana Restaurant and others, tax seal Minerva unbroken, wooden sticks 5.00

18C,JWL H/I, N/S, assorted 10.00

12C,JLT H/I, N/S, assorted 8.00

1C,20S,BS 107th Kentucky Derby 4.00

1FB,30S,BS H/I, Monterey, California, oceanfront scene (F), (DBE/LBE) 2.00

1FB,30S,BS H/I, Monterey, California, The Crows Nest Restaurant (F), (TN/BN) 2.00

30C,30S,MS H/I, N/S, assorted 20.00

40C,20S,MS H/I, N/S, assorted 15.00

4C,20S H/I, Orlando, FL, four color set 5.00

1FB,24S H/I, Hotel Oris, Licencja,30-150 Krakow, striker (I), unusual 18.00

1FB,20S,FS H/I and Penthouse Restaurant, Myrtle Beach, SC, H/I shield logo (B), (DGN/LGN) 3.00

1FB,30S,FS H/I The Pinnacle, Chicago, Ill, drawing (B) (RD/GD) 3.00

1C,30S H/I, Holiday Plaza, N/S, Merrillville, IN 2.00

1FB,30S,BS H/I Pyramid, San Francisco, drawing (F) 3.00

20C,20S H/I, all w/Cities (RD) (stock) 7.00

4B H/I, Rick's Bar 11.00

1C,30S H/I, N/S, Teddy's, Denver, CO 2.00

4C,20S,FS H/I, Valdosta, GA, four color set 4.00

30C,20S,BS H/I (WE), assorted 5.00

20C,20S,FS H/I, w/Cities (YW), assorted (stock) 4.00

2C,20S 1-N/S-H/I, YW, Kansas City, 2-HI, Eindhoven, The Netherlands (KB) 2.00

20B H/I 1.00

35C,10S,FS H/I, N/S 10.00

20B H/I [1952-present] 2.50

50C,20S,MS H/I, All w/Cities (BK) (stock) 7.00

50C,30S,BS H/I, N/S, assorted 15.00

25C,30S,BS H/I, N/S, assorted 4.00

50C,20S,BS H/I, N/S, assorted 8.00

50C,20S,BS H/I (stock) 7.00

50C,20S,BS H/I, N/S, assorted 15.00

25C,20S,FS H/I, four color, assorted 10.25
10C,20S,FS H/I, (GN), assorted 15.00
70C,20S,FS H/I, all numbered 13.75
95C,20S,FS H/I, many out-of-business (stock) 20.00
25C,20S,FS H/I, assorted (stock) 5.00
20C,20S,FS H/I, w/some Christmas, All w/ Cities (WE) (stock) 7.00
22C,20S,MS H/I, w/some Christmas, All w/ Cities (GN) (stock) 6.00
50C,20S,MS H/I from various series (stock) 6.75
25C,MZ,MS H/I [1952-present] 3.00
100C,MZ,MS H/I, assorted locations 8.00
100C,MZ,MS H/I, assorted locations 10.00
110C,30S,MS N/S H/I 23.50
100C,MZ,MS H/I, assorted locations 7.00
25C,30S,UNI/FOI N/S H/I, Uniglo & foilites 6.00

Hilton Hotel Chain

3C,20S,BS Nile Hilton, Cairo, Egypt; Berlin Hilton; Las Brisas Hilton, Acapulco, Mexico (foreign)
(stock) 5.00
3C,20S,BS Caribe Hilton, San Juan, PR; Hotel Carrera, Santiago, Chile; El Panama Hilton, Panama
(foreign) (stock) 5.00
2C,30S,FS N/S, Mainz Hilton, International 4.50
3C,20S,BS Virgin Isle Hilton, St. Thomas; Habana Hilton, Havana, Cuba; Continental Hilton,
Mexico City (foreign) (stock) 6.00
3C,20S,BS The Athens Hilton, Athens, Greece; Tel Aviv Hilton, Tel Aviv, Israel; Istanbul Hilton,
Istanbul, Turkey (foreign) (stock) 5.00
1C,30S,FS Hilton International Hotel in Egypt 2.00
2C,24S Bangkok Hiltons, N/S 7.00
2C,20S,BS (U) El Panama Hilton and Queen Elizabeth Hilton 2.25
30C,30S,BS Non-Stock Issues 3.00
30C,MS,BS N/S Hiltons including Set #4 Canadian Hiltons 8.00
1C,24S Budapest Hilton, N/S 5.00
9C,20S,BS Canadian Hilton Set #1 [1989], light print, Eddy Match Co. Pembroke Ont. Edmonton-
Montreal-Montreal (Bonaventure)-Montreal Airport-Quebec-Saint John-Toronto-Toronto
Airport-Windsor 2.00
9C,20S,BS Canadian Hilton Set #2 [1989], dark print, Quebec in smaller print Edmonton-
Montreal-Montreal (Bonaventure)-Montreal Aeroport-Quebec-Saint John-Toronto-Toronto
Airport-Windsor 2.00
10C,20S,BS Canadian Hilton Set #3 [1989], Halifax added Edmonton-Halifax-Montreal-Montreal
(Bonaventure)-Montreal Aeroport-Quebec-Saint John-Toronto-Toronto Airport-Windsor
.... 4.00
10C,20S,BS Canadian Hilton Set #4 [1990], new Hilton logo, locations (B) above logo, Eddy
Match Co- Ltd. Pembroke Edmonton-Halifax-Montreal-Montreal (Bonaventure)-Montreal
Aeroport-Quebec-Saint John-Toronto-Toronto Airport-Windsor 2.75
9C,20S,BS Canadian Hilton Set #5 [1990], U.S. locations, has printer's mark (+) (I), 7.5mm width
striker, Made in Canada added to manumark Boston-Chicago-Minneapolis-Newark-New
York Vista-New York World Trade Center-Ojai Valley-Pittsburgh-Washington 1.75
9C,20S,BS Canadian Hilton Set #6 [1990], U.S. locations, no printer's mark (I), Boston picture
is reversed, Made in Canada added to manumark Boston-Chicago-Minneapolis-Newark-
New York Vista-New York World Trade Center-Ojai Valley-Pittsburgh-Washington 1.75
11C,20S,BS Canadian Hilton Set #7 [1991], Ottawa added, locations (B) above logo, Eddy Match
Pembroke Ont. 3.00
100C,20S,FS International themes, no U.S., assorted 25.00
100C,20S/30S,FS Non-Stock Issues 5.00

4C,20S,BS Hilton Hotels from Hong Kong, B.C.C.; Hartford, CT; Denver, CO and Dorado, PR, (stock) 3.25
1B Kuwait Hilton 3.00
7C,20S,MS London Hiltons, N/S, assorted 20.00
4C,20S,BS Hilton Hotels from Madrid, Spain; St. Thomas, VI; Los Angeles, CA and Rabat, Morocco, (stock) 3.25
1C,24S Manila Hilton, N/S 7.00
4C,20S,BS Hilton Hotels from Maui, HI; New Orleans, LA; Republic of Panama and Rome, Italy, (stock) 3.25
4C,20S,BS Hilton Hotels from Mayaguez, PR; Kansas City, MO; San Francisco, CA and London, EN, (stock) 5.00
1C,30S,FS Memphis Hilton [   ], 3-D matchcover 2.00
38C,20S,BS Set #1, [   ], 4 New York, no Pittsburgh 2.00
39C,20S,BS Set #2, [   ], 4 New York, has Pittsburgh 2.00
40C,20S,BS Set #3, [   ], 3 New York, has San Antonio 2.00
38C,20S,BS Set #4, [   ], 3 New York, no San Antonio 4.00
40C,20S,BS Set #5, [1961], 3 New York, has Sydney 2.00
44C,20S,BS Set #6, [1961], Assoc. Australian Hotels 4.00
53C,20S,BS Set #7, [   ], has no Tokyo, Diamond Match 3.00
53C,20S,BS Set #8, [   ], has Tokyo 3.00
53C,20S,BS Set #9, [   ], Tunis added 2.00
57C,20S,BS Set #10, [1963], dated 9-63 (I) 5.00
60C,20S,BS Set #11, [1964], dated 5-64 (I) 5.00
57C,20S,BS Set #12, [1965], dated 1-65 (I) 5.00
64C,20S,BS Set #13, [1965], dated 5-65 (I) 5.00
64C,20S,BS Set #14, [1965], dated 10-65 (I) 5.00
67C,20S,BS Set #15, [1966], dated 1-66 (I) 5.00
72C,20S,BS Set #16, [1966], 10/7 (I) 7.00
72C,20S,BS Set #17A, [1967], 4-28-67 (I), (WE) 4.25
72C,20S,BS Set #17B, [1967], 4-28-67 (I), (BE) 4.25
72C,20S,BS Set #18, [1967], 12-15-67 (I) 4.00
40C,20S,BS Set #19, [1968], 6-6-68 (I) 2.00
41C,20S,BS Set #20, [1969], 12-3-69 (I) 3.00
43C,20S,BS Set #21A, [   ], small square boxes 3.00
43C,20S,BS Set #21B, [   ], large square boxes 3.00
125C,20S,BS Set #22, [1971], Rent A Buick 4.00
82C,20S,BS Set #23, [1972], no date, For Reservations 4.00
74C,20S,BS Set #24, [1972], 10-72 (I), For Reservations. 5.00
54C,20S,BS Set #25, [1973], 1-73 (I), For Reservations. 2.00
78C,20S,BS Set #26, [1973], 3-73 (I), For Reservations. 3.00
59C,20S,BS Set #27, [1973], 10-73 (I), For Reservations. 4.00
4C,20S,BS Montreal, CN; Mexico City, MX; San Diego, CA and Rotterdam, Holland (stock) 3.25
25C,20S,MS Non-Stock Issues 4.00
3C,24S,FS Paris Hiltons, N/S, assorted 4.00
1C,24S Rotterdam Hilton, N/S, assorted 15.00
4C,20S,BS San Juan, PR; Santiago De Chile; New York, NY and Jamaica, W.I. (stock) .. 3.25
1FB,20S,FS Tehran Hilton Made in Iran 8.00
4C,20S,BS Tel Aviv, Israel; Cincinnati, Oh; Guadalajara, Mexico and Istanbul, Turkey (stock)
.... 4.00
4C,20S,BS Tokyo, Japan; Tarrytown, N.Y.; Vancouver, B.C. and Tunis, Tunisia (stock) .. 3.25
15C,30S,BS Hiltons, N/S, assorted 2.25
10C,20S,FS Hiltons, N/S, assorted 5.00
15C,MZ,MS Hiltons N/S, assorted 7.00

Hyatt Hotel Chain

30B Assorted 6.00
13C,30S,BS N/S, assorted 8.00
28C,20S/30S,MS Assorted 3.00
40C,30S,MS Assorted 3.00
25C,30S,MS N/S, assorted 7.50
100C,30S,MS Assorted 32.00
15C,30S,MS Assorted, different cities 3.00
25C,MZ,MS Assorted 5.00
1C Odd size, Hong Kong 2.00

Sheraton Hotel Chain

4B,AA Four Stages, Sheraton-Universal Hotel, Universal City, CA 4.00
15B N/S, assorted 8.00
30B,AA, assorted 7.00
50B assorted 6.00
50C,30S,BS N/S, assorted 12.00
50C,20S/40S,FS N/S, assorted 2.00
50C,30S,FS N/S, assorted 12.00
395C,MZ,MS, N/S, assorted, album 45.00
80C,MZ,MS N/S, assorted 5.00

Hotels/Motels   (Miscellaneous)

12C,20S,FS AAA motels, motor lodges, association (some FL), assorted 2.50
50C,MZ,MS Atlantic City Casinos, assorted 2.00
10C,20S,FS Hotel Bellevue [1937], numbered 12.00
20B Best Westerns and Hiltons 2.00
50C,20S,BS Best Westerns, N/S 12.00
50C,30S,FS Best Westerns, N/S 14.00
50C,30S,MS Best Western, N/S, assorted 10.00
325C,20S,FS California Hotels/Motels, different cities 22.00
10C,20S,FS California Hotels & Restaurants, assorted 3.00
20C,30S,FS California Lodgings 2.50
100C,MZ,MS Chain N/S Hotels & Motels, different cities 5.00
50C,30S,MS Chain Hotels/Motels, different cities 3.00
9C,20S,FS Chicago Hotels, assorted 15.00
1FB,20S,FS World Famous Cocoanut Grove (restaurant) (F), The Ambassador, LA (B) 5.00
1C,20S,FS,FL Colburn Hotel, Denver, Colo., Crown Match Co. manumark 3.00
1C,20S,FS Hotel Cominos and Grill, Salinas, California, Crown Match Co. manumark 2.00
50C,20S,FS Congress Inns, different cities 2.50
56C,30S,FS Del Webb Hotels 6.00
1FB,40S,FS DeWitt Operated Hotels [ca. 1938], archives sticker (I), Universal Match Corp. 3.00
1C,20S,FS,FL Fred Harvey, Hotel El Tovar, Grand Canyon 1.50
1C,20S,FS,FL Fred Harvey, Hotel La Fonda, Sante Fe, NM 1.50
4C,40S,RF Set of Fred Harvey Restaurants & Hotels 5.00
4C,30S,FS Fred Harvey Restaurants & Hotels, Cowboy hat (F), Bronc Rider (B) 1.50
10C,MZ,MS Foreign, 8 are hotels 6.25
15C,MZ,MS Foreign hotels, assorted 2.25
15C,MZ,MS Hawaii Restaurants/Hotels (includes Don Ho) 10.00
30C,20S,FS Howard Johnson Motels 9.00
5C,20S,FS Howard Johnson Set #1 [   ] 1.00

5C,20S,FS Howard Johnson Set #2 [1963], restaurants (F) 1.00
1C,30S,BS Riyadh Inter-Continental 2.00
20C,MZ,MS Inter-Continental Hotels 10.00
15C,MZ,MS Foreign Inter-Continental Hotels 12.00
6C,20S,BS Knights Inn, stock designs 3.00
15C,20S,FS Older Maine Hotels 7.00
100C,20S,FS Master Hosts, different cities 2.00
380C,20S,FS Illinois-Indiana-Iowa Hotels/Motels, different cities 20.00
25C,20S,FS Older Missouri Hotels, assorted 10.00
15C,20S,FS Older Montana Hotels, assorted 6.00
50C,20S,FS Motels, different cities 5.00
1C,20S,FS National Hotel Week [1942], stock design 1.00
15C,20S,MS Old New York State Hotels, assorted 10.50
15C,20S,MS New York Hotels, assorted 15.00
8C,MZ,MS Outrigger Hotel, assorted designs 4.00
2C,20S,MS Outrigger Canoe Club, Waikiki Beach, Hawaii 2.00
14C,30S,FS Overland Hotel, Gunfighters Black Bart-Billy the Kid-O.M. Clanton-J. Courtright-
    Wyatt Earp-Pat Garrett-Wes Hardin-Bill Hickok-Doc Holiday-Jesse James-B. Masterson-
    J. Murrietta-John Ringo-Luke Short, Type 1, [   ], (GY) building, 5 signs on t 25.00
14C,30S,FS Overland Hotel, Gunfighters Black Bart-Billy the Kid-O.M. Clanton-J. Courtright-
    Wyatt Earp-Pat Garrett-Wes Hardin-Bill Hickok-Doc Holiday-Jesse James-B. Masterson-
    J. Murrietta-John Ringo-Luke Short, Type 2, [   ], (BE) building, 3 signs on t 15.00
1FB,40S Panther Room, College Inn, Hotel Sherman, Chicago, Panther (F), nice 3.25
100C,20S,FS Quality Court, different cities 6.00
25C,20S,FS Quality Court, different cities Blue stock design 3.00
30C,20S,FS Quality Courts Motels, Inc., assorted colors and designs 4.00
235C,20S,FS Quality Court Motels, different cities, album 8.00
40C,20S,FS Quality Courts Motels, Inc. (BE) 4.00
39C,20S,MS Quality Court Motels, different cities 4.00
390C,MZ,MS Quality Court Motels, different cities 15.00
1C,30S,FS PSA Hotel, Queen Mary, Long Beach, CA 5.00
25C,30S,MS Ramada Hotel, different cities 4.00
25C,20S,FS Ramada Inns, different cities 2.50
125C,MZ,MS Ramada Inns, stock & non-stock 6.00
1C,20S,FS Rual's Worm Ranch, Casper Wyoming 1.50
13C,20S Superior Courts, assorted 2.50
60C,20S,FS Superior Courts, different cities 4.50
10C,20S,FS Town House Los Angeles Set [ca. 1928], numbered 60.00
1C,20S,BS 1867-1967 Canada Centennial, Town House Motor Hotel (RD) 2.00
105C,20S,FS Travelodges, assorted cities 11.00
30C,20S,MS Travel Lodges, assorted 3.00
1FB,20S,FS The Waldorf Astoria, New York City (DBE/WE) 1.25
300C,20S,MS Motels, different cities 14.00
100C,20S,BS Hotels & Motels, assorted 8.00
20C,30S,FS California lodgings, assorted 4.25
600C,20S,FS Hotels/Motels, different cities, album 62.00
60C,30S,MS Hotels, Matchoramas, assorted themes 12.00
160C,20S/30S,MS Hotels/Motels, different cities 11.00
20C,MS Resorts and Vacation Places, assorted 8.00
6C,20S,FS Hotel Set [1949], (stock), design issue 5.00

Hillbilly Sets

Hillbilly Sets—A stock design category of sets with Martin Garrity's Hillbilly Humor. These matchcover sets were originally produced by the Chicago Match Co. in the late 1940s and 1950s, and by other companies later in the decade. Their humor and comic adaptations are funny in an ethnic sense only.

4C,20S,FS Canadian Set #1 [1970], Pappy's on them..-Thank goodness..-Were you..-You should.. .... 4.00

4C,20S,FS Canadian Set #2 [1974], Can't Budge..-I Feel Like..-OK! Fish Ainit..-She Cooks.. 4.00

4C,20S,FS Canadian Set #3 [   ], Premier Match Co., Have You Been..- + 3 others? 3.00

4C,20S,BS Canadian Set #4 [   ], Have You Been..- + 3 others? 3.00

2C,20S,FS Chicago Set #1 [1948], And Then She Said'-Wal—I'll Tell Ya 1.00

6C,20S,FS Chicago Set #2 [1950], Gran'pappy ain't..-I shore..-Lem Hawkins finally..-Maw, com'n git..-See Pa, thats..-Them buckshot. 3.00

6C,20S,FS Diamond Set #1 [1957], Hillbilly Hollow, Beware of Dog-Carrying TV set-Checking the still-Go to sleep Luke!..-Painting Fence-Wallpaper sure looks.. .... 2.00

4C,20S,FS Lion Set #1 [1962], Looks like a Bumper Crop..-No Wonder the Durn Thing..-Shut Her off Zeb..-You Young'uns Bin At, My, Vitym's.. .... 2.00

4C,20S,FS Maryland Set #1 [1957], A Deal is a Deal-Can't Budge Granpaw..-I Know, Let's..-If You'd Stop Whittling..-Nothing like Spending.. .... 2.00

4C,20S,FS Maryland Set #2 [1968], But You Said..-Have You Been..-Pappy's on Them..-Thank Goodness, They..-You Should See.. .... 2.00

4C,20S,FS Maryland Set #3 [   ], Can't Budge..-I Feel Like..-OK! Fish Ain't..-She Cooks.. 2.00

4C,20S,FS Match Corp. Set #1 [1954], Hilarious Hillbilly Ifin That's A Gurl..-She's a Coy?..-Too Bad Ye -Well Stacked H'Aint It? Hain't..-Wal, Thar She Be.. .... 2.00

4C,20S,FS Match Corp. Set #2 [1956], Hilarious Hillbilly Feller's a Farm Agent..-For Heavens Sake..-Gosh, Juney..-Looks like a Nervous..-Ye Don't Get Washin'. 2.00

4C,20S,FS Match Corp. Set #3 [1958], But Doc It's Clem..-Gawsh! Wotcha Use..I-Looks like a..-Wal, He's Clean But Bruised-Wrap 'Er Up, Sonny! 2.00

4C,20S,FS Match Corp. Set #4 [1962], Looks like a Bumper Crop..-No Wonder the Durn Thing..-Shut Her off Zeb..-You Young'uns Bin At My Vitym's.. .... 2.00

6C,20S,FS Republic Set #1, Gran'pappy ain't..-I shore..-Lem Hawkins finally..-Maw, com'n git..-See Pa, thats..-Them buckshot.., Type 1, [   ] 2.00

6C,20S,BS Republic Set #1, Gran'pappy ain't..-I shore..-Lem Hawkins finally..-Maw, com'n git..-See Pa, thats..-Them buckshot.., Type 2, [   ] 2.00

4C,20S,FS Superior Set #1 [1948], Blabbermouth!-Come On..Drop!-Maw's Gettin' Fancy-Spry.. Ain't She!-What's It For? 6.00

4C,20S,FS Superior Set #2 [1949], Come to Pappy!-Find Paw!-Hawgtied!-Purty Eyes, Too!-Swapped the Mule! 1.25

5C,20S,FS Superior Set #3 [1950], it and I quit Chawin'!-Can't figure it out!-Duded Up..Ain He!-No Likker..Pull the Trigger!-Not Unless You Shave 3.00

4C,20S,FS Superior Set #4 [1951], Martin Garrity Can't read Sheriff!-Careful Zeke, It's Full!-Goin' my way!-Kinda Sloppy Kissin'!-Quit Pickin' on me! 4.75

4C,20S,FS Superior Set #5 [1952], And Who's Fishin'!-Bath Again this Year?-How'll I get them off?-Hurr Paw, I can't Wait!-Kissin' Booth, Kisses 25cts 5.25

4C,20S,FS Superior Set #6 [l953], Corn Squeezins!-Durned Right ... he says YES!-Headin' fer the Hills!-Pretty Sunset ... Ain't it?-Time Out, Fellers! 5.75

4C,20S,FS Superior Set #7 [1954], Better Than Granny's!-Breakin' Her in Right-I'll Make Lem Fit-Private Property, Sonny!-Swing yore partner! 3.50

4C,20S,FS Superior Set #8 [1955], Sup Characters, A Rattling Surprise!-Guard Duty, Mountain Style-Hogging The Picture!-Lem, At Your Age?-Stop Wigglin' Hector! 3.00

4C,20S,FS Superior Set #9 [1956], Ah Kin Wait!-Better Explain T'Paw..-Make Sure This Time..-Won't Be Long Now!-Yep ... Pickled Again! 5.25

4C,20S,FS Superior Set #10 [1957], Don't Want None!-Fetch Me A Clothespin, Ma!-Hold 'Er In The Rut Granpa!-Kissin' Cousin!-Might Not Be Hongry! 5.50

4C,20S,FS Superior Set #11 [1958], Be Right With Ya!-Hey Thar, Watch Yo' Aim!-Hurry Maw, We..-Thanks Fer Th' Showah..-Zeke's Tryin' T' Impress.. .... 4.75

4C,20S,FS Superior Set #12 [1959], Awful Powerful Stuff..-Dang Woman Drivers!-Fellas, Git Up..-Git In Fo' Yo' Bath..-Hey, Ma, Git Th' Preacher.. .... 2.00

4C,20S,FS Superior Set #13 [1960], Howdy, Sheriff!-It Ain't Loaded!-Wash Your Own Durn Back!-Whut's Brakes?-Whut's Your Name, Maw? 3.25

4C,20S,FS Superior Set #14 [1962], Hey! Yore Ringin' Thuh Revenomer!-Paw's Dustier Than..-Whar Yuh Got..-Yuh Been Samplin'..-Zeke, See If You All. 6.00

4C,20S,FS Superior Set #15 [1965], same as Set #3 And I quit Chawin'!-Can't figure it out!-Duded Up..Ain't He!-No Likker..Pull the Trigger!-Not Unless You Shave! 1.25

4C,20S,FS Superior Set #16 [1970], same as Set #8 & Set #14 A Rattling Surprise!-Hogging The Picture!-Lem, At Your Age?-Yuh Been Samplin'..-Zeke, See If You All.. .... 1.25

Hunt's Recipe Sets

Hunt's Recipe Sets—This category involves relative large recipe sets with common fronts. A number of supermarket sets evolved during the 1950s. Known mostly as the Hunt's Sets, others are referred to as Hunt's for the Best, Mamma Mia!, and the Peaches Set. Note: Although these are supermarket sets, they have uniquely large numbers and are therefore difficult to collect.

50C,20S,FS Hunts Set [1948], Bacon 'n Beans-Baked Macaroni-Barbecued Chicken-Barbecue Sauce-Beef Mexicana-Chili Con Carne-Dutch Meat Loaf-Fish Fillets-Frankfurter Casserole-Halibut Steak-Hamburger Quickies-Hungarian Goulash-Hunt's Noodle Casserole-Liver 'n Onions-Oven Beef Stew-Rarebit Hunt Style-Rice Casserole-Savory Sausages-Shrimp Creole-Spaghetti Meat Sauce-Spaghetti & Meat Balls-Spaghetti Tuna Sauce-Spareribs-Stuffed Cabbage-Stuffed Peppers-Tomato French Dressing-Tomato Poached Eggs-Veal Cutlets-Vegetable Creole-Vegetables Hollywood 5.00

68C,20S,FS Hunts Set, All at Once Spaghetti Dinner-Baked Fish in Herb Sauce-Baked Ham 'n
Beans-Baked Spareribs 'Aloha'-Beef Porcupines-Beef Stew, Man Style-Burger Pizza-
Cheese and Macaroni Bake-Chicken Marengo-Chicken Pie-Chicken Skillet Barbecue-
Confetti Chicken-Country Steak and Chili Gravy-Cream of Tomato Soup-Delicious Pot
Roast-Dutch Meat Loaf-Easy Oven Stew-Easy Spaghetti Bake-Fancy Frank Fry-Green
Pepper Skillet Burgers-Hamburger and Potato Puffs-Hamburger Skillet Stew-Hearty Lunch
Soup-Hot Dog Loaf-Hungarian Pot Roast-Huntburgers-Lamb Stew-Liver 'n Onions-Maca-
roni Ham Casserole-Meat Loaf Barbecue Style-Minute Steak Stew-Mother's Meat Loaf-
New 30 Minute Spaghetti Sauce-Oven Baked Veal Cutlets-Peppy Stuffed Peppers-Perfect
Meat Loaf-Quick Fix Barbecue Sauce-Quick Homemade Chili-Saucepot Meat Balls-Saucy
Short Ribs-Scottish Meat Pie-7 Layer Casserole-Shrimp Creole-Skillet Barbecued Pork
Chops-Skillet Chicken-Skillet Macaroni and Beef-Skillet Spaghetti Dinner-Skillet Spanish
Rice-Skillet Twin Loaves-Southern Baked Pork Chops-Spaghetti and Meat Balls-Spaghetti
Meat Sauce-Spaghetti with Mushroom Sauce-Spanish Rice Pronto-Spanish Steak-Steak
and Potato Supper-Stuffed Cabbage Rolls-Sweet Sour Pork-Swiss Steak-10 Minute Pizza-
Tomato Soup-Tuna Potato Casserole-Vegetable Soup-Western Chuck Supreme-coupon:
Easy One Dish..(GN)-coupon: Easy One Dish..(YW)-coupon: 21 New Ways..(BN)-coupon
21 New Ways..(YW) (see below)
68C,20S,FS Hunts Set, Type 1 [1963], (S) and footer have (BK) print 4.00
68C,20S,FS Hunts Set, Type 2 [   ], (S) and footer have (GN) print 4.00
40C,20S,FS Hunts Set [1968],   Baked Beans-Batter Fried Chicken-BBQ Meatballs-Braised
Short Rib Casserole-Brownies-Burger Pizza-Chicken Cacciatore-Chili-Confetti Chicken-
Deviled Meat Loaf-Fruit Salad Dressing-Fruit Swirl Coffee Cake-Hearty Hero-Hotdog
Surprise-Huntburgers-Jiffy Frank & Rice Skillet-Little Loaves-Macaroni and Cheese-Oven
Barbecued Chicken-Oven Stew Italiano-Parmesan Fish-Pizza-Pizzaburger Loaf-Quick Dip
Sandwich-Ranch Style Hamburger-Savory French Dressing-Savory Meat Loaf-Shrimp
Salad-Skillet Beef Stew-Sloppy Joes-Spaghetti and Meatballs-Spaghetti Sauce with Meat-
Spaghetti Stew-Spanish Chicken and Rice-Stuffed Frank Fry-Stuffed Green Peppers-1000
Isle Dressing-Toasted Party Mix-Veal Scaloppine-Western Round Steak (see below)
40C,20S,FS Hunts Set [1968], Type 1 [1968], (GY) paper (I) 2.50
40C,20S,FS Hunts Set [1968], Type 2 [   ], (WE) paper (I) 2.50
46C,20S,FS Hunt for the Best, Bacon 'n Beans-Baked Hash-Barbecue Sauce-Barbecued
Chicken-Beef Mexicans-Beef Stew-Chili Con Carne-Fish Cakes-Fish Fillets-Frankfurt-
ers-French Dressing-Goulash-Halibut-Ham Slice-Hamburger Pie-Hamburgers-Lamb Stew-
Lima Casserole-Liver 'n Onions-Macaroni-Macaroni Salad-Meat Loaf-Meat Shortcake-
Noodle Casserole-Poached Eggs-Pork Chops-Pot Roast-Rarebit-Rice Casserole-Sau-
sages-Shepherd's Pie-Shrimp Creole-Spaghetti Meat Balls-Spaghetti Meat Sauce-Spareribs-Stuffed Cabbage-Stuffed Peppers-Swiss Steak-Tomato Burgers-Tomato Omelet-
Tuna Spaghetti-Veal Cutlets-Vegetable Medley-Vegetables-Vegetables Creole + Hunt for
the Best (50 years) (see below)
46C,20S,FS Hunt for the best, Type 1 Universal Match Corp., footer has (WE) background 2.00
46C,20S,FS Hunt for the best, Type 2 Universal Match Corp., footer has (YW) background 2.00
46C,20S,FS Hunt for the best, Type 3 Diamond Match Co. 2.00
46C,20S,FS Hunt for the best, Type 4 Ohio Match Co. 2.00
46C,20S,FS Hunt for the best, Type 5 Lion Match Co 2.00
6C,20S,FS Hunts Set [1958], Mamma Mia! Italian Macaroni and Cheese-Shrimp Risotto-
Spaghetti Meat Sauce-Spaghetti Tuna Sauce-Veal Parmesan-Veal Scaloppine-coupon:
Cook Italian 2.50
66C,20S,FS Hunts Set All at Once Spaghetti-All 'round Barbecue Sauce-Bacon 'n Beans-Baked
Kabobs-Baked Pork Chops-Baked Spareribs Aloha-Beef Crust Pie-Beef Mexicans-Beef
Porcupines-Beef Stew Man Style-Beef Stroganoff-Bunburgers-Burger Pizza-Captain Tom's
Fish Bake-Chicken in the Pink-Chicken Skillet BarBQ-Chili Con Carne-Country Chicken
Casserole-Creole Lamb Chops-Dutch Meat Loaf-Easy Oven Stew-Easy Spaghetti Bake-
Fancy Frank Fry-Fish Fillets-5 Minute Tomato Aspic-Friday Night Steaks-Hamburger
Quickies-Ham Cuplets-Hash 'n Hunts-Hunt Burgers-Hunt's Cassoulet-Lamb Stew-Meat

Loaf BarBQ Style-Mother's Meat Loaf-Oven Barbecue-Perfect Meat Loaf-Potato Burgers-Red Beans and Franks-Sauce Pot Meat Balls-Saucy Short Ribs-Sausage Supper Dish-Savory Goulash-7 Layer Casserole-Shepherd's Pie-Shrimp Creole-Skillet Chicken-Skillet Pork Chops 'n Rice-Skillet Spanish Rice-Spaghetti & Meat Balls-Spaghetti Meat Sauce-Spaghetti Mushroom Sauce-Spanish Omelet-Spanish Rice Pronto-Spanish Steak-Steak and Potato Supper-Swiss Steak-Tamale Joe-10 Minute Pizza-Tomato Luncheon Quickie-Tossed Spaghetti-Veal Cutlets-Veal Goulash-Western Lima Bake-Western Round Ups-coupon: Easy One Dish..-coupon: 21 New.. (see below)

66C,20S,FS Hunts Set [1958], Mamma Mia! Type 1 [1960], Wesson Oil suggested in recipes 3.00

66C,20S,FS Hunts Set [1958], Mamma Mia! Type 2 [   ], Wesson Oil specified in recipes 3.00

6C,20S,FS Heavenly Hunt's Peaches Set, peach with wings Codfish Cakes-French Dressing-Hamburger Quickies-Oven Beef Stew-Rice Casserole-Spanish Rice, Type 1 [   ], Diamond 2.00

6C,20S,FS Heavenly Hunt's Peaches Set, peach with wings Codfish Cakes-French Dressing-Hamburger Quickies-Oven Beef Stew-Rice Casserole-Spanish Rice, Type 2 Ohio, (BK) striker 2.00

6C,20S,FS Heavenly Hunt's Peaches Set, peach with wings Codfish Cakes-French Dressing-Hamburger Quickies-Oven Beef Stew-Rice Casserole-Spanish Rice, Type 3 Ohio, (BN) striker 2.00

17C,20S,FS Heavenly Hunt's Peaches Set, 3 houses (B) Baked Fish-Baked Hash-Chuck Steak-Croquettes-Fish Loaf-Ham Cuplets-Ham Slice-Hamburgers-Lamb Chops-Lamb Stew-Meat Loaf-Pork Chops-Pot Roast-Sausages-Spaghetti-Spareribs-Swiss Steak (see below)

17C,20S,FS Heavenly Hunt's Peaches Set, 3 houses (B) Type 1, Ohio, (GN) curved ground (B) 2.00

17C,20S,FS Heavenly Hunt's Peaches Set, 3 houses (B) Type 2, Diamond, (GN) curved ground (B) 2.00

17C,20S,FS Heavenly Hunt's Peaches Set, 3 houses (B) Type 3, Diamond, (BK) curved ground (B) 2.00

22C,20S,FS Heavenly Peaches Set for dessert.. Acorn Squash-Bacon 'n Beans-Beans-Bean Casserole-Beef Bundles-Beef Mexicana-Chicken-Chili Con Carne-Deviled Eggs-Fish Fillets-Frankfurters-Goulash-Halibut Steak-Lamb Kabobs-Macaroni-Noodles-Peppers-Rarebit-Seafood Sauce-Shepherd's Pie-Tomato Omelet-Veal Cutlets (see below)

22C,20S,FS Heavenly Peaches Set for dessert.. Type 1 Diamond 2.00

22C,20S,FS Heavenly Peaches Set for dessert.. Type 2 Ohio 2.00

10C,20S,FS Hunt's Heavenly Peaches Set Anemone-Azalea-Camellia-Cosmos-Crinum-Daffo-dil-Easter Lily-Iris-Orchid-Rose, Type 2 [   ], 2 line manumark (I), Made in USA added 2.00

10C,20S,FS Hunt's Heavenly Peaches Set Anemone-Azalea-Camellia-Cosmos-Crinum-Daffo-dil-Easter Lily-Iris-Orchid-Rose, Type 1 [1955], 1 line manumark (I) 2.00

60C,20S,FS Hunt's Set 15 recipes in each of 4 background colors (BK/GN/PK/YW) Black: Bacon 'n Beans-Baked Pork Chops-Barbecued Chicken-Codfish Cakes-Creole Lamb Chops-Fish Fillets-Lamb & Lima Stew-Lamb & Rice-Lamb Shanks-Lamb Stew-Mock Lamb Chops-Oven Beef Stew-Pot Roast-Shrimp Creole-Special Shrimp.. Green: Baked Beef & Beans-Barbecued Tongue-Beef Liver Creole-Beef Mexicans-Canned Hash Cups-Chuck Wagon Beans-Cornbread Pie-15 Minute Meat Loaf-Hamburger Quickies-Hamburger Rice Pie-Hunt's Tomato Rice Soup-Macaroni Loaf-Quick Tomato Aspic-Short Ribs of Beef-Stew 'n Biscuits Pink: Baked Macaroni-Barbecue Sauce-Chili con Carne-Cream of Tomato Soup-Dutch Meat Loaf-Fancy pants Hamburgers-Rice and Beef Porcupines-Rice Casserole-Spaghetti Hunt Style-Spanish Omelet-Spanish Rice-Stuffed Cabbage-Stuffed Peppers-Tomato French..-Tomato Soup Yellow: Hearty Chowder-Lima Bean Casserole-Meat Balls & Noodles-Meat Loaf-Meat Loaf Gems-Shepherd's Pie-Spaghetti & Meat Balls-Spaghetti Meat Sauce #1-Swiss Steak-Tomato Cheese Omelet-Tomato Clam Chowder-Veal & Bacon Patties-Veal & Noodles-Veal Cutlets-Veal Leaflets (see below)

60C,20S,FS Hunt's Set 15 recipes in each of 4 background colors (BK/GN/PK/YW) Type 1 [1957], (BK) striker 4.50

60C,20S,FS Hunt's Set 15 recipes in each of 4 background colors (BK/GN/PK/YW) Type 2 [   ], (BN) striker 4.50

42C,20S,FS Hunt Series No. 2 Set, Ohio Match Co., Baked Acorn Squash-Barbecued Chicken-Bean Furters-Cheese Delight-Chili Con Carne-Chuck Wagon Beans-Creole Lamb Chops-Creole Shrimp-Fish Casserole-Halibut Steak-Ham Cuplets-Hamburger Rice Pie-Hamburg-ers Creole Style-Hash Sandwich-Hunt's Noodle Casserole-Lamb Kabobs-Macaroni in Pepper Shells-Macaroni Loaf-Meat and Bean Loaf-Meat Loaf Hunt Style-Noodles and Sausages-Oven Beef Stew-Oven Croquettes-Pot Roast Steak Roll-Pot Roasted Steak-Rolled Fish Fillets-Salmon in Baked Potatoes-Sausages Hunt Style-Savory Goulash Hunt Style-Sea Food Sauce-Shrimp Creole-Spaghetti Hunt Style-Spaghetti with Vegetable Sauce-Spanish Omelet-Stuffed Cabbage-Succotash Hunt Style-Tomato Aspic-Tomato Scrambled Eggs-Tuna Casserole-Vegetables Creole-Western Casserole-Western Spa-ghetti 6.50

10C,20S,FS Hunt's kettle-simmered Tomato Sauce Set [1955], Anemone-Azalea-Camellia-Cosmos-Crinum-Daffodil-Easter Lily-Iris-Orchid-Rose 2.00

7C,20S,FS Wesson Oil Set, Banana Nut Bread-Brownies-Fried Onion Rings-Fruit Salad Dressing-Fruit Swirl Coffee Cake-Green Pepper Steak-Lettuce (see below)

7C,20S,FS Wesson Oil Set, Type 1 [1968], (GY) paper (I) 2.00

7C,20S,FS Wesson Oil Set, Type 2 [   ], (WE) paper (I) 2.00

90C,20S,FS Hunt's Recipes Supermarket, some w/applications (B) 8.50

Indians

Indians—Indians have been popular in the American imagination since anyone can remember. Their depiction on match-covers comes in every related fashion, including artifacts, symbols, designs, names, and, of course, the brave, chief, and squaw motifs. Rarely portraying Indi-ans in a derogatory way, Indian matchcov-ers usually symbolize purity, strength, courage, and beauty. Both sets and singles are popular in this category.

12C,30S,BS American Indian Set [1979], Ohio Match Co. Col Lee-Geronimo-Joseph-Kicking Bird-Manuelito-Medicine Crow-Osceola-Ouray-Quanah Parker-Red Cloud-Sitting Bull-Washakie 5.00

10FB,20S,FS Indian Set, each showing different craft, Universal Match Corp. 15.00

6C,30S,FS Arizona Bank Indian Dolls Set, Matchoramas, Ogre Kachina, Morning Kachina, The Maiden, Long hair, Antelope Kachina, and Hummingbird Kachina, colorful, history of each (I) 7.50

1C,20S,FS The Nat'l Shawmut Bank, Indian (B) 2.25

10FB,20S,FS Indians of the Southwest [1955], Basket Maker-Basket Maker Kindling..-The Bow..-Hopi Kachina..-Hopi Pottery..-Navajo Rug..-Navajo Silversmith..-Pueblo Corn..-Pueblo Girl..-Pueblo Mother.., Universal Match Corp. 21.00

15C,20S,FS American Indian Themes, very colorful 22.50

45C,20S/30S,FS Indians, assorted 4.50

175C,20S/30S,MS Indians, assorted 40.00

50C,MZ,MS Indians, assorted 5.00

Insurance

Inside cuts used by insurance companies.

17C,20S,MS Continental Insurance Comapnies (WE), different cities (stock) 2.25
6C,40S,FS Eagle Star Insurance [   ], England 8.00
7C,20S,FS GEICO Set #1 [1953], (BK) striker Capitol Building-Jefferson Memorial-Lincoln
    Memorial-Mount Vernon-Tomb of the Unknown Soldier-Washington Monument-White
    House 4.25
7C,20S,FS GEICO Set #2 [1959], (GY) striker Capitol Building-Jefferson Memorial-Lincoln
    Memorial-Mount Vernon-Tomb of the Unknown Soldier-Washington Monument-White
    House 4.00
20C,20S,BS Hartford Insurance Companies (WE), assorted 2.50
21C,MZ,MS Insurance Brokers 3.00

Split the Cost or The Co-operative Plan Idea, as it was sometimes called, encouraged advertisers (businesses or individuals) to share the cost of matches, allowing both to "enjoy the same advertising returns at a tremendous savings."

The first plan involved two or more places of business which do not conflict. On the front cover, a drug store might carry its advertising message and on the inside, a hardware store might have its ad.

The plan worked for advertisers in the late 1940s and 1950s, and as hobbyists we have benefited from this idea. The category is called conjunctives, and it represents any matchcover which advertises for two different kinds of businesses. Two popular sets that came from this idea are the Chiclet/Airlines sets and the Pepsi/Disney sets. Both are enjoyed by serious collectors and are valuable additions to any collection.

Jello Sets

36C,20S,FS Jello Set #1 [1952], 4 different fronts, each outside has 3 different recipes on the back, each of these 12 covers has 3 diff. offers inside (ring mold-star mold-6 molds), Baby: Jell-o Fluff, Jell-o Orange Cubes, Jell-o Twinkles/ring mold; Baby: Jell-o Fluff, Jell-o Orange Cubes, Jell-o Twinkles/star mold; Baby: Jell-o Fluff, Jell-o Orange Cubes, Jell-o Twinkles/ 6 molds; Man & Cookbook: Quick Set Jell-o, Quick Tomato Aspic, 30 minute Jell-o/ring mold; Man & Cookbook: Quick Set Jell-o, Quick Tomato Aspic, 30 minute Jell-o/star mold; Man & Cookbook: Quick Set Jell-o, Quick Tomato Aspic, 30 minute Jell-o/6 molds; Man & Scales: Grapefruit Salad, Jell-o Fruit Bowl, Vegetable Salad/star mold; Man & Scales: Grapefruit Salad, Jell-o Fruit Bowl, Vegetable Salad/6 molds; Woman & Book: Amber Russet, Apple Fluff, Harvest Salad/ring mold; Woman & Book: Amber Russet, Apple Fluff, Harvest Salad/star mold; Woman & Book: Amber Russet, Apple Fluff, Harvest Salad/6 molds, coupon expires 6-30-1953, (RD) printing 7.50

36C,20S,FS Jell-o Set #2 (as above), coupon expires 6-30-53, (BK) print 3.00
36C,20S,FS Jell-o Set #3 (as above), coupon expires 12-31-53 .... 3.00
36C,20S,FS Jell-o Set #4 (as above), coupon expires 12-31-54 .... 3.00
9C,20S,FS Jello Recipe Series, baby crying 1.50
9C,20S,FS Jello Recipe Series, man cooking 1.50
9C,20S,FS Jello Recipe Series, man on scale 2.00
9C,20S,FS Jello Recipe Series, woman in plaid 1.50

On the other side of the "Co-operative Plan Idea," matchbook companies had a second way to save. It was unofficially titled the Dealer and Jobber Idea. A manufacturer, distributor, or jobber would contract to order a large number of matchbooks to be received over a period of time--say one year. One stock ad would be used for the back, front, or inside, as the manufacturer wished. As his distributors, dealers, jobbers, salesmen, etc. needed matches, their names or organizations would be printed on the opposite face. These salesmen, jobbers, dealers, etc., would receive smaller units, say 2,500 matchcovers with the manufacturer's logo or design on the back and their name on the front.

Manufacturers were encouraged to control distribution of these matches or charge a nominal fee of $3.00 (remember, these were the early 1950s) for the case. In this way a manufacturer could place his ad in different markets, enabling his dealers to benefit by the powerful name or logo of the larger company.

Hobbyists enjoy this matchcover, commonly known as a stock design. Stock designs appear for every business, service, and product imaginable, including matchbook company stock (generic) designs offered to individual businesses. The difference between them is company stock designs (i.e. Schlitz Beer, Florsheim Shoes, Chevrolet, etc.) and the matchbook company stock designs (i.e. Sea Food, Dinner & Dancing, The Best Service in Town).

Jewelites

Jewelites—A general category of matchcovers whose trademark appears on the inside with the Universal Match Corp. logo. Not to be confused with the Lion Contour, Universal started production of the Jewelites in the early 1950s. Shaped like an hour glass and die-cut to standard, rather than custom designs, production of the nearly 7,000 varieties drifted toward sports themes, especially football helmets and baseballs in the 1970s and 1980s. Production terminated in 1987. This was such a popular category that a sub-category, Jewelite Schedules, formed around sports.

25C,JLT,BS Jewelites [1951-1987], Universal Match Corp., non-sports themes 3.00
50C,JLT,FS Jewelites [1951-1987], Universal Match Corp., assorted theme 7.50
800C,JLT,MS Jewelites [1951-1987], assorted themes 140.00
250C,JLT,MS Jewelites [1951-1987], Universal Match Corp., assorted theme 30.00
35C,JLT,MS Jewelites, no sports, assorted advertisers 14.00
500C,JLT,MS Jewelites [1951-1987], Universal Match Corp., assorted theme 90.00
8C,JLT,FS Telephone Company Set 11.00

Jewels

Jewels—A Universal Match Corp. trademark for an often elaborately decorated, elongated matchcover measuring 5 1/6" X 1 7/8". Production began in 1955 and ended in 1987 with over 5,000 varieties known. The logo and trademark can be found on the lower inside. Matchcover dimensions are exactly the same as the Jewelite, but the sides are straight instead of being die-cut.

120C,JWL,MS Jewels [1955-1987], Universal Match Corp., Dodge Transmission dealers 18.00
1C,JWL,FS The Princess Phone (Telephone) 10.00
100C,JWL,BS Jewels, assorted themes 23.00
100C,JWL,FS Jewels [1955-1987], Universal Match Corp., assorted themes older issues 20.00
50C,JWL,FS Jewels, assorted themes 8.50
200C,JWL,MS Jewels [1955-1987], Universal Match Corp., assorted themes 14.50

Knotholes (Lion Match Co.)

Knotholes—A general category for various sized matchcovers with a display hole in the front cover. Produced almost exclusively by Lion Match Co., knotholes often were coupled with highly decorated Features, the brightly colored sticks of which could be viewed through the knothole in the front. Die-cut holes were shaped round, square, rectangular and triangular, with an assortment of custom shapes included. Note the round and triangular knotholes (left).

1C,20S,FS Marvel Cleaners & Laundries, knothole is triangular hanger (F) 3.50
1C,20S,FS Phil Ahn's Moongate, circular knothole (F) 2.50
1C,30S,FS Admiral Motel, Mt. Clements, Michigan, duck (B), knothole is center of life preserver (BE/WE) 5.00
1C,30S,FS Benjamin's, La Cienega Restaurant, knothole is glass door, which says, Open This Door for the World's Finest Chicken 5.50
1C,30S,FS The 400 Show Bar, girlies (B), knothole is cutout of number 400 (F) 5.00
1C,30S,FS Heinrich Envelope Company, Boone, Iowa, knothole is #10 envelope (F) 3.00
1C,30S,FS Marineland Restaurant, knothole is center of life perserver, porpoise (B) 4.50
1C,30S,FS Royal Crest, knothole is crest (F), also easelback 4.00
10,30S,FS Knotholes, assorted themes 15.50
10C,30S,FS,FEA Knotholes, assorted themes 12.50

Manumarks

Manumark is a hobby term for the area of the cover which displays the manufacturer's mark. Only the most serious matchcover collectors study, research, and collect manumarks rather than the obvious advertising themes which appear on most matchcovers. Matchbook companies call this line(s) the footline, and usually use their own company name here. In the early 1930s, larger advertising specialty companies began to insist that their name be placed in the footline area, thus creating a plethora of different manumarks for hobbyists today. The Lion Match Co. Features, for example, has over 130 different manumarks which are standard for this category.

This is not to be confused with the hobby term "footer" which is the area at the bottom front (opposite end from the striker) of the matchcover. Both advertisers and matchbook companies used this area for safety warnings, product and service advertisement, and patent information.

1C,20S,FS Advance Match, Lewis Drug Store & Coal and Coke 2.50
5C,20S,FS Advance Match Co., assorted themes 4.00
4C,20S,FS Albert Pick Co./ Chicago manumark, assorted themes 12.00
1C,20S,FS Arrow Match Co., Bos Fuel & Material, Koppers Chicago Coke 4.00
7C,20S,FS Crown Match Co. Flats, 3 stock designs 2.00

10C,20S,FS Crown Match Co. manumark, assorted themes 15.00
20,20S,FS Crown Match Co., dynamic graphics, assorted themes 27.50
100C,20S,FS Crown Match Co. [1933-1942], Los Angeles CA 90.00
8C,20S,FS Crown Match Co. manumarks, All Gas Stations 8.00
10C,20S,FS Federal Match Corp. [1923-1940], Bellefonte, PA 10.00
100C,20S,FS Federal Match Corp. [1923-1940], Bellefonte, PA 75.00
1C,20S,FS Federal Match Corp., ad: Keller Printing Co, New York City 1.50
1C,20S,FS Green Hat Footer, Albert Pick manumark, dated 1926 .... 19.00
1B Green Hat Issues [1926-   ], Lion Match 26.00
10C,20S,FS Jersey Match Co., assorted themes 15.00
15C,20S,FS King Midas manumark, assorted themes 12.00
1C,20S,FS King Midas Match Co., photo (B), Elect 'Al' Eagler 1.50
1FB,FS Licensed Match, The Diamond Match Co., N.Y., ca. 1900, 6 matches remain 35.00
4C,20S,FS Lion Match Co. [1917-present], Chicago IL Christmas [1956] 1620-1776-1865-1920
    .... 1.50
1C,20S,FS Patented Sept. 27, 1892, Licensed Matches by Diamond, Holbrook's Varsity,
    Columbus Ohio 22.50
1C,20S,FS Patented Sept 27, 1892, Robert Burns Cigars, Straiton & Storm Co., New York 19.00
4C,20S,BS Cowpokes [1980], stock design, Republic Match Co. [-present], Arlington TX, Ace
    Reid 'If They Ever..'-'Nope, It Wuzn't..'-'Now From Here..'-'Say, Reckon When. . . 2.50
4C,20S,FS Sportsman Set, Republic Match Co. [-present], Arlington TX, Old Faithful-On The
    Wing-Quick Action-The Break 1.00

Mennen for Men Sets

Mennen Products Sets—A series
of sets promoting use of various skin
products issued by the Mennen Company in the 1950s. Sets were usually
put out in six matchcover increments,
most of which had a dated coupon on
the inside for sending in to receive a
sample of the product. At least six sets
are known as well as several single
matchcovers which preceded the issu-
ance of the sets.

6C,20S,FS D.D. Bean Set #1 [1952], Are You Sure..-Dims Face Shine..-If You Have..-The Proof
    Is..-Trouble Shaving In..-Wake Up Tingle. 2.00
6C,20S,FS D.D. Bean Set #2 [1953], offer ends 7-30-54, Are You Sure..-Dims Face Shine..-Is
    Shaving Slaving..-Mister, Can Your..-Quicker Than Brushless..-Wakes Up Your.. ... 2.50
6C,20S,FS Universal Set #1 [1954], Mennen for Men, offer ends July 15, 1954 Man in theater -
    5 others 2.00
6C,20S,FS Universal Set #2 [1955], Mennen for Men, offer ends July 15, 1955 Man on top of bus
    -5 others 2.75
6C,20S,FS Universal Set #3 [1957], Mennen for Men, offer ends July 15, 1957 'Face on Fire'
    Shaves -5 others 2.00
6C,20S,FS Universal Set #4 [1958], Mennen for Men, offer ends July 15, 1958 Are You Sure..-
    Dims Shine!..-He Man Aroma!..-Keeps Hair in Place..-New Mennen Afta..-Smoothest
    Shaves on.. .... 3.00

Midget & Midget-Type

Midgets—A Lion Match Co. trademark matchbook designed in 1934 to accompany the clutch style evening purse popular at the time. The midget or midget-type (as produced by other companies) was an exact size reduction of the 20 stick matchbook. Over 7,500 varieties are known including midget-type matchbooks made by Diamond Match Co., and Ohio Match Co. Only Lion Match Co. matchbooks, which produced over 60% by volume of the known varieties, can be called Midgets.

1FB,FS Lion, The New Automatique, Scharf's New York (BN/TN) 2.00
1FB,FS Lion, Barney Gallant, Manhattan (RD/WE/BK) 4.00
1FB,FS Lion, The Brass Rail, New York City (BE/RD/GD) 2.00
1FB,FS Ohio, Brass Rail, Youngstown, Ohio, (WE/RD/SR/BK) 2.00
1FB,FS Ohio, Castleholm Swedish Restaurant, New York (BE/YW/SR) 10.50
1FB,FS Lion, Leon & Eddie's, New York, w/ both (F) 2.00
1FB,FS Ohio, Mayflower Restaurant, no city, (WE/RD) 4.00
1FB,FS Diamond, Peck & Peck, New York et al 2.25
1FB,FS Lion, Tip Toe Inn, New York (RD/BK/GD) 3.00
2FB,FS Diamond, 1-The Belvedere, Baltimore, 2-Edwoud Optician, DC 5.50
1FS,FS Lion, The Girl of the Golden West 11.50
1FB,FS Lion, Leon and Eddie's, 12 E. Second St., Reno 4.00
1FB,FS Lion, The Lombard Bar, New York City (RD), ca. 1938 .... 2.25
1FB,FS Diamond, Mayfair, Washington, D.C., midget-type, Diamond Match Co. 2.00
4FB,FS Lion, Regetta Midget Set (BE/GN/RD/YW) Type 3, 8 lines of print inside and REGETTA
    in lighter (BK) print and smaller than Type 2 .... 8.00
4FB,FS Lion, Regetta Midget Set (BE/GN/RD/YW) Type 2, 8 lines of print inside and REGETTA
    in bold print and larger than Type 3 .... 8.00
4FB,FS Lion, Regetta Midget Set (BE/GN/RD/YW) Type 1, 12 lines of print inside 9.00
2FB,FS Lion, 1-Twenty-One Bermuda, 2-The Sky Room 3.75
10FB,FS Lion, Diamond & Ohio, assorted themes 22.00
10FB,FS Lion, assorted themes 15.00
25FB,FS Lion, assorted themes 18.00
25FB,FS Lion [1934-1943], assorted themes 15.00
6FB,FS Lion [1934-1943], assorted themes 5.50
10FB,FS Lion, assorted businesses 18.00
10FB,FS Lion [1934-1943], assorted themes 16.00
150FB,FS Midgets [1934-1943], Album of Lion, Diamond & Ohio 90.00

Military

Military—Popular since WWII, this category includes all services (i.e. Air Force, Army, Coast Guard, Merchant Marine, Marines and Navy) but not U.S. Naval Ships. Groups within include messes, camps, forts, ships, ports, bases, PXs, NCO and Officer's clubs, fields, encampments, and all 176 Veteran's Administration Hospitals. Although not a sub-classification, NCO and Officer's facilities are sometimes separated into different categories. All military events, functions and services are also included in this category.

Military   (Messes)

50C,MZ,MS Officer's Mess and Clubs 14.00
9C,20S,FS NCO Messes, etc., Based in Philippines 6.00
10FB,20S,FS Military Messes, all services 6.00
35C,20S,FS NCO, Messes, etc., based in Japan 16.50
1C,20S,FS US Air Force, Bedford Officers Club, Bedford, MA 2.00
1C,20S,FS Colonial Dac Open Mess, Yokohama, Japan, The Finest In Food And Entertainment
    (B) 2.00
1FB,20S,FS NCO Open Mess, Fort Detrick, MD, drawing of bar (B), hand dated 3/20/60, GD/
    BK 4.00
1FB,20S,FS Commissioned Officers' Mess Open, U.S. Naval Station, Guam, M.I., The Pump
    Room Annex (B), hand dated 4/8/62,(BE/WE) 1.00
1C,20S,FS Hickam Officers' Open Mess, Pacific Division, photo (F), LBE 4.00
1FB,20S,FS Fort Sam Houston Officers' Open Mess, U.S. Army insignia (F), hand dated 11/17/
    61,(WE/GD/RD) 1.25
1FB,20S,FS Officer's Open Mess, Kelly Air force Base, San Antonio, Texas, SAAMA logo (B),
    hand dated 3/17/63, (BE/WE) 1.00
1FB,20S,FS Non-Commissioned Officer's Club, McGuire A.F.B., (BK/WE), hand dated 11/5/59
    .... 2.00
10FB,20S,FS Officer's Messes, all services 9.00
1FB,20S,FS Officers' Mess, Camp Joseph H. Pendleton, Oceanside, Calif, bull dog (B), Marine
    Corp insignia (F), hand dated 7/19/60 (RD/YW) 1.50
1C,20S,FS Petty Officer Club, Yokosuka, Patronize Your Club (S), BE 1.25
1FB,20S,FS Presidio Officers' Open Mess, Presidio of San Francisco, guardsmen w/logo (F),
    hand dated 4/8/62, (RD/BK/YW) 1.00
1FB,20S,FS Sandia Base Officers Open Mess, Albuquerque, NM, nuclear symbol (F), Sandia
    logo (F), hand dated 4/15/63, (WE/GD) 4.50
25C,30S,MS U.S. Navy Messes 15.00

Military (U.S. Navy Ships)

US Navy Ships—A separate category divided into pre-WWII (prior to December 7 1941) and post-WWII (after August 1945) ships. Mostly singles but some sets exist in this category, with a few ships producing several dozens of matchcovers over a period of time. Not included in this category are foreign and Canadian Navy ships.

1FB,30S,BS U.S.S. Alabama, color photo (F/B) 4.00
1FB,30S,FS U.S.S. Alabama, color photo (F/B) 5.25
1C,40S,FS U.S.S. Albany 2.00
1C,30S,FS U.S.S. Amphion AR-13 .... 2.50
2C,20S,FS U.S.S. Antares, Stores Issue Ship, Diamond (BE), & U.S.S. Brazos, Diamond, (SR)
    .... 6.00
2C,20S,FS,FL U.S.S. Argonne (Flagship, Commander Base Force) and U.S.S. William Ward
    Burrows 3.00
2C,20S,FS U.S.S. Aulick and U.S.S. Altair (SR) 2.50
1FB,G,FS U.S.S. Bache DDE-470, Christmas 11.00
1FB,20S,FS U.S.S. Badger, (BE/SR) 5.25

1C,40S,FS U.S.S. Bayfield APA-33 .... 3.25
1C,20S,FS U.S.S. Beaver, Pre-War, COMBINE #B122C 3.50
1C,40S,FS U.S.S. Bennington CVA-20 .... 3.25
3C,40S,FS U.S.S. Block Island CVE-10 .... 12.00
3C,20S,FS U.S.S. Boise, U.S.S. Wichita, and U.S.S. Arctic (BK) 4.50
1C,12S,FS USS Boxer, LPH-4, Post-War, COMBINE #B35B 1.25
2C,20S,FS Robert J. Boynton, Fire Controlman Third Class, U.S. Navy (F), U.S.S. Mississippi, Huntington Park (S), Leona Pearl Barnaby, H. Pk. High School (B), from color set of 4 2.50
3C,40S,FS U.S.S. Cabildo (LSD-16), U.S.S. Kearsarge (CVA-33) and U.S.S. Leyte (CV32) 13.00
2C,20S,FS,FL U.S.S. Chicago (BE) and U.S.S. Cassin (GD) 5.25
1C,20S,FS U.S.S. Charleston (BE) 5.00
1C,20S,FS U.S.S. Charleston, Pre-War, COMBINE #C242C 3.50
1C,P36,FL U.S.S. Coral Sea CVB-43 .... 5.75
1C,20S,FS U.S.S. Dobbin, Pre-War, COMBINE #D147C 3.50
2C,20S,FS U.S.S. Eagle 27, Federal (BE) & U.S.S. Bowditch, Hydrographic Survey, Diamond (SR) 4.00
1C,40S,FS U.S.S. Endicott DMS-35 .... 4.25
1C,P36 U.S.S. FDR, CVB-42, caricature FDR (F), ship (B) 7.25
1C,40S,FS U.S.S. Franklin D. Roosevelt (CVA-42), caracture of FDB w/sailor (F) 10.00
1FB,G,FS U.S.S. Fremont APA 44, Santa Claus across sticks, Christmas tree (B) 12.00
7C,40S,FS U.S.S. Fulton AS-11 (all same) 14.00
50C,20S,FS U.S. Navy Service 20.00
1C,20S,FS U.S.S. Gregory (BE) 3.25
2C,20S,FS U.S.S. Gwin (DM33) and U.S.S. Antares (AK258) 3.00
1C,20S,FS U.S.S. Halfbeak 3.00
1C,20S,FS U.S.S. Harder, postwar US Navy ship 2.00
2C,40S,FS U.S.S. Hector (AR-7) and U.S.S. Cavalier (APA-37) 7.00
2C,20S,FS U.S.S. Hopkins/13, Lion (BK),& U.S.S. Relief (Red Cross Ship), Diamond (GN) 4.00
100C,40S,FS US Navy Shore Stations, Hospitals & Air Stations, mounted pages 29.00
12C,20S,FS Naval Aviation Jargon Set [1943], Ace-Ballooning-Fat Dumb and Happy-Flat Batting-Give It The Gun-Ground Loop-Pancake-Pulling It Off-Shooting The Circle-Three Point Landing-Wheel Landing-Wrap It Up 11.50
3C,20S,FS U.S.S. Jason (ARH-1), U.S.S. Stansbury, and U.S.S. Stringham (cartoon) (WE) 5.00
1C,20S,FS U.S.S. King (GD) 3.50
8C,20S,FS Know Your Navy #2,3,4,5,6,9,10,16 .... 4.00
1C,20S,FS U.S.S. Laramie (BE) 3.00
1C,20S,FS U.S.S. Leary (BE) 3.50
3C,40S,FS U.S.S. Leyte CV-32, Air Craft Carrier (all same) 9.00
24FB,40S,FS U.S.S. Leyte, All (all same) 21.75
1C,20S,FS U.S.S. Livermore (GD) 5.00
1FB,20S,FS U.S.S. George K. MacKenzie, DD836, striker (I) 8.25
1C,30S,FS Great Lakes Icebreaker, U.S.C.G. Cutter Mackinaw 3.00
4C,20S,FS Olan Jackson McMillian U.S.N., U.S.S. Mississippi, Bat. Div. 3 Bat. Force, Long Beach, Calif. 12.00
3C,30S,FS U.S.S. Midway, Air Craft Carrier (all same) 9.00
1C,30S,FS Midshipman's Cruise [1949] 3.00
5C,20S,FS U.S.S. Mississippi Set from the Barber Shop, 'Joe' Markovich, Head Barber 17.00
5C,20S,FS U.S.S. Mississippi, Carpenter Shop w/list (B) 4.00
5C,20S,FS U.S.S. Mississippi Set from the Cobbler Ship, H.W. Henderson, Ship's Cobbler 16.50
5C,20S,FS U.S.S. Mississippi, Crew's Galley, w/list (B) 4.00
1C,20S,FS Dog Fighters, U.S.S. Mississippi, Pearl Harbor, T.H., Flight Leaders, 6 men listed (B) 4.50
5C,20S,FS U.S.S. Mississippi, Executive Officers, 5 color set 6.50
5C,20S,FS Elvgren Girlie Set #5, [1940], Laundry, U.S.S. Mississippi, Pearl Harbor, Oahu, Ter. of Hawaii, G.B. 'Toby' Yates Mgr., L.A. Williams, Asst. Mgr. 11.50
5C,20S,FS U.S.S. Mississippi, Laundry, Honolulu, Oahu, T.H., 5 color set 16.00

5C,20S,FS Elvgren Girlie Set #5, [1940], Laundry, U.S.S. Mississippi, Honolulu, Oahu, Territory of Hawaii, Gilbert B. Yates, Manager 17.00
5C,20S,FS U.S.S. Mississippi, Olan Jackson McMillian, USN, 5 color set 7.75
5C,20S,FS U.S.S. Mississippi, Photo Shop, Long Beach, Calif., 5 color set 7.75
5C,20S,FS U.S.S. Mississippi Set from the photo shop, Willis H. Spell, Jr., Ship's Photographer 16.50
5C,20S,FS U.S.S. Mississippi, Police Force, New York City, 5 color set 6.50
5C,20S,FS U.S.S. Mississippi, VO-3 Squadron, Postmaster, NYC, 5 color set 6.50
3C,20S,FS Elvgren Girlie Set #5 assorted mc from Ship's Service & Anti Aircraft maintenance Dept, U.S.S. Mississippi, Honolulu, Oahu, Territory of Hawaii 6.50
5C,20S,FS Elvgren Girlie Set #5, 1940, 7th Div. U.S.S. Mississippi, Honolulu, Oahu, Ter. of Hawaii, 'Suicide Seventh' Ens. P.T. Krez, Div. Officer 20.00
4C,20S,FS Willis H. Spell Jr. Ship's Photographer, U.S.S. Mississippi, Honolulu, T.H., Representing Superior Match Co, color set of 4 .... 12.75
5C,20S,FS U.S.S. Mississippi Set from Patrick A. Walsh, Coxwsain, USN, Oahu, T.H. . 16.50
1C,20S,FS U.S.S. Missouri 3.00
4C,20S,FS U.S.S. Mullany, DD-528, color set 5.75
5C,20S,FS U.S.S. Mullany, DD-528, 5 color set, postwar US Navy ship 6.00
1C,20S,FS U.S.S. Nautilus, postwar US Navy ship 3.00
5C,20S,FS Petty Girlie Set #4, 1950, GMC p. 29, ad: George R. Newitt Detachment Navy & Marine Corps Club, Kingston, PA 16.50
1C,20S,FS U.S.S. Northampton, Pre-War 2.75
1C,20S,BS U.S. Navy w/Owl (B), early back striker 1.75
1C,20S,FS U.S.S. Plunkett, Pre-War US Navy 2.00
1C,20S,FS U.S.S. Potomac (BE) 3.00
1C,20S,FS U.S.S. Quincy (BE) 4.00
2C,20S,FS U.S.S. Gen. G.M. Randall (TAP-115) and U.S.S. Lofberg (DD-759) (BK) 2.50
1C,20S,FS U.S. Naval Receiving Barracks, Aiea, T.H. 3.00
1C,20S,FS U.S.S. Repose, postwar US Navy ship 2.00
1C,20S,FS United States Naval Reserve, Girlie - Miss Placed Confidence, (S) says - REMEMBER PEARL HARBOR 3.50
1C,20S,FS U.S.S. Rhind, Pre-War US Navy 2.00
2C,20S,FS,FL U.S.S. Richmond (DBE) and U.S.S. Gwin (DD433) Chief Petty Officer's Mess (SR) 2.00
1C,P36 U.S.S. F.D. Roosevelt 3.00
1C,40S,FS U.S.S. Franklin D. Roosevelt, CVA 42(S), FDR w/sailor 11.00
2C,40S,FS U.S.S. Sabalo (SS302) and U.S.S. Tarawa (CV40) 9.00
2C,20S,FS U.S.S. Sacramento and U.S.S. John W. Weeks (DD701), both (GD) 3.00
10C,20S,BS U.S. Navy 'Be Safe - Be Shipshape' Safety Set 7.00
2C,20S,FS,FL U.S.S. San Francisco (DBE) and U.S.S. Oklahoma (DBE/GD) 8.00
20C,40S,FS U.S. Navy Stations, Schools 5.00
20C,40S,FS U.S. Navy Stations, Schools 5.00
2C,20S,FS U.S.C.G./U.S.S. Sebago, Diamond, (BE), & U.S.S. Niblark Christmas mc, Federal (WE) 4.00
1C,20S,FS U.S.S. Stansbury (WE), Mine Division 19 .... 5.00
1C,20S,FS Ship's Store Ashore U.S. Naval Base, Guantanamo Bay, Cuba, ship (B), (DBE) 2.00
25C,20S,FS U.S. Naval Training Stations 17.50
15C,20S,MS U.S. Naval Stations 7.00
25C,40S,MS U.S. Naval Training Stations 16.00
1C,10S,FS U.S.S. Tabberer, postwar US Navy ship 3.00
1C,40S,FS U.S.S. Tarava CV-40 .... 4.25
1C,20S,FS U.S.S. Trenton, Pre-War US Navy 2.75
3C,40S,FS U.S.S. Vesole DDR-878 (all same) 6.00
1FB,20S,FS U.S.S. Wasp, (S) drawing of aircraft carrier (B), Bomb (F), post WWII 6.00
2C,20S,FS U.S.S. Wichita and U.S.S. Richard E. Krause (EDD-849), both (RD) 6.50

2C,20S,FS U.S.S. West Virginia and U.S.S. Argonne 8.00
2C,20S,FS U.S.S. Yarnall and U.S.S. William Ward Burrows (SR) 3.00
15C,20S,FS Postwar US Navy Ships, all starting w/letter 'A' 13.00
150C,20S,FS U.S. Navy Ships 115.00
15C,20S,FS Pre-WWII U.S. Navy Ships 21.50
585C,20S,FS Post-WWII U.S. Navy Ships 275.00
50C,20S,MS Post-WWII U.S. Navy Ships 38.00
25C,20S,FS U.S. Navy Ships, Battleships 50.00
50C,20S,FS,FL Pre & Post WWII U.S. Navy ships, assorted 50.00
20C,20S,FS U.S. Prewar Ships [prior to 1/05/42], assorted 27.00
30C,30S,FS U.S. Navy Ships 30.00
10C,40S,FS U.S. Navy Ships 19.00
30C,20S,FS U.S. Navy Ships, Federal Match Corp. 23.00
3C,P36 U.S. Navy Ships 7.50
15C,20S,FS Postwar US Navy Ships, all starting w/letter 'B' 18.00
29C,20S,FS Postwar US Navy Ships, all starting w/letter 'C' 32.00
10C,20S,FS Postwar US Navy Ships, starting w/letter 'D' 7.00
5C,20S,FS Postwar US Navy Ships, starting w/letter 'E' 4.50
1C,20S,FS U.S.S. Zellars, Post-War U.S. Navy 2.50
20C,20S,FS Postwar US Navy Ships, all starting w/letter 'F' 21.00
25C,20S,FS Postwar US Navy Ships, all starting w/letter 'G' 26.00
30C,20S,FS Postwar US Navy Ships, all starting w/letter 'H' 31.00
5C,20S,FS Postwar US Navy Ships, starting w/letter 'I' 3.50
10C,20S,FS Postwar US Navy Ships, starting w/letter 'J' 9.75
10C,20S,FS Postwar US Navy Ships, starting w/letter 'K' 11.00
20C,20S,FS Postwar US Navy Ships, all starting w/letter 'L' 21.00
21C,20S,FS Postwar US Navy Ships, all starting w/letter 'M' 24.00
5C,20S,FS Postwar US Navy Ships, starting w/letters 'Mc' 3.50
10C,20S,FS Postwar US Navy Ships, all starting w/letter 'N' 14.00
10C,20S,FS Postwar US Navy Ships, starting w/letter 'O' 5.00
15C,20S,FS Postwar US Navy Ships, all starting w/letter 'P' 15.50
20C,20S,FS Postwar US Navy Ships, all starting w/letter 'R' 24.00
25C,20S,FS Postwar US Navy Ships, all starting w/letter 'S' 26.00
20C,20S,FS Postwar US Navy Ships, all starting w/letter 'T' 32.50
2C,20S,FS Postwar US Navy Ships, starting w/letter 'U' 1.00
5C,20S,FS Postwar US Navy Ships, starting w/letter 'V' 6.50
20C,20S,FS Postwar US Navy Ships, all starting w/letter 'W' 19.00
5C,20S,FS Postwar US Navy Ships, starting w/letter 'Y' 5.00

Military (Disney/Pepsi)

Pepsi/Disney—In sets only, this group of sets has been sought after by avid military collectors since WWII. A Pepsi-Cola conjunctive, three distinct sets exist, each with different inside printing. All are 20 strike and there are 48 matchcovers in each set. The reason for picking the various organizations for each matchcover isn't known, although all the logos are credited to Walt Disney.

1FB,20S,FS Disney/Pepsi, 1st Marine Brigade (Penguin) 5.00
1C,20S,FS Disney/Pepsi, 8-line, 3rd Recon Sq (Donkey in truck) 5.50
1C,20S,FS Disney/Pepsi, 7-line, 3rd Recon. Squadron, (donkey driving toy truck) 3.75
1C,20S,FS Disney/Pepsi, 10-line, 4th Field Artillery Battalion (Donkey w/cannon) 6.25
1C,20S,FS Disney/Pepsi, 10-line, Sixth Reconnaissance Squadron, w/Dumbo & looking glass
     .... 7.75
1C,20S,FS Disney/Pepsi, 7-line, 6th Recon Sq (Flying elephant) 3.25
1C,20S,FS Disney/Pepsi, 8-line, 6th Reconnaissance Squad. (Dumbo w/Telescope) 4.50
1C,20S,FS Disney/Pepsi, 10 line (I), No. 11, Sixth Reconnaissance Squadron 5.25
1FB,20S,FS Disney/Pepsi, 7th Bombardment Sq (Scottie Dog) 5.00
1C,20S,FS Disney/Pepsi, 10-line, 22nd Pursuit Squadron w/ eagle & lightening bolts 7.75
1FB,20S,FS Disney/Pepsi, 26th Mat'l Sq, 19th Air Base (Tiger) 5.00
1FB,20S,FS Disney/Pepsi, 37th Pursuit Sq (Pelican) 8.75
1FB,20S,FS Disney/Pepsi, 40th Bombardment Gp, USAC (Elephant) 8.75
1C,20S,FS Disney/Pepsi, 10-line (GY), 42nd Bombardment Group, 75th Squadron, w/helmeted
     hawk riding bomb 5.50
1FB,20S,FS Disney/Pepsi, 45th Air Base Sq. 46th Air Base Gp (Donkey) 9.50
1C,20S,FS Disney/Pepsi, 10-line, 46th Bombardment Group (L), w/kangaroo dropping bombs
     .... 5.50
1C,20S,FS Disney/Pepsi, 7-line, 48th Pursuit Sq (Cat chasing bug) 4.25
1C,20S,FS Disney/Pepsi, 8-line, 48th Pursuit Sq (Cat chasing bug) 3.75
1C,20S,FS Disney/Pepsi, 56th Pursuit Squad. GHQ (Cock in Police Uniform) 10 Line 5.25
1C,20S,FS Disney/Pepsi, 10-line, 57th Signal Battalion, w/bee riding lightening bolt 6.50
1C,20S,FS Disney/Pepsi, WWII, Co. C, 69th Q-Master Battalion (Running Wrench) 4.00
1FB,20S,FS Disney/Pepsi, 72nd QMaster Battalion (Cat) 9.50
1C,20S,FS Disney/Pepsi, 85th School Squad. (Skeleton Dropping Bombs) 10 Line 2.00
1C,20S,FS Disney/Pepsi, 114th Field Artilery, Bat D (Bear Shooting Cannon) 10 Line ... 5.25
1C,20S,FS Disney/Pepsi, 10-line, Company F, 114th Infantry (cricket w/rifle & bayonet) 4.00
1C,20S,FS Disney/Pepsi, 121st Air Corps Observation Squad. (Bear w/Telescope) 10 Line 4.00
1C,20S,FS Disney/Pepsi, 10-line, First Marine Brigade, (penguin w/cannon) 4.00
1C,20S,FS Disney/Pepsi, 10 line (I), No. 18, Battery 8, 206th Coast Artillery 5.25
1C,20S,FS Disney/Pepsi, 7-line, 251st Coast Artillery, (Lion w/ship's logo) 2.00
1C,20S,FS Disney/Pepsi, 8-line, 251st Coast Artillery (Lion and ship) 4.00
1C,20S,FS Disney/Pepsi, WWII, 10-line, 251st Coast Artillery (Lion & ship) 2.50
1C,20S,FS Disney/Pepsi, 10-line, 331st School Squadron, (angel w/pilot's goggles) 4.00
1C,20S,FS Disney/Pepsi, 10-line, 40th Bombardment Group, (elephant w/shot put) 4.00
1FB,20S,FS Disney/Pepsi, 503rd Parachute Battalion (Cat) 8.75
1C,20S,FS Disney/Pepsi, 10-line, 56th Pursuit Squadron, (bird in police uniform w/baton) 4.00
1C,20S,FS Disney/Pepsi, 10-line, 72nd Quartermaster Battalion, (cat with wrench) 4.00
1FB,20S,FS Disney/Pepsi, 751st Tank Battalion (Elephant) 8.75
1C,20S,FS Disney/Pepsi, 10-line, 8th Air Corps Area Service Command, (owl riding bicycle) 4.00
1C,20S,FS Disney/Pepsi, 10-line, Air Base Detachment, (ant w/tools) 4.00
1FB,20S,FS Disney/Pepsi, Air Base Detachment (Hornet) 8.75
1C,20S,FS Disney/Pepsi, 10-line, Air Corps Training Detachment, (Thumper playing with
     airplane) 4.00
1C,20S,FS Disney/Pepsi, WWII, 10-line, Alternate Aviation Arm U.S.S. Carolina (Donkey on
     surfboard) 3.00
1FB,20S,FS Disney/Pepsi, USN Aviation Stn, Aviation Cadets (Chipmunk) 8.75
1C,20S,FS Disney/Pepsi, 10 line (I), No. 17, Jackson Air Base 5.25
1C,20S,FS Disney/Pepsi, 10-line, Mosquito Fleet, Am. Motor Torpedo Boat w/mosquito on bomb
     .... 10.25
1FB,20S,FS Disney/Pepsi, Patwing Spt Force Avn Repair Unit No. 1 (Pig) 5.00
1C,20S,FS Disney/Pepsi, 7-line, U.S. Naval Reserve Aviation Base, (Donald Duck w/parachute)
     .... 10.00
1C,20S,FS Disney/Pepsi, U.S. Naval Reserve Aviation Base (Donald Duck w/Parachute) 8 Line
     .... 12.50

1C,20S,FS Disney/Pepsi, 8-line, U.S.S. Blue (Pelican) 6.75
1C,20S,FS Disney/Pepsi, 10 line (I), No. 16, U.S.S. Hornet 5.25
1C,20S,FS Disney/Pepsi, 10-line, Utility Squadron No. 5, U.S. Naval Air Station, w/Donald Duck
    flying plane 10.25
1FB,20S,FS Disney/Pepsi, Woman's Ambulance & Defense Corp (Centor) 8.75
1C,20S,FS Disney/Military from YW set, 23rd Pursuit Squadron, w/flying hawk wearing helmet
    .... 3.00
1C,20S,FS Disney/Military from YW set, 40th Bombardment Group, w/elephant & shot put 4.50
1C,20S,FS Disney/Military from YW set, 58th Pursuit Squadron, w/rooster with boxing gloves
    .... 5.25
1C,20S,FS Disney/Military from YW set, 133rd Field Artillery, w/bulldog dressed as cowboy
    .... 4.50
1C,20S,FS Disney/Military from YW set, 165th Field Artillery, w/ape shooting cannon .. 3.00
1C,20S,FS Disney/Military from YW set, U.S. Naval Reserve, w/Donald Duck dragging
    parachute 3.00
1C,20S,FS Disney/Military from YW set, U.S.S. Blue, w/pelican holding bombs in beak . 4.50
1C,20S,FS Disney/Military from YW set, Utility Squadron, w/Donald Duck flying plane . 2.25
31C,20S,FS Disney/Pepsi, Designed Insignias (10 line variety only) 122.50
12C,20S,FS Disney/Pepsi, Designed Insignias, assorted mixed 7 & 8 line variety 50.00
48C,20S,FS Pepsi-Cola Walt Disney Insignia, numbered, Type 1 [1942], 10 lines of type inside
    .... 60.00
48C,20S,FS Pepsi-Cola Walt Disney Insignia, numbered, Type 2 [1943], 8 lines of type inside
    .... 165.00
48C,20S,FS Pepsi-Cola Walt Disney Insignia, numbered, Type 3 [1943], 7 lines of type inside
    .... 175.00
20C,20S,FS Maryland Match Disney Insignia Set Type 2 [1942], cover surface has no glazing
    .... 30.00
20C,20S,FS Maryland Match Disney Insignia Set Type 1 [1942], cover surface is glazed 35.00

Military (Veterans Administration Hospitals)

5C,40S,FS Veterans Administration Hospital Set #1 [1963], Universal Match Corp. (St. Louis)
    Capitol-Iwo Jima-Lincoln Memorial-Mount Rushmore-Unknown Soldier's Tomb 3.50
5C,40S,FS Veterans Administration Hospital Set #2 [1963], (LBE), Universal Match Corp.,
    Capitol-Iwo Jima-Lincoln Memorial-Mount Rushmore-The Tomb of the Unknown Soldier
    .... 3.50
5C,40S,FS Veterans Administration Hospital Set #3 [1964], (DBE), Universal Match Corp.
    Capitol-Iwo Jima-Lincoln Memorial-Mount Rushmore-Tomb of the Unknowns 2.50
5C,40S,FS Veterans Administration Hospital Set #4 [1966], Umc to left of manumark, Universal
    Match Corp. (Washington D.C.) Capitol-Iwo Jima-Jefferson Memorial-Liberty Bell-Lincoln
    Mem. 2.50
9C,40S,FS Veterans Administration Hospital Set #5 [1967], (BK) FS Maryland Match Co.,
    Alamo-The Capitol-Independence Hall-Iwo Jima Monument-Jefferson Memorial-Liberty
    Bell-Lincoln Memorial-Mount Vernon-Washington Monument 3.50
10C,40S,FS Veterans Administration Hospital Set #6 [1967], Universal Match, (no CORP) in
    manumark Capitol Building-Gateway Arch-Independence Hall-Iwo Jima..- Jefferson Memo-
    rial-Liberty Bell-Monticello-Mount Rushmore- Statue of Liberty-Statue of Lincoln ...3.50
9C,40S,FS Veterans Administration Hospital Set #7 [1970], reddish (BN) Maryland Match Co.
    Alamo-The Capitol-Independence Hall-Iwo Jima Monument-Jefferson Memorial-Liberty
    Bell-Lincoln Memorial-Mount Vernon-Washington Monument 3.50
10C,40S,BS Veterans Administration Hospital Set #8 [1971], light (BE), Universal Match Corp.,
    Capitol Building-Gateway Arch-Independence Hall-Iwo Jima..-Jefferson Memorial-Liberty
    Bell-Monticello-Mount Rushmore-Statue of Liberty-Statue of Lincoln 3.50

10C,40S,BS Veterans Administration Hospital Set #9 [1972], (DBE), Universal Match Corp., Capitol Building-Gateway Arch-Independence Hall-Iwo Jima..-Jefferson Memorial-Liberty Bell-Monticello-Mount Rushmore-Statue of Liberty-Statue of Lincoln 5.50
10C,40S,BS Veterans Administration Hospital Set #10 [1976], Close Cover..at foot of front cover, Superior Match American Revolution..-Betsy Ross-Independence Hall-Liberty Bell-1776 1976-1776 Bicentennial 1976-Signing the Declaration Spirit of '76'-Statue of Liberty-White House 3.50
10C,40S,BS Veterans Administration Hospital Set #11 [1976], For Safety.. at bottom of front cover, Superior Match The American..-The Bell's..-Betsy Ross-The First-Franklin's..-The Gettysburg..-Hiawatha's..-Let Us Have..- The Mayflower..-Writing the Declaration.. 2.50
10C,40S,BS Veterans Administration Hospital Set #12 [1980], Superior, blank (S) The American..-The Bell's..-Betsy Ross-Declaration of..-The First..-Franklin's..-The Gettysburg..-Hiawatha's..-Let Us Have..- The Mayflower 2.50
10C,40S,BS Veterans Administration Hospital Set #13 [1984], Superior Match Co., (S) has Smoking Is Considered Dangerous to Your Health The American..-The Bell's..-Betsy Ross-Declaration of..- The First..-Franklin's..-The Gettysburg..-Hiawatha's..-Let Us Have..- The Mayflower 3.50
4B Veterans Administration Hospital Box Set Diamond Pocketboxes America's First Locomotive-Communications in Space-Old Ironsides-The Wright Brothers 2.00
50C,40S,FS Veterans Administration Hospitals 15.00
6C,30S,BS Veterans Administration Set w/smoking message (S) 6.00

Military   (Miscellaneous)

1C,20S,FS Secretary of the Air Force, Dining Room 2.00
1C,40S,FS postcard (B) (no writing), U.S.N. Amphibious Training Base, Little Creek, VA, show cartoon alligator eating tank (B), (WE/BE)(BK/RD) 1.50
8C,20S,FS Armed Services Set, Lion Match Co. [1942] 5.00
1C,20S,FS Make the US Army your Career 1.75
1C,20S,FS Army Air Base, Batista Airport, San Antonio de Los Banos, Cuba 11.00
5C,20S,FS Famous Battles in American History, complete (BE) set 3.50
14C,20S,FS Famous battles [1935], 5 different, various colors, United Matchonian club offer 16.50
5C,20S,FS American Battles 1st Series [1942], Bunker Hill-Cowpens-Kings Mountain-New Orleans-Pittsburg.. .... 2.00
5C,40S,FS 2nd Series [1945], Boston Massacre-Manila Bay-San Jacinto-Santiago Harbor-Washington's March 2.00
3B Military sample box labels, Camp J.H. Pendleton, Camp Stewart, Ft. Du Pont. Made by Universal Match Corp. 3.00
1C,40S,FS postcard (B) (no writing), Carlisle Barracks, Carlisle, PA, caduceus (B) 1.00
1C,40S,FS postcard (B) (no writing), Clearfield Naval Supply Depot, Clearfield, Utah, battle ship (B), U.S.N. insignia (F) (DBE/WE) 1.00
1C,40S,FS postcard (B) (no writing), U.S. Coast guard 8th Naval Dist., pat logo (B), U.S.C.G. cutter w/lighthouse (F), (DBE/WE) 1.00
2C,30S,FS Coast Guard ships at sea, photo (B) 2.00
1C,40S,FS postcard (B) (no writing), U.S. Marine Corps Air Station, Eagle Mountain Lake, TX, U.S. Marine plane (B), insignia (F) (DBE/YW) 2.00
1C,40S,FS postcard (B) (no writing), Gowen Field, Boise, ID, airfield scene (B), Air Force insignia (F), colorful 3.00
10C,20S,FS Military service bases in Japan 12.00
20C,20S,FS Know Your Army Set [1943], numbered, Brigadier General, Colonel, Major, Captain, 1st Lieutenant, 2nd Lieutenant, Master Sergeant, 1st Sergeant, Technical Sergeant, Staff Sergeant, Technician 3rd Grade, Sergeant, Technician 4th Grade, Corporal, Technician 5th Grade, Private, 1st Class 6.00

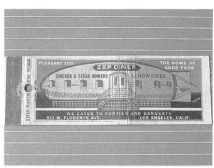

2.

1.

3.

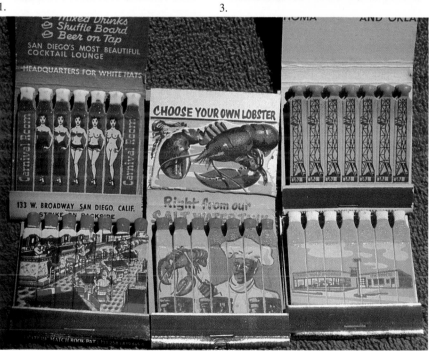

4.

5.

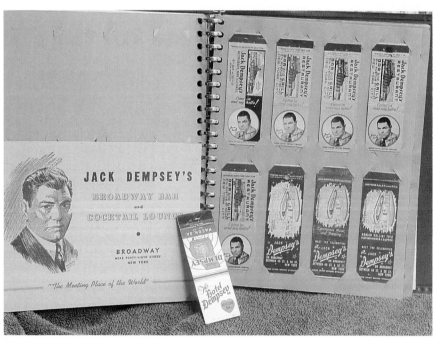

6.

7.

8.

9.

10.

11.

12.

13.

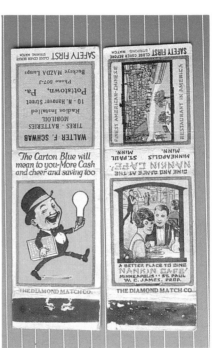

14.

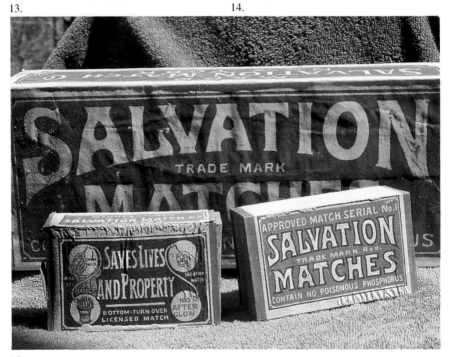

15.

16.

17.

18.

19.

20.

21.

22.   23.

24.

25.

26.

27.

28.

29.

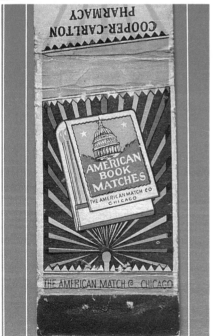

30.

31.

32.

20C,20S,FS Know Your Marines Set [1943], numbered, Lieutenant General, Major General, Brigadier General, Colonel, Lieutenant Colonel, Major, Captain, 1st Lieutenant, 2nd Lieutenant, Chief Warrant Officer, Sergeant Major, Master Technical Sergeant, 1st Sergeant, Technical Sergeant, Platoon Sergeant, Staff Sergeant, Sergeant, Corporal, Private First Class, Sergeant-Band Musician 9.00

16C,20S,FS Know Your Navy Set [1942], numbered, Admiral, Vice Admiral, Rear Admiral, Commander, Captain, Lieutenant Commander, Lieutenant, Lieutentant/JG, Chief Warrant Officer, Ensign, Warrant Officer, Chief Petty Officer, Petty Officer 1st Class, Petty Officer 2nd Class, Petty Officer 3rd Class, and one more 5.50

1C,20S,FS MacArthur Memorial 1.50

1C,100S,BS Souvenir of The MacArthur Memorial, Norfolk, VA, w/portrait at age 66, urns from Japan, The Memorial, Hat, Pipe & Glasses 5.00

1C,20S,FS U.S. Marine Corps, Okinawa, Camp Butler Clubs System (B), RD 1.00

1C,20S,FS Marine Barracks, Subic Bay, Philippines, Semper Fidelis (S), RD 2.00

1FB,20S,FS Notice: Mosquito Bites Cause Malaria, etc., ca. WWII, F&F Lozenges ad (I) 2.00

1C,30S,FS,FL Welcome to Vietnam [   ], USARV NCO/EM Open vertical FL of Vietnamese woman 7.00

1C,40S postcard (B) (no writing), U.S.N. Hospital, Newport, R.I., oval w/hospital (B), U.S.N.H. insignia (F), postcard perforation (F) 1.50

1C,40S postcard (B) (no writing), U.S. Naval Training Station, Norfolk, VA, colorful Destroyer Escort (B), U.S.N. insignia (F) 1.00

1C,20S,FS Chief Petty Officers Club, Barbers Point, Oahu, T.H. 5.50

6C,20S,FS Set of Military District of Washington, Colorful 2.50

1C,20S,FS Women's Ambulance Corp, San Francisco Unit 2.00

10C,10S,FS Military, assorted 1.50

100C,20S,FS World War II issues Military, assorted including bases, stations, & messes 25.00

30C,30S,FS Military, assorted 2.50

20C,40S,FS Military, assorted including bases, stations, & messes 8.25

5C,40S,MS Military, assorted bases, no hospitals 7.25

100C,40S,FS,RF Military, World War II issues 12.00

600C,MZ,MS Military, assorted, album 42.50

50FB,MZ,MS Military themes, assorted 25.00

1C,40S,FS postcard (B) (no writing), Purdue Naval Training School, W Lafayette, Ind (DBE/ WE), U.S.N. (S) 5.50

20C,RF,FS World War II issues, Universal Match Corp. 3.00

12C,20S,FS Navy Safety Hints Set [1943], numbered Around Ammunition-Around Machine Guns-Around Propellers-Fighting Fires-Flight Gear-Fueling-In General-Moving Planes-On Flight Deck-On Shipboard-On The Job-Starting Engines 10.00

1FB,20S,FS U.S. Medical Replacement Training Center, Camp Grant, Illinois (MN) 2.00

1C,40S postcard (B) (no writing), U.S. Navy (DBE/WE), battle ship (B), no station noted 6.00

Miscellaneous (Size & Type)

Miscellaneous—This section contains a listing of matchcover prices for groups or singles not sold in sufficient numbers to make up a listing. Many will fit into collections and are worth finding. All have been sold in a live or mail auction, or private sale.

1C,20S,FS Centurylites [1964-   ], Universal Match Corp. 5.50

19C Classiques (only 31 known) 6.00

7C,20S,FS Displays [1940-   ], assorted themes, Lion Match 12.00

40C,MS,FS Displays [1940-   ], assorted themes, Lion Match 40.00

18C,20S/30S,FS Displays [1940-   ], assorted themes, Lion Match 12.00

15C,30S,FS Displays [1940-   ], assorted themes, Lion Match 9.00

21C,20S/30S,BS Extend 'n Ad [1982-1987] 2.00

4C,30S,BS Extend 'n Ad [1982-1987], Universal Match 2.00
300C,20S,FS Flats, old issues 15.00
25C,BS Forty Strikes 2.00
50C,40S,BS Forty stick size, assorted themes 14.50
25C,FS Forty Strikes 3.25
25C,40S,FS Forty stick size, assorted themes 12.50
100C,MS Forty Strikes 10.50
50FB,30S,BS Full books, assorted themes 6.00
50FB,30S,FS Full books, assorted themes 9.00
50FB,20S,MS Full Books, assorted advertisers 7.00
250C,MZ,MS Mixed strikers, assorted themes 10.00
50C,40S,MS Mixed strikers, assorted advertisers 5.00
1FB,100S,FS The Denmead Match Book, Pat No. 1763763, Pat. June 17, 1930, advertising same,
     round wooden sticks, rare 38.75
1C,100S,BS I Made It! Summit House - Alt. 14,100 .... 2.50
1C,100S,FS Windmill Island, Holland Michigan 6.00
5C,JUP,BS Jupiter 18, [1984-1987], Universal Match Corp., assorted themes 1.25
10C,MZ,BS Jutes, assorted themes 4.00
3370L Labels, world wide, assorted themes, some duplicates 90.00
25C,20S/30S,BS Matchtones [1979-1987], Universal Match Corp., assorted themes 5.00
10C,20S,BS Matchtones [1979-1987], Universal Match Corp., assorted themes 2.50
25C,10S,FS Matchtones, assorted themes 7.00
20C,MZ,MS Matchtones, assorted themes 3.00
120C,30S,MS Matchtones, assorted themes 26.00
30C,40S,MS Matchtones, assorted themes 9.25
25C,30S,BS Pearltones, assorted themes 5.25
30C,30S,FS Pearltones, assorted themes 3.25
35C,20S,FS Pearltones, assorted themes 3.75
100C,30S,MS Pearltones, assorted themes 4.50
20C,40S,MS Pearltones, assorted themes 3.25
400C,MZ,MS Album Pearltones, assorted themes 16.00
50C,20S,MS Pearltones, assorted themes 2.00
50C,RF,FS Royal Flash [1936-present], Universal Match Corp., assorted advertisers ... 5.00
50FB,40S,FS,RF Royal Flash, assorted themes 8.00
1FB,30S,FS Safety Tab, ad: Afran Transit Co., Ship Line 4.00
4C,30S,FS Allen Bradley Set, Safe-T-Lite [1949-   ] Universal Match Corp., Keep Aisles..-Keep
     Guards..-Wear Proper..-Wear Your.. .... 3.50
1FB,20S,FS Maryland Match Co. Safety-T, ad: Chantre Soapless Oil Shampoo, very scarce 5.00
5C,20S,FS Safe-T-Lite [1949-   ] Universal Match Corp. 4.00
50C,30S,FS Satins, assorted themes 11.00
50C,20S,MS Satinkote, assorted themes 5.00
10C,30S,FS Signets, assorted themes 5.00
35C,20S,MS Signets [1963-1987], Universal Match Corp 3.00
25C,30S,BS Silktones [   ], Diamond Match Co 2.25
40C,30S,FS Silktones [   ], Diamond Match Co. 3.25
30C,20S,MS Silktones [   ], Diamond Match Co. 2.50
24C,10S/12S,BS Ten & twelve strike, assorted themes 4.00
1FB,10S,FS Universal ad: Arpeako Tenderized Ham, colorful 2.00
25C,10S,FS Ten stick size, assorted themes 9.50
1FB,10S Honey Bear Farm, Genoa City, WI, show bear watering flower (F), bear (B), (BE/WE/
     BK) 2.00
25C,10S,MS Ten stick size, assorted themes 5.00
1FB,10S Vanessi's, San Francisco, goldola in moon light (B), phone (S) (PE/RD/BK/YW/WE)
     .... 1.00
25C,12S,FS Twelve stick size, assorted themes 3.00

50C,12S,FS Twelve Strikes [1952-1989], Maryland Match, assorted themes 4.75

30C,12S,MS Twelve Strikes [1952-1989], Maryland Match, assorted themes 1.00

40C,12S,FS 12 Ups [1940-1950], Arrow Match Co 10.00

20C,24S,BS Twenty-Four Stick [1980-   ] Columbia Match Co 4.00

110C,24S,BS Twenty-Four Stick [1980-   ] Columbia Match Co. 20.00

9C,24S,FS Twenty-four stick size, assorted themes 3.00

1FB,240S,FS B&G Vending Company, Try matching us for service, The World's Largest Match Book (B) 2.00

1FB,240S,BS Greetings from Cape Breton, N.S. Canada, 'Ciad Mile Failte' 5 color photos of area 3.00

1FB,240S,FS Clark Transport Co., Illinois' Newest Most Modern Truck Stop, Phone C.H. 3843, services (F/B) 5.00

1FB,240S,FS Greetings from Franconia Notch NH, route map w/photo (F), 5 color photos (B) 2.50

1FB,240S,BS Indiana, The Hoosier State, (BK/WE) drawing of Amish Buggy, Indy 500, Notre Dame, State Capital (F), The World's Largest Match Book (B) 2.00

1FB,240S,BS Fabulous Las Vegas, color photos of 12 famous hotels & landmarks all around 2.00

1FB,240S,FS Greetings from the Massachusetts Turnpike, map w/stops (F) Howard Johnson logo, 3 color photos of turnpike (B) 4.00

1FB,240S,FS Greetings from Miami Beach Florida, color photos (F/B) 3.00

1FB,240S,BS Michigan, (BK/YW) drawing of Mackinac Island, Tahquamenon Falls, Mackinac Bridge, State Capital (F), The World's Largest Match Book (B) 2.00

1FB,240S,BS Greetings from Missouri, Land of a Million Smiles, the Show Me state, 5 color photos (F/B) of Missouri landmarks 2.50

1FB,240S,BS Niagara Falls Canada, One of the Seven Natural Wonders of the World, technicolor falls (F), other scenes (B) 3.00

1FB,240S,FS See Niagara Falls from the Skylon Observatory, Niagara Falls, Ontario, Canada, falls (F), Skylon (FL) (B) 2.00

1FB,240S,BS RMS 39th Annual Convention, August 15-18, 1979, Milwaukee, Wisconsin (RD/WE) 2.00

1FB,240S,FS Roxy Card and Gift Shop, 131 West 50th Street, New York 19, N.Y., SOL (F), Souvenir of New York City (B), Advance Match & Printing Corp, Chicago, Ill, Made in U.S.A. 7.00

1FB,240S,BS The Seagram Tower, Souvenir of Niagara Falls, Canada, (FL) Seagram Tower (B), Falls (F) 3.00

1FB,240S,FS Old Museum Village of Smith's Clove, Monroe, NY, drawing of pioneer activities (F), The World's Largest Match Book (B) 2.50

1FB,240S,BS Stream Line Tools, Inc, Conover, North Carolina, 12 inch ruler & ad (F), 6 tools pictured (B) 2.00

1FB,240S,FS National Capital Trolley Museum, Wheaton, MD, 3 Trolleys (F) w/area map, The World's Largest Match Book (B), (BK/WE) 2.50

1FB,240S,FS United States Military Academy, West Point, New York, (BK/WE) drawing of WP (F), The World's Largest Match Book (B) 2.00

1FB,200S,FS Duff Truck Lines, 200 Stick, Universal Match Corp. 3.00

1FB,200S,BS Cave of the Winds, Manitou Springs, Colo, Heart of the Pikes Peak Region, 4 sections of caves (B) 2.50

1FB,240S,BS Visit Chinatown in New York, again!, w/Chinese dragons (F), Ling Sing Temple, 7 Chinese Gods/Goddesses (B) 3.00

1FB,240S,FS The Empire State Building, the world's tallest building, day time (F), night time (B) 2.00

1FB,200S,BS For Its Panorama Of Old World Culture-Milwaukee's Holiday Folk Fair is Matchless...So light one of these! (F), Universal Match Corp., Milwaukee 3.00

1FB,200S,BS Royal Palm, Brown's Lake, Burlington, Wis., show all conveniences (F/B) (LBN/GN/WE) 2.50

1C,200S,BS Seattle World's Fair [1962], World of Tomorrow 2.50

40C,40S,BS Uniglos [1972-1987], Universal Match Corp., assorted themes 7.75

50C,20S,FS Uniglos [1972-1987], Universal Match Corp., assorted themes 8.25
50C,40S,MS Uniglos [1972-1987], Universal Match Corp., assorted themes 7.00
100C,20S/30S,MS Woodgrains, assorted themes 8.00
50C,20S,FS Woodgrains, assorted themes 9.00

These Attractive Saddle Slogans shown below and on the following pages, were created expressly for the use of our Customers. They will greatly improve the appearance of your Book Matches. Use them not only for the Saddle of the Matches, but also on the Inside Covers; that extra touch more than repays the small extra charge of $1.50 per case of 2,500 for Inside Printing.

USE SADDLE SLOGANS FOR RESULTS

Saddle Slogans added that extra bit of punch to every matchbook advertisement and few customers didn't find a satisfactory slogan to go with their ad. Hundreds of Saddle Slogans were available to every customer and were usually printed free with the order.

Miscellaneous

Miscellaneous (size)—This section contains a listing of matchcover prices (by size) for groups and singles not sold in sufficient numbers to make up a listing. Miscellaneous sizes not affiliated with other categories in the book include 10 (or half) strike, 12-Up, 15 strike, 18 strike, 22 strike, 24 strike, 28 strike, 40 strike, super 45, 48 strike, 60 strike, 80 strike, Centurylite, 100 strike, 200 strike and the souvenir (also called Jumbo King) or 240 strike matchbook.

1C,ACTION Certified Oil Company, Mobilheat Furnace Oil, colorful Mobilgas truck (I), rare 22.50
1FB,FS Action [1940-1941], Universal Match 24.00
10C,20S,FS Aladdin Mfg. Set #1,[1962], (BE/BK) Buss Stop: Danger Curves Ahead-Dear Crossing-Yield Right. Divided Highway: Danger Curves Ahead-No Passing. Tunnel Dim Lights: Dear Crossing-Yield Right of Way. Watch Out for Falling Rocks: 2.50
10C,20S,FS Set #2 [1962], (RD/BK) Bottoms Up-Down the Hatch-I am Not Loaded-I can Drink..-I Only Have..-No More for Me..(back: I Only Have..)-No More for Me..(back: Who Says I'm..)-This One's on Me(back: I Am Not..)-This One's on Me..(back: I Can Drink..)-Who Says I'm.. .... 4.50
4C,20S,FS All American Series [1953], Chicago Match Co. Abr. Lincoln-Geo. Washington-Our. Capitol-S.O.L. (stock) 1.50
8C,20S,FS The American Scene, Central Retailer, Northlake, Ill 1.25
8C,30S,FS Andersen Windowalls Set #1 [1959], Beauty Line-Casement-Flexivent-Flexivent Flexiview-Gliding- Patio-Pressure Seal-Strutwall (stock) 3.00
6C,30S,FS Andersen Windowalls Set #2 [1959], Bedroom-Chairs-Kitchen Cab.-Kitchen Sink-Living Room-Sofa (stock) 2.00
5C,30S,FS Andersen Windowalls Set # [   ], Diamond Match, Awnings-Double Hung Windows-Gliding Doors-Gliding Windows-Windows (stock) 2.00
30C,20S,FS Mexican Archaeological Treasures, numbered 5.00
1FB,20S,FS Ardrossan Refinery w/plastic match holder, (B/W) photo of refinery (F) 2.00
4C,40S,FS Arrowsmith Tool & Die Co. [1952], Scenic Ducks-Fish-Sailboat-Skier 1.00
5C,20S,FS The Young Set, 5 infants w/expression, Not Spinach Again!, We Wuz Robbed, Sweet or Hot?, Washday Blues!, Some Party, ad:Yeingst and Brenneman Barber Shop 12.00
300C,20S,MS Barber Shops, different cities 8.00
30C,20S,FS 11-Barber Shops,19-Beauty Salons 6.50
2BAR Small, no advertisement 4.00
5BAR Large w/different ads on each 12.00
39BAR Barrels, assorted sizes and shapes 46.50
1C,20S,BS IT IS YOUR RIGHT TO OWN AND BEAR ARMS, Phoeniz Sportsmens Assn. 1.00
40C,MS/MZ Beauty Shops, different cities 5.00
8C,20S,FS Bethlehem PA Bicentennial Set 1941-2 [1940], Series #1: Brickers Bread-Lipkin Furniture-Modern Cleaners-Union Bank and Trust Co. 5.00
8C,20S,FS Bethlehem PA Bicentennial Set 1941-2 [1940], Series #2: Boderman Bros.-Brickers Bread-Ruth's Funeral Home-Young's Drug Stores, Inc. 5.00
25C,MZ,MS Bi-centennial covers 5.00
6C,30S,BS American Revolution Bicentennial 1776-1976 set, patriotic scenes 2.50
1 Book, 1939 New York World's Fair Matchcovers, Second Edition, 1989, w/Price Guide, by Bill Retskin 8.00
6C,20S,FS Cessna Set #1 [1956], (stock) 3.50
5C,40S,FS Cessna Set #2 [1957], Two Ladies Driving-Two Farmers-Two Golfers-Two men in boat-Two Businessmen (stock) 1.50
25C,30S,MS Nite Clubs, assorted 4.75
25C,20S,FS Coal Companies, Koppers Coke 7.50
1C,40S,FS Doublelength [-   ], Universal Match 3.00
9C,20S,FS Detroit, MI, assorted themes 5.00
1FB,20S Schulze's Dolly Madison Cakes (F), ButterNut Bread (B) 1.50

30C,20S,FS Drug Stores, Reliable Drugs (GY) (stock) 3.00

16C,20S,FS Drug Stores, Prescription specialists, assorted colors (stock) 2.25

20C,20S,FS Drug Stores, Reliable Drugs (LGN) (stock) 3.00

30C,20S,FS Drug Stores, Reliable Drugs (YW) (stock) 3.00

6C,30S,FS Easel Backs 6.25

20C,MZ,FS Easelbacks, Lion Match 8.00

12C,20S,FS Eggbert Set [1962], Monogram of Calif. Dear Lord..-I Go Out..-'It's Got Something..'-It's You Dames..-Kennedy Made it..-'Near As I.'-One More Kiss..-Sure, You
Miss..-The Way She's..-Think I'll Bark..-What a Cutie..-Who's Calling. 7.50

50C,26S,MS Embossed.. 1.25

10C,40S 10 Wonders in Engineering (colorful) 3.00

2 items, full figural matchcover, 1FB ad: Gordon's Gin, (GN), English 15.00

1FB Figural, Shape of Grist Mill, ad: Old Engine House 3.00

4C,30S,FS Museum of Fine Arts, Boston 15, Mass., w/art work (F) of each 18.00

1FB,20S,FS Forest City Material Co., truck (F), trees (B) 1.25

10C,20S,MS Gay related.. 22.00

1C,30S,MS Gay Related, Jewel Box Lounge shows 6 photos of female impressionists in color 4.00

10C,20S,FS Gay Related 5.00

1FB Gucci, non-traditional shape, long w/wide Feature-like sticks, no printing, quote (I), (BK/
CM) 5.00

65C,20S,FS Hallmark, assorted themes 5.00

4C,20S,FS Adam Hats Set, contest set, A-D-A-M 5.00

8C,20S,FS Adam Hats Set, contest set, A-D-A-M H-A-T-S, offer expires April 1, 1948, on the
(I) Type #1 [1947], space for advertiser on (F) 10.00

Type #2 [1947], ADAM a better word for hat (F) 10.00

12C,20S,FS Historic Virginia Set, Captain Orr's..-James Galt..-The James Geddy..-Ludwell
Paradise..-Pitt Dixon..-The Public..-The Quarter..-The Raleigh..-St. George..-Travis House-
The Wren..-The Wythe.., Type 2, [1950], narrow striker 5.00

12C,20S,FS Historic Virginia Set, Captain Orr's..-James Galt..-The James Geddy..-Ludwell
Paradise..-Pitt Dixon..-The Public..-The Quarter..-The Raleigh..-St. George..-Travis House-
The Wren..-The Wythe.., Type 1, [1940], wide striker 4.00

50C,20S,MS Hospitals, different states 7.00

25C,20S,BS Hospitals (no Military), assorted 6.25

1FB,20S,FS Smith Bros. Ice Cream (WE/BE) 2.00

5C,20S,MS Ice Cream Company Ads, assorted 1.50

6C,20S,FS International Distributors Set [   ], Are We Planting..-Ghosts of..-Hold It, Jack!..-Let's
Team..- One Word..-'Pals, I'm Supposed..' 5.50

6C,30S Kilgore Fixtures, Aristocrat by Universal Match Corp., photos (B/F) 2.00

6C,20S,FS Lexington Historical Set, [1956] 2.50

1C,30S,FL,BS LIFE magazine, (RD,WE) 2.00

22C,20S,MS Liquor Stores, assorted 10.00

25C,20S,BS Lobsters 8.00

25C,20S,FS Lobsters, assorted restaurants 12.25

170C,MZ,MS Lobsters, assorted themes, in album 30.00

100C,20S,FS w/phone numbers below 1000 .... 23.00

15C,20S,FS Markets and Groceries 4.00

12C,20S,FS Metalart Set #1 [1958], Creepy Hollow..-Fruity Acres..-Grand Central..-Happy
Acres..-Harbord School..-Hiltin Mau Mau..-Old Sox..-Old Reefer..-Passion Pit..-Red Star..-
Sing Sing..-Ye Red Lamp.. .... 5.00

12C,20S,FS Metalart Set #2 [1960], The Lite of the Party set Arguing with you..-Bottoms Up!..-
Down the hatch!-Here's lookin' at..-I don't trust..-I think I have..-I think I'll..-I used to be..-
Mirror, mirror,..-Why can't you..- You make me..-Your enough 5.00

4C,20S,FS Metalart Set #3 [1962], Manhattan-Martini-Old Fashioned-Whiskey Sour 1.50

4C,20S,FS Metalart Prison Set [1962], multicolored Alcatraz..-Fort Leavenworth..-San Quentin..-
Sing Sing.. .... 3.50

30C,30S,MS Metallic Finish, assorted advertisers 3.25

5C,20S,FS Set of Monkeys by Lawson ad: SARA Hats 2.00

5C,20S,FS Superior Monkey Stock Design Set [1950], Lawson Wood He's Here Pop!-Hold ....
Everything!-The Old Skate!-Step on the Gas!-Where's Elmer? 2.00

4C,20S,FS Superior Monkey Stock Design Set [1974], Monkey Shines! 'For Once I'm Not..'-'Just
Wait Until They..'-'One Goes on My Hand..'-'Remember, A Good Trainer..' 2.50

4C,20S,FS Superior Monkey Stock Design Set [   ], Monkey Shines! 'Josephine, You've Got..'-
'I'm Sure Having Fun..'-'My Poker Face Is..'-'What Do You Mean..' Type 1 [1975] 2.00

4C,20S,BS Superior Monkey Stock Design Set [   ], Monkey Shines! 'Josephine, You've Got..'-
'I'm Sure Having Fun..'-'My Poker Face Is..'-'What Do You Mean..' Type 2 [   ] ... 2.00

12C,30S,FS Monogram Co. Set #2 [   ], A Jane Is..-Bottoms Up!..-Cheer Up..-Cute Indeed Is..-
Divorced Are Mr....-Girls Who Act..-Girls Who Claim..-Girls Who Keep..-How Old Aren't..-
If At First..-Many A Girl..- People who Live.. 5.00

12C,30S,FS Monogram Co. Set #1 [   ], A Contrary Model..-A Fool and..-A Girl When..-A Girl
Who..- A Kiss That..-A Little Flattery..-A Loving Cup..-After All..-Eat, Drink and..-It's A
Great..-People Don't Care..- 'Tis Better To.. .... 5.00

25C,40S,FS Namecraft Corp. Set [1947], Wisecrack Set Advice is..-Alimony is..-A Bachelor is..-
A Bore is..-A budget is..-A Committee is..-A Conference is..-Conscience is..-A Consultant
is..-A Coordinator is..-The Cost of Living Index is..-Diplomacy is..-An Economist is..-An
Efficiency Expert is..-Fishing is..-A Flirt is..-Genius is..-A Kiss is..- An Oboe is..-Oratory
is..-A Professor is..-Punctuality is..-A Specialist is..-A Statistician is..-A Sweater is.. 13.50

14C,20S,FS Nature Set [1955], Ducks-Hunter-Man fishing below falls-Man fishing along a tree
lined stream-Man netting fish-Sailing ship-Snow along stream & bridge-Sleigh & church-
Snow scene, moon in (BE) sky-Snow scene, moon in (PE) sky-Snowy mountains shown
reflected in lake-Snowy stream & lighted house-Snow scene, people entering lighted house-
Waterwheel behind houses.. 2.50

1FB,20S,FS Rival Dog Food, great Dog w/ship's wheel (B) 4.50

1C,20S,FS NRA Issues [6-16-1933 to 1-1-1936] 3.00

1C,20S,FS Bohack Stations, [1933-1936], (RD) NRA (BE) eagle (F), manumark, Lion Canada
1929 .... 10.00

6C,20S,FS Otis Engineering Corp. Set 2.00

4C,20S,FS Outer Space Set [1963], Chicago Match Co. (stock) 3.00

1FB,20S,BF Frank M. Page Flowers, Springfield, Mass (BK/WE) 2.00

8C,20S,FS Pageant of America Set [1935], numbered Columbus at..-The First American-The
Battle..-Declaration of.- De Soto's Death-Ceding of..-Surrender of..-Lewis & Clark in.. 13.00

10C,20S,FS Filippo Berio Olive Oil Set [1940] 18.00

10C,20S,FS Leon and Eddie [   ], Panorama Set, numbered, Entertainment-Singing-Music-
Specialty Acts-Leon & Eddie-Revue-Dancing-Dinner-Banquets-Good Drinks 55.00

11C,MZ,MS All with Penguins 7.00

20C,MS,FS w/Pigs, assorted advertisers 15.00

1FB,30S,FS GM Powerama, [August 31 - September 25, 1955], dated 5.00

50C,20S,FS Private Clubs, assorted 3.50

4C,20S,FS Monogram of California Prison Set [1959], (BK/WE) Alcatraz..-Leavenworth..-San
Quentin..-Sing Sing.. .... 3.00

4c,20S,FS Monarch Match Prison Set [   ] Alcatraz..-Leavenworth..-San Quentin..-Sing Sing..
.... 3.25

4B Fancy in plastic case, raised Jewish Menorah on each in GD, flames are cut glass ... 22.50

1C,20S,FS It Is Your Right To Own And Bear Arms 1.00

20C,40S,FS,RF Universal Match Corp. Salesman's Covers, Colorful (I) 3.00

8C,30S,FS Schafer Equipment Set Series A [1956], railroad engines Stourbridge Lion 1829-Tom
Thumb 1829-Best Friend of Charleston 1830-DeWitt Clinton 1831-Atlantic 1832-Brother
Jonathan 1832-Old Ironsides 1832-George Washington 1836 .... 5.00

8C,30S,FS Schafer Equipment Set Series B [1957], railroad engines Sandusky 1837-Mercury
1842-Mud Digger 1844-Chesapeake 1847-Camel 1848-General 1855-Tiger 1856-Mogul
1863 .... 5.00

10C,20S,FS Seagrams Detectograms Set #2, [1942], numbered 11 through 20 .... 10.00
8C,MZ,MS Ski Resorts and Lodges, different states 2.00
259C,4B,MZ,MS Album of Statue of Liberty theme covers and boxes 22.50
4C,20S,FS Sportsman Set [1950], Chicago Match Co. The Break-Old Faithful-On the Wing-Quick
  Action (stock) 1.75
6C,40S,FS St. Louis Convention City Set [1949], MirroGloss Bear Pits-Mississippi River-
  Municipal Auditorium-Municipal Opera-Shaw's Garden-Soldier's Memoria 12.00
5C,20S,FS 12th Annual Central Penna. Stamp Get-Together, May 18th, 1957 (5 colors) .. 1.25
6FB,20S,FS caddy of six, ad: Steel Suspension Desks, ca. 1930, bridge (B) 5.00
12C,20S,FS Sunmaid Raisins Set [1936], recipes (I) Caramello Squares-Old Fashioned Pound
  Cake-Raisin Carrot Mold-Raisin Carrot Sandwich-Raisin Cheese Biscuits-Raisin Cream
  Pie-Raisin Nut Bread-Raisin Oatmeal Cookies-Raisin Sandwiches-Spiced Raisin Pie-Sun
  Maid Muffins-ad for recipe book Superior Match Co. [1938-present], Chicago IL 10.00
12C30S,FS Syracuse China Set [1958] Black: Adobe Econorim-Cadet-Cardinal Line-De Ville-
  Sundown-Webster 2.00
12C30S,FS Syracuse China Set [1958] Gray: Berkeley-Colonial-Driftwood-Millbrook-Roxbury-
  Sandlewood 4.00
1FB,20S,BF The Tarbell-Watters Co., Springfield, Mass (BN,BK) 2.00
1C,30S,FS The Princess Phone 'it's little - it's lovely - it lights' 1.50
13C,30/40S,FS Telephone Company, assorted themes 18.50
1FB,20S,BF Diamond Match, Pat. 2,101,111 on footer(WE) 2.00
2FB,20S,BF no printing, testers for regular 20 strike and friction strike, Diamond, ca. 1930 3.00
50C,20S,FS Thank Yous, assorted businesses 2.00
1C,40S,FS,FL Smoothie Ties w/Leggy Girl & Slogan, Colorful 2.25
12C,20S,FS Time Magazine Set #1 [1954], Capt. Kidd-Cleopatra-Don Quixote-Godiva-Hamlet-
  Jessie James-Julius Caesar-Lucretia Borgia-Marie Antoinette-Napoleon-Nero-Sherlock
  Holmes 3.00
12C,20S,FS Time Magazine Set #2 [1955], Capt. Kidd-Cleopatra-Don Quixote-Godiva-Hamlet-
  Jessie James-Julius Caesar-Lucretia Borgia-Marie Antoinette-Napoleon-Nero-Sherlock
  Holmes, more printing (I) 3.00
20C,20S,FS Tire and Service Sales 5.00
30C,30S,FS True-Color [1956-present], Lion Match, assorted themes 3.50
40C,20S Utilities, Gas and Electric Companies, assorted 8.00
??C,20S,FS (1659) Views of Chicago 1.00
??C,20S,FS (1655) [   ], Views of Washington 1.00
18C,20S,FS Wichita, KS, assorted themes 8.00
5C,20S,FS Famous Women [1944] in history including J.W. Howe, F.E. Willard, J. Addams, H.B.
  Stowe and C. Barton, (BK/WE) 3.00
9C,30S,BS Women of Distinction Set [1980], Anthony-Barton-Beth-Bethune-Blackwell-Earhart-
  Keller-Mead-Roosevelt-Tubman 3.00
10C,40S,FS Wonders of Engineering Set, The Colossus..-Golden Gate..-The Great Sphinx..-The
  Lighthouse.. Palomar..-The Pyramid..-The Statue of Zeus..-The Temple.. The Tomb of Kin
  Mausolus-The Walls of Babylon 6.00
10C,40S,FS Wonders of Engineering Set Type 1 [1956], Arrowsmith Tool and Die Corp.,
  telephone number ORegon 8-3793 .... 5.50
10C,40S,FS Wonders of Engineering Set Type 2 [   ], Arrowsmith Tool and Die Corp., telephone
  number SPring 6-0890 .... 4.00
10C,40S,FS Wonders of Engineering Set Type 3 Arrowsmith Tool Mfg. Corp., (GY) striker 10.00
10C,40S,FS Wonders of Engineering Set Type 4 Arrowsmith Tool Mfg. Corp., (BN) striker 10.00
1FB,20S,FS F.W. Woolworth Co., Main St., Buffalo, New York (RD/GD/WE) 1.25
10C,30S,FS Yacht Clubs 10.00
35C,20S,MS Yacht Clubs 16.00

Matchoramas

Matchoramas—A Universal Match Corp. design employing a four color photographic process somewhere on the front. Production of this beautiful matchcover design began in 1955 and ended in 1987. Other company trademarks, such as Vista-Lite and Tru-Color, can be found on the inside. Black and white photos (real photo matchcovers) are not included in this category.

6C,30S,FS El Paso Natural Gas Set [1958] 2.00
300C,30S,FS [1955-present], assorted themes 22.00
50C,20S,FS,FL [1955-present], assorted themes 8.00
40C,40S,MS Automobile and Truck issues 17.00
100C,30S,MS [1955-present], assorted themes 3.75
100C,40S,MS [1955-present], assorted themes 15.00
6C,30S,FS North Pole Set [ ], numbered 2.50
1C,30S,FS Ron Bacardi Rum, Matchorama 1.50
10C,40S,FS Stephen Foster Songs Set [ ] Beautiful Dreamer-Camptown Races-Happy Hours
    at Home-Jeanie with the Light..-The Merry, Merry Month..-My Old Kentucky..- Oh! Susanna-
    Old Black Joe-Old Dog Tray-Old Folks at Home 4.75
50FB,20S complete sets of panorama, Western Scene w/sample picture, full caddy 12.00
20C,MZ,BS Assorted themes 7.25
10C,MZ,FS Assorted themes 2.00
25C,20S,MS Assorted themes 5.00

Everyone . . . uses and reads book matches

One time or another in your business career you have given quite a bit of thought to WHAT you can use to best advantage to attract people to your establishment. Maybe you have considered cards, blotters—and quite likely advertising novelties, such as billfolds, ash trays, key chains, or something else in that line.

We present no argument against the use of ANY advertising novelty because they ARE good. But the cost! You have probably investigated to find that while you'd like to use ash trays, billfolds, key chains or something else in the novelty line, the cost made it prohibitive.

Moreover, it is a bit difficult to hit upon an advertising novelty that has definite appeal to men and women alike.

There's where Book Matches come in. Smokers and non-smokers alike use—and read—Book Matches. They are found in men's pockets, in women's purses, on bridge tables in the home, on desks and tables in the office, factory and shop.

You are using an advertising medium which not only carries your story to everyone—you are passing out something that has a definite value and which will bring a "Thank You" from those to whom you pass out your Matches. **Monarch Match Co. (ca. 1950)**

Newspapers & Magazines

Newspaper—Matchcovers which advertise newspapers or magazines, to include specialty sets, such as the Ernie Pyle—Chicago Sun Set which was popular during WWII. Other singles include famous personalities as they appeared in the news or columnists. Popular magazines, such as Cornet and TV Guide used matchcovers to advertise their publications.

18C,20S,FS Chicago Sun Set [1943], Brown-Douglas-Downing-Eliot-Fodor-Grafton-Hanna-Kent-Knickerbocker-Kuh-Landis-Lardner-Lasch-Lippman-Mowrer-Pyle-Smothers-Sullivan 10.00

6C,20S,FS Chicago Sun Set [1946], The Berrys..-Chicago Page..-Dale Harrison..-Inside Washington..-Only 1cts A Day..-Warren Page.. .... 5.00

39C,20S,FS Los Angeles Daily News Set [1944], 13 features each in 3 colors (GN/PK)-turquoise) Complete Financial-Donald Duck-Drew Pearson- Eleanor Roosevelt-Ernie Pyle-Joe Palooka-Manchester Boddy-Matt Weinstock-Raymond Clapper-Red Ryder-Samuel Grafton-Tarzan-Women's Activities 22.50

8C,20S,FS Los Angeles Times Set [1943], American Leaders Arnold-Eisenhower-Halsey-King-Leahy-MacArthur-Marshall-Nimitz 27.50

12C,G,FS New York Times Set [1955], Actress-Advertising Man-Banker-Broker-Clubwoman-Executive-Gourmet-Hostess-Lawyer-Salesman-Social Leader-Sportsman 25.00

12C,30S,BS State Times Set [   ], Bayou Bengals..-Bengals Find..-Finis To..-Five Million..- Huey Long..-Louisiana State..-Nixon To..-One Small Step..- Peace..-Scopes Convicted..-Tigers Bowl..-War.. .... 5.50

Odd Strikers

Odd Strikers—A Lion Match Co. trademarked matchbook, this scarce style of matchbook used unusual shaped strikers placed on the outside of the matchbook as part of the design. Introduced in 1942, the style lasted 20 years and became an instant category at its inception. These are also known as odd strikers, spot strikers or misplaced abrasives.

Odd Strikers

2C,20S American Shippers, We Ship Anything, Anywhere, striker is back of panties of woman being carried by eagle 7.25
1C,20S Attleborough S & L Ass'n, Attleboro, MA, striker is roof of building (B) 5.00
1C,20S Attleborough Savings & Loan Ass'n, Attleboro, MASS, shows striker as roof of building 5.50
1C,20S Beaver Construction, striker is tail of beaver wearing overalls and fidora 6.50
1C,20S Billy Fry 'The Ham King' shows striker as womans back underwear 8.00
1C,20S El Sombrero Restaurant, Portland, OR, striker is donkey's back side (B) 5.00
1C,20S Fort Park Recreation, Lincoln-Park, MI, striker is seat of large blonde bowler's pants 8.00
2C,20S,CON Georgie Rudin's, Dayton, Ohio, striker is wide (BE/WE) bow tie on man . 10.00
1C,20S The Grizzly Bar, show bear scratching tree (striker) 6.00
1C,20S Jack Fischer's Restaurant & Caterers, Brooklyn, NY, striker is moulded plate of chopped liver 6.25
1C,20S Jolly Spot, shows strikers as head of drum held by clown 7.50
1C,20S Kunz's, Louisville, KY, striker is grill 5.00
2C,20S,CON Eat A Pig (S), Mr. Pig Goes To Town, striker is back of pig, pig (F/B) 10.00
2C,20S,CON Mr. Pig Sandwich Shop, Hammond, Ind, striker is back of pig 10.00
1C,20S Pizzarama, Glendale, striker is center of pizza (F) 5.00
2C,20S The Plainsman, shows cowboy on rail lighting cigarette, striker is side of pants ... 7.00
1C,30S Apple Tree Shanty, Denver, CO, striker is side walk up to building 8.00
2C,30S 1) Joe Beaver says, striker on beaver tail, 2) Shell Synthetic Rubber w/Indian, 2 strikers on arrows 12.00
1C,30S Butterfield Theatres, striker is marching band bass drum, says August is the Greater Movie Season 10.00
1C,30S Fort Delaware Hotel, Delaware, Ohio, Phone 31276, striker as center of large star (B) 7.50
1C,30S Gardena Bowl, Gardena, California, striker is bowling ball (F) w/pins 7.00
1C,30S Ray Jackson's, Milwaukee, signed baseball (F), striker is baseball diamond (B) 15.00
1C,30S King's Fare Cocktails, Kenosha, WI, striker is top of grill 8.00
1C,30S Schodorf Truck Body & Equipment, Columbus, OH, striker is parking lot near building (B) 8.00
1C,30S Shell Synthetic Rubber, striker is arrow held by Indian (F/B) (unusual) 7.50
1C,30S T-35 Asphalt Paving Co., mentor, OH, striker is asphalt lot w/steam roller 9.25
1C,30S X-L Laundromat, striker is back of woman's skirt, girlie (F) 10.00
25C,MS Odd Strikers, Lion Match Co., assorted themes 32.50
4C,30S,FS Odd Strikers, Lion Match Co., 1 Display, assorted 15.00

Owname Products Corp.

Owname Products Corp.--A highly specialized and different kind of matchbook, Owname Products Corp. produced a 15 match comb/30-strike size matchbook with a single grommet attachment from 1925 to the beginning of WWII. The striker was detachable and later issues replaced the grommet with one staple. About 500 different are known.

1FB Bonwit Teller, Fifth Avenue, New York (WE/BE/SR) 5.00
1FB Chevrier's Grill, Solana Beach, Cal, Tel. Del Mar 43 (RD/SR) 5.00
1FB EJB initials on (SR) (F) 5.00
1FB Fruehauf Trailer Co, New York (WE/BE/RD) 5.00
1FB Jane Davies, Luncheon-Dinner (RD/WE) 5.00
1FB Lord & Taylor, (BK/SR) 5.00
1FB Martha Levine Gowns, New York (SR/BE) 5.00
1FB Ratye Allen, Inc, New York (GN/BK) 5.00
1FB,FS Spivy's Roof, NYC 1.00
1FB Yama's Tea Room, New York (BK/SR) 5.00

Parks (State & National)

Parks—Matchcovers which use the theme of national, state, or regional parks, depicted by drawings or photos. Both sets and singles exist in the category with some being produced by railroads. Park sets were usually souvenir matchcovers which were purchased directly from the park.

5C,20S,FS Arkansas Set 1.25

5C,20S,FS Souvenir of White's City - Carlsbad Cavern Nat'l Park 5.75

8C,20S,FS Carlsbad Caverns Set #1 [1938], Cavern Sup. Celery Formation-Entrance of Carlsbad Caverns-The First Spring-Fountain of the Fairies-Rock of Ages-Temple of the Sun-Totem Poles-Twin & Giant Stalagmites 3.00

6C,20S,FS Carlsbad Caverns Set #2 [   ], White's City, Match Corp. Entrance to..-Giant Dome-Rock of Ages-Temple of the Sun-Totem Poles, Big Room-Twin Domes and Giant Stalagmites 3.50

6C,20S,FS Carlsbad Caverns Set #3 [1949], Souv. of White's City Entrance..-Rock of Ages-Temple..-Totem Poles..-Twin Domes..-White City Deluxe Courts 2.25

4C,20S,FS Dells of Wisconsin Set [1940], Chimney Rock-The Narrows-Stand Rock-A Winnebago Brave 2.00

4C,20S,FS Colonel Denning State Park Set 3.00

6C,20S,FS Our National Parks Set #1 [   ], (BK) manumark Big Bend-Hawaii Volcanoes-Hot Springs-Mammoth Cave-Olympic-Petrified Forest 5.00

6C,20S,FS Our National Parks Set #2 [   ], (BE) manumark, (BN) printing (B) Acacia-Crater Lake-Grand Canyon-Yellowstone-Yosemite-Zion 1.00

6C,20S,FS Our National Parks Set #3 [   ], (BE) manumark, (BK) printing (B) Bryce Canyon-Carlsbad Caverns-Great Smoky Mountains-Mount Rainier-Rocky Mountain-Sequoia 2.00

6C,20S,FS Our National Parks Set #4 [   ], (BK) manumark, (BK) striker Everglades-Glacier Park-Grand Teton-Isle Royale-Shenandoah-Virgin Islands 3.00

8C,20S,FS Grand Canyon Set [1940], Diamond Match At Bright Angel ..-Clear Creek ..-El Tovar Hotel-From Hopi Point-The Hopi House-Moran Point-The Watchtower-Yavapai Pt. 6.00

8C,20S,FS Kentucky State Parks Set 9.00

8C,20S,FS Kentucky State Parks 5.00

6C,20S,FS Kentucky Set #1 [1950], (BK) striker, Mirro-Gloss finish, (WE) paper (I) Carrollton-Corbin-Dawson Springs-Gilbertsville-Murray-Slade 2.50

6C,20S,FS Kentucky Set #2, (GY) striker, Mirro-Gloss finish Carrollton-Corbin-Dawson Springs-Gilbertsville-Murray-Slade, Type 1 [1952], (WE) paper (I) 1.00

6C,20S,FS Kentucky Set #2, (GY) striker, Mirro-Gloss finish Carrollton-Corbin-Dawson Springs-Gilbertsville-Murray-Slade, Type 2 [   ], (GY) paper (I) 1.00

8C,20S,FS Kentucky Set #3 [1954], (GY) striker, Mirro-Gloss finish, (WE) paper (I) Carrollton-Corbin-Dawson Springs-Gilbertsville-Henderson-Murray-Olive Hill-Slade 2.50

9C,20S,FS Kentucky Set #4, Kromekote finish Carrollton-Corbin-Dawson Springs-Gilbertsville-Henderson-Jamestown-Murray-Olive Hill-Slade, Type 1 Henderson phone is 7-1893 2.00

9C,20S,FS Kentucky Set #4, Kromekote finish Carrollton-Corbin-Dawson Springs-Gilbertsville-Henderson-Jamestown-Murray-Olive Hill-Slade, Type 2 Henderson phone is VAlley 6-2247 .... 2.00

9C,20S,FS Kentucky Set #4, Kromekote finish Carrollton-Corbin-Dawson Springs-Gilbertsville-Henderson-Jamestown-Murray-Olive Hill-Slade, Type 3 (Do Not Mail Matches) added on (I) 2.00

9C,30S,FS Kentucky Set #5 Set [1958], Universal Match Corp., Carrollton-Corbin-Dawson Springs-Gilbertsville-Henderson-Jamestown-Murray-Olive Hill-Slade 3.00

9C?,20S,FS Kentucky Set #6 [   ], Louisville manumark, Carrollton-Corbin-Dawson Springs-Jamestown-Murray-Olive Hill-Prestonsburg- 3.50

2C,20S,FS Mammoth Cave Set #1, Frozen Niagara-Ruins of Karnak, Type 1 [1935], (BK) single line Diamond manumark 1.00

2C,20S,FS Mammoth Cave Set #1, Frozen Niagara-Ruins of Karnak, Type 2 [1938], (BK) 2 line Diamond manumark 1.00

4C,20S,FS Mammoth Cave Set #2 [1936], (WE) manumark Cave Entrance-Echo River-Hindoo Temple-Onyx Colonnade 3.00

4C,20S,FS Mammoth Cave Set #3 [   ], (BK) manumark Echo River-Frozen Niagara-Onyx Colonnade- 2.50

3C?,20S,FS Meramec Caverns Set [   ], Onyx Mountain-Stage Curtain-Wine Table 2.00

12C,20S,FS Our National Parks, Diamond Match (BE) 4.50

6C,20S,FS Oklahoma Set #1 [1954], Ardmore-Broken Bow-Pawhuska-Watonga-Wilburton-Woodward 2.50

7C,20S,FS Oklahoma Set #2 [1955], Altus-Braggs-Durant-Freedom-Gore-Poteau-Wagoner 3.25

6C,40S,FS Rock City Set [   ] 5.00

4C,20S,FS,FL Shenandoah National Park Set Moonlight View from Crescent Rock-Stony Man Peak along Skyline Drive-View of Skyline Drive..-Winter along.., Type #1 [1938], Made in U.S.A/The Diamond.. manumark 2.00

4C,20S,FS,FL Shenandoah National Park Set Moonlight View from Crescent Rock-Stony Man Peak along Skyline Drive-View of Skyline Drive..-Winter along.., Type #2 [1949], The Diamond../Washington D.C. manumark 2.00

3C,20S,FS Wonder Cave Set [1936?], Entrance to Wonder Cave-Priest at Altar-The Devil's Play 2.50

14C,20S,FS Yosemite National Park 3.50

120C,20S,FS Souvenir, Parks, Ski, Museums, etc. 12.00

(above left) Even before the **Diamond Quality** period (ca. 1923-1936), Diamond Match Co. led the way with footer statements enhancing the quality of their matchcovers. The Safety First footer with the single line The Diamond Match Co manumark is one of the earliest examples of this. (above right)Three pre-Diamond Quality manumarks: Robert Burns Segars, with a manumark reading Patented Sept. 27, 1892; Holbrook's Varsity added the Diamond Match Co. name and Licensed Match; and the Hunt's Oxford Hotel, Chicago added Approved Match No. 7.

Patriotic

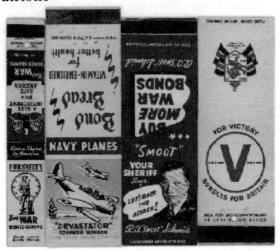

Patriotic—One of the most prolific categories known, considering the short period of time in which they were made. Thousands of singles, sets and series are known. Patriotic themes can be found on everything from Airplanes to Zoos and is a category of its own, not to be confused with Military.

4C,20S,FS Arrow Match Set [1942], stock design, For Freedom's Sake..-This Man May Die..-Volunteer for Victory.. .... 3.00

1C,20S,FS 10% Everybody Every Payday, Arrow Match, generic 5.50

1C,20S,FS Defend America, ad: Bentz Drug Store, Pottstown, PA 3.25

12C,20S,FS Bond Bread Set #1 [1942], airplanes (B) Lion Match, Avenger-Buccaneer-Catalina-Corsair-Dauntless-Devastator-Helldiver-Kingfisher-Mariner-Seagull-Vindicator-Wildcat 38.00

12C,20S,FS Bond Bread Set #2 [1943], airplanes (F) Lion Match, Avenger-Buccaneer-Catalina-Corsair-Dauntless-Devastator-Helldiver-Kingfisher-Mariner-Seagull-Vindicator-Wildcat 22.00

1C,20S,FS Bond Bread Navy Planes (B) Avenger 5.00

1C,20S,FS Bond Bread Navy Planes, 'Buccaneer,' (B) 3.50

1C,20S,FS Bond Bread Navy Planes, 'Catalina,' (B) 1.25

1C,20S,FS Bond Bread Navy Planes (B) Dauntless 3.00

1C,20S,FS Bond Bread Navy Planes, 'Devastator,' (B) 4.00

1C,20S,FS Bond Bread Navy Planes (B) Helldiver 6.25

1C,20S,FS Bond Bread Navy Planes, 'Kingfisher,' (B) 1.25

1C,20S,FS Bond Bread Navy Planes, 'Mariner,' (B) 1.25

1C,20S,FS Bond Bread Navy Planes, 'Seagull,' (B) 1.00

2C,20S,FS Bond Bread Navy Planes, Vindictor & Wildcat, photo (F), ad: Bond Bread 6.00

1C,20S,FS Bond Bread Navy Planes (B) Wildcat 6.00

1FB,20S,FS Bundles for Britain, dated 1941, Coat of Arms on F by Universal Match Corp. 6.50

1C,20S,FS The British War Relief Assn of S. Calif, Ambassador Hotel, LA 3.00

1C,20S,BS The British War Relief Society, dated: 1948, early (BS) 4.00

1C,20S,BS The British War Relief Society, Washington, DC, dated 1941 .... 5.75

1C,20S,FS The British War Relief Assn. of Southern California 1.00

1C,20S,FS The British War Relief Society, Copyright 1941 .... 1.25

1FB,20S,FS Bromo-Seltzer (F), For Victory!, Buy Bonds (B) 1.25

1FB,20S,FS Bundles for Britain, dated 3.50

1C,20S,FS Buy Bonds 2.00

1C,20S,FS For Safety Buy Defense Bonds-Stamps (generic) 2.00

1C,20S,FS Buy More War Bonds* Stamps, no ad 1.25

1C,20S,FS Buy U.S. War Stamps and Bonds Regularly 2.75

1FB,20S,FS V for Victory, Buy US War Savings Bonds 1.25
1C,20S,FS Buy U.S. War Stamps and Bonds Regularly (generic) 2.00
1FB,20S,FS V for Victory, Buy Bonds 2.75
1C,20S,FS Buy War Bonds, SOL, Jersey Match Co 2.50
1C,20S,FS Keep 'em Flying, Buy War Bonds, Jersey Match Co. 3.50
1C,20S,FS Be Careful on the Job! Safety Set (part) Use Safety Devices 4.00
1C,20S,FS Careless Lips...Can Sink Ships, ad: Drs. Smith & Rippetoe 1.50
1C,20S,FS Carless Lips...Can Sink Ships, ad: Drs. Smith & Rippetoe, Kansas City, KS .. 2.25
10C,20S,FS Czech Set [1941] 5.00
1C,20S,FS Defend America, ad: Bentz Drug Store, Pottstown, PA 2.50
1C,20S,FS Defend America, ad: J.H. Pereue Equipment Co., Memphis, TENN 1.75
6C,20S,FS Defense Set [1941], Universal Match Corp. The Arson Bug..-5th Column..-Knock the
    Props..-Laugh at Goliath..Saboteur..-Watch Your Talk.. (stock) 3.50
1C,20S,FS Don't Talk, Chew Gum, Topps Gum 5.25
1B Ft. DuPont, 1940s 5.25
1C,20S,FS Save Fats, Help Win the War 4.25
1C,20S,FS For Safety, Buy War Bonds-Stamps 4.00
1C,20S,FS France A.O.F., w/flag (F) 5.25
1C,20S,FS Greek War Relief Assn, Inc., New York City - Help GREECE Now! 5.00
1C,20S,FS Help Greece Now! Contribute, Greek War Relief Assn 4.75
12C,30S,BS Happy Birthday, America, colorful, ad: East Cheyenne Nat'l Bank (I) 3.00
1C,20S,FS Work Will Win (part of set) There's a Happy Jap for Every Gap (etc.) 3.50
12C,30S,BS Happy Birthday America Set [1975-1976], panorama, over 300 different advertisers
    known, Colonization-Road to Independence-Establishing the new Nation-The Western
    Frontier-The Civil War Period-The Turn of the Century-The Industrial Revolution-World
    War I-World War II and the Great White Way-America as We Know It Today-The Space
    Age-Happy Birthday, America! 3.00
1FB,30S,FS Promotional, The New '30' Book Match w/CN tax stamp, Hitler Cartoon (B), (RD/
    WE) 10.00
1C,20S,FS Stop Hitler, w/Hitler crossed out, (RD/WE/BE) 14.00
1FB,20S,FS Stop Hitler, Defend America by Helping Britain 9.00
1FB,20S,FS,FEA 'Strike at the seat of Trouble', (B) shows Hitler holding globe, Spot Striker
    is his backside 65.00
1C,20S,FS Hold That Line, ad: Penn State Diner, Bethlehem, PA 2.75
1C,20S,FS Keep 'Em Rolling, Keep 'Em Flying, ad: El Patio Auto Court 2.00
1C,20S,FS Keep 'Em Rolling, ...Flying, Keep Democracy From Dying, ad: El Patio Auto Ct,
    Holbrook, AZ 2.00
1C,20S,FS Keep 'em Rolling/Keep 'em Flying, ad: Mary Ann's Eat Shop, Cedar Rapids, IA 3.25
1C,20S,FS Keep On Punching 2.75
1C,20S,FS Let's Go America, ad: Buck's Sandwich Place, Cheyenne, Wyo 2.75
5C,20S,FS Lion Set [   ] 3.00
1FB,20S,FS MacArthur [1944], I Shall Return 50.00
1B MacArthur, I Shall Return, Type 1 Universal Match Corp. manumark 55.00
1B MacArthur, I Shall Return, Type 2 no manumark 70.00
2C,20S,FS Gen. Douglas MacArthur (B), Give 'em Both Barrels (F), different colors ... 11.00
1C,20S,FS V for Victory, ad: Main Buffet 1.25
1C,20S,FS The Maple Leaf Fund, Inc. New York City, Maple Leaf (F) 2.25
5C,20S,FS Match Corp. Set #1 [1942], stock design Defend America-For the Nation..-Keep 'em
    Rolling..-Keep Them Flying-Let's Go America 3.50
6C,20S,FS Match Corp. Set #2 [   ], stock design Careless Lips-God Bless America-Smash the
    Axis-Step on It-Total Eclipse-We Shall Not Fail Her 4.50
1C,20S,FS The United Merchant Seamen's Service Club, Phila., PA 5.00
1C,20S,FS GD 'V' w/ ..._ (Morse code, below) 5.00
1C,20S,FS 'Remember Pearl Harbor', ad: Shoop's Grill, Corpus Christi, TX 22.50

12C,20S,FS Remember Pearl Harbor Set General Match, Damn the Torpedoes..-It's Up to Us..-Keep 'em Flying-More Power..-Remember Pearl..-Send Us..-The Tanks are Coming-Taps for the Japs-They Asked..-Tokens for Tokyo-V for Victory-We Won't Forget.., Type 1 [1942], ad for matches (I) 16.00

12C,20S,FS Remember Pearl Harbor Set General Match, Damn the Torpedoes..-It's Up to Us..-Keep 'em Flying-More Power..-Remember Pearl..-Send Us..-The Tanks are Coming-Taps for the Japs-They Asked..-Tokens for Tokyo-V for Victory-We Won't Forget.., Type 2 [   ], (I) blank 5.00

1C,20S,FS Russian War Relief, Inc, New York 5.50

1C,20S,FS A Safe Investment for a Safe America, no ad 2.25

1C,20S,FS Safety First (part of set) Use Your Head—Save Your Hands! 1.25

1C,20S,FS Safety First (part of set) Protect Your Feet-Wear Safety Shoes 4.00

1FB,20S,FS Get in the Scrap Save Waste Paper & Old Rags, WWII (RD/WE/BE) 2.00

1C,20S,FS Get in the Scrap ** SAVE ** Waste Paper and Old Rags 4.25

1C,20S,FS Service Men's Center, V-J Day, Sept. 2, 1945 .... 2.00

1C,20S,FS Step on it! ad: Anchorage Grill 3.50

1C,20S,FS Step on it! Buy War Bonds and Stamps 2.25

1C,20S,FS Total Eclipse! Buy More Bonds, ad: D & R Café 1.75

1C,20S,FS Total Eclipse! Buy More Bonds, ad: R & D Café, Kansas City, KS 1.50

1C,20S,FS Uncle Sam, Lion Match, For Victory 3.50

1C,20S,FS USO Kansas City, Missouri, Universal Match Co 6.00

1C,20S,FS USO Nat'l Catholic Community Service, Kansas City, MO 3.50

1FB,20S,FS V for Victory, V (F), minuteman & Buy Bonds (B) (RD/WE/BE) 5.00

1FB,20S,FS 'V' (F/B), Diamond Match, rubber stamped Jun 12 1942 (I) 6.50

1FB,20S,FS generic 'V' (RD/WE/BE) (F/B) WWII Patriotic 3.00

1C,20S,FS Patriotic, large 'V' (F/B) RD/WE/BE 4.75

10C,40S,FS Veterans Administration National Landmarks 10.00

1FB,20S,FS V for Victory 4.00

1C,20S,FS V for Victory, (BK/WE), no ad 1.50

1C,20S,FS V for Victory, ad: Main Buffet, Butte, Mont. 2.25

1FB,20S,FS For Victory Buy United States War Savings Bonds & Stamps, 'V' (F)(RD/WE/BE) 4.25

1FB,20S,FS V for Victory 5.00

1FB,20S,FS for Victory, For Victory Buy U.S. War Savings Bonds... .... 1.25

1C,20S,FS,FL Service Men's Center Celebrates Official V-J Day, September 2, 1945, Ft. Worth, TX 3.00

1C,20S,FS Patriotic, W.A.D.C.A. San Francisco Unit 6.25

1C,20S,FS Buy U.S. War Stamps and Bonds Regularly, no ad 1.25

1C,20S,FS 5th War Loan, 'V', (BK/WE) 6.00

1C,20S,FS 'We Shall Not Fail Her', ad: Woody's Café, Birmingham, ALA 2.50

1C,20S,FS,FL Weinstein Co. Dept Store, Minute Man 3.00

1C,20S,FS We Must Win! Buy More War Bonds-Stamps (generic) 1.50

1C,20S,FS Women's Ambulance & Defence Corps of America (WWII) 2.00

6C,20S,FS Work Will Win Set [1943], stock design Every Minute..-Give the Axis..-Keep Production..-Speed up.. Stay on the Job..-The Production Line.. .... 3.50

20C,20S,FS World War II Patriotic themes 4.50

380C,20S,FS World War II Patriotic themes, album 100.00

Perfect "36" (Diamond Match Co.)

Perfect 36—A limited production Diamond Match Co. trademark matchbook, it is known for its unusual size. Measuring 4 3/8" by 2 1/2", the Perfect "36" was made to compete with the double-size 40 stick matchbook popular with other match companies. Introduced in 1948, it lasted four years and over 400 varieties are known. The logo (left) appears on the inside.

1FB Compliments of The Diamond Match Company, ca. 1950 .... 3.00
1FB Green Star Gift & Souvenir Store, Watkins Glen, NY, photo of Cavern Cascade (B) 3.00
1FB Murray Motors, Inc., Chelsea 50, Mass. 3.25
1FB Southern Express Inc, (SR/RD/BK), metallic, truck (F), cities (B) 6.00
10FB,FS Perfect 36 [1948-1951], Diamond Match Co., assorted themes 17.50

Perkins Americana

Perkins Americana—A long series of color sets designed and manufactured by Edgar A. Perkins, an insurance salesman from Washington, D.C. First introduced in 1957, Perkins made them with the matchcover collecting hobby in mind. All appeared with the word "Americana" on the outside and frequently featured businesses and attractions in remote Virginia and Maryland towns. They were made in the 20 strike size.

The Americana with Indian appeared on all matchcover saddles and became the trademark of this series of sets.

5C,20S,FS Sketch 1, John N. Ball, Tourists, King & Queen, VA 9.00
5C,20S,FS Sketch 2, Eastville Inn Gift Shop, Eastville, VA 5.00
5C,20S,FS Sketch 7, Buddy's Place, Amelica C.H., VA 2.00
5C,20S,FS Sketch 8, Finney's Restaurant, Saluda, VA 3.75
5C,20S,FS Sketch 10, Mineral Tea Room, Mineral, VA 3.75
5C,20S,FS Sketch 15, Bank of Goochland, Goochland C.H., VA 5.00
5C,20S,FS Sketch 20, 360 Motel Restaurant, AAA, Chesterfield, C.H., VA 3.00
5C,20S,FS Sketch 21, Twin Oaks Tourists Restaurant, Charlotte C.H., VA 4.00
5C,20S,FS Sketch 24, J.R. Carson, General Merchandise, Texaco, Nottoway, C.H., VA ... 4.00
5C,20S,FS Sketch 26, Lake Manahoac Motel, Washington, VA 3.25
5C,20S,FS Sketch 27, Earl & Tal's Restaurant, Standardsville, VA 4.00
5C,20S,FS Sketch 30, Francis E. Tilman, Powhatan C.H., VA 3.00
5C,20S,FS Sketch 31, J.L. Oliver, General Merchandise, Wicomico, VA 3.00
5C,20S,FS Sketch 32, Princess Anne Soda Shop, Princess Anne, VA 3.00
5C,20S,FS Sketch 40, 17th RMS Convention 1957, Wilkes-Barre, Penna. 3.25
5C,20S,FS Sketch 52, Penn-Daw Hotel, Alexandria, VA 3.75
5C,20S,FS Sketch 68, Hoyt's Restaurant, Yellville, AR 3.00

5C,20S,FS Sketch 82, 2nd Eastern Matchcover Swapfest, June 12, 13, 14, 1959, Ocean Grove, NJ 5.00
5C,20S,FS Sketch 87, Inwood Motel & Restaurant 5.00
5C,20S,FS Sketch 92, Ruth's Camellia Motor Lodge 1.25
5C,20S,FS Sketch 97, Georgia Welcomes You!, W.B. Moulton Grocery, Knoxville, GA ... 3.00
5C,20S,FS Sketch 98, Louisiana Welcomes You!, St. John Club, Edgard, LA 2.75
5C,20S,FS Sketch 99, Mississippi Welcomes You!, Pittsboro Hote & Café, Pittsboro, MS 2.50
5C,20S,FS Sketch 101, First State Bank, Paint Rock, TX 2.75
5C,20S,FS Sketch 104, Griffith's Sinclair, Danielsville, GA 4.25
5C,20S,FS Sketch 109, North Carolina Welcomes You, Mack's Café, Southport, NC 3.00
5C,20S,FS Sketch 114, Andrews Field Motel, Upper Marlboro, MD 4.25
5C,20S,FS Sketch 120, Fonda R. Smid, Berwyn, Ill 6.00
5C,20S,FS Sketch 124, Ilene B. Ferguson, Lu-Ma-Ro Mobile Estates, Gambrills, MD 3.50
5C,20S,FS Sketch 130, Chat & Chew Drive In, Eaton, IN, Tank or Tummy We Fill Both . 4.50
5C,20S,FS Sketch 169, Civil War (1861-1865), Mosby's Rangers 6.50
5C,20S,FS Sketch 170, Civil War (1861-1865), Philippi Motel, Philippi, WV 7.50
5C,20S,FS Sketch 171, Civil War (1861-1865), Gen. Lee Assumes Command 6.00
5C,20S,FS Sketch 172, Civil War (1861-1865), Battle of New Market, VA 7.00
5C,20S,FS Sketch 206, S. Chelmsford, Mass Welcomes You 3.75

Photo (Real Photo, Black & White)

Photo (Real Photo)—A relative recent category promoted by the author of this book, real photo matchcovers use only black and white photos of persons, places, things, events, animals, buildings, or settings, etc. Enjoyable sub-classifications include women, babies, men with hats, couples, families, chefs, dogs, etc. Real photo matchcovers skew into other categories such as sports, VIP, and political, but these are generally collected alone.

1C,20S,FS Black Angus Motel, ad (B), AAA (S), (BK/WE) photo of large Black Angus Cow (F) 2.25
1C,20S,FS San Canter's Restaurant, 624 Penn Ave, Phone Grant 9253 (F), Yes-I Thank U (S), photo of Sam (B), (RD/WE) 1.75
1C,20S,FS Dave's Delicious Beefburgers, Hollywood, CAlif, Phone HO. 0513 (F), large (BK/WE) full face photo of Dave w/chef's cap printed DAVE (YW/BK) 2.25
1C,20S,FS Doyle Freight, Saginaw, Michigan (F), (BK/WE) photo captioned 'Eleven of the Reasons why Dave Doyle needs your business' shows family in studio post, (BK/WE) 2.50
1C,20S,FS Empress Theatre, 9th St, N.W. w/Hebrew translation (F), Moishe Oysher in Overture to Glory with Helen Beverly, (BK/WE) photo of Oysher (B) (BE/WE) 5.00
1C,20S,FS Dr. Flinn's Dentists, 703 Canal St, New Orleans, LA, suspicious (BK/WE) photo of Dr. Flinn (F/B), (RD/YW/GD) 4.00
1C,20S,FS Gem Jewelry & Loan, Los Angeles 2, Calif, (BK/WE) photos of Bessie & Carl (B), (BE/WE) 2.00

1C,20S,FS The Ken, Boston, (BK/WE) photos of the Arnold Brothers at The Ken (B), Phone HAN. 0400 (S), BE/WE) 1.50

1C,20S,FS,FL Michener's, Bakersfield, Calif, shows entire staff in color photo across (O), waiters & waitresses 4.00

1C,20S,FS New York Telephone Company w/logo (F), three female operators working old-fashioned switchboard, (BK/WE) photo, (BE/WE) 3.50

1C,20S,FS O'Lexey's Restaurant, Ft Geor. G. Meade, MD, ad (B), Phone Crain 91-W-1 (S), smiling (BK/WE) photo of John H. O'Lexey (F), (BN/WE) 2.00

20C,20S,FS Photo Match Set [1956], San Francisco Scenes 10.00

10C,20S,FS,FL Photo Match of San Francisco 5.75

1C,20S,FS Lobby of Hotel Vendome, Evansville, Ind, w/PEP III and paw print (F), (BK/WE) photos of 'Pep' himself (a dog) (B) (BK/WE) 2.25

(above) Political stock cuts used in the 1950s

(above) Elect Willkie is a Lion Match Co. display with a pop-up of Willkie inside. Note the Lady Bird Johnson matchcover (lower right). Few First Ladies had matchbooks. At present, matchbooks are not being made for the White House and smoking is forbidden.

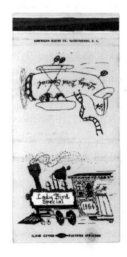

Political (National & Minor)

Political—A generous category of matchcovers with rich historical significance. Major or national categories include Presidential (over 500 known), Congressional, and Senatorial candidates and incumbents. Minor or local political matchcovers include Governor, School Council Member, Dog Catcher, Mayor, Comptroller, etc., where elected. Peripheral political matchcovers can include aircraft, yachts, homes, pets, wives, museums, vacation resorts or conjunctives (a local political coatailing a national figure). Candidates and campaigns are usually separated from incumbents and post-term matchcovers (i.e. restaurants owned by political personages after their term) are considered in the VIP category.

Political (Dated)

1C,P36,FS Truman/Barkley Inaugural Dinner, [1/19/49], photos of both (F), U.S. Seal (B), Mayflower Hotel 46.50

5C,30S,MS Inaugural Dinners, [1949/1953/1961/1965/1981] 15.00

1C,30S,FS Eisenhower-Nixon Inauguration [Jan. 20, 1953], Diamond Match Co 6.00

1C,30S,FS Kennedy-Johnson Inauguration [Jan. 20, 1961], Diamond Match Co. 8.00

1C,40S,FS Johnson-Humphrey Inauguration [Jan. 20, 1965], American Match Co., photos (F) 14.00

1FB,30S,FS The Inaugural Ball, January 20, 1969 (on B), Inauguration Seal (F), (WE) w/(GD) lettering 8.50

1C,30S,FS Nixon-Agnew Inauguration, foilite-type, Diamond Match Co., Type 1 [Jan. 20, 1969], 4 lines of printing (I) 7.00

1C,30S,FS Nixon-Agnew Inauguration, foilite-type, Diamond Match Co., Type 2 [Jan. 20, 1969], blank (I) 8.00

1C,30S,FS The Inaugural Ball, [January 20, 1969], Nixon/Agnew, Inaugural Seal (F) 6.50

1C,30S,FS Carter-Mondale Inauguration [1977] foilite-type, Diamond Match Co., Type 1 [1977], shiny plain finish 6.00

1C,30S,FS Carter-Mondale Inauguration [1977] foilite-type, Diamond Match Co., Type 2 [1977], pearltone finish 7.50

1FB,30S,BS Presidential Inauguration [1981] (B) Inauguration Seal on (B), (WE/GD) lettering, Universal Match Corp. 6.75

1FB,30S,BS 50th American Presidential Inauguration 1985, seal (F) 5.00

2C,30S,BS The President's Dinner, (1) [May 21, 1986] (2) [April 29, 1987], Washington, D.C. w/embossed (GD) logo of Reagan (F) (by Universal Match) 12.25

1FB,30S,BS 51st American Presidential Inauguration [1989], seal (F), foilite type 3.00

Political (Aircraft & Yachts)

1C,30S,FS H.H.H. under aircraft (B), Johnson Administration [1963-1969], American Match Co. 5.25

1C,30S,FS Aboard the Presidential Aircraft, Kennedy Administration [1961-1963], Universal Match Corp. 2.50

1C,30S,FS Air Force One, Kennedy Administration [1961-1963] 5.00

1C,30S,FS Air Force Two, Kennedy Administration [1961-1963] 2.50
1C,30S,FS Army One [   ] Kennedy Administration [1961-1963] 5.00
1FB,20S,FS Kennedy for president, (B/W) photo (B/F) 6.50
1C,30S,FS Marine One [   ] Kennedy Administration [1961-1963] 15.00
1C,30S,FS The Columbine, President's seal, Eisenhower Administration, (F), 4-prop plane w/
    flower (B) 6.00
1C,30S,FS The Columbine [   ], Eisenhower Administration, Presidential seal (F) 5.00
1C,30S,FS The Columbine [1955], Plane (S), no name, Lion Match Co., Eisenhower Adminis-
    tration 4.75
1C,30S,FS The Columbine [1954], D.D.E. across Presidential seal, Eisenhower Administration
    .... 6.00
1C,30S,FS The Columbine [1954], D.D.E. below Presidential seal, Eisenhower Administration
    .... 7.50
1C,30S,FS The Columbine [1954], Lt. Col. William G. Draper, Eisenhower's pilot 3.50
1FB,30S,FS The Columbine [   ], MDE (Mrs. Eisenhower's initials) (F), The Columbine (S),
    plane & flower (B) 12.00
1C,30S,FS Air Force One (GN) Jimmy Carter [1977-1981] Administration 1.75
1C,30S,FS Air Force One (WE) Jimmy Carter [1977-1981] Administration 3.00
1C,30S,FS Lady Bird Special plane, Johnson Administration [1963-1969] 3.00
1C,30S,FS LBJ under aircraft (B), Johnson Administration [1963-1969], Universal Match Corp.
    .... 5.00
1C,30S,BS Marine One, Presidential Helicopter 5.00
1C,30S,BS Air Force One, seal (F), plane (B) (WE) 3.00
1FB,30S,FS Aboard the Presidential Aircraft, seal (F) (BE) 4.00
1FB,30S,BS Aboard the Presidential Aircraft, Presidential Seal (on F), Aircraft (B) (WE) (GD)
    seal 5.00
1C,30S,BS Air Force One, Reagan Administration [1981-1989] 3.00
1C,30S,BS Air Force Two, Welcome Aboard, V. Presidential Seal, Reagan Administration [1981-
    1989] 1.75
1C,30S,BS Marine One, Reagan Administration [1981-1989] 5.00
1C,30S,FS The Spirit of '76, Aboard the Presidential Aircraft (LBE) 5.50
1C,20S,(old)BS Harry S. Truman's The Independence, Plane (F) 4.00
1C,20S,FS h.T.s. above aircraft, Truman Administration (BE/GD), Diamond Match Co., Type 1
    (BK) striker 5.00
1C,20S,FS h.T.s. above aircraft, Truman Administration (BE/GD), Diamond Match Co., Type 2
    reddish (BN) striker 7.25
1C,20S,FS The Independence, Truman Administration 20.00
1C,30S,BS Welcome Aboard Air Force Two (B), w/Vice Presidential seal (F) (Universal Match
    Corp.) 6.25
1C,30S,FS Honey Fitz [   ] Kennedy Administration [1961-1963] 7.50
1FB,20S,BS U.S.S. Sequoia, Presidential Yacht (BE/WE), seal (F) 7.00
1FB,30S,FS U.S.S. Sequoia, Presidential Yacht, Seal (F) (BE/WE) 6.00
1C,20S,FS USS Williamsburg, Presidential Yacht, Type 1 [1948], (GY) paper (I), (BK) 5.00
1C,20S,FS USS Williamsburg, Presidential Yacht, Type 2 [1949], (WE) paper (I), wide (BN)
    .... 5.00
1C,20S,FS USS Williamsburg, Presidential Yacht, Type 3 [1950], (WE) paper (I), narrow (BN)
    .... 5.00

Political (Presidential)

Bush
1C,30S,FS The President's Dinner, [June 12, 1990], George Bush [1989-1992] 20.00
1C,30S,FS The President's Dinner, [June 13, 1991], George Bush [1989-1992] 15.00

4C,20S,BS Bush for President Set (no photos) dated: [Nov 8, 1988] (RD,GN,BE,YW) .. 3.00
1C,30S,BS Bush for President, photo (F), dated: [Nov. 8, 1988] 2.25
1C,20S,BS George Bush for President [1988] (BE/WE) 3.00
1FB,20S,BS He Led Us To Victory In Kuwait, Re-elect Bush in [1992] (PE/WE) 2.25
50FB,30S,FS President George Bush & Vice President Dan Quayle [1989] Inauguration, Inaugural Seal (F) w/names, GD/WE 32.50
1C,30S,FS The White House, seal (B), George Bush Administration, Type 1 [1989], Made In Canada in manumark 6.00
1C,30S,FS The White House, seal (B), George Bush Administration, Type 2 [1990], has no Made In Canada in manumark 5.00

Carter

1C,20S,BS Carter Official Campaign, (B/W) photos (F) 2.75
1C,20S,FS Carter for President 4.00
1C,20S,BS Make it a Democratic Year, Jimmy Carter photo (F) 5.75
1C,20S,BS Jimmy Carter/Our 39th/President, (B/W) photo (F) 5.00
1C,30S,FS Jimmy Carter [1977-1981] Presidential Seal (B) 3.50
1C,20S,FS ReElect Jimmy Carter for President 1980 .... 2.00
1C,30S,BS Jimmy Carter Presidential, embossed White House (F), seal (B) 7.75

Eisenhower

1C,30S,FS M.D.E. (F) [1953], embossed portico (B) Eisenhower Administration 3.00
1C,30S,FS Sherman Adams [1953], The Assistant to the President, Eisenhower Administration 7.00
1C,30S,FS Col. Paul T. Carroll [1953], Eisenhower Administration, White House (F) 5.00
1C,30S,FS Camp David, Eisenhower term, White House (B), Eagle seal (F) 4.00
1C,30S,FS D.D.E. (F) [1954], seal (B) Eisenhower Administration, Diamond Match Co., manumark 9.00
1C,20S,FS Salute to Eisenhower Dinner, January 20, 1956, (B/W) photo (B), The Man of Peace 13.00
1FB,30S,FS Lt. Col. Wm. G. Draper, Air Force Aide to the President (Ike) (F), Columbine airplane (B) 6.25
1C,20S,FS DDE (Eisenhower) personal Golf, crossed clubs with initials (F), (WE/BE/GD) 15.75
1C,30S,FS Robert K. Gray [   ], Secretary to the Cabinet 3.00
1C,30S,FS James C. Haggerty [1953], Press Secretary of the President, Eisenhower Adminis-tration 7.00
1C,20S,FS I Like Ike(RD/WE/BE) (F), Eisenhower for President Club, Washington, D.C., (B) 5.00
1C,20S,FS I Like Ike, Eisenhower for President Club 1.25
1C,20S,FS I Like Ike, Jackson Birthplace G.O.P. 10.00
1C,20S,FS I Like Ike, photo (B), Keep Ike in the White House (S) (RD/WE/BE) 5.75
1C,20S,FS I Like Ike (F), Rhode Island Committee for Eisenhower/Nixon (B), (RD/WE/BE) 4.50
1C,30S,FS Mary Jane McCaffree [1953], White House (F) Eisenhower Administration 3.00
1C,30S,FS Eisenhower/Nixon (photo front) 1953-1957, Compliments of the PRESIDENTIAL ELECTORS * Washington, D.C. Tuesday, January 20, 1953 .... 7.00
1C,20S,FS In Ohio We Like Ike 3.00
1C,20S,FS Ohio Likes Ike (F/B), Ike & Dick (S) (RD/WE) 5.00
1C,30S,FS Dwight D. Eisenhower (F) [1953], seal (B) 3.50
1C,30S,FS Maxwell M. Rabb [1953], White House (F) Eisenhower Administration 3.00
1C,30S,FS R.L.S. (F) [1953], sketch of White House, Eisenhower Administration 3.00
1C,20S,FS Salute to Eisenhower Dinner, Jan. 20, 1956 .... 5.00
1C,30S,FS Thomas E. Stephens [1953], Special Counsel to the President, Eisenhower Admin-istration 3.00

1C,20S,FS Stick with IKE (Sticky Back) For peace and Prosperity (S), Copyright 1955 - Atlas Advertising Co., Brookline, Mass. (RD/WE/BE) 8.00
1C,20S,FS I Still Like Ike, (F) only (RD/WE) 5.75
1C,20S,FS State Game Lodge, Summer White House Coolidge-1927, Eisenhower-1953 .. 6.75
1C,20S,FS,WG State Game Lodge, Summer White House Pres. Coolidge 1927, Pres Eisenhower 1953, Hermosa, S. Dak 9.00
1C,20S,FS Los Angeles Times General Dwight D. Eisenhower 4.00
1C,20S,FS I Like Ike, Vote and Save America 4.00
1C,20S,FS We Like Ike! map of New York w/state name (F/B), New York State (S), display of Eisenhower (I), (RD/WE/BE) 7.00
1C,20S,BS We're Fore 'Ike', Suits U.S.—To a 'T', photo, dated 1956 (B) 4.75
1C,20S,BS We're Fore Ike and Dick, (B/W) photo of Ike (B), dated 1956, Matchless Partners (I) 11.75
1C,30S,FS Dwight D. Eisenhower White House, Presidential seal (B), white house w/name (F), tape mark (I) 12.00

Ford

1C,30S,BS Gerald R. Ford, personal, signature on footer, seal (F) 3.00
1FB,30S,BS Gerald R. Ford (DBE) White House (B), Seal (F) 5.00
10C,20S,BS Gerald R. Ford, President of the United States, Filigree 2.50
1C,30S,BS The President and Mrs. Ford, (LBE) rare as never issued, White House, seal (F), never distributed 20.00
1FB,30S,BS The President & Mrs. Ford, White House (B) (BE) satin 4.00
1C,30S,FS The President and Mrs. Ford, (GD/BE) silktone 6.00
4FB,30S,BS Gerald R. Ford Presidential Museum Sleeve, each w/embossed White House (F) & name, presidential seal (B) 5.00
1C,30S,FS Gerald R. Ford Presidential seal (B) 1.00
1C,30S,FS Gerald R. Ford, (GD/BE) silktone Maryland Match Co 2.25
1C,30S,FS Gerald R. Ford (F), Reproduction G. R. Ford Museum, 1983 .... 2.25
4FB,30S,FS Gerald R. Ford (F), Reproduction G. R. Ford Museum, 1983, in presentation sleeve 6.25
1FB,30S,BS The President & Mrs. Ford, tan, White House (B) 6.25
1FB,30S,BS Gerald R. Ford (White House (F), Seal (B)) (WE) Universal Match Corp., St. Louis 5.00

Hoover

1C,20S,FS Hoover for President [1928], Hoover and Curtis 35.00

Kennedy

1C,30S,FS John F. Kennedy [1961-1963] (SR/BK) 2.50
1C,20S,FS Kennedy for President, side photo (F/B) 10.00
1C,20S,FS Kennedy for President, Johnson for VP, photo of each 18.00
1C,20S,FS Kennedy for President, photo (F), Johnson for Vice President, photo (B), (RD/WE/BE) 4.00
1C,30S,FS Leadership in the 60's, Kennedy & Johnson, January 20, 1961, both photos (F) 5.50
1C,30S,FS John F. Kennedy [1961-1963] (F), Presidential seal (B) 5.50
1C,30S,FS The President's House, Kennedy Administration [1961-1963] 2.00
4FB,30S,FS John F. Kennedy [1961-1963], Presidential Museum & Library, embossed White House (F), Presidential Seal (B) 7.00

1C,20S,FS Kennedy for President (F/B), Vote Democratic (S), (RD/WE/BE) 4.00
1C,20S,FS Kennedy for President, Johnson for V. President. 3.00
1C,30S,FS John F. Kennedy White House, seal (B), White House (F) 10.25

Johnson

1C,30S,BS Leadership in the 60's, photo JFK & LBJ (F), Washington, D.C., January 20, 1961 w/
    seal (B) (Diamond Match Co.) 5.00
1C,20S LBJ for the USA HHH, both photo (F), Vote Democratic (S) 4.00
1C,30S,FS Lady Bird Special train Johnson Administration [1963-1969] 3.00
1C,20S,FS LBJ for the USA (photo on F), Vote Democratic (RD/WE/BE) 3.25
1C,20S,FS LBJ for the USA, Vote Democratic 2.50

Nixon

8C,40S,FS Richard M. Nixon Series No. 1 thru 8, RMS made, photo (F), historical note (B) 36.00
1C,30S,FS Spiro T. Agnew, January 18, 1973, Nixon Administration [1969-1974], Universal
    Match Corp 3.00
1C,30S,BS Spiro Agnew, [January 18, 1973], VP seal (F) 3.00
5C,20S,FS Superior set of Capitol themes - NIXON for PRESIDENT (F), Nixon — '68 (S),
    Superior Match Co., Chicago, U.S.A. 5.75
1C,20S,FS Nixon for President, Flag & SOL (B), Nixon— '68 (S) 4.50
1C,20S,FS Nixon for President/Vote Dick Nixon for President (B/W photo (F/B) (Universal
    Match Corp., Washington, D.C.) 5.00
1C,20S,FS Nixon/Lodge (B/W) (F) Vote Republican Nov. 8th 1960 'The Matchless Ticket'
    (Universal Match Corp. Washington, D.C.) 9.25
1C,20S,FS Nixon/Lodge, Experience counts! (S) (RD/WE/BE) 5.25
1C,20S,FS NIXON LODGE, 'The Matchless Ticket', Nov. 8, 1960, photo (F) 6.75
1C,20S,FS Nixon for President (F/B) w/photo, 'The Matchless Man' (S) (RD/WE/BE) . 6.00
1C,20S,FS Nixon for President, The Matchless Man, AFL-CIO 24122 .... 4.50
1C,20S,FS Nixon for President, The Matchless Man, Union Label 3.25
1C,30S,FS Nixon Agnew (F) only, (RD) w/(WE) lettering, elephant (B) 3.25
10C,20S,FS Nixon Agnew 1968 (F), Joe Blatchford for U.S. Congress, San Pedro, CAlif (B) 15.00
1FB,20S,FS Nixon Now, large lettering (BE/RD) (F/B) 5.00
1FB,20S,FS President Nixon, Now more than ever. (F/B) (RD/WE/BE) 6.50
1C,30S,FS Richard M. Nixon [1969-1974] (F), Presidential seal (B) 5.00
1C,30S,FS President Richard M. Nixon 5.00
1C,20S,FS Nixon Now [1972], Financial Committee for Re-Elect Pres. 2.00
1C,20S,FS Nixon's, Whittier, California (F), Nixon's, Complete Market, Coffee Shop, Drive-in
    Restaurants 5.00
4FB,30S,FS from San Clemente Inn, 3 say Home of the Western White Hous 6.00
1C,20S,FS Nixon's the One!, Feeley & Wheeler Inc. 3.50
1C,20S,FS Nixon's the One, For President 2.00
1C,20S,FS Nixon's the One!, Van's Advertising 2.00
1C,20S,FS Nixon's The One, large (RD) lettering (F), This Time Vote Like Your Whole World
    Depended On It (I) 8.00
1C,20S,FS Nixon's The One! (F) small (RD) lettering (Diamond Match Co.) 5.25
1C,30S,FS The Western White House, Nixon Administration [1969-1974], Union Made manumark
    .... 2.50
1C,30S,FS Richard M. Nixon, White House, seal (B) 5.75
1C,20S,FS Nixon/Lodge, Experience counts! (S),(RD/WE/BE) 5.50
1C,20S,FS Nixon/Lodge, photos of both (F), Vote Republican, Nov. 8th, 1960 (B), 'The Matchless
    Ticket' (S) (RD/WE/BE) 6.50

Reagan

1C,30S,FS CA [   ], seal (B), Ronald Reagan signature 1.00
1C,30S,BS The President's Dinner, May 21, 1986, Universal Match Corp. 5.25
1C,30S,BS The President's Dinner, April 29, 1987 .... 5.00
1C,30S,BS The President's Dinner, [May 11, 1988], Washington, D.C., Reagan likeness (F) 7.25
1C,20S,BS Reagan/Bush '84 (BE/WE/RD) 4.25
1C,20S,BS Reagan Bush '84 (F/B/S) (RD/WE/BE) 2.50
1C,30S,BS Reagan/Bush - Leadership 80 (F) United Airlines logo (B) (Columbia Match Co.,
    Mentor, OH 44060) 4.00
1C,30S,BS Reagan/Bush Leadership 1980, United Airlines 6.00
1C,30S,BS Reagan/Bush 1984 .... 2.50
1C,30S,BS Camp David, (WE) Reagan Administration [1981-1989] 3.00
6FB,30S Dixon's Favorite Son, Ronald Reagan, bank matchbook, cellopack (TN/BN) 3.25
1FB,30S Reagan's 50th American Presidential Inaugural, 1985 .... 5.00
1C,30S,BS Ronald Wilson Reagan above striker, official White House 4.00
1C,30S,BS Ronald Wilson Reagan above striker, official White House, autographed by president,
    only 50 known 250.00
1C,20S,BS Reagan/Bush 84 (RD,WE,BE) 3.25
1C,30S,BS Ronald Wilson Reagan White House, Presidential Seal (B), White House embossed
    (F) 6.00

Rockefeller

1C,30S Nelson A. Rockefeller (signature on footer), VP, Capitol (B) 15.00
1C,20S,FS Rockefeller [1964], Vote Rockefeller March 10th 3.00
1FB,30S Nelson Rockefeller, Capitol (B), VP seal (F) 3.00

Roosevelt (Franklin D.)

1C,20S,FS Blair-Lee House [1942], Roosevelt Administration [1933-1945] Diamond Match Co.
    .... 3.00
1C,30S,FS Churchill & Roosevelt, Canadian Tax 3/10 cent, Bookmatch (manumark), rare 22.00
1C,20S Roosevelt and Humanity (B) w/photo, Retain James M. Slattery, U.S. Senator (F), (RD/
    WE/BE) 12.50
1FB,20S,FS Franklin D. Roosevelt [1933-1945] personal match book (not museum issue), (DBE/
    GD) initials woven into sale of sail boat (F) 25.00
1C,20S,FS FDRs initials creating the sail of a sailboat, (I) exact replica of his match book 3.50
6FB,20S,BS President Roosevelt's Personal Book Matches, show FDR on sleeve, w/exact
    replica of his matches, disclaimer (I) 6.25
1C,20S,FS FDR [   ] Stolen from the White House, Roosevelt Administration [1933-1945] 5.00
1C,20S,FS Roosevelt [1936], United Behind the President 11.00
1C,30S,FS Churchill & Roosevelt [1942] 5.00

Truman

1C,20S,FS Blair-Lee House [1949], Truman Administration, Dept. of State seal (F) 3.00
1FB,20S,FS HTS, personal matchbook of Harry S. Truman (BE) 32.00
1C,20S,FS HTS, Truman Administration, letters in (WE) oval (F) 15.00
1C,20S,FS HTS, Truman Administration, intertwined raised lettering (F) 18.00
1C,20S,FS President's House (GD/BE), Truman Administration, Diamond Match Co. ... 3.50
1C,20S,FS President's House (GD/RD), Truman Administration, Diamond Match Co. 3.50

1C,20S,FS President's House (GD/WE), Truman Administration, Diamond Match Co. .. 3.50
1C,20S,FS Stolen from Harry S. Truman, (GD/RD) 3.50
1C,20S,FS Swiped from Harry S. Truman, Same signature not diagonal, (GD/RD) 4.00
1C,20S,FS Swiped from Harry S. Truman, Same signature not diagonal, (GD/WE) 4.00
1C,20S,FS Swiped from Harry S. Truman, (GD/WE) 4.00
1C,20S,FS Swiped from Harry S. Truman, (RD/WE) Universal Match Corp. 4.00
1C,20S,FS Swiped from Harry S. Truman, (SR/BE) 3.50
1C,20S,FS Swiped from Harry S. Truman, (WE/RD) Universal Match Corp. 4.00
1C,20S,FS Swiped from Harry S. Truman, (WE/BE) Universal Match Corp. 4.00
1C,30S,FS,FL The White House [1949], Truman Administration, Diamond Match Co. 3.00

Presidential Candidates

1C,20S,FS Dewey [1948] in '48, photo (F) 15.00
1FB,20S,BS Vote Bob Dole, President 1988, elephants (S) (BN/WE) 2.00
1C,20S,BS Vote Bob Dole President 1988, Republican (WE) 2.00
1C,30S,FS Mike Dukakis for President, Vote Nov. 8, 1988 .... 3.50
1C,20S,FS Goldwater in '64 (B/W) photo (F/B) (Universal Match Corp., Washington, D.C.) 2.50
1C,20S,FS Goldwater for President 1964 .... 2.50
1C,20S,FS Goldwater in '64 for President 3.00
1C,20S,FS GOP 1964, Goldwater for President 3.00
1FB,20S,FS Goldwater in '64, photo (F), Make a Note to Vote for ... (B),(RD/WE/BE) 2.00
1FB,20S,FS Goldwater in '64 (GD/BK) metallic, photo of Goldwater (F/B) 2.50
1C,20S,FS Goldwater—'64, White House picture (B) 2.50
1FB,20S,FS Goldwater—'64 (S), color photo (F), White House (he was dreaming) (B) .. 4.50
1C,20S,FS Goldwater—'64, color photo (F), White House (B) 6.25
1C,20S,FS,FL Desert Fashions Goldwaters, Phoenix & Prescott 15.00
1C,20S,FS Goldwater for President 2.50
1B GOParty 1964 (F), foil label, small, Made in Sweden 5.25
2C,20S,FS GOParty 1964, Goldwater for President, (B/W) photo, candidate wearing glasses (B)
    (Aldine Co., L.A., Calif.) 8.00
1C,20S,FS Goldwater for President, photo (F), Liberty Bell (B) 4.25
1FB,20S,FS Goldwater in '64, (BK/WE) photo (F), Make A Note To Vote for ... (B), DBE/RD/
    WE) 4.00
1FB,20S,FS Goldwater in '64, photo (F/B) (GD) metallic 3.50
1FB,20S,FS Goldwater for President, photo (F) 2.00
1C,30S,BS Barry Goldwater, Jr, signature (F), Nat'l seal (B) (BE) 1.00
1C,20S,FS Goldwater for President, photo (B), Why Not Victory? (S) 4.50
1C,30S,FS Goldwater for President 1964, Miller for VP 1964, both photos 7.50
1C,30S,FS Goldwater for President (F), Goldwater, Miller (B) (DBE) (Aldine Co., L.A. Calif)
    .... 5.00
1C,30S,FS Goldwater for President Goldwater/Miller, no manu 2.50
1C,30S,FS Goldwater for President (F), Goldwater Miller (B), DBE 3.00
1FB,40S 1972 G.O.P. Nat'l Convention Hq, Royal Inn Hotel—(but it never happened there!), rare
    .... 10.50
1C,20S,FS Humphrey for President, HHH, photo (F) 10.25
1C,20S,FS HHH for President 2.00
1C,20S,FS Kefauver for President, A Great American 3.00
1FB,20S,FS Estes Kefauver for President (B/W) photo (F), seal w/donkey (B), Lion Match Co.
    .... 2.50
1FB,20S,FS Adlie Stevenson (B/W) photo (F), WELCOME DELEGATES (B) (Match Corp.
    of America) 3.50
1C,20S,FS I Like McCarthy and his Methods (F), I am with Joe McCarthy in his fight against
    Treason and Dishonor (B) 8.00

1C,30S,FS McGovern - President '72, Right From The Start! 3.00
1C,20S,FS Rockefeller for President, Vote March 10th (F), photo of Rocky (B) 6.00
1FB,20S,FS Vote for Bob Taft for President, photo (B), Vote Republican (S) 7.75
1C,20S,FS WALLACE in '68, photo (F) 5.00
1FB,20S America Needs Wallace!, photo (F), Stand up for America!, Wallace for President (F),
    Wallace in '68 (S) 6.25
1C,20S Wallace in '68, Stop Red Trade (S) 5.00
1C,20S,FS Wallace in '68, Stand Up For America! 2.50
1C,20S,FS Wallace in '68, Support Your Local Police 2.50
1C,20S Wallace in '72 (B/W) photo (F), Stop Red Trade (S), Wallace Stands Up For
    America....(B), Monarch Match San Jose, Calif 7.50
1C,20S Stand Up for Alabama WALLACE (F), Confederate Flag (B) (Superior Match Co.,
    Chicago, U.S.A.) 4.75
1C,20S C.J. Wallace photo (F), American Family Insurance ad (B) 2.00
1C,20S Elect Geo. Wallace, Constitutional Government (B), photo (F) 4.00
1C,20S,FS Governor Wallace w/photo (F), Wallace (S), Stand-Up for Alabama (B), (RD/WE/
    BE) 4.50
1C,20S,FS Wallace, Stand-Up for America, photo of Governor Wallace (F), Elect Geo. Wallace
    .... 5.00
1C,20S Wallace 'Wah-Wah' Jones for Congress, photo (B) 5.00
1PQ Pull for Willkie, Pullmatch 8.00
1C,20S,FS Win with Wendell Willkie, display match 14.00
1FB,20S,FS Win with Willkie, vote for Jobs Work, not charity, different photo of Willkie (F/B),
    Columbia Match Co 17.50
1FB,20S,FS Wendell Willkie, No Third Term-ites, Let's Go! (B), (B/W) photo (F) 16.25
1C,20S,FS Elect Willkie (popup), Preserve Your Freedom 11.50
1PQ Wendell Willkie [1940], Pull for Willkie, Pullmatch 14.00
1PQ Pull for Willkie, for President, Wendell Willkie, photo (F), (RD/WE/BE) book-form pull quick
    .... 24.50

Presidential   (Miscellaneous)

1FB,20S,FS The President's House (F), all (WE) 3.50
36C,30S,FS Diamond Set #2 [1972], Nixon is last one 6.00
36?C,30S,FS Diamond Set #1 [1972]... 6.00
37C,30S,BS Diamond Set #3 [1975], Ford is last one 4.00
40C,30S,BS Diamond Set #4 [1992], Bush is last one 4.00
16C,20S,FS Maryland Set #1 [1960], Presidents 8.50
1C,20S,BS Presidential seal on F, Blair House/The president's guest House (B)
    (BE)(BS)(Universal Match Co., Washington, D.C.) 9.25
1FB,20S President's House w/Seal (F), (GD/RD) 2.25
1FB,30S,FS The President's House (F), all (WE) 3.00
1C,20S,FS President's House, seal (F) (BE) 2.75
1C,20S,BS Blair House/The President's Guest House (B), Seal of Department of State (F) 3.00
1FB,20S President's House w/Seal (F), (GD/WE) 2.00
31C,20S Supermarket Presidential Set, 1941, including 'Old Hickory' for #7 .... 26.25
32C,20S,FS Diamond Set #1, numbered, Type 1 [1941] wide striker, Stonewall Jackson error
    included 45.00
32C,20S,FS Diamond Set #1, numbered, Type 1 [1941] wide striker, John Q. Adams error, John
    Adams picture/J. Q. Adams data 48.00
32C,20S,FS Diamond Set #1, numbered, Type 1 [1941] wide striker, Woodrow Wilson error, May
    6 1917 instead of Apr. 17 1917 .... 50.00
32C,20S,FS Diamond Set #1, numbered, Type 2 [1942] narrow striker 50.00
1FB,30S Seal of the President (F), White House (B), (WE), (GD) lettering 3.00
4C,20S,FS Chicago Match Co. Liberty Set, G. Washington, Our Capitol, Statue of Liberty, A.
    Lincoln, ad: Vapo-Swat Vapo-Tab 5.00

16C,20S,FS Maryland Match Co. President Set (2 presidents on each) 4.25
1C,30S,FS Camp David, Presidential Seal (F) 6.00
1C,20S,FS National Capital Democratic Club, emblem (F/B) 2.00

Gubernatorial (General)

1C,20S,BS Spiro T. Agnew for Governor/on Nov.8 AGNEW on (F), Ted Agnew is your kind of
    man for Governor! (B) ad: Auth: Tilton H. Dobbin, Treas. 7.00
1C,20S,FS MT [   ], The Executive Mansion, Forrest Anderson 1.00
1C,30S,FS WV [   ], seal (F), William Wallace Barron 1.00
1C,30S,FS IN [   ], The Governor's Residence, Otis R. Bowen 1.00
1FB,30S Christopher S. Boyd, State seal MO (B), Gov. Mansion (F) 2.00
1C,40S,FS IN [   ], Governor's Mansion, Roger Branigin 1.00
1C,20S,FS Vote for Governor Brown, Keep California First! (S), photo (B/F) 2.00
1C,20S,FS Pat Brown, Governor, Glenn M. Anderson, Lt. Governor, both photo (F/B) ... 2.25
1C,20S,FS Vote for Governor Brown, 'A Matchless Record' same photo (F/B) 2.25
1C,20S,FS Vote for Governor Brown, 'A Matchless Record' (B/W) photo (B/F), Keep California
    First! (I) 3.25
1C,30S,FS CO [   ], Colorado Executive Residence, blank (I) 1.00
1C,30S,FS CO [1963], Colorado Executive Residence, Aristocrat trademark (I) 1.00
1C,30S Governor's Mansion Gov. and Mrs. Jimmie H. Davis (F), State of Louisiana (B) 2.00
1C,30S,FS Governor of Mississippi, Cliff Finch, Autograph (I), Uniglo 3.00
1C,30S,FS OK [   ], The Executive Mansion, foilite, David Hall 1.00
1C,20S Richard J. Hughes, re-elect Governor, dated Nov. 2, 1965 .... 3.00
1C,30S,BS IL [   ], Executive Mansion, seal (B), Superior 1.00
ÍC,30S,BS KS [   ], The Executive Mansion, seal (B) 1.00
1C,30S,BS KY [   ], Governor's Office, seal (B), Superior 6.00
1C,20S,FS KY [   ], Governor's Mansion, seal (B) 1.00
1FB,30S Governor's Mansion, Jackson MS 1.50
1C,30S,BS MS [1975], picture (F), Opening Ceremonies 1.25
1C,30S,FS Office of the Governor of Mississippi, signature (I) 1.25
1C,30S,FS Arch A. Moore, Jr., Governor, West Virginia State Seal (B) 3.00
1C,30S,FS WV [   ], Arch A. Moore, Jr., Governor, matchorama 1.00
1C,30S,BS,RAMA WV [   ], Arch A. Moore, Jr., Governor 1.00
1C,30S,FS,CA WV [   ], Arch A. Moore, Jr., Governor 2.00
1FB,30S Arch & Shelley Moore, WV seal (B), state house (F) 2.00
1C,30S The Governor's Mansion (F), N.C. State Seal (B) 2.00
1C,30S,BS OK [   ], George Nigh (I), The Governor's Mansion 1.00
1C,30S,BS OK [   ], George Nigh, Caring and Sharing 1.00
1C,30S,BS OK [1982], George Nigh, Diamond Jubilee 1907-1982 .... 1.00
1C,30S,FS Nixon for Governor (F) (DBE) 6.25
1C,30S,FS NC [   ], The Governor's Office, seal (B) 2.00
1C,20S,FS PA [   ], Executive Mansion, (GD/BE) 2 line Diamond manumark 1.00
1C,20S,FS PA [   ], Executive Mansion, (GD/BE) 1 line Diamond manumark 1.00
1C,20S,FS PA [   ], Executive Mansion, (BE/GY) Diamond 1.00
1C,20S,FS Reagan for Governor, photo (F), For Common Sense Answers to Ca Problems ....
    .... 6.50
1C,30S,FS Gov. Ronald Reagan, Gov. of the State of California 5.00
1C,20S,FS Reagan for Governor, Vote Nov. 8, 1966 (S), photo (F) 4.00
1C,20S,FS Reagan for Governor, Vote Republican (S), photo (F) 4.00
1C,20S,FS Ronald Reagan for Governor, The Taxpayer's Choice 3.75
1C,20S,FS Reagan for Governor, photo (F) 5.50
5C,20S,FS Ronald Reagan for California's Governor, Nov. 8. 1966, color set 10.00
5C,20S,FS Ronald Reagan for California's Governor, Nov. 8. 1970, color set 5.00
1C,30S,BS Governor and Mrs. John D. Rockefeller IV (B), Governor's Mansion (F),GD 5.00

1C,20S,FS WA [   ], seal (F), Albert Rosellini (B) 1.00
1C,20S Enjoy WASHINGTON STATE (on B) Allen D. Rosellins, GOVERNOR (F) w/(B/W)
    photo 2.25
1C,20S Vote for Sawyer, Democrat for Governor, Nevada, photo (F) 3.00
1C,20S Re-elect Wm G. Stratton, A Good Governor, photo (F) 3.00
1C,30S,FS AL [   ], Office of the Governor, George Wallace 2.00
1C,30S,BS AL [   ], Office of the Governor, George Wallace, blank (I) 2.00
1C,30S,BS AL [   ], Office of the Governor, George Wallace, 2 line Superior manumark (I) 2.00
1FB,20S Governor of Washington State, photo (F) 2.00
1C,30S,FS IN [   ], seal on (B), Edgar D. Whitcomb (F) 2.00
1FB,30S,FS Governor's Mansion, Jackson, Mississippi, William Winter, home (F), seal (B) 2.00
1FB,30S,BS William Winter, Governor, State of Mississippi 2.25
1C,30S,FS WV [   ], West Virginia Governor's Mansion, cameo 2.00
1C,20S,FS Governors' Conference [1960], Montana's Glacier N.P. 2.00
13C,RF,FS Southern Governors' Conference [1965] 20.00
1C,20S,FS Republican Governors' Conference [1969], Lexington 2.00
1C,30S,FS Southern Governors' Conference [1972] 1.00
1C,20S,BS Midwest Governors' Conference [1976] 1.00

Senatorial

1C,20S,FS U.S. Congressman Alphonzo Bell, House of Representatives (F), PE 2.00
1C,20S Re-elect Styles Bridges, US Senator, photo (F) 8.50
1C,20S,FS United States Capitol/ The Restaurant of the United States Senate, Washington,
    D.C.(Diamond Match Co.) 2.50
30C,30S,MS Stock U.S. Congressional w/various Congressmen & Senator's names (I) (some
    photos) 7.00
1C,30S,FS Official Capitol, Senator Barry Goldwater - Arizona (I) 4.75
1C,20S Re-Elect US Senator Ernest Gruening, photo (B) 2.00
1C,20S Compliments of Keith Kelly Your State Senator, photo (B) 1.50
1C,30S,FS Sen. George Murphy 3.00
1C,20S,FS George Murphy for U.S. Senator (F), California needs this great American in the
    United States Senate (B)(no manumark) 3.50
1C,30S Official Capitol, Claiborne Pell, US Senator RI (I) 1.00
1C,20S,BS Senator Percy '84, U.S. Senator (DBE/WE) 3.75
1FB,20S Pierre Salinger for U.S. Senator (F&B), Democrat (S) (Made in U.S.A.) (RD/WE/BE)
    .... 3.25
1C,20S,FS Leverett Saltonstall, US Senator Mass (DBE) 2.50
1C,20S,FS Elect Hugh Scott for U.S. Senator, Member of Congress since 1941, photo (F) 2.00
1C,20S,FS Re-elect Stuart Symington, US Senator, photo (F) 2.50
1C,20S,FS Elect Democrat Waggoner Carr, U.S. Senator, photo (B) 3.25
1C,30S,BS Official Capitol, Milton R. Young, US Senator, photo (I) 2.75
1C,20S,FS The Restaurant of the United States Senate/Washington D.C. (on B), U.S. Capitol
    (on F) 1.25
1C,30S US Senate Restaurant, Washington, DC 5.00

Political (Minor, Etc.)

8C,30S,FS National Political, assorted 12.00
9C,20S,MS Minor Political (dated) 2.50
12C,30S,FS National Political, assorted 14.00
1C,30S,FS Congressman Bill Ayres, photo (I) (stock) 1.50

1C,20S,FS Stick with Bender, Sticky-Back, Copyright 1955, Atlas Advertising Co., Brookline, Mass (manumark) 2.50
1C,30S,FS Congressional, w/Garry Brown, 3rd District, Michigan (I) (photo) (stock) 3.00
1C,30S,FS Re-Elect ALAN CRANSTON our State Controller, photo (F) 4.00
1C,20S,FS Re-elect Thomas D'Alesandro, Jr. for Mayor, photo (B) 1.50
1FB,20S,FS Go Onward Pennsylvanians! with Duff-Fine, U.S. Seante & Governor (YW/WE/ BE) 2.00
1C,30S,BS CT [1975], Inaugural Ball, Ella Grasso 1.00
1C,30S,BS Official Capitol, Wayne L. Hays, 18th Dist Ohio (I) 2.00
1C,20S We Want Hoffman, New Jersey, photo in star (F) 3.00
1C,20S,BS U.S. Hostages in Iran Released, January 20, 1981 .... 5.50
1C,30S,BS,Rama Official US Congress, Congressman Walter B. Jones 2.50
1C,20S JR for President 3.75
1FB,20S,FS Re-Elect Mayor La Guardia, photo (F), City Fusion Party Park Central Hotel (S), shamrock (B) 4.25
1C,30S,Rama Official US Congress, Season's Greetings from Tom Lane 2.75
1C,30S,FS NV [   ], Paul Laxalt & seal (F), American 1.00
1C,30S,BS Rama Official US Congress, Congressman Lucien N. Nedzi 3.00
1C,30S,FS Official Capitol, James G. O'Hara, 7th Dist Michigan (I) 3.00
1C,20S,FL Pat Paulsen for President Committee (I), Pat (F),YW 4.00
1C,20S,FS George W. Roberts for Attorney General, photo (F) 3.25
1C,30S,FS Official Capitol, H. Allen Smith, 20th Cong Dist (I ....) 2.25
1C,30S,FS Re-Elect Harley Staggers, Jr. to Congress (S) ...Working for You. (JRB Assoc. Grafton, WV) 8.25
1FB,20S,FS Stick with Utt, Sticky Back, copyright 1955 .... 6.75
1C,30S,BS Voice of America, seal (F), USIA seal (B), Broadcasting since 1942 .... 1.75
1FB,20S,FS FAKE 'Vote for Jimmy' (Walker) dated November 1925, made as a promotion, photo (B/F) 2.50
1C,20S,BS American Right of Way Association., Boston, Mass, [May 21-26,1967] 2.50

Political (Foreign)

42C,20S,FS Organization of African Unity [1974], set 35.00
3C,40S,BS Andi & Fergi, dated: 23 July, 1986 .... 5.25
1C,20S,FS Inauguracao da Embaixada Dos Estados Unidos Da America, Brasilia, Abril 1961, Embassy seal (F) 2.75
1C,20S,FS U.S. Embassy in Brazil, Dated April 1961 .... 3.25
1C,20S,FS H.M. The King's Silver Jubilee, 1935 .... 7.50
1C,20S,FS Foreign Head of State Forbes Burnham of Guyana, photo (F), National Flag of Guyana (B ....) 3.25
1C,20S,FS Foreign Head of State Charles de Gaulle, photo (F), Strike one in support of the Free French, etc. (B) 3.25
1FB,24S L.M. le Roi Hassan II personal matchbook (RD/GD) 5.25
1FB,24S L.M. le Roi Hassan II personal matchbook (BE/GD) 5.25
1C,30-SS, FS,Tel Aviv Israel 5.00
1C,20S,FS Foreign Head of State T.H. Maharaja & Maharani of Kapurthala, (B/W) photo of both (F), Jagatjit Palace Kapurthala (B) 3.25
1C,20S,FS Foreign Head of State of Republique du Mali, President Modibo Keita, (B/W) photo (B), state crest (F), Un Peuple-Un But-Une Foi (S) 3.25
1C,30S Embassy Of Kuwait, Moscow (GD/WE) 5.25
1C,20S,FS Foreign Head of State of the Republic of Dahomey, President Hubert Maga, (B/W) photo (B), state flag (F), Fraternite-Justice-Travail (S) 3.25
1C,20S,BS Foreign Head of State, shows Benito Mussolini and Comm. G. Dieni in (B/W) photo (B), M.S.I. Commendatore G. Dieni, 209 Dante & telephone number (F) 3.25

1C,20S,FS Foreign Head of State of Niger, no name, (B/W) photo of president (B), state flag (F), Fraternite-Travail-Progres (S) 3.25
1C,20S,FS Foreign Head of State of Ghana, Dr. Kwame Nkrumah, (B/W) photo (B), state crest (F), Ghana's First President.. 3.25
1C,20S,FS Foreign Head of State President Quirino, The Champion of Clean, Honest and Just Government, Philippines, (B/W) photo (F) 3.25
1 Pocket Box, Royal Embassy of Saudi Arabia, Washington, DC 2.00
10C,20S,FS Foreign political, Made in Spain, assorted.. 2.50
1C,20S,FS Foreign Head of State of the Dominican Republic, Generalismo R.L. Trujillo, (B/W) photo (F), flags (B) w/Yate 'Ramfis'.. 3.50
1C,30S,BS Foreign Head of State of Liberia, President William V.S. Tubman, (B/W) photo (B), state crest (F), Africa's Oldest Republic (S) 3.50
10C,20S,MS Non US Political, 5 w/photos, 1 woman.. 2.50

Port Authority (New York)

Port Authority—A series of matchcovers which promoted use of various ways of access into New York City. First issued in the mid 1930s, these matchcovers reportedly were put out one every 30 days, with a yearly distribution of over one million. Most are colorful full lengths, some having coupon offers on the inside or lists of various Port Authority facilities. There is a complicated numbering system on the inside of this series which has yet to be figured out, as the Port Authority has no records of these listings.

1C,20S,FS,FL Long Islanders go to Football Games via Staten Island............................ 3.50
1C,20S,FS,FL I'm Keeping My Speed Down! w/trucker & soldier................................... 2.50
1C,20S,FS,FL Hicksville Airpark 3.25
1C,20S,FS,FL Keep Tires properly Inflated 3.00
1C,20S,FS,FL Time Savers—Free Maps of Metro Area, w/sea gull, etc. 4.25
1C,20S,FS,FL Avoid Philadelphia Traffic, Chester/Bridgeport Ferry 3.00
1C,20S,FS,FL Between NY-NJ, Any Season Any Hour (4 Minute Crossings)................. 3.00
1C,20S,FS,FL (4 Minute Crossings) Save Time for Fun!, w/woman & beach hat............ 3.00
1C,20S,FS,FL Use the Short Route . . Save Gas (w/map).. 5.00
1C,20S,FS,FL Keep Tires Properly Inflated 71057 .... 3.75
1C,20S,FS,FL Wonder.. 71956 .... 4.00
1C,20S,FS,FL Let's Go and See 60088 .... 2.75
2C,20S,FS,FL Use the 4 minute Crossings-Use the Official World's Fair.. 51526............ 8.00
5C,20S,FS,FL Bayonne Bridge-George Washington Bridge-Goethals Bridge-Holland Tunnel-Outerbridge Crossing 36343 [1936] 22.50
1C,20S,FS,FL Don't Mark Time-Four minute crossings-Lincoln Tunnel-On time with time to spare 47223 .... 3.75
1C,20S,FS,FL Be Time Thrifty-See Port Authority Exhibit 52486 .... 3.75
1C,20S,FS,FL George Washington Bridge 32653 .... 4.50
1C,20S,FS,FL Wonder if Pop.. 71957 .... 3.50
1C,20S,FS,FL Between NY NJ..-By Pass Heavy Traffic.. 53655 .... 4.50
1C,20S,FS,FL Bayonne Bridge 35838 .... 3.50
1C,20S,FS,FL Check Your Tires Now-Keep 'Em Recapped 70178 .... 3.50
1C,20S,FS,FL I'm Keeping My Speed Down-Thanks, Bud, You're.. 70906 .... 3.00

Pull Quick & PullMatches

Pull Quick—This category of match container was popular during the 1930s and 1940s, but is rarely seen today. Made under the name of Pull Quick by Diamond Match Co. and Pullmatches by the American Pullmatch Co., the principle involved the quick removal of the match from a striker insulated compartment, thus igniting the match upon removal. Pull Quicks were made in single and double cards, attached to business cards, in folded cards and in thicker packs with wooden sticks. The principle was relatively safe, however, accidents did happen.

5PQ PullMatch, Type 1 [1936-1939], American Pullmatch Corporation, Tipp City, OH, assorted 5.00

5PQ PullMatch, Type 2 [1939-1949], American Pullmatch Division, Piqua, OH, assorted 5.00

1PQ PullMatch, American Pullmatch Div., Westerville, Ohio ad: U.S. (F), Insignia of United States Army (B),(RD/WE/BE) 4.00

1PQ PullMatch, American Pullmatch Div., Westerville, Ohio ad: Associated Piping, Los Angeles 11, Calif.,(WE/BE) 4.00

1PQ PullMatch, American Pullmatch Div., Westerville, Ohio ad: W.D. Chandler Realtor, HollyWood Beach, Florida, double row of sticks, YW/RD/BE) 7.00

1PQ Associated Piping, Los Angeles 11, Calif, complete, single row, from American Pullmatch Div 4.00

1PQ Badger Restaurant, Wisconsin Dells, WI (GN) 4.00

1PQ Pull Quick, Pat. Pending, No. 1,694,864, Diamond Match Co., ad: The Boar & Castle, Greensboro, Kendall Oil ad (B) (RD/BK/WE) 5.00

1PQ British Pullmatch Co., Ltd, Made in England, no ad, drawing of woman in costume,(WE) 6.00

1PQ Pull Quick, Pat. Pending, No. 1,694,864, Diamond Match Co., ad: The Brown Derby, 3 CA addresses (B) (BN/YW) 4.25

1PQ Custom Made, Canadian PQ Corp., w/3/20 Tax Stam 1.50

1PQ Diamond, ad: Diamond Pullquick Matches 4.75

1PQ ad: Diamond PullQuick [ca. 1940], stapled sides, possibly test book 6.00

3PQ Diamond Match Co., assorted themes 3.25

1PQ Diamond Match Co., NY (Pat. Pending), Drawing of Sailing Ship (F/B) 5.00

1PQ Diamond, Drawing of sailing ship (F/B) 3.00

2PQ The Eat Shop & The Kenesaw Café 9.25

1PQ Electronical Merchandise Crop. 8.00

1PQ Pat. Pending, No. 1,694,864, Diamond Match Co., ad: Fred W. Miller's Café, Philadelphia, PA, 1 stick remaining 2.50

1PQ Pull Quick, Pat. Pending, No. 1,694,864, Diamond Match Co., ad: Geiss' Restaurant, Evansville, IN, all sticks, MN/GN/BK 8.00

1PQ The Glass Hat, Shreveport, LA, complete, slight bend in corner of book 6.50

1PQ Ye Golden Lion Tavern, San Diego, Calif., standing Lion (B), colorful, Diamond Match Co. 6.50

1PQ Graham's Cocktail Bar 4.00

1PQ Pull Quick, Pat. Pending, No. 1,694,864, Diamond Match Co., ad: Hatton's Restaurant, Cleveland (BK/RD/WE) 7.00

2PQ 1. Hob Tea Room, Wilmington, DE, 2. Celebrity Club w/Blondie and her Gang (7 women) (B) 7.25

1PQ Diamond, Picture of Dog w/From 'The Invader' 5.00

1PQ ca. 1930, Kendall, The 2000 Mile Oil, can (B) 6.50
1PQ The Kenesaw Café 2.50
1PQ The Koffee Kup, very colorful 7.00
1PQ McCool's Ice Cream, two cones & child (B) 5.00
1PQ Miller's Café, Globe & Safford, AZ 3.50
1PQ double fold, Mt. Joy Insurance, Mt. Joy, PA 4.00
1PQ United States Navy (Press Lightly Here/Pull Quickly) 5.00
1PQ Olney Inn, Olney MD & Miami Beach, Fla 5.00
2PQ 1. The Oriental, Charlotte, NC, 2. Tips, Los Angeles, CA 3.75
2PQ 1. The Plaza Steak House, Durham, NC 2. Kendall Oil 3.75
1PQ New Rocky Mountain Café, Butte, MT (OE) 4.50
1PQ Pat. Pending, No. 1,694,864, Diamond Match Co., generic w/2 Scottie dogs (F/B) diff, Colgate
    design, 5 sticks remaining 3.00
1PQ Two Scottie Dogs playing (F/B), Diamond Match Co. 4.75
1PQ Phil Smidt & Sons, Roby Indiana 4.50
1PQ Thick Steaks, Thin Pancakes, Tip's 6.00
1PQ Pull Quick, Pat. Pending, No. 1,694,864, Diamond Match Co., ad: Susan Palmer Restaurant
    & Oyster Bar, (BK/WE, probably NY, no sticks remaining 3.00
1PQ U.S. on F, Insignia of United States Army (b) (RD/WE/BE) 4.25
1PQ U.S. Marine Corps, American PullMatch Division 3.25
1PQ U.S. Navy American PullMatch Division 3.00
2PQ The Schooner, New York, NY 3.25
1PQ Wivel's Special Six Course Diner 3.00
1PQ Y.M.C.A. Cafeteria, Coatesville, Pa (RD) 4.00
25PQ Pull Quick, assorted Themes 22.00

PATRIOTIC DESIGN STOCK CUTS

Patriotic Stock Cuts were presented as the "sensational America Victorious series" and accompanied advertisements from Airlines to Zoos. Dedicated to "Our Country At War," every matchbook company had a reservoir of designs, frequently borrowed from competitors. Match Corp. of American used the following to sell this line: Masterly in creative drawing, their colors are bright, attractive and compelling with all the strength of the nation's own red, white and blue predominant.

Who could refuse? Although orders for patriotic matchbooks began to taper off after the surrender in Europe, many designs portraying our Pacific theatre were still popular.

Radio & TV Stations

Radio & TV Stations—The category of matchcovers whose advertisement refers to any radio or television station by call letters or number, or radio or television personality by name, drawing or photo, to include news, variety, music or program management. One popular set from 1965 was the Canadian Radio Station Series of 92 Canadian Radio Stations. American series includes the CBS and NBC stars of the 1930s and the KPHO television set from Phoenix, AZ. One very difficult set to find is the Town Talk Bread Set of 20 matchcovers, featuring "20 Great Radio Stars."

80C,20S,FS C.B.S. Radio Stars Set [1935], 20 stars each in four colors (BE/GN/PE/RD) Diamond Match Co., including: Allen-Barlow-Edwards-Gates-Givot-Green-Guizar-Hulick-Husing-Kostelanetz-Marshall-Neisen-Ponselle-Ross-Rothafel-Smith-Stoopnagle-Van-Warnow-Williams 175.00

1C,FS,JLT KCBQ Radio 2.50

72C,20S,FS KFOX Radio Series [   ] 30.00

24C,20S,FS KPHO-TV Set [1956], Take 5 for.. Abbott & Costello-Amos 'n Andy-Annie Oakley-Arizona Newsreel-Colonial March-Confidential File-Cook's Corner-Five Star Playhouse-Goldust Charlie-Guy Lombards-Highway Patrol-I Am the Law-It's Wallace?-Judge Roy Bean-Jungle Jim-Man Behind Badge-Movietime-Passport to Danger-Ray Milland-Secret File-Stories of the Century-This is Your Music-Three Star News-Trailtime 30.00

6FB,30S,FS KXGO-RV, Channel 11, Fargo-Moorhead ND, CBS eye (B), ABC (F), cellopack, all same, (BK/RD/WE) 6.25

24C,20S,FS N.B.C. Radio Stars Set [1935], Diamond Match Co., Albini-Barclay-Bond-Cook-Cozzi-Goldman-Gordon-Grauer-Havrilla-Kirberry-Knight-Lundell-Luther-McCoy-McNamee-Olsen-Perkins-Reser-Robinson-Ross-Shilkret-Small-Steinke-Thomas ... 35.00

1C,40S,FS Queen for a Day [   ], 20th Anniversary Year 8.00

20C,20S,FS Town Talk Bread Set Match Corp. Bradley-Campbell-Carpenter-Cross-Des Autels-Doyle-Goodwin-Grauer-Hamp-Hanlon-Martin-McGeehan-McKee-Meyers-Mueller-Neblett-Niles-Roberts-Wilcox-Wilson 20.00

1C,20S,FS Radio Station WMAQ, 670 on your Dial, Chicago 3.00

1C,20S,FS Radio Station WMGM, 1050, Ted Brown and that crazy Redhead 3.00

1C,20S,FS Radio Station WMGM, 1050, Your Hits of the Week w/Phil Goulding 3.00

1C,20S,FS Radio Station WMIE, Dial 1140, Miami 1.50

1C,20S,FS Radio Station WMTR 1250 on the Dial, Morristown, NJ 3.25

10C,20S,FS WPEN Radio, Series A [1956], numbered, Smith-Allison-Brees-Farren-check cashing-Goukas-Pancho-Pat & Jack-Bennett-O'Reilly 4.50

10C,20S,FS WPEN Radio, Series B [1956], numbered, Smith-Allison-Brees-Farren-check cashing-Goukas-Pancho-Pat & Jack-Milner & Brown-Ford 4.25

10C,20S,FS WPEN Radio, Series C [   ], numbered, x-x-x-Farren-x-Guokas-x-x-x-x 5.00

10C,20S,FS WPEN Radio, Series D [   ], numbered 5.00

10C,20S,FS WPEN Radio, Series E [1957], numbered, Smith-McGuire-Brees-Farren-check cashing-Guokas-Raymond-Benson-check cashing-O'Reilly 10.00

10C,20S,FS WPEN Radio, Series F [   ], numbered 5.00
10C,20S,FS WPEN Radio, Series G [1957], numbered, Smith-McGuire-Brees-Farren-check
    cashing-Guokas-Raymond-Pat & Jack-Milner & Brown-Ford 12.00
10C,20S,FS WPEN Radio, Series 1164 [   ], numbered, O'Reilly-x-Benson-Raymond-Guokas-
    Farren-Brees-Smith-Ford-x 10.00
1C,20S,FS WPEN Radio personality, set has 10, photo (F), Steve Allison, 'the man who owns
    midnight' 3.00
1C,20S,FS WPEN Radio personality, set has 10, photo (F), Fred Bennett, 'Mr. Music and Mirth'
    .... 2.25
1C,20S,FS WPEN Radio personality, set has 10, photo (F), Bud Brees, 'Melody Midas' 4.25
1C,20S,FS WPEN Radio personality, set has 10, photo (F), Bill Farren, 'Front Page' 2.75
1C,20S,FS WPEN Radio personality, set has 10, photo (F), Matt Guokas, 'Big Matt' ... 3.25
1C,20S,FS WPEN Radio personality, set has 10, photo (F), Pancho, 'the man in the Black
    Sombrero' 2.00
1C,20S,FS WPEN Radio personality, set has 10, photo (F), The Pat & Jack Show 3.00
3C,20S,FS WPEN Radio No. 8 Pat & Jack, No. 9 Fred Bennett, No. 10 Jack O'Reilly 3.00
2C,20S,FS WPEN Radio No. 1 Bill Smith, No. 2 Steve Allison 3.00
1C,20S,FS WPEN Radio personality, set has 10, #5, no photo, 10 cent coupon 2.00
10C,20S,FS WPEN Radio personalities, parts of Series A & B, including Frank Ford, Bill Farren
    & Pancho, photo (B), history (I) 12.00
30FB Radio & Radio related (some Features, some Printed Sticks) 12.00
750C,MZ,FS Radio Stations, assorted, album (some duplicates) 115.00
325C,MZ,FS Radio Stations, assorted, album 37.50
100C,30S,MS Radio Stations, assorted 28.00

Railroad

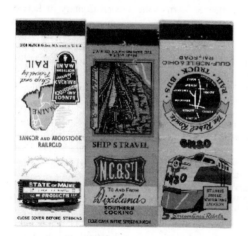

Railroad—Any single or set which advertises or mentions a railroad company, station, commercial train, or service. Not usually collected as trains alone, railroads emphasize commercial names and services. There are thousands of railroad matchcovers known. The same railroad might produce large numbers of different matchbooks, depending on how railway routes changed over the years, with slight variations in cities served, and the coloration of the matchbooks themselves. Collectors should check every detail for these variations.

1FB,30S,FS A.C. & Y Railroad, The Road of Service (logo) (B), The Friendly Road (S) (BK/WE)
    .... 5.00
6FB,20S Ann Arbor Railroad, Dependable Double A Serivce, cellopack, all same (RD,WE,BE)
    .... 10.00
1FB,20S,FS Ann Arbor Railroad, (BE/WE/RD), flag logo (F), Linking East-North-West (B) 3.00
1C,G,FS Merry Christmas and Happy New Year Baltimore & Ohio RR, carolers (B) 10.00
3C,30S,MR B&O Railroad singles 15.00
1FB,20S,FS Baltimore & Ohio Railroad, train (F), On Time Dependability (B), map (I) (BE/OE)
    .... 6.00

1C,20S,FS Bangor & Aroostook Railroad, State of Maine box car (F), logo and map (B) 2.50

1FB,20S,FS Bessemer and Lake Erie R.R. Co. (GD/BE) metallic, Traffic Department phone (F), map (I) 3.25

4FB,30S,FS Blue Streak Service, Cotton Belt Route, St. Louis SW Railway Lines, cellopack, all same, train & globe (F) (BK/BE/WE) 5.00

1C,20S,FS Burlington Railroad [1948] 5.00

1C,20S,FS California Western RR, Ft Bragg, Calif w/locomotive (F), Ride the Skunk Trains (S), skunk w/train (B) 3.00

8C,20S Canadian National Railroad, Eddy Match Co., CN 5.00

1FB,20S,FS The Chessie Line, sleeping kitten (F), C&O and B&O logos (B) 3.25

6FB,20S,FS The Chessie Route, sleeping kitten, presentation sleeve, all same (F), train (F) sleeve, all the same 15.00

4FB,30S,FS Detroit Toledo Ironton Railroad, Dearborn, Michigan, name (B), logo (F), cellopack, all same, (RD/BK/WE) 10.50

3 Containers 3 railroad cars 7.00

1C,20S,FL,FS Railroad, Frankfort & Cincinnati RR Co., colorful 6.00

3C,20S,FS Frisco Lines, N & W The Powhatan Arrow, Sun Valley Idaho 10.00

1C,40S,FS Central Georgia RR, Map & Truck (I), colorful 7.00

1FB,20S,FS Great Northern Railway (GN/WE) color photo of train (B), Mtn. Goat logo (F) 5.00

1FB,20S,FS Monon, The Hoosier Line, (MN/WE), logo (F/B), map (I) 3.00

6FB,20S,FS Illinois Central, Main Line of Mid-America, cellopack, all same (RD/BK/WE) 15.00

6FB,20S,FS L&N Louisville & Nashville R.R., (BE/RD), cellopack, all same 18.00

6FB,20S LACKAWANNA RAILROAD display sleeve w/train (B), The Route of Scenic Charm between The Great Lakes and The Sea 10.00

1FB,20S,FS Louisville & Nashville R.R. (DBE/RD/WE) logo (F/B), map (I) 4.00

1FB,20S,FL The Milwaukee Road, shows train & logo, (SR/RD/WE) 4.50

6FB,20S,FS MKT Katy Lines (F), map w/route (B), cellopack, all same, (GN/RD/YW/BK) 12.75

6FB,20S Monon - The Hoosier Line display sleeve, Starting the Second Century of Service, cellopack, all same 10.50

3C,20S,FS N&W, Symbol of Precision Transportation, Erie Railroad, Northern Railway (Photo of train (B) 6.00

1C,20S,FL,FS Railroad, Nancy Hanks, II/Man O' War, colorful 7.00

4FB,20S,FS Cello-pak, Northern Pacific Railway 12.00

1FB,20S,FS Northern Pacific Railway, (RD/BK/WE), logo (F/B) 3.00

1FB,20S,FS Northern Pacific RR, The Streamlined North Coast Ltd., logo (F/B) 6.00

30C,20S,FS New York Central 7.50

6FB,20S Rio Grande Fast Freight, Main Line Thru the Rockies, cellopack, all same (OE/BK) 14.00

6FB,20S,BS Santa Fe RR Six-Pack, 2 Indians (F) 21.00

6FB,20S,FS Seaboard RR Presentation Sleeve 18.50

1FB,30S,FS Holland-America (ship) Line, port list (B), (GN/WE) 5.00

6FB,20S,FS Soo Line Railroad, cellopack, all same (DBE/RD/WE), map (I) 16.00

1C,20S,FS Soo Line RR, Dated Anniversary 1883-1958, map (I) 5.00

1FB,20S,FS Soo Line Railroad, (DBE/RD/WE), logo (F/B), map (I) 4.00

1C,20S,FS Railroad, Southern Bell, photo of girl (F) 6.00

1FB,20S,FS Southern Pacific Streamlined, deco train (B) 3.00

24C,M,FS Southern Railways Set [1940] Barnes-Berkely-Davis-Elkins-Engbarth-Fulger-Fulmer-Furbner-Furbner(name omitted)-Gay-Howard-McFall-Myers-Myers(new pose)-Rollins-Sandford-Sandlin-Smith-Stollard-Sullivan-Tipping-Ware-Warren-West 60.00

21C,20S,FS Southern Railways Set [   ], daytime view Bateler-Carney-Collins-Conduff-Foster-Free-Gainer-Griffin-Hunt-Keiser-Lyle-McClellan-McRae-Myers-Pearce-Reins-Springer-Vann-Ward-West-Wilson 25.00

19C,20S,FS Southern Railways Set [   ], nighttime view Anderson-Bible-Blanton-Briscoe-Conduff-Edwards-Hunt-Mayhall-Mitchell-Myers-Rippetoe-Sanford-Singer-Stallard-Stone-Ward-Warnock-Watts-Westerberg 25.00

6FB,20S,FS T&P Texas & Pacific Railway, Route of the Eagles, cellopack, all same, (RD/WE/ BK) 15.00

6FB,20S,FS Tennessee Central Railway, Nashville Route, tracks (B), map w/route (F), cellopack, all same (TN/BN) 12.50

7C,30S,FS,RAMA Union Pacific, numbered Yellowstone-Domeliner-Grand Teton-Bryce Canyon-Hoover Dam-Catalina Island-Sun Valley, Type #1 [1956], M-1102 .... 5.00

7C,30S,FS,RAMA Union Pacific, numbered Yellowstone-Domeliner-Grand Teton-Bryce Canyon-Hoover Dam-Catalina Island-Sun Valley, Type #2 [1956], M-1282 .... 5.25

4C,20S,FS Union Pacific Agents, name on each 4.50

1FB,20S,FS Union Pacific Railroad, (YW/BE/RD) train (F) (RD/WE/BE) shield (B) 2.00

8FB,30S,FS Union Pacific Railroad, name (F), shield (B), (WE), celo pack 20.00

1FB,30S,FS Sun Valley Lodge (F), Union Pacific Railroad (B) (MN/RD/WE) 2.00

8C,30S,FS Union Pacific Set [1956] 5.00

7C,30S,FS,RAMA Union Pacific Railroad Set [1956] 7.00

1FB,30S,FS Union Pacific Railroad (RD/GD), name (F), shield (B), Get The Right Connection (I) 4.00

7C,30S,MS Union Pacific Railroad 15.00

6FB,20S,FS Wabase Fine Passenger Service, 2 trains (F), cellopack, all same, (DBE/GD/RD) 13.50

1FB,20S California Zephyr Railroad, name only (F/B) (SR/BK) 5.00

8C,30S,FS Old Time Locomotives Set [1957], stock, DeWitt Clinton 1831-8 Wheel..1876-General 1862-Mogul Freight..1878-Mogul Tank..1872-10 Wheel Double Ender..1883-10 Wheel Double Ender..1885-10 Wheel Freight..1880, Universal Match Corp., ... 2.00

5C,20S,FS Railroads including: MKT/Katy, Souther Pacific, L&N, Kansas City Souther, Union Pacific 8.00

3C,20S,FS Richmond, Fredericksburg & Potomac RR Co., Bangor & Aroostook RR, Southern Pacific Streamlined (train (B) 7.00

5C,20S,FS Railroads including: North Western, Missouri Pacific, N&W, Streamliner 8.00

6FB,20S,MS Railroads including Illinois Central, Canadian Pacific, Union Pacific, Erie, Santa Fe and Burlington Northern 21.00

50C,20S,FS Railroads, colorful, assorted 65.00

5C,20S,BS Railroads including: Santa Fe, SCL/L&N, Algoma Central, Frisco 8.00

6C,20S,MS Railroads including Milwaukee Road, Katy Lines, Missouri Pacific, Southern Pacific, Amtrak & Norfolk & Western 15.00

6FB,20S,MS Railroads including L&N, NY/New Haven/Hartford, Pennsylvania, Soo Line, Southern Pacific & Southern RR System 22.00

5C,20S,FS Railroads, (L&N, N&W, Streamliner, Pacific Electric, Union Pacific) 11.75

5C,20S,FS Railroads including: Chessie, Illinois Central, Union Pacific, Souther Pacific, Missouri Pacific 8.00

5FB,20S,FS Railroads (Belfast & Moosehead Lake, Bangor & Aroostook, L&N, Western RR, Wabash Red Ball) 16.00

5FB,20S,FS Railroads (New Haven, Atlantic Coast Line, Rio Grande Freight, Zephyr, Rio Grande) 20.00

3C,20S,FS L&N Railroad, Kansas City Southern Lines, map (B), North Western, (train (F) 3.50

5C,20S,FS Railroads including: Union Pacific, REA, Great Western, Monon & N&W 11.25

5C,20S,FS Railroads including: T&P, EJ&E, Central of Georga, Frisco, Great Northern 13.50

6FB,20S,FS Railroads including Santa Fe, L&N, Milwaukee Road, Illinois Central, Hoosier Line and Wabase 18.00

5FB,20S,FS Railroads (Atlantic Coast Line, NY Central, N&W, Edavile RR, NY Central) 19.00

5C,20S,FS Railroads including: Great Western, T&P, Chessie, EJ&E, P&WV 8.00

3C,20S,FS Railroads including: B&O, train (F), N&W RR The Scenic Route, Lehigh Valley Trains, train (F) 5.50

6C,20S,MS Railroads including: Northern Pacific, Katy, Atlantic Coast Line, Wabash, Union Pacific & Frisco 12.00

5C,20S,FS Railroads including: Wabash, Missouri Pacific, Union Pacific, N&W, Rio Grande 12.25

6FB,20S,MS Railroads including Atlantic & Danville, Chssie, Frisco, Ontario Northland, Great Northern, & Lackawanna 25.00
5C,20S,FS Railroads (South Shore Line, West Point Route, Illinois Central, Sandersville RR Co., Atlantic Coast Line) 13.50
3C,20S,FS L&N Railroad, Kansas City Southern Lines, MAP (B), North Western, train (F) 10.00
20C,20S,BS Railroads, assorted 22.00
380C,20S,FS Railroads, assorted lines, album, no duplicates 135.00
25C,20S,FS Railroads, assorted 38.00
21C,20S,FS Railroads, assorted lines 10.00
20C,20S,MS Railroads, assorted 35.00
25C,30S,MS Railroads, assorted lines 15.00
30C,MZ,MS Railroad, assorted themes 50.00
20C,40S,FS Railroads, assorted lines 26.00
8C,30S,FS 1966 Universal Match Corp., Trains Set 4.25
12C,30S,BS 1981 Ohio Match Co., Trains Set 3.25

Restaurants

Restaurants—The single largest and probably most popular category of matchcovers throughout the history of the hobby, restaurants include any eating place (i.e. restaurants, fountains, coffee shops, drive-ins, snack bars, donut shops, tea rooms, inns, cafés, cafeterias, diners, delicatessens, automats, lunches, lunchrooms, confectioneries, Bar-B-Ques, grills, etc.). Several sub-classification methods for this category are popular, including ethnic divisions, the most popular of which include Chinese, Japanese, Thai, Korean, French, Mexican, Spanish and Greek. Restaurants can also be sub-classified by meal, including Pizza, Fast Food, Hamburger, Coffee and oriental. Taverns, cocktail lounges, bars, dairies, and ice cream parlors are usually collected separately.

Restaurants (General)

15C,20S,MS Bonanza Restaurants (BN) 2.00
15C,20S,MS Bonanza Sirloin Pit (OE) 2.00
1FB,20S,FS The Brown Derby, Los Angeles, Hollywood, Beverly Hills 3.00
6FB,20S,FS The Original Buckhorn Saloon, San Antonio, Texas, longhorn (F), colorful drawing of bar (B), celo 6-pack (all same) 4.00
425C,MZ,MS Cafés, different cities, all USA 26.00
730C,20S,FS California Restaurants 50.00
1FB,40S,FS from Heros Restaurant, Movie Stars photos (F/B & I) 5.50
10C,20S,FS Leon & Eddie's Panorama Set [ca. 1940], They make a picture when placed side by side 41.00
1FB,20S,FS The Rainbow Room, Rockefeller Center 1.25
20C,20S,BS Smuggler's Inn, same (F), different (I), assorted addresses 4.00
1FB,20S,FS Stork Club, New York City 3.25
315C,20S,MS Taverns, assroted 13.00
1B Top of the Mark 2.50

1FB,20S,BF The Village Restaurant, Lancaster, PA, (WE/BK,YW/RD) 1.50
100C,MZ,FS Bars, including taverns, assorted 5.00
20C,20S,MS Tuscon Arizona Restaurants 3.00
640C,20S,FS Illinois Restaurants 65.00
15C,30S,BS New York City Restaurants 6.00

Restaurants (Ethnic)

40C,20S,BS Oriental Restaurants, different cities 7.00
50C,20S,FS Chinese Restaurants 8.00
15C,20S,FS,FL Chinese Restaurants 3.00
50C,20S,MS Oriental Restaurants, different cities 12.00
20C,30S,BS Chinese Restaurants 9.00
50C,20S/30S,FS Chinese Restaurants 4.00
35C,MZ,MS Chinese Restaurants 4.00
5C,30S,BS Italian Restaurants 2.00
50C,20S,BS Italian Restaurants 3.00
128C,20S,MS Japanese Restaurants 8.00
11C,30S,BS Mexican Restaurants, different locations 5.00
200C,20S,FS Mexican Restaurants 13.00
50C,20S,MS Mexican Restaurants 3.00
14C,30S,BS Oriental Restaurants 3.50
100C,30S,MS Oriental Restaurants 4.00
50C,20S,BS Oriental Restaurants 6.50

Restaurants (Miscellaneous)

65C,20S,BS Mostly NE cities 12.00
100C,20S,FS Assorted locations 23.00
375C,20S,FS Assorted types, different cities, album 27.50
100C,20S,MS Different cities 15.50
560C,20S,MS Assorted types, different cities, album 65.00
575C,30S,FS Assorted types, different cities, album 50.00
480C,30S,MS Assorted types, different cities, album 65.00
100C,30S,MS Assorted types, different cities, album 17.50
285C,40S,MS Assorted types, different cities, album 37.50
40C,30S,MS Matchorama, assorted styles 8.00

Stock cuts used for restaurant matchcovers from the 1940s and 1950s. Every kind of eating place had a stock cut and many used them to reduce the cost of their matchbooks.

RMS Conventions

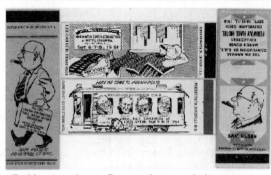

RMS Convention—A category of singles and sets associated with the annual meeting of the Rathkamp Matchcover Society. Sets are made by individuals, clubs or businesses, promoting congratulatory messages to the host club. These are usually dated and can be placed as conjunctives in other categories such as girlies, scenic, Perkins Americana, flowers, dogs, patriotic, etc.

6C,20S,FS 11th Convention Set [1951], Empire Matchcover Club, Empire State Bldg (B), color set 3.00

25C,40S,FS 12th Convention Set [1952], Keystone Matchcover Club 5.00

4C,20S,FS 13th Convention Set [1953], Universal Dog Set, Edith Cooper/Horace Rush, Universal Match Corp. 3.25

5C,20S,FS 14th Convention Set [Sept 9-11, 1954], Mercury Match Co. Dog Set 1.75

6C,20S,FS 14th Convention Set [1954], Raynor's Advertising Specialty Dog Set 10.00

4C,20S,FS 15th Convention Set [1955], Universal Match Corp. Dog Set, Bill Jarboe, Paul Thornburg 7.00

5C,20S,FS 16th Convention Set [1956], Edith M. Cooper, RMS logo (B), color set 3.00

5C,20S,FS 19th Convention Set [1958], Old Dominion Matchcover Club, Mt Vernon (B), color set (club now defunct) 4.00

5C,20S,FS 19th Convention Set [Aug. 24-30, 1959], Keystone Matchcover Club, Sun City Motel, Miami Beach, Fla. 6.50

4C,20S,FS 29th Convention Set, Las Vegas, NV, [1969], Girlie Set 6.00

4C,40S,FS 19th Convention Set [1959], Frank Tripodi, shows hobby room (B), category list (I) 4.00

5C,20S,FS 20th Convention Set [1960], Paul Revere Mall and 'Old North Church' 6.00

5C,20S,FS 22nd Convention Americana Set, [Aug. 19-25, 1962] 1.25

5C,20S,FS 22nd Convention Americana Set, [Aug. 19-25, 1962] 2.00

10C,20S,FS 25th Convention Set [1965], H. Froud & C. Gilson, Vista-Lite Toronto scenes, Princess Gates, Centre Island, Casa Loma, GNE Grounds, Skyline, Moose, Mountain Sheep, Bear, Squirrel, Buffalo, (B) of each, colorful 5.00

5C,20S,BS Long Beach MC, 9th Annual Christmas Party Set [1965] 2.00

4C,20S,BS 5th Annual Spring Swap-Fest Set [March 26-27, 1966], Forest City MC, Cleveland, OH 2.00

5C,20S,BS 25th Convention Set [1965], Great Lakes Matchcover Club, Americus Hotel   4.00

4C,20S,BS 27th Convention & AMCAL Set [1967], Fresno, CA, metallic finish 2.00

5C,20S,BS 27th Convention Set [Aug 16-20, 1967], Forest City MC, Long Beach, CA 2.00

4C,20S,FS 27th Convention Set [1967], Girlie Set, Charles L. Wolf, Long Beach, CA 6.00

6C,20S,FS 28th Convention Set (Cleveland, OH) Set, [May 16-19, 1968] & AMCAL (Fresno, CA) 2.00

5C,20S,FS 28th Convention Set [1968], Berks Cty Matchcover Club 3.50

5C,20S,FS 28th Convention Set [1968], Don DeGunia & Paul Ferguson, Water Fowl designs, Cleveland, OH 2.00

4C,20S,FS 28th Convention Set [1968], Empire Matchcover Collecting Club, Cleveland, OH 4.00

4C,20S,FS 28th Convention & AMCAL Set [1968], Evelyn Hovious 4.50

10C,20S,FS 28th Convention & AMCAL Set [1968], Redwood Empire Matchcover Club 10.00

4C,20S,FS 28th Convention Set [1968], Trans-Canada Matchcover Club, Cleveland, OH 4.00

5C,20S,FS 28th Convention Set [1968], Western Reserve MC, Sheraton-Cleveland Hotel, Cleveland, OH 2.00

5C,20S,FS 29th Convention Set [1969], Bailey, Bailey, Mackie & Fisher 2.00

4C,20S,FS 29th Convention Set [Aug. 13-17, 1969], Lorne Branton, Stardust Motel, Las Vegas, NV 5.00

5C,20S,FS 29th Convention [1969], Western Reserve Matchcover Club, Las Vegas, NV, Girlie Set 5.50

4C,20S,FS 30th Convention [Aug. 19-22, 1970], Lorne Branton, Marriott Motor Hotel, Newton, MA 2.25

4C,20S,FS 30th Convention [1970], Newton, MA, officers list (I) 2.00

3C,20S,FS 30th Convention Set [1970], Newton, MA, Girlie Set 6.50

5C,20S,FS 31st Convention & AMCAL Set [1971], Angelus Matchcover Club 4.00

5C,20S,FS 31st Convention Set [Aug. 18-22, 1971], El Cortez Hotel, San Diego, CA 2.00

8C,40S,FS 31st Convention Nixon Series Set [1971] 2.00

5C,20S,FS 31st Convention Set [Aug. 1971], San Diego, officers list (I) 2.00

4C,30S,BS 32nd Convention Set [1972], Wray Martin, outhouse (B), color set, Eddy Match Co. 3.00

5C,20S,BS 32nd Convention Set [1972], MARVA Matchbook Collecting Club, Montreal, CN 1.50

8C,40S,BS 32nd Convention Set [1972], HMS Queen Mary Set 4.00

7C,20S,BS 32nd Convention Set [1972], Trans Canada Matchcover Club, Montreal, Que 2.00

7C,20S,BS 34th Convention Set [Aug. 14-18, 1974], Cleveland, OH, Manley Brudvig 2.00

4C,20S,BS 34th Convention Set [1974], Fry, Fuller, Harpster, Mils & Quinn, Girlie Set .. 4.00

4C,20S,BS 34th Convention Set [1974], International Matchcover Club, Girlie Set 4.00

4C,20S,BS 36th Convention Set [1976], Empire Matchcover Club 7.50

10C,40S,BS 38th Convention Set [1978], Orange County Set 1.00

12C,40S,BS 39th Convention Set [1979], Natural Landmarks USA Set 6.00

6C,20S,BS 40th Convention Set [Aug. 20-23, 1980], Lorne Branton & Frank Ralph 2.00

4C,20S,BS 40th Convention Set [Aug. 20-23, 1980], 9 Lehigh Valley Matchcover Club Members, listed (B) 1.25

5C,20S,BS 40th Convention Set [Aug. 20-23, 1980], Mel Reese & Marilyn Reese 1.25

5C,20S,BS 40th Convention Set [Aug. 20-23, 1980], Alice B. Riel 2.50

4C,20S,BS 41st Convention Set [Aug. 18-23, 1981], Keystone Matchcover Club 1.25

5C,20S,BS 41st Convention Set [Aug. 18-23, 1981], Mel Reese & Marilyn Reese 1.25

5C,20S,BS 41st Convention Set [Aug. 18-23, 1981], Harry Trankner 1.25

5C,20S,BS 42nd Convention Set [Aug. 18-22, 1982], Berks County Matchcover Club 1.25

4C,20S,BS 42nd Convention Set [Aug. 18-22, 1982], Brewster, Ferguson & Swope, Girlie Set 3.25

4C,20S,BS 42nd Convention Set [Aug. 18-22, 1982], 4 Keystone Matchcover Club collectors listed (B) 1.25

5C,20S,BS 42nd Convention Set [Aug. 18-22, 1982], Mid South Matchcover Club & International Matchcover Club 1.25

4C,20S,BS 42nd Convention Set [Aug. 18-22, 1982], Monumental Matchcover Club 1.25

4C,20S,BS 43th Convention Set [1983], Badger State Matchcover Club 2.50

4C,20S,BS 43th Convention Set [1983], Bill Furlong, International Matchcover Club 2.50

4C,20S,BS 43th Convention Set [1983], Alice Riel & David Riel, color photos (B) 3.50

5C,20S,BS 44th Convention Set [1984], Berks County Matchcover Club 2.50

7C,20S,BS 44th Convention Set [1984], T.J. Gray, Ames, IA 2.50

4C,20S,BS 44th Convention Set [1984], David Riel & Alice Riel, color photos (B) 3.50

5C,20S,BS 45th Convention Set [1985], Alma & Bob Adams 2.50

5C,20S,BS 45th Convention Set [1985], Andy & Ellie Anderson 2.50

6C,20S,BS 46th Convention Set [1986], Gateway Matchcover Club 2.50

5C,20S,BS 47th Convention Set [1987], Bill Retskin 2.50

5C,30S,BS 49th Convention Set [1989], Lyle & Penny Smith, Girlie Set 5.00

5C,20S,BS 49th Convention Set [1989], Bill Retskin 3.50

4C,30S,BS 53nd Convention Set [1993], American Matchcover Collecting Club & Bill Retskin, girlie set, (BK/WE) photos, nude 3.50

10C,40S,FS Orange County Series, RMS, numbered & dated 3.00
50C,20S,MS RMS Conventions, assorted 2.50
5C,20S,FS Forest City Matchcover Club, 2nd Annual Christmas Party Set [1962] 2.00
9C,20S,FS Forest City Matchcover Club, 4th Annual Christmas Party Set [1964], Cleveland, OH
.... 4.00
4C,20S,BS Int'l Matchcover Club, Bi-Centennial Celebration Set [1776-1976], officers listed (F),
metallic 1.50
5C,20S,FS Keystone Matchcover Collecting Club [1968], 17th Anniversary Set 2.00
4C,20S,FS William Reid, Member, Trans-Canada Matchcover Collecting Society Set [1970] 1.50

Safety Sets

Safety Sets—A category specializing in color and designer sets and series of matchcovers featuring slogans or messages concerned with various kinds of safety procedures. They were popular during WWII, with slogans and designs relating to ship and ordinance safety. Civilian safety sets include areas of auto, job, home, and product safety messages.

12C,20S,FS The A B C of Safety Set Always Wear..-Better Looking..-If You're Not Sure..-Lift With..-No Horseplay-No Smoking-Pile Material..-Report all Injuries..-Throw Waste..-Watch Out For.. Type 1 [   ], (BK) 5.00
12C,20S,FS The A B C of Safety Set Always Wear..-Better Looking..-If You're Not Sure..-Lift With..-No Horseplay-No Smoking-Pile Material..-Report all Injuries..-Throw Waste..-Watch Out For.. Type 2 [1955], (GY) 5.00
12C,20S,FS The A B C of Safety Set Always Wear..-Better Looking..-If You're Not Sure..-Lift With..-No Horseplay-No Smoking-Pile Material..-Report all Injuries..-Throw Waste..-Watch Out For.. Type 3 [   ], 2 dots either side of manumark 5.00
10C,20S,FS Arcade Pontiac Safety Set [   ] Jack Blank says.. .... 3.00
4C,20S,FS Cotton Safety Set [1956] 1.00
4C,20S,BS Monsanto Safety Series, Early Back Strikers 1.00
10C,20S,FS First Federal S&L numbered, Rules of the Road At A..-If 2 Drivers..-If There's..-Driver Making..- Drivers on..-Driver Should..-Driver Should..-When You Approach An..-Watch For..-If You Hear.. .... 3.00
19C,20S,FS R.A. Humphries Safety Set [1958] 3.00
10C,20S,FS Jefferson FS&L Safety Set [1959] 3.00
5C,20S,FS Match Corp. #1 [1956], stock, Be Patient Today..-Better Wait Than Never!-Don't Gamble With Safety-It Won't Kill You!..-Stop Look and Live! 2.00
5C,20S,FS Match Corp. #2 [1961], stock, Alert Today Alive Tomorrow-Children Should Be Seen..-Drive Slow Kids Move Fast-Safety Is A Job..-Stop, Drive As If.. .... 2.00
6C,20S,FS National Lead Co. [1952], Titanoxers The emergency safety..-For your safety keep..-For your safety know..-If you don't..-Well stacked..-Which valve?.. .... 22.00
10C,20S,FS Northwest FS&L 3.00
8C,20S,FS Ohio [1953], stock, Accidents Happen..-Be Careful-Clean up for..-Make today..-Monkey business..-Prevent fires..-Prevent foot..-Protect your.. .... 3.50
8C,20S,FS Ohio [1953], stock, Be Sure They're Not..-Don't Go Home..-Don't Stick Your..- I'm Really a Careful..-Look Out Keep..-Taint Funny Don't.. This'll Floor Ya..-Watch Your Step.. .... 2.50
5C,20S,FS Ohio [1957], stock, Be Sure..-Don't Get Caught..-Look Both Ways..-Take It Easy..-These Children Are.. .... 2.00
5C,20S,FS Superior #1 [1950], stock, Never Ignore This Signal!-Obey Traffic Rules!-Respect the Job He's Doing..-You Must Think and..-Will Your Brakes Hold 3.00
5C,20S,FS Superior #2 [1952], stock, Be Extra Careful on Rainy Days..-Drive As Though..-Face Traffic When Walking-Good Advice..-X Marks the Spot 2.75
5C,20S,FS Superior #3 [1954], stock, He Knows Best-Look Before Backing!-Look Both Ways!-Play Safe! Away From Traffic-Watch For Cars Turning! 2.50

5C,20S,FS Superior #4 [1955], stock, Courtesy Costs So Little!-Don't Gamble With Your Life!-Slow Down at This Sign!-Teach Your Child..-They'll Heed Older.. .... 3.25

5C,20S,FS Superior #5 [1956], stock, Be Courteous While Driving-Don't Be a Road Hog-Don't Jump the Signals-Look Before Backing (Giraffe)-Stay in Your Own.. .... 4.25

5C,20S,FS Superior #6 [1957], stock, Don't Crawl in Traffic-Don't Horse Around..-Flying Low is for the Birds-Keep a Safe Distance!-Slow Down When It's Wet 3.25

5C,20S,FS Superior #7 [1958], stock, A Minute for Safety..-Always Think for Two..-Clean Clothes Are Important..-Every Child Pedestrian..-Never Mind Who's.. .... 3.00

5C,20S,FS Superior #8 [1959], stock, Alert Motorists..-Don't Learn Traffic Laws..-For Traffic Safety..-Safety is a Job..-There's No Place Like Home.. .... 2.50

5C,20S,FS Superior #9 [1961], stock, A Good Look Can Mean..-Always Use the Proper..-Beware Your Smoke..-Bicycles Aren't Built for Two-They Don't Mix 3.00

5C,20S,FS Superior #10 [1962], stock, A Safe Car Means A Safer Ride-Close Doesn't Count..-Don't Gamble With..-Give Them The Break!-In Daylight Use Hand.. .... 2.50

5C,20S,FS Superior [1965], stock, Be Extra Careful..-Drive as Though..-He Knows Best-Slow Down at this Sign!-Will Your Brakes Hold? 2.25

5C,20S,FS Superior [1973], stock, A Safe Car Means A Safer Ride-Close Doesn't Count..-Don't Gamble With..-For Traffic Safety..-Give Them The Brake! 2.50

20C,20S,FS Safety Set #1,2,3,4 (5 in ea. set) 5.00

6C,20S,FS Universal [1941], Safety First, stock, Be Careful-Check Carefully-Safety First, Carelessness..- Safety First, Protect Your Eyes..-Safety First, Protect Your Feet..-Safety First, Use Your.. .... 3.50

10C,20S,FS Washington FS&L [   ] 3.00

7C,20S,FS Wright Aeronautical [1943] 4.00

The inside covers of your book matches contain valuable advertising space. Use it effectively and productively to emphasize your "ad" on the outer cover . . . for special offers . . . as a reply coupon . . . for charts or tables of useful information . . . or any sound, attractive copy that will fit.

Inside cover copy draws the attention of the book match user every time he strikes a match. It's "point of use" advertising that should produce splendid results.

Wise advertisers will exploit it to the utmost.

A page from a WWII Salesman's Sample book from Match Corp. of America. This article promotes inside printing for advertisers. Usually not costing more than $1.50 per thousand in the early 1940s, inside printing today costs more than a full case did then.

Although not a regular category, many speciality collectors keep examples of inside cuts related to their field. Girlies, beverages, sports schedules, and cartoons were popular after WWII.

Today, inside printing leans mostly toward more information about the advertiser. Words have replaced graphics and more emphasis is put on delivering a message rather than entertaining the matchbook user.

Scenic Sets

Scenic—Any matchcover single or set that mentions or advertises natural wonders, vacation spots, outdoor locations, vistas or outdoor historical attractions.

5C,20S,FS Match Corp. Set [1949], Scenic America Blue Ridge Mountains-Lake Louise-Lake Tahoe-New England Coast-Yosemite Valley 2.50

12C,20S,FS Match Corp. Set [1953], Scenic America A Minnesota Lake-Blue Ridge Mountains-Dells of Wisconsin- Falls of the Yellowstone-Grand Canyon-In Northern Michigan-Lake Louise-Lake Tahoe-New England Coast-Niagara Falls-Old Faithful-Yosemite Valley 3.50

5C,20S,FS Match Corp. Set [1956], Scenic America Bryce Canyon-Grand Canyon-Mount Rainier-Niagara Falls-Yosemite Falls 2.25

5C,20S,FS Match Corp. Set [   ], Cypress Gardens-Grand Teton-Mt. Hood-Mt. Rushmore-Wisconsin Dells.. 2.00

5C,20S,BS Maryland Set [1976] Scenarama Alpine Lake-Capitol-Desert Rocks-Falls on River-Mt. Rushmore 2.00

4C,20S,FS Republic Set [1974], Vacationland USA Dunes & mountains-Lake & mountains-Shoreline-Trees & swamp 2.00

5C,20S,FS Superior Set #2, 1942, ad: Pat: Forward U.S.A., Japs' Rising Sun is Setting ... 3.50

5C,20S,FS Superior Set #3, 1943, ad: A. A. Steiner, match cover collector 2.00

5C,20S,FS Superior Set #4, 1944, ad: Pat: Co-operation w/donkeys pulling together 2.25

5C,20S,FS Superior Set #7, 1947, ad: Abdulkader Hobby Exchange Club, Dar Es Salaam, T.T. East Africa 1.75

5C,20S,FS Superior Set #9, 1949, ad: G.H. Emberson, Ringgold, GA, match cover collector 2.25

Ship Lines

Ships—This watery category includes sets and singles from cruise, passenger, or freight lines, and usually advertise services or products. Included in this category are single tugs, ferry boats, hover craft, riverboats, or water jitneys.

As with railroad and airline matchcovers, four color designs with catchy slogans and promotional messages were standard. Many of the old ships are gone now and ship collectors look for any paper with drawings or photos of the older liners.

1C,20S,FS American President Lines, ship (B), flag (F) 3.00
1FB,30S,FS American President Lines (RD/WE/BE) eagle logo (F/B) 2.25
1C,20S,FS Chester/Bridgeport Ferry, Ferry (F/B), very colorful 1.25
1FB,20S,FL Cunard Line w/printed sticks 4.00
1FB,20S,FS Cunard Line, printed sticks 2.25
1B,W Cunard Lines, Bryant & May, Special Safety Match 1.25
2FB,20S,FL Cunard Line w/printed sticks, 1-YW, 1-BE 5.00
8B Cunard Ship Lines Set 11.00
6C,20S,FS Furness Lines Set [1964] 12.00
2FB,20S,FS Furness Lines, 1-Universal, 1-Bryant & May (printed sticks) 3.00
6C,20S,FS Furness Lines [1964], Anchor-Flag-Sextant-Shield-Smokestack-Wheel 7.00
1C,20S,FS Grace Line to Hanover Square (S), globe (F/B) 2.00
1C,20S,FS Matson Line to Hawaii, ship (I), girl w/lei (B) 6.00
4FB,30S,FS Pacific Transport Lines, Inc., presentation sleeve of four, OE-BK-WE, line flag on
    sleeve, full size ship (B) of sleeve 7.50
1C,40S,FS Queen Mary [1967], final voyage 14.00
2C,20S,FS Queen Mary, maiden voyage [5-27-36] & final voyage [1967] 75.00
6C,MZ,MS Queen Mary Ship Line, assorted 10.50
1C,20S,FS Quaker-Line, California Eastern Line, flag (F) 2.25
1FB,CLK Swedish American Line by Saffa, Italy 2.75
1FB,20S,FS SS United States/SS America, liner (F/B) 2.50
1FB,20S,FS United States Lines, To and From All Europe, Colorful 2.00
1FB,20S,FS United States Lines, S.S. United States-S.S. America 3.00
5C,30S,BS Cruise Lines 2.50
100C,20S,FS Ship Lines, assorted 28.00
50C,30S,MS Ship Lines, assorted 5.25
10C,MZ,MS Ship Lines 4.50
45C,20S,FS Ships of the Past Set, Maryland Match Co. [1957], 9 ships in 5 different colors (BE/
    GN/OE/PK/YW) Caravel..-East Indiaman..-Grain Ship..-Incas..-Mayflower-Northern Eu-
    ropean..-Roman Galley-Ship of..-Spanish Galleon.. Type 2 [   ], (BN) 3.00
45C,20S,FS Ships of the Past Set, Maryland Match Co. [1957], 9 ships in 5 different colors (BE/
    GN/OE/PK/YW) Caravel..-East Indiaman..-Grain Ship..-Incas..-Mayflower-Northern Eu-
    ropean..-Roman Galley-Ship of..-Spanish Galleon.. Type 1 [1957], (BK) 3.00
8C,30S,BS Ships Set [   ], Brigantine-Clipper Ship-Five Masted Schooner-Four Masted
    Barkentine-Four Masted Schooner-Great Lake Schooner-Square Topsail Schooner-Three
    Masted Schooner, Universal Match Corp. 3.00
6C,30S,FS Famous Mississippi Steamboats Set [1966], Eclipse-Morning Star-Natchez-Prin-
    cess-Queen of the West-Robert E. Lee 1.00

VOTE-GETTING POLITICAL SADDLE SLOGANS

The dynamic political slogans on the saddle cuts pictured below have
been designed to tell a complete story in a flash. The hand drawn lettering
presents each message in attractive dress and with powerful effect.

All these cuts bear the INTERNATIONAL PHOTO ENGRAVERS UNION
LABEL.

When ordering cuts printed on the saddle or top fold of book match covers always check the cover design selected to make sure that space is allowed for such cuts.

Book Matches Are Real
Vote-Builders . . Use Them

Small Towns

10C,20S,BS California, assorted themes	3.00
25C,MZ,FS Hawaiian, assorted themes	14.00
35C,30S,FS Hawaiian, assorted hotels & motels	3.25
25C,MZ,MS Hawaiian, assorted themes	2.00
370C,MZ,MS Hawaiian, older issues	50.00
50C,20S,MS Hawaiian, assorted themes	2.00
16C,20S,FS Illinois	4.00
18C,20S,FS Iowa	3.00
22C,20S,FS Kansas	3.00
29C,20S,FS Kansas City & St. Louis, Missouri	5.25
15C,20S,FS Michigan	3.25
9C,20S,FS Detroit, Michigan, assorted themes	2.75
10C,20S,FS Mississippi	3.00
10C,20S,FS Missouri	3.00
27C,20S,FS Montana	5.00
40C,20S,FS Miles City, Great Falls, Billings, Butte & Bozeman, Montana	10.00
14C,20S,FS Nebraska	3.00
10C,20S,FS Omaha Nebraska, assorted businesses & hotels	3.00
20C,20S,FS Wichita, KS, assorted themes	4.00
26C,20S,FS Assorted states	8.00
150C,20S,FS Assorted themes	9.00

Soda

Soda—The category of matchcovers which features commercial advertising for soda or soft drink products including Coke, Pepsi, Dr. Pepper, and hundreds of others. Sometimes included in this category are mixers and a few conjunctives actually showing a liquor or beer product.

1C,20S,FS 7UP, the 'Exciting' diet Drink (B), square logo (F) 1.25
1FB,20S,FS 7Up RD/WE) (F) Drink Like (GN/YW) (B) 4.25
1C,20S,FS 7UP, long neck bottle (B), round logo (F) 1.25
1C,20S,FS 7UP, Nothing does it like 7UP (F), square logo (B) 1.25
1C,20S,FS 7UP, peacock (B), 7UP Likes You (F) 1.25
1FB,20S,FS Seven-Up, 'Rye' and Seven-Up (BK/RD) 4.00
1C,20S,FS 7Up, round logo (F) short bottle (B), Take Smoe Along! 3.00
1C,20S,FS 7UP, The Uncola (B), 7UP (F) 8.00
2C,20S,FS Belfast Old Fashioned Mug Root Beer, overflowing mug (F), ad (B) (BN, BE) 2.50
1C,20S,FS Drink Bob's Cola, blonde w/cola glass (F), 'You'll enjoy its tempting tasty flavor'
     (B) 3.25
1C,20S,BS 100 Great Years '86, Coca-Cola 8.00
1C,20S,FS Coca-Cola [1936], 50th anniversary 5.00
1B Coca-Cola repro w/1901 calendar, large w/6 small (I) 7.00
1C,40S Compliments of The Coca-Cola Bottling Company of Fort Smith, colorful Santa (F) w/
     older Coca-Cola round sign 15.00
1FB,20S,FS Drink Coca-Cola,(RD/WE) small bottle (B) w/Have a Coke 7.50
1FB,20S,FS Enjoy Coca Cola w/wave, (BK/RD), modern, Superior manumark 3.00
1C,20S,FS Coca-Cola, wave (F), 'it's the real thing' (B) 3.50
1FB,20S,FS Coca-Cola, wave (F),(RD/BK) logo (F) only 4.00
1C,FS,J Coca Cola w/wave, (RD/WE), Chattanooga, Tenn bottler (B) 3.00
5C,20S Coca-Cola, assorted advertisers 5.00
1C,20S,FS It's Cott to be good, 7 cans (B), 'In Cans . . .' (F) 4.00
1C,20S,FS Canada Dry Grapefruit Beverage (F), seal (B) 4.00
1C,20S,FS Dr. Pepper (RD/YW) ad: Frank's Café, Great Bend, KS 3.00
1C,20S,FS Dr. Pepper (DBE,RD) 3 bottle (B), Taste That Flavor (S) 4.00
1C,20S,FS Drink Dr. X, The Tempting Beverage, same ad (F/B) 4.00
1C,20S,FS Drink Gold Vine as a mixer 'The Best What Gives' (YW/GN) 3.50
1C,20S,FS America's Taste Sensation, Nichols Kola 5c, (LBE/RD) 3.50
1C,ACTION Drink NuGrape Soda, 2 sticks remain, bottle on gusset (I), rare 8.00
15C,20S,FS Orange Crush, assorted advertisers 9.00
6C,20S Pepsi-Cola, assorted advertisers, one advertising Pepsi @ 5 Cents 12.00
1FB,20S,FS Pepsi-Coca Cola logo (F/B), (RD/WE), modern, Superior manumark 3.00
1C,20S Pepsi-Cola, long neck bottle (F/B), 5 cents 1.25
6C,20S,FS Pepsi Cola, older issues 3.00
1FB,20S,FS Pepsi-Cola (RD/WE) a remake of an earlier design 3.00
15C,20S,FS Soda Pop, assorted 2.50
1C,20S,FS Royal Crown Cola (F), Nehi (B),(RD/YW/BE), Good Housekeeping seal (S) 4.00
1FB,20S Royal Crown Cola, big bottle w/pyramids (B) 3.00
1C,20S Squirt, It's 'In the Public Eye', bottle (F), elf (B) 5.00
1C,20S,FL Sun Spot, 'Bottled Sunshine,' 5 cents, FL bottle 8.00
9C,20S,Soda (inc.Orange Crush, Nutri-Cola, Bob's-Cola, Coca-Cola, High Rock) 9.00

Souvenir & Education Sets

Souvenir Views Sets—These sets were popular during the 1930s and are differentiated by title, scene, and the number of rays on the saddle. All were made by the Diamond Match Co. Variations of some exist. Popular souvenir view sets include the cities of: Atlantic City, Chicago, Cleveland, Florida, Grand Coulee, Milwaukee, New England, New York, San Francisco, Texas, Washington, and Williamsburg.

Souvenir

Atlantic City Souvenir Views

Atlantic City Souvenir Views; A Popular Spot..-Along The Beach-Atlantic City..-Beach View..-Elephant Hotel-General View-Steel Pier-View From..(see below)

8C,20S,FS Set #1 [1935], 4 (GN) 4 (RD), (BN) print, 12 narrow rays (S), 1 line Diamond manumark 2.50

8C,20S,FS Set #2 [1937], 4 (GN) 4 (RD), (BK) print, 13 wide rays (S), 2 line Diamond manumark 3.00

8C,20S,FS Set #3 [1938], 4 (GN) 4 (RD), (BK) print, 13 narrow rays (S), 2 line Diamond manumark 3.00

8C,20S,FS Set #4 [1938], 4 (BE) 4 (RD), (BK) print, 12 wide rays (S), 2 line Diamond manumark, colored tip 5.00

8C,20S,FS Set #5 [1941], 4 (BE) 4 (RD), (BK) print, 12 wide rays (S), 2 line Diamond manumark, (BK) tip 2.50

8C,20S,FS Set #6 [1942], 4 (BE) 4 (RD), (BK) print, 12 narrow rays (S), 2 line Diamond manumark, narrow striker 3.00

Cleveland Souvenir Views

Cleveland Souvenir Views, Two sets of 8, Airport..-Boat Landing..-Cleveland's Public Square..-Garfield Memorial..-Museum of Art..-Public Auditorium..- Severance Hall..-Union Terminal..(see below)

8C,20S,FS Set #1 [1935], 4 (GN) and 4 (RD) covers, (BN) print, 13 narrow rays (S), 1 line Diamond manumark 7.25

8C,20S,FS Set #2 [1936], 4 (GN) and 4 (RD) covers, (BK) print, 13 narrow rays (S), 1 line Diamond manumark 5.00

Florida Souvenir Views

Florida Souvenir Views, 10 sets of 8, A Bit of Skyline..-Cocoanuts..-February Beach Scene..-Fort Marion..-North View of..-Oranges and Blossoms..-Palm Walk..- Venetian Pool..(see below)

8C,20S,FS Set #1 [1935], 4 (GN) 4 (RD), (BN) print, 13 wide rays (S), 1 line Diamond manumark 3.00

8C,20S,FS Set #2 [1936], 4 (GN) 4 (RD), (BN) print, 13 narrow rays (S), 1 line Diamond manumark 3.00

8C,20S,FS Set #3 [1937], 4 (GN) 4 (RD), (BK) print, 13 wide rays (S), I line Diamond manumark 13.00

8C,20S,FS Set #4 [1938], 4 (GN) 4 (RD), (BN) print, 12 wide rays (S), 2 line Diamond manumark 3.00

8C,20S,FS Set #5 [1938], 4 (GN) 4 (RD), (BN) print, 12 narrow rays (S), 2 line Diamond manumark 3.00

8C,20S,FS Set #6 [1938], 4 (GN) 4 (RD), (BK) print, 12 wide rays (S), 2 line Diamond manumark 3.00

8C,20S,FS Set #7 [1939], 4 (GN) 4 (RD), (BK) print, 12 narrow rays (S), 2 line Diamond manumark 3.00

8C,20S,FS Set #8 11940], 4 (BE) 4 (RD), (BK) print, 12 wide rays (S), 2 line Diamond manumark, color tip 3.00

8C,20S,FS Set #9 [1940], 4 (BE) 4 (RD), (BK) print, 12 wide rays (S), 2 line Diamond manumark, (BK) tip 3.00

8C,20S,FS Set #10 [1942], 4 (BE) 4 (RD), (BK) print, 12 narrow rays (S), 2 line Diamond manumark, narrow striker 3.00

Milwaukee Souvenir Views

Milwaukee Souvenir Views 2 sets of 8, Beautiful Washington..-Court House and..-Court of Honor,..- 'Downtown' View of..-Hotel Schroeder..-Juneau Park Vista..- Public Library and..-Tripoli Temple Shrine..(see below)
8C,20S,FS Set #1 [1937], 4 (GN) 4 (RD), 13 wide rays (S), 2 line Diamond manumark .. 2.00
8C,20S,FS Set #2 [1939], 4 (GN) 4 (RD), 12 narrow rays (S), 2 line Diamond manumark 1.50

New England Souvenir Views

New England Souvenir Views, five sets of 41, Conn: Across the Green..-Harkness Memorial..-Connecticut River Near..-State Capitol..-The Yale Bowl..-Ye Olde Town..NOTE: Connecticut River Near.. is title in (GN), while the same scene in (BE) is titled Picturesque Valley of.. Maine: Longfellow's Home..-Maine Potatoes-Old Orchard Beach..-Portland Headlight..-State Capitol..-Todd Head.. Mass: Bunker Hill Monument..-Copley Square..-Faneuil Hall..- The Hairpin Turn..-Old North Bridge..-Old South Church..-Old State House..-Plymouth Rock..-Public Gardens..-State Capitol..-Tremont Gardens..-N.H.: Echo Lake..-Lake Winnipesaukee..-Mills at Manchester..-Old Man of the Mountain..-State Capitol..-White Mountains.. R.I.: Betsy Williams Cottage..-Cliff Walk..-Memorial Arch..- Narragansett Pier..-Pawtucket, R.I.-State Capitol..Verm: Bennington Monument..-Coolidge Homestead..-Granite Quarr Maple Sugar..-'On Lake Champlain'..-State Capitol..(see below)
41C,20S,FS Set #1 [1936], 21 (GN) 20 (RD), (BK) print, 13 narrow rays (S), 2 line Diamond manumark 19.50
41C,20S,FS Set #2 [   ], 21 (GN) 20 (RD), (BK) print, 13 wide rays (S), 2 line Diamond manumark 19.50
41C,20S,FS Set #3 [1938], 21 (BE) 20 (RD), (BK) print, 12 wide rays (S), 2 line Diamond manumark, color tip 18.50
41C,20S,FS Set #4 [1938], 21 (BE) 20 (RD), (BK) print, 12 wide rays (S), 2 line Diamond manumark, (BK) tip 17.50
41C,20S,FS Set #5 [1942], 21 (BE) 20 (RD), (BK) print, 12 narrow rays (S), 2 line Diamond manumark, narrow striker 17.50

New York Souvenir Views

New York Souvenir Views 6 sets of 8 American Fall..-Bear Mountain..-Lake George..-New Lake Champlain..-Saratoga Race Track..-State Capitol..-Toll House..-U.S. Military Academy..(see below)
8C,20S,FS Set #1 [1937], 4 (GN) 4 (RD), (BK) print, 13 wide rays (S), 2 line Diamond manumark 3.00
8C,20S,FS Set #2 [1937], 4 (GN) 4 (RD), (BK) print, 13 narrow rays (S), 2 line Diamond manumark 3.00
8C,20S,FS Set #3 [1938], 4 (BE) 4 (RD), (BK) print, 12 wide rays (S), 2 line Diamond manumark, color tip 3.00
8C,20S,FS Set #4 [1938], 4 (BE) 4 (RD), (BK) print, 12 wide rays (S), 2 line Diamond manumark, (BK) tip 3.00
8C,20S,FS Set #5 [1942], 4 (BE) 4 (RD), (BK) print, 12 narrow rays, 2 line Diamond manumark, color tip, narrow striker 3.00
8C,20S,FS Set #6 [1942], 4 (BE) 4 (RD), (BK) print, 12 narrow rays, 2 line Diamond manumark, (BK) tip, narrow striker 3.00
9C,20S,FS New York State Set, Type A, 12 Wide Rays 2.00
6C,20S,FS New York Souvenir Set from 1930s, 12 ray, Type B, complete 35.00

San Francisco Souvenir Views

San Francisco Souvenir Views 2 sets of 4, Ferry Building..-Palace of Fine Arts..-San Francisco's City Hall,..-San Francisco's War Memorial..(see below)
4C,20S,FS Set #1 [   ], 2 (BE) and 2 (RD) covers, (BK) print, 12 wide rays (S), 2 line Diamond manumark 2.25
4C,20S,FS Set #2 [1942], 2 (BE) and 2 (RD) covers, (BK) print, 12 narrow rays (S), 2 line Diamond manumark, narrow striker 1.50
16FB,20S,FS Souvenir Set of San Francisco, in original celo pack, 2 sets 10.50

Golden Gate Bridge Souvenir Views

San Francisco Golden Gate Bridge Souvenir Views, 2 sets of 4 Bridging San Francisco's..-..Looking toward the Marin..-..Looking toward San..-Spanning the Golden Gate (see below)
4C,20S,FS Set #1 [1939], 2 (BE) 2 (RD), (BK) print, 12 wide rays (S), 2 line Diamond manumark 1.50
4C,20S,FS Set #2 [1942], 2 (BE) 2 (RD), (BK) print, 12 narrow rays (S), 2 line Diamond manumark, narrow striker 1.50

San Francisco Oakland Bridge Souvenir Views

San Francisco Oakland Bridge Souvenir Views, 4 sets of 4, Descriptive..-From Yerba Buena..-This great..-West Bay..(see below)
4C,20S,FS Set #1 [1937], 2 (GN) 2 (RD), (BK) print, 13 narrow rays (S), 2 line Colgate manumark 7.00
4C,20S,FS Set #2 [1939], 2 (GN) 2 (RD), (BK) print, 12 narrow rays (S), 2 line Colgate manumark 1.50
4C,20S,FS Set #3 [1939], 2 (BE) 2 (RD), (BK) print, 12 wide rays (S), 2 line Diamond manumark 1.50
4C,20S,FS Set #4 [1942], 2 (BE) 2 (RD), (BK) print, 12 narrow rays (S), 2 line Diamond manumark, narrow striker 1.50

Texas Souvenir Views

Texas Souvenir Views, Three sets of 4, The Alamo..-Bronk Riding..-The Oil Fields..-State Capitol..(see below)
4C,20S,FS Set #1 [1937], 4 (BE) covers, (BK) print, 12 wide rays (S), 2 line Diamond manumark 2.00
4C,20S,FS Set #2 [1942], 4 (BE) covers, (BK) print, 12 wide rays (S), 2 line Diamond manumark, color tip, narrow striker 2.00
4C,20S,FS Set #3 [1942], 4 (BE) covers, (BK) print, 12 wide rays (S), 2 line Diamond manumark, (BK) tip, narrow striker... 2.00

Washington Souvenir Views

Washington Souvenir Views, 7 sets of 8, Arlington..-George Washington..-Japanese..-Lincoln Memorial..-Mount Vernon-United States ..-Washington Monument..-White House..(see below)
8C,20S,FS Set #1 [1935], 4 (GN) 4 (RD), (BN) print, 12 wide rays (S), 1 line Diamond manumark 2.00

8C,20S,FS Set #2 [1937], 4 (GN) 4 (RD), (BK) print, 13 narrow rays (S), 2 line Diamond manumark 2.00

8C,20S,FS Set #3 [   ], 4 (BE) 4 (RD), (BK) print, 12 wide rays (S), 2 line Diamond manumark, color tip 2.00

8C,20S,FS Set #4 [   ], 4 (BE) 4 (RD), (BK) print, 12 wide rays (S), (BK) 2 line Diamond manumark (BK) tip 2.00

8C,20S,FS Set #5 [   ], 4 (BE) 4 (RD), (BK) print, 12 wide rays (S), (SR) 2 line Diamond manunumark (BK) tip 2.00

8C,20S,FS Set #6 [   ], 4 (BE) 4 (RD), (BK) print, 12 narrow rays (S), 2 line Colgate manumark 2.00

8C,20S,FS Set #7 [1942], 4 (BE) 4 (RD), (BK) print, 12 wide rays (S), 2 line Diamond manumark, narrow striker 2.00

Miscellaneous Souvenir Sets

8C,20S,FS Chicago Souvenir Views, [1935] 4 (GN) 4 (RD), (BN) print, 12 narrow rays (S), 1 line Diamond manumark Adler Planetarium..-Clarence Buckingham..-Field Museum..- Looking North..-Looking South..-North State..-University Chapel..-Upper Michigan Avenue 10.00

4C,20S,FS Williamsburg Souvenir Views Set [   ], Royal Governor's Palace, (RD), (BK) print, 12 narrow rays (S), 2 line Diamond manumark 2.00

7C,20S,FS GEICO scenes of Washington, DC Set 3.00

2C,20S,FS Grand Coulee Souvenir Views Set [1942], 1 (BE) 1 (RD), (BK) print, 12 wide rays (S), 2 line Diamond manumark Grand Coulee Dam (BE)-Grand Coulee Dam (RD) . 2.00

1FB,20S,FS Souvenir Set ca. 1930, Mark Hopkins Hotel (BE) 2.25

1C,20S,FS Single [1942], colored oranges and blossoms 1.00

1FB,20S,FS Souvenir Series - 13 rays - State Capitol - Augusta, Maine (RD) 2.75

1FB,20S,FS Souvenir Series - 13 rays - Bunker Hill Monument - Charlestown, Mass. (RD) 2.00

1FB,20S,FS Souvenir Series - 13 rays - Old State House - Boston, Mass. (RD) 2.25

1FB,20S,FS Souvenir Series - 13 rays - Old Man of the Mountain - Franconia Notch, N.H. (GN) 1.75

1FB,20S,FS Souvenir Series - 13 rays - Cliff Walk - Newport, R.I. (GN) 2.25

1FB,20S,FS Souvenir Series - 13 rays - Coolidge Homestead - Plymouth, Vermont (GN) 2.25

1FB,20S,FS Souvenir Series - 13 rays - Harkness Memorial - Quadrangle - Branford Court. Yale University - New Haven, Conn. (GN) 2.50

Educational Sets

Educational Sets—There are several Educational Sets, each consisting of varying numbers of matchcovers with a few variations. All were made by the Diamond Match Co. and come in various colors.

Santa Catalina Educational Set

Santa Catalina Educational Set; A Pretty..-Avalon-Avalon Bay-Catalina Airport-Catalina Bird Park-Descanso..-El Encanto-Glass..-Palm Fronds..-Santa Catalina Island-Santa Catalina Isthmus-Scenic..-Seals-Swordfish-the Catalina Casina-Wild Mountain Goats (see below), 17C,20S,FS Set, Type 1 [1934], blank (I) Additional cover is Avalon with (RD) background, printed in error 7.50

16C,20S,FS Set, Type 2 [1937], ad (I) 5.00

33C,20S,FS Set, Type 1 and 2 .... 27.50

Educational Series

1FB,20S,FS Photo (B), Desc. (F), Ambassador International Bridge 1.25
1FB,20S,FS Photo (B), Desc. (F), Arlington Memorial Bridge 1.25
1FB,20S,FS Photo (B), Desc. (F), Betsy Ross' Home 1.25
1FB,20S,FS Photo (B), Desc. (F), Brooklyn Bridge 2.00
1FB,20S,FS Photo (B), Desc. (F), Georgia State Capitol 1.25
1FB,20S,FS Photo (B), Desc. (F), Kennebec River Bridge 1.25
1FB,20S,FS Photo (B), Desc. (F), Merchandise Mart 1.25
1FB,20S,FS Photo (B), Desc. (F), Scene in New England 1.25
1FB,20S,FS Photo (B), Desc. (F), Beautiful New England 1.25
1FB,20S,FS Photo (B), Desc. (F), Old Man's head Rock 1.25
1FB,20S,FS Photo (B), Desc. (F), San Francisco Bay Toll Bridge 2.00
1FB,20S,FS Photo (B), Desc. (F), Capitol at Washington, D.C 1.25

New England Educational Set

44C,20S,FS 12 Wide Rays, Type A 24.50
43C,20S,FS 12 Thin Rays, Type B 25.00
43C,20S,FS 13 Wide Rays, Type C.. 17.50
43C,20S,FS 13 Thin Rays, Type D 18.00

New York State Educational Set

9C,20S,FS 12 Wide Rays, Type A 7.50
6C,20S,FS 12 Thin Rays, Type B 7.25
8C,20S,FS 13 Wide Rays, Type C... 5.50
8C,20S,FS 13 Thin Rays, Type D 6.25

Miscellaneous Educational Sets

100C,20S,FS Educational Sets, Diamond Match, Type 1 [1932], 34 (BE), 33 (RD), 33 (WE) 200.00
1FB,20S,FS Educational Series, photo (B), Desc. (F), New York State Capitol 1.25

Space

Space—The category devoted to aerospace sets and singles, the most noteworthy of which is the Apollo series, dating from Apollo 7 in October 1968 to Apollo 17 in December 1972. Airlines, flight services, or commercial freight carriers are not included in this category.

Apollo

1C,30S,FS,FOI Apollo 7 - Oct. 11-22, 1968, color photo of Eisele, Schirra, & Cunningham on F
.... 12.00
1C,30S,FS,FOI Apollo 7 [10-11 to 10-22-1968] 40.00
1FB,30S,FS Apollo 7, Eisele, Schirra, Cunningham, Oct. 11-22, 1968 RCA Set 6.00
1FB,J Apollo 8, Borman, Lovell, Anders, logo (F), name & number (B) 7.25
1C,30S Apollo 8, Dec 21-27, 1968, Lovell, Anders, Borman, photo (F), seal (B) 10.00
1C,JL,FS,CAM Apollo 8 [12-21 to 12-27-1968], RCA, Type 1, Miami manumark 5.00
1C,JL,FS,CAM Apollo 8 [12-21 to 12-27-1968], RCA, Type 2, Orlando manumark, Astronautics
Specialties 2.00
1FB,30S,FS Apollo 09, McDivitt, Scott, Schweickart, March 3-13, 1969, RCA Set 6.00
1FB,J Apollo 9, McDivitt, Scott, Schweickart, logo (F), name & number (B) 5.50
1C,30S Apollo 9, McDivitt, Scott, Schweickart, Mar 3-13, 1969, photo (F), seal (B) 8.00
1C,JL,FS,CAM Apollo 9 [3-3 to 3-13-1969], RCA, Type 1, Miami manumark, 9 (B) 5.00
1C,JL,FS,CAM Apollo 9 [3-3 to 3-13-1969], RCA, Type 2, Miami manumark, (B) blank .. 2.25
1C,JL,FS,CAM Apollo 9 [3-3 to 3-13-1969], RCA, Type 3, Orlando manumark, Astronautics
specialties 2.00
1FB,30S,FS Apollo 10, Cernan, Young, Stafford, May 18-26, 1969, RCA Set 6.00
1C,30S,FS,CAM Apollo 10 [5-18 to 5-26-1969], Miami manumark 2.00
1C,30S, Apollo 11 - July 16-24, 1969, color photos of Armstrong, Collins & Aldrin on F ... 7.50
1C,30S,FS,CAM Apollo 11 [7-16 to 7-24-1969], Miami manumark, Type 1 [1969] 2.00
1C,30S,FS Apollo 11 [7-16 to 7-24-1969], Miami manumark, Type 2 [1969], Cameo trademark
with smooth finish 2.00
1C,30S,CAM Apollo 12, Conrad, Gordon, Bean 7.75
1FB,30S,FS,CAM Apollo 12 Conrad, Gordon, Bean, no dates given, RCA 6.00
1C,30S,FS,CAM Apollo 12 [11-14 to 11-24-1969], RCA, Type 1, Miami manumark 4.00
1C,30S,FS,CAM Apollo 12 [11-14 to 11-24-1969], RCA, Type 2, Miami manumark, Cameo
trademark, smooth finish 2.25
1C,30S,FS Apollo 12 [11-14 to 11-24-1969], RCA, Cameo Type 3 [   ], Orlando manumark,
Astronautics Specialties 2.00
1C,30S,FS Apollo 13 [4-11 to 4-17-1970], Type 1, Miami manumark, RAM Associates, Lowell-
Haise-Mattingly 2.25
1C,30S,FS Apollo 13 [4-11 to 4-17-1970], Type 2, Orlando manumark, Caesars Palace, Lowell-
Haise-Swigert, space for number (I) 2.00
1FB,30S,FS,CAM Apollo 14, Shepard, Roosa, Mitchell, Jann. 31-Feb 9, 1971, RCA Set . 6.00
1C,30S,FS Apollo 14 - Jan. 31-Feb 9, 1971, color photo of Roosa, Shepard & Mitchell on F 9.50
1FB,30S,FS Apollo 14 [1-31 to 2-9-1971], Miami manumark, 30S, FS, Cameo 2.00
1C,30S,FS,CAM Apollo 15 Scott, Worden, Irwin, no photo, no date 6.50
1C,30S,FS,CAM Apollo 15 [7-26 to 8-7-1971], Type 1 [   ], Miami manumark 3.00
1C,30S,FS,CAM Apollo 15 [7-26 to 8-7-1971], Type 2 [   ], Orlando manumark, Wayne Newton
.... 2.25
1C,30S,FS Apollo 15 [7-26 to 8-7-1971], Type 3 [1971], no manumark, (PK), RCA info (I) 2.00
1C,30S,FS Apollo 16 - April 16-27, 1972, color photo of Young, Mattingly & Duke on F . 6.50
1FB,30S,FS Apollo 16, Young, Mattingly, Duke, April 16-27, 1972, RCA Set 6.00
1C,30S,FS,CAM Apollo 16 [4-16 to 4-27-1972], Type 1, Miami manumark, Del Webb Hotels
International, Astronautics Specialties, space for number 2.00
1C,30S,FS,RAMA Apollo 16 [4-16 to 4-27-1972], Type 2, Philadelphia manumark, RCA 2.50
1C,30S,CAM Apollo 17, Cernan, Evans, Schmitt, no photo 6.50
1FB,30S,CAM Apollo 17, Cernan, Evans, Schmitt, logo (B) 4.50
1C,30S,FS,CAM Apollo 17 [12-7 to 12-19-1972], Orlando manumark, Del Webb Hotels
International, Astronautics Specialties 2.25
1FB,30S,FS,CAM Apollo 17 Cernan, Evans, Schmitt, no dates given, RCA Cameo Set .. 6.00

12C,30S,FS,FOI Apollo Commemorative Series Set [1972], by RCA, 7-8-9-10-11-12-13-14-15-
16-17- For the benefit of mankind 4.00
??C Apollo Set [   ], Astronautics Specialties, framed by company 130.00

Space   (Miscellaneous)

8C,40S,FS Neil Armstrong, First Man on the Moon, July 20, 1969 Space Exploration Series, photo
(F) of each 17.00
1C,40S,FS Neil Armstrong, First Man on the Moon, July 20, 1969 .... 15.00
1C,30S,FS Kennedy Space Center, seal (f), blast-off (b) 1.75
2C,30S,BS Space Shuttle, Type 1 Orlando manumark, (BK) striker, (S) blank 1.50
2C,30S,BS Space Shuttle, Type 2 Orlando manumark, (BK) striker, Kennedy Space Center FL
(S) 1.50
2C,30S,BS,FL Space Shuttle, Type 3 Orlando manumark, (GY) striker, Kennedy Space Center
(S) 1.50
2C,30S,BS,FL Space Shuttle, Type 4 Made in Canada manumark, (GY) striker, Kennedy Space
Center (S) 1.50
9C,30S,FS Space Age U.S.A. Set [1970], 3 (F) views each combined with 3 different (B) views
Man's first step: Command unit-LEM & module-2 astronauts Rocket taking off:. Command
unit-LEM & module-2 astronauts View of earth: Command unit-LEM & module-2 as 1.00

Stock Cuts used for sports related matchcovers.

  Puzzle or game matchcovers were always
popular, but are very rare. Here, Ole's Waffle Shop
in Oakland and Alameda asks, "My Girl & Her
Mother. Do You See Both?" That's one way to keep
the customer looking at your advertisement!
  Do you see them both? Once you do, you'll
always see them.

Sports

Sports—One of the most popular categories of matchcover collecting, Sports matchcovers are collected as a side line by many Sports memorabilia collectors. The category is very broad, encompassing teams, individuals, VIPs, stadiums, schedules, foreign sports, olympics, and special events. Pioneered in the mid-1930s by Diamond Match Co., Group One sports matchcovers number in the thousands.

Sports (Auto Racing)

12C,20S,FS Champion Spark Plug Winners [c. 1955] including F. Agabashian, D. Carter, R.
    Crawford & E. Iglesias, J. Flock, J. McGrath, P. O'Connor, J. Parsons, L. Petty, J. Reece, J.
    Rutherford, B. Sweikert, and P. Walters 65.00
1C,40S,FS Official Pace Car, 51st Indianapolis 500 Mile Race, Chevrolet Camaro, May 30, 1967,
    car (F) 5.00
12C,20S,FS Champion Spark Plugs, Set #1 [1956], Agabashian-Carter-Crawford-Flock-McGrath-
    O'Connor-Parsons-Petty Reece-Rutherfurd-Sweikert-Walters (stock) 8.00
10C,20S,FS Champion Spark Plugs, Set #2 [1957], Andrews-Cross-Davies-Flaherty-Linden-
    Dick Rathman-Jim Rathman-Thomson-Wallard-Ward (stock) 7.50
1C,20S,FS Champion Spark Plus Indy 500, 1955, Art Cross, w/photo of car & driver (B) 5.00
1C,20S,FS Champion Spark Plus Indy 500, 1955, Jimmy Davies, w/photo of car & driver (B) 5.00
1C,20S,FS Champion Spark Plus Indy 500, 1956, Pat Flaherty, winner, w/photo of car & driver
    (B) 5.00
1C,20S,FS Champion Spark Plus Indy 500, 1955, Andy Linden, w/photo of car & driver (B) 5.00
1C,20S,FS Champion Spark Plus Indy 500, 1956, Dick Rathman, w/photo of car & driver (B) 5.25
1C,20S,FS Champion Spark Plus Indy 500, 1955, Jim Rathman, w/photo of car & driver (B) 5.00
1C,20S,FS Champion Spark Plus Indy 500, 1955, Johnny Thomson, w/photo of car & driver (B)
    .... 5.00
1C,20S,FS Champion Spark Plus Indy 500, 1951, Lee Wallard, winner, w/photo of car & driver
    (B) 9.25
1C,20S,FS Champion Spark Plus Indy 500, 1955, Rodger Ward, w/photo of car & driver (B) 6.25
6C,30S,FS Sport Cars of Yesteryear Set [1967], Kissel Speedster-Mercer Raceabout-Roamer
    Sport Touring-Stutz Sport Roadster-Templar Sport Roadster-Velie Sport Car 2.00

Sports (Baseball Teams)

Montreal Expos

7C,30S,BS Set [1970] 12.00
7C,30S,BS Set [1971] 12.00
7C,30S,BS Set [1973] 12.00
7C,30S,BS Set [1974] 12.00
7C,30S,BS Set [1975] 12.00
7C,30S,BS Set [1976] 16.00
7C,30S,BS Set [1977] 12.00
7C,30S,BS Set [1978] 9.50

Famous Senators, 1st Federal Savings & Loan Set

10C,20S,FS Set [1952], w/O. Bluege, J. Cronin, L. Goslin, C. Griffith, S. Harris, W. Johnson, J.
Judge, C. Milan, E. Rice, and R. Sievers 79.00
10C,20S,FS Set [1959], no dots on either side of the manumark, Bluege-Cronin-Goslin-Griffith-
Harris-Johnson-Judge-Milan-Rice-Sievers 35.00
10C,20S,FS Set [1960], 2 dots on either side of the manumark, Altrock-Crowder-Killebrew-
Kuhel-Lewis-Jyer-Peckinpaugh-Spence-Vernon-West 35.00
1C,20S,FS Nicholas (Nick) Altrock, P, Most Famous Baseball Clown, photo (F) 6.25
1C,20S,FS James (Mickey) Barton, Batting Champ. 1946 & 1953, photo (F) 5.25
1C,20S,FS Ossie Bluege, 3B, Mgr, All-Time Fielding Star, photo (F) 7.75
1C,20S,FS Joe Cronin, Shortstop, Manager, HOF 1956, photo (F) 9.75
1C,20S,FS Alvin Floyd (General) Crowder, P, Won 88 Games for Washington, photo (F) 6.25
1C,20S,FS Leon (Goose) Goslin, Outfield, AL Batting Champion, 1928, photo (F) 11.50
1C,20S,FS Clark C. Griffith, Pitcher, HOF 1946, photo (F) 9.00
1C,20S,FS Stanley (Bucky) Harris, 2B, First Famous 'Boy Manager', photo (F) 9.25
1C,20S,FS Walter Johnson, Pitcher, Manager, HOF 1936, photo (F) 14.25
1C,20S,FS Joe Judge, 1st Base, Coach, photo (F) 8.25
1C,20S,FS Harmon Clayton Killebrew, AL Home Run Champ, 1959, HOF 1984, photo (F) 16.25
1C,20S,FS Joseph Anthony Kuhel, 1st Base, Manager, photo (F) 5.25
1C,20S,FS Famous Senators Baseball, 1st Federal Set, photo (F), John (Buddy) Lewis, Lifetime
Average .297 .... 5.25
1C,20S,FS Clyde Milan, Outfield, Manager, Coach, photo (F) 9.00
1C,20S,FS Famous Senators Baseball, 1st Federal Set, Charles (Buddy) Myer, 2nd Base,
Batting Champion 1935, photo (F) 9.25
1C,20S,FS Roger Thorpe Peckinpaugh, Short Stop, AL/MVP 1925, photo (F) 10.00
1C,20S,FS Edgar (Sam) Rice, Out Field, Lifetime Average .322, HOF 1963, photo (F) 10.00
1C,20S,FS Roy Sievers, Outfield, 1st Base, AL Home Run King 1957, photo (F) 9.00
1C,20S,FS Stanley Orville Spence, CF, All-Star Team for 4 years, photo (F) 5.25
1C,20S,FS James Barton (Mickey) Vernon, 1st Base, Batting Champion 1946 & 1953 ... 6.75
1C,20S,FS Samuel Filmore West, Center Field, Lifetime Batting Average .299, photo (F) 5.75

Minnesota Twins, F&M Savings Bank Set

10C,20S,FS Set [1961], Allison-Battey-Bertoia-Gardner-Green-Killebrew-Lavagetto-Lemon-
Pascual-Ramos 41.00
10C,20S,FS Set [1962], Allison-Battey-Green-Kaat-Killebrew-Kralik-Lemon-Pascual-Ramos-
Versalles 45.00
1C,20S,FS Camillo Alberto (Potato) Pascual, Pitcher, photo (F), stats (I) 6.75
1C,20S,FS William Robert (Bob) Allison, Out Field, photo (F), stats (I) 7.50
1C,20S,FS Earl Battey, catcher, photo (F), stats (I) 8.50
1C,20S,FS Reno Bertoia, 3rd Base, photo (F), stats (I) 7.50

1C,20S,FS William Frederick 'Billy' Gardner, 2nd Base, photo (F), stats (I) 8.75
1C,20S,FS Lenny Green, outfielder, photo (F), stats (I) 7.50
1C,20S,FS Harmon Clayton (Harm) Killebrew, In Field, HOF 1984, photo (F), stats (I) 28.00
1C,20S,FS Harry A. (Cookie) Lavagetto, Manager, photo (F), stats (I) 8.00
1C,20S,FS James Robert (Jim) Lemon, Out Field, photo (F), stats (I) 9.00
1C,20S,FS Camilo Pascual, photo (F), stats (I) 6.75
1C,20S,FS Pedro (Pete) Ramos, Pitcher, photo (F), stats (I) 7.50

Sports   (Baseball—Miscellaneous)

1C,20S,FS Attend every game of the '53 World Series, ad: Rum & Maple Tobacco, rules (I) 5.50
1C,40S The Swinging A's, AL Champions 1972, Charlie O. Finley, Owner, Dick Williams, Mgr,
    plate scene (B) 11.00
4C,20S,BS 1982 thru 1985 Cincinnati Reds at Riverfront Stadium (I), team ad & dates (F/B) 5.00
15C,20S,FS California Angels [1965], County Nat'l Bank, Chance-Clinton-Fregosi-Kirkpatrick-
    Knoop-Latman-Lee-McBride-Newman-Piersall-Reichardt-Rigney-Rodgers-Satriano-Smith
    .... 30.00
15C,20S,FS California Angels [1965], Sata Fe Savings, Chance-Clinton-Fregosi-Kirkpatrick-
    Knoop-Latman-Lee-McBride-Newman-Piersall-Reichardt-Rigney-Rodgers-Satriano-Smith
    .... 30.00
15C,20S,FS California Angels [1966], County Nat'l Bank, Chance-Clinton-Fregosi-Kirkpatrick-
    Knoop-Latman-Lee-McBride-Newman-Piersall-Reichardt-Rigney-Rodgers-Satriano-Smith
    .... 30.00
1C,30S,FS Baltimore Orioles, Championship Flags (B), logo (F) 6.00
24C,30S,FS Baltimore Orioles Set [1970], Belanger-Blair-Buford-Cuellar-Dalrymple-Etchebarren-
    Floyd-Hall-Hardin-Hendricks-Johnson-Leonhard-McNally-Motton-Palmer-Phoebus-
    Powell-Richert-Rettenmund-Brooks Robinson-Frank Robinson-Salmon-Watt-Weaver 55.00
1B titled Big League, Made in U.S.A., Safety Matches, National Safety Match Corp., wooden
    penny box, showing batter, catcher & umpire, ball in air 6.00
13C,JWL Boston Red Sox Baseball 5.50
1C,20S,FS Dean Chance, Los Angeles Dodgers, (B/W) photo in uniform (B), ad: Santa Ana
    Savings & Loan (F) 8.75
1C,30S,BS Baseball Hall of Fame 4.50
1C,20S,FS Jim Fregosi, Los Angeles Dodgers, (B/W) photo in uniform (B), ad: County National
    Bank 5.00
1C,20S,FS Bobby Knoop, I, Angels, County Nat'l Bank Set 5.00
1C,20S,BS Legends Restaurant & Sports Bar, New York, (BK/WE) 1.75
1C,20S,FS Ken McBride, Los Angeles Dodgers, (B/W) photo in uniform (B), ad: Santa Ana
    Savings & Loan (F) 8.75
12C,JWL Milwaukee Brewers Baseball 5.00
1C,20S,FS Macke Vending Machine, Baseball Player (F/B), Jersey Match Co. 3.25
1C,20S,FS Macke Machines, Special World Series mc, ad: cigarettes 4.50
1C,20S,FS 1953 World Series by Rum & Maple Smoking Tobacco 10.00
6C,20S,FS Pedro's Rum Set [   ], Names to Remember Corbett-Fitzsimmons-Mathewson-
    McGraw-Rockne-Sullivan 35.00
2C,30S,FS Kansas City Royals 1. Stadium Club, 2. The Aladdin Hotel 2.25
1C,20S,FS Clemson House, Home of the Tigers, Tiger (F), Clemson House (B) 5.00

Group One Baseball

24C,20S,FS 2nd Baseball Set [1935], (BK) border, Allen-Berger-Carey-Chiozza-Dean-Frisch-
    Grimm-Hafey-Hogan-Hubbell-Klein-Lombardi-Lopez-Maranville-Moore-Mungo-Ott-Slade-
    Stengel-Thevenow-Waner, L.-Waner, P.-Warnecke-Wilson 75.00
546C,20S,FS 3rd Baseball Type 1 [1935-6], 236 reported, 182 players each in 3 colors (BE/GN/
    RD) 1200.00

69C,20S,FS 3rd Baseball Type 2 Set [1936], 23 players in 3 colors (BE/GN/RD), (BN) ink Bryant-Carleton-Cavaretta-Collins-Davis-Dean-Demaree-French-Frey-Galan-Garbark-Hack-Hartnett-Herman-Jurges-Lee-Marty-O'Dea-Parmelee-Root-Shoun-Stainback-Waner 125.00

69C,20S,FS 3rd Baseball Type 3 Set [1936], 23 players each in 3 colors (BE/GN/RD), (BK) ink, Bryant-Carleton-Cavaretta-Collins-Davis-Dean-Demaree-French-Frey-Galan-Garbark-Hack-Hartnett-Herman-Jurges-Lee-Marty-O'Dea-Parmelee-Root-Shoun-Stainback-Warner 150.00

42C,20S,FS 4th Baseball [1937], 14 players each in 3 colors (BE/GN/RD) Carey-Cuccinello-Fitzsimmons-Frisch-Grimm, ((WE) shirt, (BK) print))-Grimm ((WE) shirt, brown print)-Grimm (dark shirt)-Hubbell-Jordan-Klein-Lopez-Medwick-Mungo-Ott 75.00

1C,20S,FS Richard 'Dick' Bartell, Philadelphia Phillies, (RD) 3.00

1C,20S,FS Aloysius Bejma, St. Louis Browns 3.50

1C,20S,FS Walter Berger, Boston Bees (RD) 7.00

1C,20S,FS Claiborne Bryant, Chicago Cubs (GN) 7.00

1C,20S,FS Tommy Carey, St. Louis Browns (GN) 7.00

1C,20S,FS James A. Collins, Chicago Cubs (BE) 7.00

1C,20S,FS James A. Collins, 3rd/Type II, Chicago Cubs (BE) 3.50

1C,20S,FS James A. Collins (BE), 1st Baseball 6.00

2C,20S,FS Curt Davis, 3rd/Type II, Chicago Cubs (GN/BE) 7.50

2C,20S,FS Jerome 'Dizzy' Dean, 3rd/Type II, St. Louis Cardinals, HOF 1953 (GN,BE) 40.50

2C,20S,FS Frank Demaree, 3rd/Type II, Chicago Cubs (GN,BE) 15.00

1C,20S,FS Elwood G. English, Chicago Cubs 5.50

1C,20S,FS Freddy Fitzsimmons, 3rd/Type II, New York Giants (RD) 27.50

1C,20S,FS Freddy Fitzsimmons, New York 'Giants' (RD) 8.00

1C,20S,FS Larry French, 3rd/Type II, Chicago Cubs (RD) 3.50

1C,20S,FS Benny Frey, Cincinnati Reds (RD) 10.50

1C,20S,FS Frankie Frisch, 3rd/Type II, St. Louis Cardinals, HOF 1947 (RD) 7.75

3C,20S,FS August Galan, 3rd/Type II, Chicago Cubs (BE,RD,GN) 15.50

3C,20S,FS Bob Garbark, 3rd/Type II, Chicago Cubs (BE,RD,GN) 15.50

1C,20S,FS Group 1 Baseball Charles Grimm, Chicago Cubs (BE) 7.00

1C,20S,FS Stanley Hack, 3rd/Type II, Chicago Cubs (GN) 10.00

1C,20S,FS Charles Hartnett, Chicago Cubs (RD) 7.50

2C,20S,FS Charles 'Gabby' Hartnett, 3rd/Type II, Chicago Cubs, HOF 1975, (BE/RD) .. 7.00

1C,20S,FS William Herman, Chicago Cubs 5.50

1C,20S,FS Carl Hubbel, P, New York Giants, HOF 1947 .... 22.50

1C,20S,FS Sylvester Johnson, Type II, Cincinnati Reds (RD) 7.00

2C,20S,FS Baxter Jordan, Boston Bees (RD,GN) 5.00

2C,20S,FS William F. Jurges, 3rd/Type II, Chicago Cubs (BE,GN) 11.00

1C,20S,FS Charles Klein, Phila Phillies (GN) 7.00

1C,20S,FS Mark Koenig, New York Giants 5.50

1C,20S,FS Joe Moore (OE), 1st Baseball 6.00

1C,20S,FS Joe Moore, New York Giants (RD) 7.50

1C,20S,FS Glenn Myatt, New York Giants 5.50

1C,20S,FS Melvin 'Mel' Ott, OF, New York Giants, HOF 1951 (RD) 18.00

1C,20S,FS Le Roy Parmelee, St. Louis Cardinals (RD) 6.00

1C,20S,FS Charlie Root, Chicago Cubs 5.50

1C,20S,FS Fred Schulte, Pittsburgh Pirates (RD) 7.00

1C,20S,FS Clyde Shoun, Chicago Cubs (RD) 6.00

1C,20S,FS Walter, Stephenson. Chicago Cubs 3.25

1C,20S,FS William H. Walker (BE), 1st Baseball 6.00

Sports (Basketball)

1C,20S,FS Basketball's Museum & Shrine, Springfield, MA 4.00
1C,20S,FS Baltimore Bullets, ad: ticket information, no schedule 5.00
1C,20S,FS Baltimore Bullets, player (B).. 5.25
1C,20S,FS Baltimore Bullets Professional Basketball 4.00
1C,JLT Kansas Jayhawks w/football helmet (F), Basketball (B)..................................... 2.75
1C,20S,FS New York Nicks, New York Rangers w/information number.......................... 3.75
1C,20S,FS New York Nicks, no schedule, Basketball (F), logo (B)................................ 3.00

Sports (Bowling)

1C,20S,FS Metro Bowl, Home of the 1960-1961 State Tournament, Lansing, Mich 3.25
10C,30S,FS Bowling Lanes, mostly older, assorted 4.75
10C,20S,FS California Bowling Lanes 2.75
15C,20S,FS Illinois Bowling Lanes 3.50
5C,20S,FS Indiana Bowling Lanes 3.00
10C,20S,FS Michigan Bowling Lanes 3.00
10C,20S,FS New Jersey Bowling Lanes... 4.00
20C,20S,FS New York Bowling Lanes 5.00
20C,20S,FS Ohio Bowling Lanes 6.25
10C,20S,FS Pennsylvania Bowling Lanes 9.00
25C,20S,FS Wisconsin Bowling Lanes.. 7.75
33C,20S,FS Wisconsin and Ohio Bowling Alleys 5.00
24C,20S,FS New Jersey, Michigan & Indiana Bowling Alleys 5.00
20C,20S,FS New York and New York State Bowling Alleys 5.00
50C,20S,FS Bowling Alleys, assorted cities 4.00
50C,30S,MS Bowling Alleys, assorted cities 5.00
40C,20S,MS Bowling Alleys, assorted cities 4.00
100C,MS Bowling Alleys, assorted cities 11.00

Sports (Boxing)

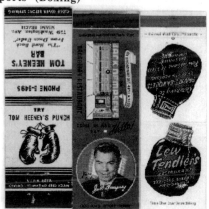

Boxing—A popular sub-classification of Sports, Boxing matchcovers tend to be difficult to find. They either mention or depict a boxing personality in the ring or as a VIP (i.e. his restaurant, liquor store, etc.). Adam Hats published sets of 30 ring personalities with approximately 40 different dealer imprints which are also known as Sam-Taub's Ring Personalities sets. This category may have singles or sets not directly related to a boxer, but to the sport itself, (i.e. The Ring Bar, or The Square Ring Tavern, etc.).

1C,20S,FS Primo Carnera's Liquor Store, 513 1/2 So. Brand Blvd, Glendale, cartoon of Carnera
(F), phone (S)... 8.00
1C,20S,FS Jack Dempsey's Restaurant, Bar and Grill, New York City, photo of young Dempsey
(F), restaurant (F) 8.50

1FB,30S,FS Jack Dempsey's Restaurant, New York, restaurant matchbook, seated family (B/
W) photo (F) 6.75

1C,20S,FS Jack Dempsey, circular middle-aged looking (BK/WE) 'Yours truly, Jack Dempsey'
photo w/(BE) background (F), Come in and say Hello! (S), drawing of front of restaurant
w/ on Broadway Bet. 49st & 50 St. 10.00

1C,20S,FS Jack Dempsey's Restaurant, New York City, signed photo (F), restaurant (B) 16.00

1C,20S,FS Jack Dempsey's Broadway Restaurant, (LBE) w/boxing gloves (F), photo of Jack
looking to side, ring scene (B) 13.00

1C,30S,FS Jack Dempsey's on Broadway, display of JD (I) 4.00

1C,20S,FS Jack Dempsey's Broadway Restaurant, (DBE) w/boxing gloves (F), photo of Jack
facing front, ring scene (B) 13.00

1C,20S,FS Jack Dempsey, Come in and Say Hello! (S) (SR) 7.00

1FB,30S,FS Jack Dempsey's Restaurant, New York, restaurant matchbook, pretty girl (B/W)
photo (F) 6.75

1FB,30S,FS Jack Dempsey's Restaurant, New York, restaurant matchbook, pretty girl (B/W)
photo (F) 5.25

1FB,20S,FS Jack Dempsey's Broadway Restaurant, older (BK/WE) photo (F) w/Boxing glove,
Demspey/Williard 1919 fight scene (B) 10.00

1C,20S,FS Jack Dempsey, Gloves (F), Ring (B) 2.00

1C,20S,FS Jack Dempsey's Restaurant opposite Madison Square Garden. Bar and Grill 8th
Avenue at 50th St. New York City. 'Yours truly, Jack Dempsey' color photo (F) Come in
and say Hello! (S) (RD) 7.50

1C,20S,FS Meet the Celebrities at Jack Dempsey's on Broadway between 49th. & 50 St. New
York (F), last name in script and underlined. Drawing of Broadway Bar & Lounge (B) 6.50

1C,20S,FS Jack Dempsey, Miami Beach, Fla. (S) (SR) 5.75

1C,20S,FS Jack Dempsey, Miami Beach, Fla. (S) (RD) 4.25

1C,20S,FS Jack Dempsey's Restaurant, circular photo w/Yours truly, Jack Dempsey (F),
restaurant (B) 3.00

1C,20S,FS Jack Dempsey's Restaurant, Bar & Grill, NYC, photo (F) 5.00

1C,20S,FS Jack Dempsey Vanderbilt Hotel, Miami Beach, square photo w/Yours truly, Jack
Dempsey (F), drawing of hotel (F), (DBE border 12.00

1C,20S,FS Jack Dempsey Vanderbilt Hotel, Miami Beach, round photo w/Yours truly, Jack
Dempsey (F), drawing of hotel (F), (RD) border 12.50

1C,20S,FS Vince Dundee Cocktail Lounge & Liquor Store, Glendale, Calif, Ex-Middle Weight
Champion, gloves (F) 7.00

1C,20S,FS Lew Fendler's Restaurant, Fendler (F), (Boxing), w/Manny's Delicious Waffles (B)
.... 4.00

1C,20S,FS Abe Kaplan Sportsmen Café, Yermo, Calif, full face (BK/WE) photo (B) 6.50

1C,20S,FS Jake la Motta's Lounge & Package Sotre, 2300 Collins Ave, Miami Beach, FL, (B/
W) photo of Jake as boxer (B) 15.00

1FB,20S,FS,FEA Jake LaMotta's Lounge & Package Store, 2300 Collins Ave, Miami Beach, FL,
(BK/WE) photo in boxing trunks (B), 'Where Celebrities Meet' (S) 12.00

1FB,G,FS Joe Louis/Max Schmeling Fight [6-18-1936], Type 1, [1936], (BE) behind fighters,
(WE) (F) flap and wording on 2 lines 45.00

1FB,G,FS Joe Louis/Max Schmeling Fight [6-18-1936], Type 2, [1936], (BE) behind fighters,
(WE) (F) flap and wording on 1 line 55.00

1FB,G,FS Joe Louis/Max Schmeling Fight [6-18-1936], Type 3, [1936], (BE) behind fighters,
(OE) (F) flap and wording on 2 lines 45.00

1FB,G,FS Joe Louis/Max Schmeling Fight [6-18-1936], Type 4, [1936], (WE) behind fighters,
(OE) (F) flap and wording on 2 lines 65.00

1FB,G,FS Joe Louis/Max Schmeling Fight [6-18-1936], Type 5, [1936], (WE) behind fighters,
(OE) (F) flap and wording on I line 45.00

1C,20S,FS Rocky Marciano's Italia Supper Club, Cleveland, Ohio, no photo 6.50

1C,20S,FS,CON The Rocky Marciano Room, 591 Lexington Ave, NYC, large(BK) glove (F/B)
.... 7.50

1C,20S,FS Nick Peters' Main Event, Los Angeles, photo of Nick Peters (B) 7.25

1C,20S,FS,FL Nick Ranieri, Int'l Golden Gloves champion, (BK/WE) photo in trunks, full length 7.25

1C,20S,FS 'I'll meet you at Ringside' 3.25

1C,20S,FS Jack Sharkey Tavern, Booths for Ladies (S), head photo (B) 15.00

1C,20S,FS Jack Sharkey's signature in (BK) on (SR), no other markings 12.50

1C,20S,FS Jack Sharkey's Ringside Bar, 156 Canal St., Boston w/phone (S), bar (B), photo of Jack (F), Federal Match Corp, New York 7.50

1C,20S,FS Slapsy Maxie's, San Francisco, CA 2.50

1C,30S,FS Billy Soose's Mountain Retreat, Tafton, PA, photo of Soose (F), Retired Middle-weight Champion of the World 12.00

1C,20S,FS Gene's Ringside Tavern, 533 N. Clinton Ave, Trenton, photo (S), (FL) (BK/WE) photo (B), Your Host, Gene Takach (F) 3.50

1C,20S,FS Lew Tendler's Restaurant, Atlantic City, N.J.(F), Mammy's Delicious Waffles (B), photo of Lew (F) 9.00

Sports (Sam-Taub's Ring Personalities w/stock ad for Adam Hats (F))

30C,20S,FS Sport Shorts Set, Sam-Taub's Ring Personalities (I), Attell-Braddock-Burns-Canzoneri-Carpentier-Chocolate-Corbett-Dempsey-Donovan-Joe Dundee-Johnnie Dundee-Fitzsimmons-Gans-Griffo-Jeffries-Ketchel-Leonard-Louis-Lynch-McAuliffe-McCoy-McGovern-McLarnin-O'Brien-Ross-Siki-Sullivan-Tunney-Walcott-Wilde, Type #1 [1943], (BN), Adam Hats & Long's Hats (B), advertiser (F) 150.00

30C,20S,FS Sport Shorts Set, Sam-Taub's Ring Personalities (I), Attell-Braddock-Burns-Canzoneri-Carpentier-Chocolate-Corbett-Dempsey-Donovan-Joe Dundee-Johnnie Dundee-Fitzsimmons-Gans-Griffo-Jeffries-Ketchel-Leonard-Louis-Lynch-McAuliffe-McCoy-McGovern-McLarnin-O'Brien-Ross-Siki-Sullivan-Tunney-Walcott-Wilde, Type #2 [1943], (YW), Adam Hats (B) space for advertiser (F) 150.00

1C,20S,FS Abe Attell, (WE) tip 5.25

1C,20S,FS James J. Braddock, (RD) tip 5.25

1C,20S,FS Tommy Burns, (WE) tip 4.00

1C,20S,FS Tony Canzoneri, (WE) tip 3.75

1C,20S,FS Georges Carpentier, (WE) tip 4.00

1C,20S,FS Kid Chocolate, (WE) tip 3.75

1C,20S,FS Gentleman Jim Corbett, (RD) tip 4.50

1C,20S,FS Jack Dempsey, (RD) tip 8.00

1C,20S,FS Bob Fitzsimmons, (WE) tip 3.50

1C,20S,FS Joe Gans, (RD) tip 4.50

1C,20S,FS James J. Jeffries, (WE) tip 3.75

1C,20S,FS Benny Leonard, (WE) tip 5.25

1C,20S,FS Joe Louis, (WE) tip 7.75

1C,20S,FS Joe Lynch, (RD) tip 4.25

1C,20S,FS Jack McAuliffe, (WE) tip 4.00

1C,20S,FS Kid McCoy, (WE) tip 4.50

1C,20S,FS Terrible Terry McGovern, (RD) tip 4.25

1C,20S,FS Jimmy McLarnin, (RD) tip 4.25

1C,20S,FS Philadelphia Jack O'Brien, (WE) tip 4.50

1C,20S,FS Barney Ross, (WE) tip 5.00

1C,20S,FS Battling Siki, (WE) tip 4.50

1C,20S,FS John L. Sullivan, (RD) tip 5.75

1C,20S,FS Gene Tunney, (RD) tip 7.50

1C,20S,FS Joe Walcott, (WE) tip 4.50

1C,20S,FS Jimmy Wilde, (WE) tip 4.50

Sports (Football)

1C,JLT 1973 Sugar Bowl, Notre Dame 24-Alabama 23, Irish helmets (F/B) 6.00
1C,20S,DQ All America Board of Football Official Seal 1.50
1C,20S,FS Detroit Lions Leon Hart (F), ad: Ray White Chevrolet 6.00
1C,20S,FS Detroit Lions Doak Walker (F), ad: Mello Crisp Potato Chips, Detroit, MI ... 6.00
1C,40S,FS Louisiana's Annual Football Classic, L.S.U. vs. Tulane, no date 12.00
1C,20S,FS Oshawa Hawkeyes Football Club, Support Junior Football in Oshawa 3.00

Sports (Washington Redskins Football)

Washington Redskins 1939 Autograph Set

The 1939 Washington Redskins Set pioneered the way for commercially sponsored sports sets. A set of twenty matchcovers, this set was sponsored by Ross Jewelers, Washington, D.C. Each player's autograph and personal statistics appears on the inside along with his photo. The Sammy Baugh matchcover from this set is the key.

18C,20S,FS 1939 Washington Redskins Football, including Baugh, Bradley, Carroll, Ericksen, Filchock, Flaherty, Irwin, Justice, Karcher, Krause, Malone, Masterson, Millner, Parks, Pinckert, Stralka, Tarkas, and Turner 382.00
1C,20S,FS Sam Baugh, HB, Texas Christian 45.00
1C,20S,FS Vic Carroll, Center, U. of Nevada 30.00
1C,20S,FS Bud Ericksen, Center, U. of Wash 30.00
1C,20S,FS Ray Flaherty, Coach, Gonzaga 25.00
1C,20S,FS Don Irwin, FB, Colgate 24.00
1C,20S,FS Ed Justice, HB, Gonzaga U 30.00
1C,20S,FS Charlie Malone, E, Texas A&M 27.50
1C,20S,FS Wayne Millner, E, Notre Dame 30.00
1C,20S,FS Clem Stralka, Georgetown U. 17.00
1C,20S,FS Andy Tarkas, HB, U. of Detroit 27.50

Washington Redskins 1940 Autograph Set

20C,20S,FS 1940 Washington Redskins, including Barber, Baugh, Carroll, Edwards Forman, Hoffman, Irwin, Malone, Masterson, Millner, Parks, Pinckert, Russell, Shugart, Slivinski, Stralka, Tarkas, Todd, Young and Zimmerman 342.00
1C,20S,FS Jim Barber, U. of San Francisco 5.25
1C,20S,FS Sam Baugh, HB, Texas Christian 38.00
1C,20S,FS Vic Carroll, U. of Nevada 14.50
1C,20S,FS Glen Edwards, Tackle, Washington State 12.75
1C,20S,FS Bob Hoffman, H. Back, So. California 9.50
1C,20S,FS Jim Karcher, Guard, Ohio State... 15.00
1C,20S,FS Charles Malone, E, Texas A&M 12.50
1C,20S,FS Bob Masterson, E, U. of Miami 17.50
1C,20S,FS Mickey Parks, U. of Oklahoma 9.25
1C,20S,FS Ernie Pinckert, S. Calif. 13.00
1C,20S,FS 'Bo' Russell, Auburn U. 7.00
1C,20S,FS Clem Shalka, Guard, Georgetown U. 12.50
1C,20S,FS Clyde Shugart, Guard, Iowa State, ad: Ross Jewelry Co 14.25
1C,20S,FS Steve Slivinski, Guard, U. of Washington 17.50
1C,20S,FS Clem Stralka, Guard, Georgetown U. 15.50
1C,20S,FS Dick Todd, HB, Texas A&M 14.50
1C,20S,FS Bill Young, U. of Alabama... 13.50
1C,20S,FS Leroy Zimmerman, San Jose State 7.00

Washington Redskins 1941 Autograph Set

The 1941 Washington Redskins Set came with 20 matchcovers. The front was in (GD) printing on a (DBN) background. This set was sponsored by Home Laundry and featured a six game home schedule on the front. Each player appeared on the inside with his statistics, photo and autograph.

18C,20S,FS 1941 Redskins Football, including Aldrich, Barker, Baugh, Bowman, Carroll, Davis, Farkas, Filchock, Flaherty, Kralka, Masterson, McChesney, Millner, Moore, Seymour, Shugart, Titchenal, and Todd 350.00
1C,20S,FS Hi Aldrich, Texas Christian 5.25
1C,20S,FS Jim Barber, U. of San Francisco 5.25
1C,20S,FS Autograph Set, Sam Baugh, HB, Texas Christian 42.50
1C,20S,FS Vic Carroll, Guard, U. of Nevada 9.50
1C,20S,FS Andy Farkas, Fullback, U. of Detroit 9.50
1C,20S,FS Frank Filchock, H. Back 13.00
1C,20S,FS Robert Fitchenal, San Jose State 13.00
1C,20S,FS Ray Flaherty, Coach, Gonzaga U. 15.00
1C,20S,FS Bob Masterson, E, U. of Miami 22.50

1C,20S,FS Bob Mc Chesney, E, U.C.L.A. 15.00
1C,20S,FS Wilbur Moore, HB, Minnesota 14.50
1C,20S,FS Bob Seymour, FB, (I), Oklahoma 15.00
1C,20S,FS Clem Shalka, Guard, Georgetown 15.00
1C,20S,FS Clyde Shugart, Guard, Iowa State 11.50
1C,20S,FS Bill Young, T, U. of Alabama 15.50
1C,20S,FS Gary Zimmerman, H., B, San Jose State 13.00

Washington Redskins 1942 Autograph Set

20C,20S,FS Washington Redskins 1942 Autograph Set, including Aldrich, Barman, Baugh, Beinor, Carroll, Cifers, Davis, Edwards, Farkas, Flaherty, Kralka, Kruger, Masterson, McChesney, Moore, Seymour, Shugart, Todd, Wilken, and Young 300.00
1C,20S,FS Hi Aldrich, C, Texas Christian 13.00
1C,20S,FS Sam Baugh, HB, Texas Christian 35.00
1C,20S,FS Ray Flaherty, Coach, Gonzaga 13.00
1C,20S,FS Clyde Shugart, G, Iowa State 10.00
1C,20S,FS Dick Todd, HB, Texas A&M 44.50

Washington Redskins Arcade Pontiac Autograph Set

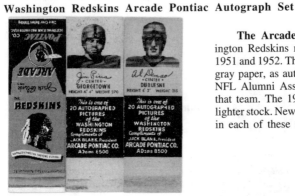

The Arcade Pontiac Set of Washington Redskins matchcovers appeared in 1951 and 1952. The 1951 set was printed on gray paper, as authenticated by Jim Ricca, NFL Alumni Association and member of that team. The 1952 set was printed on a lighter stock. New football players appeared in each of these sets.

17C,20S,FS Arcade Pontiac Redskins Autograph Set, photo & signature (I) (20 in series) 275.00
1C,20S,FS Herman Ball, Head Coach, Davis Elkins 18.00
1C,20S,FS Sammy Baugh, QB, Texas Christian 67.50
1C,20S,FS Dan Brown, E, Villanova 18.00
1C,20S,FS Ed Burang, E, Villanova 18.00
1C,20S,FS Al Demao, Center, Duquesne 18.00
1C,20S,FS Chuck Drazenovich, FB, Penn State 21.75
1C,20S,FS Bill Dudley, HB, Virginia 17.00
1C,20S,FS Harvey Gilmer, QB, Alabama 18.00
1C,20S,FS Robert Goode, FB, Texas A&M 18.00
1C,20S,FS Lou Karras, Tackle, Purdue 18.00
1C,20S,FS Paul Lipscomb, Tackle, Tennessee 18.00
1C,20S,FS Laurie Niemi, Tackle, Washington State 19.25
1C,20S,FS James M. Peebles, E, Vanderbilt 18.00
1C,20S,FS James B. Staton, Jr., Tackle, Wake Forest 21.75
1C,20S,FS Hugh Taylor, E, Oklahoma City U 16.75
1C,20S,FS Joe Tereshinski, E, Georgia 16.50
1C,20S,FS Ed Tuirk, Center, Missouri 14.50

Famous Redskins Sets

The **Famous Redskins** series of four sets appeared in the late 1950s and early 1960s. These sets of 10 shows front photos of famous players on the team. This set was sponsored by the First Federal Savings and Loan Association of Washington, DC. The first two sets were printed on a gray stock, which the later sets appeared on a lighter paper.

17C,20S,FS 1952 Redskins Football, including Ball, Baugh, Berrang, Brown, Demao, Drazenovich, Dudley, Gilmer, Good, Karras, Lipscomb, Niemi, Pebbles, Quirk, Staton, Taylor, and Tereshinski 326.00

10C,20S,FS 1961 Famous Redskins, 1st Fed S&L of Washington D.C., series No. 1, including Drazenovich, Dudley, Fiorentino, Irwin, Schrader, R. Smith, Sommer, Todd, Wilkin, and Witucki 165.00

10C,20S,FS 1963 Famous Redskins, 1st Fed S&L of Washington D.C., series No. 2, including Anderson, Drouse, Guglielmi, Hecker, James, Lemek, Olszewski, Paluck, Schrader, and Stephens 125.00

1C,20S,FS Steve Bagarus, HB, Notre Dame 18.00

1C,20S,FS Cliff Battles, HB, WV Wesleyan 17.00

1C,20S,FS Sammy Baugh, QB, Texas Christian 47.50

1C,20S,FS Don Bosseler, FB, Miami (FL) 14.00

1C,20S,FS Gene Brito, E, Loyola U (L.A.) 12.00

1C,20S,FS Jim Castiglia, FB, Georgetown 11.50

1C,20S,FS Al Demao, C, Duquesne 12.50

1C,20S,FS Turk Edwards, T, Wash State 17.50

1C,20S,FS Bill Hartman, HB, Georgia 17.50

1C,20S,FS Dick James, HB 10.75

1C,20S,FS Charlie Justice, HB, North Carolina 14.00

1C,20S,FS Eddie Lebaron, QB, U. of Pacific 12.00

1C,20S,FS Wayne Millner, E, Notre Dame 17.50

1C,20S,FS Tommy Mont, QB, Maryland 12.50

1C,20S,FS Wilbur Moore, HB, Minnesota 14.50

1C,20S,FS Jim Peebles, E, Vanderbilt 13.00

1C,20S,FS Bo Russell, T, Auburn 15.00

1C,20S,FS Red Stephens, OG, San Francisco 15.00

1C,20S,FS Ed Sutton, HB, North Carolina 14.00

1C,20S,FS Joe Tereshinski, E, Georgia 12.00

1C,20S,FS Bob Toneff, T, Notre Dame 14.50

1C,20S,FS Lavern Torgeson, LB, Wash State 15.50

1C,20S,FS The Redskins, side portrait of brave (F), name (B) 10.00

1C,30S,FS The Redskins, side portrait of brave (F), name (B) 10.00

1C,30S,FS The Redskins, side portrait of brave (F), name (B) 10.00

Sports (Group One College Football Rivals,1933-1934)

Football College Rivals—Appearing in several types, this sub-classification of Sports (Football) featured specific games played between selected college rivals. There are 24 matchcovers in all, naming 12 teams with two different color backgrounds (tan and black) for each. A set of 24 appeared in 1934 followed by sets of 24 and 12 in 1935.

1C,2OS,FS 1934 Army vs. Navy 8.00
1C,2OS,FS 1934 Fordham vs. St. Mary's 9.00
1C,2OS,FS 1934 U. of Georgia vs. Georgia Tech 11.00
1C,2OS,FS 1934 Holy Cross vs. Boston College 17.00
1C,2OS,FS 1933 College Football Rivals, Group 1, U. of Michigan vs. Ohio State 9.00
1C,2OS,FS 1934 Notre Dame & Army, 1935 .... 15.00
1C,2OS,FS 1934 Football Rivals, Group I, Notre Dame vs. Southern California 11.50
1C,2OS,FS 1934 U. of Pennsylvania vs. Cornell 11.00

1C,2OS,FS USMC Recruit Depot, Bulldog w/football, leather helmet & blanket (B) 2.50

Sports (Group One Football)

Group One Sports came out in 1934, featuring three different sports: Baseball, Football and Hockey. In general, the players represented on the front of each matchcovers were limited to popular teams of the period. Singles and color sets were popular and each matchcover had a photograph and short biography of the player on the front and back. A number of sub-types were made for all three sports, helping collectors with a wide variety of players.

1C,2OS,FS 1933 Official Seal, All America Board of Football, from Group One Football (SR) set
.... 17.00
3C,2OS,FS Arvo Antilla, University of Illinois (GN/TN/RD) 13.00
2C,2OS,FS Morris Badgro, New York Giants (RD/TN) 9.00
1C,2OS,FS Harry Benson, Philadelphia Eagles (GN) 5.50
2C,2OS,FS Jack Beynon, University of Illinois (GN/TN) 8.00
1C,2OS,FS Delbert Bjork, Tackle, Chicago Bears (GN) 4.50
2C,2OS,FS Morry Bodenger, Detroit Lions (GN/TN) 8.00

3C,20S,FS John Bond, University of Georgia (GN/TN/RD) 13.50
1C,20S,FS Bill Brian, Philadelphia Eagles (RD 4.00
1C,20S,FS Carl Brumbaugh, Chicago Bears (TN) 4.00
1C,20S,FS Ray Buivil, Chicago Bears (RD) 3.00
1C,20S,FS Dale Burnett, New York Giants (RD) 4.00
1C,20S,FS Art Buss, Philadelphia Eagles (RD) 4.00
1C,20S,FS John Canella, New York Giants (RD) 3.00
1C,20S,FS Myers 'Algy' Clark, Cincinnati Reds, ca. 1935 (TN) 4.00
1C,20S,FS William Conkright, 3rd/Type V, Chicago Bears 4.50
1C,20S,FS Orien Crow, Boston Redskins (RD) 4.50
1C,20S,FS John Doehring Chicago Bears (GN) 2.00
1C,20S,FS Gary Famiglietti, Chicago Bears (RD) 3.00
1FB,20S,FS Beattie Feathers, Chicago Bears (RD) printing error 5.25
1C,20S,FS Daniel Fortmann, Chicago Bears (RD) 4.25
1C,20S,FS Daniel Fortmann, Chicago Bears, ca. 1935 (GN) 4.00
1C,20S,FS Harrison Francis, 3rd/Type V, Chicago Bears 2.50
1C,20S,FS Frank Froschauer, U. of Illinois, (RD), photo (F), history (B) 3.50
2C,20S,FS Dave McCollough, University of Georgia (TN/RD) 2.75
2C,20S,FS Al Minot, University of Georgia (TN/GN) 2.75
1C,20S,FS Leonard Grant, New York Giants, ca. 1935 (RD) 8.75
1C,20S,FS Ed Gryboski, U. of Ill, ca. 1935 (RD) 4.00
1C,20S,FS Clark Hinkle, Green Bay Packers 3.50
1C,20S,FS Bert Johnson, Chicago Bears (RD) 3.00
1C,20S,FS Green Bay Packers, Joe Kurth 3.00
1C,20S,FS Gil Lefebvre, Cincinnati Reds ca. 1935 (GN) 8.75
1C,20S,FS Jim Leonard, Phila. Eagles (GN) 3.50
1C,20S,FS Les Lindberg, U. of Illinois, ca. 1935 (RD) 4.00
1C,20S,FS John Manders Chicago Bears (GN) 2.50
1C,20S,FS John Manders, Chicago Bears (RD) 3.25
1C,20S,FS Joe Maniaci, Chicago Bears (RD) 3.25
1C,20S,FS Ed Manske, Philadelphia Eagles (TN) 4.00
1FB,20S,FS Edgar Manske, End, Chicago Bears (RD) 5.50
1C,20S,FS Bernie Masterson, 3rd/Type V, Chicago Bears 2.50
1C,20S,FS Dave McCollough, U. of Georgia (RD), photo (F), history (B) 3.50
1C,20S,FS Dave McCollough, 2nd/Type I, U. of Georgia (TN) 8.00
1C,20S,FS Lester McDonald, Chicago Bears (RD) 3.00
1C,20S,FS John McKnight, U. of Georgia (RD), photo (F), history (B) 3.50
1FB,20S,FS James McMillen, Chicago Bears 5.25
1C,20S,FS Forrest McPherson, 3rd/Type III, Philadelphia Eagles 2.50
1C,20S,FS Edward Michaels, 3rd/Type III, Chicago Bears (RD) 3.50
1C,20S,FS Charles Miller, 3rd/Type II, Chicago Bears (RD) 3.25
2C,20S,FS Al Minot, 2nd/Type I, U. of Georgia (GN,TN) 6.00
1C,20S,FS Keith Molesworth, 3rd/Type V, Chicago Bears 2.50
3C,20S,FS Jim Mooney, Cincinnati Reds (RD/TN/GN) 6.75
2C,20S,FS LeRoy Moorehead, 2nd/Type I, U. of Georgia (RD/TN) 15.00
2C,20S,FS Bill Morgan, 2nd/Type I, New York Giants (RD/TN) 14.00
1C,20S,FS George Mulligan, 3rd/Type I, Philadelphia Eagles (RD) 4.00
2C,20S,FS George Munday, 3rd/Type I, Cincinnati Reds (RD/GN) 5.00
1C,20S,FS George Musso, Chicago Bears, (GN), photo (F), history (B) 3.50
2C,20S,FS George Musso, 3rd/Type IV, Chicago Bears, HOF (GN,TN) 12.50
2C,20S,FS Harry Newman, 2nd/Type I, New York Giants (RD/GN) 16.00
1C,20S,FS Raymond Nolting, 3rd/Type IV, Chicago Bears (GN) 4.50
1C,20S,FS Raymond Nolting, Chicago Bears (GN), photo (F), history (B) 3.50
1C,20S,FS John Oehler, 3rd/Type I, Pittsburgh Pirates (RD) 8.25
1C,20S,FS John Oehler, Pittsburgh Pirates (CM), photo (F), history (B) 3.50

1C,20S,FS John Oehler, Pittsburgh Pirates (RD), photo (F), history (B) 3.50
1C,20S,FS Bill Owen, 2nd/Type I, New York Giants (GN) 5.00
1C,20S,FS Bert Pearson, Chicago Bears 3.50
2C,20S,FS Tom Perkinson, 2nd/Type I, U. of Georgia (RD/TN) 4.00
1C,20S,FS Joe Pilconis, Philadelphia Eagles (GN), photo (F), history (B) 3.50
1C,20S,FS William H. Pollock, Chicago Bears 5.25
1C,20S,FS Glenn Presnell, Detroit Lions (GN), photo (F), history (B) 3.50
1C,20S,FS Raymond Nolting, Chicago Bears (GN) 4.00
1C,20S,FS Henry 'Hank' Reese, Philadelphia Eagles (CM), photo (F), history (B) 3.50
1FB,20S,FS Chicago Bears, Ray Richards 5.25
1C,20S,FS Theodore Rosequist, 3rd/Type III, Chicago Bears (GN) 2.50
1C,20S,FS John Schneller, Portsmouth Spartans 3.50
1C,20S,FS John Sisk, 3rd/Type III, Chicago Bears (RD) 2.50
1C,20S,FS Ben Smith, Pittsburgh Pirates (GN), photo (F), history (B) 3.50
1C,20S,FS Dave Smukler, 3rd/Type III, Philadelphia Eagles (TN) 7.50
1FB,20S,FS James Stacy, Detroit Lions (RD) 5.25
1C,20S,FS Pete Stevens, 3rd/Type III, Philadelphia Eagles (GN) 4.50
1C,20S,FS Frank Sullivan, Chicago Bears (RD) 4.25
1C,20S,FS Robert Swisher, Chicago Bears (RD) 4.00
1C,20S,FS Ray Tesser, 2nd/Type I, Pittsburgh Pirates (RD) 15.00
1C,20S,FS 'Stumpy' Thomason, 2nd/Type I, Brooklyn Dodgers (TN) 4.50
1C,20S,FS John Griffin Thomason, 3rd/Type III, Philadelphia Eagles (TN) 2.50
1FB,20S,FS Russell Thompson, Chicago Bears (RD) 6.25
1C,20S,FS Milton Trost, 3rd/Type III, Chicago Bears (TN) 2.50
1FB,20S,FS Claude Urevig, Philadelphia Eagles 5.25
1C,20S,FS John Vaughn, 2nd/Type I, Pittsburgh Pirates (RD) 15.00
1C,20S,FS Henry Wagnon, 2nd/Type I, U. of Georgia (RD) 4.50
1C,20S,FS John West, 2nd/Type I, U. of Georgia (GN) 4.50
1FB,20S,FS Joseph Zeller, Chicago Bears 5.25

Sports (Football Miscellaneous)

7C, JWL Monday Night Football 4.00
12BL Complete set of Chinese Women's Football World Championships in 1991 .... 5.00
1B All American Safety Match, Made in U.S.A. show place kicker w/leather helmet (wooden) 4.50
1B titled All American, Made in U.S.A., Safety Match , Capitol Safety Match Corp., wooden penny
     box, showing leather helmeted place kicker in action 5.00

Sports (Golf)

1C,30S,FS Golf Coast Magazine, Coral Gables, Florida 2.25
1C,30S,FS 1967 Supertest Ladies' Open w/photos of Mickey Wright, Althea Gibson, Kathy
     Whitworth, Susie Maxwell & Sandra Haynie, rare 17.00
1C,JLT,BS 1982 PGA Tour Schedule (I), PGA logo (F), ad: First State Bank of Greenville (MI)(B)
     .... 1.50
1C,30S Firestone Country Club, PGA Championships & CBS Golf Classic 5.50
4BL Nosega Match Factory, Golf related, Made for U.S.S.R. 2.00
20C,30S,MS Golf & Country Clubs, assorted 19.00
20C,20S,BS Golf Clubs 12.00

Sports (Group One Hockey, Tan Set)

Group One Hockey serials accompanied the other two major sports of the decade, namely baseball and football. With a slight alteration in pattern, the entire group repeats itself in various ways with Type I through Type IV. Pictured here is the part of the Type IV Tan set. A Silver Set was also made with a different pattern around the photos.

70C,20S,FS Group One Hockey, Tan Type I, [1935], has team name or position, single line Diamond manumark Aitkanhead-Ayres-Beveridge-Bowman-Brydge-Byrdson- E. Burke-M. Burke-Carr-Carson-Chabot-Chapman-Conn-Connolly-B. Cook-T. Cook-Coulter-Couture-Cowley-Cude-Dutton-Finnigan-Frew-Goldsworthy-Gottselig-Gracie-Heller-Hines-Howe-Jenkins-Johnson-Joliat-Kumsinsky-Keeling- Kendall-Klein-Lamb-Larechelle-Lepino-Locking-G. Mantha-S. Mantha-March-Mason-McFayden-McGill-McVeigh-Mondoe-Morens-Murdoch-Murray-Oliver-Pusie-Raymond-Riley-Ripley- D. Roche-E. Roche-Ronnez-Schriner-Seibert-Shannon-Smith-Starke-Stewart-Thompson-Trudel-Voss-Wisbe-Worters 90.00

65C,20S,FS Group One Hockey, Tan Type II, [1936], has no team name or position, single line Diamond manumark Anderson-Ayres-Boucher (2)-Brydge-Burke-Carr-Chabet- Chapman-Connelly-Bill Cook (2)-Bun Cook-T. Cook-Coulter-Couture-Cude-Dillon (2)-Dutton-Emms-Frew-Gagnon- Goldsworthy-Gottselig-Haynes-Heller-Jaffee-Jarwa-Johnson- Joliat-Keeling-Kendall-Kerr-Klein-Larochelle-Lepine- Lesieur-Levinsky (2)-Locking-G. Mantha-S. Mantha-Marsh-Mason-McFaydon-McGill-Monden-Morenz-Murdoch-Murray-Oliver-Ouellette-Patrick (2)-Runge-Schriner-Somers-Starr-Stewart-Thompson-Trudel-Voss-Wiebe-Worters 80.00

60C,20S,FS Group One Hockey, Tan Type III, [1937], 2 line Diam. manumark, Anderson-Ayres-Boucher-Brydge-Burke-Bushwell-Carr-Chabet-Chapman-Connelly-Bill Cook-Bun Cook-T. Cook-Coulter-Couture-Cude-Dillon-Dutton-Emms-Frew-Gagnon-Goldsworthy-Gottselig-Haynes-Heller-Jarwa-Johnson-Joliat-Karakas-Keeling-Kerr-Klein-Larochelle-Lepine-Lesieur-Levinsky-Locking-G. Mantha-S. Mantha-Marsh-Mason (2)-McFaydon-McGill-Monden-Morenz-Murdoch-Murray-Oliver-Ouellette-Patrick-Runge-Schriner-Starr-Stewart-Thompson-Trudel-Voss-Wiebe-Worters 80.00

15C,20S,FS Group One Hockey, Tan Type IV, [1937], has player's team name, Blair-Brydson-Burke-Cook-Gottselig-Jackson-Karakas-Larchelle-Livinsky-Loughlin-March-Seibert-Thompson-Trudel-Wiebe 20.00

14C,20S,FS Group One Hockey, Tan Type V, [1938], (TN) tips, Brydson-Burke-Cook-Dahlstrom-Gottselig-Heyliger-Karakas-Livinsky-March-Seibert-Stewart-Thompson-Trudel-Wiebe 20.00

14C,20S,FS Group One Hockey, Tan Type VI, [1939], (BK) tips, Brydson-Burke-Cook-Dahlstrom-Gottselig-Heyliger-Karakas-Livinsky-March-Seibert-Stewart-Thompson-Trudel-Wiebe 20.00

60C,20S,FS Hockey Issues Silver [1934], Abel-Barry-Beattie-Boucher-Brenman-Brydge-E. Burke-M. Burke-Carson-Chabot-Chapman-Clapper-Conacher-Conn-Bill Cook-Bun Cook-T. Cook-Couture-Davie-Dillon-Dutkowski-Dutton-Gagnon-Gardiner-Gottselig-Gracie-Gross-Heller-Hitchman-Jackson-Jenkins-Joliat-Keeling-Kendall-Klein-Lamb-Larochelle-Lepine-Loswick-G. Mantha-S. Mantha-March-Martin-McVeigh-Morenz-Murdoch-Oliver-Patterson-Picketts-Ripley-Ronnes-Sheppard-Shore-Somers-Speyer-Stewart-Thompson-Trudel-Worters 295.00

1C,20S,FS Glenn Brydson, Type VI, Chicago Black Hawks 4.50
1C,20S,FS Martin A. Burke, Chicago 'Black Hawks' 3.50
1C,20S,FS Martin A. Burke, Type VI, Chicago Black Hawks 3.00
1C,20S,FS Tommy Cook, Type VI, Chicago Black Hawks 3.25
1C,20S,FS Carl Dahlstrom, Chicago Black Hawks 3.25
1C,20S,FS Johnny Gottselig, Chicago Black Hawks 3.25
1C,20S,FS Vic Heyliger, Type VI, Chicago Black Hawks 4.50
1C,20S,FS Michael Karakas, Chicago Black Hawks, ca. 1935 .... 4.25
1C,20S,FS Michael Karakas, Type VI, Chicago Black Hawks 4.50
1C,20S,FS Alex Livinsky, Type VI, Chicago Black Hawks 3.00
1C,20S,FS Harold March, Chicago Black Hawks 4.50
1C,20S,FS Earl Seibert, Chicago Black Hawks 3.25
1C,20S,FS William J. Steward, Manager, Chicago Black Hawks, ca. 1935 .... 4.00
1C,20S,FS Paul Thompson, Chicago Black Hawks 3.25
1C,20S,FS Louis Trudel, Type VI, Chicago Black Hawks 3.00
1C,20S,FS Art Wiebe, Type VI, Chicago Black Hawks 2.00

Sports (Olympics & Games)

1C,20S,FS,FEA Los Angeles 1932 (summer) Olympics, Pig 'n Whistle 3.00

British Empire and Commonwealth Games
1C,20S,FS 1954 British Empire Games, Vancouver, BC 2.00
1C,20S,FS British Empire Games, 1954 .... 3.50
1C,20S,FS 1954 British Empire and Commonwealth Games, Vancouver, B.C. w/dates ... 4.00
1C,20S,FS British Empire Games, 1954, Eddy Match, CN 3.00

Melbourne 1956 (summer)
1C,20S,FS Olympic Training Fund, Amateur Swimming Association 2.00

Squaw Valley 1960 (winter)
1FB,20S,FS Squaw Valley Lodge, Site 1960 Winter Olympics Games, five ring design (B), two
    caricature Indians skiing (F) 9.00
1C,20S,FS Silver Spur Casino & Café, Carson City 1.00

Mexico City 1968 (summer)
30FB Olympics Set 10.00
1C,20S,FS Olympiada 1968, ad: Hotel Ritz, Mexico, D.F. 6.50
1C,20S,FS Visit Mexico, Site of the Olympics 1968, ad: Hotel Alameda (OE/BK/WE) ... 6.50

Munich 1972 (summer)
36C?,30S,FS Olympics Set, Jupiter size, Factory 18, 9? sports each in 4 colors (BE/GN/RD/YW)
    Bogenschiessen-Gewichtheben-Radfahren-Segeln-Turnen-+ others?? 50.00
7FB Olympics Set 7.00
21C,20S,BS Olympics Set 20.00
15B Olympics Set 37.75
20B Olympics Set 5 designs each in 4 colors 20.00
36C?,30S,FS Olympics Set, Jupiter size, Factory 1, 9? sports each in 4 colors (BE/GN/RD/YW)
    Basketball-Boxen-Gewichtheben-Handball-Kanu-Radfahren-Reiten-Schwimmen-Turnen
    .... 50.00

Montreal 1976 (summer)

21C,30S,BS 21 (OE) from set of 105 .... 24.00
105C,30S,BS 21 sports each in 5 colors (BK/BE/GN/OE/RD) Archery-Athletics-Basketball-
Boxing-Canoeing-Cycling-Equestrian-Fencing-Football-Gymnastics-Handball-Hockey-
Judo-Modern Pentathlon-Rowing-Shooting-Swimming-Volleyball-Weight Lifting-Wrestling-
Yachting 75.00

Lake Placid 1980 (winter)

15C,20S,FS Portuguese Set, XIII Olympics Winter Games 22.50
1C,20S,BS American Airlines, Official Air Carrier... 1.00
1C,20S,BS Turf-Inn, Winter Olympic Tours 1.00
15C,20S,BS Portugal, numbered 25.00
1C,30S,BS The Official Bank of the 1980 Olympic Winter Games, Irving Trust Co., One Wall St,
NY 5.00

Moscow 1980 (summer)

14B Australia, numbered, Carlton Sponsors Post Office Hotel-xx-Cecil Hotel-x-Capalaba
Tavern- + ... 20.00
18B Great Britain, numbered, Cornish Match Co. Cycling-Track & Field-Shooting-Swimming &
Diving-Gymnastics-Weightlifting-Boxing-Judo-Football-Yachting-Equestrian Sports-Ar-
chery-Basketball-Wrestling-Hockey-Fencing-Rowing-Canoeing 42.50

Los Angeles 1984 (summer)

14L for the 1984 Los Angeles Olympics, colorful 8.25
1B Australia, Willy, Hanna Match 1.75
26B Australia, Olympic Redheads 1896-1900-1904-1908-1912-1920-1924-1928-1932-1936-1948-
1952-1956-1960-1964-1968-1972-1976-1980-1984-Good Luck-+ 5 others 25.00
18B Great Britain, numbered, Cornish Match Co. Sprint-Middle Distance-Hurdles-Marathon-
Relay-High Jump-Long Jump-Triple Jump-Hammer-Discus-Shotput-Javelin-Pole Vault-
Weight Lifting-Decathlon-Swimming-Diving-Gymnastics 20.00
10C,20S,BS Safeway Set 4.00

Seoul 1988 (summer)

30C Seoul 1988 (summer) Olympics, Portugal 35.00

Olympics (Miscellaneous)

1B titled Sport, Safety Matches Impregnated, Made in Esthonia, wooden penny box, showing 1920
style discus thrower in Olympic stadium 4.75
16L Chinese origin, made 1985 with Olympic Sports Events 4.25
45L+1 Chinese Olympic Matchbox Labels, issued 1987 .... 7.25
25C,20S,FS Portugal Set, numbered 35.00
120L History of the Olympics, issued by Szeged Match Factory, Budapest in 1961 .... 15.00

Sports (Dog Racing & Horse Racing)

1C,20S,FS Biscayne Kennel Club, photo of Greyhound (F)..................................... 2.50
1C,20S,FS West Flagler Kennel Club, Miami, Greyhound (F)............................... 2.00
1C,30S,BS Geneva Lakes Kennel Club, Greyhound (F), Delavan, Wisc 3.25
1C,20S,FS Hollywood Dog Races, opening dates (F), Hollywood, FL 2.00
3C,20S,FS Dog Racing from Florida Palm Beach, Hollywood, Daytona Beach 4.00
1C,20S,FS Palm Beach Kennel Club, Florida, racing dog (F) 3.00
1C,20S,FL Randall-Thistledown-Cranwood Dog Racing, Cleveland, OH 2.00
5C,20S,MS Dog Race Tracks.. 2.00

(above) An inside cut of a map to the
Daytona Beach Dog Racing Kennel Club,
Route 92 in Daytona Beach.

24C,20S,FS Horses Set, 6 horses each in 4 different colors (BE/BN-GN/RD) Cow Pony-Hunter-Indian Pony-Jumper-Race Horse-Trotter Type 1 [1961], Greenwich manumark, blank (B) 2.75

24C,20S,FS Horses Set, 6 horses each in 4 different colors (BE/BN-GN/RD) Cow Pony-Hunter-Indian Pony-Jumper-Race Horse-Trotter Type 2 New York NY manumark 2.00

24C,20S,FS Horses Set, 6 horses each in 4 different colors (BE/BN-GN/RD) Cow Pony-Hunter-Indian Pony-Jumper-Race Horse-Trotter Type 3 New York 17 manumark, blank (B) 3.00

1C,30S,FS Beaumont Horse Racing, Belgrade, Montana, Horse & Jockey (F), 'There's only one!' (S) 3.25

2C,20S,FS Del Mar Turf Club & Sunshine Park Horse Racing 4.00

8C,24S,FS French Horses [1977], Air Landais-Ashmore-Beau Dad-Duc De Vrie-Empery-Equileo-Faker Du Vivier-Furdanne-Grandval-Hasty Love-Infragreen-Ivanjica-Lagunette-Les Roseaux-Paiute-Pawneese-Riverqueen-Youth 10.00

10C,20S,FS Harnass Racing Tracks, Horses on each 16.50

1C,30S,FS Miami Jockey Club, Hialeah Park, Miami, Florida 2.50

1C,20S,FS National Museum of Racing, Hall of Fame, Saratoga Springs, N.Y. 3.75

1C,20S,FS Rob Roy (trotter) (BK/WE) photo (F), Terry Says! 'I Am Waiting' (B), w/statistics 3.00

1C,20S,FS photo of trotter Rob Roy 2.09 1/4 (F), Terry Says 'I am waiting' (B) 2.50

1C,30S,BS Jimmy Shoughro's Derby Turf & Sports, Las Vegas, Horses (B) 3.25

10C,20S,MS Horse Racing Tracks 5.25

35C,20S,MS Horse Race Tracks, assorted 8.50

1C,30S,FS Saratoga, New York Racing Association, Horse & Jockey (F) w/name 2.00

Sports (Stadiums)

Sports Stadiums—Most matchcovers in this sub-classification of Sports show drawings of stadiums or give information about seasonal events. Some indicate prices for performances. Some are conjunctives with home teams and sometimes feature sports schedules. (below) Inside cut used for a stadium matchcover.

1C,20S,FS Detroit Sports Park, Largest Amateur Sports Stadium in America 4.25
1C,20S,FS Detroit Sports Park, drawing of park (B)... 6.25
1C,30S,FS NY Jets, Shea Stadium (B), logo (F)... 7.00
1C,20S,FS N.Y. Mets logo (F), Shea Stadium (B), striker stained 2.50
1C,30S,FS New York Yankees, (WE) w/Stadium (F), letters NY (B) 6.00
1C,20S,old BS, The Nittany Lions Inn, State College, Pa. 5.50
1C,30S,BS Rose Bowl Race & Sports Book, Las Vegas, Nevada 2.00
1C,30S,FS Rose Bowl, color photo (F), ad: Pasadena Federal Savings (B) 6.50
1C,30S,FS 1959 Rose Parade, dated: January 1, ABC-TV, Live from Pasadena, by Quaker Oats, parade floats (F) 13.00
1C,30S,FS 1960 Rose Parade, dated: January 1, ABC-TV, Live from Pasadena, by Quaker Oats, parade floats (F) 12.75
1C,30S,FS 1961 Rose Parade, dated: January 2, ABC-TV, Live from Pasadena, by Quaker Oats, hand and rose (F) 8.00
1C,30S,FS 1962 Rose Parade, dated: Monday-January 1, CBS-TV, Live from Pasadena, by Quaker Oats, roses (F) 11.50
1C,30S,FS New York Jets Shea Stadium, Flushing Meadows, helmet (F), stadium (B) . 2.50
1C,20S,FS Yankee Stadium Club (F/B) 6.00

Sports (VIP)

VIP Sports—Separated from VIPs, VIP Sports features ex-ball players and gridiron celebrities in their businesses or post career activities. Most are popular night spots, restaurants, liquor stores, taverns, and bars.

The VIP Sports name and photo are often present, along with the city and state, however, a number of these establishments have no reference to the celebrity who owns it. Some research may have to be done in order to build a successful VIP Sports category; however, it is frequently well worth the effort.

1C,30S,FS John David Crow's (#44) Fountains Steak House, Football (F) 8.00
1C,20S,FS World Famous Di Maggio's on Fisherman's Wharf, San Francisco, (B/W) photo w/ bat (B), HOF 1955 .... 42.50
1C,30S,FS Di Maggio's on Fisherman's Wharf, San Francisco, (B/W) photo (F), restaurant (B), HOF 1955 .... 26.00
1C,20S,FS Joe Di Maggio's Grotto, San Francisco, Christmas Theme Season's Greetings (B) 9.50
1C,20S,FS Joe Di Maggio's Grotto Fisherman's Wharf, San Francisco, drawing w/cap & New York Yankees (B), HOF 1955 .... 27.50
1C,20S,FS Don Drysdale's Dug Out, Van Nuys, CA, P, HOF 1984 (BK) 22.50
1C,20S,FS Don Drysdale's Dug Out, Van Nuys, CA, P, HOF 1984 (WE) 21.00
1C,30S,FS Eisenhower Golf Course, USAF Academy, Colorado, drawing (B), greens layout (I) 6.00
1FB,30S,FEA Freddie Fitzsimmons Bowling Lanes & Restaurant, w/bowling pins on sticks, popup of baseball player Fitzsimmons (I) 14.00
1C,30S,ODD Ray Jackson's, Milwaukee, signed baseball (F), striker is baseball diamond (B) 15.00
1C,30S,FS Mickey Mantle's Holiday Inn, Joplin, MO, (B/W) photo looking away from camera w/ H/I sign (F), hotel (B) (GN) (I) 57.00
1C,30S,FS Mickey Mantle's Holiday Inn, Joplin, MO, photo of Mickey (F), motel layout (F), map in (GN)(I) 27.00
1C,30S,FS Mickey Mantle HI, Joplin MO, (BK) w/(BK) (I) 29.00
1C,30S,FS Mickey Mantle HI, Joplin MO, (BK) w/(WE) (I) 25.00
1C,20S,FS New York Yankee's George McQuinn's Restaurant, (B/W) photo of George (B) 6.50
1C,30S,BS Stan Musial & Biggies Hotel, Resort and Restaurant, St. Louis, MO 6.50
1C,30S,FS Joe Namath's Restaurant, photo of Namath (B) 19.00
1C,20S,FS Lefty O'Doul's Cocktail Lounge, (BK/WE) photo (B), Baseball (F), EXbrook 3004 (S) 7.50
1C,20S,BS from Walter Payton's Thirty Four's, A Sporty Place, (BE/WE) 3.00
1C,30S,FS Ron Perranoski's Stadium Club, baseball player, Sepulveda, CA 5.50
1C,20S,FS Johnny Schiechl, All America, photo (I), phone GArfield 591 .... 6.00
1C,30S,FS Toots Shor Restaurant, New York 3.00
1C,20S,FS Capt. Gus Suhr, Pittsburgh Pirates, Liquor Store, Millbrae, CA, photo (F) (SR/BK/ WE) 6.00
1C,20S,BS Joe Theismann's Restaurant (DBE) 3.00
1C,20S,BS Joe Theismann's Restaurant (TN) 3.00
1C,20S,BS Joe Theismann's Restaurant (DBE/S 3.00
1C,20S,FS Johnny Unitas' Golden Arm Restaurant, Unitas (F/B) 10.00
1C,30S,FS The Home Plate Restaurant, w/Dougout Room, Vancouver, Wash 3.50
1C,20S,FS Doak Walker, Detroit Lions by Mello Crisp Potato chips, photo (F) 9.25
1C,20S,FS Bill Zuber's Major League Restaurant, Homestead, IA, (B/W) photo w/Yankee's uniform (F), address (B) 3.75

Sports (Schedules)

Baseball Schedules

1C,20S,FS 1938 Philadelphia Athletics Baseball Schedule (I), elephant (F), reservations number (B) 6.00
1C,20S,FS 1939 Philadelphia Athletics American League Baseball Home Game Schedule (B) 8.75
1C,20S,FS 1940 Blues Baseball Schedule (I), ad: Arnold's Army Store, Kansis City, MO (F/B) 5.00

1C,20S,FS 1940 Philadelphia Athletics Baseball Schedule (I), elephant (F), reservations number (B) 4.00

1C,20S,FS 1941 San Francisco Baseball Club, The Seals, Home Game Schedule (B) 6.25

1C,20S,FS 1941 Philadelphia Athletics American League Baseball Schedule (B), elephant (F) 6.50

1C,20S,FS 1943 Philadelphia Athletics Baseball Schedule (I), elephant (F), reservations number (B) 4.00

1C,20S,FS 1944 American League Tigers Home Schedule (I), WWII Patriotic, ad: Shar-Lay's Cocktail Lounge, Detroit 5.00

1C,20S,FS 1948 White Sox, Comiskey Park Welcomes You, Schedule (I) 6.00

1C,20S,FS 1950 Washington Nationals Baseball, Home Game Schedule (I) 5.50

1C,20S,FS 1955 Washington American League Baseball Club, Schedule (I), logo (F) 6.25

1C,40S,FS 1955 Columbus Jets Home Games Schedule (I), ad: City Nat'l Bank (F/B) ... 7.00

1C,40S,FS 1959 Buffalo Bisons Home Games Schedule (I), ad: Mansion House Cocktail Lounge, Buffalo, NY (F/B) 7.00

1C,20S,FS 1960 Goldeye Home Games (I), ad: Labatt's Beer 2.00

1C,20S,FS 1963 Detroit Tigers Schedule (I), team ads (F/B) 5.00

1C,20S,FS 1963 Detroit Tigers Baseball Schedule (I), Tigers logo (B) 10.00

1C,20S,FS 1965 St. Louis Cardinals Home Game Schedule (I), World Champions & Busch Stadium ad (F), prices (B) 6.50

1C,20S,FS 1966 Elkhart High School Baseball Schedule (I), ad: Volcano Pizza, Elkhart, Indiana 3.50

1C,20S,FS 1966 Boston Red Sox, Home Schedule (I) 6.00

1C,20S,FS 1969 Minnesota Twins Baseball Club, Schedule (I) team ad outside 6.50

1C,20S,FS 1970 Minnesota Twins Baseball Club, Schedule (I) team ad outside 6.25

1C,20S,FS 1971 Minnesota Twins Baseball Club, Schedule (I) team ad outside 8.00

1C,20S,FS 1972 Minnesota Twins Baseball Club, Schedule (I) team ad outside 5.50

1C,20S,FS 1973 Minnesota Twins Baseball Club, Schedule (I) team ad outside 5.50

1C,20S,FS 1974 Minnesota Twins Baseball Club, Schedule (I) team ad outside 5.50

7C,30S,BS 1978 Montreal Expos Home games Schedule (I), (B/W) action photos (B), logo (F) 25.00

1C,JLT,BS 1979 Cincinnati Reds Schedule (I), Go Reds-79 (B), logo (F) 3.00

25C,JLT,BS 1980s (mostly) Pro Baseball Schedules 22.00

2C,JLT,BS 1981 & 1982 New York Yankees Schedules (I), Yankees logo (F) 5.00

2C,JLT,BS 1981 & 82 California Angels Schedules (I), team ad (F/B) 2.50

1C,20S,BS 1982 Cincinnati Reds, Schedule (I), logo (F) 2.75

1C,20S,BS 1983 Cincinnati Reds, Schedule (I), logo (F) 2.75

1C,20S,BS 1984 Cincinnati Reds, Schedule (I), logo (F) 2.75

1C,20S,BS 1985 Cincinnati Reds, Schedule (I), logo (F) 2.75

3C,JLT,BS 1983, '84 & '85 Kansas City Royals Home Games Schedules (I), team ads (F/B) 3.50

3C,JLT,BS 1983, '84 & '86 Milwaukee Brewers Home Games Schedules (I), team logo (F) 4.00

1C,20S,BS Milwaukee Brewers 1986 Home Schedule (I) 3.00

1C,30S,BS St. Louis Cardinals (F), Lou Brock Sports Shop (B), 1987 Home Game Schedule (I) 4.75

9C,30S,BS Schedules, 1987 thru 1990 Football and Baseball Schedules 3.50

3JLT,BS Milwaukee Brewers home games schedules (I) each, 1983, 1984 and 1986, baseball & logo (F), different ads 4.00

1C,20S,BS 1960 Goldeye Schedule (I), Labatt's Prix d'Excellence ad (F) 3.00

15C,JLT,MS Sports Jewelites, w/Baseball Schedules 8.00

1C,20S,FS Washington Nationals Baseball Club, ball, bat, & capital (F), player (B), 1957 Home Game Schedule (I) 15.00

3JLT,BS Kansas City Royals home games schedules (I) each, 1983, 1984 and 1985, Baseball & logo (F) 4.00

1C,20S,FS Washington 'Senators' Schedule on calendar (no year given)(B), ad: Northwestern Federal, Washington, D.C. 17.00

1C,20S,FS Washington Senators (F), 1949 Home Game Schedule (I) 10.00

Basketball Schedules

1C,20S,FS 1955-56 South Carolina Trojans Basketball Schedule (I), SC Bookstore (F) .. 2.00
1C,20S,FS 1960-61 South Carolina Trojans Basketball Schedule (I), SC Bookstore (F) .. 2.00
1C,20S,FS 1968-69 Lakers Schedules at the Forum (I), ad: Fletcher's Chevrolet, Encino, CA (w/ Zip code) 2.50
11C,JLT,MS Pro Basketball Schedules 1970s & 1980s 13.00
1C,30S.BS 1975-76 Pan American Basketball Schedule (I), University ads (F/B) 3.25
2C,JLT,BS 1976-77 Moline Sr. H.S. Basketball Schedule (I), different, BB (B), Go! Maroons (F) 3.00
1C,JLT,BS 1977-78 U. of Akron Zips Basketball Schedule (I), Go! Zips Go!, BB (F/B)] . 2.50
10C,JLT,BS College Basketball Schedules mostly 1980s 4.50
1C,JLT,BS 1984-85 Boston Celtics Basketball Schedule (I), ad: Adams Co-operative Bank (B), Celtics man (F) 2.75
1C,20S,FS Baltimore Bullets Basketball, no schedule 3.00
1C,20S,FS New Your Knicks (F), New York Rangers (B), (DBE/RD/WE/OE), no schedule 4.00
10JLT,BS Basketball home schedules (I) of each (2 Baseball), logos & some ads (F) 5.00
10C,JLT,MS Basketball Teams w/schedules (I), assorted 11.00
25C,JLT,BS Basketball schedules 6.00
10C,JLT,MS Sports Jewelites, w/Basketball Schedules 8.00

Football Schedules

Football Schedules appear on the inside of sports matchcovers as well as non-sports matchcovers--it pays to check. Both professional and collegiate, home and away games are found along with advertisements from supporting organizations and businesses.

1C,20S,FS 1933 WV U. Varsity Schedule (I), ad: Palace Rest, Fairmont, W. Va., dated 1933 12.50
1C,20S,FS 1946 U. of Notre Dame Football Schedule (I), ad: Thrift Food Market, girlie . 9.50
1C,20S,FS 1948 U. of Miami Hurricanes Booster, Schedule (B), kicker (F) 20.00
1C,20S,FS 1955 U. of Penn Football Schedule 1.50
1C,20S,FS 1954 U. of Pennsylvania, Schedule (B), date w/player (F), coupon (I) 8.00
1C,20S,FS 1956 U. of Pennsylvania, Schedule (B), date w/player (F), coupon (I) 3.00
1C,40S,FS 1957 Florida Gators Football Schedule, home games (F), away games (I) ... 10.00
1C,20S,FS 1957 U. of Pennsylvania Football Schedule 1.50
1C,20S,FS 1958 Brownfield Cubs Football Schedule (B), ad: Brownfield State Bank, Brownfield, TX (F) 4.25
1C,20S,FS 1958 U. of Pennsylvania, Schedule (B), date w/player (F), coupon (I) 5.00
1C,20S,FS 1958 U. of Villanova Cats Football Schedule (B), Tiger jumping goal post (F) 7.25
1C,20S,FS 1959 U. of Pennsylvania, Schedule (B), date w/player (F), coupon (I) 6.00
1C,20S,FS 1959 South Carolina Trojans Football Schedule (I), SC Bookstore (F) 2.00
1C,20S,FS 1960 U. of Pennsylvania, Schedule (B), date w/player (F), coupon (I) 3.00

1C,20S,FS 1960 U. of Pennsylvania Football Schedule, player (F), schedule (B) 6.00
1C,20S,FS 1962 U. of Pennsylvania, Schedule (B), date w/player (F), coupon (I) 3.00
1C,20S,FS 1962 South Huntingdon High Golden Eagles Football Schedule (I), Zip's Place, Waltz Mill, PA (F) 5.00
1C,20S,FS 1963 U. of Pennsylvania Football Schedule 1.50
1C,20S,FS 1963 U. of Pennsylvania, Schedule (B), date w/player (F), coupon (I) 3.00
1C,30S,FS 1964 Giants Stadium Club, Candlestick Park, Home Schedule (I)................... 7.00
1C,20S,FS 1964 U. of Pennsylvania, Schedule (B), date w/player (F), coupon (I) 6.00
1C,20S,FS 1965 U. of Pennsylvania, Schedule (B), date w/player (F), coupon (I) 6.00
1C,20S,FS 1966 U. of Pennsylvania, Schedule (B), date w/player (F), coupon (I) 6.00
1FB,20S,FS 1972 CU Football Schedule (B), Go Buffs Go! (S), Buffalo w/We're Trying Harder, metallic (GD) 4.00
1C,20S,FS 1973 Opp, Alabama Bobcats Football Schedule (I), Joe's Steak House (F)... 4.00
1C,40S,BS 1974 Memphis Southmen, WFL, schedule (I), Royal Flash 3.00
4C,JLT,MS 1974 Schedules for Sikeston HS Bulldogs, Texas Longhorns, TCU Frogs, & Fighting Illini (I) 8.00
1C,40S,FS 1974 Brazoswood Buccaneers Football Schedule (I), color team photo (B), ad: Lake Jackson Bank (F)... 6.00
2C,JLT,BS 1975 & 1979 Oklahoma Sooners Schedules (I), helmets (F/B) 4.00
2C,JLT,BS 1976 New Mexico Eagles & Michigan State Schedules (I), helmets (F/B) 4.00
7C,JLT,BS 1977 Schedules for Pittsburgh Steelers, Kent State Golden Flashes, Texas Longhorns, Ohio State Buckeyes, U. Tenn Vols, Fighting Illini & Notre Dame 8.00
1C,JLT,BS 1978 Illini Schedule (I), helmets (F/B).. 2.00
1C,JLT,BS 1978 Murray State University Football Schedule (I), helmet (F), Racers (B) .2.00
9C,40S,BS 1978-81 Arkansas Razorback Schedules (B), ads & team ads (F/B) 3.00
3C,JLT,BS 1980, '85 & '86 Missouri Fighting Tigers Schedules (I), helmets & ads (F/B) 3.50
2C,JLT,BS 1980 & '81 U. of Michigan Football Schedules (I), 1979 & '80 Schedules (B), helmets (F) 4.00
3C,JLT,BS 1980, 1984, 1985 Los Angeles Rams Schedules (I), helmets (F/B) 3.00
2C,JLT,BS 1981 Houston Oilers Schedule (I), helmets (F/B) 3.00
4C,JLT,BS 1982, '84, '85 & '86 Monday Night Football Schedules (I), NFL logo helmets (F/B) 2.75
2C,JLT,BS 1982 'Ole Miss' Schedule (I), helmets (F/B) & 1982 Blue Devils Schedule (I), helmets (F/B)... 3.00
3C,JLT,BS 1983, '84 & '85 Fighting Illini Schedules (I), team ads (F/B) 2.50
2C,JLT,BS 1983 Notre Dame Schedule (I), helmets (F/B) & 1980 U.S.C. Trojans Schedule (I), helmets (F/B) 4.50
2C,JLT,BS 1984 New Jersey Generals, Schedules (I), helmets (F/B) 13.00
1C,30S,BS 1987 Washington Redskins Schedule (I), ad: Super Bowl II Pub, helmets (F/B) 7.25
30C,JLT Football Schedules, assorted teams.. 8.25
10C,JLT,MS Schedules (I), Rams, Missouri Fighting Tigers, Michigan Blue 3.00
25C,JLT,MS College Football Schedules, 1970s & 1980s.. 27.00
25C,JLT,MS Football, some with Schedules, assorted 4.50
25C,JLT,BS Pro Football Schedules, mostly 1980s.. 26.00
25C,JTL,MS Sports Jewelites, w/o Schedules (Football)... 10.00
10C,JTL,MS Sports Jewelites w/College Football Schedules 2.00
10C,JTL,MS Sports Jewelites, w/Football Schedules 2.00
1C,30S,FS Detroit Lions schedule, away games (B), home games (I), ad: Swedish Crucible Steel 9.00
14C,JLT,MS L.A. Rams, some with schedules 10.00
12C,JLT,MS Pittsburgh Steelers, some with schedules 15.00
1C,20S,FS Don't talk chum . . . chew Topps gum, w/Yankee Stadium games schedule (B), prices (F), rare... 12.00
30C,JLT,MS Football, some with schedules, assorted 12.00
20C,JLT,MS Football Related... 15.00

Hockey Schedules

1C,20S,FS 1939-1940 St. Louis Flyers, schedule (I) 6.25
1C,20S,BS 1970-71 NHL Vancouver Canucks Home Game Schedule (I), ad: The Inn Service,
Powel River, B.C. (F/B) 7.75
1C,30S,BS 1972-73 NHL Hockey Pittsburgh Penguins Schedule (I), team ad (F/B) 8.00
1C,JLT,BS 1977-78, U. of Wisconsin Badger Hockey Schedule (I), Badger w/stick (F/B) . 2.50
1C,JLT,BS 1979 U. of Wisconsin Badgers Hockey Schedule (I), Badger (F/B) 3.25
3C,JLT,BS 1980-81, 1981-82 & 1982-83 Hartford Whalers Home Games Schedules (I), ads &
logos (F/B) 7.00

Soccer Schedules

1FB,G,FS 1975 Dallas Tornado Soccer Club w/Schedule on Matches 3.00
1C,JLT,MS 1979 Tulsa Roughnecks Soccer Schedule (I), mascot (F), Soccer Ball (B) 3.50

Jewelites w/Schedules

Jewelites—A sub-classification by size of Sports, Jewelites lent themselves to popular helmet and ball design by virtue of their rounded front and back. Team schedules often appear on the inside, and on occasion a commercial ad will appear opposite the teams logo.

20C,JLT,MS Schedules (I), assorted ads & helmets F/B 11.50
20C,JLT,MS Sports Related 8.00
30C,JLT,MS College Sports Jewelites, some with schedules 12.00
20C,JLT,MS Sports Related 5.00
200C,JLT,BS Schedules 47.50
100C,JLT,BS Jewelites with sports schedules 9.50
20C,JLT,MS Schedules 13.00

Sports   (Miscellaneous)

10C,20S,FS U.S. Athletic Clubs 2.50
4C,30S,FS The Athlete Set by Diamond Match Co. 6.00
15C,20S,MS Recreation & Billiard related 4.00
1C,30S,MS Outrigger Canoe Club, Honolulu, Hawaii 5.00
1C,30S,MS The Avalon Card Club, Emeryville, CA 1.25
1C,20S,BS Enrique Freeman, New York World Checkers Champion, (BK/WE) photo (F), name
(B), brief story of checkers (I) 2.00
14C,20S,BS Christie's Sports Spoofs 1.50

15B Complete set of Finnish Skillets w/Cricket Club Badges 4.00

12C,30S,BS Sports History Series Set [1984], Ohio Match Co. Baseball-Basketball-Billiards-Bowling-Football-Golf-Hockey-Olympic Games-Ping Pong-Racquet Ball-Soccer-Tennis .
.... 5.00

1C,20S,FS 1965 World Horseshoe Tournament, July 31-Aug 10, Keene, N.H. 7.75

5C,20S,FS Jai Alai Games, 3-Tijuana, Mexico, 1-New Orleans, 1-Miami 5.00

1C,20S,FS Macke Vending Machines, shows Baseball player w/ball (F/B) 2.00

10C,20S,FS Fishing Related, one Rod & Reel Club, Bait & Supplies 5.50

11C,20S,FS Fishing Related, Rod & Reel Club, Sorting Goods 6.50

1C,20S,FS Winchester Public Shooting Center, Ft. Lauderdale, FL, logo (F) 2.00

1C,30S,FS Rockridge Rod & Gun Club, Marietta, Georgia 1.50

18BL Rugby players in England (set), Made in Finland 4.00

28B Sport Championships Set, from Russia 36.00

10B Swedish Sports Set, drawing on each 4.00

5C,20S,FS Sports Set [1962], Match Corp.[-1966], Baseball-Basketball-Boxing-Football-Horse Racing stock design 2.00

9C,20S,FS Roller Skating related, some colorful 8.00

15C,MS Ski and Skiing Sportswear Related 3.00

18C,30S,FS W. German Set, Soccer Club 'FC Bavara, w/circular sticker on ea 18.00

10C,20S,FS Sportmen's Series Set [1953], Canadian Geese-Deer-Ducks on ground-Ducks flying-Fox-Grouse-Pheasant-Quail-Rabbit-Trout 2.00

6C,20S,FS Sportsmiles Set [1962], stock Bowler-Diver-Fisherman-Golfer-Hunter in boat-Skier
.... 2.00

30B Swedish Sports Parade Matches, 1952, in presentation box, colorful designs 7.00

5C,20S,MS Tennis & Racquet Clubs, assorted 4.50

1C,30S,FS Davis Cup Finals [1964] 3.25

5C,20S,FS Sports Set Western Match Co., Vancouver, BC Fishing-Golf -Hunting -Water Skiing-Winter Skiing 2.00

10B Full Swedish Sports Set, drawing on each 3.75

14B Ohio Match sports scenes (ca. 1955) 4.00

45C,JWL Pro Sports Teams 12.50

240C,20/30S,MS General Recreation, assorted sports 6.00

30C,JWL College Sports 12.00

28FB,JLT Football Helmets Set in (WE) presentation box 11.00

6C,30S,JLT Pro Western Football Helmets 3.00

45C,JLT,FS St. Louis Sports Teams 5.00

20C,JLT,BS Sports, no schedules (I), assorted ads & helmets (F/B) 7.50

1C,20S,FS Irving Jaffee, World's Champion Skater 3.50

1C,20S,FS Mineola Skating Rink Fairgrounds, skaters (F), time schedule (B) 1.50

Walter Payton's Thirty Four's club in Chicago, IL, a popular night spot whose matchcovers are easily available to patrons. Many gridiron greats retired to secure incomes after their heyday on the field. This matchcover falls into the select category of Sports VIPs.

Sticky Backs

Sticky Backs—Also known as Piggybacks, this category of matchcovers had a relatively short life (about 400 varieties known). Each matchcover has a covered sticky back which was supposed to be exposed and stuck to your pack of cigarettes. Although made by several companies, including Universal Match Corp. and Lion Match Co., the most popular manumark seen is that of the General P-R Corp. of Brookline, Mass, which was manufactured by D.D. Bean & Sons, Co., Jaffrey, NH.

1C,20S,FS Stick with Bender, Sticky-Back, Copyright 1955, Atlas Advertising Co., Brookline, Mass (manumark) 2.50
1C,20S,FS Sticky Back, The International House of Pancakes, Universal Match Corp. 4.00
1C,20S,FS Stick with IKE (Sticky Back) For peace and Prosperity (S), Copyright 1955 - Atlas Advertising Co., Brookline, Mass. (RD/WE/BE) 8.00
1C,20S,FS Sticky Back, Stick with Kearns for Congress, (RD/WE/BE), General P-R Corp 3.50
1C,20S,FS Sticky Back, Chris Spinosa and his Orchestra, Featuring Ralph Spinosa 3.50
1FB,20S,FS Stick with Utt, Sticky Back, copyright 1955 .... 6.75
1FB,20S,FS Sticky Back, Welex Jet Perforating, patent (B) 5.00
25C,20S,FS Sticky Backs, assorted 28.00
25C,20S/30S,MS Sticky Backs, assorted 12.00
25C,20S/30S,MS Sticky Backs [1955-], D.D. Bean, ... 12.00

Super Market Sets

Super Market Sets—This category includes a wide number of commercial and non-commercial matchcovers with generic designs and pictures. Many advertise nationally known products (Nationals) and some advertise specials for various grocery chains. Although known as a common or easy matchcover to collect, super market sets have been the mainstay of many collections. In this book, the Hunt's Recipe Set and the Eddy Nature Sets fall into this category.

18C,20S,FS Ancient Sea-craft Set [1962], 1600 B.C.-500 B.C. Chinese-500 B.C. Grecian-200 B.C.-600 A.D.-1000 A.D., 6 ships each in 3 colors (GN/PK/RD) 1.25
4C,30S,FS The Athlete Set [   ], Discus Thrower-Skater-Skier-Swimmer 1.00
6C,20S,FS Autumn Season Set [1967], Corn Shocks-Ears of Corn-Fruit Stand-Man carrying Leaves-Trees and Water-Yellow Trees and House 1.00
4C,30S,BS American Revolution Bicentennial Set [1976], stock design (Eagle & Shield-Liberty Bell-Minute Man-Spirit of 76) 1.00

6C,30S,BS American Revolution Bicentennial Set [1976], The Battle of Bunker Hill-The Boston Tea Party-Cornwallis Surrenders at Yorktown-The Midnight Ride of Paul Revere-Washington Crossing the Delaware-Winter at Valley Forge Type 1 [1976], wide reddish 1.00

6C,30S,BS American Revolution Bicentennial Set [1976], The Battle of Bunker Hill-The Boston Tea Party-Cornwallis Surrenders at Yorktown-The Midnight Ride of Paul Revere-Washington Crossing the Delaware-Winter at Valley Forge Type 2 [1976], narrow (GY) striker 1.00

6C,30S,BS American Revolution Bicentennial Set [1976], The Battle of Bunker Hill-The Boston Tea Party-Cornwallis Surrenders at Yorktown-The Midnight Ride of Paul Revere-Washington Crossing the Delaware-Winter at Valley Forge Type 3 [1976], wide (GY) striker 1.00

30C,20S,FS Capitol Scenes Set [1967], 6 buildings each in 5 different colors Capitol Building-Jefferson Memorial-Lincoln Memorial-Mount Vernon-Washington Monument-White House 2.00

12C,30S,FS Chess Set [1967], 6 chess pieces, each in 2 colors (BK/WE) Bishop-King-Knight-Pawn-Queen-Rook 2.00

24C,20S,FS Circus Day! Set of 6 scenes each in 4 colors (BE/GN/OE/YW), Calliope-Clown-Elephant-High Wire-Lion Tamer-Ringmaster Type 1 New York manumark, (GY) (I) 4.25

24C,20S,FS Circus Day! Set of 6 scenes each in 4 colors (BE/GN/OE/YW), Calliope-Clown-Elephant-High Wire-Lion Tamer-Ringmaster Type 2 New York 17 manumark, (WE) (I) 6.00

5C,20S,FS The Cyclists Set [1955], Auto & Bicycle-Dog, Cat, & Bicycle-Man greeting Lady-2 on bicycle heading to left-2 on bicycle heading to right 1.00

6C,20S,FS Do It Yourself! Set [1956], Boat Builder-Carpenter-Chair Maker-Painter-Picture hanger-Plumber 1.00

6C,30S,BS Famous Dates in History Set [1974], 1492-1776-1869-1903-1920-1969 .... 1.00

6C,30S,FS Early American Fire Engines S 1.00

6C,30S,BS Early American Fire Engines Set [1981].. 1.00

6B Fishing Set [1955], Scene-Horse Head-Hunting Spaniel-Indian-Pointer-Sailing Ship .. 1.00

36C,20S,FS (6 of each), American Folklore, colors (BE/BN/GN/OE/RD/TN) Johnny Appleseed-Paul Bunyan-Davy Crockett-Casey Jones-Joe Magarac-Ri Van Winkle, Type 1 [1960], (GY) paper (I) 2.00

36C,20S,FS (6 of each), American Folklore, colors (BE/BN/GN/OE/RD/TN) Johnny Appleseed-Paul Bunyan-Davy Crockett-Casey Jones-Joe Magarac-Rip Van Winkle, Type 2 [1961], (WE) paper (I) 2.00

6C,20S,FS Historic America Set [1974], Concord Bridge-Faneuil Hall-Independence Hall-Plymouth Rock-Spanish Mission-The Alamo 1.00

6C,30S,BS Historic America Set [   ], The Alamo-Concord Bridge-Cumberland Gap-The Gold Rush-Independence Hall-The Pony Express 1.00

24C,20S,FS Homes of Great Americans Set [1958], 6 houses each in 4 different colors (BE/BN/GN/YW) Benjamin Franklin-Patrick Henry-Andrew Jackson-Thomas Jefferson-William Penn-George Washington 3.50

6C,30S,BS How It Began Set, The Airplane-The Automobile-The Book Match-The Box Camera-Mardi Gras-Mother's Day Type 1 [1976], Diamond Match Division, New York 1.00

6C,30S,BS How It Began Set, The Airplane-The Automobile-The Book Match-The Box Camera-Mardi Gras-Mother's Day Type 2 Diamond Match Division, Springfield 1.00

6C,30S,BS How It Began Set, The Airplane-The Automobile-The Book Match-The Box Camera-Mardi Gras-Mother's Day Type 3 Diamond Match Company, Springfield 1.00

6C,30S,BS How It Began Set, The Airplane-The Automobile-The Book Match-The Box Camera-Mardi Gras-Mother's Day Type 4 Diamond Brands, Mpls 1.00

6C,30S,BS How It Began Set, The Airplane-The Automobile-The Book Match-The Box Camera-Mardi Gras-Mother's Day Type 5 Diamond Brands Inc., Product of Canada 1.00

6C,20S,FS Manmade Wonders Set [   ], Gateway Arch-The Golden Gate Bridge-Hoover Dam-Mount Rushmore-Statue of Liberty-Washington Monument 1.00

24C,20S,FS The Old West Set, 6 scenes each in 4 colors (BE/GN/OE/RD) Chuck Wagon-The General Store-Last Gasp Well-Smoke Signals-Square Dancing-Stage Coach, Type 1 [1958], New York manumark 2.00

24C,20S,FS The Old West Set, 6 scenes each in 4 colors (BE/GN/OE/RD) Chuck Wagon-The General Store-Last Gasp Well-Smoke Signals-Square Dancing-Stage Coach. Type 2 [1959], New York 17 manumark 3.00

53C,20S,BS Playing Cards Set [1983], 52 cards plus joker 3.25

6C,30S,FS Proverbs Set #1 [   ], A Stitch..-April Showers..-Faint Heart..-He Who..-Out Of Sight..-Where There's.. .... 2.00

6C,30S,FS Proverbs Set #2 [   ], reddish FS All The..-Good Things..-Home Is..-It Never..-Too Many..- Two Heads.. .... 2.00

4B Scenic America Set [   ] 1.00

4C,20S,BS The Scenic West Set [   ], Buffalo-Cable Car-Dam-Log Train 1.00

4C,30S,FS The Seasons Set [   ] Spring-Summer-Autumn-Winter 1.00

6C,20S,FS Ships Set [1956] Constitution-Half-moon-Leif Ericson-Lightning 1854-Mayflower-Santa Maria 1.00

30C,20S,FS Ships of Yesterday Set [1967], 6 ships each in 5 different colors (GN) (S) & compass-(YW) (S) & compass-(BE) (S) & compass-(GN) (S) & (RD) compass-(YW) (S) & (RD) compass) Brigantine-Chinese Junk-Clipper-Schooner-Sloop of War-Whaling Bark ... 5.00

48C,20S,FS Old Timepieces Set, Type 1 [1970] 4.00

48C,20S,BS Old Timepieces Set, Type 2 [   ] 4.00

6C,20S,FS Winter Season Set [1967], Blowing Wind-Snowflake-Snowman-Snowshoes & Skates-Stove-Thermometer 1.00

6C,20S,BS Word Origins Set, Boycott-Curfew-Derby-Ferris Wheel-Figurehead-Tank Town, Type 1 -1977], New York manumark 1.00

6C,20S,BS Word Origins Set, Boycott-Curfew-Derby-Ferris Wheel-Figurehead-Tank Town, Type 2 Springfield manumark, Diamond Match Div 1.00

6C,20S,BS Word Origins Set, Boycott-Curfew-Derby-Ferris Wheel-Figurehead-Tank Town, Type 3 Springfield manumark, Diamond Match Co. 1.00

6C,20S,BS Word Origins Set, Boycott-Curfew-Derby-Ferris Wheel-Figurehead-Tank Town, Type 4 Diamond Brands 1.00

6C,20S,FS World Landmarks Set, Arc de Triomphe-Big Ben-Eiffel Tower-Leaning Tower of Pisa-Sphinx-Taj Mahal Type 1 (BN) striker, (BE) print 4.00

6C,20S,FS World Landmarks Set, Arc de Triomphe-Big Ben-Eiffel Tower-Leaning Tower of Pisa-Sphinx-Taj Mahal Type 2 reddish (BN) striker, (BE) print 4.00

6C,20S,FS World Landmarks Set, Arc de Triomphe-Big Ben-Eiffel Tower-Leaning Tower of Pisa-Sphinx-Taj Mahal Type 3 (BK) striker, BE/GN print 4.00

12C,20S,FS America's Yesteryear Bicycle: Electric Trolley-Gazebo-Horse Drawn Car ... 1.00

12C,20S,FS America's Yesteryear Electric Trolley: Bicycle-Gazebo-Horse Drawn Car ... 1.00

12C,20S,FS America's Yesteryear Gazebo: Bicycle-Electric Trolley-Horse Drawn Car ... 1.00

12C,20S,FS America's Yesteryear Horse Drawn Car: Bicycle-Electric Trolley-Gazebo ... 1.00

9?C30S,FS Zanies Set, Type 1 [1970] 2.00

9?C30S,FS Zanies Set, Type 2 [   ] 2.00

6C,20S,FS Zany Zoo Set, Dog-Frog-Giraffe-Pelican-Penguin-Turtle, Type 1 [1960], (WE) paper
.... 1.00

6C,20S,FS Zany Zoo Set, Dog-Frog-Giraffe-Pelican-Penguin-Turtle, Type 2 [   ], brownish paper
.... 1.00

6C,20S,FS 'Do it Yourself', Diamond Set (PK) 3.00

5C,20S,FS Superior Match Co., Dog's Best Friend 6.00

18C,20S,FS Dots/Stripes Set [1963], Ohio Match Co. 2.00

10C?,30S,FS Ecology Set [1969], Ohio Match Co. 2.00

6c,30S,FS Old Locomotives Set [1956], Elite Set #108, De Witt Clinton 1831-General 1862-Mogul Tank 1872-Eight wheel..1876-Ten wheel..1883-Ten wheel..1885, Universal Match Corp. 2.00

5C,20S,FS A&P Set Good Meals Good Deals ...From the Dairy-...From the Garden-...From the Orchard- ... From the Range-...From the Sea, Type 1 Diamond Match Co. 2.00

5C,20S,FS A&P Set Good Meals Good Deals ...From the Dairy-...From the Garden-...From the Orchard- ... From the Range-...From the Sea, Type 2 Ohio Match Co. 2.00

10C,20S,FS Food Club Set [1955] 1.00

8C,20S,FS King Scopers Set Air Force..-Colorado National..-Denver-The Great..-Mesa Verde..-
Narrow Gauge..-Rocky Mountain..-Royal Gorge, Type 1 .... 2.00

8C,20S,BS King Scopers Set Air Force..-Colorado National..-Denver-The Great..-Mesa Verde..-
Narrow Gauge..-Rocky Mountain..-Royal Gorge, Type 2 .... 2.00

25C,20S,FS Kroger Set Apples-Butter-Cabbage-Candy-Cheese-Chicken-Coffee (mill)-Coffee
(pot)-Eggs-Fish-Flour-Fondue-Grapes-Ice-Lobster-Milk-Onions-Oranges-Peaches-Pine-
apple-Pork-Shishkabob-Steak-Strawberries-Vegetables, Type 1 [-1976], Kroger Brands
.... 5.00

25C,20S,FS Kroger Set Apples-Butter-Cabbage-Candy-Cheese-Chicken-Coffee (mill)-Coffee
(pot)-Eggs-Fish-Flour-Fondue-Grapes-Ice-Lobster-Milk-Onions-Oranges-Peaches-Pine-
apple-Pork-Shishkabob-Steak-Strawberries-Vegetables, Type 2 [   ], Big K Soft Drinks 5.00

25C,20S,FS Kroger Set Apples-Butter-Cabbage-Candy-Cheese-Chicken-Coffee (mill)-Coffee
(pot)-Eggs-Fish-Flour-Fondue-Grapes-Ice-Lobster-Milk-Onions-Oranges-Peaches-Pine-
apple-Pork-Shishkabob-Steak-Strawberries-Vegetables, Type 3 [1983], 1883-1983 (I) 5.00

25C,30S,FS Kroger Set Apples-Butter-Cabbage-Candy-Cheese-Chicken-Coffee (mill)-Coffee
(pot)-Eggs-Fish-Flour-Fondue-Grapes-Ice-Lobster-Milk-Onions-Oranges-Peaches-Pine-
apple-Pork-Shishkabob-Steak-Strawberries-Vegetables, Type 4 [   ], Kroger Brands (I) 5.00

5C,20S,FS Kroger Set A Baseball Bat..-Father Wants..-Mother Needs..-Top Value Stamps..-
Where Can You.., Type 1, Diamond Match 2.00

5C,20S,FS Kroger Set A Baseball Bat..-Father Wants..-Mother Needs..-Top Value Stamps..-
Where Can You.., Type 2, Columbia Match... 2.00

10C,20S,FS Pic-n-Pay Set [1956] 2.00

10C,20S,BS Ralphs Set [1974], Nutrition Tips 2.00

12C,20S,FS Shurfine Set [1956] 3.00

36C,20S,BS Topco Set [   ], 6 designs each in 3 colors (BE/OE/WE) and reversed colors on the
(F) Converging lines go down-Converging lines go left-Horizontal lines-Smaller circle is
down-Smaller circle is up-Vertical lines 3.00

5C,30S,FS Topco Set [   ] 1.00

6C,20S,BS Winn Dixie [1978], Astor Coffee-The Beef People(meat on cutting board)-The Beef
People(with mushrooms)-Harvest Fresh Produce-Super Brand Dairy Products-Thrifty
Maid Canned Goods 2.00

6C,30S,BS, Early American Fire Engines, Diamond Match Co., NY 4.25

6C,30S,FS, Early American Fire Engines, Diamond Match Co., NY 5.00

4C,30S,FS Historic Fire Fighting Equipment, numbered, Series A, stock, 1830 Red Rover..-1838
Hope..-1841 Southwark..-1848 Big Six.. Universal Match Corp., Type 1 [1956] picture (F),
title (S) 10.00

4C,30S,FS Historic Fire Fighting Equipment, numbered, Series A, stock, 1830 Red Rover..-1838
Hope..-1841 Southwark..-1848 Big Six.. Universal Match Corp., Type 2 [   ] picture and title
(B) 5.00

6C,20S,FS Ohio Match Co. 1955, Fish 2.75

10C,20S,FS Fish Set [1955], Ohio Match Co. (SR), name (S) and picture (F) Angel Fish-
Firemouth-Green Swordtail-Guppies-Paradise Fish-Pompadour Fish-Ruby Jewel Fish-
Siamese Fighting Fish-Tiger Barb-Variatus 2.00

5C,20S,FS Folk Art Collection, Cooperstown, NY 2.50

10C,20S,BS Eddylites Folk Art Collection 2.50

20C,20S,FS Giant Food Set #1 (numbered) [   ], Super Giant, Universal Match Fort McHenry..-
Monument Erected..-Chesapeake &-Ohio..- Bancroft Hall..-Barbara Fritchie's..-Chesa-
peake Bay..- Eastern Shore..-United States..-The White House..-The Supreme Court..-State
Capitol..-Library of Congress-Dumbarton Oaks..-Virginia..-Colonial Capitol..-Jamestown..-
Mount Vernon-National Cemetery..-Natural Bridge-Nation.. .... 3.50

20C,20S,FS Set #2 [1962], The Quality Food People Baltimore Oriole-Baltimore & Ohio Railroad-
Cardinal- Cornwallis..-District of..-First Commercial..-George Washington..-The Great
Falls-Home of..-Japanese Cherry..-Lord Baltimore-Mason Dixon..-Monitor & Merrimack-
National Gallery..-Norfolk Naval..-The Reaper-Smithsonian..-University of Maryland-Uni-
versity of Virginia-Washington.. .... 2.00

20C,20S,FS Set #3 [   ], Diamond Match Across the..-Airships to..-Alone Across..-Apollo VIII-A Walk..-Balloons, Then..-Dreams of..-First Liquid..-Freedom VII-Friendship VII-First Non Stop..-Lighter Than..-Mail Delivery..-Man on..-Parachutes-Passenger Service..-'Round the..-The 'Comet'-World War..-Wright Brothers 10.00

??C,20S,BS Set #? [   ], Nutrition Tips Cereals Rice & Pasta- others 5.00

15C,20S,FS Giant Supermarket set (partial) points of interest 3.00

50FB,20S,FS Giant Food, assortment, 1 caddy 2.00

34C,20S,FS Grand Slam Set, Anemone-Baltimore Oriole-Banded Purple-Bluebird-Blue Jay-Buckeye-Camellia-Chipmunk-Daisy-Dog Face-Goatweed-Hairstreak-Kentucky Cardinal-Leopard Frog-Lily-Lovebirds-Monarch-Mourning Cloak-Painted Bunting-Painted Turtle-Pansy-Parakeets-Petunia-Redheaded Woodpecker-Robin-Rose-Ruby Jewel Fish-Siamese Fighting Fish-Tiger Barb-Tiger Swallowtail-Variatus-Western Tanager-Wood Duck-Zinnia, Type 1 [1955], Ohio Match Co. 1955 manumark 3.00

34C,20S,FS Grand Slam Set, Anemone-Baltimore Oriole-Banded Purple-Bluebird-Blue Jay-Buckeye-Camellia-Chipmunk-Daisy-Dog Face-Goatweed-Hairstreak-Kentucky Cardinal-Leopard Frog-Lily-Lovebirds-Monarch-Mourning Cloak-Painted Bunting-Painted Turtle-Pansy-Parakeets-Petunia-Redheaded Woodpecker-Robin-Rose-Ruby Jewel Fish-Siamese Fighting Fish-Tiger Barb-Tiger Swallowtail-Variatus-Western Tanager-Wood Duck-Zinnia, Type 2 [1957], Ohio Match Co. 1957 manumark 3.00

12FB,30S Happy Birthday America in original plastic case 12.50

6C,30S,BS Historic America Series 9.25

24C,20S,FS Homes of Great Americans set by Diamond Match Co 2.00

6C,20S,FS Horses Set, Diamond Match Greenwich, Conn. (BE) 2.25

6C,20S,FS Horses Set, Diamond Match Greenwich, Conn. (GN) 2.25

12C,30S,BS Iron Horse Set [1981], Ohio Match Co. Dewitt Clinton-Dorothy-John Hancock-Minnetonka-999-Old War Horse-Pioneer-Teakettle-Union Pacific 119-William Crooks-Willie-0 4 OT Switcher 1.50

5C,20S,FS Our Kids Set [1949], Match Corp. [-1966], All For One-Finishing Touch-Loose Ends-Me and My Pal-Unlucky Star stock design set 2.00

11C,40S,BS Natural Landmarks, numbered, McLaughlin Ent. 5.50

1C,20S,BS 1000 Islands Skydeck, St. Lawrence River 2.00

20C,20S,FS Giant Food Set, Famous scenes in Metro DC area 2.00

50C,30S,FS Atlas 4 Color [   ], Atlas Match 3.00

28C,20S,FS 12-1953 Jello Series, 10-1955 Ohio Birds, 6-assorted airlines 10.00

32C,20S,FS 4-1953 Jello Series, 6-Circus Day, 10-1955 Ohio Birds, 12-Old Timepieces .. 5.00

5C,30S,FS L'Opera Set of Famous Musicians 4.00

5C,20S,FS Visit Scenic Oklahoma 2.75

50FB,20S,FS Old Time Pieces, 1 caddy 2.00

??C,30S,FS Poems Set [1971], Ohio Match Co. A Bursting..-Born Free..-Crystal Waters..-In A Wondrous..- Life Is..-On Leafy..-Proud Ruler..-Rolling Meadows..- Sunlit Blossoms..-The Wondrous.. .... 1.50

??C,30S,BS Poems Set, It Flies..-We Could Feel.. Type 1 [1971], Ohio Match Co. blank (I) 1.00

??C,30S,BS Poems Set, It Flies..-We Could Feel.. Type 2 [   ]. Ohio Match Co. (I) says Please Keep Matches.. .... 1.00

32C,20S,FS 1941-2 Presidential Set w/Extra Jackson (#7) error 30.00

6C,30S,FS Proverbs Set [   ], A Stitch..-April Showers..-Faint Heart..-He Who..-Out of Sight..-Where There's.. .... 2.00

12C,30S,BS Proverbs Set [1978], Ohio Match Co. A bird..-A fool..-A stitch..-Beware of..-Birds of..-Don't count..-Don't put..-If you hear..-Never fish..-One rotten..- Time brings..-Where there's smoke.. .... 2.00

5C,20S,FS 10 Provinces Set, Eddy Match (BN) 1.00

4C,30S,FS Sailing Vessels Set [1959], stock, Barkentine-Brig-'Flying Cloud'-Schooner, Universal Match Corp., ... 2.00

6C,20S,FS Set of Ancient Sea-craft, Supermarket Set of Ancient Sea-Craft 2.00

17C,20S,FS Smile Set [   ], Ohio Match Co. 1.50

8C,30S,FS Space Age U.S.A. (scenes from space) 3.00

50C,20S,BS 50 States [1987], set 8.00
12C,20S,FS Supermarket Set, (GY/WE) Statues 1.25
10C,40S,FS Ten Wonders in Engineering Set, colorful & educational 8.50
8C,30S,BS Think of Tomorrow Set Conserve Energy-Conserve Fuel..-Conserve Gas-Conserve
    Oil-Keep America Beautiful-Keep Fit-Recycle..-Use Pesticides.., Universal Match Corp.,
    Type 1 [1981] 1.00
8C,20S,BS Think of Tomorrow Set Conserve Energy-Conserve Fuel..-Conserve Gas-Conserve
    Oil-Keep America Beautiful-Keep Fit-Recycle..-Use Pesticides.., Universal Match Corp.,
    Type 2 [1984] 1.00
36C,20S,FS Old Timepieces, 6 sets of six 1.00
4C,20S,FS Totem Series Set, The Bear-Graveyard Post-The Thunderbird-The Wolf, Type 2 (BK)
    striker, rough creamy paper (I) 1.50
4C,20S,FS Totem Series Set, The Bear-Graveyard Post-The Thunderbird-The Wolf, Type 3 (GY)
    striker, (GY) paper (I) 1.50
32C,30S,BS How's Your Trivia, Universal Match Corp., All for one..-Appeared in..-Austin..-Bell
    X 1-Building boys..-Bullet..-California..-Can do-Cannonball..-Casa Loma.. plus others 3.00
66C,20S,BS Trivia [1974], Ohio Match Co. numbered, numbers run #1 through #67, #40 was
    withdrawn prior to distribution 5.00
17C,20S,BS Trivia, Type 1 [   ], Ohio Match Co., (I) has Please Keep Matches..Checkerboard..-
    Chili-Dr. John S..-Florence..-Frank..- Golden..-Graf Spee-In God we..-Jay Gorney..-Johnny
    Mack..-Knute..-Lepidoperist-Lorne Green..-Motto on..-P.T. Barnum-Seven-Six-Who?
    What?..-World War II-102-206-1933 .... 3.50
17C,20S,BS Trivia, Type 2 [1985], Ohio Match Co., (I) doesn't have Please Keep
    Matches..Checkerboard..-Chili-Dr. John S...-Florence..-Frank..- Golden..-Graf Spee-In God
    we..-Jay Gorney..-Johnny Mack..-Knute..-Lepidoperist-Lorne Green..-Motto on..-P.T. Barnum-
    Seven-Six-Who? What?..-World War II-102-206-1933 .... 3.50
40C,20S,BS How's Your Trivia? (RD) Universal Match Corp.,print 5.00
30C,20S,BS How's Your Trivia? (BK) Universal Match Corp., print 3.50
17C,20S,BS Trivia Set, Alfred..-American..-Bus..-Eleanor..-Haberdasher-Jesse..-Joe..-Kentucky..-
    Miami..-Pyramids..-Sir..-Spirit..- Theodore..-Tin..-Washington..-W.C...-8 Universal Match
    Corp., Type 1 [1989], Kenner manumark, (WE) paper (I) 1.00
17C,20S,BS Trivia Set, Alfred..-American..-Bus..-Eleanor..-Haberdasher-Jesse..-Joe..-Kentucky..-
    Miami..-Pyramids..-Sir..-Spirit..- Theodore..-Tin..-Washington..-W.C...-8 Universal Match
    Corp., Type 2 [1989], St. Louis manumark, (BN) paper (I) 1.00
17C,20S,BS Trivia Set, Alfred..-American..-Bus..-Eleanor..-Haberdasher-Jesse..-Joe..-Kentucky..-
    Miami..-Pyramids..-Sir..-Spirit..- Theodore..-Tin..-Washington..-W.C...-8 Universal Match
    Corp., Type 3 [1989], St. Louis manumark, (WE) paper (I) 1.00
66C,20S,BS Trivia Set, Ohio Match [1974] 4.00
18C,30S,FS Trolly Car Memories Set, 3 sets in (RD), (YW) & (GN) 10.00
9C,20S,BS Vote Set [1972], Ohio Match Co. 2.00
6C,20S Supermarket Set, Winter Scenes, Diamond Match Co. 2.00
50FB,20S,BS Word Origins, 1 caddy 2.00
17C,20S,BS Word Origins Set #1 [1981], Ohio Match Co. Clue-Dixie-Etiquette-Hobo-Idiot-
    Magazine-Mail-Marathon-Paddy Wagon-Poll-Postman-Scapegoat-Soldier-Steeplechase-
    Travel-Umbrella-Villain 1.50
17C,20S,BS Word Origins Set #2 [1984], Ohio Match Co. Alcatraz-Alphabet-Canary-Dictionary-
    Easel-Elbow-Erase-Fender-Infantry-Ink-Maverick-Paragraph-Scholar-Skeleton-Televi-
    sion-Window-Yacht 2.00
6C,30S,FS Set of Zanies 2.00
24C,20S,FS 12-America's Yesteryear, 6-Do It Yourself, 6-Historic America 5.00
58C,MZ,MS Grocery & Food Stores 10.00
34C,20S,FS 10-1955 Ohio Birds, 12-Ohio 1969 Zodiac Set, 12-Our National Parks 5.00
10B Original Paper Caddy, [1963] Ohio Match Co. designs of boat, sports, train, horses, etc. 3.00
34C,20S,FS Ohio Match Co. [1957], Flowers and Wildlife 9.00
18C,20S,FS 6-Capital Scenes, 6-Our National Parks, 6-World Landmarks 7.25
24C,20S,FS 6-World Landmarks, 6-Capital Scenes, 12-1969 Ohio Zodiac Set 3.00

Theatre

Theatres—Any matchcover naming a popular movie or stage theatre. This ad may be accompanied by a specific program offering, date, city, or ticket price. Early theatres advertised air conditioning and special showings. Stock theatre matchcovers advertised a film with the name of the theatre printed on the front. A single film can have dozens of theatres on different matchcovers. These are not considered sets or series, but stock theatre matchcovers.

1C,20S,FS Play: Noel Coward's Best Comedy, Blithe Spirit staring Clifton Webb & Peggy Wood 6.00

1C,20S,FS Play: Brother Rat by John Monks, Jr. & Fred F. Finklehoffe 5.00

1C,20S,FS Eddie Cantor in Banjo Eyes, black-face Cantor (F), commentary (B) 35.00

1C,30S,FS David O. Selznick Presents Duel in the Sun (B/W) photo (B) w/star 5.50

1C,20S,FS Play: The Egg and I staring Claudette Colbert & Fred Mac Murray 7.75

Theatre (Group One)

Theatre (Movies, Group One)—After the first Test Set of 10 Motion Picture Stars was produced by Diamond Match Co. in 1934/35, the matchcover sets became enormously popular. Hundreds of stars appeared in singles and color sets of two and four. Printed in an assortment of types, these sets featured a short, current biography on the back with the star's photo on the front. Sets ranged from 10 (Test Set) to over 100, considering the color variations.

10C,20S,FS 1st Movies Type 1 [1934], Test Set Arlen-Bennett-Dee-Dunne-Harding-Hepburn-Pitts-Raft-Stuart-Summerville 125.00

32C,20S,FS 1st Movies Type 2 [1934], Arlen-Ayres-Barrymore-Beery-Cooper-Crawford-Cromwell-Dix-Dressler-Dunne-Durante-Furness-Gable-Gibson-Grant-Harding-Harlow-Hayes-Hepburn-Holt-Jordan-Karloff-McCrea-Miles-Montgomery-Park-Pitts-Raft-Stuart-Summerville-Tracy-Wray 85.00

95C,20S,FS 1st Movies Type 3 [1935], Ames-Arlen-Arliss-Armstrong-Astaire-Ayres-Bancroft-J. Barrymore-L. Barrymore-Beery-Bennett-Boles-Brook-Buck-Connolly-Cooper-Crabbe-Crawford-Cromwell-Dee-Dix-Dressler-Dunne-Durante-Etting-Furness-Gable-Harding-Harlow-Hayes-Henry-Hepburn-Holt-Howard-Knapp-LaRue-Laughton-Lederer-LeRoy-Lyman-Maynard-McCrea-Montgomery-Raft-Rogers-Scott-Sullavan-L. Tracy-S. Tracy-Wing-Wray-Young + Buck-Rogers 175.00

48C,20S,FS 2nd Movies Type 1 [1935], Arliss-Astaire-Beal-Beery-Blackmer-Bradley-Colman-Crawford-Dee-Dix-Donat-Drake-Evans-Gable-Grant-Harlow-Hepburn-Hopkins-Hyams-Larocque-Laughton-March-Merman-Morgan-Nugent-Oakie-Oberon-Raft-Ralston-Rogers-Scott-Shirley-Stanwyck-Stevens-Stone-Tone-Twelvetrees-Wing-Young 110.00

16C,20S,FS 2nd Movies Type 2 [1935], 8 stars each appearing in 2 colors—Astaire-Beery-Gable-Harlow-Hopkins-Rogers-Stanwyck-Tone 35.00

176C,20S,FS 2nd Movies Type 3 [1936], star's name in script on a (WE) saddle Astaire-Barnes-Barrymore-Beery-Benny-Bradley-Brebt-Chevalier-Churchill-Colman-Crawford-Denny-Dix-Dunne-Evans-Fairbanks-Fox-Gable-Harding-Healy-Hepburn-Hull-Jane-Jones-Karloff-Karnes-Knight-Lowe-Lukas-March-Montgomery-Moore-Morris-Neagle-Pryor-Raft-Rogers-Stevens-Stone-Sullavan-Taylor-Wing-Wyatt 325.00

16C,20S,FS 2nd Movies Type 4 [1936], 8 stars each in 2 colors, same as Type 2 except (WE) saddle Astaire-Beery-Gable-Harlow-Hopkins-Rogers-Stanwyck-Tone 42.00

185C,20S,FS 2nd Movies Type 5 [1936], 46 stars each in 4 colors (BE/GN/OD/RD) + 1 single Arnold-Arthur-Bergner-Blore-Boyer-Broderick-Bruce-Crabbe-Crawford-Dietrich-Downs-Eddy-Erikson-Fairbanks-Fonda-Foster-Gaynor-Gleason-Grahame-Hall-Hepburn-Hilliard-Hopkins-Howard-Jones-Karns-Landi-Laughton-Leigh-Loy-MacDonald-March-Meredith-Merkel-Milland-Moore-Oakie-Oberon-Overman-E. Powell-W. Powell-Rainer-Rogers-Sidney-Tallichet-Tapley + Gaynor 400.00

85C,20S,FS 2nd Movies Type 6 [1936], 21 stars each in 4 colors (BE/GN/OD/RD) + 1 single Arnold-Autry-Baker-Calloway-Carrillo-Clark-Coghlan-Cooper-Courtney-Dvorak-Keene-Lamour-Leeds-Lewis-Logan-McCarthy-McKinney-Menjou-Movita-Randall-Regan + Gurie 195.00

4C,20S,FS 2nd Movies (Type 1), photo (F), Edward Arnold, Jr., (BE/GN/RD/OD) 14.00

2C,20S,FS Jean Arthur (OD/RD), ca. 1935 .... 10.00

2C,20S,FS Gene Autry (BE/GN) 2.00

2C,20S,FS Kenny Baker (RD/GN) 7.75

1C,20S,FS Elisabeth Bergner (RD) 5.25

1FB,20S,FS Eric Blore (RD), 2nd Movies, Type 1 .... 3.50

1C,20S,FS Charles Boyer (GN/RD), ca. 1935 .... 11.00

1C,20S,FS Helen Broderick (OD), ca. 1935 .... 3.00

4C,20S,FS Cab Calloway, color set of 12.00

1C,20S,FS Cab Calloway (only African-American on Group I Movie Set) (BE), ca. 1935 (GN) 6.00

2C,20S,FS Groups 1, Second Movie, Type 1, Leo Carrillo (RD/BE), photo (F) 9.50

2C,20S,FS Bobby Clark (RD/GN) 4.00

2C,20S,FS Frank Coghlan, Jr., 2nd Movies, Type 2 (OD/RD) 5.75

1C,20S,FS Jackie Cooper (RD) 10.00

1C,20S,FS Sigrid Gurie & Gary Cooper, 2nd Movies, Type 1V 9.50

1C,20S,FS Inez Courtney (GN) 3.75

1C,20S,FS Larry 'Buster' Crabbe (BE), ca. 1935 .... 4.25

1C,20S,FS Marlene Dietrich (RD) 7.75

2C,20S,FS Ann Dvorak (GN/BE) 4.25

1C,20S,FS Nelson Eddy (OD) 5.75

1C,20S,FS Preston Foster (RD) 3.00

1C,20S,FS Preston Foster (BE), ca. 1935 .... 3.00

1C,20S,FS Janet Gaynor, 2nd Movies, Type V (the oddity) 5.50

1C,20S,FS Margot Grahame (RD), ca. 1935 .... 3.00

2C,20S,FS Porter Hall, 2nd Movies, Type 1 (LBE/RD) 7.75

1C,20S,FS Ted Healy (OD) 7.00

1C,20S,FS Harriet Hilliard (GN) 7.00

4FB,20S,FS Miriam Hopkins, 2nd Movies, Type 1 (OD/GN/LBE/RD) 14.50

2C,20S,FS John Howard (OD/RD) 8.75

1C,20S,FS Roscoe Karns (LBE) 4.25

1C,20S,FS Evelyn Kaye (OD) 3.00

4C,20S,FS Tom Keene (OD/LBE/RD/GN) 13.50

1C,20S,FS Dorothy Lamour (GN) 5.00

1C,20S,FS Elissa Landi, 2nd Movies, Type 1 (GN) 3.50

1FB,20S,FS 2nd Movies, Type 1, Charles Laughton (RD) 6.50

1C,20S,FS Viven Leigh (GN) 6.00

2C,20S,FS Ella Logan (GN/LBE) 7.00

1C,20S,FS Lucille Manners (PK) 3.75

1C,20S,FS Frederic March (OE) 10.00

1C,20S,FS Janet Gaynor & Frederick March 6.25

1C,20S,FS Charlie McCarthy, 2nd Movies, Type 1 (BE/GN/OD/RD), photo (F) 17.50

3C,20S,FS Florine McKinney (RD/GN/BE) 9.00

4C,20S,FS Ray Milland (BE/RD/OD/GN) 16.00

1C,20S,FS Douglass Montgomery (lavender) 8.00
1FB,20S,FS Victor Moore, 2nd Movies, Type 1 (LBE) 5.50
1C,20S,FS Movita (OD), ca. 1935 .... 12.00
1FB,20S,FS Jack Oakie, 2nd Movies, Type 1 (RD)...................................... 40.00
4C,20S,FS Merle Oberon, color set of 4 .... 8.00
1FB,20S,FS Merle Oberon, 2nd Movies, Type 1 (LBE) 7.00
3C,20S,FS Jack Randall (GN,LBE,RD) 10.50
2C,20S,FS Phil Regan (LBE,GN) 5.00
1FB,20S,FS Ginger Rogers, 2nd Movies, Type 1 (LBE) 10.00
1FB,20S,FS Sylvia Sidney, 2nd Movies, Type 1 (RD) 4.50
1FB,20S,FS Margaret Sullavan (OR)... 8.75
3C,20S,FS Colin Tapley (GN/RD/LBE)... 9.00

Theatres (Movies)

1C,20S,FS Golden Boy by Clifford Odets with Luther Adler and Frances Farmer, Belasco Theatre, NYC...12.00
1C,20S,FS Betty Grable in Down Argentine Way, photo of Grable (F) 11.00
1FB,40S,RF Republic Pictures, (I) ad: 'I'll Always Love You', studio (B) 25.00
1FB,40S,RF Republic Pictures, ad:(I) 'I've Always Loved You' 2.00
1C,20S,FS Johnny Johnson, A Group Theatre Production, A Play with Music 8.00
400C,20S,FS Amsterdam Movie Stars Set [1938] 900.00
1C,20S,FS Down Argentine Way [1940], Betty Grable 5.50
10C,20S,FS Movie Stars, Crown Match Co., ... 60.00
10C,30S,FS Duel in the Sun Set [1947].. 95.00
1C,40S,FS Gone with the Wind [1967] 9.00
11C,40S,FS Republic Pictures Set [   ], Bells of Rosarita-The Cheaters-Dakota-Earl Carroll Vanities-Flame of Barbary Coast-I've Always Loved You-Lake Placid Serenade-Mexicana-Murder in the Music Hall-In Old Sacramento-Rendevous with Annie 40.00
1C,20S,FS Play: The Private Afairs of Bel Ami staring George Sanders & Angela Lansbury 5.00
1C,20S,FS Movie: Thief of Bagdad 2.25
1C,20S,FS Ethel Barrymore Theatre, 'Whistling in the Dark' w/Ernest Truex 7.00
1C,20S,FS Play: Yiddle with his Fiddle, starring Molly Picon 12.00

Theatre (Theatres)

1C,20S,FS Star Theatre Inc, Bar Harbor, Maine, Season's Greetings w/candled wreath (B) (RD/GN/BE) 7.50
1C,20S,FS Tall Lion Match, Cameo Theatre, Vitaphone Talking Pictures, Bridgeport, Conn, Direction Warner Bros (OE/BE) 12.00
1C,20S,FS Elmiro Theatre, phone Santa Monica 23344 (S), dynamic graphics by Crown Match Co.. 6.00
1C,20S,FS,FL Tall Lion Match Co., Loew's State for Good Shows, Singing & Talking Pictures (RD/BK/YW) 15.00
1C,20S,FS Tall Lion Match, Netoco New Show World Theatre by World's Greatest Producers (RD/BK/YW) 10.50
1C,20S,FS,FL Pantages Theatre, Just for Fun - See a Movie Today!!, Minneapolis, Minn (BE/YW/RD) 4.75
1C,20S,FS Paramount Theatre, The Home of 2 for 1 Shows, Times Square, NYC, LO 3-1100 (BE/WE) 5.50
1C,20S,FS Attend the 'Pickfair' for the Pick The Picture Fare, Kernersville, NC (stock). 4.25
1C,30S from Ziegfeld Follies (the Movie), Stars Names (B)... 5.00
30C,20S,FS Theaters w/drive-in locations, stock design 9.00

Theatres   (Miscellaneous)

4B marked 40 Fosforos, Victoria photos of different female movie star, Santiago, ca. 1920 6.00
3B marked 40 Fosforos, w/female movie stars, foreign 3.00
2B marked 40 Fosforos, Marca Victoria, each with female movie star, foreign 7.00
4B marked 40 Fosforos, female movie star, foreign 4.00

Vitaphone Varieties   (left) was an early sound picture process popular in the late 1920s. The wide striker and single line large-lettered Lion Match Co. manumark places this matchcover around that period. (center) The famed Brooklyn Paramount where so many learned about rock n' roll in the mid 1950s. (right) A matchcover showing the admission ($1.20) to Harry T. Dixon's Academy Theatre. Some matchcovers can be dated by determining the period low-digit phone numbers were used in a certain area. Note: WA 9424 was the Academy's.

Theatre (Group One Nite Life & NBC/CBS Stars)

The First Nite-Life (left) set of famous personalities was produced by Diamond Match Co. in 1938. Colored in pastels, 24 matchcovers made the complete set. (right) A matchcover each from the NBC (a total of 24 in this set) and CBS (a total of 80 in this set) radio personality matchcover set, produced in 1935 by Diamond Match Co. A phantom picture of the Radio City building is imprinted over the history on the back of each matchcover.

First Nite Life   NBC & CBS Stars

24C,20S,FS Night Life Sets Arthur-Baker-Clinton-Crosby-Dorsey-Frost-Jessel-Jolson-Kay-
      Kaye-Kennedy-Manners-Marlow-Marsala-Martin-Morgan-Reichman-Riley-Rogers-
      Sharbutt-Small-Spitalny-Van Steden-Wilkens Type 1 [1938], (BK) tips 30.00
72C,20S,FS Night Life Sets Arthur-Baker-Clinton-Crosby-Dorsey-Frost-Jessel-Jolson-Kay-
      Kaye-Kennedy-Manners-Marlow-Marsala-Martin-Morgan-Reichman-Riley-Rogers-
      Sharbutt-Small-Spitalny-Van Steden-Wilkens Type 2 [1938], (WE) tips, 24 persons each
      in 3 colors (GN/OR/RD) 90.00
1C,20S,FS Group 1 Nite Life, Tommy Dorsey (OD) 7.00
1C,20S,FS Group 1 Nite Life, Buddy Rogers (GN) 2.25
1C,20S,FS Group 1 Nite Life, Mary Small (TN) 3.00
1C,20S,FS Group 1 Nite Life, Dorothy Wilkens (PK) 3.00

Tobacco Related

Tobacco—This popular category is made up mostly of singles or series, advertising popular tobacco products, including cigarettes, pipe tobacco, pipes, cigars, and chewing tobacco. Tobacco advertising appeared on matchcovers in the teens and has continued to be popular for most of this century. Without addresses, tobacco advertising matchcovers are often considered as Nationals, but collected separately.

(above) Stock cuts used for advertising tobacco, pipe stores, and cigarettes. It is surprising that very few stock cuts are found in the literature for this category.

1FB,20S,FS Ascot Aromatic Pipe Mixture (F), Koppers Chicago Coke (B) 8.00
1B Benson & Hedges 100's 100 Hostess Matches 3.00
36C,20S,BS Camel Cigarettes Set #1 [1991], featuring Joe Camel 13.50
48C,20S,BS Camel Cigarettes #2 Set [1992], featuring Joe Camel 11.00
1B pre-Castro Cuban, Chesterfield Wax Matches 2.00
1B pre-Castro Cuban, 1/2 Centavo tax seal, 'El Varadero' 2.00
4C,20S,FS Chesterfield Set, Like Your Pleasure Big? Type 1 [1957], Big game hunter-Fisherman-
    Golfer-Mexican siesta D.D. Bean 2.00
4C,20S,FS Chesterfield Set, Like Your Pleasure Big? Type 2 [1957], Big game hunter-Fisherman-
    Golfer-Mexican siesta Lion Match 2.00
4C,20S,FS Chesterfield Set, Like Your Pleasure Big? Type 3 [1957], Big game hunter-Fisherman-
    Golfer-Mexican siesta Match Corp. 2.25
4C,20S,FS Chesterfield Set, Like Your Pleasure Big? Type 4 [   ], Big game hunter-Fisherman-
    Golfer-Mexican siesta Universal Match 2.50
4C,20S,FS Chesterfield Set, Like Your Pleasure Big? Type 5 [   ], Big game hunter-Fisherman-
    Golfer-Mexican siesta Maryland Match 2.00
15C,20S,MS Cigarette Brand related 5.50
33C,MZ,MS Cigarette, Cigar, & Tobacco advertisers 12.00
15C,20S,MS Cigarette Brand related 5.50
15C,20S,MS Cigar Brand related 5.50
20C,20S,FS Cigar Stores 2.00
20C,MZ,MS Cigarettes, assorted British advertisers 2.75
1FB,20S,FS Hit Parade Cigarettes, Full King Size! (S), pack (F/B) 1.50
1C,20S,FS Lion Match, ad: J.A. Quality Cigars 2.00

1FB,20S,FS L&M Low in tar, More taste to it, Miracle Tip logo (B) 2.00
4C,20S,FS Marlboro Set [   ], Advertised in.. Look-Popular Science-Time-TV Guide 2.00
1FB,20S,FS Oasis, Menthol-Mild, pack (B), palm tree (F) 1.50
1C,20S,FS Lion Match, ad: King Perfectos & Lion Book Matches 3.00
1C,40S,FS Humphrey Bogart, from Raleigh 903 Set [1947], set of 6 .... 23.00
1C,40S,FS Joan Crawford, from Raleigh 903 Set [1947], set of 6 .... 18.00
1C,40S,FS Linda Darnell, from Raleigh 903 Set [1947], set of 6 .... 20.00
1C,40S,FS Douglas Fairbanks Jr., from Raleigh 903 Set [1947], set of 6 .... 16.00
1C,40S,FS Paulette Goddard, from Raleigh 903 Set [1947], set of 6 .... 14.00
1C,40S,FS Hedy Lamarr, from Raleigh 903 Set [1947], set of 6 .... 12.00
1C,20S,FS R.J. Seidenberg Co, Exceptional Cigars, address (B) 2.00
1FB,20S,FS United Cigar Stores, tall book, wide striker, excellent condition 9.50
1FB,20S,FS Ukemco Shaving Cream, United Cigar Stores, wide striker, single line Diamond
      manumark 5.00
95C,20S,FS Tobacco, assorted advertisers 17.00
25C,20S/30S,FS Tobacco, assorted advertisers 2.75
100C,20S,FS Cigar and Tobacco related 23.00
35C,30S,MS Tobacco, assorted advertisers 4.00
15C,20S,MS Cigarettes, assorted advertisers, colorful 6.50
350C,MZ,MS Cigar and Tobacco related 38.00

Transportation

Transportation—A general category with advertisements for any public or private conveyance of passengers or freight. Although large sub-classifications are separate (e.g. railroads, airlines, ships), this category includes automobiles, trucks, taxi cabs, jitneys, buses and other land transportation. This category usually doesn't include accessories, body repairs, glass or break service, loans, painting, tires, service, tune-up, or wrecker service.

Transportation (Automobile Sets)

1C,40S,RF 1948 Packard, Car (B), Blank (F) 2.50
1B,E pre-Castro Cuban, Sante Motors, photos of 1949 Buick & Chevy, nice 5.50
1C,40S,RF 1952 Buick, Car (B), Ad (F) 2.75
1C,40S,RF 1953 Buick, Car (B), Ad (F) 2.75
15C,20S,FS Chevrolet Dealers [1953 to 1967], one each, each dated 9.75
1C,40S,RF Plymouth [1953], Car (B), Ad (F) 2.50
20C,20S,FS Auto Dealers [1954/55], Chevy, assorted 1.00
10C,40S,RF Chevy Trucks [1954-60], assorted advertisers 5.00
30C,20S,FS Auto Dealers [1956/57], Chevy, assorted 1.00
20C,20S,FS Auto Dealers [1956], Ford, assorted 2.50
9C,30S Oldsmobile [1956], assorted advertisers & car photos 8.00
6C,30S Pontiac [1956], assorted advertisers, stock 5.00

10C,30S,FS De Soto [1957-58], assorted advertisers 5.00

25C,20S,FS Auto Dealers [1957], Ford, assorted 75

10C,30S,FS Oldsmobile [1957-60], assorted advertisers & car photos 11.00

8C,30S,FS Pontiac [1957], assorted advertisers, stock 8.00

5C,30S,FS Buick [1958], assorted advertisers (I), stock 3.25

15C,30S,BS Pontiac Set [1958], Match Corp., Pontiac Guardian Maintenance Aquamarine-Cameo Ivory-Caravan Gold-Yuma Beige + 11 .... 2.25

6C,30S,MS Buick, Pontiac, Oldsmobile [ca. 1959], assorted advertisers, stock 5.00

10C,30S,BS Pontiac [1959], assorted colors and advertisers, stock 3.00

15C,30S,BS Pontiac Set [1959], Match Corp., dated Cameo Ivory-Canyon Copper-Castle Blue-Concord Blue-Dundee Green-Gulf Stream Blue-Jademist Green-Mandalay Red-Regent Black-Royal Amethyst-Seaspray Green-Shoreline Gold-Silvermist Gray-Sunset Glow-Vanouar Blue 3.00

15C,30S,BS Pontiac Set [1960], Match Corp., dated Berkshire Green-Black Pearl-Caribe Turquoise-Coronado Red-Fairway Green-Mahogany-Newport Blue-Palomino Beige-Regent Black-Richmond Gray-Shelltone Ivory-Shoreline Gold-Sierra Copper-Skymist Blue-Stardust Yellow 3.00

15C,30S,BS Pontiac Set [1961], Match Corp., dated Bamboo Cream-Bristol Blue-Cherrywood Bronze-Dawnfire Mist- Fernando Beige-Rainier Turquoise-Regent Black-Richelieu Blue-Richmond Gray-Tradewind Blue + 5 others 2.25

15C,30S,BS Pontiac Set [1962], Match Corp., Wide Track.. Aquamarine-Bamboo Cream-Belmar Red-Burgundy-Cameo Ivory- Caravan Gold-Ensign Blue-Kimberley Blue-Mandalay Red-Seafoam Aqua-Silverleaf Green-Silvermist Gray-Starlight Black-Yorktown Blue-Yuma Beige 2.00

15C,30S,BS Pontiac Set [1963], Match Corp., Tempest Aquamarine-Cameo Ivory-Caravan Gold-Cordovan-Grenadier Red-Kimberley Blue-Marimba Red-Marlin Aqua-Nocturne Blue-Saddle Bronze-Silverleaf Green-Silvermist Gray-Starlight Black-Yorktown Blue-Yuma Beige 2.00

15C,30S,BS Pontiac Set [1964], Match Corp., 23 models Alamo Beige-Aquamarine-Cameo Ivory-Grenadier Red-Gulfstream Aqua-Marimba Red-Nocturne Blue-Pinehurst Green-Saddle Bronze-Silvermist Gray-Singapore Gold-Skyline Blue-Starlight Black-Sunfire Red-Yorktown Blue 2.25

15C,30S,BS Pontiac Set [1965], Match Corp., 32 models Blue Charcoal-Cameo Ivory-Capri Gold-Fontaine Blue-Iris Mist-Mayfair Maize-Mission Beige-Montero Red-Nightwatch Blue-Palmetto Green-Reef Turquoise-Starlight Black-Teal Turquoise + 2 others 1.25

4C,30S,BS Chrysler [1966], New Yorker, 300, Sport 300, Windsor, color photo (B) Canadian advertiser 4.00

4C,30S,BS Chrysler Dealer Set [1966], color photo (B), Vista-Lite, CN, assorted advertisers 3.00

5C,30S,BS Ford [1966], Fairlane, Mustang, Ford, Thunderbird, Falcon, color photo (B) Canadian advertiser 5.00

5C,30S,FS Ford Dealer Set [1966], color photo (B), Vista-Lite, CN, assorted advertisers 5.00

4C,30S,BS Plymouth [1966], Belvedere II, Satellite, Sport Fury, Sport Fury (yes! 2 different), color photo (B), Canadian advertiser 5.00

4C,30S,BS Plymouth Dealer Set [1966], color photo (B), Vista-Lite, CN, assorted advertisers 2.00

15C,30S,BS Pontiac Set [1966], Diamond, 40 models Barrier Blue-Blue Charcoal-Burgundy-Cameo Ivory-Candlelite Cream-Fontaine Blue-Marina Turquoise-Martinique Bronze-Mission Beige-Montero Red-Nightwatch Blue-Palmetto Green-Platinum-Reef Turquoise-Starlight Black 2.00

16C,20S,FS Chevrolet [1952-1967], one for each year, stock 5.00

4C,30S,BS Chrysler [1967], New Yorker, 300, Town & Country, Newport Custom, color photo (B) Canadian advertiser 4.00

4C,30S,BS Chryslers [1967], color photo (B) of each 6.50

4C,30S,BS Chrysler Dealer Set [1967], color photo (B), Vista-Lite, CN, assorted advertisers 3.00

8C,30S,BS Chrysler [1967], color photo (B) of each 6.00

4C,30S,BS Dodge [1967] trucks, color photo (B) of each, Canadian, (RD) footer & (F), by Vista-Lite, CN 5.00

4C,30S,BS Dodge [1967] trucks, Fargo Tilt, Fargo Medium-Heavy, Fargo Sweptline, Fargo Transivan, color photo (B) Canadian advertiser, (BE) footer 4.00

4C,30S,BS Dodge [1967] trucks, Fargo Tilt, Fargo Medium-Heavy, Fargo Sweptline, Fargo Transivan, color photo (B) Canadian advertiser, (RD) footer 4.00

4C,30S,BS Dodge [1967] trucks, color photo (B) of each, Canadian, (BE) footer & (F) by Vista-Lite, CN 5.00

4C,30S,BS Fargo Truck Dealer Set [1967], color photo (B), (BE) Set, Vista-Lite, CN, assorted advertisers 2.25

5C,30S,BS Ford [1967], La Fairlane, La Thunderbird, La Ford, La Falcon, La Decapotable Mustang, color photo (B) Canadian advertiser 4.00

5C,30S,BS Ford Dealer Set [1967], French, color photo (F), Vista-Lite, CN 3.75

5C,30S,BS Mercury [1967], Meteor Montcalm, Montclair 4 Door, Falcon Futura, Cougar, Caliete 2 Door, color photo (B), Canadian advertiser (all but Ranchero GT) 6.00

4C,30S,BS Mercury Dealer Set [1967], color photo (F), Vista-Lite, CN, assorted advertisers 4.00

8C,30S,BS Plymouth [1967], Belvedere Satellite, Sport Fury Hardtop, Sport Fury Fast Top, Belvedere GTX, Valiant, Fury III SW, Belvedere II Convertible, Fury VIP, color photo (B), Canadian advertiser 7.00

8C,30S,BS Plymouth Dealer Set [1967], color photo (B), Vista-Lite, CN, assorted advertisers 3.25

15C,30S,BS Pontiac Set [1967], Diamond, 35 models Burgundy-Cameo Ivory-Champagne-Fathom Blue-Gulf Turquoise-Linden Green-Mariner Turquoise-Montego Cream-Montreux Blue-Plum Mist-Regimental Red-Signet Gold-Silverglaze-Starlight Black-Tyrol Blue 1.25

4C,30S,BS Chrysler [1968], color photo (B) of each, Canadian 2.50

8C,30S,BS Ford [1968], Thunderbird, Country Squire, 100 Pickup, Torino GT, Mustang Convertible, Falcon Futura, Ranchero, Galaxie 500 XL, color photo (B) Canadian advertiser 6.00

8C,30S,BS Ford/Mercury Dealer Set [1968], color photo (F), Vista-Lite, CN, assorted advertisers 5.00

8C,30S,BS Ford Dealer Set [1968], color photo (F), Vista-Lite, CN, assorted advertisers 2.00

8C,30S,BS Ford [1968], color photo (B) of each, Canadian 5.25

8C,30S,BS Mercury [1968], Meteor Montcalm, Montclair 2 Door, Cyclone, Falcon Futura, Cougar, Montego MX, 100 Pickup, Ranchero GT, color photo (B), Canadian advertiser (all but Ranchero GT) 6.00

15C,30S,BS Pontiac Set [1968], Lion, 34 models Aegena Blue-Aleutian Blue-Alpine Blue-April Gold-Cameo Ivory-Flambeau Burgundy-Mayfair Maize-Meridian Turquoise-Nightshade Green-Nordic Blue-Primavera Beige-Solar Red-Springmist Green-Starlight Black-Verdoro Green 2.00

12C,30S,BS Chrysler [1969], fleet sales, Newport, Coronet, Sport fury, Pickup D100, Barracuda, Charger, Valiant, Newport, Monaco, Dart, Chrysler 300, Road Runner, color photo (B) 8.00

12C,30S,BS Chrysler [1969], assorted, Newport, Coronet, Sport fury, Pickup D100, Barracuda, Charger, Valiant, Newport, Monaco, Dart, Chrysler 300, Road Runner, color photo (B) no advertiser 6.00

13C,30S,BS Chrysler [1969], fleet sales, color photo (B) of each, Canadian 5.75

13C,30S,BS Chrysler [1969], color photo (B) of each, Canadian 6.75

12C,30S,BS Chrysler Dealer Set [1969], French, color photo (B), Western Match, CN, assorted advertisers 2.00

8C,30S,BS Ford [1969], Mustang Mach 1, Ford LTD, Landau Thunderbird, Supervan Econoline, Country Squire, Coupe Sport Falcon Futura, Pick-Up Ranger, Torino GT, color photo (B) Canadian advertiser 5.00

8C,30S,BS Ford [1969], Mustang Mach 1, Ford LTD, Landau Thunderbird, Supervan Econoline, Country Squire, Coupe Sport Falcon Futura, Pick-Up Ranger, Torino GT, color photo (B) United States advertiser 5.00

8C,30S,BS Ford Set [1969], photo (F) 4.00

8C,30S,BS Ford Dealer Set [1969], French, color photo (F), Western Match, CN, assorted advertisers 3.50

8C,30S,BS Ford Dealer Set [1969], color photo (F), Western Match, CN, assorted advertisers 2.00

8C,30S,BS Ford [1969], color photo (B) of each, Canadian 4.50

18C,30S,BS Pontiac Set [1969], Lion, dated Antique Gold-Burgundy-Cameo White-Carousel Red-Champagne Crystal Turquoise-Expresso Brown-Goldenrod Yellow-Liberty Blue-Limelight Green-Matador Red-Mayfair Maize-Midnight Green-Palladium Silver-Starlight Black-Verdoro Green-Warwick Blue-Windward Blue 2.75

16C,30S,FS Chrysler Set [1970] 8.00

5C,30S,BS Pontiac Set [1970] 2.00

15C,30S,BS Pontiac Set [1970], Diamond Match Co., Pontiac Safety.. Atoll Blue-Baja Gold-Bermuda Blue-Burqundy-Cardinal Red-Granada Gold-Mint Turquoise-Palladium Silver-Palomino Copper-Palisade Green-Pepper Green-Polar White-Sierra Yellow-Starlight Black-Verdoro Green 2.00

10C,30S,FS Chrysler Set [1971] 6.00

14C,30S,FS Ford Set [1971] 8.00

20C,30S,BS Pontiac Set [1971] Lion Match Co., dated Adriatic Blue-Aztec Gold-Bluestone Gray-Bronzini Gold-Cameo White-Canyon Copper-Cardinal Red-Castillian Bronze-Laurentian Green-Limekist Green-Lucerne Blue-Nordic Silver-Quezal Gold-Regency Blue-Rosewood-Sandalwood-Starlight Black-Tropical Lime + 2 others 2.75

20C,30S,BS Pontiac Set [1972] Diamond Match Co., dated Cardinal Red-Cumberland Blue-Julep Green-Quezal Gold-Wilderness Green + 12 others 1.00

14C,30S,FS Ford Set [1973] 8.00

14C,30S Ford [1973] dated Auto w/full length color photo of car 10.00

20C,30S,BS Pontiac Set [1973], Diamond Match Co., Wide Track.. Admiralty Blue-Ascot Silver-Brewster Green-Buccaneer Red-Burma Brown-Burnished Umber-Cameo White-Desert Sand-Florentine Red-Golden Olive-Mesa Tan-Navajo Orange-Porcelain Blue-Regatta Blue-Slate Green-Starlight Black-Sunlight Yellow-Valencia Gold-Verdant Green 3.00

14C,30S,FS Ford Set [1974], 7 Ford and 7 Mercury Ford: Ltd-Maverick-Mustang-Pickups-Pinto-Thunderbird-Torino Mercury: Capri-Comet-Cougar-Marquis-Meteor-Montego-Pickups 5.00

20C,30S,BS Pontiac Set [1974], Lion, Test Drive..Aquamarine-Bahia Green-Berkshire Green-Brentwood Brown-Buccaneer Red-Buckskin Metallic-Cameo White-Fiesta Orange-Firethorn Red-Mojave Tan-Nautilus Blue-Royal Lime-Starlight Black-Sterling Silver 2.00

22C,30S,BS Pontiac Set [1975], Lion, Astre Alpine Green-Arctic Blue-Augusta Green-Bimini Blue-Buccaneer Red-Cameo White-Carmel Beige-Copper Mist-Fire Coral Bronze-Ginger Brown-Graystone-Honduras Maroon-Lakemist Green-Oxford Brown-Persimmon-Roman Red-Sandstone-Starlight Black-Sterling Silver-Sunstorm Yellow-Tampico Orange + 1 other 3.00

22C,30S,BS Pontiac Set [1976], Lion, dated Athena Blue-Bavarian Cream-Buckskin Tan-Cameo White-Carousel Red-Cordovan Maroon-Durango Bronze-Firethorn Red-Goldenrod Yellow-Metalime Green-Polaris Blue-Starlight Black-Sterling Silver 2.00

22C,30S,BS Pontiac Set [1977], Diamond Match Co., Pontiac Ventura..Admiralty Blue-Buccaneer Red-Cameo White-Carmel Beige-Colonial Gold-Denver Gold-Fernmist Green-Fire Coral Bronze-Gulfmist Aqua-Porcelain Blue-Regatta Blue-Starlight Black-Sunstorm Yellow 2.00

24C,30S,BS Pontiac Set [1978], Diamond Match Co., dated Berkshire Green-Cameo White-Carmine-Chesterfield Brown-Claret-Desert Sand-Dresden Blue-Ember Mist-Glacier Blue-Laredo Brown-Martinique Blue-Mayan Red-Mayfair Green-Nautilus Blue-Platinum-Roman Red-Seafoam Green-Starlight Black-Sundance Yellow + 5 others 2.00

22C,30S,BS Pontiac Set [1979], Diamond Match Co., dated Atlantis Blue-Blue Metallic-Burnished Gold-Cameo White-Carmine-Claret-Dark Charcoal-Glacier Blue-Heritage Brown-Jadestone Green-Mayan Red-Mission Beige-Montego Cream-Nocturne Blue-Platinum-Redbird Red-Sierra Copper-Sky Mist Blue-Solar Gold-Starlight Black-Sundance Yellow-Willow Mist Green 2.00

22C,30S,BS Pontiac Set [1980], Lion Match Co., dated Yellow Bird Yellow + 21 others . 2.25
22C,30S,BS Pontiac Set [1981], Lion Match Co., dated Yellow Orange + 21 others 2.00

Automobile Sets, Miscellaneous

4C,20S,FS Superior Antique Cars Set [1974], Stanley Steamer 1910-Maxwell 1912-Packard
    1912-Stutz..1914 .... 1.00
4C,20S,FS Superior Antique Cars Set, Type 1 [1975], Cadillac 1906-Reo 1906-Stearns 1910-
    Simplex 1912 (stock)... 1.00
4C,20S,BS Superior Antique Cars Set, Type 2 [1976], Cadillac 1906-Reo 1906-Stearns 1910-
    Simplex 1912 (stock)... 1.00
6C,20S,FS Antique Cars Set [1957], 2 autos each with the same wording on the (S) Be Polite-
    Drive Safely-Speed Kills, Eddy Match Ltd, CN 1.25
12C,30S,BS Ohio Antique Autos Set [1977].. 2.00
12C,30S,BS Classic Car Series Set, Ohio Match Co., 1977 .... 3.25
24C,20S,FS Old Time Autos Set [1956], 6 cars each in 4 colors (BE/GN/OE/RD) Duryea's Motor
    Wagon 1895-First Chevrolet 1913-Ford Model T 1908-Hudson 1909-Maxwell 1908-
    Oldsmobile Runabout 1903 .... 4.00
5C,20S,FS Early Autos Set [1955] 1.00
12C,30S,FS Holland Antique Autos Set [   ].. 14.00
4C,30S,BS Vintage Cars Set, manumark; Printed in Canada-Matches Inserted in U.S.A. 2.75
6C,20S,FS Cesare, Quebec Antique Autos Set [   ], 1893-1902-1908-1912-1917-1924, D.D. Bean
    & Son.. 1.00
24C,20S, Antique Autos Set, Diamond Match Co. 7.75
12B WIMCO Safety Matches, Old Cars Set, (flattened) 4.00
12C,20S,FS Oldsmobile Set, 'Safety keeps you In the Picture', (GN) 1.25
20C,20S,FS Portuguese Automobiles Set 15.00
15C,40S,FS Portuguese Antique Clubs Set.. 12.50
15C,40S,FS Portuguese Antique Autos Set 10.00
15C,20S,FS Portuguese Antique Autos Set 15.00
10C,40S,FS Portuguese Antique Autos Set 12.50
25C,20S,DS Portuguese Dated Antique Autos Set, numbered 12.50
18C,20S,FS Early American Automobiles Set, 6 autos each in 3 colors (BE/BN/GN) Buick 1908-
    Cadillac Automobile 1903-First Chevrolet 1913-Ford Model T 1908-Stanley Steamer 1908-
    Studebaker Elec..Type 1 Greenwich manumark 2.00
18C,20S,FS Early American Automobiles Set, 6 autos each in 3 colors (BE/BN/GN) Buick 1908-
    Cadillac Automobile 1903-First Chevrolet 1913-Ford Model T 1908-Stanley Steamer 1908-
    Studebaker Elec..Type 2 New York 17 manumark, (B) is blank 2.00
18C,20S,FS Early American Automobiles Set, 6 autos each in 3 colors (BE/BN/GN) Buick 1908-
    Cadillac Automobile 1903-First Chevrolet 1913-Ford Model T 1908-Stanley Steamer 1908-
    Studebaker Elec..Type 3 New York 17 manumark, (B) has cartoon 2.00
12C,30S,BS Automobiles Set [1977], Ohio Match Co. 1906 Franklin-1907 Craig..-1907 Gale-1908
    Buick-1908 Stanley Steamer-1909 Oakland-1909 Rambler-1910 Velie '40'- 1910 1911
    Studebaker '40'-1911 Moline '35'-1912 Reo the Fifth-1920's Stutz Bearcat 2.50
5C,20S,FS Antique Cars Set Western Match Co., Vancouver, BC 1908/09 Mercedes..-1910 Ford-
    1911 Rolls..-1912 Mercer..- 1921 Locomobile 2.00
1FB,20S,FS Harris Auto Sales, 109 South Cherry, Eaton, Ohio Phone 293, (DBE,SR) ... 2.00

Auto Dealers, Miscellaneous

1FB,20S,CON ad: Charlie Irish Chevrolet, Shamrock (F/B) 5.00
2C,30S,ODD Odd Strikers 1) Bill Kuhn Chevrolet, striker on car logo, 2) Pacific Abrasive Supply
    Co, San Francisco, striker on wheel 10.00
9C,30S,BS Pontiac [1959], single advertiser, assorted colors, stock 3.00
20C,20S,BS Pontiac Motor Division, 'Look and Live!' Safety Set, (GN) 6.00
35C,30S,BS Auto Dealers, Pontiac covers, assorted 10.00
55C,MZ,MS Auto Dealers, dated, assorted 7.00
15C,20S,FS Auto Dealers [1950], dated, assorted 3.25
25C,20S,MS Car Dealers, assorted advertisers 7.00
100C,20S,FS Auto Dealers, assorted 9.00
25C,20S,FS Auto Dealers, old dealer imprints 6.00
20C,30S,MS Car Dealers 3.00
50C,30S,MS Auto Dealers, assorted 5.00
250C,40S,MS Auto Dealers, assorted 65.00
30C,30S,RAMA Auto Dealers, assorted 5.00

Transportation (Brown & Bigelow Sets)

4C,20S,FS Brown & Bigelow [   ], Antique Cars Set, 1902 Studebaker..- + 3? others 1.00
4C,20S,FS Brown & Bigelow [   ], Antique Cars Set, 1906 Success..- + 3? others 1.00
4C,20S,FS Brown & Bigelow [1965], Antique Cars Set, 1910 Brush..-1911 Stanley..- + 2 others
.... 1.00
4C,20S,FS Brown & Bigelow [1971], Antique Cars Set, 1904 Duryea Phaeton - 3? others 1.00

Transportation (Powers Regulator Sets)

4C,30S,FS Set #1 [1954], Maxwell-Mercedes-Mercer-Stanley 1.00
4C,30S,FS Set #2 [1954], American-Ford-Rambler-Rolls 2.00
4C,30S,FS Set #3 [1955], Apperson-Moon-Overland-Simplex 2.00
4C,30S,FS Set #4 [1955], Cadillac-Peerless-Stutz-Thomas 2.00
4C,30S,FS Set #5 [1955], Buick-Franklin-Hupmobile-Marmon 2.00
4C,30S,FS Set #6 [1956], Brewster-Lozier-Studebaker-Winton 2.00
4C,30S,FS Set #7 [1956], Chevrolet-Kissel-Oldsmobile-Pierce 2.00
4C,30S,FS Set #8 [1957], Brush-Cartercar-Premier-Templar 2.00
4C,30S,FS Set #9 [1957], Hudson-Locomobile-Maytag-Pope 2.00
4C,30S,FS Set #10 [1957], Abbott-Garford-International-Interstate 1.00
4C,30S,FS Set #11 [1958], Daniels-Doble-Glide-Packard 2.00
4C,30S,FS Set #12 [1958], Autocar-Chalmers-Reo-Saxon 2.00
4C,30S,FS Set #13 [1959], Chadwick-Cunningham-Stevens-Stoddard 2.00
4C,30S,FS Set #14 [1959], Monitor-Mora-National-Sturtevant 2.00
4C,30S,FS Set #15 [1960], Biddle-Knox-Lincoln-White 2.00
4C,30S,FS Set #16 [1960], Camden-Elcar-Oakland-Wolverine 2.00
4C,30S,FS Set #17 [1961], Briggs-Clark-Dodge-McFarlan 2.00
4C,30S,FS Set #18 [1961], Aerocar-Dixie-Duesenberg-Zachow 2.00
72C,30S,FS Sets, 18 sets of 4 each. [1954-1961] 25.00

Taxi Cabs & Buses

1C,20S,FS Sunset Cab Co, drawing (B) 1.50

2C,20S,FS DeLuxe Taxi, (BK/YW) & East Orange Cab Co., little boy (B) 5.00

2C,20S,FS Gray Top Cabs, MA 49-49, no city,(RD/BK/WE/GY) & Langton Taxi, Tel. 243
Ossining, Advertizit Match Co. manumark (OE/BK) 5.00

1C,20S,FS Simon's Taxi, Phone 191, 2 Way Radio, Adams, Mass 5.00

2C,20S,FS Skyline Cab, taxi (F), Charlestown, WV & Sky-View Cab, Asbury Park, NJ (RD/YW)
can (B)... 8.00

1C,20S,FS Strop Taxi, Dial 5811, Raleigh, NC 3.50

1C,20S,FS Strop Taxi, Phone 3800, Raleigh, NC 5.00

2C,20S,FS Town Taxi, Williamstown, MA, Tel 653 & Public Taxi, Schenectady, NY 5.00

1FB,20S,FS Yellow Cabs, TUxedo 1234, big cab (B) 5.00

1C,20S,FS Yellow Cab, Low Fares, ATlantic 9000, Omaha 4.25

1C,20S,FS Yellow Cab, Baggage Service, Phone 440 .... 5.00

10C,20S,FS Yellow Taxi Cabs, assorted.. 12.50

30C,20S,MS Taxi cabs, assorted companies 4.00

35C,20S,FS Taxi cabs, assorted companies 12.50

10C,20S,FS Taxi Cabs, assorted.. 13.00

10C,20S,FS Gray Line Set [1955], Jefferson Memorial-Library of Congress-Lincoln Memorial-
Mount Vernon-Pan American Union Building-The Supreme Court Building-Tomb of the
Unknown Soldier-United States Capitol-Washington Monument-The White House .. 4.00

20C,20S,FS Bus Lines 12.00

Trucks & Truck Lines

4C,20S,FS Allied Van Lines Set [1952], stock design, Local moving-Long distance moving-
Packing-Storage 2.00

1C,20S,FS Atlas Transit, Serving Arkansas, Fast Freight Service (RD/BK/WE) 2.75

1C,20S,FS Boweil, North American Van Lines, Cincinnati, Ohio, Billy Beaver (B), (YW/GN/WE)
.... 4.00

1C,20S,BS Boyce Motor Lines Inc., truck (B), (RD/WE/BK) 2.50

1C,20S,BS The CCC Highway Inc, Cleveland, Ohio, photo of truck (B), (GN/YW) 3.25

1C,20S,FS Dearmon Inc., Transportation Company, Mansfield, Ohio, (GN/WE/YW) 2.00

1C,20S,FS Johnson Motor Lines System, truck (B) (OR/BK/WE.SR) 2.25

1C,20S,FS La Biondo Brothers Motor Express, Inc, Bridgeton, NJ, stock truck (B) (YW/GN/BK)
.... 3.00

1C,20S,FS,FL J.D. Leonard Long distance Moving, closed van-truck w/sign on side (BK/WE/RD)
.... 5.00

1C,20S,BS Lifschultz Way, Freight Forwarders, (BE/WE) 2.00

1C,20S,FS Michigan Motor Friengh Lines, truck (B) (YW/BK/RD) 3.00

1C,20S,FS Miller & Miller Motor Freight, Texas Panhandle since 1923, truck (B) (SR/GN) 4.00

1C,20S,FS North Penn Transfer, Landsale, PA (YW/RD) 2.25

1C,20S,FS Palmer Lines Inc, Great Barrington, Mass, truck (F), terminal (B) (GN/WE) 3.00

1C,20S,FS Security Cartage Co. Inc, logo w/eagle (F) (GN/RD/SR) 2.75

1C,20S,FS,FL Southern Transfer & Storage Co, San Antonio, TX (RD) truck 5.00

1C,20S,FS United Security Association Warehouses, Inc., New York, NY, truck w/map (F) (YW/
RD/GN/WE) 2.50

100C,MZ,MS Truck Lines, assorted 14.00

35C,20S,FS Truck Lines, terminals & cities Acme Fast Freight, assorted 5.00

50C,30S,FS Truck Lines, terminals & cities, assorted 22.00

120C,20S/30S/40S,MS Truck Lines, terminals & cities, assorted 17.00

50C,40S,MS Truck Lines, terminals & cities, assorted 13.00

350C,40S,MS Truck Lines, terminals & cities, assorted, album 75.00

Transportation (Miscellaneous)

1C,20S,FS Auto Allied Mutual Assn, John Hippen, Agt., Kanawaha, Iowa 3.50

1C,20S,FS It saves to/AAA /Belong, $5000.00 Bail Bond $1000.00 Personal Accident Insurance
(SR/BK) 2.50

1C,20S,FS National Automobile Club, Ride Worry Free with N.A.C.! (B) (RD/WE/BK) . 3.25

30C,20S,FS Trolley Car Memories Set [1966], 6 cars each in 5 different colors (GN/GN with (GY)
frame on (B)-RD/RD with (GY) frame (B)-YW), 1873-1901-1905-1922-1926-1949 3.00

4C,20S,FS The Dream Highway Set [1941], Diamond Match Mt. Dallas Cut-Overpass-Ticket
Booth-Tunnel 4.00

4C,20S,FS Pennsylvania Superhighway Set [   ], Diamond Match By Way of..-Part of 13..-The
Pennsylvania..-There are 11. .... 3.25

265C,20S,FS Transportation, assorted, rail and ship 50.00

48C,20S,FS Transportation, assorted, 6 rail/6 ship/18 air/18 Truck 13.00

360C,20S,FS Transportation, assorted, 135 rails/117 air/108 ships, album 90.00

20C,20S,FS Transportation, assorted, air and ship, 20C 2.50

20C,20S,MS Transportation, assorted carriers 8.50

25C,30S,MS Transportation, assorted 3.50

100C,MZ,MS Transportation, assorted, ... 11.00

20C,20S,FS Transportation in the '90's Set [1956], 5 scenes each in 4 colors (BE/BN-GN/RD)
Ferryboat-Horse Drawn Trolley-Steam Train-Surrey-Victoria 3.00

10C,20S,FS AAA Approved lodging & restaurants 2.50

10C,20S,MS AAA Approved 1.25

Tums for the Tummy Sets

Tums for the Tummy—A series of sets issued in the early to mid 1950s by the Universal Match Corp., promoting the use of Tums for the Tummy. Two sets of six featuring fish lures were followed by two sets of six birds. Later, six matchcover releases depicted animals in sets labeled Series #1 and Series #2. The fish lures and birds sets also have large and small letters A, B, and C on the inside, the meaning of which is not known, although it may have something to do with the area where the sets were distributed or a code to identify the customer who ordered the sets.

12C,20S,FS Tums Wild Animal Set (partial) 9.00
6C,20S,FS Animals Set [1956], Series #1, African Elephant-African Gorilla-African Lion-Bengal Tiger-Black Panther-Canadian Moose 3.50
6C,20S,FS Animals Set [1956], Series #2, African Leopard-African Rhinoceras-African Zebra-American Buffalo-Brown Bear-German Boar 3.00
12C,20S,FS Tums Wild Bird Set, 6 from series A, 6 from series C, colorful 11.50
6C,20S,FS Birds Set, no letter.. 2.25
6C,20S,FS Birds Set, small letter A 2.50
6C,20S,FS Birds Set, Canada Goose-Mallard Drake-Mourning Dove-Pintail-Redhead-Ringneck Pheasant, Type 1 [1953], large letter A 1.00
6C,20S,FS Birds Set, Canada Goose-Mallard Drake-Mourning Dove-Pintail-Redhead-Ringneck Pheasant, Type 2 [   ], large letter C 2.00
6C,20S,FS Birds Set, Bob White Quail-Canvasback-Prairie Chicken-Wild Turkey-Woodcock-Wood Duck, Type 1 small letter B 2.00
6C,20S,FS Birds Set, Bob White Quail-Canvasback-Prairie Chicken-Wild Turkey-Woodcock-Wood Duck, Type 2 large letter C 3.00
12C,20S,FS Fly Fishing Set, from series A,C, and blank, colorful 9.00
6C,20S,FS Fish Lures, Gray Hackle Orange Body-Pale Evening Dun-Parmacheene Beau-Professor-Scarlet Ibis-Silver Doctor, Type 1 [1950], no letter................................... 3.00
6C,20S,FS Fish Lures, Gray Hackle Orange Body-Pale Evening Dun-Parmacheene Beau-Professor-Scarlet Ibis-Silver Doctor, Type 2 large letter A 3.00
6C,20S,FS Fish Lures, Gray Hackle Orange Body-Pale Evening Dun-Parmacheene Beau-Professor-Scarlet Ibis-Silver Doctor, Type 3 large letter B 3.00
6C,20S,FS Fish Lures, Gray Hackle Orange Body-Pale Evening Dun-Parmacheene Beau-Professor-Scarlet Ibis-Silver Doctor, Type 4 large letter C 2.25
6C,20S,FS Fish Lures Set Tums Sets, Black Gnat-Col Fuller-Logan-Montreal-Parmacheene Belle-Royal Coachman, Type 1 small letter B 2.50
6C,20S,FS Fish Lures Set Tums Sets, Black Gnat-Col Fuller-Logan-Montreal-Parmacheene Belle-Royal Coachman, Type 2 large letter C 2.50

VIP (non sports)

VIP—A popular category among more experienced collectors, VIP, or Personality matchcovers include the name or business of any well known personality. Sometimes divided into sports and non-sports VIPs, headings include movie stars, theatre actors and national political figures.

1C,20S,FS Gene Autry Hotels, Hotel Continental, Hollywood California, crest (F/B) 7.75
3C,20S,FS Bonanza Set w/Ben Cartwright, Hoss, & Little Joe on each 15.00
1C,20S,FS The Pat Boone Country Inn, (B/W) photo (F) 2.25
1C,20S,FS Salesman's Blank, The Eddie Cantor Comedy Theatre, photo of EC (F/B), place (B) for local listing, unusual 22.00
111C,30S,FS Celebrity Set [1951], Lion Match, set 111.00
40C,20S,FS Celebrity Contest Set, picture of person inside, 6 names at bottom (I), 2 different photos for each group of 6 names Names in sequence are: Carillo-Allen-Benny-Blue-Haley-Baker-Dempsey-Gomez-Hope-Hubbell-Jolson-Rogers-Raft-Rubinoff-Regan-Penner-Nagel-Murry-Linden-Lehr-Carillo.. Type #1 [1940], space for ad on front 50.00
40C,20S,FS Celebrity Contest Set, picture of person inside, 6 names at bottom (I), 2 different photos for each group of 6 names Names in sequence are: Carillo-Allen-Benny-Blue-Haley-Baker-Dempsey-Gomez-Hope-Hubbell-Jolson-Rogers-Raft-Rubinoff-Regan-Penner-Nagel-Murry-Linden-Lehr-Carillo.. Type #2 [1940], has no space for ad on front 50.00
2C,20S,FS Character Set [1950], Chicago Match Co. And Then She Said..-Wal, I'll Tell Ya.. (stock) 1.50
1C,30S,FS Bob Cummings Motor Hotel, AAA, Joplin, Missouri 6.00
1C,30S,FS Polynesian Palace, Home of the Don Ho Show 2.00
1FB,30S,BS Arthur Fiedler, Conductor, photo (F), The Boston Pops (B), (BK/WE) 4.00
1C,30S,BS Pete Fountain's French Quarter Inn, New Orleans, La., photo (B) 2.50
1C,20S,FS Betty Grable in 'Down Argentine Way,' photo (B) 14.00
1C,30S,JWL OZ..A Private Club, San Diego, Ca.,drawing of Jean Harlow on (F/B) 3.50
1C,20S,FS The Palladium Ballroom-Café, (B/W) photo of Woody Herman (F), Crown Match Co. 4.25
1C,20S,BS I Luv to Hate JR 3.00
1C,20S,FS Duke Kahanamoku, Hawaii's first, and greatest Olympic Champion 2.50
1C,20S,FS Los Angeles Times Admiral Ernest J. King 4.00
1C,20S,FS Julius La Rosa's Restaurant, Hollywood, Florida, shows La Rosa (F/B) 3.00
1FB,20S,FS Jack La Rue Restaurant, Studio City, CA 3.00

1C,20S,BS Alan Ladd's Spanish Inn, 840 N Indian Ave, Palm Springs, CA 92262 .... 2.00
1C,30S,FS Frances Langford's Outrigger Restaurant, Jensen Beach, FL, Hawaiian themes (B) 3.00
1C,30S,FS Ted Lewis 'Just Wonderful Food' Restaurant in Wash, D.C. 2.00
1C,40S,FS Roberta Linn & Freddie Bells - Inn Place in Corona Del Mar, CA. 10.00
1C,30S,FS Guy Lombardo at the Roosevelt Grill, photo (F) 9.00
1FB,20S,FS Guy Lombardo, East Point House, photo (F), printed sticks 7.50
1C,20S,FS Guy Lombardo's, Long Island, photo (F) 3.75
1C,20S,FS Los Angeles Times General Douglas Mac Arthur 4.00
1C,20S,FS Audie Murphy in To Hell and Back, in French 4.00
1C,20S,FS Louis Nye, Appearing at Pacific Playhouse, (B/W) photo (F) 4.00
1C,20S,FS Pat O'Brien's, New Orleans, Shamrock (F) 3.50
1C,20S,BS Paul Rigby, Cartoonist for Daily News 1.50
1C,20S,FS Frank Sinatra's Italian American Restaurant, Perth Amboy, NJ (RD/WE) 5.00
1C,30S,FS Red Skelton Show, sponsor Johnson's Wax, CBS-TV, photo (F) 10.00
1C,30S,BS Tracy's w/Spencer Tracy (B), MGM Grand Hotel w/Lion (F) 3.00
20C,MS Personalities & VIPs, assorted 5.00
1C,30S,FS Duke Zeibert's Restaurant, Washington, DC 2.00
12C,20S,FS Tip and Twinkle Set [1957], V.I.P. Alcatraz..-Alcoholics Unanimous..-Buckingham Palace..-Golden Naval..-Happy Daze..-Hunting College..-Infernal Revenue..-Last Chance..-Mabel's House..-Nudist Camp..-The Happy Dream..- The Kremlin.. .... 5.00
12C,20S,FS V.I.P. II Set [1958], A message to..-Bernies Flophouse..-Devil's Island..-If You Died..-Kill Joy..-Mau Mau..-Next Summer..-Purple Passion..- Things are a..-The Jayne..-The Snow White..-The Tiltin'.. .... 4.00
12C,MS,FS V.I.P. III [1961], 8-20S,2-10S, 1-30S,1-JL, A message to..-Bernies Flophouse..-Devil's Island..-If You Died..-Kill Joy..-Mau Mau..-Next Summer..-Purple Passion..- Things are a..-The Jayne..-The Snow White..-The Tiltin'.. .... 4.00

VIP (Chez Paree Issues)

VIP Chez Paree—This series is considered one of the finest to own. Beginning on June 12, 1955 with Marion Marlow and ending on April 17, 1960 with Sammy Davis, Jr., each matchcover has a promotional (BK/WE) still of the star, and is dated. All performed at the Chicago theatre restaurant which bears the name of this category.

3C,20S,FS [1954], Nov 21-Dec 05-Dec 28 .... 7.50
6C,30S,FS [1955], Jan 19-Feb 9 Feb 27-Mar 22-Apr 7-May 13 .... 7.50
11C,20S,FS [1955], undated-Jun 12-Jul 5-Jul 22-Aug 5-Sep 7-Sep 22-Oct 16-Nov 11-Nov 27-Dec 28 .... 10.00
14C,20S,FS [1956], Jan 17-Feb 7-Mar 29-Apr 23-May 10-Jun 10-Jun 20-Jun 28-Sep 10-Sep 21-Oct 12-Nov 2-Nov 16-Dec 27 .... 10.00
14C,20S,FS [1957], Jan 10-Jan 30-Feb 26-Mar 19-Apr 21-May 10-May 24-Jun 16-Jul 24-Sep 10-Oct 3-25th Anniversary-Dec 1-Dec 27 .... 12.50
12C,20S,FS [1958], Jan 31-Feb 27-May 16-Jun 4-Jun 18-Aug 7-Sep 25-Oct 12-Nov 2-Nov 16-Nov 30-Dec 26 .... 12.50
9C,20S,FS [1959], Feb 18-Mar 22-Apr 16-May 3-May 21-Sep 7-Oct 2-Oct 23-Nov 13 .. 12.00
6C,20S,FS [1960], Jan 15-Mar 11-Apr 17-May 27 .... 7.50
1C,20S,FS Tony Bennett, (B/W) photo (F) 5.50
1C,20S,FS Red Buttons, (B/W) photo (F) 5.50

1C,20S,FS	Nat 'King' Cole, (B/W) photo (F)	6.50
1C,30S,FS	Nat 'King' Cole, (B/W) photo (F)	8.50
1C,20S,FS	Sammy Davis, Jr., (B/W) photo (F)	5.50
1C,20S,FS	Sam Levenson, (B/W) photo (F)	5.50
1C,20S,FS	Lou Monte, (B/W) photo (F)	5.50

VIP (Al Hirt singles)

1C,30S,FS	Drawing of Al (B)	2.00
1C,30S,FS	Bourbon Street, New Orleans, drawing (B), trumpet (F), foilite (BK/WE)	2.50
1C,30S,FS	New Orleans The Happy Trumpet	2.25
1C,30S,FS	New Orleans The Horn meets The Hornet	1.75
1C,30S,FS	New Orleans Live at Carnegie Hall	2.25
1C,30S,FS	New Orleans, record ad: The Best of Al Hirt	3.00
1C,30S,FS	@ Dan's Pier 600, photo (B)	5.00
1C,30S,FS	New Orleans 'Pops' goes the Trumpet	1.75
1C,30S,FS	New Orleans The Sounds of Christmas	1.75
1C,30S,FS	New Orleans Sugar Lips	1.75

World's Fairs

World's Fairs—Any set or single matchcover which advertises or mentions any internationally recognized World's Fair or Fair event. Peripherals include commercial products, services, businesses and events related to the World's Fair. The earliest World's Fair sets come from the 1933 Chicago Century of Progress, although the founding of the hobby is synonymous with the 1939 New York World's Fair.

3C,20S,FS Washington Bicentennial Set [1932] 5.00

1933-34 Century of Progress, Chicago, Ill

10C,20S,FS Gold Set [1933], numbered, Birdseye..-Administration..-Replica..-Travel and..-Hall of..-Electrical..-U.S. Government..-Hall of Science, North Facade-The Hall of Science Tower-Replica of the. 35.00

10C,20S,FS Silver Set [1934], numbered, Birdseye..-Administration..-Replica..-Travel and..-Hall of..-Electrical..-U.S. Government..-Hall of Science, North Facade-The Hall of Science Tower-Replica of the.. .... 75.00

1C,20S,FS,FL Gold Set, shows two buildings, dated: [1934] 12.00

1C,20S,FS	'I Will' (F) (stock)	10.25
1C,20S,FS,FL	Administration Building	4.50
1C,20S,FS,FL	Bird's Eye View, (B/W) drawing	5.25
1C,20S,FS,FL	ad: Canadian Club Whiskey (F), Canadian Club Café at WF (B)	12.25
1C,20S,FS,FL	generic	3.00
1C,20S,FS,FL	Electrical Group	9.75
1C,20S,FS,FL	Replica of Fort Dearborn	6.00
1C,20S,FS,FL	The Hall of Science Tower	6.25
1FB,20S,FL	Hall of Science, North Facade	9.00

1C,20S,FS,FL Replica Golden Pavilion of Jehol 6.00
1FB,20S,FS No. 5 - Tower 4.25
1C,20S,FS,FL Travel and Transport Building 5.25
1C,20S,FS,FL U.S. Government Building 4.50
1C,20S,FS 1933-34 Old Heidelberg World's Fair, Randolph near State Street 10.25
1FB,20S,FS Canadian Club Café, tall Universal, colorful, dated 1934 .... 12.00

1935-36 California-Pacific Int'l Exposition, San Diego, CA

6C,20S,FS Diamond Set [1935], (YW) Building in Palisades..-Café of the World-Lily Pond..- San Diego Museum..-Spanish Section-Ultra Moderne Section 35.00
8C,20S,FS Diamond Set [1935], (OE/GN/GD) Building in Palisades..-Café of..-Cairo Oriental..- Lily Pond..-Palace of..-San Diego..-Spanish Section..-Ultra.. .... 38.00
8C,20S,FS Diamond Set [1936], (OE/GN/GD) Building in Palisades..-Café of..-Cairo Oriental..-
Lily Pond..-Palace of..-San Diego..-Spanish Section..-Ultra.. .... 35.00
8C,20S,FS Lion Set [1935] 30.00
1C,20S,FS,FL Café of the World 3.00
1C,20S,FS,FL Miss California w/map & seal 3.00
1C,20S,FS,FL Palace of Better Housing, (OE) set 10.25
1C,20S,FS,FL Palace of Science, colorful 10.00
1C,20S,FS,FL Travel and Transportation Building, colorful 10.00
1C,20S,FS,FL Women's Palace, Palace of Education 13.50

1935 Detroit & Michigan Exposition, Detroit, MI

1C,20S,FS Detroit-Leland Hotel 12.00
1C,20S,FS Hotel Detroiter, Your Headquarters 12.00
1C,20S,FS Eddystone Hotel, Parks Ave. at Sproat 12.00
1C,20S,FS Hotel Fort Shelby, Detroit 10.00

1936 Texas Centennial, Dallas, TX

6FB,20S,FS Administration-Food and Agricultural-Live Stock-Petroleum Products-Poultry-Varied Industries, Electrical and Communications. This set occurs with a wide and a narrow (SR) (S) 30.00
1C,20S,FS Administration Building (SR/BE)..
.... 9.50
1C,20S,FS Electrical & Communications Building (SR/BE) 9.00
1C,20S,FS Food & Agriculture Building (SR/BE) 8.00
1C,20S,FS Live Stock Building (SR/BE) 7.50
1C,20S,FS The Petroleum Products Building (SR/BE) 8.50
1C,20S,FS Poultry Group (SR/BE) 7.50
1C,20S,FS Live Stock Building 5.00
1C,20S,FS Varied Industries, Electrical and Communications Building 6.00

1937 Paris Expo

1C,20S,FS Jersey Match Co. 3.00
1C,20S,FS Jupiter size 5.00

1939-40 Golden Gate Exposition, San

12C,20S,FS Diamond Set [1939], Court
of..-Federal Building..-The Gayway-
Night Scene..- Pacific Nations..-
Pacifica at Night-Portals of..-Rain-
bow Fountain-South Towers-Towers
of the East..-Tower of the Sun-Trea-
sure Isle 55.00
5FB,G,FS Lion Set [1939], San Francisco,
(BE/GD/RD/SR) 27.50
1C,20S,FS Drink Brazilian Coffee .. 5.25

1C,20S,FS Cinnabar Cocktail Lounge 3.75
1FB,20S,FS Court of the Moon Gardens 3.50
1FB,20S,FS The Gayway 1.75
1FB,G,FS 1939 San Francisco 6.00
1FB,20S,FS The Majestic Federal Bldg 3.25
1C,20S,FS Old Gold Cigarettes, Double-Mellow 7.00
1FB,20S,FS Pacific Nation's Exhibit 3.50
1FB,20S,FS Pacific at Night 1.75
3C,20S,FL Portals of the Pacific, Treasure Island, Court of the Moon Garden 6.50
3C,20S,FL Rainbow Fountain, Federal Building, Pacific Nations' Exhibit 6.50
1C,20S,FS Larkspur Rose Bowl 5.00
1FB,20S,FS The South Towers 3.50
1C,20S,FS Souvenir Golden Gate Int'l Expo on San Francisco Bay 1939 .... 5.25
3C,20S,FL Towers of the East at Night, The GayWay, The South Towers 6.50
3C,20S,FL Night Scene Tower of the Sun, Tower of the Sun, Pacifica at Night 6.50
1FB,20S,FS Treasure Island 5.50
34C,20S,FS San Francisco, assorted themes 65.00
1C,20S,FS ad: Drink Brazilian Coffee (dated: 1940) 1.50
1C,20S,FS ad: Old Gold Double-Mellow Cigarettes (dated: 1940) 2.25
1C,40S,FS,RF,FL (dated: 1940), (stock) 3.00

1939-40 New York World's Fair, New York City, NY

20C,20S,FS Diamond Match Co. (SR) Set [1939], Administration..-Aviation..-Business Systems..-Con-
sumer.- Cosmetics..-DuPont..-Food & Sports..-
Food Building..-Ford Motor..-Gas Exhibits..-Hall
of Communications-Maritime..- Medicine & Public..-Railroad..-R.C.A...-Textile..-Theme Center-
Transportation..-United States Gov't...-U.S. Steel
.... 165.00
9C,20S,FS Diamond Match Co. (BE) Set [1939], Aviation-Business Systems-Food Building #2-Ford
Motors- Lucky Strike-Maison Coty-Medical-
R.C.A.-U.S. Steel 50.00

20C,20S,FS Diamond Match Co. (SR) Set [1939], Administration..-Aviation..-Business Systems..-Consumer.- Cosmetics..-DuPont..-Food & Sports..-Food Building..-Ford Motor..-Gas Exhibits..-Hall of Communications-Maritime..- Medicine & Public..-Railroad..-R.C.A...-Textile..-Theme Center-Transportation..-United States Gov't...-U.S. Steel 165.00

9C,20S,FS Diamond Match Co. (BE) Set [1939], Aviation-Business Systems-Food Building #2-Ford Motors-Lucky Strike-Maison Coty-Medical-R.C.A.-U.S. Steel 50.00

9C,20S,FS Diamond Match Co. (OE) Set [1939], Administration-Chrysler Motors-Communications-Consumers-DuPonts-Gas Exhibits-Railroad-Trylon & Peri.-U.S. Government. 50.00

4C,20S,FS Lion Regulars [1939], Federal Building-Gas Industries Building-Theme Center-U.S. Steel Building 9.50

4C,20S,FS Lion Giants Set [1939] 32.50

4C,M Lion Midgets [1939], (BE/GN/MN/OE) 26.00

1C,20S,FS Albanian Continental Restaurant, logo (F/B) (BK/RD) 6.50

1C,20S,FS Hotel Albert, Where Courtesy Dwells 4.00

1C,20S,FS,FL Albert Pick Hotels, All Along Your Way 3.25

1C,20S,FS,FL Albert Pick Hotels (map of Northeast) (OE) 6.50

1C,20S,FS Anacin Tablets (B), T&P (F) (YW/RD/WE/BK) 3.00

1C,20S,FS Ballantine Three Ring Inn (Full Length) display (I) 10.50

1C,20S,FS Aviation Building (BE) set 7.25

1C,20S,FS Business Systems and Insurance Building, (BE) set 8.00

1C,20S,FS Ride the Blue Coach, Manhattan Line, bus (F/B) 2.50

1C,20S,FS Flame Restaurant, Gas Exhibit Building 5.25

1C,20S,FS Medical & Health, Science & Education Exhibits (BE) 3.25

1C,20S,FS R.C.A. Building (BE) 6.00

1C,20S,FS The United States Steel Building (BE) 6.25

1C,20S,FS U.S. Steel Building, (BE) 4.75

1C,20S,FS Belgian Pavilion Restaurant, Constitution Mall 6.50

1C,20S,FS Bell System, Anywhere Inexpensively (F), 50c call (B), (DGN/BK/WE) 4.00

1C,20S,FS Visit the Bell System, Call Anywhere 50 cents 7.25

1C,20S,FS Bell System, photo (F), rate chart (I), (GN/WE/KB) 11.00

1C,20S,FS Visit the Bell System Exhibit...Back Home 4.75

1C,30S,FS The Beverly Hotel, 50th & Lexington Ave, food prices (B) 3.50

1C,20S,FS The Biltmore, drawing (B) 5.25

1C,30S,FS Chr. Bjelland & Co. Sardines, Stavanger, Norway 7.75

1C,20S,FS Bloomingdale's at the Gateway to the World's Fair T&P (B) (BK/WE/RD) .. 5.25

1C,20S,FL Borden's Dairy World of Tomorrow 5.50

1C,20S,FS Boulevard Rotisserie Bar & Grill 5.00

1C,20S,FS Brazilian Pavilion, The Restaurant, (YW) 6.25

1C,20S,FS The British Pavilion (CM) 4.00

1C,20S,FS The British Pavilion (YW) 5.50

1C,20S,FS (BE) Set, Business Systems & Insurance Building (DBE/WE) 1.50

1C,G,FS Statue (B), Canada Pavilion (F) 7.50

1C,20S,FS Hotel Capitol, Opposite Madison Square Garden 5.25

1C,20S,FS Hotel Carteret, Every Room with Bath 5.25

1C,20S,FS Caruso Restaurants, rest (B) 4.00

1C,20S,FS The Hotel Chelsea, Complete One-Room Homes 5.25

1C,20S,FS Chrysler Motors Bldg (OE) set 3.25

1C,20S,BS,FL The City of Light, early back striker 5.25

1C,20S,FS,FL Columbus Memorial Lighthouse, Dominican Republic 5.00

1C,20S,FS The Commodore, Right at Grand Central 6.75

1C,20S,FS Cornish Arms, 350 Comfortable Rooms with Bath, NYWF ad (I) 5.25

1C,20S,FS ad: Crystal T&P Set in Colorful Genuine Leather Disc 4.75

1C,20S,FS Cuban Pavilion Restaurant, 'Visit Beautiful Havana' (BE/WE/RD) 9.75

1C,20S,FS Cuesta-Rey Havana Cigars, Florida State Exhibit 5.00

1C,20S,FS Dawn of a New Day, (BE/OE/WE) 9.00

1C,20S,FS De Camp Lines, Suburban Essex, Bus (B) 5.75

1C,20S,FS The De Witt Clinton Hotel, Albany, NY 6.00
1C,20S,FS Hotel Dixie, In the Center of Everything 5.25
1C,20S,FS Dodes Restaurant, T&P logo (B), taped 2.50
1C,20S,FS Dubrow's Cafeteria, Eastern Parkway, Brooklyn, T&P (B) (RD/BE/WE) 3.75
1C,20S,FS Ever Ready Label Corp., 25 Label Years 5.25
1C,20S,FS World of Fashion (OE) set 6.25
1C,20S,FS Federal Government Bldg 5.00
1C,20S,BF (BE), Federal Area (F), Chrysler Bldg (B) 3.50
1C,20S,FS Firestone Exhibit & Private Lounge, tire (B) 3.00
1C,G,FS Forecast of Transportation (B), Sunrise (F) 2.00
1C,20S,FS Forest Hills Inn, Forest Hills L.I. 4.00
1C,20S,FS Forrest Hotel, Excellent Food and Choice Liquors 5.25
1C,20S,FS Four Star Café, Flushing, L.I., Mithrana, stock (B) T&P (F) (MN/BE) 4.25
1C,M Franklin Simon's, T&P (B) (MN/WE) 9.50
1C,20S,FS from orange set, Gas Exhibit Building (OE/WE/BE) 5.00
1C,20S,FS General Motors Highways & Horizons, seal (F/B) (YW/BK) 9.50
1C,G,FS Glass Center Bldg (on B), Railroad Bldg & Electrical Products Bldg (F) 2.75
1C,20S,FS Gimbels, 15 Minutes from the World's Fair, Adjoining Penn Station 6.25
1C,20S,BF (OE), Hall of Comm (F), Glass Bldg (B) 3.50
1C,20S,FS Gulistan Rugs & Carpets 2.50
1C,20S,FS George Washington Bridge, Holland/Lincoln Tunnel, Open April 30, 1939 ...... 4.75
1C,20S,FS Heineken's on the Zuiderzee, Famous Holland Beer, Beer Glass (I) (PE/WE) 7.25
1C,20S,FS Holland/Lincoln Tunnel, Open April 30, 1939 .... 10.00
1C,20S,FS Horn & Hardart Automats, Welcome Visitors! (OE/DBE) 7.50
1C,20S,FS The Huddle Diner, (GD) 3.00
1C,20S,FS Hungarian Restaurant, Hungarian Pavilion, Magyat Etterem Gundel's Heart (F) 5.25
1C,20S,FS,FEA Iraq Pavilion, Garden of Eden Café, colorful 15.00
1C,20S,FS Japanese Tea Garden & Formosa Oolong Tea 5.75
1C,20S,FS Jewish Palestine Pavilion, Café Tel Aviv (DBE/WE) 12.50
1C,20S,FS w/search lights, ad: Kent-Ley Garage (F), Fair (B) (stock) 5.25
1C,20S,FS Kew Gardens Hotel 6.00
1C,20S,FS King Cotton Hotel 5.00
1C,20S,FS,FL Le Restaurant Francais, French Pavilion (BK) 5.00
1C,20S,FS The Lobster Oyster & Chop House Welcomes you to the NYWF, lobster (B), T&P
     (F) (DBE/RD/WE) 4.50
1C,20S,FS ad: Lone Star Tavern, San Francisco 5.00
1C,20S,FS Café Loyale, 525 5th Ave, T&P in ad 3.00
1C,20S,FS Cigarette Making, Lucky Strike Building (DBE/WE) 5.50
1C,20S,FS Mamaroneck Express Cruisers - Avoid City Traffic, drawing (B) 7.75
1C,20S,FS Manhattan Line, Blue Coach (B), (RD) bus (F), terminals (I) 5.00
1C,20S,FS,FL Marine Transportation Exhibit, colorful, message (I) 6.00
1C,20S,FS Hotel Martinique, Broadway & 32nd Ave 4.75
1C,20S,FS Hotel McAlpin, hotel (B), WF ad (I) (BW/WE) 4.75
1C,20S,FS Mee Wah Chinese & American Restaurant, Brooklyn, NY 5.00
1C,20S,FS Midway Inn at the Amusement Area 5.00
1C,20S,FS Mohawk Coach Lines, (BE) bus (B), Coach Lines ad w/cities (F), terminals (I) 5.00
1C,30S,FS The Narragansett Bar Restaurant, 2510 Broadway, NYC 4.25
1C,20S,FS Hotel New Weston, (DBE), drawing (B) 5.25
1C,20S,FS Hotel New Weston, (DRD) 5.25
1C,20S,FS World's Fair Nite Club, The Nite Club of Tomorrow (OE/WE) 3.75
1C,20S,FS O.K. Snyder Insurance, Mount Joy, PA 5.50
1C,20S,FS Administration Building (OE) 5.00
1C,20S,FS Communications Bldg (OE) 5.00
1C,20S,FS The Consumers Bldg (OE) 5.00
1C,20S,FS Gas Exhibits Building (OE) 4.75
1C,20S,FS T&P (OE) (stock) 5.00

1C,20S,FS Theme Center (OE)... 4.75
1C,20S,FS United States Government Building (OE) 5.25
1C,20S,FS Pabst Blue Ribbon Beer, Blue Ribbon girl w/long neck bottle (F), Pabst Blue Ribbon Gardens (B), colorful.. 6.00
1C,20S,FS Paprin's, Roosevelt Ave., 61st St. 5.00
1C,20S,FS Hotel Paramount, New York, colorful T&P (B), Home of Billy Rose's Diamond Horseshoe (I) 6.00
1C,20S,FS,DQ Hotel Pairs, ad (I).. 7.00
1C,20S,FS Pennsylvania Railroad, A Fleet of Modernism... 10.50
1C,20S,FS Hotel Pennsylvania, T&P (F), cities (B) (DBE) 5.75
1C,20S,FS Hotel Piccadilly, 227 W 45th St, New York, colorful...................................... 5.75
1C,20S,FS (I), Hotel Pickwick Arms, Moderate Weekly and Daily Rates, 230 E 51st St., New York.. 5.25
1C,20S,FS (I), Hotel Plymouth, 49th E. of Bway... 5.25
1C,20S,FS Polish Restaurant at the Polish Pavilion, girl w/ham (B), waiter (B) 5.75
1C,20S,FS POlymol Products, New York, colorful.. 5.00
1C,20S,FS Powers Hotel, Single $2, Double $4 .... 5.25
1C,20S,FS Hotel President, drawing (B).. 5.25
1C,20S,FS Professional Club, checker board (F)... 4.25
1C,20S,FS Professional Club... 4.00
1C,20S,FS Port Authority George Washington Bridge/Holland Tunnel, colorful 8.75
1C,20S,FS Port Authority Holland Tunnel 6.00
1C,20S,FS,FL Port Authority #51548, Drive Your Car Direct, colorful 6.25
1C,20S,FS Port Authority Drive Your Car Direct, 4 Minute Crossings, colorful 6.50
1C,20S,FS Port Authority Don't Mark Time, 4 Minute Crossings, colorful 6.25
1C,20S,FS Port Authority Be Time Thrifty, 4 Minute Crossings 5.75
1C,20S,FS from orange set, Railroad Building (OE/WE/BE) 13.50
1C,20S,FS Rheingold Extra Dry Lager Beer, short bottle (F), Winter Wonderland (S) ... 5.25
1C,20S,FS Rothmann's East Norwich Inn, NYWF ad (I) 4.00
1C,20S,FS Ruby Foo's 'Sun Dial' at the Perisphere 5.00
1C,20S,FS U.S.S.R. Pavilion Restaurant 8.75
1C,10S,FS S.S. Grandview Point Hotel & Allegheny Mountains 3.00
1C,20S,FS Hotel Sanford, Flushing, New York (I) 4.75
1C,20S,FS Schaefer Center, center (B), glass of beer (F) 6.25
1C,20S,FS Schlitz Palm Garden, long neck bottle (B), T&P (F) 7.25
1C,20S,FS Schlitz Aviation Grill (T&P (F), logo (B) 8.00
1C,20S,FS Shelton Hotel 5.00
1C,20S,FS Silhouette Room... 5.00
1C,20S,FS Statue of Liberty (B) 2.50
1C,20S,FS,FL Sonoco Services the World Paper Carriers, T&P made from paper cones (F) (LBE/BK/RD).. 6.25
1C,20S,FS General souvenir matchcover (BE/OE/WE) SOL (B), T&P (F) 9.00
1C,20S,FS Administration Building (SR) 5.00
1C,20S,FS Aviation Building (SR) 5.00
1C,20S,FS Business Systems and Insurance Building (SR)... 5.00
1C,20S,FS Hall of Communications (SR) 1.25
1C,20S,FS Consumer Interests Bldg (SR) 3.25
1C,20S,FS Cosmetics Building (SR).. 5.00
1C,20S,FS DuPont Bldg (SR).. 3.00
1C,20S,FS Food & Sports Bldg (SR) 3.75
1C,20S,FS Gas Exhibit Building.. 5.25
1C,20S,FS Hall of Communications (SR) 3.25
1C,20S,FS Hall of Marine Transportation (SR) 1.25
1C,20S,FS Medicine & Public Health Science & Education Exhibits (SR) 4.25
1C,20S,FS R.C.A. Building (SR) 3.50
1C,20S,FS Railroad Transportation Building (SR).. 4.75

1C,20S,FS Textiles Bldg (SR) 3.50
1FB,20S,FS Theme Center (SR) 4.25
1C,20S,FS The World of Tomorrow (SR), (stock) 2.00
1C,20S,FS T&P (B) (SR), stock 5.75
1C,20S,FS United States Gov't Bldg (SR) 3.25
1C,20S,FS Hotel St. George, Brooklyn, NY, WF map (I), T&P (B) (GD/RD/BK) 5.75
3C,20S,FS General Souvenir (GD/SR), (stock) 9.00
1C,20S,FS T&P (F), SOL (B) (stock) 5.25
1C,20S,FS (BE/OE), (stock) 8.75
1C,20S,FS (MN/WE) Deco figures (F/B) (stock) 3.00
1C,20S,FS Sunchester Hotel, Exquisitely Furnished 4.50
1C,20S,FS Swiss Pavilion Restaurant (RD/WE) 3.75
1C,20S,BS Abstract (GD) design of T&P (F) 5.00
1C,20S,FS Terminal Café, Always Open (S), Tel. WOrth 2-8298, T&P (F/B) 3.75
1C,30S,FS The Terrace Club, T&P (B), large letter T (F) 5.25
1C,20S,FS Hotel Times Square, Towers of Hospitality, map (B) 6.25
1C,20S,FS Toffenetti Restaurant, ham plate (B), (B/W) photo of Toffenetti (F) 4.75
1C,20S,FS Thomas Torrent, Brooklyn, NY, personal, T&P (B), collector's ad (F) (DBE/OE),
     (stock) 3.00
1C,20S,FS Triangle (Hof-Brau) Restaurant 2.50
1C,20S,FS Turf Trylon Café (opposite Perisphere) 2.25
1C,20S,FS Hotel Tudor, In Beautiful Tudor City 4.00
1C,20S,FS Visit the Turf Trylon Café, (SR) no drawing 5.00
1C,20S,FS Star & Crescent Restaurant, Turkish Pavilion, sickle & star (F/B) (RD/WE) 8.75
1C,20S,FS The Union News Company 5.00
1C,20S,FS Valencia Gardens, spanish Restaurants and Lounge, drawing (B) 4.00
1C,20S,FS The Vanderbilt Hotel, drawing (B) 5.25
1C,20S,FS Washington Hall, erected by Messmore Kendall, (YW/DBE) 4.75
1C,20S,FS Hotel Wellington, hotel (B), (RD/MN/YW), NYWF message (I), 7th Ave @ 55th
     St, New York 5.00
1C,20S,FS,FL World's Fair Restaurant, John W. Wexler, Managing Director 4.25
1C,20S,FS New White Owl Cigar Exhibit (DBE/OE) 4.75
1C,20S,FS,FL Windsor Diner, shows full length diner, When you visit the World's Fair . . .(stock)
     .... 7.50
1C,20S,FS (I), The Winslow Bar, Madison Ave @ 55th, New York 5.25
1C,20S,FS Hotel Winthrop, 47th & Lex, New York 5.00
1C,20S,FS Hotel Woodstock, drawing (B) 4.25
1C,20S,FS Wrigley's Spearmint Gum, Come and Enjoy... .... 4.25
1C,20S,FS,FL Wrigley's Spearmint Chewing Gum, T&P 5.50
1C,20S,FS The Wyndham Hotel, New York City 5.25
1C,20S,FS ad: Zeidler Bros., Medford, L.I. 6.25
1C,20S,FS Zucca's Restaurant, T&P (B), shield (F) 5.00

1939-40 New York World's Fair, New York City, NY (dated 1940)

6C,20S,FS Diamond Match Co. (BE) Set, Aviation Building-Business Systems..-Food Building..- Lucky Strike..-Medical and Public Health..-United States 22.50
6C,20S,FS Diamond Match Co. (OE) Set, Administration..-DuPont Wonder..-Railroad..-Theme Center-United States Government..-World of Fashion 20.00
1C,20S,FS,FL Ballantine Three Ring Inn display (I) 7.50
1C,20S,FS,FL Ballantine Three Ring Inn clown & inn, display (I)
     .... 8.00
1C,20S,FS Business Systems & Insurance Building (BE) set
     (DBE/WE) 5.25
1C,20S,FS Belgian Pavilion Restaurant Constitution Mall 3.00

1C,20S,FS,FL Falcetta Royal Pastry Shoppes Welcome Fair Visitors WF logo (B) (OE/DBE) 5.00
1C,20S,FS Firestone Exhibit & Private Lounge tire (B) 5.00
1C,20S,FS w/search lights, ad: Hollis Diner, Forest Hills L.I. (stock) 6.25
1C,20S,FS Horn & Hardart Automats 5.00
1C,20S,FS Japanese Tea Garden Formosa Oolong Tea 7.50
1C,20S,FS Lion Match Co. (BN) (dated: 1940), (stock) 5.00
1C,20S,FS Mee Wah Chinese and American Restaurant Brooklyn, NY 6.25
1C,20S,FS Norway Restaurant, Viking Ship (B) flag (F) 6.25
1C,20S,FS O.K. Snyder Insurance, Phone 15, Mount Joy, Pennsylvania 5.00
1C,20S,FS Dupont Wonder World of Chemistry (OE) Set 5.00
1C,20S,FS Railroad Building (OE) Set 5.25
1C,20S,FS ad: Hotel Paramount (F) Fair (B) 4.75
1C,20S,FS For Peace and Freedom w/opening dates (B) T&P logo (F) 3.75
1C,20S,FS for Peace and Freedom w/opening dates 6.00
1C,20S,FS POlymol Products (dated: 1940), (colorful) 3.50
1C,20S,FS Collector's Cover Sylvia M. Sewards Matchcover Collector 5.00
1C,20S,FS Business Systems and Insurance Bldg (SR) set 5.00
1C,20S,FS Souvenir, Peach and Freedom w/opening dates (B) T&P (F) 3.50
1C,20S,FS Souvenir mc, Admission...50c 8.00
1C,20S,FS Hotel Taft, New York, T&P (B) (DGN,BK/WE) 2000 Rooms (I) 5.00
1 Book, (non match) *1939 New York World's Fair Matchcovers, Second Edition*, 1989, w/Price Guide, by Bill Retskin 7.00

1939 Sacramento Golden Empire Centennial, Sacramento, CA

1C,20S,FS Hotel Lenhart, western scene w/stage coach (B) 3.00

1958 Exposition de Bruxelles

1C,20S,FS Allumettes de Union Allumettiere 2.25
1C,20S,FS Souvenir Matchcover 4.50
1C,20S,FS Pabellon de Venezuela (WE/BK/BE/RD/YW) 7.00

1962 Seattle World's Fair, Seattle, WA

6C,20S,FS Century 21, Boulevards of the World-Coliseum 21-The Gayway-Monorail-Mt. Rainier-United States Science Pavilion 22.50
3C,20S,FS U.S. Science Pavilion, The Gayway, Monorail 3.00
1C,200S,BS World of Tomorrow 2.50
1C,20S,FS Coliseum 21 .... 1.50
1C,20S,FS The Gayway 7.00
1C,20S,FS Monorail 1.75
1C,20S,FS Mt. Rainier 1.50

1964-65 New York World's Fair, New York City, NY

1FB,100S,FS Peace Through Understanding
.... 6.75
1C,30S,FS Festival/65 The American Restaurant (F), Festival of Gas Pavilion, NYWF w/phone (I), (DBE/GN/WE 3.00
1C,30S,FS The Balcony Bar & Lounge (F), A Place to Relax (S), piano (B), WF message (I) 3.00
1C,20S,FS 42nd St. Cafeteria, 110 W 42nd St 3.50
1C,30S,FS Caribbean Pavilion, dates (B), sun design (F), (BN/TN) 4.00
1FB,20S,FS Coca-Cola Tower, logo (F) 5.50

8C,20S,FS Peace through Understanding, Coca Cola Bldg.-Federal Building-Fountain of the Planets-Missouri Building-Monorail-Pool of Industry-Stadium-Unisphere 12.00
1C,20S,FS . . . things go better with Coke, pavilion (B) 8.00
1C,20S,FS Fair Le Chalet Restaurant, Switzerland (RD/WE,BK) 2.50
1C,20S,FS House of Japan Restaurant & Theatre (BN/BK/WE)................................... 2.00
1C,30S,FS Ford Motor Company Exhibit (I), (WE) cover w/Fair logo (F) 3.00
1C,20S,FS Pavilion of Greece (WE/BE) 1.00
1C,30S,FS Harmonia Savings Bank w/logo (F), dated 1851-1964, Visit the State of New Jersey Tercentenary Pavilion, NYWF (B), message & dates (I) 4.00
1C,30S,FS HGT (initials), House of Good Taste (F), New York World's Fair (B), host's name (I)... 2.50
1C,20S,BS Hilton, stock 2.00
1C,30S,FS Jul's North Star Smorgasbord, Cocktail Lounge (F), phone (S), Morgan & Jerry Minnesota Pavilion World's Fair-New York (B), message (I), (WE/BE/GD) 3.50
1C,20S,FS Long Island Railroad 5.75
1C,20S,FS The Millstone Restaurant and Lounge, (TN/BN).. 2.50
1C,30S,FS Moultray's Polynesian Restaurant (F), phone (S), The New York World's Fair (B) (DBN/GD) 3.00
1C,30S,FS Parker Pavilion, NYWF (B), Pen (F), colorful 5.00
1C,20S,FS Parkway Tavern, Queens Village, NY 2.50
8C,20S,FS New York World's Fair [1964-1965], Peace through Understanding, Astral Fountain-Amphitheater-The Coca Cola Company Pavilion-Main Mall-Monorail 10.00
1C,20S,FS Post House Greyhound Bus 1.00
1C,20S,FS The Rutland County Bank, Unisphere (F) 1.25
1C,30S,FS,RAMA San Miguel Beer (F), Souvenir NYWF 1964-65 (B) 7.00
1C,30S,FS Schaefer Beer logo (F), Schaefer Center, New York World's Fair 1964-65 (B), original Schaefer Brewery, New York City, 1842 (I) 8.00
8C,30S,FS New York World's Fair [1964] Set, colorful, assorted aristocrats 5.00
5C,40S,FS Souvenir Set 15.00
3C,20S,FS Top of the Fair Restaurant (WE/GD/BE) 3.25
1C,20S,FS Unisphere (F), dates (B), (stock) 6.00
1C,100S Universal Match Corp. 3.00
1C,30S,FS,RAMA Meet the New Yorker, White Owl Cigars, See Hall of Magic at World's Fair, Free Admission (I)... 3.00

We Are
**ALWAYS BENT
ON PLEASING
YOU**

1967 Montreal Expo, Montreal, CN

4C,30S,FS Ports of Call, C-534, (BE/GN/RD/YW)
.... 5.00
13B Australia-Canada-Ceylon-France-Germany-
Great Britain-Israel-Italy-Japan-Ontario-Que-
bec-Russia-United States 11.50
12C,20S,FS General Souvenir Matchcover.... 5.00
1C,20S,BS Westinghouse, 'Dancing Water' .. 2.00
1C,20S,BS Discover New York State 7.00
1C,20S,BS Dot's Variety Shop, Ltd., Burns Lake, BC
.... 5.00
1C,20S,BS Embassy Terrace, Montreal, Que 2.00
1C,20S,BS Jamaica, out of many...one people, seal
(F) 1.25

4C,30S,FS Ports of Call, C-534, (BE/GN/RD/YW) 5.00
13B Australia-Canada-Ceylon-France-Germany-Great Britain-Israel-Italy-Japan-Ontario-Que-
bec-Russia-United States 11.50
12C,20S,FS General Souvenir Matchcover 5.00
1C,20S,BS Westinghouse, 'Dancing Water' 2.00
1C,20S,BS Discover New York State 7.00
1C,20S,BS Dot's Variety Shop, Ltd., Burns Lake, BC 5.00
1C,20S,BS Embassy Terrace, Montreal, Que 2.00
1C,20S,BS Jamaica, out of many...one people, seal (F) 1.25
1C,20S,BS Klondike Steak House, Ft. Edmonton 2.00
1C,20S,BS,FL Mexican Food, Mexico City (I) 2.00
1C,20S,BS Northern Electric (OE/BE) 2.75
1C,20S,BS Canada Pulp and paper Pavilion 2.00
1C,20S,BS The House of Seagram 2.00
1C,20S,BS Montreal Expo[1967], The House of Seagram (WE/PE) 5.00
1C,20S,BS dated: April 28 - October 27, 1967 .... 1.25
1C,20S,BS Terre Des Hommes/Man and His World, Montreal 3.25
1C,20S,BS Westinghouse 'Dancing Waters' (PE/WE) 6.00
1C,20S,BS Sel Windsor Salt, (RD/WE/BE) 2.50
20C,30S,BS Montreal Canada, assorted themes & businesses 18.00

1968 Hemisfair, San Antonio, TX

8C,20S,FS Set, H.E.B. 3.00
1C,20S,FS Lone Star Beer (WE/RD) 6.50
5C,20S,FS Set, Motoring America (Sketch 229) 1.00
8C,20S,FS Set, Piggly Wiggly 3.00

1970 Osaka Expo, Osaka, Japan

1C,20S,FS Osaka Daiwa Bank 1.50
7B Osaka Set..3.00
20B Osaka Set, pavilions Australia-Belgium-Brazil-Canada-France-Hong Kong-Indonesia-
Italy-Japanese-Korea-Malaysia-New Zealand- Philippines-Republic of China-Switzerland-
Thailand-United Kingdom-United Nations-U.S.A.-West Germany 25.00

1974 Spokane World's Fair, Spokane, WA

1C,20S,BS Boeing Amphitheater 3.00
1FB,20S,FS Falls Gondola Ride 2.25
1FB,20S,FS U.S. Pavilion 3.00
1FB,20S,FS Washington State Pavilion 3.00
4C,20S,FS Boeing Amphitheater-Falls Gondola Ride-U.S. Pavilion-Wash. State Pavilion 6.50

1982 Knoxville World's Fair, Knoxville, TN

1C,20S,BS Coca-Cola 7.50
1C,30S,BS Dated October 1982 .... 2.25
1C,30S,BS Stroh's Light, Official Beers 1982 World's Fair, same ad (F/B) 3.25

1986 Vancouver Expo, Vancouver, CN

4C,30S,BS Delta Hotels Set, Delta Puts..-Delta Sports..-The Grand Piano..-Taste the.. .. 5.00
30C,20S,FS Assorted 20.00
5C,20S,FS Set [1986], mixed (B) panel slogans 7.00
6FB,G,BS 6 different (F) scenes each with 3 different (B) panels, B.C. Place Dome-Canada Place-Expo Centre-Fireworks-Highway 97-Main Gate and clock, Type A, Don't miss it ... for the World! 15.00
6FB,G,BS 6 different (F) scenes each with 3 different (B) panels, B.C. Place Dome-Canada Place-Expo Centre-Fireworks-Highway 97-Main Gate and clock, Type B, Transportation and Communication 15.00
6FB,G,BS 6 different (F) scenes each with 3 different (B) panels, B.C. Place Dome-Canada Place-Expo Centre-Fireworks-Highway 97-Main Gate and clock, Type C, World in Motion ... World in Touch! 15.00

World's Fairs (State Fairs, dated)

State Fairs—Any local, county, state or minor fair or expo which produced matchcovers for publicity or souvenirs. These are usually dated and feature the name of the fair and town. A further listing of State Fairs can be found in the glossary. Conjunctive matchcovers are often made by local restaurants or hotels, but are not strictly fair matchcovers. Series of state matchcover (same design, different year) become a record of the event. Minor event may also fit into this category.

State Fairs

1C,20S,FS Robeson County Fair, Lumberton, NC, [Sept. 20-23, 1938], (YW/BK) 5.50
1C,20S,FS Oklahoma Free State Fair, Muskogee, [October 1-7, 1939] (DGN/GD) 5.50
1C,20S,FS North Montana State Fair and Rodeo, [Aug. 4-9, 1941] (GN/LTN) 5.50
1C,20S,FS Kimberton Fair, [July 23 - August 2, 1941], Kimberton, PA (OE/WE/BK) 4.50
1C,20S,FS Kansas State Fair, [Sept. 19-24, 1943], Hutchinson, SOL (F) (RD/We/BE) . 5.00
1C,20S,FS Oklahoma Free State Fair, Muskogee, [Sept 28 - Oct. 4, 1947] (BE/WE) 4.75

1C,20S,FS Rhode Island State Fair, Kingston, R.I. [August 28 - September 6, 1948] (RD/WE) 3.50
1C,20S,FS State Fair of West Virginia, Lewisburg, Ronceverte, [August 22-27, 1949] (BK/WE) 4.00
1C,20S,FS Calumet County Fair, [September 2,3,4,5, 1949], (Wisconsin) (BE/WE) 3.50
1C,20S,FS 1949 Shelby County Fair, Shelbyville, Ind. [Aug 2-7, 1949] trotter (B) 4.25
1C,20S,FS Calumet County Fair, [September 1,2,3,4, 1950], (Wisconsin) (BE/WE) 3.50
1C,20S,FS Huron County Fair, [Aug. 12-16, 1952], stock County Fair (B) 2.50
1C,20S,FS 1952 Illinois State Fair, ad: City Service Airmaster Tires (RD/BK/GN) 3.00
1C,20S,FS 98th Annual Green County Fair, Monroe, Wis. [July 30,31-Aug. 1-2-3] (1952) (GN/WE) 2.00
1C,20S,FS 99th Annual Green County Fair, Monroe, Wis. [August 5-6-7-8-9] (1953) (GN/WE) 2.00
1C,20S,FS 1953 Illinois State Fair, ad: City Service (RD/BK/GN) 3.00
1C,20S,FS 100th Annual Green County Fair, Monroe, Wis. [August 4-5-6-7-8, 1954] (GN/WE) 2.00
1C,20S,FS 1954 Illinois State Fair, ad: 5-D Premium Gasoline 3.00
1C,20S,FS 101th Annual Green County Fair, Monroe, Wis. [August 3-4-5-6-7, 1955) (GN/WE) 2.00
1C,20S,FS 96th Annual Tioga County Fair, Owego, NY, [July 24-30, 1955] (RD/YW/BK/BE) 4.75
1C,20S,FS 4-H Show Kansas State Fair [Sept 17-22, 1955] (BK/YW) 2.50
1C,20S,FS Great Allentown Fair, [Sept. 19-24, 1955], America's Greatest County Fair, (RD/We/BE) 3.00
1C,20S,FS 102th Annual Green County Fair, Monroe, Wis. [August 1-2-3-4-5] (1956) (GN/WE) 2.00
1C,20S,FS 4-H Show Kansas State Fair [Sept 15-20, 1956] (BK/YW) 2.50
1C,20S,FS 102th Annual Green County Fair, Monroe, Wis. [July 31 - August 1-2-3-4] (1957) (GN/WE) 2.00
1C,20S,FS Merced County's Spring Fair & Livestock Show, [May 1-5, 1957] (GN/WE) 1.50
1C,20S,FS 4-H Show Kansas State Fair [Sept 14-19, 1957] (BK/YW) 2.50
1C,20S,FS Calhoun County Fair, Marshall, Mich, [Aug. 20-25, 1962] (YW/BK) 2.00
1C,20S,FS Arizona State Fair [Nov. 6-15, 1964] 1.75
1C,20S,FS San Mateo County Fair & Floral Fiesta, [July 31 - Aug 8, 1964] (GN/WE) ... 2.00
1C,20S,FS Arizona State Fair [Nov. 5-14, 1965] 1.75
1C,20S,FS Fairtime Funtime, Santa Clara County Fair, [Aug 14 - 23, 1970] (RD/WE/BE] 2.00
1C,20S,FS Fairtime Funtime, Santa Clara County Fair, [Aug 13 - 22, 1971] (RD/WE/BE] 2.00
1FB,20S,FS Welcome to the Empire State Grotto Convention [1940] 2.50
1C,20S,FS Playland at the Beach, San Francisco (shows carnival scene on the beach) ... 4.25
25C,MS/MZ County & State Fairs, assorted 5.00

Wood Sticks

Wooden Sticks—Any match book which contains wooden sticks, which may be glued or stapled into the matchcover. Most are of foreign manufacture.

1FB,24S Wood Sticks Amsterdam Hilton 3.00
1FB Wood sticks, Le Boulevardier, Inter-Continental Hotel, Manila (RD/BK) 4.00
1FB Wood sticks, El Pollo Dorado, Santiago De Chile (BK/WE/YW) 4.00
1FB Wood sticks, Jupiter, Hast Du Zundholzer-Hast Du Feuer! (WE/RD) 3.25
1FB Wood sticks, Marchi's Restaurant, New York (WE/BE) crest (F) 2.25

Zodiac

Zodiac matchcovers are mostly a sub-classification of super market sets, but can also include any stellar feature or name (i.e. Orion's Pub, The Big Dipper Restaurant, etc.).

12C,20S,FS Zodiac/Constellation Set [1969] 2.00
20C,20S,FS Zodiac/Constellation Set, Type 1 [1970] 3.25
12C,20S,FS Zodiac, Type 1 [1969], Ohio Match Co., solid background color 1.00
20C,20S,BS Zodiac/Constellation Set, Type 2 [1972] 3.25
12C,20S,FS Zodiac, Type 2 [1971], Ohio Match Co., split background colors 1.00
12C,20S,BS Zodiac, Type 3 [1975], Ohio Match Co. 1.00
50FB,20S,FS Zodiac caddy [1970], dated, Ohio Match Co. 9.00
50FB,1 CADDY Zodiac Matchbooks from 1969, Ohio Match Co. Still in original caddy wrapper. 5.00
12C,20S,FS, Zodiac Set [1969], Ohio Match Co. 5.50
12C,30S,BS Signs of the Zodiac Set [1976], Universal Match Corp. 3.25

Zoos

Zoos--A category featuring the name, photo, design or drawing of any of the major zoos or zoological centers. These matchcovers were often produced for sales in zoo souvenir shops and sometimes include photos or drawing of their animals. Both sets and singles are known.

8B Cincinnati Zoo Set [1988], American Ace boxes by Universal Match Corp., Bald Eagle-Orange Bengal Tiger-White Bengal Tiger-Lowland Gorilla (facing left)-Elephant & Hippo-Polar Bear-Red Panda-Walrus 3.50
6B Cincinnati Zoo Set [1981], American Ace boxes by Universal Match Corp., Betsy Ross-Lowland Gorilla (facing right)-Masai Giraffe-Red Eyed Tree Frog-White Cheeked Gibbon-White Tiger 3.00
4B Columbus Zoo Set [1984], American Ace boxes by Universal Match Corp., Carousel-Giraffe-Gorilla-Tiger 3.00
10C,JLT,FS Erie Zoological Society Set [1963] Alligator-Bear-Deer-Duck-Elephant-Giraffe-Lion-Monkey-Owl-Pig 2.50
3C,20S,FS San Diego Zoo Set [1955], Jaguar-Koala-Zebra 1.00

POCKET MATCH SAFES

Friction matches were invented by John Walker in 1827. These matches ignited very easily and had to be kept dry. Therefore, a container was necessary to protect the user from harm and the matches. Hence, the match safe came into existence. The first known match safe was used by John Walker. It was a cylindrical tin container with a friction top.

Early match safes were simple and often nothing more than a snuff box with added serrations for striking a match. Match safes came into their own in the 1850's. They were containers specifically made to hold matches of various lengths, on which there was usually a serrated or ribbed area to strike the match. By the 1870's, match safes began their heyday. It lasted into the early 1900's until their use began to dwindle with the invention and popularity of the paper match book.

Match safes were made of virtually every type of material known at that time. They included sterling silver, brass, plated metal, thermoplastics, ivory, gold, wood, leather, tortoiseshell, etc. They were made by the tens of thousands and the common ones sold for a few cents each. Sterling silver ones sold for a couple of dollars each and gold safes were higher, depending on whether diamonds, rubies, and other jewels were used.

In the 1890s match safes became a popular means of advertising and were used by a number of companies to advertise their businesses or products. Their advertising appeal was further enhanced with the invention of celluloid and celluloid-wrapped match safes. The celluloid provided a good surface to print an advertising message.

The popularity of match safe collecting has grown greatly in the last 15-20 years. Common match safes still sell for a few dollars each. Sterling safes are generally in the $40-$125 range. Figural, enameled, and fancy match safes are usually in the $100 plus range depending on their rarity, quality, and maker. It is not unusual to find quality enameled safes made by a company such as Sampson Mordan selling in excess of $1000. Tortoiseshell safes with gold pique designs or presentation match safes also command a premium. Specialized collectors such as advertising and political collectors will usually pay a premium for safes in their category vs. a general match safe collector.

Numerous match safes were made that incorporated other features such as cigar cutters, knives, stamp holders, sovereign holders, and corkscrews. Some included a miniature sterling mechanical pencil and a sterling toothpick. Others were trick opening or included a compartment with several miniature dice.

Match safes were made and used around the world. Therefore, their variety is endless. The novelty and uniqueness of these tiny containers usually fascinates the average person and excites the collector. George Sparacio.

Match Hardware

Match Hardware—The given term for any item (excluding invoices or other paper) which is related to the match industry or hobby. This includes match box holders, slides and grips, match safes, shipping boxes, tin and counter boxes, vending machines, ash trays, salesman's sample books, tax stamps and other matchcover related accouterments. Although an interesting peripheral, tramp art made of match sticks is not strictly match hardware.

Match Hardware (Adveraps)

Big Joe Flour, colorful 6.00
Blue Room, Lowell, MA (DBE) 6.00
Adverap & Matching FB, The Camellia House, The Drake, Chicago (PK) 11.00
Long Beach, CA, Play Spot of the Pacific, w/1-20S matching full book 9.00
The Theo. Schmitt Co, Toledo, OH 6.00
[1939-1942], Universal Match, matched set of matchcover and sleeve that slides over a cigarette
    pack 15.00
Hand-pick (cardboard sleeve that slips around a cigarette pack) 7.00

Match Hardware (Ashtrays)

Ceramic, box/cover holder in middle, Hotel Statler 6.00
Glass, triangular, 2 matchcover slots on sides 10.00
Porcelain, round box slide in middle 6.00
Metal, round, raised box support in middle 7.50
Glass, box/cover holder in middle, raised sides 7.00
Glass, round, upright matchcover slot, advertising 7.00
Tin for match rolls ashtray, American Pullmatch Corporation, Piqua, Ohio, hold two rolls, (RD/
    WE/BE) 28.00
For match rolls ashtray, American Pullmatch Corporation, Piqua, Ohio, Refil No. 250, 'Pull Quickly
    to Light', (BE/WE) 10.00
For match rolls ashtray, Standard Radio, Chicago, ILL. Jerry King & Milt Blink on paper label w/
    Keep 'Pulling' for us!, (RD/WE) 10.00
Ceramic, cover slot in middle, D. M. Co. 5.00
Glass, round w/molded match book holder, embossed Diamond Match Co. bottom 12.00
The Hamilton Match Co., Cincinnati, Ohio, Pat'd. Apr. 23, 1935 & Pats. Pend. U.S.P.O., For Match
    Rolls cast embossing on bottom, (BK) w/PullMatch roll, no striker 25.00

The Hamilton Match Co., Cincinnati, Ohio, Pat'd. Apr. 23, 1935 & Pats. Pend. U.S.P.O., For Match
    Rolls printed on bottom, (RD) w/match roll and regular matches, striker on top 25.00
Glass, solid box support at back, Holophane Co. 7.50
Glass, cover slot at back, Lion Match Co. 6.00
Glass, solid box support at back, Hotel Martinique 3.50
Ceramic, upright box slide, advertising White Rock 10.00
Match Roll Ashtray, ceramic, black, Hamilton Match Co. 28.00
Match Roll Ashtray, custard glass, Hamilton Match Co. 32.00
Pullmatch Ashtray, ceramic base, plastic blue top 30.00
Pullmatch Ashtray, aluminum base and top 26.50
Pullmatch Ashtray, plastic black base, plastic yellow top 21.00
Pullmatch Ashtray, chrome base and top, AP logo on top 30.00
Pullmatch Ashtray, refill roll No. 250 .... 3.00

Match Hardware (Books)

Report to Stockholders of The Diamond Match Company at the Annual Meeting, May 4th, 1910,
    18 pages, (GY) cover 10.00
A Match for the World! The Diamond Match Company, Ltd., London, Liverpool, Belfast, 5 3/8"
    X 8 3/8", Brithis & American flag (F), 32 pag 15.00
Report to Stockholders of The Diamond Match Company at the Annual Meeting, May 6th, 1914,
    18 pages, (GY) cover 10.00
Diamond Book Matches, Stock Designs and Backgrounds, dated November 1, 1933, 4 1/8" X 6
    5/8", approx. 100 pages, (BN/GD) 25.00
Fifty Years of Match Making (1878-1928) by Herbert Manchester, copyright 1928, The Diamond
    Match Co., 20 pages, 6 3/8" X 9 1/2", multicolor (F), Seaman's Metal (B) 28.00
Mr. Match at Home, The Story of the Match, copyright 1953, Ohio Match Co., 8 pages w/photos,
    publication No. 1054, 8 1/2" X 11", (BK/WE) 15.00
The Story of a Match, Ohio Match Co., no date, 28 pages, 3 7/8" X 7", (GN/RD/WE/BE) 15.00
The Romance of the Match by Herbert Manchester, The Diamond Match Co., copyright 1926, 45
    pages, 6 1/4" X 9 3/8" 25.00
The Matchcover Collector's Resource Book & Price Guide, by Bill Retskin, 1988 .... 30.00
Annual Report, Ohio Match Company, 1966 booklet 15.00

Knapsacks

The Diamond Match Co. 7.50
The United Machine & Supply Co. 8.50
Bryant & May Limited 5.00
Diamond Deutsche Zundholzfabr. AG 8.00

Match Box Slides and Grips

Slide, Brass, flower design on front and back 7.50
Slide, Metal, Japanese torii and mountain, marked JAPAN 5.00
Slide, Metal, raised flower on top 9.00
Slide, Cloisonne, green w/white flowers, marked CHINA 11.00
Slide, Cloisonne, black w/white flowers, MADE IN CHINA 15.00
Slide, Ceramic, raised bunch of flowers on top 8.00
Grip, safety size, metal, black, Ulm Germany 5.00
Grip, safety size, metal, coat of arms & FRANCE on front 7.00
Grip, safety size, aluminum, hammered finish, goose on back 7.00
Grip, safety size, metal, green, Washington DC scenes 8.00

Match Holders

Wall type, iron, three acorns at back, small open type 55.00
Wall type, glass, amber colored, boot shaped 13.00
Table type, chalk, Amos & Andy.. 75.00
Wall type, iron, coal bucket advertising Anchor & Bellair Block, Ottumwa IA 85.00
Wall type, brass, basket style single open 100.00
Wall type, iron, basket w/handle and ivy 65.00
Table type, terra-cotta, bear sitting w/three smaller bears................................. 60.00
Table type, metal, standing bear.. 5.00
Wall type, iron, coal bucket, advertising Beck Walker Coal Co., St. Louis 65.00
Table type, metal, figure of bird on a limb 40.00
Wall type, metal, bird & rabbit w/open pouch and gun...................................... 30.00
Table type, terra-cotta, woman wearing a bonnet standing w/a bucket 30.00
Table type, iron, pair of high topped boots 40.00
Wall type, brass, boots w/tassels & mouse.. 160.00
Table type, cast iron, black lady's boot 40.00
Wall type, metal, boot top rolled down, spur at bottom 160.00
Wall type, iron, pair of boots, 'For Sale' 60.00
Table type, iron, boot, and bootjack... 150.00
Wall type, brass, bucket, and well... 140.00
Wall type, iron, large butterfly 460.00
Wall type, silver, head of cat and trough below 155.00
Wall type, metal, cat climbing wall w/a bucket at the well 230.00
Wall type, iron, lattice style, small open single, cathedral shaped 47.50
Wall type, iron, cherub w/wings spread, open single type 90.00
Wall type, iron, cherub kissing woman, double lidded type, Matches on side 25.00
Wall type, iron, embossed head of Grover Cleveland, open single type 160.00
Table type, brass, small coal shuttle on base 37.50
Wall type, tin, DeLaval Cream Separators 85.00
Wall type, metal, devil in basket 120.00
Wall type, metal, embossed head of horned devil, signed Muller NY 50.00
Wall type, iron, lidded type w/pointer dog, Pat. Mar. 12, 1863, by Stevens 180.00
Wall type, brass, man climbing wall w/bucket and dog 130.00
Wall type, tin, bulldog head, and double pipe rack on decorated background 35.00
Wall type, iron, puppy begging, signed Nacht.. 280.00
Table type, iron, two donkeys and 'When Shall We Three Meet Again' 50.00
Wall type, iron, IOOF w/hand & heart along w/two dragons and a horseshoe................ 45.00
Wall type, nickel on iron, advertising E&C Gurney fireplace stoves............................ 200.00
Wall type, iron, advertising Eclipse, double large open holders 110.00
Table type, standing elephant in a suit smoking a cigar.. 110.00
Wall type, steel, Foyer Steel Stamping Co 8.50
Wall type, iron, wall telephone advertising Ring Up Frisco Line 380.00
Table type, iron, frog on a log.. 65.00
Wall type, iron, Dutch girl carrying two pails... 90.00
Table type, terra-cotta, girl sitting w/lamb 45.00
Wall type, iron, coal bucket, advertising Glenwood Day & Co. 70.00
Table type, coal, carved barrel inscribed 'Good Luck' 40.00
Wall type, nickel on iron, advertising Goodman the Clothier.................................... 80.00
Wall type, iron, head of Gen. Grant, Civil War w/flags and cannon............................. 170.00
Wall type, iron, large lidded box w/cluster of grapes and original finish...................... 140.00
Table type, boy in straw hat standing beside 2 barrels.. 50.00
Wall type, wood, homemade 5.00
Wall type, iron, three hooks, painted red single open type 60.00
Wall type, lead, hunting pouch 17.50

Wall type, lead, hunting pouch w/gun and other items on a board fence 40.00
Table type, iron, hunting pouch w/crop and powder flask 30.00
Wall type, lead, hunting horn w/pouch and rifle on a board fence 45.00
Wall type, pewter, Indian head 35.00
Wall type, chalk, Indian chief's head w/full headdress 32.50
Table type, papier-mache, Indian w/gun 25.00
Table type, chalk, Indian chief w/headdress 45.00
Wall type, metal, embossed Indian w/feather headdress, double basket top, signed N. Muller
.... 80.00
Table type, iron, Indian sitting by stove, by Zimmerman 50.00
Wall type, iron, advertising Keen Kutter Tools & Cutlery, large single open type w/red paint 105.00
Kitchen Wall type, 2 pocket 8.00
Wall type, iron, lattice style, small open single 40.00
Wall type, iron, double lidded, Pat. 1870 .... 105.00
Table type, iron, mechanical lighthouse 70.00
Wall type, iron, Match Safe Looking Glass & Friction Surface, Cummings Pat. July 21, 1863 260.00
Wall type, iron, head of man w/feather in his hat, small open type 55.00
Wall type, chalk, man w/a hood 22.50
Wall type, chalk, head of man in a cap 15.00
Wall type, bronze, man w/barrel on his back standing on a ledge 120.00
Wall type, brass, handmade painted (BEGN), Matches & 1919 on front 60.00
Wall type, tin, mechanical match dispenser 50.00
Wall type, nickel on iron, lidded mechanical pocket, Pat. Nov. 21, 1899 .... 130.00
Wall type, iron, large lidded box w/heart Medallion and cluster of grapes 125.00
Wall type, metal, two men, 'The Young Husband' 170.00
Table type, milk glass, round upright 18.00
Wall type, chalk, seven large hooded monks 35.00
Wall type, iron, monkey and basket on fence 80.00
Wall type, chalk, three hooded monks 20.00
Wall type, metal, monkey climbing on clock 120.00
Wall type, chalk, four larger hooded monks 25.00
Wall type, chalk, five hooded monks 20.00
Table type, iron, mechanical monkey 180.00
Wall type, chalk, moon face 25.00
Wall type, iron, National Match Co. name on open type 75.00
Wall type, chalk, Negro boy w/red hat 45.00
Wall type, chalk, seven comical heads including Satan and a Negro 90.00
Wall type, iron, decorated double acorn w/double oak leaf and acorn back 90.00
Wall type, nickel on iron, advertising Olney & Payne Wood & Coal, coal bucket on front 60.00
Table type, iron, hornet advertising Wm. Page Boiler Co., Norwich, CT 65.00
Table type, iron, man under a palm tree 65.00
Wall type, iron, parasol on wall 90.00
Wall type, chalk, sailor smoking pipe 20.00
Wall type, chalk, sailor w/black jacket smoking pipe 20.00
Table type, metal, Negro boy smoking a pipe and sitting on a basket 80.00
Wall type, chalk, sailor w/blue jacket smoking pipe 20.00
Table type, metal, colonial man w/hat & clay pipe sitting between two barrels 40.00
Wall type, chalk, devil's head and pipe holder 5.00
Wall type, chalk, pirate 10.00
Table type, iron, rat w/pistol in a cape 80.00
Table type, terra-cotta pumpkin ware, young boy sitting w/a ram, small damage 80.00
Table type, pumpkin 230.00
Wall type, metal, rat climbing down a wall, double holder 140.00
Wall type, iron, wall telephone advertising Ring Up Dyeing & Cleaning Co. 160.00
Wall type, metal, saddlebag style, striker in middle, C. Parker, Oct. 6, 1868 .... 55.00
Wall type, iron, star in circle, Standard Clark open style 80.00

Table type, iron, tilting acorn by Stevens, patent dated 1862 .... 90.00
Table type, iron, tilting acorn by Stevens, patent dated 1862, portrait of a woman on front 60.00
Wall type, nickel on iron, advertising Anchor Stoves & Ranges, single open type 300.00
Wall type, iron, acorn and leaf, advertising Charter Oak Stoves 70.00
Wall type, iron, helmet w/shield of armor and swords, double type 55.00
Table type, walnut, square upright 11.00
Wall type, brass, tambourine 10.00
Wall type, iron, toilet paper holder, signed Toilet Requisite Co. London 110.00
Wall type, iron, small double w/painted tole floral scene 60.00
Wall type, iron, small open basket style w/triangular tulip lattice back 105.00
Table type, iron, turtle 75.00
Wall type, iron, double urn, small open type w/embossed work 130.00
Wall type, iron, single urn and two birds, signed by Zimmerman 70.00
Wall type, iron, single urn, signed Stevens, Pat. Jan. 15, 1867 .... 65.00
Wall type, iron, double urn, by Stevens, Pat. Jan. 15, 1867 .... 65.00
Wall type, iron, double urn, small open type w/roses, signed Bradley & Hubbard 80.00
Wall type, iron, Vestibule Pat. Apr. 2, '89, double lidded w/embossed scrollwork 120.00
Table type, silver, Victorian man w/barrel on back riding high wheel bicycle 300.00
Wall type, iron, open single, holder for a matchbox, strike on the box 80.00
Wall type, metal, basket of wheat w/40 cent price tag 65.00
Wall type, iron, Winchester advertising w/ gun and stars 70.00
Wall type, iron, window w/shutters, open single w/decorations 100.00
Wall type, metal, wolf head 360.00
Wall type, iron, topless woman figure 130.00
Wall type, chalk, woman smiling 35.00
Wall type, chalk, woman w/wart on cheek 30.00
Wall type, iron, lidded box w/head of a woman, Pat. 1872 .... 35.00
Wall type, chalk, woman w/bonnet 30.00
Table type, iron, mechanical woodpecker 17.50
Wall type, tin & brass, double type, wreaths and torch, drape, & tassel 30.00
Table type, iron, acorn and oak leaves w/a beetle, signed Zimmerman 140.00
Kitchen Box Holder, wall type, lid on pocket, Made in H. K. 3.00

Match Safes

Match Safes--One of two match hardware items. (1) A metal or plastic container which holds a limited number of wooden stick matches and is often highly decorated. Match safe collecting is a well respected hobby in itself and is classified here due to its relationship to matches. (2) Usually a flat metal or plastic container used for holding a book of matches. With the popularity of matchbooks around the turn of the century, match safe manufacturers soon turned their attention to what could be called a match book safe.

Art Nouveau motif, sterling 2 3/8" X 1 1/4", EX 85.00
Celluloid, advertising Burt Label Machines, Whitehead & Hoag, 2 3/4" X 1 1/2", EX 55.00
Anheuser Busch, stamped w/trademark, plated brass, falling lids, 3" X 1 5/8", VG 45.00
Pocket type, silver plated, 1893 Columbian Expo 110.00
Pocket type, Diamond Match Co. box containing a safe and 10 match books 10.00
Pocket type, plastic, double width, advertising 5.00
King Edward VII, book shaped, vulcanite, gold lettering, 2" X 1 1/2", EX 55.00
Pocket type, cylindrical, metal, Everdry 12.75
Gauntlet, figural, striker (I), copper, 2 3/4" X 1 1/4", EX 410.00
Gold, 14k, diamond, ruby, sapphire w/embossed cherubs, 2 3/8" X 1 3/8", E 550.00
Wall mounted, Holdfast Mfg. Co. 10.00
Pocket type, cylindrical, metal, Made in Hong Kong 12.75
International Tailors, heavily embossed lid, button release, dated 1904, 1 3/8" X 2 3/8", EX 45.00

Pocket type, brass, click bottom, Knights of Columbus, 1919 .... 15.00
Pocket type, cylindrical, metal, Marble's 12.75
President McKinley, figural, brass, 2 1/2" X 2 1/4", EX 275.00
Negro head, plated brass w/glass eyes, 2 1/8" X 1 1/2", EX 345.00
Advertising, Pabst/Milwaukee trademark (F), Pabst Worlds Greatest Beer (B), brass 2 1/2" X
    1 1/2", VG 50.00
Pickle, figural, brass w/green patina, 2 1/2" X 3/4", EX 295.00
Privy w/brass man, figural, plated brass 2" X 3/4" X 1/2", EX 235.00
Rebecca At The Well, embossed both sides, sterling, 2 5/8" X 1 3/4", EX 125.00
Enameled, w/4 bag pipers, Sampson Mordan, sterling 1 1/4" X 1 3/4", EX 650.00
Schlitz Beer, black leather wrapped, globe one side, cigar cutter on bottom, 2 3/4" X 1 1/2", EX
    80.00
Sea Horse, figural, brass w/glass eyes, 2" X 1 1/8", EX 325.00
Pocket type, plastic, click top, Souvenir of Nantucket 5.00
Unger, embossed cherubs, slant top, sterling, concave back, 3" X 2", EX 325.00

Match Tax Stamps

Match Tax Stamps--A revenue tax enacted by Congress in 1863 to help finance the Civil
War applied to many products, among them matches. Several hundred different ones are known
from the 18 years that the tax was in effect. The stamps were used to seal packages of match
boxes, so many copies were torn when the packages were opened. Several other countries have
used match taxes as a means of generating revenue. Some stamps are imprinted directly on the
matchcovers, while other issues have stamps affixed to either the inside or outside of the
matchcovers and boxes.

New York Match Co., 1cts green, silk paper 6.00
Barber Match Co., 1c blue, pink paper 3.00
Cramer & Kemp, 1cts black, old paper 25.00
Bousfield & Poole, 3cts black, old paper 16.00
Greenleaf & Co., 5cts orange, old paper 65.00

Match Vending Machines

Book type, upright, 2 for 1cts 75.00
Book type, round, Diamond Match Co 365.00
Box type, upright, Griswold Mfg. Co 265.00
Book type, horizontal 100.00
Book type, round w/adjustable dispensing (from 1 to 4 books) mechanism, Diamond Match Co.,
    American Made Matches, Beaton & Cadwell Co., New Britain Conn., Pat. appld. for.
    (stamped on base), 14 inches high, deep brown w/decal 350.00

Miscellaneous (Salesman's Sample Books)

Salesman's Sample Books--A very recent matchcover peripheral, collected mostly by
matchcover historians and researchers. These books were used by matchbook salesmen to show
customers various stock cuts, sample matchcovers, sales incentive plans, and prices. Printed and
used by most every matchbook manufacturing company, these books are difficult to find in good
condition.

The matchcovers glued into these books are not collectible and are called flats or friction flats,
as many didn't have the striker material attached. Few collectors will even admit to saving flats,
however, historically, they are very important.

*The author of this book has a standing order for any salesman's sample book or
accumulation of flats. He is also interested in any material related to the matchbook industry
including awards, invoices, company newsletters, documents, annual reports, etc. Send all
descriptions and prices to: AMCC, PO Box 18481, Asheville, NC 28814. Charitable
donations are also graciously accepted.*

Salesman's Sample Book (page) from the Mercury Match Co., Zanesville, Ohio, 1950. These books often contained 75 to 250 pages and were often bound in a metal or plastic spiral binder.

Admatch Corp., 1991 .... 3.00
Advance Match and Printing Corp., 814 N. Sacramento Blvd, Chicago, ca.1945, 64 pages 24.00
Arrow Match Corp., Maywood, Illinois, No. SJ-50, copyright 1950, 72 pages 25.00
Art Covers for Book Matches 20s, Madcap Maids, Champion Dogs, Floral Designs price card, copyright 1949, 10 pages, (PK/BK/WE) 10.00
Book Matches Tell the World, ca. 1942, 56 pages, 6" X 9", (RD/WE/BE), patriotic girlies & others
.... 16.00
Chicago Match Company, Libertyville, Illinois, 152 pages, 8 5/8" X 4 1/2", spiral bound, (DGN/ RD/YW) 15.00
Diamond Match Cover Designs by Geo. Steck, Arlinghaus Engraving Co., Cleveland, Ohio, (hand letters cover), approx. 34 pages, ca. 1920, Pressman's Guide Book 175.00
Firefly, Ever Brite It Glows At Nite!, no company, price card, 4 pages, 6" X 9", 2 flats (I) 8.00
Choice Matches, Trade Mark Harima, cord bound, ca. 1870, 6 1/4" X 9", (BK/WE) cover ....
.... 55.00
Kaeser & Blair Inc, Cincinnati, 1937, 185 pages, (BK) binder, 9" x 12", spiral bound 25.00
Maryland Match Company, Baltimore 30, MD, ca, 1950, 6" X 9", spiral hard bound, 130 pages, (TN/BK/RD) 22.00
New Stock Cuts, Copyright 1947, fold-out flyer, Match Corp. of America, Chicago 32, U.S.A., (BK/ WE) 3.00
Match Corp. of America, 3433-43 West 48th Place, Chicago 32, U.S.A., Salesman's Order form tablet, 6 3/4" X 8 1/4", (BK/WE), approx. 25 order sheets w/carbons 4.00
Match Corp. of America, Chicago 32, U.S.A., ca. 1945, (BK/RD), 7 X 9 3/8", 16 pages ... 15.00
Match Corp. Flash, single page ad flyer, ca. 1955, Match Corp. of America, 8 1/2" X 14", (RD/YW)
.... 2.00
Victory Models for Quicker Delivery, Copyright 1948, price card, Match Corp. of America, Chicago 32, U.S.A., (BE/WE), 3 flats (I) 4.00
Super Embosso Design Book Matches, Copyright 1947, price card, Match Corp. of America, Chicago 32, U.S.A., (RD/BK/WE), 8 flats (I), 8 pages 6.00
Match Corp. of America, 3433-43 West 48th Place, Chicago 32, U.S.A., Salesman's How To Sell Them book, 6" X 9", (BK/WE), no flats 4.00
Match Corp. of America, Chicago 32, U.S.A., ca. 1950, (BK/RD), 6" X 9", 35 pages, 30s Catalogue
.... 15.00
Royal DeLux Designs, Copyright 1947, price card, Match Corp. of America, Chicago 32, U.S.A., (RD/BK/WE), 4 flats (I), 4 pages 5.00
Mercury Match Co., Zanesville, Ohio, Safety Series price card, 5 flats (I), ca. 1955, (GN/RD/WE)
.... 4.00
Monarch Match Company, San Jose, California, ca. 1945, 8 1/2" X 10 3/4", plastic spiral hard bound, 184 pages, (BK/GD) 28.00

National Union Label Book Matches, Chicago 19, Ill, ca. 1950, 9 1/4" X 11 1/4", plastic spiral bound, 180 pages, (TN/SR/BK) 20.00
The National Line of Union Label Book Matches, Chicago, Illinois, ca. 1945, 6 1/8" X 9", spiral bound, 116 pages 16.00
3 Star Treasure Portfolio, The National Press, 1617 Lakeside Avenue, North Chicago, Ill, price card, 8 pages, 6" X 9", (MN/BK/WE), featuring George Petty, Lawson Wood, & Martin Garrity 4.00
Rex Book Matches, Fleming Calendar Company, Chicago, Illinois, 64 pages, 5 3/4" X 8 3/4", (TN/BK) 24.00
Superior Match Company, Chicago 19, Illinois, Americana Series price card, 6 page tri-fold, 6" X 9", (OE/BK), cocker spaniels (F), 8 flats (I), ca. 1955 .... 4.00
Snappy Sales Talk, newsletter, Superior Match Co., Chicago 19, Ill., April 1949, 4 pages 2.00
Superior Match Company, Chicago, Illinois 60619, 96 pages, 8 3/8" X 10 7/8", saddle stitched, Cat. No. 171 .... 6.00
Snappy Sales Talk, newsletter, Superior Match Co., Chicago 19, Ill., September, 1949, 4 pages 2.00
Snappy Sales Talk, newsletter, Superior Match Co., Chicago 19, Ill., July 1949, 4 pages ... 2.00
Superior Match Company, 7520-30 Greenwood Ave, Chicago 19, Illinois, Christmas price card, 4 pages, 3 3/4" X 8 5/8", (BE/WE) 3.00
Superior Match Company, 7524-30 S. Greenwood Ave, Chicago 19, Illinois, Ad-Display Double Book Matches and Jumbos, price card, 6 pages fold-out, 6" X 9", (BK/WE) 4.00
Superior Match Company, 7520-30 Greenwood Ave, Chicago, 208 pages (tabbed), 6 3/4" X 9", (GN/BK/GD) 4.00
3 Star Treasure Portfolio, Superior Match Company, Chicago 19, Illinois, price card, 8 pages, 6" X 9", (MN/BK/WE), featuring George Petty, Lawson Wood, & Martin Garrity 4.00
Superior Match Company, Chicago 19, Illinois, Holiday Book Matches price card, 4 pages, 6" X 9", (RD/GN/WE) 4.00
Famous Glamour Girls, Superior Match Company, Chicago 19, Illinois, price card, 4 pages, 6" X 9", 5 flats, Thompson #3, 1955 .... 5.00

Match Shipping Boxes

Diamond Match, Signal Light Brand 45.00
Diamond Match, Searchlight Brand 45.00
Diamond Match, Capitol Brand 27.50
A & P Matches, box in fair condition 18.00

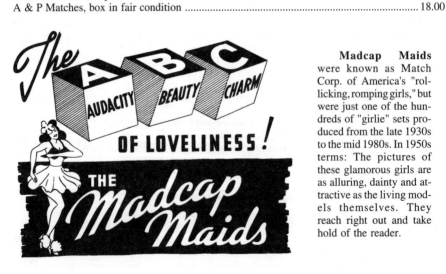

Madcap Maids were known as Match Corp. of America's "rollicking, romping girls," but were just one of the hundreds of "girlie" sets produced from the late 1930s to the mid 1980s. In 1950s terms: The pictures of these glamorous girls are as alluring, dainty and attractive as the living models themselves. They reach right out and take hold of the reader.

Diamond Match, Bird's Eye Brand 35.00
Salvation Matches, ca. 1895, Russian, lead lined for 144 kitchen size boxes, colorful printing all
    sizes 75.00

Match Tins and Tin Boxes

Countertop Match Bin, Ohio Match Co, clear plastic, square 5.00
Small tin store container, The Diamond Match Co. embossed on top, 8 5/8" X 5 3/8" X 4 7/8", (BK)
    .... 22.00
Tin store container, Safe Home Matches, 14 1/2" X 10 1/2" X 21", black w/colorful matchbox on
    lid 35.00
Wax Vesta Tin, Bell's Waterproof Wax Vestas 5.00
Tin match box, Evacuation of Ft. Ontario, 1796, Diamond Match Company, dated 1896 . 75.00
Metal match box, 4 1/2" X 2 1/4" X 1 9/16", by Ginna & Co., New York. Top shows black family
    lighting parlor match w/Their First Box of Drawing Room Matches: Paterfamilias: You
    Chillun Keep Back Deah! You Want You' Heads Blowed Off'n You' Shouldus?, coarse
    striker on side 400.00
Wax Vesta Tin, Duncan's Waterproof Wax Vestas 6.00

Match Hardware (Miscellaneous)

Disc Wheel 1 container, Give w/peasant girl and Greek flag, half moon striker 30.00
Card Matches, intact strip of 17 matches, Civil War vintage 13.50
Pocket Mirror, Ohio Blue Tip Matches and The Monypeny-Hammond Co., Columbus, O, factory
    in deep (RD) w/(BE) sky, (GN) lawn 35.00
Striker Postcard, abrasive is seat of man's pants 35.00
Pipe Rest, metal, round, includes box holder 7.00
Pipe Rest, plastic, matchcover holder in front 2.50
Poster, Cirillo's Hilton Head Lights 15.00
Poster, Cirillo's New York Lights 15.00
Poster, Cirillo's Tournament Lights 15.00
Poster, Cirillo's Washington Lights 15.00
Wall Striker Plate, rectangular strip of metal, 2" X 6" 10.00
Wrapper, 8 combs of matches plus wrapper, Diamond Match Co., 1880s 9.00

A category not yet formalized in the hobby, **stock blanks** is being promoted by the author of this book as a cross between matchcovers and flats. The open space was for the dealer or local distributor while the manufacturer or national service organization provided the stock design. This category has some interesting possibilities, especially for matchcover historians.

END OF PRICE GUIDE SECTION

Our large selection of beautiful border designs makes possible many very attractive type-set covers. They are especially adaptable when a special advertising message is desired on the back cover. All of these designs have been originated by our own Art Department, assuring the user an unusual cover for his Book Matches. Please observe the following important points when ordering these designs:

Border designs can be used ONLY on the Five-Color Stock Assortment—De Luxe —Standard color—"Super Embosso"—and Foil-Glo Metallic designs. They are NOT to be used on the Rainbow, Madcap Maids, "Our Kids," Scenic America or Sunburst Designs.

Stock Cuts cannot be used in combination with these Border Designs. There is no room for them. If desired, Stock and Saddle Cuts, Inside Cover Plates or Small Cuts may be used on the inside cover.

SADDLE CUTS or COPY can be used only on those designs where noted under the illustrations on the following pages.

USE SHORT COPY. The finished job will be much more effective if wording is as brief as possible. If more than 4 or 5 lines of copy is necessary, select one of the designs that affords the most copy space.

The use of these attractive border designs makes your "ad" look like a specially designed job at regular low stock prices.

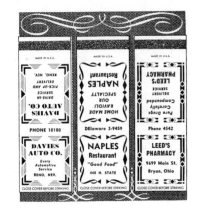

Border Designs--Found on many restaurant and small business matchcovers, and advertised to give your "ad" an attractive setting, border designs came with the warning that they could not be printed over Sunbursts, Girlie Sets, Our Kids Sets, Scenic America, or Rainbow designs. They were also "stock" in nature, insofar as nothing could be added or taken away from the original design. This selection is from a 250 page, mid-1950s Match Corp. of America generic salesman's sample book, used by small advertising specialty companies exclusively for matchbook sales.

GLOSSARY

-A-

A - (1) An abbreviation for 30 strike size (Ambassador) matchcovers, (2) An abbreviation for Aristocrat matchcovers.

AA - An abbreviation for American Ace Boxes.

AS - An abbreviation for Above Striker.

Above Striker - On back strike matchcovers, the area between the striker and the tip of the matchcover.

Abrasive - An older term used for the striker, generally referred to on matchboxes. (See Striker.)

Academies - (See Colleges.)

Accumulation - An unorganized gathering of matchcovers.

Ace - A term used to describe American Ace Boxes.

Ace Match Co. - An old, defunct match company that was located in Maywood, IL. This company used the manumark Arrow Match Co. until it went out of business in 1950. They produced three different sets of girlie matchcovers. (See Girlie, Arrow.)

Acme Match Co. - An old, defunct match company that went out of business in 1931.

Acorn Match Co. - An old, defunct match company of the 1920s.

Action Match - A Universal Match Corp. trademark for a different type of matchcover. It was the same size as the 30 Strike matchcover with added discs at the ends of the saddle, giving a satchel-like appearance. These "wings" moved in and out as the user opened and closed the matchbook. Only about 20 known designs were ever produced by Universal about 1940.

Ad Display Double Book Matches - A Superior Match Co. term for the common 40 strike matchbook. (See Delux Ad Display.)

Adaco Co. - An old, defunct match company.

Adams - A single word manumark that appears on several types of Group I matchcovers. No city, advertiser or other identification is given.

Adam Hats Contest Sets - A series of 5 letter contest sets and 2 picture contest sets issued to advertise Adams Hats between 1935 and 1948.

Adam Hats Sports Sets - Two similar 30 match-cover 20 strike sets manufactured by Universal

Match Corp., N.Y.C., with space for the dealer's imprint, advertising either Adam or Long's Hats. There were approximately 40 different dealer imprints known, making a total of about 1200 different matchcovers possible. The matchcovers with Adam Hats advertising are black on yellow background, while the matchcovers featuring Adam Hats & Long's Hats are black on a buff background. All of the outsides look the same; however the inside features the history of prize fighters, known as "Sam-Taub's Ring Personalities." The first 24 have a copyright date of 1942, while the last six show 1943, but all were distributed in 1943.

Add-ons - Any or all types of matchcovers with additional ornamentation added to the front or back cover. (See Lenticular, Novelty Match-covers.)

Admatch Corp. - Advertising specialty company with headquarters in New York City which markets a full range of Japanese-made boxes and matchcovers.

Advance Match Co. - An old, defunct match company of the 1930s and 1940s. They are credited with issuing the first 12 strike and 40 strike matchcovers. They were located in Chicago and went out of business about 1950.

Advance Match and Prtg. Corp. - An old match company located in Chicago, IL.

Adverap - Not actually a matchcover, but a cardboard cigarette pack holder that also held a pack of matches. They were a Universal Match Corp. idea (introduced in 1940) and had advertising (to match the matchbook) on all four sides. They were popular during the early 1940s. Over 250 varieties are known.

Advertising Matches: (Wellington) - A match-book manumark from New Zealand.

Advertizit Match Co. - An old, defunct match company that was located in Newark, NJ.

A-Frame - (See Tent.)

Air Force - (See Military.)

Airlines - A category of matchcovers whose advertisement mentions airline companies and includes domestic, commercial, and foreign. Both sets and singles can be collected. Around 3,000 varieties are known.

Al Ashri & Co. A.R.E. - An African matchbook manumark from Egypt.

Album (Matchcover Album) - A standard un-bound book with commercial (slotted) pages or sewn pages for displaying matchcovers. The 3-ring binder type is the most popular style.

All Round The Box - Label on a matchbox which wraps around the box instead of being one or two separate pieces on the front and/or back panels.

All Trades Match Co. - An old, defunct match company of the 1930s and 1940s, that was located in Rockford, IL.

Allenco Match Co. (Auckland) - A matchbook manumark from New Zealand.

Allis Press (The) - An old, defunct printing company located in Kansas City, MO that specialized in printing matchbooks.

Allubox - A European matchbox manumark from Switzerland.

Allumettes - French word for matches.

AMCAL - An abbreviation for the Associated Matchcover Clubs of California, which holds a convention every May. First gathering was held in 1956.

AMCC - The American Matchcover Collecting Club, P.O. Box 18481, Asheville, NC 28814. A national matchcover collecting club.

Amateur Sports - (See Sports.)

Ambassador - A Diamond Match Co. trade-mark for its 30 strike matchbooks.

American Ace - A Universal Match Corp. trade-mark for a wooden stick box match. Popular from 1977 to present, they were first issued by West Virginia Match Corp. in 1934. Over 9,300 varieties are known.

American Legion - (See Veterans Clubs, Fra-ternal.)

American Match Co. (WI), - An old, defunct match company of the 1920s and 1930s that was located in Grand Rapids, MI. Not related to a later company of the same name.

American Match Co. (OH) - An old, defunct match company located in Zanesville, OH. Began operating in 1956 and sold to Maryland Match Co. in August 1975.

American Match Council - Organization of U.S. match producers formed in 1991 "to promote awareness of the match and its value as a communications vehicle, an important inven-tion and an environmentally responsible 'light.'"

American Pullmatch Corp. - Company formed in June 1936 in Piqua, OH. Their logo read: Get the Pullmatch Habit, and showed a design of an early Pullmatch holder. Reg. under U.S. Pat. No.

2,014,182. After going bankrupt in early 1939, the company was bought by the Kilgore Manu-facturing Company of Westerville, OH, in Oc-tober, 1939.

American Pullmatch Div. - Company estab-lished in Tipp City, OH, in late 1939 by the Kilgore Manufacturing Company. After World War II, the company was moved to Kilgore's headquarters in Westerville, OH, where a 1949 bankruptcy halted production. (See Pullmatch.)

American Quality - The footer wording used on early matchcovers from the American Match Co., Chicago, IL.

Americana - A category of matchcovers show-ing scenes of American history.

Americana (Perkins) - (See Perkins Ameri-cana.)

Andorra - A box sold by the Maryland Match Corp., measuring 2" X 1 3/8" X 1/2". This type box is made in Spain.

Amvets - (See Veterans Clubs.)

Anniversary - A category of matchcovers with an anniversary or milestone number of years placed somewhere (inside or outside) (i.e. 50th anniversary, 25th reunion, etc..) (See Dated.)

Apollo - A category of matchcovers commemo-rating the various American manned space flights. It includes matchcovers issued for Apollo 7 in October 1968 through Apollo 17 in Decem-ber 1972.

Approved Match No. 7 - Very early (pre-1910) manumark wording. Second line: (Licensed Match)/The Diamond Match Co. N.Y. Said to be one of the earliest manumarks for match-books.

ARTB - Abbreviation for All Round The Box.

Aristocrat - A Universal Match Corp. trademark used for a 28 strike matchcover. Generally combined with 30 strike size matchcovers by most collectors. Introduced in February 1950.

Army - (See Military.)

Arrow Match Co. - An old, defunct match company that was located in Maywood, IL. Started in 1934, it went out of business in 1950 and is credited with issuing the first set of nude girlies, called A Study in Photo Art. Some sources believe this set hastened their demise or may even have caused it.

Arrow Press - An old, defunct match company.

Art Match Co. - An old, defunct match company, located in Grand Rapids, MI, which started business in the 1920s and went out of business in 1935.

Art Quality - The footer wording used by the Art Match Company, Grand Rapids, MI on their early matchcovers.

Athletic Clubs - (See Legitimate Clubs.)

Articulos Publictarious - A Central American matchbook manumark from Mexico.

Atlantic City Souvenir Set - This set consists of eight matchcovers (four in red and four in green) and was issued by The Diamond Match Co. about 1935. There is a one line manumark which reads: The Diamond Match Co. N.Y.C. and the saddle has 13 rays. Two variations in printing exist. Later issues have four red and four blue matchcovers.

Atlantic Match Co. - An old, defunct match company that was located in Jacksonville, FL, and operated in the 1930s. It was absorbed into Universal Match Corp. about 1941.

Atlantic Match Co. - An old, defunct match company located in Philadelphia, PA.

Atlantis Match Co. - A Chicago based match company.

Atlas Match Co. (TX) - A Texas based match company which started operation in 1960 is still in business. No relation to the earlier matchbook company of the same name. Originally in Arlington, TX, but moved to Euless, TX.

Atlas Match Co. (NJ) - An old, defunct match company that at one time was located both in Newark, NJ and New York, NY. It went out of business in the 1940s.

Atlas Four Color - Trademark of the Atlas Match Co. (TX) used on their matchbooks with color photo pictures.

Atria Lucifers - A European matchbook manumark from The Netherlands.

Auction - Any live sale of merchandise in which participants bid for various lots, in competition with each other, which will result in the purchase of that lot for the highest bid. (See Mail Auction.)

Australian Match Mfg. Co. - An old, defunct matchbox company that was in business from 1969 to 1976 in Strathpine, Queensland, Australia. Their excise mark was 10/5.

Auto Dealers - A category of matchcovers whose advertisement mentions automobile dealers. These are usually stock matchcovers. Earliest known matchcover is 1928, featuring the Hup automobile.

Auto (Dated) - (See Dated Auto.)

Auto (Stock) - A category of matchcovers whose advertisement mentions automobile dealers but has a stock design for the back. The individual dealer's ad appears on the front.

Aviation Commemoration Set - Probably one of the first Universal Match Corp. 40 strike releases with the Los Angeles manumark. They were printed on white "kromecoat" paper in 1951 and the wording and photos are sepia. The inside describes the advertiser: Artcraft Engineering Co.

Aztec - A Lion Match Co. trademark having debossed portions of the design.

-B-

B - Abbreviation for the back (not the inside) portion of a matchcover.

BPOE - An abbreviation referring to Elks lodge matchcovers. Stands for "Benevolent and Protective Order of Elks."

BS-CCBS - An abbreviation standing for Be Safe - Close Cover Before Striking. Used by Universal Match Corp. starting about 1974.

BS - A hobby abbreviation for back striker. (See RVS, SS.)

BW - An abbreviation for Best Western matchcovers.

B/W (1) - An abbreviation for "black and white" referring to the kinds of photo found on some older matchcovers. (Not to be confused with Matchoramas.) (See Matchorama.)(2) - An abbreviation for Best Western matchcovers used in category listings among collectors.

Back - The area of the matchcover between the saddle and the striker zone (on back strike matchcovers) or between the saddle and the manumark area (on front strike matchcovers.)

Back Panel - (See Back.)

Back Striker (Back Strike) - A matchcover on which the striker zone appears on the back side. (See Reverse Striker, Front Striker.)

Banks - A category of matchcovers whose advertisement mentions banks, thrift companies, savings and loans or various other types of money exchange institutions. Some collectors do not include Title and Trust Companies in this category. Collectors arrange this category according to state, then by city and then alphabetically within these groups. A collection of 15,000 different is not uncommon.

Barbecue Matches - (See Fireplace Matches.)

Barber Match Co. - Established in 1847 in Middlebury, OH, this company was one of the leaders in the merger that resulted in the Diamond Match Co.

Barber, Ohio Columbus - Nineteenth century matchmaker who was instrumental in helping found the Diamond Match Company in 1880. O.C. Barber served as company president from 1889-1909.

Barrel Box - Cylindrical matchbox that usually contains about 80 matches. The top is often transparent so the matches are visible, and the striker is located on the bottom. (See Can.)

Bars - A category of matchcovers whose advertisement mentions bars, taverns, cocktail lounges or other establishments where alcoholic beverages may be obtained (not to be confused with Liquor Stores.) (See Liquor Stores, Legitimate Clubs.)

Baseball - (See First Baseball, Second Baseball, Third Baseball, Fourth Baseball.)

Base Friction - A Diamond Match Co. trademark for matchcovers having the striker zone shifted slightly so as to be where the bottom fold usually is located. Introduced in 1937 and last produced in late 1942. Pat. #2,101,111 appears on all Base Friction matchcovers, granted on December 7, 1937.

Bases - (See Military.)

Beach - A commercial matchcover album maker, who has been around since the 1930s, and whose albums use 25 slotted pages per album. Each page has an 18-ring flexible attachment. Pages come in 20 strike, 30 strike and 40 strike slotted sizes.

Beer - A category of matchcovers whose advertisement mentions beer products, breweries, ales, beer brands or other related beer advertisement.s

Bell Machine Co. (The) - An old, defunct match company that was located in Oshkosh, WI. Operated in the 1930s.

Best Western - A category of matchcovers whose advertisement mentions locations in the Best Western hotel and motel chain. These matchcovers come in both 20 strike and 30 strike versions and are a popular category among matchcover collectors. First issued by Diamond Match Co., Chico, CA in 1948, there are over 12,000 known varieties.

Best Western Identity System - This classification system of Best Western hotels and motels stock designs contains over 28 issues, varying in color, imprint, and design.

Bicentennial - Any and all matchcovers issued to commemorate the 200th anniversary of the United States. Matchcovers came in singles and in sets and is probably the last national event to start a category of its own. Over 8,000 varieties are known.

Billboard - A Universal Match Corp. trademark for their 40 strike matchbooks. These matchbooks were exactly twice the width of the regular 20 strike matchbook (See Royal Flash, Double-Size, Forty-Strike.)

Binghampton Match Co. - An old, defunct match company that existed between 1893 and 1895. This match company produced one matchbook run for Piso's Cough Syrup and was sued by Joshua Pusey for copyright infringement, forcing it out of business in 1895.

Bitten - A slang expression for matchcovers on which the striker has been marked by striking a match stick., (See Struck, Hit, Used.)

Block Matches - Mid to late 1800s type of matches which were fastened together at the base. Typically, 100 or more would have a common base of 1 1/2" square piece of wood.

Blot-r Match - A distinct and different category of matchcovers issued by the Union Match Co. of Hudson, NY starting in December, 1928. Across the bottom of the matchcovers read: Absorbs Moisture, Keeps Matches Dry. The inside of the matchcover was a usable ink blotter.

Blue Set (The) - (See New York World's Fair - 1939.)

Bobbed - Slang for Bobtailed or Clipped. (See Bobtailed, Clipped.)

Bobtail(ed) - A front strike matchcover which

has had its striker cut off (also known as Clipped, Bob-tail(ed).) (See Clipped, Bobbed.)

Book - A single matchcover book (also means full book with all match sticks still inside.)

Book Match Co. - An old, defunct match company that was located in Chicago, IL.

Booklite Match Co. - An African matchbook manumark from the country of South Africa. The company began operations in 1966 and went out of business in 1969. It is credited for producing several lengthy sets. The factory was located in Springfield, Transvaal.

Bookmatch - A popular term for matchbooks used primarily before 1965. The matches are in a folder rather than in a box. (Also spelled Book Match.) (See Matchbook.)

Bookstores - A category of matchcovers whose advertisement mentions bookstores from colleges or universities.

Bottom Fold - The machine crease at the bottom of the matchcover. This is the area where the manumark usually appeared.

Bowling Alleys - A category of matchcovers whose advertisement mentions bowling alleys, bowling products or any recreational facility that offers the sport of bowling. Thousands are known. (See Recreational Facilities.)

Box Stand - Usually a rectangular block of metal, glass, etc., over which a matchbox fits, causing the tray to be pushed up and exposing the matches. It may be alone on a small base or it can also be found as part of an ashtray, either on the edge or in the middle. Also called Stand.

Boxes - Another popular term for matchboxes. The general classification for all size boxes from petites to presentation boxes. (See Petites, Presentation Boxes.)

Boyles - A category of matchcovers whose advertisement contains pictures or photos of slightly clad men in various stages of undress. Fewer of these sets are produced in comparison to the girlies. (See Girlies.)

Breaking - (See Broken Set.)

Breweries - (See Beer.)

Broken Set - A distribution anomaly as seen when matchbooks are given away through vending machines or sold in Supermarket Sets. (i.e. A set of 24 matchcovers will often not all be found in a single Supermarket Set caddy, and therefore, the collector must purchase several caddies in order to put a complete set together. The same is true when matchbooks are sold using a matchbook vending machine.) (See

New York World's Fair - 1964.) Sets either "break good" or "break bad." This term also refers to a partial set of matchcovers being offered for sale or trade.

Bridge Sets - A category of matchcovers issued from mid 1924 through 1943 with Bridge scoring information on the inside. They were issued from the Colgate Studios. (See Colgate.)

Brown & Bigelow - A large, mid-western advertising specialty company that has been around for a long time. Several stock design sets are attributed to this company.

Brussels World's Fair - (See Exposition de Bruxelles.)

Bryant & May - (1) A European matchbook manumark from England. (2) A foreign matchbook manumark from Australia. (3) A foreign matchbook manumark from New Zealand.

Bryant & May - This company was started in 1909 with a factory in Melbourne, Victoria, Australia. They first made matchboxes and later matchbooks. Swedish Match took over in 1987 and closed the factory in 1988.

Buckeye Match Works - Company located in North Baltimore, OH. Out of business about 1916.

Bulb - Wide portion of a match head.

Bus Lines - A category of matchcovers whose advertisement mentions bus companies or bus terminals.

-C-

CBS Stars - This matchcover set consists of Columbia Broadcasting Company radio personalities, and was issued by The Diamond Match Co. There are 80 matchcovers in this set with colors: red, blue, purple and green. Issued about 1935, 20 stars each appear in the four colors.

CC - An abbreviation for Country Clubs.

CCBS - An abbreviation for Close Cover Before Striking, the most commonly printed four word phrase since the beginning of time.

CCC Camps - A category of matchcovers whose advertisement mentions any of a series of Civilian Conservation Corps camp locations, popular in the 1930s. This category is usually collected by camp number, of which over 550 varieties are known. The first camps were established starting in March 1933 and disbanded in 1942 because of WWII.

C/S - An abbreviation for County Seats.

Caddy - A small, usually gray box of matchbooks, with 50 matchbooks to a caddy for the 20 strike and 30 strike matchbooks and 25 matchbooks to a caddy for the 40 strike variety. Usually, 50 caddies of 20 strikes make up a case of matchbooks.

California-Pacific International Exposition - This Exposition opened in 1935 in San Diego, CA. It issued a six matchbook set. Other matchcovers were issued in 1936, and a total of about 30 are known from the two years.

Cameo - A Universal Match Corp. trademark having portions of the often elaborate design debossed and printed with metallic ink. Most Cameos are 30 strike and some are Jewels. The name "Cameo" appears inside on many matchcovers. They were first produced in 1965 and over 7,500 varieties are known.

Cameo Box - A type of small round matchbox.

Camera Color - A Superior Match Co. trademark using a real four color photo as part of the design.

Camera Ready Copy - Artwork prepared for custom matchbooks. CRC, as it is sometimes written, can either be an artist's rendering or a photograph.

Camps - (See Military.)

Can - Small cylindrical box that holds about 30 matches. (See Barrel.)

Canada Match - Canadian match maker that began operations in 1963 in Downsview, Ontario, CN, and in 1973 moved to Markham, Ontario, CN. Ceased matchcover production in 1986.

Canadian - Any and all matchcovers from Canada.

Canadian Book Match Co. Ltd. - An old, defunct match company that was located in Toronto, Ontario, CN. It was bought by D.D. Bean in the 1960s. It produced 30 stick matchbooks from its beginning in 1938 to when it closed prior to 1964.

Canadian Book Match Co. - An old defunct match company that operated in Toronto, Ontario from 1933 - 1940.

Canadian Match Co. Ltd. - Formed in Ontario in the fall of 1921 by three companies: Diamond Match (U.S.), Bryant & May (British), and Maguire, Patterson & Palmer (British.) Each company had a 1/3 interest in the venture. It merged into Eddy Match Co. in 1927.

Canadian Radio Station Series - As of 1965, there were 92 Canadian Radio Stations offering a matchcover from each. All call letters begin with the letter "C." They are found from all ten Canadian provinces.

Canadian Tax Stamp - Any or all older Canadian matchcovers that have a tax stamp printed as part of the design on the matchcover. Stamps were first used around 1918 and discontinued in 1949. Matchcovers imported into Canada had actual stamps attached, usually on the inside.

Candidates - A category of matchcovers whose main theme is a person or persons running for any office (fraternal, local political, national political).

Card Matches - Early type which were fastened together at base, 17 wooden matches to a card. Discontinued about 1913.

Case - A large carton of matchbooks containing 50 caddies of 20 strike or 30 strike matchbooks (total of 2500 matchbooks). Also can pertain to matchboxes. Quantities will vary according to the matchbox size and who manufactured it.

Casinos - A category of matchcovers any or all of which advertise gambling houses. Popular from Nevada and New Jersey. Over 2,500 varieties known.

Category - A subject, topic or theme of an organized group of matchcovers being collected.

Cellopak - A closed pack of two, four, six or eight matchbooks, usually sealed in a clear plastic wrapper.

Cellophane Wrapping - The manufacturer's name for the covering of a Cellopak.

Cello-wrap - Another name for Cellopak.

Central Match & Label Co. - An old, defunct match company.

Century of Progress - (See Chicago Century of Progress.)

Century 21 Exposition - (See Seattle World's Fair.)

Centurylite - A Universal Match Corp. trademark for matchcovers containing 100 match sticks. They were introduced in 1964 but did not catch on and only a few were made.

Cerillos De Mexico - A Central American matchbook manumark from Mexico.

Cerillos "La Paz", S.A. - A Central American matchbook manumark from Mexico.

Chains - A category of matchcovers whose advertisement mentions hotels, motels, restaurants or other business establishments having many locations (i.e. Holiday Inn, Best Western, Bonanza Sirloin Pits, etc.). (See Stock Design.)

Chapman Match - An old, defunct match company that was located in Kansas City, MO.

Checklist - A listing made up by collectors or clubs to be used in checking which matchcovers are in a collection. Checklists report types of matchcovers by number rather than the actual issues. Also known as an Index. (See Lists.)

Chez Paree Serials - Advertised as America's Smartest Theater Restaurant at 610 Fairbanks Ct. in Chicago made a matchcover for a number of its headliners. Produced by Match Corp. of America, both 20 stick and 30 stick sizes are known. Each matchcover is dated and the 20 strikes start with Marion Marlow on June 12, 1955 and end with Sammy Davis, Jr. on April 17, 1960. Over 80 matchcovers have been found.

Chicago Century of Progress - This world's fair issued two sets of matchcovers. In 1933, the first set (12 matchcovers) was issued and tagged the "Gold Set." It was followed by the "Silver Set" issued in 1934, the second year of the Exposition. The Diamond Match Co. issued this set designed by Homer Colgate. It contained two Diamond Quality matchcovers (See Diamond Quality.) It is said that this fair was the "kick-off" event for serious matchcover collecting nationwide.

Chicago Match Co. - An old, defunct match company, located in Chicago, IL, which started in the 1930s and went out of business in 1968.

Chicago Souvenir Set - This set consists of only 8 matchcovers and was issued by The Diamond Match Co. around 1935. There is a one line manumark which read: THE DIAMOND MATCH CO. N.Y.C., on each matchcover, and the saddle design has 12 rays. There are four matchcovers in red and four in green.

Chicago Sun Set - (also called the Ernie Pyle - Chicago Sun Set) Manufactured during WWII by the Universal Match Corp. and made into a set of 18 matchcovers. Each matchcover features the name and biography of a famous war correspondent. The set originally sold for 50 cents and was issued in late 1944. Coloring includes white lettering with light blue background.

Chiclets - A 1940s group of at least 118 matchcovers produced by the Chiclets Peppermint Candy Coated Gum Company. These matchbooks were to be distributed during commercial airline flights and all (except one) are 20 strike size. All matchcovers (except two) have a Lion Match Co. manumark.

Chilina de Fosforos - A South American matchbook manumark from Chile.

Chinese Restaurants - A category of matchcovers whose advertisement mentions Chinese eating establishments (sometimes grouped in Oriental Restaurants).

Christmas - A popular category of matchcovers whose theme is related to Christmas. Often very fancy and highly decorated. They come as non-commercial or with business, product or service advertisement. Various sizes, thousands known.

Circle Match Co. - An old, defunct match company that was in Chicago, IL, in the early 1930s.

Class A Match Books - An early industry name for color sets of matchcovers printed with black ink on assorted color paper stocks.

Class B Match Books - An early industry name for matchcovers printed with one color on white stock.

Classique - A Universal Match Corp. trademark whose matchbook had two combs of match sticks that were glued into the matchcover. They measured 2" X 5 1/8" and only 32 varieties are known. It was introduced in 1966 and were never very popular with match company customers.

Classique 180 - A Universal Match Corp. trademark for a large style matchbox. Introduced in the late 1980s and contains 180 wooden matches.

Cleveland Souvenir Set - This set consists of only 8 matchcovers and was issued by The Diamond Match Co. about 1935. There are four matchcovers in red and four in green. There is a one line manumark which reads: THE DIAMOND MATCH CO. N.Y.C., on each matchcover, and the saddle design has 13 rays. Some sources claim this set was also issued with black and white pictures instead of brownish pictures.

Click - A product of Italy, trademarked by the Maryland Match Corp. It pertained to matchbooks with curved ends that overlapped at the top to close the matchbook. Originally imported from Italy and patented in 1949, later versions were also manufactured in the U.S.

Clipped - A front strike matchcover that has had its striker removed (also known as Bobtailed). (See Bobtail.)

Clix Advertising Co. - An old, defunct advertising specialty company located in San Francisco which sold matchbooks. Their manumark reads:

Mfg. by Lion Match Co., Inc.

Close Cover Before Striking - The warning printed at the bottom of the outside matchcover. (See CCBS, Footer.)

Clover Farm Quality - An old footer message, used by The Diamond Match Co. in the 1920s.

Clubs - A category of matchcovers whose advertisement mentions any type of club (athletic, yacht, country, Playboy, political, etc.). Not included in this category are night clubs or matchcover clubs. Some collectors include fraternal matchcovers in this category.

Coast Book Match Co. - An old, defunct match company that was located in Tacoma, WA. This is one of the companies that produced both "tall" and standard size matchbooks. (See Tall.)

Coast Guard - (See Military.)

Coast Match Co. - An old, defunct match company that was located in Los Angeles, CA. Their manumark includes the phrase Made in California.

Cocktail Lounges - (See Bars.)

Colgate - Matchcovers designed by William Homer Colgate, in the Colgate Studios, Div. of Diamond Match. Co., during the mid 1920s until about 1950. His matchcovers were known as Group I of which the Bridge Sets are the most famous. (See Bridge Set.)

Collection - A group of matchcovers which have been put into a recognizable order or arrangement.

Collectordom - A made up word meaning the whole realm of collectors.

Colleges - A category of matchcovers whose advertisement mentions institutions of higher learning (also called Colleges and Universities). Some collectors also include private schools, junior colleges and academies, but not commercial colleges or correspondence schools. Sports teams schedules are sometimes printed inside making them cross-over matchcovers. Conjunctives include fraternities and sororities. Does not include barber colleges, kiddy colleges or other commercial schools.

College Football Rivals - A set of football rival team matchcovers, issued by The Diamond Match Co. in 1934 and 1935. There were three different sets (or types) issued. (See Football.)

College Football Rivals (Type I) - A set of football rival team matchcovers, issued by The Diamond Match Co. in 1934. The historical data speaks of records in 1933. There were 24 matchcovers in this set with each of 12 rival teams shown with two different color backgrounds (tan and black). The one line manumark reads: THE DIAMOND MATCH CO. N.Y.C.

College Football Rivals (Type II) - A set of football rival team matchcovers, issued by The Diamond Match Co. in 1935. In this set, however, there are different historical background sketches than in Type I. The historical data speaks of records in 1934. There were 24 matchcovers in this set with the same rivals as in Type I listed, each of 12 rival teams shown with two different color backgrounds (tan and black). The one line manumark reads: THE DIAMOND MATCH CO. N.Y.C. There are two name changes in this set.

College Football Rivals (Type III) - A set of football rival team matchcovers, issued by Diamond Match Co. in the late fall of 1935. There were 12 matchcovers in this set with the same rivals as in Type II listed, but this set only was issued with the tan background. The two line manumark reads: Made in U.S.A./THE DIAMOND MATCH CO. N.Y.C.

College Sports - (See Sports.)

Collegiate Match Co. - An old, defunct match company whose manumark read "1928 - N. Shurr Co., Chicago."

Colorama - Monarch Match Co. name given to their ten color set, style number VM-100, which sold in assorted colors only.

Color Abbreviations - Used in mail auction legends, usually signified by the first and last letter of the color. (i.e. RD = RED, WE = WHITE, BE = BLUE, GN = GREEN, YW = YELLOW, LBN = LIGHT BROWN, DBE = DARK BLUE, B/W - BLACK & WHITE). (See Legend.)

Columbia Match Co. (CA) - A southern California based match company which makes mostly match making machinery. Previously of Ohio, it began in 1938 and has no relation to the other match company of the same name.

Columbia Match Co.(WI) - An old, defunct match company which started in 1915 and went out of business in the 1930s.

Columbia Match Co. of Canada Ltd. - This company was incorporated in 1928 and went bankrupt in 1933. The factory was located at St. Johns, Quebec, CN.

Comb - A measured section of match sticks contained in a matchbook. Combs come in all matchbooks. (See Panes.)

COMBINE - A defunct national matchcover collecting club that specialized in U.S. Navy ship matchcovers. Established in 1961 and disbanded in 1978 due to lack of new issues.

Combo - A hybrid form of collecting matchcovers in which a matchcover is saved with another item from the same establishment (i.e. a matchcover and a postcard). "Combo" is short for combination and the two items (one being a matchcover) must correspond.

Commercial Colleges - A category of matchcovers whose advertisement mentions commercial, proprietary, or trade schools, but not the schools listed under Colleges. (See Colleges.)

Commercial Lines - (See Ship Lines.)

Conjunctive - A little used generic term describing matchcovers that can apply in two or more categories (i.e. a matchcover with two advertisers). A lounge in a country club makes the lounge conjunctive to the country club; bus lines and bus terminals are conjunctives. World's Fair matchcovers printed especially for the fair, that were given out by non-pavilion restaurants and hotels, would be considered Fair Conjunctives. This term also applies to two distinctly different advertisers, disseminating information about their specific products (i.e. some older airlines matchcovers had Chiclets ads on the back).

Contact Sets - Matchcovers which form bigger pictures when put side by side. A famous set is the Leon and Eddie's night club set from New York. Another is the 12 matchcover 30 strike "Happy Birthday America" set by Universal Match, made in 1976. (See Panorama, Jig-Saw Set.)

Consumers Press - An old, defunct printing company located in Chicago, IL which specialized in printing matchbooks.

Continental Match Co. - An old, defunct match company which started in 1936 and went out of business in 1944, that was located in Chicago, IL.

Continental Match Co. (NY) - Subsidiary of Lion Match Co. that was set up in the 1950s to handle imported styles of matchcovers for which Lion Match sold orders.

Contour - A Lion Match Co. trademark for standard size matchcovers (20 strike) that were custom die-cut to the shape of the advertised product. The name Lion Contour Match

appeared on the inside matchcover. The manumark on early issues also uses the word Contour. These were top-of-the-line as far as expense and design were concerned. (See Jewelites.) Over 1050 varieties are known and collected. It was introduced in 1951 to compete with the Jewelite designs from Universal Match Corp. Discontinued in 1991.

Convention - A category of matchcovers from any kind of convention (usually pertaining to national matchcover conventions, annual meetings of local clubs, or club parties). Usually dated, these might include matchcovers issued by individual matchcover collectors, clubs, groups of collectors or other organizations within the matchcover hobby.

Convention Sets - A category of matchcovers specifically pertaining to RMS, AMCAL or local annual matchcover conventions. Both matchcover clubs, groups of collectors and individual collectors produced these sets.

Copy - Referred to as the wording of an ad or slogan used on a matchcover. Political Copy refers to the candidates credentials or platform promises.

Counter Display - A separately sold countertop plastic display box used for displaying commercial matches. The sign usually read "For Our Matchless Friends," or some slogan, and could be purchased with matchbooks from the manufacturer.

Country Clubs - A category of matchcovers whose advertisement mentions country or golf clubs. This category comes in all sizes. (See Legitimate Clubs.)

County Seats - A category of matchcovers whose advertisement specifically mentions the town and state (preferred on the front) of a business establishment, product or service from a recognized county seat. This category was originated in 1935 by Charles N. Reed, an Indianapolis pharmacist (known as Doc Reed). All county seats are 20 strike. Although their location changes from time to time, there are approximately 3400 county seats in the United States.

Cover - Slang for matchcover. (See Matchcover.)

Credit Line - (See Manumark.)

Crests - A category of matchcovers bearing a heraldry design. May be collected as hotels, restaurants, or other categories.

Cronmatch - A European matchbook manumark

from Denmark.

Cron Match - A European matchbook manumark from Finland.

Cross-Over - Any matchcover that can be placed in two or more distinct categories (i.e. a college matchcover with a football team schedule printed inside is categorized as both a College and a Sports matchcover). (See Conjunctives.)

Copy - A design term which means the wording or design of the words used in the layout of a matchcover. It is usually referred to as the advertising message; name, address, city, state, zip, phone; or any other wording that goes into the matchcover design.

Crown Match Co. - A defunct, old match company which started in 1933 and went out of business in 1942. It was noted for its spectacular graphics and sometimes captivating colors and design. There were at least twenty different manumarks used while this company was in business. The factory was located in Los Angeles, CA.

Crowns - A term used to denote matchcovers from the Crown Match Co.

Cruise Lines - A category of matchcovers whose advertisement mentions any means of sea transport for people having fun. Does not include marine products. (See Ship Lines.)

Cube - Term used to describe a wrapped package of 10 American Ace matchboxes. (See Sleeve.)

Custom Shapes - This is a minor category containing matchbooks that were made in several different shapes for specific, one time matchbook customers (i.e. Modelos Exclusivos of Rio, whose matchcovers have flat wings coming out from the back, or Gordon's Special Dry London Gin in which the matchcover is shaped like a large bottle of Gin). (not to be confused with Contours) (See Contours.)

Cut - 1. The term used for a photo, logo, graphic design, or line drawing used by a customer as art work on a matchcover. (See Stock Design.) 2. Any photo, logo, graphic design, or line drawing used as art work on a matchcover.

Cuties - The name first given to "girlies" matchcovers when they appeared commercially in England.

Cy Prisyon Co. - An old, defunct advertising specialty company located in Brooklyn, NY, that sold matchbooks.

Czecho Set - A patriotic 12 matchcover set commissioned by a Czech living in Chicago in 1942. They were sold in the Bohemian Czech district of Chicago, IL for 25 cents a set.

-D-

D.D. Bean Match Co. - A high volume, low quality matchbook company located in Jaffrey, NH which began operations in 1938.

D'Amario Girlies - A stock design set of five girlie matchcovers produced by the Superior Match Co. in 1952. The artist was Gus D'Amario.

DOT - An abbreviation for the Department of Transportation.

DQ - An abbreviation for Diamond Quality. (See Diamond Quality.)

Dated - A category of matchcovers with a date (month, day and year) appearing somewhere (inside or outside) (See Anniversary.) They were usually issued by a business or organization to celebrate an anniversary or special event. Not included in this category are matchcovers stating "Since 1905"; however, "From 1926 to 1956" is acceptable.

Dated Auto - Auto dealer matchcover with specific dates indicated for the autos advertised. (See Auto Dealers, Auto.)

David Lionel Press - An old, defunct printing company located in Chicago, IL, which special-

ized in printing matchbooks.

Dealer Imprints - A category of matchcovers having one design for all agents, outlets, dealerships, etc., of a particular business, but showing different location addresses on each. (See Stock Design.)

Debossed - A matchcover, a portion of whose design is impressed or recessed into the matchcover material. A Cameo is a famous example. (opposite of embossed) (See Embossed, Cameo.)

Defunct - Any advertised business, product, service, matchbook company, design, style, method of classification or technique which is no longer used, no longer in existence or currently popular. (i.e. Star Match Company, Bobtailing, Talls, Diamond Quality, etc.) Not to be confused with "old" as applies to matchcovers. (See Obsolete.)

Delux Ad Display - An Ad Display matchcover with process embossed Silver ink. Sometimes spelled with a hyphen between Ad and Display. (See Ad Display.)

Denmead Match Co. - An old, defunct match company located in Akron, OH in the 1930s.

Detached Striker - A matchcover with a separate striker material stapled to the matchcover. This kind of striker is seen on Scandinavian matchcovers and Owname matchcovers.

Diamond Brands - A holding company based in Minneapolis, MN, responsible for mostly Diamond box matches.

Diamond Color - A Diamond Match Co. trademark which has a real full color photo as part of the design.

Diamond Match Co. - At one time, the largest match company in the world, currently part of Diamond Brands of Minnesota. Formally established in 1880 through the amalgamation of several prominent match companies of the day.

Diamond Match - A footer used by The Diamond Match Co. after the Diamond Safety First and before the Diamond Quality footers. Probably used in the early to mid 1920s.

Diamond Quality - A Diamond Match Co. trademark issued between 1926 and 1936. (One source sites 1922 as the beginning of the Diamond Quality era and ends it with 1939, a victim of the great depression). The words "Diamond Quality" appeared on the footer (lower left portion of the front). There are seven known variations on this manumark/footer combination. (Classification expert is Bob Oliver,

Boyton Beach, FL.)

Diamond Safety First - As the popularity of the matchbook did not become dominant until 1925, early representations of this matchcover are very rare. Some surviving examples are Clown Cigarettes, the Morrison Hotel in Chicago and Que Placer Cigars. (See Safety First (DMC).)

Die-Cut - A shaped matchcover, usually in the form of an hour glass. The Jewelite is the most popular example. (See Jewelite.)

Die-Cut Hole - Covers with other than round holes punched in the front used to reveal wording or design on sticks. Holes may be shaped as products or have a geometric shape. (See Knot Hole.)

Disc Wheel Match Pack - A Unit Match Co. invention introduced in 1940. It was a wheel of matches about 4" in diameter in a square box. Wheels contained anywhere from 200 to 540 matches on the disc, which sold for about $1.00. The matches had to be struck on the friction strip which appeared on the side, front, or back of the box.

Disney (Walt) Set - This patriotic set of twenty 20 strike matchcovers was designed by Walt Disney and manufactured by the Maryland Match Co. in 1942. Each matchcover represents a different military unit. Sometimes known as The Yellow Set.

Disney (Walt) Pepsi-Cola Set - This patriotic set of 48 numbered 20 strike matchcovers was designed by Walt Disney and was manufactured by D.D. Bean & Sons, Jaffrey, NH who made them for the National Match Co. They were sold through Whelens and United Drug Stores. Each matchcover had a different Disney character and the name of a military unit. This set occurs with three different inside imprints.

Disney World - (See Walt Disney World.)

Display - A Lion Match Co. trademark which had a separate piece of pop-up cardboard advertisement attached to the upper inside. First produced in 1940. (See Pop-Ups.)

Displays - Any or all exhibits of matchcovers, full books or matchboxes, and collections at a convention or gathering of matchcover collectors.

Dogs - A category of matchcovers featuring pictures, drawings or photos of dogs.

Dominion Match Company Limited - (See Eddy Match Co. Ltd..)

Double Design - (See Errors.)

Double Dip Matches - First produced in 1886,

this type of match has phosphorus applied only to the tip of the bulb.

Double-Length - A rarely used kind of matchcover which is twice the length (1 1/2" X 8 7/8") of the regular. It was produced by Universal Match Corp. in the mid-1950s and appears in 20 and 40 stick widths. They were patented in 1957.

Double Sizes - Another older term for 40 strike matchcovers. (See Forty-Strike.)

Douglas - A single word manumark that appears on a number of Group I type matchcovers. Matchbook contained trick matches. Usually, a device to explode a cap upon opening. For this reason, no city, advertiser or other identification is evident.

Drava - The company was formed in 1909 by the takeover of the A. Reisner Match Works in Osijek, Yugoslavia.

Drawer - (See Tray.)

Drunkard's Match - A chemically treated match stick which caused the light to go out after a short period of time. These match sticks were popular in the 1920s and helped prevent drunks from burning their fingers. Made by Diamond Match Co. (See Stop Lite.)

Dummy Match - An old, defunct match company which used the Safety First footer. A surviving specimen of this matchcover is a Tall.

Dupes - An alternate term for duplicates, often used for trading stock. (See Duplicate.)

Duplicates - A second, third, etc., identical version of matchcover in a collection, often used for trading stock.

-E-

Eagles - (See Fraternal.)

Easel Back - Collector's term used to refer to Eez-l Back matchcovers by Lion Match Co.

Easy Matchcovers - A general collector's term applied to good, clean matchcovers which are generally not hard to find. This could apply to hotels, restaurants, motels, and other large, well stocked businesses. Easy matchcovers are usually found on the freebie table. (See Freebie Table.)

Eddy Match Co. Ltd. - An active match company located in Canada. Formed in December 1927 by merger of E.B. Eddy Co. Ltd., Dominion Match Co. Ltd., World Match Corp. Ltd., and Canadian Match Co. Ltd. Factory is located in

Pembrook, Ontario, CN.

Eddy Match Co. Canadian Girlie Series - Two sets of girlie matchcovers manufactured by Eddy Match Co. of Canada, and were produced in 1962 and 1969.

Eddy Quality - The footer wording used on early matchcovers produced by the Eddy Match Co. of Canada. This phrase was discontinued in the early 1940s.

Educational Set - This set consists of 100 matchcovers issued by The Diamond Match Co. There were 33 matchcovers in red, 33 matchcovers in white and 34 matchcovers in blue. The three sub sets do not repeat the same theme or description. Produced in the early 1930s. (See also Santa Catalina Educational Set.)

Edward I. Plottle Co. - An old, defunct advertising specialty company located in Scranton, PA which sold matchbooks.

Eez-l Back - A Lion Match Co. trademark for matchcovers that had a portion of the back made into a push-out easel so that the matchbook could stand by itself. They came in 20 strike, 30 strike, 40 strike and Giant sizes. Introduced in the mid 1950s.

Elks - A category of matchcovers whose advertisement mentions various Elks lodges. These come in both stock and non-stock designs. This category is usually collected by lodge number. About 2,750 lodges have been granted charters but some are no longer active.

Elvgren, Gillette - The first "girlie" artist to produce commercial drawings of partially clad women for matchcovers. He originally worked for Superior Match Co., and released his first set in June, 1938. He produced a total of 15 sets for Superior. In 1948, he went over to Match Corp. of America and later to Brown and Bigelow (an advertising specialty company).

Embossed - A matchcover, a portion of whose design is raised above the surface of the matchcover material. (The opposite of debossed.) (See Debossed.)

Empire Book Match Corp. - An old, defunct match company that was located in Brooklyn, NY. This is one of the companies that produced both "tall" and standard size matchbooks. Operated in the 1920s & 1930s.

Empire Match Co. - An old, defunct Chicago based match company that existed from the 1920s to the 1930s.

Empire Quality - The footer wording used by the

Empire Book Match Corp, New York and Empire Book Match Co. Chicago, IL. There were three versions of this footer line used, two for the IL company, one for the NY company.

Empresa Fosforera S.A. - A Central American matchbook manumark from Guatemala and Honduras.

Ephemera - The general term used for collectibles of minor documents of everyday life. Also known as "throw-away" paper collectibles. Also, this field of collecting includes short-lived or transitory printed matter of current or passing interest.

Ernie Pyle - Chicago Sun Set - (See Chicago Sun Set.)

Errors - A category of matchcovers whose design was unintentionally printed incorrectly by the manufacturer and accidentally released in an order. Errors include misprints, mis-cuts, double design, color mis-registration, color missing, 40 strikes with two 20 strike designs side by side, front designs printed inside, etc. (See Irregulars.)

Etincelle Comptoir d'Allumettes, S.A. - A European matchbook manumark from Switzerland.

Excise Marks - Australian system to identify the company which made a particular box or matchcover. Introduced about 1930 as part of a protective tariff which put a tax on imported matches.

Expo - A category of matchcovers whose advertisement pertains to the 1967 Montreal Expo. The general term can be used to annotate any exposition. Some collectors include them as World's Fairs.

Expo '67 - This Exposition opened in 1967 in Montreal, Quebec. Officially, it issued several handsome sets of matchbooks.

Expo '74 - Known as the Spokane World's Fair. (See Spokane World's Fair.)

Expo '86 - The exposition opened in 1986 in Vancouver, B.C., CN. Several dozen matchcovers are known.

Exposition de Bruxelles - The Exposition opened in Brussels in 1958 and produced a fine assortment of matchbooks (both singles and sets). Over 300 different matchcovers have been reported from this event.

Extend n' Ad - A Universal Match Corp. trademark whose matchcover had a peel-off label, either inside or outside, where additional advertising was displayed. This concept was introduced in 1982 and over 50 varieties are known.

-F-

F - An abbreviation for the front portion of a matchcover.

F.A.A. - An abbreviation for Federal Aviation Administration.

FOE - An abbreviation for "Fraternal Order of Eagles" also called "Eagles", a fraternal organization which had many varieties of matchcovers. (See Fraternal.)

FS - Abbreviation for Front Striker.

Fabrica Nacional de Fosforos - A Central American matchbook manumark from the Dominican Republic.

Face - A general term for the printed side of the matchcover.

Faces - As applied to matchcovers, it means any single design or advertising message on the front side of the matchcover. Each manufacturer's run uses a single face. (See Run.) A set of 20 matchcovers from the same advertiser will have 20 faces, while a case of 2,500 matchbooks for the same restaurant will have one face.

Fairs - Generally speaking, matchcovers from any World's Fair or Expo to include county, state or local fairs as well. Cross-overs might include hotels or restaurants outside of the fair grounds that mention the Fair.

Fancy (Types) - Any or all matchcovers with other than an ordinary size or surface finish. i.e. Jewelites, Filigrees, foilites, Uniglos, etc. (See Add-ons.)

Fairburn, William A. - President of Diamond Match Co. from 1915-1947.

Far East Match Co. - An Asian matchbook manumark from the Philippines. Their factory is located in Manila.

Features - A Lion Match Co. trademark for a matchbook containing wide match sticks that have been printed with lettering, designs or a combination of both (not to be confused with printed sticks). The standard 30 strike size matchcover held 21 wide stick feature match sticks (referred to as 21-Feature) while the 20 strike size matchcover held 15 wide match sticks. Introduced in Sept. 1930. (See Printed Sticks, Thirty Stick.)

Feature Match Book - A current manumark

owned by the Lion Corporation of America (formerly Lion Match Co. of Chicago). There are over 125 different manumark variations used for this one kind of matchbook. (See Features.)

Feature-Type Matches - Any or all matchbooks made in the style of the Lion Match Co. Feature, but without the registered trademark of that company. This kind of match was produced by Bryant & May in England after being patented in that country in 1933. Made by several U.S. Companies.

Federal Match Co. - An old, defunct match company which started in 1923, and had headquarters located in New York City. It was one of the companies that produced both "tall" and standard size matchcovers. This company was absorbed by Universal Match Corp. between 1939 and 1940. Formed by the consolidation of nine smaller match companies.

Federal Match Co., Div. Universal Match Corp. - An old, defunct company manumark used during the absorption of Federal Match Co. into Universal Match Corp. (ca. 1940).

Federal Match Co. Pty. - This Australian company was formed in 1913 in Alexandria, Sydney, New South Wales. It closed in December 1975, and used the excise mark 1/4.

Federal Prtg. Co. - An old, defunct printing company located in Chicago, IL which specialized in printing matchbooks.

Federal Trucks Girlies - A brightly colored series of seven girlie stock designs issued between 1941 and 1947 by the Ohio Match Company.

Fiat Lux - A South American matchbook manumark from Brazil.

Filigree - A Universal Match Corp. trademark for matchcovers that had a waxy surface coating, spattered in a random manner over the entire surface of the matchcover. This trademark was first used in 1969 and there are approximately 5800 different known matchcovers. (See Florentine.) In 1979, the waxy coating was changed to include three new patterned designs. Fleur de Lis consisted of the French Fleur de Lis design. Grain was slightly wavy lines running the length of the matchcover. Tear Drop was a pattern which looked like fishnet. All were discontinued in 1987.

Fireplace Matches - A relatively modern type of stick match usually over 8" long for starting conventional fireplace fires. Also called Barbe-

cue Matches.

First Baseball - A set of baseball players matchcovers issued in 1934 by The Diamond Match Co. The complete set consists of 200 different baseball players, each with four different color backgrounds including blue, green, orange and red (deep tones). Of 800 possible matchcovers, 655 have been reported by collectors.

First Football (Silver Set) - A set of football player matchcovers which was issued in 1933 by The Diamond Match Co. The football player appears on the front. The background of each player's matchcover is silver with either green or pink appearing under the descriptive data on the back. There is one oddity included with the 185 matchcovers in this set (an issue for the All-American board of Football). The data on the back of each matchcover gives the 1932 records of the various players.

First Movies (Type I) - A set of Motion Picture Stars matchcovers issued between 1934 and 1935 by The Diamond Match Co. The star's picture appears in full face on the front of the matchcover, paneled to present a picture frame in gilt and black. The star's name appears in script across the saddle, and the back gives a brief history of the star's career. Colors include: green, silver, orchid, blue and red, in deep shades. The two line manumark reads: THE DIAMOND MATCH COMPANY/NEW YORK and only ten matchcovers are known. This was also known as the "Test Set."

First Movies (Type II) - A set of Motion Picture Stars matchcovers issued by The Diamond Match Co. As in First Movies (Type I) the stars appear in full face in a rectangular gilt frame only. Several of the photos appear with hand tinted hair and clothing. Colors include green, dark blue, red, silver and orchid as in First Movies (Type I). The two line manumark read: THE DIAMOND MATCH CO./NEW YORK, and there are 32 known matchcovers in this set.

First Movies (Type III) - A set of Motion Picture Stars matchcovers issued by The Diamond Match Co. Similar to First Movies (Type II), this set included several different backgrounds for each star. Colors include: light blue, orchid, red, green and silver. The two line manumark read: THE DIAMOND MATCH CO./ N.Y.C. There are 95 known matchcovers with two oddities.

First Night-Life - A set of famous personalities

matchcovers issued about 1938 by The Diamond Match Co. Each shows a small square picture of the performer on the front with sketched champagne glasses and undulating music bars at the left and above the picture. The performer's name appears in script across the saddle, and the back gives a brief history of the performer's career, enclosed in a black border. A phantom picture of diners at a table is imprinted over the history. Colors include: green, pink, peach, orchid and red. There are 24 matchcovers in the complete set, and each has a two line manumark imprint: Made in U.S.A./THE DIAMOND MATCH CO., N.Y.C. All matchcovers in this set have black tips. (See Second Night-Life.)

Flair - A Maryland Match Corp. trademark for matchcovers with the look of a textured material. (See Pearltone.)

Flamlux - A European matchcover manumark from Switzerland.

Flasher - Another name for lenticular matchcovers or matchboxes.

Flats - Matchcover factory stock that never contained matches or were never machine creased or stapled. Used primarily as salesman's samples. Infrequently collected in the US and Canada, but more widely sought in overseas countries. (See Salesman's Samples.)

Fleur de Lis - (See Filigree.)

Flexibles - The name given to the first safety matches, invented by Joshua Pusey, with the striker on the inside of the matchbook.

Florentine - A Universal Match Corp. trademark for matchcovers that had a waxy surface coating in a specific patterned design that doesn't cover any printing on the matchcover. (See Filigree.) There are about 150 varieties known.

Florentine Gold - An American Match Co. (OH) trademark.

Florida Match Co. - An old, defunct match company.

Florida Souvenir Set - This set consists of eight matchcovers (four in red and four in green) issued by The Diamond Match Co., about 1935. At least four variations of the set exist. Later issues were produced with four red and four blue matchcovers with at least two variations.

Foilite - A Universal Match Corp. trademark for matchcovers (usually 30 strike) which had portions of the lettering or design printed with colored metallic foil. Used extensively for Christmas matchcovers, the word "foilite"

often appears on the inside, and the first letter "f" is not capitalized. Production of this matchcover stopped in 1987.

Folder - An older term for a matchcover. (See Match Folder.)

Football - (See First Football, Second Football, Third Football, Fourth Football.)

Footer - Wording which occurs at the lower portion of the front panel.

Footline - A match company's term for the manumark. This is the area on a front strike matchcover between the striker and the back where a company name was usually printed. (See Manumark.)

For Safety - A generic safety phrase placed on the footer (lower left portion of the front). It was used by various match companies. Generally followed by CCBS. Used in the 1920s in most cases, but examples from the 1930s and 1940s are known.

For Your Safety/Striking Surface on Other Side - (See SOB Warnings.)

For your Safety/ Turn Over for Striking Surface - (See SOB Warnings.)

Foreign - Any or all matchcovers, matchbooks or matchboxes that were manufactured in a foreign country (outside the United States except Canada) or advertise a business establishment, product or service for use or sale in that foreign country. The manumark should be from a foreign country and in some cases, a tax stamp may be present. For matchbooks, the sticks are sometimes straw or wooden.

Foreign Sets - Any and all sets that pertain to the definition of Foreign (See Foreign.)

Forts - (See Military.)

Forty-Strike - A matchbook size that is twice as large as the regular (20 strike) matchbook. It contains 40 match sticks. (See Royal Flash, Billboard, Double Size.) (written as 40 strike).

Fosforera Centroamericana, S.A. - A Central American matchbook manumark from Guatemala.

Fosforera el Inca - A South American matchbook manumark from Peru.

Fosforera Equatoriana S.A. - A South American matchbook manumark from Ecuador.

Fosforera Peruanna, S.A. - A South American matchbook manumark from Peru.

Fosforera Suramericana, C.A. - A South American matchbook manumark from Venezuela.

Fosforera Venezolana - A South American matchbook manumark from Venezuela.

Fosforeira Portuguese Esphino - A European matchbook manumark from Portugal.

Fosforera Espanola, S.A. - A European matchbook manumark from Spain.

Fosforos Sol, S.A. - A Central American matchbook manumark from the Dominican Republic.

Fosforos Universal - A Caribbean matchbook manumark from Cuba.

Foster, Lee - Sales manager of Superior Match Co., Chicago, IL, in the 1940s. He wrote a series of salesman's guides and Superior's "The Story of Fire."

Four Color - Any and all matchcovers that have a real photo-like color photo on the back, front or inside.

Fourth Baseball - A set of baseball players matchcovers issued in 1938 by The Diamond Match Co. The complete set consists of 42 matchcovers. Except for the fact that the historical printing on the back is smaller, it is the same set as the Third Baseball. Most of the matchcovers are printed in brown ink except for three that are printed in black ink.

Fourth Football - A set of football players matchcovers which was issued in 1938 by The Diamond Match Co. The overall background color is silver and each player is shown in a head and shoulder photo. The back of the matchcover shows a brief description of the player's history printed over a panel with a bright red (all are Chicago "Bears") background color on 12 matchcovers, and a deep blue (all are Detroit "Lions") background color on the other 12 matchcovers. The printing is in white. The saddle bears each player's name and his team, imprinted over a light tan football. The two line manumark for this colorful 24 matchcover set reads: Made in U.S.A./THE DIAMOND MATCH CO. N.Y.C.

Franklin Adv. Nov. Co. - An old, defunct advertising specialty company located in Dayton, OH which sold matchbooks. This is one of the companies that sold "tall" and standard size matchcovers.

Fraternal - A category of matchcovers whose advertisement mentions any number of national fraternal organizations (i.e. Lions, V.F.W., Eagles, American Legion, Moose, etc.). Some collectors do not include Elks in this category. Most are stock matchcovers, collected by lodge or chapter number.

Freebie Table - A table usually set aside at a meeting where members can take matchcovers or matchbooks for their collection, at no charge to themselves. Contributions in number and kind to this table are also made by members. (See Grabber, Easy Matchcovers.)

Freight Lines - (See Ship Lines.)

Friction (also Friction Strip) - Another name for striker. Also, the process that causes a match to ignite.

Friction Match - First patented in the U.S. in 1836.

Front - The outside portion of the matchcover between the saddle and the bottom.

Front Cover Striker - A matchcover design that had the striker on the front, forcing the user to close the front flap against the matchbook in order to strike the match. A relatively short lived trial judging from the number of matchcovers that have survived. Both 20s and 30s sizes are known, with about 50 varieties reported so far. Introduced by Universal Match Corp. in the mid-1950s.

Front Flap - The outermost portion at the bottom of a closed matchcover. This part of the matchcover contains the striker on front strike matchcovers.

Front Panel - (See Front.)

Front Striker (Front Strike) - A matchcover in which the striker zone appears on the front flap of the matchbook, and is in fact at the end of the matchcover. (See Back Striker.)

Front Striker Bulletin (The) - A nationally recognized newsletter concerning itself with the history of the hobby and the industry. It is the publication of The American Matchcover Collecting Club. Memberships available by writing, or mailing a copy of the application form on page 331 to: **AMCC, PO Box 18481, Asheville, NC 28814**.

Full Book - As shipped by the manufacturer, matchbooks with all of the original match sticks. For collectors, the term Full Book means the same; however the striker must be unstruck. Not widely collected due to increased space requirements and more trouble in trading by mail.

Full Length - A category of matchcovers with its message (words and/or picture(s)) running the full length of the matchcover.

Full Length (Horizontal) - A full length matchcover that has to be turned sideways in order for the message to be read.

Full Length (Vertical) - A full length matchcover whose message may be read while holding the matchcover in a vertical position (from tip to tip).

Full View - Another term for Full Length (either horizontal or vertical).

Funeral Homes - A category of matchcovers whose advertisement mentions funeral parlors, funeral homes or funeral accouterments (such as casket companies).

Fusee Matches - Name used in the mid to late 1800s for wax vesta matches.

-G-

Gambling Casinos - Any and all establishments that participate in legal gambling of any form. Primarily in Nevada and New Jersey. (See Legitimate Clubs.)

Gdanskie ZPZ - A European matchbook manumark from Poland. (See SZPZ Gdansk.)

Gem Match Co. - An old, defunct match company that was located in Chicago, IL, (ca. 1935-1938).

Gem Razor Blades Sets - A series of at least 6 sets of 6 matchcovers, each advertising Gem Razor Blades. They were issued in the mid 1940s.

General Match Co. - An old, defunct match company that was located in Cincinnati, OH. It began operations in 1890 and was reorganized in 1920. The company moved to a new plant in Reading, OH, in 1924. Matchcover production began soon after and terminated around 1951. Matchboxes were produced throughout the company's 61 years of operation.

General - A ubiquitous classification of matchcover collecting in which matchcovers can come from any category.

General Collector - A matchcover collector who collects any and all categories rather than specializing in a few. (See General.)

Getra Werbung Taunstein - A European matchbook manumark from Sweden.

Giant - A Lion Match Co. trademark for matchcovers which usually contained one large comb of wide match sticks (with or without imprint) and measured 9 1/16" by 3 3/8". It was produced in 1936 and probably earlier, and is still being made.

Giant Feature Match Books - A Lion Match Co. trademark for the Giant Matchbook (See Giant). These matchbooks contain printing or designs on the wide match sticks inside. Each match stick measured 3 1/4" x 1/4". Themes include Christmas and business establishments.

Girlies - A category of matchcovers whose advertisement contained pictures or photos of slightly clad women in various stages of undress, or nude. These designs were usually on the back, while the advertisement was on the front. Most are stock matchcovers and were usually issued in sets. Superior Match Co. issued the first sets in 1938.

Glamour Girls Sets - Three sets of girlie matchcovers made by the Advance Match Corp. between 1942 and 1950.

Glamour Girls - The generic advertising name used by various matchbook companies for their girlie sets.

Gledefri-Taendstickfabriker - A European matchbook manumark from Denmark.

Gold Set (The) - The nickname for a set of matchcovers issued at the 1933 Chicago Century of Progress Exposition.

Golden Gate Exposition - A fair that began in 1939 in San Francisco, CA. They issued numerous sets of matchcovers for both years (1939 and 1940) that it was open. There were at least 12 different fair issued matchcovers, three souvenir, a Midget and a Royal Flash.

Golden Light Match Co. - An Asian matchbook manumark from Singapore.

Golf Clubs - (See Legitimate Clubs).

Gopher Match Co. - An old, defunct match company which was in business in the late 1920s.

Gosch Taendstikfabriker A/S - A European matchbook manumark from Denmark.

Gowland Girls - Generally referred to as the series of Girlie matchcovers issued by the Republic Match Co. during the 1970s.

Gowland, Peter - World class photographer and teacher noted for his "pin-up" girls and techniques of photographing women.

Grabber - A person who industriously scoops quantities of matchcovers or matchbooks from the freebie table whether he or she can use them or not. (See Freebie Table.)

Grain - (See Filigree.)

Gral. Fosforera - A European matchbook manumark from Spain.

Granada - A Superior Match Co. trademark that has a portion of the design debossed.

Grant-Mann - A lithograph printing company located in Vancouver, B.C. It ceased operations around 1964.

Grand Coulee Souvenir Set - This set consists of two matchcovers issued by The Diamond Match Co., one is red and one is blue and the saddle has 12 rays.

Grater - Striking surface on a metal matchbox, when it is formed by a series of punctures in the metal.

Green Hat - A copyrighted (in 1926) trademark of the Albert Pick Hotel chain. This footer wording is extremely rare and is used on both stock and non-stock Albert Pick matchcovers. These were originally made by the Lion Match Co.

Green Hat Safety Book - A matchbook credited as having been manufactured by the Lion Match Co. of NY for the Albert Pick Co. of Chicago, IL, and copyrighted in 1926.

Grip - Term used to describe a 3-sided piece of metal or plastic which slides over a matchbox, leaving only one side and the two ends exposed. The grips were often highly decorated or displayed advertising. Also known as a Spring Grip.

Grocery Store Sets - Sets with very general nationally recognized product advertisement which are usually purchased in grocery stores. (See Supermarket Sets, Nationals.) This category may also include sets with designs, pictures, or words.

Gross - Unit of measure to show number of matches or boxes produced in 19th Century U.S. factories. Stands for 144 items or pieces. Shipping boxes were usually made to hold 144 boxes or one gross.

Gross Packet Label - Paper label that went on the outside of a shipping box, usually to show what the contents of the box were. The label would be a big version of whatever labels were on the boxes inside the shipping carton.

Group I - Matchcovers with no advertising of any kind (general classification) but usually pertains to movie stars, radio personalities and sports figure matchcovers popular in the 1930s. In the 1930s, W.W. Wilson invented the Group Classification System, dividing all matchcovers into five broad areas. Only the Group I term is still used. (See Colgate.) The term referred to matchcovers which were never given away but were always sold. (Also: group one.)

-H-

H/I (or H-I) - An abbreviation for Holiday Inn matchcovers.

H/M - An abbreviation for hotels and motels, as applied to classifications of categories.

H/M/R - An abbreviation for hotels, motels and restaurants, a popular combination of categories.

H.P.M. - Abbreviation for Hazardous Products Matches. Starting in 1972, Canadian made matchcovers had to carry a reference to the manufacturer on the manumark. HPM 01 through HPM 04 are known.

H.W. Stapleton Co. (The) - An old, defunct advertising specialty company located in Salt Lake City, UT that sold matchbooks.

Half Size - Another older term for Ten-Strike matchcovers. (See Ten Strike.)

Halftone - The intermediate step between a photo and a final art reproduction on a matchcover. This is an industry-wide and common printing term, not indigenous to matchcovers.

Hamilton Match Co. - An old, defunct match company that was located in Cincinnati, OH. It started in 1939 and was out of business shortly after the war in 1946.

Hanna Match Co. - A matchbook manumark from Australia. It began operating in 1969 with a plant at North Richmond, N.S.W.

Hardware - Hobby term used to describe items which are found with matches, such as slides, match holders, vesta boxes, match safes, etc.

Harrison Co. (The) - An old, defunct advertising specialty company located in Union City, IN that sold matchbooks.

Head - End of the match which is lighted. Also called Match Head.

Hellerup & Glodefri Taendstrikfabriker - A European matchbook manumark from Denmark.

Hellman Match Co. - An old, defunct match company that was located in Hollywood, CA and Los Angeles, CA.

Hemisfair '68 - (See San Antonio World's Fair.)

Henry Award - An award given in the matchcover collecting hobby, originally conceived by Edgar A. Perkins. It was given for a collection demonstrating outstanding beauty, artistry, originality and collector appeal. This award was first presented at the 1953 R.M.S. Convention in 11 categories. Only awarded for a few years. The award was named after Henry Rathkamp.

Henseleit Match Co. - An old, defunct match company that was located in Kohler, WI.

Hercules Match Co. - An old, defunct match

company that was located in New York City and Brooklyn, NY.

High Gloss White Covers - A finish applied to older front strikers which made the front appear bright white. Printing was then put over this finish.

Hill-Bigelo - An old, defunct advertising specialty company located in Grand Rapids, MI.

Hillbilly - A category of stock design matchcovers whose advertisement contained pictures of Hillbilly Humor. The artist was Martin Garrity who was published first by the Chicago Match Co. in 1948, and then by a number of matchbook companies later on. These designs were usually on the back, while the advertisement was on the front. Also spelled Hillbillies. (See Stock Designs.)

Hiltons - A category of matchcovers whose advertisement mentions the locations of the Hilton Hotel Chain (both stock and non-stock). This category's divisions include (1) matchcovers from Hilton Hotels, Inc.; (2) matchcovers from Hilton International Hotels; (3) matchcovers from Hilton Inns and franchised Hilton Inns.

Hilton I.D. System - A series of 27 different stock design issues of Hilton Hotels. On the inside, this series listed various Hilton locations around the world. Some of the issues were known as "The Pontiac Series", "The Buick Series", "The Reservations Series" and others. Want lists are used for this category. After 1973, individual locations were no longer listed, and a single national matchcover was used for all hotels.

Hilton Mini-Max - A series of about 30 different matchcovers manufactured by various match companies for the Hilton Hotel chain between the years of 1930 and 1944. It was Hilton's slogan and stood for Minimum Price — Maximum Service.

Hit - Matchcovers on which the striker has been marked by striking a match stick on it. (See Struck, Bitten, Used.)

Hobbymaster - A matchcover album maker, whose albums feature a three ring binder attachment and slit pages.

Hockey - (See Silver Hockey, Second Hockey).

Holiday Inns - A category of matchcovers whose advertisement mentions locations of the Holiday Inn Chain (both stock and non-stock.) (See N/S-H/I, H/I.) Two identity systems exist (1) The "Basic 17" (now 18)

Identity System or (2) the "Williams Holiday Inn Identity System" mostly used by advanced collectors. Over 23,000 varieties known.

Holiday Inn 4 Color Sets - A series of sets issued in the 1960s by individual locations of the Holiday Inn motel chain. Each set used the same four color combinations. (red, green, black, & yellow)

Honduras Fosforera, S.A. - A Central American matchbook manumark from Honduras.

Horizontal - A type of full length matchcovers in which the matchcover is held sideways in order to view the design or read the advertisement or message. (See Vertical, Full Length.)

Hotels & Motels - A general category classification of matchcovers which advertise places of lodging or rooms for a night (this category might also include guest houses, dude ranches, resorts, lodging inns, houses or courts). Chain hotels are usually not included in this category (i.e. Albert Pick Co. Hotels, etc.) but when they are included, they are considered a sub-category. (See Chain Hotels, H/M.)

Hundred-Strike - The third longest matchcover size, frequently reserved for vacation spots and historical places of interest. It contains 100 match sticks. (written as 100 strike). (See Souvenir, Two Hundred Strike, Two Forty Strike, Centurylite.)

-I-

I - An abbreviation for the inside portion of the matchcover.

IP - An abbreviation for "Inside Print" (See Inside Print.)

Ignia Coronica - A European matchbook manumark from Austria with the number #153 inside.

Illuminescents - An Atlas Match Co. (TX) product for both their 30 strike and 40 strike matchcovers. The message or design appears to change as you tilt the matchcover. (See Lenticular, Three-D.)

Illustro-Ad - Monarch Match Co. five style stock set (each came in four colors) including designs for food, auto service, spirits, and general customer acceptance.

Impregnated Matches - Match stick treated with chemicals to prevent afterglow when the flame is extinguished. This process was developed in 1915.

Imprint - A manufacturer's trademark generally found on the inside.

Imprint Book Match - An old, defunct match company that was located in Rochester, NY. Operated in the 1930s.

Inside Cover Plates - Stock designs that are sometimes used for inside printing. On older matchcovers, they included: Prayers, Songs, List of Birthstones, Accurate Age Finders, Distances Between Cities, etc.

Index - (See Checklist).

Indiana Match Co. - An old, defunct match company located in Crawfordsville, IN. This was one of nine companies which merged to form Federal Match Co. in 1923.

Indians - A category of matchcovers that includes a picture of an American Indian. Some collectors include matchcovers with American Indian artifacts, symbols, names and designs in this category.

Individual Sports - (See Sports).

Industria Argentia - A South American matchbook manumark from Argentina.

Industria Columbian de Fosferos - A South American matchbook manumark from Columbia.

Industria del Caribe - A South American matchbook manumark from Columbia.

Inner - The portion of a box which holds the matches. (See Tray).

Inside - The portion of the matchcover that is closest to the matches. (do not confuse "inside" with "back"). (See Back, I).

Inside Print - Any wording, design, message or advertisement that is printed on the inside of the matchcover. Also called inside printing.

Inter-Continental Hotels - A category of matchcovers and boxes from locations of this hotel chain. Established in 1946, there are over 100 locations worldwide. Over 460 varieties are known.

International Exposition - Opened in 1937 in Paris, France. Matchbooks were issued: exactly how many are not known.

Interpak - Printing company in South Africa.

Interstate Printing Service - An old, defunct printing company located in Biglerville, PA which specialized in printing matchbooks.

Inter-State Press - An old, defunct printing company located in Los Angeles, CA that specialized in printing matchbooks.

Irregulars - Any or all custom made matchbooks which in some way are blemished and cannot be sold to the customer. (See Errors, Jobbers).

Italian Tax Stamps - Italian method of making sure tax on matches is paid.

-J-

Jersey Match Co. - An old, defunct match company which started in 1935 that was located in Elizabeth, NJ and New York City, NY, and went out of business around 1948.

Jewel - A Universal Match Corp. trademark whose elongated matchcovers had parallel sides and dimensions that measured 5 1/16" x 1 7/8". The name "Jewel" is usually on the inside. An updated catalogue of numbered Jewel matchcovers has been available. Production ended in 1987 for this type, and there are over 5,000 varieties known. Introduced in 1955, early varieties have the Jewelite trademark inside.

Jewelite - A Universal Match Corp. trademark whose matchcovers had non-parallel, hourglass, die-cut sides (not to be confused with a Contour which is shorter and made by the Lion Match Co.). These matchcovers are the same dimensions as the Jewel. The first Jewelite was issued in 1951. Production ended in 1987 for this type, and there are over 7,000 varieties known.

Jewelite Sports - A sub-category of Jewelite matchcovers relating to popular team sports. All had the hour glass shape, and many contained team schedules inside.

Jig-Saw Set - Any set of matchcovers which has to be placed side by side to reveal the entire picture or motif. The Filippo Berio Olive Oil set of 10 is a wonderful example. (See Panorama, Contact Sets.)

Jobber - Any person who acts as a middle man between the manufacturer and purchaser of a product. In the matchcover industry, jobbers often handle overruns (See Overrun), miscuts, mis-prints or other merchandise, not able to be sold on the open market or to their originally intended customer.

Joshua Award - Given by the Match Industry, this award honored certain groups of advertisers for outstanding designs. The first "Joshua" went to the National Lead Company in 1952. The award was named after Joshua Pusey. This award was only given for a few years.

Jumbo King - The Monarch Match Co. name for the standard 240 strike matchbook. Actual size was 16 inches wide. (See Souvenir, Two-Forty Strike.)

Junior Colleges - (See Colleges.)

Juniors - A matchbook produced by the Ohio Match Co. in direct competition to the Lion "Midget." Most collectors use the generic category classification "midget" for this entire size grouping. (See Midgets.)

Jupiter - A trademark used by a West German matchcover manufacturer with approximate dimensions to that of a Jewel.

Jupiter 18 - A Universal Match Corp. trademark for matchcovers having 18 wooden matchsticks. Made in Belgium, it uses no staple as the combs are glued in. Introduced in the mid 1980s. About 20 different issues have been found.

Jute - A category of matchcovers having a recycled paper appearance. Over 220 varieties have been catalogued.

-K-

K.P.H.O. Set - Issued from the television station KPHO in Phoenix, AZ, the complete set contains 24 matchcovers. As they were originally issued through local vending machines, this set is extremely difficult to complete. Each matchcover is a 20 strike with the front showing a TV Screen, and the back says "Take 5 For"...followed by the various shows currently on the air.

Kaeser & Blair, Inc. - An advertising specialty company located in Cincinnati, OH that sold matchbooks. At one time, this was one of the largest advertising speciality companies in the mid-west and sold just about every imaginable Advertising Specialty item. Began operating around 1894.

Kentucky Match Co. - An old, defunct match company that was located in Evansville, IN.

King Midas Match Co. - An old, defunct match company that was located in Los Angeles, CA and was taken over by Universal Match Corp. around 1942.

Kitchen Matches - Type of box matches produced by various companies. These were popular in the kitchen for lighting the cook stove. Most were the "strike anywhere" type.

Knot Hole - A category of matchcovers with a round "knot hole" in the front revealing the match sticks inside. These were frequently found on Features and show the designs printed on the wide match sticks through the Knot Hole. (See Die-Cut Hole.)

Knoxville World's Fair - The World's Fair opened in 1982 in Knoxville, TN and only issued a handful of lackluster matchcovers commemorating the event.

Kolff Lucifers - A European matchcover manumark from The Netherlands.

Konsum-Zundholzfabrik Riesa - A European matchbook manumark from East Germany.

Konsum Zundwarenmark - A European matchbook manumark from East Germany.

Kreuger, Ivar - Managing director of Swedish Match when it was formed in 1917. Began a program to gain control of the world's match production capacity which was highly successful in the 1920s. Committed suicide in 1932 due to enormous losses due to the Great Depression. Also known as "The Match King."

Kromecoat - A type of paper stock used for making newer matchcovers (post-1965).

-L-

L.B. Herbst Corp. - An old, defunct advertising specialty company located in Chicago, IL that sold matchbooks. Their manumark included the line: Mfg. by Match Corp of America, Chicago.

La Central - A Central American matchbook manumark from Mexico.

Labels - A piece of thin paper bearing an advertisement that was glued to the outside of a matchbox. Labels can be affixed to either the front or the back of a box, both front and back, or one large label that goes all around the box. Used labels have been glued on boxes and then soaked off, while mint labels have never been attached to a box and are often found as uncut sheets as issued by the factory. (See Skillets.)

Leatherette - A type of matchcover having a leather-like appearance.

Legend - The list of abbreviations that often appears in a mail auction list. An example of a legend might include: (note: colors are the first and last letter of the word (i.e. green (GN), and appear in parentheses.) 100S-One Hundred Strike, 10S-Ten Strike, 12S-Twelve Strike, 1B-One Box, 20S-Twenty Strike, 24S-Twenty-Four Strike, 24OS-Two-Forty Strike, 30S-Thirty Strike, 40S-Forty Strike, AL-American League, AQ-American Quality, B-Back, (BK/WE)-Black & White, BAR-Barrel, (BE)-Blue, (BEGN)-Blue/Green, BF-Base Friction, (BK)-Black, BL-Box Label, (BN)-Brown, BS-Back Striker, (BF)-Buff, C-Cover, CA-Cameo, CCC-Civilian Conservation Corps, (CM)-Cream, CON-Contour, (CR)-Copper, (DBE)-Dark Blue, DOI-Declaration of Independence,DQ-Diamond Quality, E-Empty or End, EQ-Eddy Quality, F-Front, F/B-Front & Back, FEA-Lion Feature, FB-Full Book, FL-Full Length, FO-foilite, FS-Front Striker, FT-Flat (Salesman's Sample), G-Giant, (GT)-Gilt, (GD)-Gold, GGIE-Golden Gate Int'l Exposition, GMC-Girlie Matchcover Catalogue, (GN)-Green, GPF-Giant Poster Feature, (GY)-Gray, H-Horizontal, HB-Halfback, HOF-Hall of Fame, HR-Home Run, INC-Includes, JWL-Jewel, JLT-Jewelites, KB-Kitchen Box, L-Labels, LBA-League Batting Average, (LBE)-Light Blue, (LBN)-Light Brown, (LGY)-Light Gray, M-Midget, MS-Mixed Strikers, MVP-Most Valuable Player, MZ-Mixed Sizes, N/S-Non Stock, NL-National League, NM-Non Match, NYWF-New York World's Fair, O-Outside, (OD)-Orchid, (OE)-Orange, P36-Perfect "36", PAT-Patriotic, (PE)-Purple, (PH)-Peach, (PK)-Pink, PQ-Pull Quick, QB-Quarterback, RAMA-Matchorama, (RD)-Red, RF-Royal Flash, RM-Row Missing for Mounting, RR-Railroad, S-Saddle, SF-Safety First,

SG-Signet, (SM)-Salmon, SOL-Statue of Liberty, (SR)-Silver, SS-Spot Striker, T&P-Trylon & Perisphere, (TN)-Tan, U-Used or Struck, UN-Uniglo, UQ-Union Quality, V-Vertical, VIP-Very Important Person, VP-Vice President, W-Wooden, (WE)-White, WG-Woodgrain, WS-Wooden Sticks (Book Match), (YW)-Yellow.

Legitimate Clubs - A relatively sophisticated category listing which was popular some years back. It included all clubs with formal memberships (such as athletic clubs, country clubs, tennis clubs, golf clubs, yacht clubs, etc.). Other establishments that use the word "club" (i.e. night clubs, bars, gambling casinos, matchcover clubs) are not considered in this category. (See Clubs.)

Lenticular - An Atlas Match Co. (TX) trademark whose matchcover had a square of plastic glued to the front. The design on the plastic square moved from side to side as the matchcover was moved. Introduced in 1974 but did not prove to be very popular. Only a few varieties known. (See Add-ons, Illuminescents, Three-D.)

Licensed Match/The Diamond Match Co. NY - Very early (pre-1910) manumark wording. Said to be one of the earliest manumarks for matchbooks.

Lightning Bolt (Holiday Inn Series) - An early four color set (in red, yellow, black and green). The saddle reads: "Your Host From Coast To Coast", and the inside key words were "Facsimile matches." There were more than 20 different series of this type matchcover.

Lion Match Co. - A currently active match company, located in Chicago, IL, now known as Lion Corporation of America. It originally started business in 1917 in Brooklyn and began using the Safety First footer wording in 1922.

Lion Match Co. (Durban), (Capetown) - A African matchbook manumark from South Africa.

Lion Match Co. Glamour Gals Set - Four sets of girlie matchcovers manufactured by the Lion Match Co. of Chicago, IL, were produced in 1951, 1952, 1953 and 1955.

Lion Match (Safety First) - (See Safety First (Lion Match Co.).)

Lions - (See Fraternal.)

Lipstick Box - Term used to describe a square matchbox that contains about 22 matches. Dimensions are 2 1/4" long by 3/4" square.

Liquor Stores - A category of matchcovers which advertises any business establishment that sells hard liquor or wine. Stock design matchcovers for this category may have a single product advertised on the back and the business name on the front.

Lists - A description and assignment of reference numbers by collectors and/or matchcover clubs to which matchcovers have been reported in specific categories. (See Checklist.)

Listings - Any or all attempts by serious or well-intended collectors to assign a reference number to each different matchcover of a particular type, set, series or category.

Lite-Rite Match Co. - An old, defunct match company from Garwood, NJ.

Live Model - A Girlies category in which the subject is photographed rather than drawn. These subjects are usually partially nude or nude. Pornographic photos are not considered as part of this category.

Livingston Adv. Assoc., Inc. NY - An old, defunct match company that was located in New York City. Manumark also read: Mfg. by Lion Match Company, Inc.

Loco-Foco - Name for early Strike Anywhere matches used in the 1830s.

Lodges - A category of matchcovers whose advertisement mentions lodges, produced by Elks, Moose, etc.

Logo - Any trademark, registered symbol or symbol design of a business, company, newsletter or match club.

Lone Star Match Co. - An old, defunct match company that was located in San Antonio, TX. Operated in the mid-1950s.

Long Beach World's Fair - Which never took place in Long Beach, CA in 1967 and 1968. Matchcovers, however, were issued.

Los Angeles Match Co. - An old, defunct match company.

Los Angeles Town House Set - Produced by the Lion Match Co. with the Safety First footer around 1930. There were 10 matchcovers in this set (numbered on the back) and only one complete set has ever been recorded. The scenes are different views of the hotel and grounds.

Louden, Thomas - Featured performer and subject of the first commercial matchbook advertisement to appear in 1895. (See Mendelson Opera Co.)

Lounges - (See Bars.)

Lucifers - An early type of match which gave off poisonous fumes when lit. First developed in the 1830s, the matches were ignited by being drawn between a folded piece of sandpaper.

Lucky Sticks - A Lion Match Corp. trademark for matches with various poker hands printed on the sticks. Sticks were similar in width to the patented Feature match stick. First issued around 1954.

Luster-Tone Process - A printing process popular in the 1940s and 1950s which used raised (embossed) ink. Larger areas were also treated with a pattern or design further enhancing the brilliance of the advertisement.

Lynx Specialty Co. - An old, defunct advertising specialty company located in Salt Lake City, UT that sold matchbooks.

-M-

MM - An abbreviation sometimes used for Manufacturer's Mark. (The more popular term is manumark) (See Manumark.)

Machine Crease - The crease produced by the scoring machine when a matchcover is machine scored (See Machine Scoring.) This is one of the factors that differentiates hand creased "fake" matchcovers from a true machine creased matchcover.

Machine Scoring - The creasing procedure facilitated by a special scoring machine to help the fold of the matchcover around the match sticks. (See Machine Crease.)

Machine Staple - The staple placed in the matchcover and through the bottom of the combs to hold the matchbook together. (See Staple.)

Mad Cap Maids - Eleven sets of girlie matchcovers made by Match Corp. between 1939 and 1958.

Made in USA - A generic manumark found on matchcovers from various match companies.

Magna Match Co. - An old, defunct match company from around the 1920s.

Magna Quality - A little known footer line used on matchcovers by the Magna Match Co. (See Magna Match Co..)

Magnet Match Works - A match company that was located in London, England, SW14, not related to the Magna Match Co.

Maguire & Paterson Ltd., Dublin - A European matchbook manumark from Ireland.

Maids in Baltimore - Fourteen girlie matchcovers, 11 singles and a set of three, produced in the late 1940s by Diamond Match Co., Universal Match Corp., and Maryland Match Co.

Mail Auction - Any auction that is carried on through the mail. (See Auction.)

Mailer - A specially designed foil-lined box for sending full book matches through the U.S. Postal Service.

Mainostikku Hamina - A European matchbook manumark from Finland.

Major - A Bryant & May trademark for matchbooks of approximately 30 sticks. Introduced in 1960.

Manhattan Match Co. - An old, defunct match company which started in 1936 that was located in New York City, NY and Elizabeth, NJ. It ended its operations around 1940 and was taken over by Universal Match Corp.

Manu - An abbreviation for the term "manumark" meaning manufacturer's mark. (See MM, Manumark.)

Manumark - The collector's term for the wording usually near the striker that indicates what company manufactured the matchcover or which company sold or produced the matchcover for distribution or sale. Also called the credit line. (See Footline, MM.)

Marines - (See Military.)

Marlin Blades - Nine sets of six matchcovers with cartoons on the back panel which advertised Marlin Blades. Issued in the mid 1940s.

Maryland Match Corp. - A match company formerly in Baltimore, MD, but relocated to Canada in January 1980. It started operations in 1934.

Master Display Portfolio - The Chicago Match Co. name for their salesman's sample kit.

Match - The device that catches fire when drawn across a rough surface: may be cardboard, wood, or other flammable substance. (See Match Stick.)

Match Company United - An old, defunct match company located in Montreal, Canada. It began operations at the Berthierville, Quebec, plant in May 1922. The name was changed to World Match Corp. Ltd. in May 1923.

Match Corp. - An old, defunct match company which started business around the mid-1920s that was located in Chicago, IL. This company was absorbed by the Lion Corp. of America around 1970. (See Lion Match Co..)

Match Cuts - Match industry talk meaning standard or stock match designs placed on the front or back panel of the matchcover. (See Stock Design).

Match Folder - A cardboard holder used to protect a book of matches during prolonged usage. Also, another name for a matchcover.

Match Head - (See Head.)

Match S.A. - A South American matchcover manumark from Uruguay.

Match Safe - Usually a metal holder for a matchbook or single wooden matches (considered a separate collecting category from matchcovers). Sometimes made out of other materials such as plastic.

Match Stand - Another name for Box Stand.

Match Stick - The portion of the matchbook which is struck on the striker to produce the needed fire. Any or all of the individual matches in a comb, matchbook or box of matches. Also known as a pane. (Also spelled Matchstick.) (See Pane, Match.)

Match Tax - U.S. law in effect from 1864-1883 which taxed matches at the rate of 1 cent per 100 matchsticks.

Match Tax Stamps - Stamps affixed to packages of matches produced during the 1864-1883 period to show payment of the match tax. Different stamps are also found on more recent issues of some other nations.

Matchbook - A matchcover surrounding combs of match sticks stapled together into a "book." It is also written as two words - Match Book. Matchbooks are what is sold to businesses by match companies and matchcovers are what is generally collected. Manufacturers do not sell matchcovers. (See Full Book.)

Matchbox Publicity - A European matchbook manumark from England.

Matchcover - The actual piece of cardboard or shinekote used to imprint the advertisement which surrounds the match sticks. (Also spelled Match Cover.) Does not include matchboxes. (See Shinekote.)

Matchcover Club - Any body of collectors that have come together to share matchcover collecting information.

Matchcover Collecting - The hobby of bringing together like designs, styles, sets, etc. of matchcovers and organizing them into classifications according to loosely dictated national standards.

Matches (Australia) Ltd. - An old, defunct company located in Sydney, Australia. The factory operated between 1927 and 1952, producing both book matches and safety match-boxes. Their excise mark was 2/4.

Matchmakers - A European matchbook manumark from England (Made in U.S.A.). This trademark was also used by Match Corp. for their matchbooks sold in England.

Matchorama - A Universal Match Corp. trademark which used a real four color photograph as part of the design usually printed on the back and front of the matchcover. Matchcover sizes were usually 30 strike or 40 strike. Production on this style was begun in 1955 and concluded in 1987. (See Ramas, Vista-Lite, Tru-Color.)

Matchstriker - A small container, usually ceramic, which sat on a table or stand and was hollow in the center for holding matches. The striker surface was usually a series of rough concentric rings around the outside of the object.

Matchtone - A Universal trademark whose matchcovers had contrasting types of material on either side of the striker. Production was begun in 1980 and halted in 1987. There are at least 650 varieties known. Advertisers could order any of eight different combinations of material.

Mendelsshon Opera Co. (also Mendelson) - In 1895, this small traveling light opera company was credited with making and using the first commercial advertisement on a matchcover. There were about 200 blank matchcovers used, and hand decorated with pasted pictures of the opera star, Thomas Louden (also spelled Lowden), who appeared on the front and back. Hand lettering said, "A cyclone of fun - powerful caste - pretty girls - handsome ward-robe - get seats early." and included opening dates and accolades for the star. They were passed out by hand to the audience. There is only one surviving specimen of this matchcover known today.

Mercury Match Co. - An old, defunct match company which operated in Zanesville, OH between 1946 and 1955 and finally went out of business in the early 1960s.

Merchant Marine - (See Military.)

Merchants Ind(ustries) - An advertising specialty company located in Bellefontaine, OH that sold and manufactured matchbooks. Sales began in 1921 and terminated in the early 1970s.

Merit Match Co. - An old, defunct match company that was located in Elizabeth, NJ.

Merlin Girls Series - Six sets of girlie matchcov-ers drawn by the artist Merlin, were produced in 1940, 1949, 1952, 1955, 1962 and 1968. These sets were produced by the Maryland Match Co.

Metallic - (1) A Universal Match Corp. trademark for matchcovers which have a thin sheet of aluminum on which the wording is printed and bonded to the outside of a matchcover. Introduced in 1940, their shiny appearance made them very popular until the supply of aluminum dried up due to government defense work in mid-1941. (2) After WWII, the term has meant any matchcover with a colored metallic appearance. This style of matchcover was issued by many companies, usually in sets. Standard colors included gold, silver, red, green, and copper and were printed in black ink.

Midget - A Lion Match Co. trademark whose matchbooks contained 14 match sticks in two combs and measured 3 3/16" by 1 1/8". These matchbooks were produced between 1934 and 1943 for the popular clutch purse style evening bag. In 1943, the O.P.A. (Office of Price Administration) ruled a single size staple for all matchbooks thus ending the production of Midgets, 10 strike and 12 strike matchcovers. There are over 7,500 varieties known. It is generally believed that this size was made 60% by Lion, 30% by Ohio and 10% by Diamond Match Companies. (See Ten Strike, Twelve Strike, Half Sizes, Juniors.)

Military - A category of matchcovers whose advertisement mentions any branch of the Armed Services to include Air Force, Army, Coast Guard, Merchant Marine, Marine and Navy (not U.S. Naval Ships). They can include bases, ports, forts, camps, officer's messes, NCO clubs, PXs or any military function that issued a matchcover. This category is usually sub divided into individual services and sub divided again into individual establishments and then sorted alphabetically. (See Service.)

Milwaukee Souvenir Set - This set consists of eight matchcovers (four in red and four in green) issued by The Diamond Match Co. The set was reissued with four red and four blue matchcovers.

Mini-Max - (See Hilton Mini-Max.)

Minnesota Match Manuf. Co. - An old, defunct match company located in Duluth, MN. One of the nine companies that merged to form the Federal Match Corp. in 1923.

Minor Fairs - A listing of some of the minor fairs that issued matchcovers follows: 1949 - Kansas State Fair (And continuing years); 1951 - The Festival of Britain (London, England); 1952 - The Illinois State Fair (Covers in all successive years); 1954 - The British Empire Games, Vancouver, B.C.; 1956 - The California Silver Jubilee, Fresno, CA; 1961 - The Kansas Centennial Fair; 1962 - The U.S. Government Century of Agriculture; 1962 - The California Mid-Winter Fair, Imperial, CA (also in 1965); 1963 - The West Virginia Centennial; 1964 - the Arizona State Fair (also continuing years); 1967 - the Northwest Washington Fair (repeated in 1973); 1967 - The Alaska Exposition; 1967 - The Oregon 100th Anniversary; 1971 - The British Columbia Exposition (and the list goes on).

Mirro-Gloss - A Universal Match Corp. trademark whose matchcovers had a laminated finish on an acetate background. Introduced in 1941 and apparently did not meet with much success as only a few are known to have survived.

Miscellaneous Categories - There are hundreds of minor categories that are mostly personal fancies of individual collectors. These are valid categories and frequently included in collector's category lists; however, they are not recognized as national categories. Some of these include: owls, frogs, cats, pigs, tall matchcovers, towns with certain names, a word on the matchcover that is the same as your name, etc.

Misplaced Abrasive - An early term used for Odd Striker matchcovers. (See Odd Striker.)

Model - A Lion Match Co. trademark whose matchcovers appeared in the shape of the company's products that were being advertised and looked like a giant version of the Lion Contour. First introduced in 1952 and apparently not very successful as only a very few varieties are known.

Monarch Match Co. - A match company located in San Jose, CA which operated from 1946 to 1966. This company merged with Superior Match Co. and continued to produce matches under its own name into the late 1970s.

Monkeys - A category of matchcovers whose advertisement portrays monkeys in various human situations. The artist was Lawson Wood.

Monogrammed Match Packs - Special low quantity matchbook orders featuring stylized personal initials. Match companies offered this kind of matchcover to attract small orders of as few as 50 matchbooks.

Moose - (See Fraternal.)

Motion Picture Stars - (See Movie Stars.)

Mounting - The process of placing matchcovers in albums.

Movies - (See First Movies, Second Movies.)

-N-

NBC Stars - A set of National Broadcasting Company radio personalities matchcovers issued by The Diamond Match Co. around 1935. The star's picture appears in a round frame on the front of the matchcover, the frame being ringed with a black and silver circle. The star's name appears in script across the saddle, and the back of the matchcover gives a brief history of the star's career. A phantom picture of the "Radio City" building is imprinted over the history. There are 24 total matchcovers in this set with the colors (blue, green, pink and peach - all in light shades). Each star appears with one color. A single line manumark reads: THE DIAMOND MATCH CO. N.Y.C.

NCO Clubs - (See Military.)

N.V. Amsterdamsche Lucifersfabrieken - A European matchbook manumark from The Netherlands.

N/S - An abbreviation for Non-Stock.

N/S-H/I - An abbreviation for Non-Stock Holiday Inn matchcovers (See H/I, Holiday Inn.)

Name-On Match Co. - An old, defunct match company that was located in Cleveland, OH.

National Match Book Adv. Co. - An old, defunct advertising agency that was located in both Chicago, IL and New York City, NY. It was

formed in 1947 to act as a distribution agency for nationally advertised products on match-covers.

National Match Co. - An old, defunct match company that was located in New York City, and went out of business in the 1940s.

National Press - An old, defunct printing company located in Chicago, IL which specialized in printing matchbooks.

Nationals - A general category of matchcovers whose advertisement mentions products or services that are sold nationally. (i.e. Camel Cigarettes, Be a Shoe Salesman, Rival Dog Food, Draw This Picture - Win a Scholarship, etc.) Unless pre-1960, this kind of matchcover is not collected by serious collectors. Within the last 40 years more than one half of this nation's matchbook production has been Nationals. (See Vending Machine Matchbooks, Supermarket Sets.)

Nationwide Match - An old, defunct match company that was located in Chicago, IL.

Navy - (See Military).

Navy Ships - In general, any matchcover from a U.S. Naval vessel. They were originally issued only through the ship stores and were not available to the general public. There are two major sub categories: (1) Pre-War (WWII) U.S. Naval Ships and (2) Post-War (WWII) U.S. Naval Ships. No Navy Ship matchcovers were issued during World War II. Some collectors use a third sub-category called Canadian Naval Ships. This category is generally collected alphabetically and major listings are available for all sub categories. Over 3,000 known varieties.

Navy Ships, Canadian - Matchcovers issued by Canadian Navy Ships and shore stations. Over 400 varieties are known.

Nested Category - An organizational tool in which a subject can first be organized into a major classification and then broken down into sub-classifications. (i.e. Restaurants can be broken down alphabetically into kinds of restaurants, within kinds into states, within states into towns and within towns alphabetically.)

New England Souvenir Sets - This set consists of 86 matchcovers (two sets of 43 each), known as the First and Second New England Souvenir Set, issued by The Diamond Match Co. The First set has 21 green and 22 red matchcovers and the Second set has red and blue matchcovers. The red matchcovers of both sets are very

much alike. The primary difference between these two sets were that the First set had thirteen colored rays on the saddle while the second set had 12.

New York State Souvenir Set - This set consists of eight matchcovers (4 red & 4 green) issued by The Diamond Match Co. around 1937. A red and blue background set was issued in 1938, and reprinted in 1942 with a narrow wartime striker.The pictures on both sets are identical; however the red and blue background matchcovers have 12 rays on the saddle while the green and red background matchcovers have 13 rays on the saddle. There is a two line manumark on each matchcover.

New York World's Fair (1939) - Opened in 1939 in New York City and issued several different sets of matchbooks for both years (1939 and 1940) that it was open. Besides the official World's Fair matchcover sets (The Blue Set, The Orange Set and The Silver Set), there were scores of business, service and peripheral World's Fair matchcovers to be found. There were at least 39 different Fair issued matchcovers that are dated 1939 and a set of four that are dated 1940. Matchcovers came in 20 strike, 30 strike, 40 strike, 10 strike and Midgets. This is the World's Fair at which Bob Oliver and a group of matchcover collectors first developed the concept of a national match-cover organization, later to become the Rathkamp Matchcover Society. (See RMS.)

New York World's Fair (1964) - Opened in 1964 and went into 1965. This World's Fair issued many sets and singles, along with a host of peripheral business, product and service matchcovers. The official sets (1) a five piece 40 strike set and (2) an eight piece 30 strike set, were produced by Universal Match Corp. Both of these sets are Panoramas (See Panorama.) Poorly "broken" sets were sold in vending machines throughout the fair.

Night Clubs - (See Legitimate Clubs.)

Night-Life - (See First Night-Life, Second Night-Life).

Nile Match Co., Alexandria (The) - An African matchbook manumark from Egypt. The company was formed in 1933 by the Swedish Match Group.

Non-Specific - A national type of matchbook without an advertisement. A vending machine matchbook might say "Thank You" and nothing else.

Non-Stock - An adjective placed before some categories to denote that those matchcovers produced by advertisers were not stock designs (i.e. Non-Stock Holiday Inns.) (See Stock.)

Northwestern Prtg - An old, defunct printing company located in Chicago, IL which specialized in printing matchbooks.

Novaca Fabrica, A.B., Halmstad - A European matchbook manumark from Sweden.

Novelty Matchcovers - Odd ball, limited production matchcovers with items glued to them. Interesting, but not widely collected. (See Lenticular, Add-ons).

Nudies - Another name for girlie matchcovers of no specific classification or design. Pertains to women with no clothes instead of partially clothed. (See Girlies.)

Nur Match Co. - A Middle Eastern matchbook manumark from Israel. It is believed to have commenced operating about 1939.

-O-

Obsolete - Any advertised business, product, service, match company, design, style, method of classification or technique which is no longer used, in existence or popular (i.e. Crown Match Company, Midgets, Classiques, etc.) Not to be confused with "old" as applies to matchcovers. (See Defunct.)

Odd Sizes - Any or all types of matchcovers other than standard sized 20 strike, 30 strike or 40 strike. This classification includes 10 strike, 12 strike, 100 strike, 200 strike, 240 strike, Contours, Jewels, Jewelites, Midgets, Perfect 36s, Giants and all custom cut or custom shaped matchcovers. Most of these classifications comprise separate collecting categories. (See listing for all of the categories mentioned above).

Odd Striker - A category of matchcovers whose advertisement includes an unusually shaped and/or placed striker zone, frequently incorporated into the message on the matchcover. This was also a trademark of the Lion Match Co. which made these matchcovers between 1942 and 1962. (See Spot Strikers.)

Oddity - Any single matchcover that belongs to a set by virtue of its origin, but doesn't look anything like the other members of the set.

Officer's Mess - (See Military.)

Ohio Match Co. - A match company located in Wadsworth Ohio which started operations in 1895 and went out of business in 1987. Matchcover production was started around 1924. Matchboxes were made throughout the company's production years.

Olpha Match - A European matchbook manumark from Holland.

One Hundred Strike - (See Hundred-Strike, Centurylite.)

Orange Set (The) - (See New York World's Fair - 1939.)

Oriental Restaurants - A category of restaurants including Japanese, Chinese, Thai, Korean and other Far East eating places. (See Chinese Restaurants.)

Orleans - A Superior Match Co. trademark for matchcovers that had a waxy surface coating, spattered in a random manner over the entire surface of the matchcover. (See Filigree.)

Oshkosh Match Works - An old match company located in Oshkosh, WI. Operated in the late 1800s.

Outer - The portion of the box which has the design on it and which surrounds the tray containing the matches.

Overruns - Quantities of matchcovers that are in addition to the regular or usual quantity of ordered matchcovers. Overruns are usually handled by jobbers (See Jobber), or may be purchased, at a reduced price, by the original customer.

Owname - An Owname Match Co. trademark, usually seen on 30 strike size matchbooks issued between 1935 and 1945. It has a detached striker which separates from the matchcover when the staple is removed. It was reported that one collection had over 500 varieties and contained one comb of 14 matches. Trademark was granted for this name in March, 1925.

-P-

PX - (See Military.)

Pacific International Livestock Exposition - This Exposition took place in the state of Washington. Several matchcovers were issued.

Packet Label - Paper label which goes on the outside of a package of matches to show the contents.

Pageant of America - An Exposition which took

place in the Black Hills of South Dakota in 1935. This Exposition issued an eight matchbook set.

Pageant Match Inc. - An old, defunct match company that was located in San Francisco, CA.

Palmer, Lloyd C. - First collector to make a comprehensive listing of Pre-War U.S. Navy ships. He was a civil engineer and died in 1952.

Palmer Match Co. - An old, defunct match company located in Akron, OH. Began operating in 1922.

Pan-Am New Zealand Movie Set - A set of 50 matchcovers, which were released in 1977 and sold in New Zealand. Profits from the sale went to local charities. The inside features Pan-Am advertising and some were issued on board Pan-Am flights. Each matchcover depicted a first run movie which was shown in-flight aboard Pan-Am aircraft.

Pan-Am Sets - A series of at least 15 colorful sets issued in the 1950s and 1960s by the Pan American airline company.

Pana Match Corp. - An old, defunct match company that was located in New York City, NY.

Panamanian Fosfora el Gallo - A Central American matchbook manumark from Panama.

Pane - Another term for a single match stick. (See Match Stick.)

Panel - Referring to the outside of the matchcover, (i.e. the "front panel" and "back panel"). (See Front, Back.)

Panorama - Two or more matchcovers, which, when brought together side by side, form parts of a bigger picture. (See Jig-Saw Sets, Contact-Sets.)

Parlor Match - First made in 1857, this match type used paraffin instead of sulphur in order not to cause an odor in the family parlor.

Parlor Matches - It was a mid-size stick match (between a kitchen and fireplace match), used primarily to light kerosene or gas lamps. Produced during the time when match heads were relatively unstable, they were known to "pop" off the stick and shoot across the room. Taken off the market in 1912.

Passenger Lines - (See Ship Lines).

Patented Sept. 27, 1892 - One of the earliest manumarks known. Later versions had a second and third line which read: (Licensed Match)/ The Diamond Match Co. NY.

Patriotic - A category of matchcovers whose message portrays any number of scenes, word-

ing or phrases, or places compatible with American patriotism. This category does not include Military. World War II patriotics is a sub-category.

Pats - A short form of "Patriotic" as applied to matchcovers.

Pearltone - A Superior Match Co. trademark whose matchcover surface appears to have a textured, rib-like linen finish with horizontal striations across the matchcover.

Pennsylvania Match Co. - An old, defunct match company located in Bellefonte, PA. This was one of the nine companies which merged to form Federal Match Co. in 1923. The factory was closed in 1947.

Perfect 36 - A Diamond Match Co. trademark whose matchbooks contained 36 match sticks and measured about 4 3/8" by 2 1/2". This matchcover style was designed to replace their double-size matchbook of 40 matches. It was introduced in 1948 and manufactured until 1952. Over 400 varieties are known.

Perkins Americana - A series of sets sponsored by Edgar A. Perkins, Washington D.C. depicting American cities, places and events. The matchcovers were 20 strike only and most came in sets of five colors each. Matchcovers show an American Indian and the word "Americana" with advertising on the front and a historical sketch on the back. They were first introduced in 1957 in conjunction with the Jamestown Festival. (See Americana.)

Personalities - A category of matchcovers whose message or advertisement is (1) the personal matchcover of a well known personality (i.e. Paul Whiteman's personal matchcover) or (2) matchcovers issued by businesses, services or products owned by celebrities or known personalities (i.e. Lew Tendler's Steak House or Guy Lombardo's Port-O'-Call Hotel) or (3) matchcovers issued while famous personalities are performing at noted establishments (i.e. Chez Paree presents Julius La Rosa or Johnson's Wax presents The Red Skelton Show). (See VIP.)

Personality Products - A European matchbook manumark from England (Made in Japan.)

Personalized - Matchcovers that have been imprinted with a person's name. (See Personals).

Personals - Any or all matchcovers that are made up for special occasions (i.e. weddings, bar mitzvahs, graduations, etc.) and include the name of the person(s).

Petite - A type of small matchbox. (See Boxes.)

Petty, George - An early American girlie artist who is credited with producing a total of eight girlie sets. He was a featured artist at Esquire Magazine and won international acclamation with his picture of Miss Chicago for the 1933 Chicago World's Fair. He also designed for calendars and playing cards.

Petty Girls - Five sets of girlie matchcovers issued by the Superior Match Co. between 1948 and 1951. The artist was George Petty.

Philippine Match Co. - An Asian matchbook manumark from the Philippines. (See PHIMCO).

Phillumenist - The generally accepted scientific name for matchcover collectors.

Phillumeny - The art and hobby of matchcover collecting.

PHIMCO - An abbreviation for Philippine Match Co.

Phosphorus - White phosphorus fumes in match factories caused a large number of deaths due to phosphorus necrosis (phossy-jaw.) Poisonous white phosphorus was replaced by non-poisonous yellow phosphorus around 1911-1912.

Photo Color - A Maryland Match Corp. trademark which has a real, full-color photo as part of the design.

Picked - A collection of matchcovers which has been picked over or gone through by previous collectors for the purpose of buying only those matchcovers from the collection which are needed. This generally lessens the collection value of the remaining matchcovers.

Piggyback - A slang expression used to describe Sticky Backs. Name used by some companies in marketing their version of the Sticky Back. (See Sticky Back.)

Pillboxes - Cylindrical boxes used for holding wax vesta matches in the late 1800s and early 1900s. They were very popular in Australia and New Zealand.

Pillow - Smaller version of a Pouch which contains about 15 matchsticks. (See Pouch.)

Pixlite Book Matches - An old, defunct match company manumark used by the Albert Pick Co., Chicago, IL.

Plastic Matchboxes - First produced in Germany in 1964.

Playboy Clubs - A category of matchcovers whose advertisement mentions various Playboy Club locations. At least eight sets have been made since their introduction in 1961 as well as several single issues.

Playgirls - Generally referred to as the series of girlie matchcovers issued by the Superior Match Co. in the 1970s. In 1983, Superior made available single poses instead of sets and called them Playgirl Halftones.

Please Strike on Back/for Safety's Sake - (See SOB Warnings.)

Plyfiber Match Co. - A matchbook manumark from Australia. Ceased production in mid-1962.

Pocketbox - A Diamond Match Co. trademark for one style of its matchboxes. Introduced in 1959, there are over 8,000 reported varieties. The box measures 2" X 4" when opened and flattened.

Pocketbox Slim - A Diamond Match Co. trademark for one style of its matchboxes that is slimmer than the standard Diamond matchbox. Introduced in 1980, this box measures 2" X 3.5" when opened and flattened. Over 3,100 varieties have been reported.

Pocket Wallet - Produced by Lion Match Co. in the early 1920s, it looked like a regular size matchcover but had two flaps of cardboard which folded inward and were stapled together. This formed a "pouch" which contained loose wooden stick matches.

Political - A category of matchcovers whose advertisement or message mentions the current status of a political candidate or the candidacy of a potential office holder. Generally broken down into (1) Local Political, (i.e. Mayor, Examiner, School Council, Registrar, Dog Catcher, also known as Minor political); and (2) National Political (i.e. The President, Congressional and Senatorial Seats, etc., also known as Major political). (See Presidential.) Campaigns, politicians, and current office holders are considered part of this category and a real photo matchcover is preferred.

Pop-Ups - Another name for Display Matchcovers. (Also spelled Pop Up.) (See Display.)

Portland Star Match Corp. - An old, defunct match company which was founded in 1866. In 1890 it was the second largest match company in New England, having built the first "fireproof" factory out of brick, with a tin roof and concrete floors in 1870. It was purchased by The Diamond Match Co. of NY in 1908 and the "instantaneous blaze match" soon put it out of business.

Portuguese Comedian Sets - Three sets of

matchcovers totaling 228 pieces.

Portuguese Comedian Set (First Set) - This 1971 set contains a total of 96 matchcovers, the backgrounds of which are: 24 in pink, 24 in white, 24 in yellow and 24 in blue. The edges are black and the matchcover has a single striker. The manumark says Fosforeira Portugesa Esphino and this set advertises Portuguese overseas colonies, Angola and Mocambique.

Portuguese Comedian Set (Second Set) - This 1971 set contains a total of 48 matchcovers, the backgrounds of which are: 24 in pink and 24 in blue. The edges are blue and the matchcover has a double striker. The manumark says Fosforeira Portugesa Esphino and this set advertises Portuguese overseas colonies, Angola and Mocambique.

Portuguese Comedian Set (Second Set, variation) - This 1971 set contains a total of 12 matchcovers, There is a black bar beneath the second striker. The edges are blue and the matchcover has a double striker. The manumark says Fosforeira Portugesa Esphino and this set advertises Portuguese overseas colonies, Angola and Mocambique.

Portuguese Comedian Set (Third Set) - This 1972 set contains a total of 72 matchcovers, 24 have a red edge on a blue background, 24 have a blue edge on a yellow background and 24 have a red edge on a white background. The manumark says Fosforeira Portugesa Esphino and this set advertises "Districts" with descriptions on the back panel.

Poster - A Lion Match Co. trademark whose matchcovers were about as wide as a postcard. The matchcover measured 9" long by 6" wide when spread out. It was introduced in 1956 and apparently not widely accepted as only a few types are known.

Post War Ships - A category of matchcovers whose theme is U.S. Navy ships that were issued after World War II. Generally, ships that were commissioned after August, 1945.

Pouch - Flat match container open at both ends which holds about 24 match sticks. The striker is located on the outside of the sliding center portion which contains the matches. (See Pillow.)

Pre-Cut Pages - Any or all slotted album pages used for mounting matchcovers.

Premier Match Co. Ltd. - A match company located in Montreal, Quebec, Canada which commenced operations in 1946.

Premier Match Co. Canadian Girls Series - Two sets of girlie matchcovers manufactured by the Premier Match Co. of Canada, and were produced in 1951 and 1952.

Presidential - A category of matchcovers whose message pertains to or were issued by U.S. Presidents. Over 500 known varieties. (See Political.)

Presentation Boxes - Any or all of the category of boxes that are highly decorated and possibly used for special occasions. (See Boxes.)

Press - (1) A method of flattening matchcovers after the matches have been removed. (2) Referring to the device used to hold matchcovers in place when flattening them.

Press-Back - (See Sticky Back.)

Pre-War Ships - A category of matchcovers whose theme is U.S. Navy ships that were issued before World War II. Generally, any ship commissioned before December 7, 1941.

Printed Stick - Standard size match sticks that have words or designs on each stick (not to be confused with Features). (See Features.)

Private Schools - (See Colleges.)

Productos Parafinados, S.A. - A Central American matchcover manumark from Guatemala.

Professional Sports - (See Sports.)

Progress Cal. Co. - An old, defunct printing or advertising specialty company located in San Antonio, TX which specialized in printing matchbooks.

No Cover Charge

Proprietary Schools - (See Commercial Colleges).

Prudential Art Cal. - An old, defunct printing or advertising specialty company located in Chicago, IL which specialized in printing matchbooks.

Publifosforos Madrid - A European matchbook manumark from Spain.

Publix Printing Corp - An old, defunct printing company located in Oakland, CA and Chicago, IL which specialized in printing matchbooks.

Pullmatches - These matches are flat cardboard stems which light by being pulled between two pieces of cardboard which make up the booklet. Refills for this unusual match came in round (2 7/8" diameter) spools of pullmatches, frequently with an advertisement (i.e. Standard Radio, Jerry King and Milt Blink.) Their motto - "Keep Pulling for Us." (See American Pullmatch Co.)

Pullquick - A Diamond Match Co. trademark whose containers used a hidden ignition striker strip to light the round match stick as it was quickly pulled out of its place in the container. Dimensions were 1 7/8" X 2" X 1/4". Popular in the 1930s and 1940s, they were also referred to as "Pull Quicklies."

Pusey, Joshua - Received Patent Number 483166 on Sept. 27, 1892 for "the object of this invention is to provide a friction match device, which shall be cheap, readily made, convenient to use and efficient, and which may be safely carried in the pocket." He sold his patent to The Diamond Match Co. (for around $4,000) and remained on The Diamond Match Co. payroll until his death in Lima, PA in 1906. He was 64 years old.

-R-

R - An abbreviation for regular (20 strike) size matchcovers.

RR - An abbreviation for any railroad matchcovers.

RF - An abbreviation for Royal Flash matchcovers. (See Royal Flash.)

RMS - Standard abbreviation for the Rathkamp Matchcover Society. (See Rathkamp Matchcover Society.)

RVS - An early 1970 collector-dubbed abbreviation for "Reverse Strikers", meaning a matchcover with the striker on the back. (See SS.)

Radiant Match - An old, defunct match company manumark used by the Radiant Safety Match Corp.

Radio/TV - A category of matchcovers whose advertisement mentions any radio or TV station or radio or TV personality (disc jockey, etc.). The call letters and/or call number of the station are usually present on the front, back or inside.

Radio Stars - (See CBS Stars, NBC Stars).

Railroad "Pullquick" Matches - The three known matchcovers of this style are from the Katy Lines, the Susquehanna & N.Y. Railroad and the Texas and Pacific Railroad. (See Pullquick.)

Railroads - A category of matchcovers whose advertisement mentions railroad companies, railroad stations, railroad trains, etc. This category came in both sets and singles and in all matchcover sizes.

Rainbow - A Universal Match Corp. trademark whose matchcovers had an oily looking, multicolored surface appearance, incorporated into the design of the advertiser. Introduced in 1979, over 290 varieties are known by collectors. Discontinued in 1987.

Rainbow Stock Designs - Used by various match companies in the 1940s. These color pattern designs overlaid the advertisement and usually came in five colors (red, pink, purple, green and yellow). Not to be confused with Rainbow matchcovers by Universal Match Corp.

Raised Ink - A category of matchcovers whose message or advertisement wording or design is printed with a heavy ink, thus raising the design above the surface of the matchcover. These are not embossed.

Rama - An abbreviation for Matchorama. (See Matchorama.)

Rathkamp, Henry - Namesake of the Rathkamp Matchcover Society (the national matchcover organization) and early matchcover collector.

Rathkamp Matchcover Society (RMS) - Founded in 1941, the club takes its members from all over the world, but is a single based organization without member clubs.

Real Photo - (1) Any matchcover that includes an actual photograph of a person, place or thing as part of its message or advertisement. In color, these matchcovers have special names such as Matchoramas and Tru-Color. (2) Any matchcover that includes an actual black and white photograph of a person, place or thing.

The name was borrowed from the postcard collecting term.

Recreational Facilities - A loosely clad matchcover category which gathers all kinds of facilities that are used for recreation or sporting fun. This category might include bowling alleys and stadiums, as well as swimming pools and gymnasiums.

Refill Pages - Packages of extra slotted pages sold by album manufacturers for their products.

Regal Book Match Co. - An old, defunct match company that was located in Chicago, IL.

Regal Match & Prtg. Co. - An old, defunct printing company located in Chicago, IL which specialized in printing matchbooks.

Regie Francaise - A European matchbook manumark from France.

Regular - Another traditional term for the standard 20 strike size match. (See Standard.)

Reliable Match Co. - An old, defunct match company formed in Ashland, OH, in 1903. This company was one of the nine who merged in 1923 to form the Federal Match Corp. The factory was closed in 1930.

Repeat Order - The manufacturing term used when a customer wishes to have another run of his matchcover design printed. (See Run). He may want to change a phone number, reverse a design or alter a color for the new run.

Republic Match Co. (TX) - A match company located in Euless TX. It was originally formed in the early 1960s, as a subsidiary of Atlas Match Co. (TX) to handle smaller orders. Originally located in Arlington, TX.

Republic Match Co. (WI) - An old, defunct match company that was located in Plymouth, WI. No relation to the Texas company. Operated in the 1930s.

Rest - An abbreviation for the category of restaurants.

Restaurants - A category of matchcovers whose advertisement mentions a kind of eating establishment or business that offers a meal (i.e. restaurants, fountains, coffee shops, drive-ins, snack bars, donut shops, tea rooms, inns, cafés, cafeterias, diners, delicatessens, automats, lunches, lunchrooms, confectioneries, bar-b-ques, grills, etc..) This is probably the largest single category in the hobby and an excellent category for the beginner due to the ease in which these matchcovers may be obtained. Suggested collecting method is alphabetically within cities, within states. Also, they may be categorized according to the sub-categories as mentioned above.

Reverse - (1) Another term used for the back panel of the matchcover. (2) An obsolete term used for the inside portion of the matchcover itself.

Reverse Plate Designs - A design in which the type matter, wording, or cuts appear in the color of the matchcover stock, with a background of the color ink in which the matches are printed.

Reverse Striker - A matchcover on which the striker zone appears on the back. (See Back Striker, SOB.)

Reward Cuts - Any stock matchcover which offers a reward and "see inside cover." Used in the 1940s and 1950s, rewards ranged from $1 to $15.

Rex Match Co. - An old, defunct match company.

Rhapsody - A Maryland Match Corp. trademark for matchcovers that had a waxy surface coating, spattered in a random manner over the entire surface of the matchcover. (See Filigree.)

Royal Flash - A Universal Match Corp. trademark whose matchbooks contained 40 match sticks. These matchbooks were twice the width of the regular 20 strike matchbooks. They were introduced into the market in 1937. (See Billboard, Double Size.)

Run - A manufacturing term which means the printed material in a specific order. A run can be one case or 1,000 cases, usually for the same customer and with the same design.

-S-

S - An abbreviation for the saddle portion of the matchcover.

SAW - Abbreviation used in match production to indicate Strike Anywhere Matches.

S.A.S.E. - An abbreviation for Self Addressed Stamped Envelope. An S.A.S.E. should be sent to a correspondent to whom you are asking a question or requesting information. This is an unwritten rule in collecting and common courtesy.

S.E.I.T.A. - A European matchbook manumark from France. An abbreviation for Service D'exploitation Industrielle des Tabacs et des Allumettes. It is the match monopoly of the French Government.

S&L - An abbreviation for Savings and Loan Association matchcovers. (See Savings and Loan.)

SOAL - A term which refers to the return guarantee on letters or packages, often saying "Return and Forwarding Postage Guaranteed." Means "Stamp on all Letters."

SOB - An abbreviation for "Strike on Back." In the late 1930s, certain match companies experimented with SOBs, but were not very successful. All American-made matchcovers produced after July 1, 1978 had to be SOBs.

SOB Warnings - The following is a list of the SOB (Strike on Back) warnings that were placed in the old striker zone area to encourage patrons to strike their matches on the back. Safety Match/Strike on Back; For Your Safety/ Striking Surface on Other Side; Strike on Back Cover; Strike on the Back Cover; Turn Over for/ Striking Surface; Turn Over to Strike; For your Safety/ Turn Over for Striking Surface; Striking Surface/on Back for Safety; Scratch My Back; Safety Feature/Turn Over for Striking Surface; Strike on Back; Wise Man Strike on Back/Save Temper & Hands from Igniting; Please Strike on Back/for Safety's Sake; Turn Over/Scratch My Back;"Scratch My Back"/For Safety.

SS - An early 1970 collector abbreviation for "Straight Strikers." This abbreviation was used to denote a matchcover with the striking surface on the front. (See RVS).

SZPZ Gdansk - A European matchbook manumark from Poland. (See Gdanskie ZPZ).

Saddle - The outside area between the front and back portions of the matchcover. This area is usually used for short worded messages or a stock cut.

Safe-T-Lite - (See Safety Tab).

Saddle Slogan - Any specific stock cut design offered to the matchbook customer to be placed on the saddle. Such slogans as "The Right Place", "Always a Friendly Welcome", and "Free Parking" were popular.

Safety - A category of matchcovers whose message or advertisement includes safety or accident prevention themes.

Safety Feature/Turn Over for Striking Surface - (See SOB Warnings).

Safety First - A generic safety phrase placed on the footer (lower left portion of the front). It was used by several match companies in the 1920s and 1930s.

Safety First (Art Match Co.) - A seldom seen

footer from the Art Match Co.

Safety First (Diamond Match Co.) - This footer was popular between 1916 and the early 1920s. It preceded the DIAMOND MATCH footer on Diamond Match Co. matchcovers.

Safety First (Lion Match Co.) - This was a popular footer wording on early Lion Match Co. matchcovers. There are five known versions of the Lion Match Co. Safety First footer. Variations in type size and style are notable differences. Lion Match Co. began using this wording on its footers in 1922 and terminated it in 1930.

Safety Match/Strike on Back - (See SOB Warnings).

Safety Matches - Invented in Sweden in the early 1860s.

Safety Series - The general name for safety sets made by various matchcover companies. They usually contained five matchcover stock designs on the back, with slogans referring to auto, job, and home safety. Advertiser's name and address were usually printed on the front.

Safety Tabs - A Universal Match Corp. trademark whose matchbook provided a safety tab on the front and back of the matchcovers which had to be torn out to remove the matches. First made by Universal in 1949, there are over 75 varieties known. (See Safe-T-Lite.)

Safeway Matches - An Australian company located in Sydney, New South Wales. They used the excise mark 3/4.

Saffa Magenta - A European matchbook manumark from Italy.

Salesman's Samples - Matchcover stock that never contained matches or was never machine creased or stapled. Some businesses advertised on salesman's samples never existed but were invented by matchcover salesmen just for show. (See Flats.)

San Antonio World's Fair - Opened in 1968 in San Antonio, TX. It was lamely dubbed "The 1968 World's Fair", and issued several matchcovers. About 40 matchcovers and matchboxes have been found.(See Hemisfair '68.)

San Francisco Souvenir Set - This set consists of only four matchcovers and was issued by The Diamond Match Co. in 1939. There are two matchcovers in red and two in blue. There is a two line manumark which reads: Made in U.S.A./ THE DIAMOND MATCH CO. N.Y.C. on each matchcover, and the saddle design has 12 rays. The historical description on the back is in black ink on a yellow field. The set was also reprinted with a narrow wartime striker in 1942.

Santa Catalina Educational Set (Type I) - This set consists of 17 matchcovers issued by The Diamond Match Co. The background colors are either red or blue. The Avalon Bay matchcover in red was issued in error with the picture from the Avalon matchcover, and later corrected. The two line manumark reads: THE DIAMOND MATCH CO./ NEW YORK. This set has colored tips as opposed to Type II which has white tips. Matchcovers are blank inside. It was issued in the early 1930s. (See Educational Set.)

Santa Catalina Educational Set (Type II) - This set consists of 16 matchcovers issued by The Diamond Match Co. The background colors are either red or blue and none repeat. The two line manumark reads: Made in U.S.A./The Diamond Match Co. N.Y.C. This set, issued around 1937, has white tips as opposed to Type I which has colored tips. Matchcovers have printing inside. (See Educational Set.)

San Francisco-Oakland Bridge Souvenir Set - This set consists of only four matchcovers and was issued by The Diamond Match Co. There are two matchcovers in red and two in green. There is a two line manumark on each matchcover which reads: Made in U.S.A. Colgate Studios Division/The Diamond Match Co. N.Y.C. The saddle has a 13 colored ray design.

San Francisco-Oakland Bay Bridge Souvenir Set - This set consists of only two matchcovers and was issued by The Diamond Match Co. One matchcover shows a section of the bridge at night and the other shows it by daylight. Each has a red background. There is a two line manumark on each matchcover which reads: MADE IN U.S.A. /The Diamond Match Co. N.Y.C. The historical description on the back is in black ink against a blue field.

Satin - A category of matchcovers having horizontal satin threads across the entire surface of the matchcover.

Satinkote - A Diamond Match Co. trademark for matchcovers having a silk or rayon looking finish. (See Silktone.)

Satintone - A category of matchcovers that feels like satin or rayon. These matchcovers may come in any size.

Savings & Loan - A category of matchcovers which advertises savings and loan institutions. Usually categorized under banks as a sub category. Some collectors include credit unions.

At least 10,000 varieties known. (See S&L).

Scenic - A category of matchcovers whose advertisement mentions various outdoor locations, natural wonders, vacation spots, etc. and is often produced in sets.

Scored - The manufacturer's machine crease on either side of the saddle and at the manumark area to ease folding. (See Machine Crease.)

Scratch My Back - (See SOB Warnings).

"Scratch My Back"/For Safety. - (See SOB Warnings.)

Season's Greetings - (See Christmas.)

Seattle World's Fair - This World's Fair opened in 1962 in Seattle, WA. Officially, it issued a six matchbook set in a 20 strike, non descriptive style. The Fair's official name was The Century 21 Exposition.

Second Baseball - A set of baseball players matchcovers issued in 1935 by The Diamond Match Co. The set consists of one each of 24 different baseball players (background colors are eight in red, eight in blue and eight in green). Each matchcover in this set has a black border entirely around the picture on the front, with the history on the back.

Second Football (Type I) - A set of football players matchcovers which was issued in 1934 by The Diamond Match Co. This set differs from the First Football (Silver Set) in that each player appears on four background colors including: blue, green, red and tan. The one line manumark reads: THE DIAMOND MATCH CO., N.Y.C. and there are 456 matchcovers in this set.

Second Football (Type II) - A set of football players matchcovers which was issued in 1936 by The Diamond Match Co. This set differs from the First Football (Silver Set) in that the descriptive data changes and each player appears in one of three background colors including green, red and tan. The two line manumark reads: Made in U.S.A./THE DIAMOND MATCH CO. N.Y.C. and there are 96 matchcovers in the complete set.

Second Hockey (Tan Hockey) (Type I) - A set of hockey players matchcovers which was issued by The Diamond Match Co. Each player is shown in a frame on the front. The back of the matchcover gives a brief history of the player's career. The player's name appears at the top of the history and either the name of his team or his position appears between his name and this history. The single line manumark reads: THE

DIAMOND MATCH COMPANY, N.Y.C. and the set is comprised of 70 known matchcovers.

Second Hockey (Tan Hockey) (Type II) - A set of hockey players matchcovers which was issued by The Diamond Match Co. early in 1936. It is similar to Second Hockey (Type I) except that the name of the player's team or his position has been omitted from his record. Same manumark as Tan Hockey (Type I) and 65 known matchcovers are in this set.

Second Hockey (Tan Hockey) (Type III) - A set of hockey players matchcovers which was issued by The Diamond Match Co. issued in late 1936. This known set of 60 is similar to Second Hockey (Type II) except that the manumark is two lines and reads: Made in U.S.A./THE DIAMOND MATCH CO. N.Y.C.

Second Hockey (Tan Hockey) (Type IV) - A set of hockey players matchcovers which was issued by The Diamond Match Co. early in 1937. This set is similar to Second Hockey (Type III) except that the player's team name appears between the player's name and history record (similar to Second Hockey (Type I)). All of the players are from the Chicago Black Hawks. There are 15 known matchcovers in this set and the two line manumark reads: Made in U.S.A./ THE DIAMOND MATCH CO. N.Y.C.

Second Hockey (Tan Hockey) (Type V) - A set of hockey players matchcovers which was issued by The Diamond Match Co. late in 1938. This set is similar to Second Hockey (Type III and Type IV) except that the player's team names do not appear on the back. Instead of the team's name, the nickname of the town is used. All of the players are from the Chicago Black Hawks. The matchcover tips are tan. The manumark is the same as Second Hockey (Type III) but the set only contains 14 matchcovers.

Second Hockey (Tan Hockey) (Type VI) - A set of hockey players matchcovers which was issued by The Diamond Match Co. This is the same as Second Hockey (Type V) except that this set of 14 matchcovers has black tips. All of the players are from the Chicago Black Hawks.

Second Movies (Type I) - A set of Motion Picture Stars matchcovers issued by The Diamond Match Co. The stars appear in an oval frame with silver side pieces and base, resembling a swing picture frame. The star's name is in script on the saddle between silver bars. The history of the star's career is on the back of the matchcover without a frame effect and with a phantom cameraman and director in a chair, printed over the wording. Several stars appear on more than one matchcover but with different histories. Colors include green, red, light blue, and orchid. The one line manumark reads THE DIAMOND MATCH CO., N.Y.C. and there are 48 known matchcovers in this set.

Second Movies (Type II) - A set of Motion Picture Stars matchcovers issued by The Diamond Match Co. The appearance of this set is the same as Second Movies (Type I) except for the absence of the phantom cameraman and director printed over the history on the back of the matchcover. There are 16 matchcovers known in this set.

Second Movies (Type III) - A set of Motion Picture Stars matchcovers issued by The Diamond Match Co. This set is known as the "White Saddle Set" because the star's name in script appears across a white background. Each star appears in four different colors including blue, green, orchid and salmon. The one line manumark reads: THE DIAMOND MATCH CO., N.Y.C. and there are 152 known matchcovers in this set.

Second Movies (Type IV) - A set of Motion Picture Stars matchcovers issued by The Diamond Match Co. issued around 1935. This set is similar in appearance to Second Movies (Type III) except that there is no phantom cameraman and director printed over the history on the back of the matchcover. In other words it is a duplicate to the Second Movies (Type II) except that it has a white saddle. Each star appears in only two colors of the four assigned to this set including: orchid, blue, red, or green. There are 16 matchcovers known in this set and the one line manumark reads: THE DIAMOND MATCH CO., N.Y.C.

Second Movies (Type V) - A set of Motion Picture Stars matchcovers issued by The Diamond Match Co. in 1936. This set differs from the Second Movies (Type I) set in that each star appears four times in different colors. Colors include: blue, green, orchid, and red. The history of the star also differs from the Second Movies (Type I) set. There are 185 matchcovers in this set with one oddity (Janet Gaynor). The two line manumark reads: Made in U.S.A./THE DIAMOND MATCH CO., N.Y.C.

Second Movies (Type VI) - A set of Motion Picture Stars matchcovers issued by The Diamond Match Co. This set differs from Second Movies (Type V) in that there are different stars appearing on the front. There are 85 matchcovers known in this set with one oddity. Colors include: blue, green, orchid, and red. The two line manumark reads: MADE IN U.S.A./ THE DIAMOND MATCH CO., N.Y.C.

Second Night-Life - A set of famous personalities matchcovers issued about 1938 by The Diamond Match Co. This set is similar to the First Night-Life in that the same performers appear on the fronts of the matchcovers. Twenty four stars appear in three colors: (green, orchid, and red), making a complete set of 72 matchcovers. The tips above the strikers are white in this set, as in the first Night-Life they are black. The two line manumark reads: Made in U.S.A./THE DIAMOND MATCH CO., N.Y.C.

Separated - Matchboxes that have been taken apart and flattened for mounting in albums or displays.

Series - Two or more matchcovers issued at different times by the same advertiser, which are subject or message related.

Serrated Gold - The Universal Match Corp. version of Taffeta. (See Taffeta, Serrated Sil-ver).

Service - A category of matchcovers whose message involves non-military government employment, stations, activities or involvement of any kind. (i.e. Public Service work). Some collectors include Military matchcovers in this category. (See Military.)

Sets - Two or more matchcovers issued at the same time by one advertiser which are subject or message related. Most sets are issued in groups of 6, 8, 10, or 12 matchcovers. Some foreign sets run as high as 50 or more matchcovers. Sets fall into two major categories (1) Commercial - with product, service, business or advertising message on the matchcover (i.e. 1941 Washington Redskins Football Team sponsored by Home Laundry Service or the Syracuse China Set) or (2) Non-Commercial - without a product or commercial advertisement (i.e. The Silver Hockey Set). A popular subdivision of this category are stock design sets (i.e. girlie, safety, or hillbilly sets) where the advertisement is on the front and the stock design is on the back.

Sewn Pages - Handmade album pages which are sewn by a collector, using a strong, flexible thread, cotton string, or fishing line.

Shelling - (See Shucking.)

Sheratons - A category of matchcovers whose advertisement mentions locations of the Sheraton Hotel Chain. Over 1,300 varieties known.

Shinekote - The trade name given to the white matchcover stock which is used on most post-1975 back strike matchcovers. (See Matchcovers, Kromecoat.)

Ship Lines - A category of matchcovers whose advertisement mentions any and all methods of sea transport to include commercial lines, passenger lines, or freight lines. Also tugs, riverboats, and ferry boats. (See Cruise Lines.)

Shipping Box - Wooden container used for getting matchboxes from the match factory to the customer or distributor. Dimensions were 24" long X 18" wide X 12" high and the box usually held 144 kitchen size matchboxes.

Shucking - Any or all methods of removing the staples and match sticks from a book of matches, leaving the matchcover separated in preparation for framing, mounting, or storing. (See Stripping.)

Signet - A Universal Match Corp. trademark whose matchcovers provided the advertisement in a wedge-shaped, debossed gold or silver metallic foil finish. Most come in 30 strike size and are often Jewels. Made from 1963 to 1987. This category is often combined with foilites by matchcover collectors.

Silktone - A Universal Match Corp. trademark whose matchcovers had a silk or rayon looking finish. This matchcover usually had silk threads fraying at top and bottom. They came in a variety of sizes. (See Satinkote.)

Silver Hockey Set - A set of hockey players matchcovers which was issued by The Diamond Match Co. reportedly in 1934. This set has a silver background with a green and black set of bars running vertically from top to bottom on the left side of the matchcover. The players are shown in their playing positions and in various colors. The player's history appears in black on green on the back of the matchcover. There are 60 matchcovers known in this set and the two line manumark reads: THE DIAMOND MATCH CO./NEW YORK.

Silver Set (The) - (1) Group I Football, made in 1933. (See First Football), (2) (See Silver Hockey), (3) A set of matchcovers issued at the 1934 Chicago Century of Progress Exposition. This was a carry-over set from the year before, (4) (See New York World's Fair - 1939.)

Single - (1) One matchcover, matchbook or matchbox in a display by itself. (2) One matchcover, as opposed to a series or set.

Sirius Zundholz Fabric - A European matchbook manumark from Austria.

Sixteen-Strike - Very short lived matchbook size, with 16 match sticks. These were reported as being made by Ohio Match Co.

Skillet - A matchbox which has the message, wording or design printed directly on the matchbox itself rather than on the matchbox label (removable). (See Labels.)

Sleepy Bear (The) - (See Travelodge.)

Sleeve - (1) A cardboard container open at both ends which can hold four, six or eight matchbooks. The sleeve can be either plain or with die-cut windows to exemplify the product's name on the matchcovers. They were used for mailing sample matchbooks or presentation matchbooks by matchbook salesmen. (2) A term used by collectors to signify one of the wrapped packages which make up a case of American Ace boxes. One sleeve contains 12 cubes, and six sleeves make up one case. (3)

A term used to describe the other portion of a matchbox.

Slide - Open frame which goes around a matchbox, providing decoration and stability. Usually made of metal.

Slit Pages - Commercial matchcover album pages which are available to the collector for various matchcover sizes. (See Albums.)

Small Stock Cuts - Any reduced size design or logo art work which is used on the front, back or inside of the matchcover. Every matchcover company offers several hundred small stock cuts to be used to emphasize a customer's business or message.

Small Towns - A category of matchcovers whose advertisement or message has the locality (town with state) on the matchcover and generally comes from a town of 250 people or less (See Towns.) This category is a spin off from County Seats. Any product, business or service may be advertised. Only 20 strike matchcovers are accepted in this category. Some collectors include Americana. (See County Seats, Perkins Americana.)

Snap Lid Box - Type of box made in Italy which has a tray with a pull tab for pulling it out. When the tray comes out a certain distance, an elastic band attached to the split upper lid causes part of the lid to open. There is often advertising attached to the part of the lid which becomes visible.

Soc. Nacional de Fosforos, Lisboa - A European matchbook manumark from Portugal.

Society de Fosferos - A European matchbook manumark from Portugal.

Societe Allumettiere Marocaine - An African matchbook manumark from Morocco.

Solo - A European matchbook manumark from Czechoslovakia.

Solo Coronica - A European matchbook manumark from Austria.

Solo Jupiter - A European matchbook manumark from Czechoslovakia.

Solo Zundholz GMBH - A European matchbook manumark from Austria. The company was formed in 1903 by the merger of the seven largest companies in Austria.

Southern Match Corp - An old, defunct match company that was located in Jacksonville, FL. Operated in the 1930s.

Southern Railways Hostess Sets - There were three sets printed, one on Midget matchcovers and two on 20 strike matchcovers by Lion

Match Co. in the 1940s. On the inside of each of the 24 Midgets (known number to exist) there is a picture of the hostess with her signature. Both the first and last name of each hostess is shown. One hostess had two different pictures.

Southern Railways Hostess Sets (Daytime) - One of the 20 strike sets was a daytime view with blue sky. Each of the 21 known hostesses for this set was titled "Miss" and her last name only.

Southern Railways Hostess Sets (Nighttime) - The other 20 strike set was a nighttime view with a black background. Each of the 18 known hostesses for this set was titled "Miss" with her last name only. The pictures in the set are smaller than the Daytime set.

Souvenirs - A category of matchcovers which comes from famous places, states, cities or other locales.

Souvenir - A size class of matchcovers which pertains mostly to the 100 strike, 200 strike and 240 strike matchbook. This type of matchbook is sold primarily in souvenir shops and may or may not include a commercial message. (See Two Forty Strike, Two Hundred Strike.)

Souvenir Views (Souvenir Sets) - (See Atlantic City S.V., Chicago S.V., Cleveland S.V., Florida S.V., Grand Coulee S.V., Milwaukee S.V., New England S.V., New York S.V., San Francisco S.V., Texas S.V., Washington S.V., Williamsburg S.V.)

Sovereign - A Bryant & May trademark for a 40 stick size matchbook. Introduced in 1967 and discontinued in 1979.

Space - A category of matchcovers whose advertisement or message pertains to aerospace activities including rockets, satellites, etc. (both product and event).

Splint - The portion of the match usually held when striking the match head.

Spokane World's Fair - This World's Fair opened in 1974 in Spokane, WA but issued poorly designed, average looking matchcovers.

Sports - A popular category of matchcovers whose message pertains to college, amateur or professional athletic team or individual sports. This might include events, schedules, players, coaches, stadiums, etc. Sets, series and singles are found. Sports personalities' businesses, products or services as related to this category, is the collector's personal choice.

Spot Strikers - Another term used for Odd

Strikers. (See Odd Strikers, Misplaced Abrasive).

Spring Grip - (See Grip.)

Standard - (See Regular.)

Standard Match Co. - An old, defunct match company that was located in Chicago, IL and went out of business around 1941 or 1942.

Stand - (See Box Stand.)

Standard - A Bryant & May trademark used to describe 20 strike matchcovers.

Stanwood-Hillson Corp. (The) - An old, defunct advertising specialty company located in Brookline, MN that sold matchbooks.

Staple - The metal wire that holds the match stick combs in place within the matchcover. (See Machine Staple, Comb.)

Star Match Co. - An old, defunct match company. This is one of the companies which produced both "tall" and standard size matchcovers and was absorbed by Universal Match Corp. in the mid 1930s. Some of their matchcovers read: "Patented Sept. 27, 1892," the use of such wording which may have been granted by The Diamond Match Co.

Starline Girlies - Eight sets of girlie matchcovers made by Bryant & May (England) from 1970 through 1984.

Stem - Another term for match stick.

Sterns Co., Chicago (The) - An old, defunct advertising specialty company located in Chicago, IL that sold matchbooks. A second line on the manumark read: Mfg. by Lion Match Company, Inc.

Sticky Back - A category of matchcovers, introduced about 1955, which has an adhesive strip on the back of the matchcover for fastening it to the side of a cigarette pack. This idea remained popular only for a few years. There are over 400 varieties known. (See Press Back, Piggyback).

Stipple Finish - A Lion Match Co. trademark for matchcovers that had a waxy surface coating, spattered in a random manner over the entire surface of the matchcover. (See Filigree.)

Stock - Pertaining to the matchcovers that a collector has on hand at any one time.

Stock Design - A standard matchcover design produced by advertisers for all of their locations. This was typical for auto dealers, chain hotels, motels and restaurants. (See Cuts).

Stock Matchcover - A cooperative advertising matchcover which is shared by advertisers over a wide area of the country. The price of this kind of matchcover to the advertiser is less expensive than a non-stock design. Match companies often took an order for 1 million stock matchcovers and printed local dealer's names on lots of 50,000.

Stop Lite - A Diamond Match Co. trademark that used chemically treated match sticks which caused the light to go out after a short period of time (usually within 10 seconds.) This sometimes prevented drunks or distracted patrons, from burning their fingers. Also written Stoplite. (See Drunkards Match.)

Strike Anywhere - Wooden matchstick which will ignite when drawn over any rough surface.

Strike on Back - (See SOB Warnings).

Strike on Back Cover - (See SOB Warnings.)

Strike on the Back Cover - (See SOB Warnings.)

Strike on Box - Wooden matchstick which requires being struck on the striker surface of the box in order to ignite.

Strike Rite (NZ) Ltd. - A company which made matchcovers in New Zealand.

Strike-Rite Match Co. - A match company located in London, Ontario, Canada. It began operating in 1939 and was sold to Maryland Match Co. in 1959 but continued operations under its original name. Factory was closed in 1988.

Strike-Rite Glamour Girl Sets - Also called Strike-Rite Canadian Girlie Sets. Four sets of girlie matchcovers manufactured by the Strike-Rite Match Co. of Canada, and were produced in 1950, 1961, 1965 and 1969.

Striker - The part of the matchbook where the matches are struck in order to light them. This is usually a chemically treated, abrasive surface also known as the Striker Zone.

Striker Zone - Another term for the striker.

Striking Surface/on Back for Safety - (See SOB Warnings.)

Striking Tape - A part of the inside of a WWII vintage 40 strike matchcover near the bottom tip. The manumark appeared at this location.

Stripping - The practice of removing match sticks from matchbooks in order to prepare them for mounting. (See Shucking).

Struck - A matchcover which has match abrasions on the striker. Matchcovers on which the striker has been marked by striking a match stick. (See Used, Hit, Bitten.)

Sunburst Stock Designs - Used by various match companies in the 1940s, this design pattern augmented the advertisement. The

matchcovers were usually varnished and came in red and green only.

Super 45 - An Atlas Match Co. (TX) trademark for matchcovers which were the same width as the 30 stick issues, but contained three combs of matches rather than the usual two combs. The saddle is also wider to hold the increased bulk of the three combs.

Super Giant - Another term for the 240 strike matchbooks.

Superba Quality - A little known footer line used on Diamond Match Co. matchcovers around 1920.

Superior Match Co. - A match company located in Chicago, IL, which started in 1932 and is still a working match company.

Superior Live Models - Twelve sets of girlie matchcovers manufactured by the Superior Match Co., were produced in 1958 (2 sets), 1960, 1961, 1962 and 1969, 1971, 1973, 1976 (2), and 1977 (2).

Supermarket Sets - Two or more matchcovers of similar design that are usually purchased in a supermarket. These sets have either generic designs, generic pictures, nationally known product advertisement or wording of some kind or another. (See Grocery Store Sets, Nationals.)

Svenska Tandsticks Aktiebolaget - A European matchbook manumark from Sweden.

Swapping - The traditional exchanging of duplicate matchcovers with other collectors. (See Trading.)

Swap Fest - A local or national event at which matchcover collectors come together from all over an area or the nation to exchange matchcover information and swap or trade.

Swedish Match - Formed in December, 1917, by merger of the leading Swedish match groups. Ivar Kreuger was its first managing director.

-T-

TS - An abbreviation for 10 strike matchcovers and matchbooks.

Taffeta - A Lion Match Co. trademark whose surface exhibited horizontal striations across the entire metallic background.

Taffeta Foil - A Lion Match Co. trademark whose matchcovers had portions of the design printed with metallic foil.

Tall - Any or all matchcovers produced prior to

the beginning of the vending machine period (ca. 1940), which measured at least 4 7/8" long. Full books of this kind of matchcovers frequently had rounded saddles (no machine scoring).

Tan Hockey - (See Second Hockey.)

Taper Slim - A type of container imported by Lion Match Co. and distributed by their subsidiary Continental Match Co. It was a thin flat case of wooden match sticks, usually containing one row of sticks placed upright in the holder.

Taverns - A category of matchcovers whose advertisement mentions bars or other known places serving alcoholic beverages. (See Bars.)

Taxi Cabs - (See Transportation.)

Team Schedules - (See Colleges.)

Tear Drop - (See Filigree).

Tear-Out Tabs - (See Safety Tabs.)

Tehran Match Co. - A Middle Eastern matchcover manumark from Iran.

Telegraph Matches - A type of matches produced in the mid to late 1800s.

Temper & Hands from Igniting - (See SOB Warnings.)

Ten Strike - A smaller matchbook (one half the width of the regular 20 strike matchbook) which contains 10 match sticks (written as 10 strike). This size matchbook was first manufactured by Universal Match Corp. around 1938 and was designed to appeal to women who carried small or clutch purses. Production stopped for three years during WWII due to O.P.A. regulations. (See Half Size, Midget.)

Tenorama - Monarch Match Co. name for their color set of ten, process embossed in Silver. The set was sold in assorted colors only.

Tent - Type of matchbox whose sides come to a peak. Also known as an "A-Frame" which sums up the shape. (See A-Frame.)

Terza - A European matchbook manumark from Switzerland.

Test Set - (See First Movies (Type I).)

Texas Centennial Exposition - This Exposition opened in 1936 in Dallas, TX and issued a six matchbook set to commemorate its opening.

Texas Souvenir Set - This set consists of four blue matchcovers issued by The Diamond Match Co. The saddle has 12 rays.

Thai Match Co. - An Asian matchbook manumark from Thailand.

Thank You - A category of matchcovers whose message usually contains the words "Thank

You." (See Nationals, Vending Machine Matchbooks.)

Third Baseball (Type I) - A set of baseball players matchcovers issued in 1935 and 1936 by The Diamond Match Co. The set consists of 544 known matchcovers, but not considered complete. Players generally appeared in three colors: green, blue and red. Distinguishing characteristic for this set is a baseball appearing in the saddle area with the player's name and team only.

Third Baseball (Type II) - A set of baseball player matchcovers issued around 1938 by The Diamond Match Co. The complete set consists of 69 matchcovers, and 23 baseball players, each player appearing on three different colors: green, blue, and red. Distinguishing characteristics for this set is a baseball appearing in the saddle area with the player's name and team only. Most of the pictures are bust pictures. Two complementary sets exist, one printed in black ink and the other printed in brown ink, making a grand total of 138 matchcovers in both sets.

Third Football (Type I) - A set of football players matchcovers which was issued in 1936 by The Diamond Match Co. This set differs from the Second Football set in that the player's appear in a standing "picture frame." Background colors include: green, red, and tan, with each player appearing in only one color. Only

Now whatsh the matter with thish dad-gummed SHOWER!

members of the Philadelphia "Eagles" appear in this set. Printing is in black. The two line manumark reads: Made in U.S.A./THE DIAMOND MATCH CO. N.Y.C. and 17 matchcovers are known to comprise this set.

Third Football (Type II) - A set of football players matchcovers which was issued in 1936 by The Diamond Match Co. This set differs from Third Football (Type I) in that the player's position on the team appears between the player's name and the description on the back of the matchcover. Background colors are the same as in Third Football (Type I): green, red and tan and each player appears in only one color. All players are members of the Chicago "Bears" with the exception of Don Jackson. This set of 30 known matchcovers is printed in black with a two line manumark that reads: Made in U.S.A./THE DIAMOND MATCH CO. N.Y.C.

Third Football (Type III) - A set of football players matchcovers which was issued in 1936 by The Diamond Match Co. It is practically the same as Third Football (Type I) except that it is printed in brown. Some of the background colors also differ for each player. All 17 of the players in the set are members of the Philadelphia "Eagles" and the two line manumark reads: Made in U.S.A./ THE DIAMOND MATCH CO. N.Y.C.

Third Football (Type IV) - A set of football players matchcovers which was issued in 1937 by The Diamond Match Co. It is practically the same as Third Football (Type II) except that the color of the ink used in printing is brown. The list of players is exactly the same as Third Football (Type II) with the exception of Raymond Nolting appearing in two background colors. All players are members of the Chicago "Bears" with the exception of Don Jackson. The two line manumark for this 31 matchcover set reads: Made in U.S.A./THE DIAMOND MATCH CO N.Y.C.

Third Football (Type V) - A set of football players matchcovers which was issued in 1937 by The Diamond Match Co. This set is similar to Third Football (Type IV) except that the printing size of the descriptive data is smaller and the color of the printing is brown. Players are members of the Chicago "Bears" and each appears three times in background colors: green, red and tan. The two line manumark for this 72 matchcover set reads: Made in U.S.A./THE

DIAMOND MATCH CO. N.Y.C.

Third Football (Type VI) - A set of football players matchcovers which was issued in 1938 by The Diamond Match Co. This set is similar to Third Football (Type V) except the printing is black instead of brown. The two line manumark for this set of 24 matchcovers (each player appears in only one color) reads: Made in U.S.A./THE DIAMOND MATCH CO. N.Y.C.

Thirty-Stick - (30 Stick) - A Lion Match Co. trademark for its 30 stick matchbooks.

Thirty-Strike - A matchcover, just a little larger than the regular matchcover, containing 30 match sticks (written as 30 strike). There are several slight variations to the exact size of this matchcover, depending on the manufacturer. Packs sometimes contained 28 match stems. The Ohio Match Co. issued the first 30 stick matchbook in 1948.

Thompson Models - Five sets of girlie matchcovers drawn by the artist Thompson, were produced in 1953, 1954, 1955, 1956, and 1957. Produced by Superior Match Co.

Three-D (3D) - Matchcovers having a three-dimensional picture design. (See Lenticular.)

Tip - On front strike matchcovers, the end of the matchcover nearest the striker zone. Also, the end of the head of a matchstick.

Town - A category of matchcovers which encompasses any and all locations that have the city or town (with the state) as part of the message or advertisement. (See Small Towns).

Town Talk Bread Set - This 20 strike, 20 matchcover set was manufactured by Match Corp of Chicago, IL. The set contained popular radio broadcasters of the time. This set is also known as "20 Great Radio Stars." It came out in the mid-1940s.

Trade Schools - (See Commercial Colleges.)

Trademark - The manufacturer's brand name of the matchcover often appearing in the manumark, but also can appear inside. The trademark, however, may not be present at all. (See Manumark, Inside).

Trader - (1) Another collector with whom a collector exchanges matchcovers. (2) A matchcover used for trading.

Trading - Exchanging duplicate matchcovers (usually without charge to either collector) with other collectors. (See Swapping.)

Trading Stock - Any and all dupes or extra matchcovers used for swapping.

Tramp Art - Non-commercial items that are

made out of match sticks, matchcovers or various other commonplace items (popsicle sticks, bottle caps, etc.). These items can include lamps, jewelry boxes, statues, covered cigar boxes and ladies purses. (This style of American art is also known as Prison Art or Folk Art.)

Transportation - A general category of matchcovers whose advertisement mentions any form of commercial or paid travel or transportation, including (1) Class One Transportation - airlines, commercial ship lines (steamships), railroads and (2) Class Two Transportation - bus lines, truck lines, cruise lines, jitneys, taxi cabs, etc. A number of collectors do not include Railroads in this general category.

Travelodge - A category of matchcovers whose advertisement mentions the Travelodge Motel chain. Each matchcover features "The Sleepy Bear" symbol. This category became generic in 1960 (no individual sites mentioned).

Tray - The sliding center portion of a matchbox, which holds the match sticks. (See Inner.)

Trivia - A specific set of 66 numbered matchcovers issued by the Ohio Match Co. This is a Supermarket Set. The matchcovers are numbered 1 through 67, but number 40 was not issued due to the death of Charles Lindbergh a few weeks before release of the set in 1974. (See Supermarket Sets.)

Truck Lines - A category of matchcovers whose advertisement mentions any and all forms of cargo haulers or carriers. Also spelled Trucklines. (See Transportation.)

Tru-Color - A Lion Match Co. trademark whose matchcovers have a four color photograph as part of the design, printed both on the back and front of the matchcover. Production began in 1956. Early issues were marked as "True-Color" instead of "Tru-Color." (See Matchoramas, Vista-Lite).

Tulip Match Co. - An old, defunct match company that was located in Newark, NJ.

Tulip Match - The footer wording used by the Tulip Match Co.

Turkay Istinye - An Asian matchcover manumark from Turkey.

Turn Over for/Striking Surface - (See SOB Warnings.)

Turn Over to Strike - (See SOB Warnings.)

Turn Over/Scratch My Back - (See SOB Warnings.)

Twelve-Up (12-Up) - An Arrow Match Co. trademark whose matchbooks had 12 match sticks inside. First made in 1940, production stopped during WWII due to O.P.A. regulations. (See Midget.)

Twelve Strike - A smaller matchbook containing 12 match sticks (written as 12 strike). This size was made by the Maryland Match Corp. starting in 1951 and is still in production.

Twenty-Four Strike - A matchbook holding 24 match sticks, made by Columbia Match Co. in the late 1970s and early 1980s.

Twenty-One Feature (21-Feature) - A Lion Match Co. trademark for its 30 strike size matchcovers that contained 21 wide stick panes. Production started in the mid 1930s. (See Features.)

Twenty Strike - The regular (or standard) size matchcover with 20 match sticks. This is the most popular size matchcover in the hobby, normally measuring 1 1/2" X 4 1/2". (Written as 20 strike.)

Twin Packs - A marketing device used by various companies in the 1930s and 1940s. Two matchbooks were packaged in cellophane and distributed to retailers. Wartime restrictions on cellophane eventually resulted in a thin strip of glue being used to fasten the two backs of the matchcovers together.

Two-Forty Strike - The longest size matchcover (nearly 13" long), generally reserved for souvenir shops and vacation spots. Contains 240 match sticks. Earliest dated examples of this matchcover are from 1939. (written as 240 strike) (See Souvenir, Jumbo King.)

Two-Hundred Strike - The second longest size matchcover, generally reserved for souvenir shops and vacation spots. Contains 200 match sticks. (written as 200 strike). (See Souvenir.)

-Type - A suffix used to denote matchcovers similar to a trademark style but made by other companies. Matchcover collectors usually group similar matchcovers under one name for ease of listing. Thus, a Uniglo is made by Universal and a Uniglo type matchcover is a similar style made by any other company. (See Feature-Type.)

-U-

UES - An abbreviation for United Eastern Swapfest, held annually in Hagerstown, MD.

USPS - An abbreviation for the United States Postal Service.

UPS - An abbreviation for United Parcel Service.

U.S. Pat. No. 1,735,258. Patented in Canada 1929 - The first part of an older Lion Match Co. manumark. The second line reads: Lion Match Co., N.Y. Made in U.S.A. An earlier version of the second line reads: Lion Match Co. New York.

U.S. Stationery Corp. - An old, defunct advertising specialty company located in Elizabeth, NJ that sold matchbooks.

U.S. Business Card Co. - An old, defunct advertising specialty company located in New York City that sold matchbooks.

U.S. Novelty Co. - An old, defunct advertising specialty company located in New York City that sold matchbooks.

Ultraslim - A Diamond Match Co. trademark for a style of matchbox, smaller than the pocketbox slim, measuring 2" X 2 3/4" when opened and flattened. This box was first introduced in 1984. Over 2,000 varieties have been reported.

Uniglo (Uni-Glo) - A Universal Match Corp. trademark whose matchcover surface appears to be like styrofoam or melted silk and seems to glow with bright colors. There are more than 9,000 varieties known. The Uniglo II is a later version of this style with a slightly different surface appearance. Produced from 1972 to 1987.

Union Allumettiere, S.A. - A European matchbook manumark from Belgium.

Union Match - A European matchcover manumark from Belgium.

Union Match Co. - An old, defunct match company that started in 1926 and was located in New York City and Hudson, NY. It went out of business in 1938 and was absorbed by Federal Match Corp. They made principally "Tall" matchcovers. (See Tall.)

Union Match Co. - An old, defunct match company that was located in Duluth, MN, around 1900. It mostly produced kitchen boxes.

Union Label - A part of the manumark indicating the symbol of a union shop. This symbol is offered to the matchbook customer but is not frequently required.

Union Quality - The wording used on the footer line of matchcovers produced by the Union Match Co., of New York City and Hudson, NY, used between 1929 and 1934.

Unit Match Co. - An old, defunct match company that produced Disc Wheel matches in the late

1930s or early 1940s. The factory was probably located in Elizabeth, NJ.

United Eng. Corp - An old, defunct printing or advertising specialty company located in Kenilworth, NJ that specialized in printing matchcovers. This company operated in the early 1930s.

United Match Co. - Another name for the U.S. Match Co., an old, defunct match compnay.

United Matchonians - A matchcover club which started in 1936 and was organized by Colonel Ernest Damron, Sistersville, WV. This club never held a meeting. It ceased operating in 1951.

United States Match Corp. - An old, defunct match company that was located in New York City .

United States Match Co. - An old, defunct match company that was located in Detroit, MI.

Universal Match Corp. - An active match company which was located in Missouri until 1987, and started production in 1925. Now part of Diamond Brands. Primarily a matchcover producer, but boxes were issued during World War II and after 1977.

Universal Match Corp., Sao Paulo - A South American matchbook manumark from Brazil. Universal Match began operating in Brazil in 1955.

Universities - (See Colleges.)

Unscored - A matchcover which does not have traditional saddle machine creases, but is still considered a true matchcover.

Unstruck - Matchcovers that have not been struck by a match. (See Unused.)

Unused - Matchcovers that have no marks on the strikers. (See Unstruck.)

Used - Matchcovers on which the striker has been marked by striking a match stick against it. (See Struck, Hit, Bitten.)

-V-

V.A. Hospitals - A category of matchcovers whose advertisement mentions the various Veterans Administrations Hospitals (not Military Hospitals) around the country. These are generally seen as blue 40 strike matchcovers. (Some are known in silver). At their peak, there were 176 V.A. Hospitals, with at least one in every state including Washington, D.C. and Puerto Rico.

VIP - A category of matchcovers whose message or advertisement mentions a very important person or celebrity. This might include his/her place of business or just a personal matchcover. (See Personalities.)

V.F.W. - (See Veterans Clubs, Fraternal.)

Vargas Girlies - One set of girlie matchcovers made by the Ohio Match Company in 1953. The artist was Alberto Vargas.

Vending Machine Matchbooks - Any or all matchbooks that come from a vending machine, usually with a national advertisement or a Thank You on the matchcover. (See Nationals, Thank You.)

Vertical - A full length matchcover with its message or design laid out so that you have to hold the matchcover vertically in order to read it.

Vesuvian - A type of match made in the mid 1800s.

Veterans Clubs - A category of matchcovers whose advertisement mentions any or all veterans organizations (i.e. VFW, Amvets, American Legion, etc.). (See Fraternals.)

Vista-Lite - A Western Match Co. trademark which used a four-color photograph as part of the design on some issues. Most have a serial number from C-1 to C-1127. Not all Vista-Lites have numbers. Series introduced around 1964 and ran to 1971. (See Matchorama, Tru-Color.)

Vista-Lite Canadian Girls Series - A single set first issued in 1964 (the panel above the manumark was blank). Later, they were reissued with "Memories of Summer" and finally with "Souvenirs Estivaux" added under the English. This manumark read: Western Match Co.

-W-

W.A. Match Co. - An Australian company formed in 1930 with a factory in West Perth, Western Australia. Their excise mark was 15/1.

WIMCO - An abbreviation for the Western India Match Co. Ltd.

Wagon Tongue - A older trademark used by the Lion Match Co., with "wagon tongue" inserted inside. The front must be lifted and the message read to use the matches.

Walt Disney World - A category of matchcovers which are issued for various places in the Walt Disney World area. Over 50 basic types have been produced. Opened in 1971.

Want List - A collector's personal list of matchcovers needed for sets, serials or collections. A want list can be made up of photos, photos with names, lists of names or lists of numbers. The American Ace want list is a series of 10,000 numbers. When you get a box, you simply cross off its number.

Washington, D.C. Souvenir Set - This set consists of eight matchcovers, four in red and four in blue. The saddle is made up of a 12 ray design. At least two variations exist in this set, later issues have four red and four blue matchcovers with a 12 ray design.

Washington Nov. Co. - An old, defunct advertising specialty company located in Washington, D.C. that sold matchbooks.

Washington State Apple - Subject of some early contour shaped matchcovers manufactured by The Diamond Match Co. It was a National matchcover with a coupon for a pastry knife inside.

Wax Vesta - A type of small match which is made of wax.

West Virginia Match Co - An old, defunct match company that was located in Wheeling, WV. Absorbed by Universal Match Corp. in 1939.

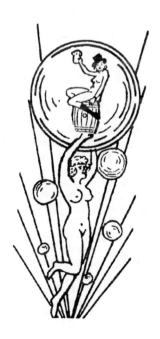

Western India Match Co. Ltd - A company that produces matchcovers in India.

Western Match Co. - An old, defunct match company. Manumarks used include Grant-Mann and Vista Lite products as well as Western Match Co. It was eventually taken over by Strike-Rite Matches, Ltd. Produced matches in the 1960s from a factory in British Columbia, CN.

Wide Stick Features - (see Features).

Williamsburg Souvenir Set - This set is believed to consist of four red and four blue matchcovers issued by The Diamond Match Co. The saddle is made up of a 12 ray design.

Willens & Co., Inc. Print - An old, defunct advertising specialty company located in Chicago, IL that sold matchbooks. Established in 1900 but match operations were in the 1930s.

Wise Man Strike on Back/Save - (see SOB Warnings).

Wooden Match Sticks - Match sticks that are made out of wood rather than cardboard. Most foreign matchbooks of earlier issue and many present foreign matchbooks use wooden sticks.

Wood Grain - A category of matchcovers having a background design (or portion thereof) in a woodgrain pattern. Printed by several match companies, these matchcovers usually appealed to owners of resorts, restaurants with a knotty pine effect, ranches and so on. Usually printed in brown ink and issued as a stock design.

Woody - Slang for Wood Grain.

World's Fair - A category of matchcovers whose advertisement mentions either an internationally recognized World's Fair or World's Fair event or may advertise a commercial product, business, or service as related to a World's Fair.

World Match - An old, defunct match company manumark used by the World Match Corp. Ltd. It was renamed from Match Co. Ltd. in May 1923 and merged with E.B. Eddy Co. Ltd, Dominion Match Co. Ltd. and Canadian Match Co. Ltd. in December 1927 to form the Eddy Match Co. Ltd. Factory was located in Berthierville, Quebec, CN.

World War I Issue - Matchcovers known to exist that were issued during WW I are: Knights of Columbus (Two issues (a) Safety First, 20 strike, (b) "Our Doughboys; American Red Cross (Safety First issue); Pennsylvania Keystone division (28th Division, with state insignia on front and back); Buy Fifth Liberty Bonds;

Cramp Shipyards (of Philadelphia, Pa.

Wrapper - A piece of paper which is used to contain matches. Used more in the 1800s for some types of matches which were not packed in boxes.

Wrigley Gum Cartoon Set - All matchcovers had a standard Wrigley Gum advertisement on the outside, but the inside had a series of at least 43 different corny cartoons drawn by Art Heifant. This 1935 set was distributed as a national (see Nationals) in a hit-or-miss fashion, and collecting started late.

-Y-

Yacht Clubs - (see Legitimate Clubs).

Yellow Set (The) - (see Disney).

York Printing Company - An old, defunct printing company located in Chicago, IL which specialized in printing matchcovers.

-Z-

ZIP Code - A USPS addressing requirement instituted on July 1, 1963 to improve on the older Zone System. (see Zone System).

Zone - (see Striker, Reverse Striker, SOB, Back Striker).

Zone Sales Co. - An old, defunct advertising specialty company located in Delray Beach, FL that sold matchbooks.

Zone System - A USPS addressing requirement instituted on May 1, 1943 and terminated on June 30, 1963. It was used to help facilitate mail delivery.

Zundholzer - The German word for matches.

Zundholzreklame - A European matchcover manumark from Switzerland.

The American Matchcover
Collecting Club

APPLICATION FORM

You are cordially invited to join **The American Matchcover Collecting Club** and continue your enjoyment of this truly great American Hobby. As of June 1993, membership fees are:

U.S. Bulk Rate ($12.50)
U.S.Regular Class & Canadian ($17.50) Overseas ($28.00)

Please include a registration fee for ALL new memberships:

$2.00 (U.S.), $2.50 (CN), $3.50 (Overseas)

Rates subject to change without notice during the life of this book

Please enter my membership in **The American Matchcover Collecting Club**. I understand that I will receive four issues of *The Front Striker Bulletin*, membership in **AMCC**, and four special political matchcovers valued at $10.00.

NAME:_____

ADDRESS: (___) _____

CITY:_____STATE:_____ZIP:_____

PHONE: (_____) _____

DATE OF BIRTH: (month & day only)_____

COLLECTING PREFERENCES: _____

_____

_____

____ - Check here if you want your phone number listed in the annual AMCC Member Directory

____ - Check here if you want to know about a local matchcover club in your area

Make Check Payable To:

The American Matchcover Collecting Club
PO Box 18481
Asheville, NC 28814

704/254-4487   24-Hour FAX: 704/254-1066

Appendix

F.A.A. Regulations for Matches

The following regulations were secured from the FAA/Office of Civil Aviation Security ACS 120, 800 Independence Ave S.W., Washington, D.C. 20591.

Matches are classified as a hazardous material. The description is as follows:

Safety Matches

Description: Matches, safety, book, card, or strike on box

Hazard Class: Flammable solid; Identification Number: UN1944; Labels required: None; Packaging Exceptions: 173.176 (see below); Packaging Specific requirements: None; Max. net quantity in one package:.

Passenger carrying aircraft or railcar: 50 pounds

Cargo aircraft only: 50 pounds

Strike Anywhere

Description: Matches, strike anywhere; Hazard Class: Flammable solid; Identification Number: UN1331; Labels required: Flammable solid; Packaging Exceptions: None; Packaging Specific requirements: 173.176a (see below); Max. net quantity in one package:.

Passenger carrying aircraft or railcar: Forbidden

Cargo aircraft only: Forbidden

Page 477 of the Research and Special Programs Administration, DOT code further expands regulation 173.176 and 173.176a as follows:

173.176 Safety Matches

(a) Safety matches (strike on box, book, and card) are matches which are intended to be ignited on a prepared surface. Safety matches, when offered for transportation, must be of a type which will not ignite spontaneously or undergo marked decomposition when subjected for eight consecutive hours to a temperature of 200 degrees Fahrenheit (93.3 degrees Celsius). As used in this section, the term "safety matches" includes matches combined with or attached to the box, book, or card.

(b) Safety matches must be tightly packed in securely closed inside packagings to prevent accidental ignition under condition normally incident to transportation, and further packed in outside fiberboard, wooden, or other equivalent type packagings. Safety matches in outside packagings not exceeding 50 pounds gross weight are not subject to any other requirement (except marking) of this subchapter. Safety matches may be packed in the same outside packaging with materials not subject to this subchapter.

173.176a Strike Anywhere Matches

(a) Strike anywhere matches are matches which may be ignited by friction on a solid surface. Strike anywhere matches, when offered for transportation, must be of a type which will not ignite spontaneously or undergo marked decomposition when one complete inside package is subjected for eight consecutive hours to a temperature of 200 degrees Fahrenheit (93.3 degrees Celsius).

(b) Strike anywhere matches may not be packed in the same outside packaging with any material other than safety matches. The safety matches must be packed in separate inside packagings.

(c) Inside packagings. Strike anywhere matches must be tightly packed in securely closed chipboard, fiber board, wooden, or metal inside packagings to prevent accidental ignition under conditions normally incident to transportation. Each inside packaging may contain no more than 700 strike anywhere matches.

(d) Outside packagings. Strike anywhere matches must be packed in specification packagings as follows:

(1) Spec. 15A or 19B (code ref: 178.191 of this subchapter). Wooden boxes, with inside packages. Gross weight must not exceed 100 pounds.

(2) Spec. 12B or 12C (code ref: 178.205, 178.206 of this subchapter). Fiberboard boxes, with inside packages. Gross weight must not exceed 60 pounds. Fill in pieces specified by code ref: 178.205 14 or code ref: 178.206 14 of this subchapter are not required.

U.S. Postal Regulations for Matches

(From the DMM (Domestic Mail Manual) Code 124.3 on Hazardous Matter.)

On page 93 of the Domestic Mail Manual (DMM), the Hazardous Matter section begins with Chemicals and Explosives (neither category of which contains matches), and about mid way down the page, starts with section 124.33 Flammable Materials. After Flammable Liquids, Combustible Liquids, Flammable Solids and Oxidizers, the code gets to section 124.335, Matches. From here on I quote chapter and verse.

a. Strike anywhere matches may not be mailed.

b. Safety matches (book, card, or strike on box) are mailable domestically only when they meet the following conditions:

(1) They will not ignite spontaneously when subjected for eight consecutive hours to a temperature of 200 degrees Fahrenheit (93.3 degrees Celsius).

(2) They will not ignite spontaneously under conditions normally incident to transportation.

(3) They can be readily ignited by friction only by striking on their own box, or similar box, card, or book.

(4) Each parcel containing matches weighs not more than 50 pounds gross weight.

(5) They are packed tightly to prevent movement within the container and to prevent ignition caused by rubbing against adjoining boxes, books, or cards.

(6) They may be packed in the same outside container with nonflammable articles if they are packed in outside fiberboard or containers or securely wrapped so as to prevent accidental ignition.

(7) When packed with nonflammable articles, shipments must be marked, BOOK MATCHES, STRIKE ON CARD MATCHES, OR CARD MATCHES.

(8) If they are not packed with other articles, no marking, labeling, or certification is required.

(9) For air transportation, a label, SHIPPER'S DECLARATION FOR DANGEROUS GOODS, is also required.

c. All matches are prohibited in the international mail.

AUCTION LEGEND:

100S-One Hundred Strike, 10S-Ten Strike, 12S-Twelve Strike, 1B-One Box, 20S-Twenty Strike, 24S-Twenty-Four Strike, 240S-Two-Forty Strike, 30S-Thirty Strike, 40S-Forty Strike, AL-American League, AQ-American Quality, B-Back, BK/WE-Black & White, BAR-Barrel, BE-Blue, BF-Base Friction, BK-Black, BL-Box Label, BS-BackStriker, C-Cover, CA-Cameo, CCC-Civilian Conservation Corps, CM-Cream, CON-Contour, DBE-Dark Blue, DOI-Declaration of Independence,DQ-Diamond Quality, DS-Double Striker, E-Empty or End, EQ-Eddy Quality, F-Front, F/B-Front & Back, FEA-Lion Feature, FB-Full Book, FL-Full Length, FO-foilite, FS-Front Striker, FT-Flat (Salesman's Sample), G-Giant, GD-Gold, GGIE-Golden Gate Int'l Exposition, GMC-Girlie Matchcover Catalogue, GN-Green, GPF-Giant Poster Feature, GY-Gray, H-Horizontal, HB-Halfback, HOF-Hall of Fame, HR-Home Run, I-Inside, INC-Includes, JWL-Jewel, JLT-Jewelites, KB-Kitchen Box, L-Labels, LBA-League Batting Average, LBE-Light Blue, LGY-Light Gray, M-Midget, MS-Mixed Strikers, MVP-Most Valuable Player, MZ-Mixed Sizes, N/S-Non Stock, NL-National League, NM-Non Match, NYWF-New York World's Fair, O-Outside, OD-Orchid, OE-Orange, P36-Perfect "36." PAT-Patriotic, PE-Purple, PK-Pink, PQ-Pull Quick, QB-Quarterback,RAMA - Matchorama, RD-Red, RF-Royal Flash, RM-Row Missing for Mounting, RR-Railroad, S-Saddle, SF-Safety First, SG-Signet, SOL-Statue of Liberty, SR-Silver, SS-Spot Striker, T&P-Trylon & Perisphere, TN-Tan, U-Used or Struck, UN-Uniglo, UQ-Union Quality, V-Vertical, VIP-Very Important Person, VP-Vice President, W-Wooden, WE-White, WG-Woodgrain, WS-Wooden Sticks (Book Match), YW-Yellow.

Matchcover Categories and Contact Persons

The following is a list of topic names, approximate number of matchcovers reported (in parenthesis), and the name of listing editor (if a list is being published). An asterisk (*) indicates that a list was once published, but has no current editor. Bracketed names are collectors who can answer basic question on the topic. For a complete address on any of these editors, send an SASE to: AMCC, PO Box 18481, Asheville, NC 28814.

Airlines (115 pages) Wray Martin; American Ace Boxes (9,150) Clem Pater; Atlas Four Color (600) Bob Hiller; Beer (555) Rich Klabacha; Best Western (120 pages) Terry Rowe; Bicentennial (1,500) John Williams/Clem Pater; Cameos (7,700) * ( ); Canadian Four Color (1,280) Wray Martin; Canadian Navy Ships (400) * (Pat Griffiths); CCC Camps (215) John Williams; Colgate Bridge Covers (2,100) John Williams; Contours (873) Emily Hiller; County Seats (3,200) Clem Pater; Disneyworld (100) Bill Thomas; Eddy Boxes (410) Larry & Carol Ziegler; Elks (BPOE) (53 pages) Seymour Shedlow; foilites (11,100) Ruth Hagan; Four Seasons Hotels (28 sets) Stan Tombs; Girlies (65 pages) Bob Borton/John Kern; Group One (66 pages) * (John Williams); Hilton Non-Stock (600) John Williams; Holiday Inn 4 Color Sets (900) John Williams; Holiday Inn Non-Stock (3,050) John Williams; Inter-Continental Hotels (417) John Williams; Japanese Boxes (6,500) Les Good; Jewels (5,000) Evelyn Hovious/Clem Pater; Jewelites (5,666) Ruth Hagan/Larry Sanger; Labels & Match Sales ( ) Bob Jones; Matchoramas (6,000) Evelyn Hovious; Midgets (4,252) Emily Hiller; Military Royal Flash (2,000) Mike Hickey; Navy Ships pre/post War (1,100/2,000) * (Steve Kovacs, Jr.); Odd Strikers (300) John Williams; Pocketboxes (7,750) Paul Moyer; Pocketbox Slims (3,100) Paul Moyer; Sports (291 pages) Bill Hubbard; Sports 30-Stick Size (400) Art Houser; Stickyback (200) John Williams; Ultraslim Boxes (1,750) Paul Moyer; Uniglos (10,200) Dorothy Fry; World's Fair (NY 1939) (370) Bill Retskin.

Company Trademarks

Trademark	Company	Trademark	Company
Action	Universal	Fire Chief	Pacific
Ambassador	Diamond	Firechief	Universal
American Ace	Universal	Florentine	Universal
American Quality	American	Foil Tab	American
Aristocrat	Universal	Foilite	Universal
Armadillo	Ohio	Giant	Lion
Atlantic	Diamond	Giant Feature	Lion
Atlas 45	Atlas	Globe	Diamond
Atlas Four Color	Atlas	Gold Medal	Diamond
Aztec	Lion	Golden State	Diamond
Big Ben	Sweden	Granada	Monarch
Billboard	Universal	Green Diamond	Diamond
Bird's Eye	Diamond	Green Goddess	Diamond
Blot-r Match	Union	Green Hat	Lion
Blue Tip	Ohio	Greenlites	Bryant & May
Brymay	Bryant & May	Grenada	Monarch
Cameo	Universal	Jewel	Universal
Camera Color	Monarch	Jewelite	Universal
Canal Zone	Sweden	Junior	Ohio
Centurylite	Universal	Jupiter One-Eight	Universal
Classique	Universal	Jute	Atlas
Classique 180	Universal	King	Lion
Clover Farm Quality	Diamond	Kohinoor	Helio
Contour	Lion	Lancer, The	Sweden
Copperhead	Diamond	La Petite	Sweden
Cordon Bleu	Sweden	Lite-King	Pacific
De-Lite	Pacific	Major	England
Dependable	Pacific	Magno Quality	Magna
Diamond Quality	Diamond	Maple Leaf	Eddy
Diplomat	Lion	Match Buds	Bell Machine
Display	Lion	Matchorama	Universal
Domino	Diamond	Matchtone	Universal
Drunkard's Match	Lion	Midget	Lion
Eagle 20	Columbia	Mirro-Gloss	Universal
Eagle 24	Columbia	Model	Lion
Eagle 30	Columbia	National Safety	Federal
Easel Back	Lion	No Name	Korea
Eddylites	Eddy	Orleans	Monarch
Emboss-O-Match	Universal	Owname	Owname
Empire Quality	Empire	Palmetto	Barber
Ever-Glo	Maryland	Peacock	England
Extend n'Ad	Universal	Perfect 36	Diamond
Feature	Lion	Pocketbox	Diamond
Filigree	Universal	Pocketbox Slim	Diamond

Trademark	Company
Poster Feature	Lion
Protecto	Diamond
Pullmatch	Am. Pullmatch
Diamond Race	Barber
Radiant	Radiant
Rainbow	Universal
Red Bird	General
RF	France
Rizla+	Sweden
Red Head	Pacific
Red Top	Diamond
Redbird	Eddy
Rosebud	Ohio
Royal Flash	Universal
Safe Home	Diamond
Safe-T-Lite	Universal
Safety Match Veil	Lion
Search Light	Diamond
Sesqui	Eddy
Signet	Universal
Silktone	Universal
Soveriegn	England
Sta-Dri	Diamond
Star	Clark/Star
Strikalite	Palmer
Stipple Finish	Lion
Stone's Pocket	Diamond
Stone's Quality	Diamond
Stop-Lite	Diamond
Sunset	Pacific
Superba Quality	Diamond
Swan	Diamond
Tacoma	Pacific
Taffeta	Lion
Taffeta Foil	Lion
Ten-Strike	Universal
Three Plumes	Trinidad
Three Torches	Trans/Match
Three Torches	Union
True-Color	Lion
Ultra Slim	Diamond
Uncle Sam	Diamond
Uniglo	Universal
Union Match Quality	Union
Union Quality	Union
Victoria	Universal
Vulcan Safety	Vulcan
Wagon Tongue	Lion

(. . . and a few additional Trademarks)

Trademark	Company
12 Up	Arrow
Black Swan	Diamond
Blue Moon	General
Blue Ribbon	Diamond
Chips	Diamond
Doubl' Book	Arrow
Home	Diamond
Hy-Grade	West Virginia
Johnny Walker	Palmer
Little Star	Diamond
Miown	Diamond
Ohio Noiseless	Ohio
Palmer	Palmer
Pla-Safe	Ohio
Real-Lite	General
Red Bird	General
Signal Light	Diamond
True American	Diamond

Yes! Even Bull Dogs

Matchcover Collecting Categories

--A--
AAA (All Kinds)
AAA Hotels
AAA Motels
Action
Adam Hats
Advance Match Co.
Adveraps
Advertising
Africa
Agriculture Related
Air Corps
Air Force (all)
Air Force One
Airlines

Airports
Alabama
Alaska
Albert Pick
Alberta
All Sizes
Alligators
American Ace Boxes
American Hotel
  Association
American Legion
American Quality
Americana
Anchors
Angels
Animals

Anniversaries
Apples
Aristocrat
Arizona
Arkansas
Army (U.S.)

Arrow Match Co.
Asia
Astronauts
Atlantic City (General)
Atlantic City Casinos

Atlas Four Color
Attorneys & Lawyers
Australia
Autographed
Automobile

Automobile (Chevy)
Automobile (Dated)
Automobile (Ford)
Automobile (Non U.S.)
Automobile (Old)
Automobile (Oldsmobile)
Automobile (Pontiac)
Automobile Dealers

--B--
Babies
Bahamas
Balloons
Bank Checks
Banks
Banks (First National)
Barber Shops

Barrels
Bars

Baseball
Bears
Beauty Shops
Beer
Bell Machine Co.
Belly Dancing
Bermuda
Best Western
Best Western (Non
  Stock)
Beverages
Bicentennial
Bicycles
Big Boy Restaurants
Billboards
Billiards
Birds
Birthdays
Black & White Photos
Black People
Black Ravens
Boats
Bowling Alleys

Boxes
Boxes (Foil)
Boxes (Intact)
Boxes (Japanese)
Boxes (Kitchen)
Boxes (Plastic)
Boxes (Swedish)
Boxes (Tent)
Boxing
Bread
Breweries

Bridge Sets
Bridges
British

British Columbia
Brothels
Buffalo/Bison
Bus Lines, Trans.

Businesses
Butterflies

--C--
Cable Cars
Cafés
California
Cameos
Canadian
Canadian Centennial
  1967
Canadian Four Color
Canadian Hotels
Canadian Navy Ships
Canadian Restaurants
Canadian Tax Stamps
Candy

Cans
Cape Cod
Carousels
Cartoon Characters
Casinos
Cats
Caves
CCC Camps
Centurylite
Chef Hats
Chewing Gum
Chimney Sweeps
Chinese Restaurants
Christmas
Cigar Related
Cigarettes
City & Town & State

Classiques
Clicks
Clowns
Clubs
Clubs (Private)
Coal

Coca-Cola
Coffee
Colgate
Colleges
Colleges & Universities
Colorado
Combos
Comical
Commemorative
Conjunctives
Connecticut
Contact Sets
Contest Sets
Contours
Cornucopia/Horn of
    Plenty
Country Clubs
Country Music
County Seats
Cowboys
Cows

Credit Unions
Crests
Crocodiles
Crown Match Co.
Crowns
Cruise Lines

--D--
Dancing/Dancers
Dated
Dealer Imprints
Delaware
Delicatessens

Department Stores
Devils
Diamond Color
Diamond Pocketboxes
Diamond Quality
Diamond Safety First
Die Cuts
Diners
Dinosaurs
Disc Wheels
Disney (General)
Disney Land
Disney World
Disney/Pepsi
Displays
District of Columbia
Doctors
Dog Racing
Dogs

Double Length
Double-Double
Drinking Establishments
    (All)
Drive-In Theatres
Drug Stores

--E--
Eagles (F.O.E.)
Easel Backs
Eating Places (General)
Eddy Match Sets
Eddy Quality
Elks (B.P.O.E.)

Embossed
Entertainment
Errors
Eskimos
Ethnic Restaurants
Europe
Extend 'n Ad

--F--
Fairs & Expos (General)
Famous Places
Fancy
Farm Implements (All)
Fast Food Restaurants

Feature Manumarks
Feature Type
Features
Federal Match Co.
Filigrees
Financial Institutions
Fire Departments
First Names
Fish
Flags
Flats
Florentine
Florida
Florists
Flowers

Say It With Flowers

Foilites
Food
Football
Foreign, non-U.S.
Fountain
France
Franklin D. Roosevelt
Fraternal
Fred Harvey (Related)
French Restaurants
Frogs
Front Strikers
Fruits & Vegetables
Full Books
Full Length
Funeral Homes
Furniture Stores

--G--
Gambling Related
Gas Stations

Gay Related
Gem Razor Blades
General
Georgia
Germany
Giants
Giants (Features)
Girlies

Girlies (Nudes)
Girlies (Risque)
Girlies (Sets)
Girlies (Singles)
Golf

Golf Courses
Gondolas
Government Agencies
Governors
Grant-Mann
Green Hat
Group One
Group One (Baseball)
Group One (Football)
Group One (Hockey)
Group One (Movies)
Group One (Sports)

--H--
Halloween
Hamburgers
Handipack
Hard Rock Cafés
Hardware Stores
Hats

Hawaii
Health & Beauty
Hearts
Hillbilly
Hiltons
Hiltons (Non U.S.)
Hiltons (Non-Stock)
Hiltons Sets
Historical
Hockey
Holiday Inn (Four Color)
Holiday Inn (Location Inside)
Holiday Inn (Non U.S.)
Holiday Inn (Non-Stock)
Holiday Inn (Stock)
Holiday Inns
Holidays (general)
Horse Drawn Vehicles
Horse Racing

Horses
Horseshoes
Hospitals
Hot Air Balloons
Hotels
Hotels (Old)
Hotels/Motels
Hyatts

--I--
Ice Cream
Idaho
Illinois

Indiana
Indians
Initials
Inns
Insects
Insurance

Intercontinental Hotels
International Harvester
Iowa
Irish Themes
Italian Restaurants

Italy

--J--
Jewelites
Jewels
Jewish Related
Jupiter 18
Jutes

--K--
Kansas
Kentucky
Keys
King Midas
Knights Inn
Knotholes

--L--
Labels
Las Vegas
Las Vegas Casinos
Lighthouses
Lincoln, Abraham
Lion Cocktail
Lips
Liquor Stores
Lobsters
Lodges
Lodging (All)

Look-A-Likes
Louisiana
Lounges

--M--
Maine
Major Chain Hotels
Major Chain Motels
Major Hotels
Major Political
Manitoba
Manumarks
Maps
Marlin Blade Sets
Maryland
Masonic
Massachusetts
Match Companies
Match Hardware
Match Safes
Matchoramas
Matchtones
Mermaids
Mermen
Metallic
Mexican Restaurants
Mexico
Michigan
Midgets
Military

Military POW Camps
Military Royal Flash
Minnesota
Mississippi
Missouri
Model Match
Monkey Sets
Monks
Montana
Moose Lodges
Motels

Motorcycles

Movie Stars
Movies
Music Related
Mustaches

--N--
Names
National Advertising
National Recovery Act
Nautical

Navy
Navy Ships (Non U.S.)
Navy Ships (Post-War)
Navy Ships (Pre-War)
Navy Ships (U.S.)
Nebraska
Nevada
New Brunswick
New Hampshire
New Jersey
New Mexico
New York
New York City Hotels
New York World's Fair
New Zealand
Newfoundland
Newspapers
Nickelodeons/Juke Boxes
Nite Clubs

North Carolina
North Dakota
Nova Scotia
Novelty
Numbers

--O--
Octopus
Odd & Unusual
Odd Sizes
Ohio
Ohio Match Co.
Oil Companies

Oklahoma
Old Covers
Old Manumarks
Olympics
Ontario
Orchestras
Oregon
Oriental Restaurants
Owls
Ownames

--P--
Pancake Restaurants
Pandas
Panning for Gold
Panorama Sets
Parks
Parrots
Patriotic

Peacocks
Pearltones
Pennsylvania
Pepsi-Cola
Perfect '36'
Perkins Americana
Personal
Personalities

Phone Area Codes
Phone Numbers (4 digit
  or less)

Piggybacks
Pigs
Pirates
Pizza Restaurants
Plaids
Plastic Boxes
Playboy Clubs
Pocketbox Slims
Police
Political

Pop-Ups
Portuguese Sets
Presidential
Prince Edward Island
Printed Sticks
Puerto Rico
Pull Quicks
Pullmatches

--Q--
Quality Courts
Quality Inns
Quebec

--R--
Race Tracks

Radio Stars
Radio Stars (CBS)
Radio Stars (NBC)
Radio/TV Stations
Railroads
Rainbows
Ramada Inns
Real Estate
Recreational
Religious

Resorts
Restaurants
Rhode Island
RMS Conventions
RMS Conventions
  (Current Year)
Roller Skating
Roses
Route 66
Royal Flash
Royalty

--S--
Safe-T-Lite
Safety First
Safety Sets
Saskatchewan
Satin
Savings & Loans, Fin'l
  Institutions

Scandinavia
Scenic
Scottie Dogs
Sea Food Restaurants
Sears & Roebuck
Seashells
Season's Greetings
Service
Sets
Seven Up (7-Up)
Shamrocks

Shells
Sheratons
Ship Lines

Signets
Silktones
Silver Dollar
Ski Resorts
Skulls
Small Towns
Smokers
Soda

South Africa
South Carolina
South Dakota
Souvenir
Souvenir Views
Space
Spain
Sports

Sports (Jewelites)
Sports Schedules
Spot Strikers (Odd)
Star Match Co.
State Capitols
State Parks
Statue Of Liberty
Stickybacks (Piggybacks)
Stock Designs
StopLites
Summits
Super 45
Supermarket Sets

Supermarkets

--T--
Taffeta
Tall Masted Ships
Taverns
Taxi Cabs

Telephone Co.
Tennessee
Texas
Thank You
Theatres
Three-D
Tigers
Tire Companies
Tobacco
Top Hats
Totem Poles
Tourist Attractions

Tourist Courts
Tractors
Transportation
Travelodges
Trees
Truck Lines
True Color

--U--
U.S. Marines
U.S. Military
U.S.O.

Ultraslims
Umbrellas
Undertakers

Uniglos
Union Match Co.
Unions
Universals
Universities
Unusual
Used
Utah

--V--
V.I.P. (All)
V.I.P. (National)
Velvet
Vermont
Vet. Admin. Hospitals
Veterans of Foreign
    Wars

Virgin Islands
Virginia
Vista-Lites

--W--
Waffle-Strikers
Walt Disney
Washington
Washington Redskins
Watermelons
Weddings

West Virginia
Western Themes

Wildlife
Wind Mills
Wine
Wisconsin
Witches
Women
Wooden Sticks
Woodgrains (Knotty
    Pines)
World War II
World's Fair (New York)
World's Fairs (General)

Worldwide
Wrigley Gum
Wyoming

--Y--
Y.M.C.A.
Y.W.C.A.

Yacht Clubs

--Z--
Zebras
ZIP Codes
Zodiac Sets
Zone Codes
Zoos

--MISC--
10 Strike
100 Strike
12 Strike
15 Stick Feature
18 Strike
20 Strike
200 Strike
22 Stick Feature
240 Strike
28 Strike
30 Strike
40 Strike
48 Strike
60 Strike
80 Strike

Each year, more categories appear on club rosters. New collectors are coming up with inventive angles on old categories. When matchcover collecting first became a formal hobby, category lists were broad (i.e. US Navy ships, Girlies, Political, Sports, etc.). Today, sports alone can have a dozen sub-categories, including stadiums, sports VIPs, individual sports (i.e. football, baseball, etc.), college sports, professional sports, playing schedules . . . and the list goes on. If you have a specific interest, such as time pieces or antique arms, there's a matchcover out there that you'd like. Write to the author with new ideas for categories, and, who knows, yours might appear in the next edition. Have fun with your categories and enjoy this wonderful hobby.

Bibliography

"A Story Behind Each Matchbook Collector," Hobbies: December 1968, p. 72.

"Acres of Matches," Literary Digest: August 1, 1936.

Advance Stock Design Book Matches Catalog S-40, Advance Match and Printing Corp: Chicago, 64 pp., IL, (ca. 1940s).

Advertise with Monarch Union Label Book Matches, Catalog 612, Monarch Match Co.: San Jose, CA, 184 pp., (ca. 1950s).

Advertise with National Union Label Book Matches Catalog No. 670, National Press: Chicago, IL, 180 pp., (ca. 1950s).

Advertise with Superior Union label Book Matches, Superior Match Co. Sales Portfolio No. 495: Chicago, IL, 1949, 208 pp.

Advertising Book Match Space Distribution Contracts, Match Corp. of America: Chicago, IL, 1945.

Advertising Book Matches Cat. No. 171, Superior Match Co.: Chicago, IL, 96 pp., (ca. 1960).

AICH, British Phillumatic Society London, England (1972-1973).

Allright, George, Bookmatch News (1965), B.P.S. Magazine (1971), County Seat Collectors Group Target, Holiday Inn Lantern (1972-3), Phillumatic (1968).

American Book Match Collector, Clarke Cameron: Colton, CA. (1941-1942).

American Matchcover Collector, Clarke Cameron: Colton, CA. (1942-1943).

The American Post, Minneapolis, MN, (1940s).

Association Vitolphilique et Phillumenique Francaise, bulletin of the Association Vitolphilique et Philumenique Francaise, Paris (in French), (1954-present).

"Boer Tradition," Nation's Business: May 1943, p. 76-7.

Book Matches for Advertising Cat. No. SJ-50, Arrow Match Corp.: Maywood, IL, 72 pp., 1950.

Bounds, Harvey, Wilmington Match Companies, Newark, DE: 1960.

BPS Magazine, British Phillumatic Society: London, England (1971-1973).

Boyer, J., "The Manufacture of Matches in France," Scientific American: May 11, 1907, p. 392-394.

California Matchcover News, California Matchcover Club, Richmond Annex, CA, (1950).

Carolina Matchcover Club Bulletin, Carolina Matchcover Club, NC, (1983-1985).

Carpenter, A.L., Provisional Catalogue of South African Matchbox Labels: 1884-1972, Durbin, South Africa: Lion Match Co., Ltd, 30 pp.

"Cartel in Matches?," Business Week: May 6, 1944, p. 23-4.

Catalog and Price List, Match Corp. of America: Chicago, IL, 250 pp., 1949.

Catalog and Price List 30's, Match Corp. of America: Chicago, IL, 35 pp, 1949.

Catalog and Price List 40's, Match Corp. of America: Chicago, IL, 39 pp, 1949.

Chicago Match Co. Advertising Book Matches, Chicago Match Co.: Chicago, IL, 72 pp., (ca. 1940s).

Collectors Forum (originally Matchonia & Hobby Advertiser), New York: Moyer Bros., (1938-?).

"Covers," New Yorker: October 13, 1956, p. 37-8.

Cruse, Alfred J., Match-Box Labels of the World; With a History of fire-Making appliances from Primitive Man to the Modern Match, together with a History of the World's Labels, London: R. Ross: 1946.

Deck, J.F., "The Match Stick Colossus," Foreign Affairs: October 1930, p. 149-156.

Diamond Book Matches Stock Designs, The Diamond Match Co.: NY, 1933.

The Diamond Years: 1881-1956, (75th anniversary publication), Diamond Match Co.: 1956.

Dick, G., "How Grownups play with matches," American Magazine: August 1950, p. 42-43+.

"Dither in Matches," Business Week: November 18, 1944, p. 88-9.

"Do You Read Match Books," Changing Times The Kiplinger Magazine: February 1953, p. 45-6.

Double Book Matches and Jumbos, Superior Match Co.: Chicago, IL, 1949.

Eichenlaub, A.J., Manufacturer's and Agent's Imprints As Used On Match Book Covers; Ohio, 1942 (revised edition by Horace Rush, Washington, D.C., 1947).

Famous Glamour Girls, Superior Match Co.: Chicago, IL, (ca. 1950s).

The Florida Matchbook, Sunshine State Matchcover Club: Winter Park, FL, (1958-1979).

The Front Striker Bulletin, The Retskin Report: Asheville, NC.: (1986-present).

Galton, L., "The Story Behind the Match Business," Science Digest: February 1946, p. 57-61.

Gateway Gazette, Gateway Matchcover Club: Kirkwood, MO, (1983-1988).

Girlie Matchcover Club Newsletter, Girlie Club: Columbus, OH, (1982-present).

"Government Monopolies," Independent: December 1, 1910, p. 1225-6.

Heaton, J.P., "Making All Matches "Safeties"," Survey: December 3, 1910, p. 384-389.

Huges, Stephen, Pop Culture Mania, McGraw-Hill: 1984, 330 pp.

International Book Match Association Bulletin, International Book Match Association: Washington, D.C., (1955-1959).

Kaeser & Blair, Inc. Advertising Specialty Catalog: Cincinnati, OH, 183 pp., (ca. 1940s).

Keystone Highlights, Keystone Matchcover Club: Allentown, PA, (1951-1987).

Lake Breezes, Great Lakes Matchcover Club: Detroit, MI, (1961-1985).

"The Last of Phossy Jaw," Survey: February 19, 1911, p. 818-9.

Laurel, Globe Correspondence Club & Worldwide Swappers Club: MA, (ca. 1940s).

The Lantern, British Phillumatic Society: London, ENG, (1972-1974).

Lehigh Valley News, Lehigh Valley Matchcover Club: Allentown, PA, (1968-1987).

Manchester, Herbert, The Diamond Match Company: A Century of Service, of Progress, and of Growth: 1835 - 1935: New York, Diamond Match Co., 1935.

Manchester, Herbert, Fifty Years of Match Making: New York, Diamond Match Co., 1928.

Manchester, Herbert, The Romance of the Match: New York, Diamond Match Co., 1926.

Marcosson, I.F., "The Match King," The Saturday Evening Post: October 12, 1929, p. 3+.

Maryland Book Matches, Maryland Match Co.: Baltimore, MD., 128 pp., (ca. 1950s).

"Match," Collectors Service Bulletin: Rochester, NY, (ca. 1940s).

"Matches: Cigarettes Light Way for Continued Diamond Profits," Newsweek: June 13, 1936, p. 34-6.

"Matches with messages," Dun's Review and Modern Industry: October 1963.

Match Covers from U.S. Naval Vessels: Post - War List: Walter Mensch, Garden Grove, CA, (ca. 1940s).

Match Folder News, Match Folder Collectors Alliance: Harrisburg, PA (1936-1937).

A Match Labelist's Notes, Bill Fontaine: Columbus, OH (1934-1939).

Match Lights, Jesse Heuszel: Kansas City, MO, (1937-1941).

Match-O-Grams, Edgar Perkins: Washington, D.C., (1946-1950).

Match Pack Notes, "Doc" Wilson: San Francisco, CA, (1936-1940).

Matchcover Adlet, Dave Pophal: Pewaukee, WI, (1978-79).

Matchcover Classified, David Hampton: Pittsburg, CA, (1985-1989).

Matchcover Club of the Carolinas Bulletin, Matchcover Club of the Carolinas: Mooresville, NC, (1986-1987).

Matchonia & Hobby Advertiser, (later Collectors Forum), Auburn, NY: Moyer Bros., (1938-?).

The Match Makers, The Story of Bryant & May, Patrick Beaver, Henry Melland Press, London: 1985, 126 pp.

Mid-West News, Mid-West Matchcover Club: St. Louis, MO, (1962-1975).

"Mixed Results for Match Makers," Financial World: March 19, 1958, p. 11-12.

Monda Lingo Bulletin, Pasadena, CA: (1907-?).

Monumental's Match-Less Chatter, Monumental Matchcover Club: Baltimore, MD, (1978-1988).

NACAMCO News, National Capitol Match Collectors Club: Washington, D.C., (1950-1970).

New Royal DeLuxe Designs, Match. Corp. of America: Chicago, IL, 1947.

New Stock Cuts for Book Match Advertising, Match Corp. of America: Chicago, IL, 1947.

Newsletter, British Matchbox Label & Booklet Society: Norwich, Great Britain, (1945-present).

ODMC Chronicle, Old Dominion Matchcover Club: MD, (1952-1970).

The Past is Prologue: Diamond International Corporation's First One Hundred Years (1881-1981), (100th anniversary publication): Diamond International, 1981.

Pasteboarder's Notes, Bob Oliver: Mira Loma, CA, (ca. 1930s).

Perkins, Edgar, American Bookmatch Collector: Washington, D.C. 1954.

Perkins, Edgar, American Bookmatch Courses: Washington, D.C., 1954.

Perkins, Edgar, Matchcover Collecting As a Finer Art: Washington, D.C., 1947.

Perkins, Edgar, Matchcovers, The World's Most Fascinating Hobby: Washington, D.C., 1956.

Personalized Book Matches, Match Corp. of America: Chicago, IL, 1947.

The Phillumenist, (independent magazine), (1940 - 1960).

"Phosphorus Poisoning in Chinese Match Factories," U.S. Bureau of Laboratory Statistics: June 1925, p. 117-8.

"Popularity of American Match Still Safe From the Safety," Business Week, April 5, 1931, p. 22 - 3.

"The Psychology of the Last Match," Overland Monthly: April 2, 1909, p. 286 - 7.

Rancier, Esther, Matchcovers: A Guide to Collecting: NY, Century House, Inc., 1976, 176 pp.

Retskin, Bill, The Matchcover Collectors Resource Book and Price Guide: Asheville, NC, The Retskin Report, 1988, 264 pp.

Rendell, Joan, The Match, the Box and the Label: London, ENG, David & Charles, 1983.

Rex Book Matches, Fleming Calendar Co.: Chicago, IL, 64 pp., 1941.

Richardson, M.A., "Match Box Labels," Hobbies, Vol. 41, #8, October 1936, p. 124.

Richardson, M.A., "Match Labels," Hobbies, Vol. 42, #8, p. 125.

Sanders, Helen & George, Roberts, Ralph, The Price Guide to Autographs, 2nd Edition, Wallace Homestead, Radnor, PA, 1991.

The Ship's Bell, COMBINE: Winter Haven, FL, (1961 - 1979).

Snappy Sales Talk, Superior Match Co.: Chicago, IL, April 1949, Sept. 1949.

Southeastern Matchcover Club, Southeastern Matchcover Club: Mooresville, NC, (1988 - 1989).

Sparkes, B., "Made in Russia; Sold in U.S.A.," The Saturday Evening Post: July 25, 1931, p. 21 +.

The Story of a Match, The Ohio Match Co.: Wadsworth, OH, 1928.

"The Story of the Match," American Forests: January 1956, p. 24 - 26 +.

The Striker, Beer and Soda Match Cover Society: Colorado Springs, CO, (1983 - 1986).

Striking News, Striking News: Goldens Bridge, NY, (1971 - 1983).

Super Embosso Design Book Matches, Match Corp. of America: Chicago, IL, 1947, 7 pp.

"Terms of License for Harmless Phosphorus," Survey: January 7, 1911, p. 523.

This Space Reserved For You, Chicago Match Co.: Libertyville, IL, 152 pp., (ca. 1940s).

Three Star Treasure Portfolio, The National Press: N. Chicago, IL, 1955.

"To Prohibit Use of Poisonous Phosphorous," Survey: June 11, 1910, p. 427-8.

"The U.S. Match Industry - Its History and Labels," Bob Jones: Indianapolis, IN, 1950, 24 pp., illus.

The United Matchonians, Ernest Damron: Sistersville, WV, (1936 - 1951).

"U.S. Kitchen and Parlor Boxes," Bob Jones: Indianapolis, IN, 1977, 43 pp. catalog, #77-074175.

Victory Models, Match Corp. of America: Chicago, IL, 1947.

Warman's Americana and Collectibles, Warman Pub. Co.: Elkins Park, PA, 1992.

Western Reserve Newsletter, Western Reverse Matchcover Club: Thompson, OH, (1967 - 1972).

INDEX

Dating from the 1940 **Rex Book Matches/Fleming Calendar Company** (Chicago, Ill.) Salesman's Sample book, this outrageous "coal man" was popular with coal companies. His eyes, nose and mouth are spelled out with the letter of the word COAL and he stands among the mountains from which he was mined. Simple, direct and clear, early matchcover messages made their point directly.

Color Photo Credits

(Color page 1)

1. Charles A. Lindbergh, Lion Match Co. Safety First. This is the highest selling matchbook of modern times and considered extremely rare, a total of three different ones are known.

2. Zep Diner. This colorful full length matchcover was both attractive and informative, giving the user enough information to compliment the color graphic.

3. Frank M. Page, Flowers, uses a base friction matchbook (note striker on the bottom of the match book). The base friction striker was invented and promoted by Diamond Match Co., but with little success.

4. Lion Match Co. Features. Upper left and right, images printed on single sticks. Center and lower left and right, panorama images.

(Color page 2)

5. Figural matchbook containers. Each contained eight matchbooks, decorated with the same colors and theme as the container.

6. After his turbulent boxing career, Jack Dempsey became an entrepreneur, operating several restaurants in New York and Florida. Displayed here are just a few of the Dempsey matchcovers (over 24 known) and a personal photo album from his Broadway restaurant in New York.

(Color page 3)

7. Fractured French Bookmatches. Comic series released with French sayings and their audacious translations on each.

8. Odd or Spot Striker. The striker material is in the shape of the model's panties. The front of this match book shows her front peeping through the curtains. Hundreds of different kinds of Odd Strikers use the striker material in various places on either front or back.

9. Display sleeves were often popular as giveaways at company functions. Note the Chessie Line (kitten) with the die-cut in the display sleeve.

10. An assortment of salesman's sample flats. Note that although a striker is present, traditional machine creases and staple holes are missing.

11. Three railroad display boxes, each representing a railroad car. Display boxes can contain either matchbooks or matchboxes.

(Color page 4)

12. Both early matchbooks, the E. Robinson's Sons (right) and the Casper's Whiskey (left) have the Sept. 27, 1892 patent date on the manumark. Casper's Whiskey also says (Licensed Match). Both pre-1910.

13. Back of the Casper's Whiskey matchbook showing the copper distillery mechanism and "Absolutely Hand Made." The E. Robin's Sons Pilsener Lager also advertises Scranton's Pure Beer.

14. Two Lion Match Co. Safety First matchcovers displaying a bold and attractive, non-cluttered approach to matchbook advertising. The graphic message was simple, direct, and easily understood with one quick glance.

15. Salvation Matches, produced in Russia before the turn of the century, were "dumped" on the United States. Shipping box was lined in lead. The crate contained 144 kitchen size boxes (F/B) showing. The paper sleeve (behind) contained 12 kitchen boxes.

(Color page 5)

16. Diamond Match Company, parlor match tin with derogatory ethnic saying and picture on front. The striker of this tin was extremely rough, indicating that both physical strength, as well as a chemical reaction, was needed to light a match.

17. American Pullmatches Corporation ashtray and holder. Each match stick was broken from the central roll and struck on the top or bottom of the ashtray.

18. Lion Match Co. Giant Features. Note the exaggerated amount of advertising space, both on the matchcovers and the sticks. This kind of matchbook is still being made today.

19. American Pullmatches Corporation refill (left) and tin mailing container (right).

(Color page 6)

20. Five colorful matchcovers representing different World's Fairs. (left) 1936 California-Pacific International Exposition (left-center) 1936 Texas Centennial; (center) 1933-34 Chicago Century of Progress; (right-center) 1939-40 New York World's Fair; (right) 1964-65 New York World's Fair.

21. Tall, Universal Match Corp. matchcovers were popular prior to WWII. Note the center advertisement for Canadian Club is a conjunctive with the 1934 Chicago Century of Progress World's Fair. Fair conjunctives from this event are scarce.

22. Three matchcovers depicting Indians. (left) One of ten from the Indians of the Southwest Set. (center) Harold's Club, Reno, NV. (right) One of the Canadian Artists (Indian Maiden) Set.

23. A sterling silver match safe with a front door that opens to reveal a gold, top-hatted man on the throne. The slanted roof of the privy opens for match storage. Corrugated striker is on the bottom. No other markings. (collection: George Sparacio)

(Color page 7)

24. Stock designs used on Diamond Quality matchcovers (mostly pre-1936). There were dozens of stock designs available to the small businessman during this period, all quite colorful and related to the type of business being advertised.

25. Ronald Wilson Reagan White House matchbook, signed by the President while in office. Fifty of these were presented to the Chief White House Steward, and are all that are known.

26. Matchcovers displaying the blue NRA symbol. This symbol dates the matchcovers between the years when the symbol was popular.

27. Sterling silver match safe as a full figural head. The eyes are stone or glass, and the rough corrugated metal striker is on the bottom. Loop appears at the back of the neck, probably to hold it on a key chain. No other markings. (collection: George Sparacio)

28. National political matchcovers including (second from left) MacGillivary's in Boston with President Harry S. Truman pinning the C.M.O. on a soldier (possibly MacGillivary himself). It is uncommon to see national political figures used for advertising public restaurants.

(Color page 8)

29. Display caddies and cello paks. These popular matchbook wrappings were found on souvenir counters and display racks in the 1930s, 1940s, and 1950s. Sets and partial sets often made up the contents.

30. An American Match Co. stock ad for its own matchbooks. Part of the ad for Cooper-Carlton Pharmacy is visible. Match companies often provided discount stock conjunctives to small companies interested in advertising on matchbooks.

31. Five different designs for Civilian Conservation Corps matchcovers. Although a majority are of one stock design (left-center) a number of non-stock CCC Camps can be found.

32. Matchcovers celebrating members of the English Royal Family.